BIOGRAPHICAL DICTIONARY OF

HISPANIC AMERICANS

SECOND EDITION

NICHOLAS E. MEYER

Facts On File, Inc.

Biographical Dictionary of Hispanic Americans, Second Edition

Facts On File, Inc.
132 West 31st Street
New York NY 10001

Library of Congress Cataloging-in-Publication Data
Meyer, Nicholas E.
    Biographical dictionary of Hispanic Americans / Nicholas E. Meyer.—2nd ed.
       p. cm.
    Includes bibliographical references (p.) and index.
    ISBN 0-8160-4330-2 (alk. paper)
    1. Hispanic Americans—Biography—Dictionaries. I. Title.
    E184.S75 M49 2001
    920'.009268'073—dc21   00-049046

Facts On File books are available at special discounts when purchased in bulk quantities for businesses, associations, institutions, or sales promotions. Please call our Special Sales Department in New York at (212) 967-8800 or (800) 322-8755.

You can find Facts On File on the World Wide Web at http://www.factsonfile.com

Text design by Joan M. Toro
Cover design by Cathy Rincon

Printed in the United States of America

VB FOF 10 9 8 7 6 5 4 3

This book is printed on acid-free paper.

To Vanesa and Solange.
And to Gustavo Ponce de León.

CONTENTS

ACKNOWLEDGMENTS

Many thanks to: Clara Albertengo, Jacqui Behrend, Nicole Bowen, Fernando Campos, Pedro and Raquel Gaska, Ricardo Goldstein, David Mackintosh, Gloria Martínez, Oscar Medina, Lidia, Solange and Vanesa Meyer, Julio Nakamurakare, Graciela Ortiz, Inés Pardal, Marisol Rocabado Paravicini, Colonel José Rodríguez (U.S. Army), Joe Schneider, Emily Spectre, Gene Springs, Mariano, Marilí and Ricardo Tepper, Carmen Valdivieso, James Warren, Eric Weil, Marcelo Zapata.

INTRODUCTION

*T*he *Biographical Dictionary of Hispanic Americans* pursues two main aims. In the first place, it provides the straightforward service implied by its title: it is a reference volume, supplying information on Hispanic notables whom the reader wishes to look up.

But at the same time, and equally or more important, its goal is to highlight the significance, richness, and variety of Hispanic participation in U.S. life, past and present.

In so doing, this volume will hopefully also achieve a number of additional goals. They are interrelated to one another and to the above but do not wholly overlap.

First, we hope this book will bolster the pride of Hispanic readers by revealing the full range and importance of Hispanic contributions to U.S. history, culture, and current affairs. Second, we trust it will remind all readers of the crucial role played by Hispanics in the early stages of U.S. history, particularly its (European) discovery and its colonization, begun many decades before Jamestown and before the *Mayflower.*

Finally, it recalls the discrimination often encountered by Hispanics and draws attention to the achievements of those who fought and overcame it.

The individuals chosen for inclusion in this biographical dictionary are approximately two hundred and fifty outstanding Hispanics of every description. Every effort was made to make the selection as wide-ranging as possible in five different ways: (1) in fields of activity; (2) in gender; (3) in time, that is, ranging from the very discovery of the United States by Juan Ponce de León in 1513, to the present day; (4) in space, that is, from coast to coast of the United States; and (5) in national origin, that is, Mexican Americans, Cuban Americans, Puerto Ricans, and so on.

To enhance the usefulness of this reference work, the names of other prominent Hispanic Americans that appear in individual entries have been set in small capital letters.

Another issue that was carefully weighed when choosing whom to include in the book is the question of definition—who, exactly, is a Hispanic? Hispanics' skin, after all, can come in any of the colors that are traditionally described as white, black, yellow, or red. Also, what percentage of "Hispanicity" is enough (e.g., is one Hispanic grandparent sufficient)?

Then there is the fact that—among the early discoverers, conquerors, and colonizers—the Hispanic influence on what was to become the United States was exercised by people who were straightforwardly Spaniards.

As for the foreign-born today, what length of residence, what percentage of life's work carried out in the United States, qualify a person as a Hispanic American, as opposed to simply a foreigner who spent some time here?

Finally, there is the question of Portuguese and Brazilians, who are sometimes excluded, when considered as a category—while the Brazilian actress Carmen Miranda (who was actually born in Portugal) is definitely considered Hispanic.

Thoughtful people tend to arrive at the conclusion that, in the ultimate instance, a person is Hispanic if he or she feels Hispanic and/or is considered Hispanic by others. People can very well feel simultaneously Hispanic and something else, in the same way that someone with an Italian mother and an Irish father, for example, may feel Italian and may feel Irish too.

With regard to terminology, although there is an awareness of the nuances involved, such words as *Hispanic* and *Latino* are here used interchangeably, alternating for variation only.

Bibliographical information is provided as a guide and encouragement to further reading.

We trust that this overview of the Hispanic-American experience, its tribulations, and its contributions to the U.S. mosaic, will be as inspiring as it is informative.

A

Adolfo (**Adolfo Sardiña**) (1933–)
fashion designer

Adolfo became a nationwide and international celebrity thanks to a United States president's wife who made it no secret that this Hispanic stylist was her favorite fashion designer. Before this, however, he was well known to a small circle of wealthy and influential clients in the United States.

Adolfo Sardiña—who prefers to go by the single name Adolfo—was born on February 15, 1933, to a prosperous family in the Cuban port city of Cárdenas. As a youth, he toyed with the idea of designing clothes but never dreamed of mentioning this to the strict Jesuit priests who were in charge of his education.

Things changed for him when he was 15. An aunt decided to take him with her to France, where she intended to buy many clothes. An important client, she introduced him to the designers. As a result, by the age of 16, Adolfo had landed a job with Cristóbal Balenciaga, one of the most important designers in the Paris fashion world. Balenciaga hailed from Spain and, like Adolfo, was known by a one-word name.

From Paris, Adolfo quickly went on to New York, where he settled. Having apprenticed at the Balenciaga Hat Salon, he initially concentrated on women's hats, designing for a succession of enterprises: Bragaard, the Bergdorf Goodman department store, and Emme Millinery. His hallmark was his capacity to give shape to a hat cleverly without using wiring or padding but solely through the stitching he employed.

It was through his work as a milliner that Adolfo caught the attention of moneyed clients, who liked such flourishes as the deep-diving "Adolfo brim." He formed his own fashion company, Adolfo, Inc., in 1962, and attracted a high-society clientele.

His customers included Babe Paley, wife of the CBS television patriarch; Jacqueline Kennedy, former first lady of the United States; and Gloria Vanderbilt, a celebrated heiress and herself a fashion designer. Vanderbilt is credited with having convinced Adolfo to branch out into also making dresses for sale. Until she encouraged him, he had only designed dresses for the models who paraded his hats at shows.

Of all the diverse styles he worked with, Adolfo made his biggest hit with women's suits fashioned in the tradition of French designer Coco Chanel. This, however, also embroiled him in controversy over who had actually launched the fashion at that moment.

Adolfo became the favored designer of important U.S. politicians' wives. One of these clients, Nancy

Reagan, was the wife of Ronald Reagan, a former actor and California governor who was elected president of the United States in 1980 and 1984.

Nancy Reagan was extremely fashion conscious, and her predilection for Adolfo clothes created additional renown for the Cuban-born designer. They became so closely identified that the remark was made and often quoted, "A vote for Ronald Reagan is a vote for Adolfo."

Adolfo has won honors for his fashion work: the Neiman-Marcus Award in 1956 and the Coty Award in 1955 and 1969.

Further Reading

Blackwell, Earl. *Celebrity Register.* New York: Celebrity Register, Inc., 1986.

O'Hara, Georgina. *The Encyclopedia of Fashion.* New York: Harry N. Abrams, 1986.

≈ Alegría, Fernando (1918–) *writer*

Fernando Alegría is a Chilean-born novelist, poet, literary scholar and teacher who has worked for many decades in California. He writes about both Chile and the United States; his work is marked by his strong, lifelong interest in social matters. He also held a diplomatic post for a few years.

Alegría (whose last name means *joy* in Spanish) was born on September 26, 1918, in the Chilean capital, Santiago. His vibrant home neighborhood of Maruri left him with strong memories as it did for another of its inhabitants, Chile's celebrated writer Pablo Neruda.

In his youth, Alegría was educated at a number of his country's best schools. Having graduated in Spanish and philosophy from the University of Chile, in 1939 Alegría became a professor at his alma mater.

His activities the previous year demonstrated his social concern: He published his first novel, *Recabarren,* a fictionalized biography of a Chilean labor leader, and was active in the Youth for Peace movement. As the world teetered on the brink of World War II, this movement held an international gathering, which Alegría attended. This meeting in New York State marked the writer's first trip to the United States.

Thereafter, he would keep a foot in each country, though when a military dictatorship in Chile forced him to stay out of that country, the United States became his permanent residence.

Alegría obtained a master's degree in literature from Bowling Green State University in Ohio and a Ph.D. from the University of California at Berkeley. Berkeley appointed him instructor in 1947 (the year he took his doctoral degree) and professor in 1949. In 1967, he took a professorship at Stanford University; he has remained there, now holding the title of professor emeritus.

A Guggenheim Fellowship, the Latin American Prize for Literature, and the Atenea prize are among the honors Alegría has garnered during his career. Further, he has had the satisfaction of being one of the pioneers in the recognition and teaching of Spanish-language literature within the United States. He has also brought American literature to Spanish-speaking countries through translations. Alegría's greatest pleasures have come from combining both of his worlds, as in his 1954 work on one of the most renowned U.S. poets, *Walt Whitman en Hispanoamérica.* In 1965, he published the fundamental *Historia de la Novela Hispanoamericana (History of the Spanish-American Novel).*

With regard to his fiction, Alegría is classified within Chile's Generation of 1938. This name was given to socially committed authors who were influenced by the 1938 election of a progressive government in Chile.

That government was created by a coalition of middle-class, socialist, and communist parties. The 1930s was a historical period associated with the full bloom of "socialist realism." This style, promoted by the Soviet Communist Party, insisted on realism within a highly heroic mold. Despite these factors, the Generation of 1938 approached realism from a poetic viewpoint.

Among Alegría's works are *Camaleón (Chameleon,* 1950), *Caballo de Copas (Queen of Hearts,* 1957), *Amerika, Amerikka, Amerikkka, Manifiestos de Viet Nam (Amerika, Amerikka, Amerikkka, Vietnam Manifestos,* 1970), and the autobiographical *Una Especie de Memoria (A Kind of Memoir,* 1983).

Alegría was a supporter of the Marxist Chilean politician Salvador Allende, and in 1970, when Allende was elected the country's president, he named Alegría to the post of Chilean cultural attaché in the United States. One of his brothers, Julio Alegría, a politician, was made ambassador to Bulgaria.

On one trip to Santiago, Fernando Alegría was supposed to have a lunchtime appointment with Allende on the very day—September 11, 1973—that a right-wing coup exploded against the president. Alegría did not go to the presidential palace because he had been tipped off early that morning that an insurrection was being planned. By afternoon, Allende was dead inside the palace, and the country was in the hands of a military dictatorship, which, among other things, persecuted intellectuals.

After that, Chile's cultural life could only continue abroad, and Alegría became one of its shepherds and leading lights. He cofounded, with a friend, a literary magazine, *Literatura Chilena en el Exilio (Chilean Literature in Exile),* in 1977 and edited an anthology, *Chilean Writers in Exile,* in 1982.

Alegría's work not only provided a beacon for Chilean exiles in the United States but also voiced constant condemnation of human-rights abuses in the country of his birth.

Further Reading
Alegría, Fernando. *Changing Centuries: Selected Poems of Fernando Alegría,* trans. Stephen Kessler. Pittsburgh, Pa.: Latin American Literary Review Press, 1988.

❧ Algarín, Miguel (1941–) *writer*

Miguel Algarín is a leader and key benefactor of the "Nuyorican" poetry literary movement. He also gave the movement a "home" at New York's Nuyorican Poets Cafe.

Born in Santurce, Puerto Rico, on September 11, 1941, Algarín might have easily turned to music instead of literature. His father taught him to play the violin, and his upbringing included plentiful exposure to classical music, including opera, and art.

His parents were neither wealthy nor members of the worlds of art, music, or literature. His father man-

aged a chain of gas stations, and his mother was a caterer who also ran a jewelry store. But Miguel Algarín Senior and his wife, María Socorro, appreciated cultural pleasures. They passed this appreciation on to their children, of whom Miguel Junior was the second of three.

After the family left Puerto Rico, Spanish Harlem in New York City became the Algaríns' home. There, they joined the large group of Puerto Ricans who had migrated to New York in the 1950s. Later, they moved to Queens, another part of New York City. While his father ran parking lots and his mother served as a community worker, Miguel Algarín continued his education. He first studied at New York's City College but completed his bachelor's degree at the University of Wisconsin and received a master's degree from Pennsylvania State University. Algarín began to teach at Brooklyn College. He went on to New York University and then Rutgers University in New Brunswick, New Jersey.

It is at Rutgers that Algarín has made the greatest strides in his career as an educator. He is a professor and chairman of the department of Puerto Rican and related studies. Indeed, Algarín built up the department, employing his drive and his strong links with the Puerto Rican community to create a lively site that fires student enthusiasm.

Since the 1960s, Algarín has written poetry that sometimes entwines both the English and the Spanish languages and occasionally French. His published books include *Mongo Affair* (1978), *On Call* (1980), *Body Bee Calling from the 21st Century* (1982), and *Time's Now/Ya es Tiempo* (1985). They explore such varied subjects as the Hispanic experience, ethical questions, Latin American politics, communication with God, and language itself.

Unlike some writers who prefer isolation, Algarín thrives within a community. He also has helped a community thrive—the community of *Nuyoricans,* a word used to refer to the Puerto Ricans of New York and, more specifically, to the artists and writers among them.

Together with another writer, Miguel PIÑERO, Algarín contributed to the creation and definition of the group's sense of identity, editing and publishing

Nuyorican Poetry: An Anthology of Puerto Rican Words and Feeling (1975).

Years earlier, Algarín took the step for which he is best known. His apartment on the Lower East Side of Manhattan had become a meeting place for literary enthusiasts. He shifted those literary meetings to an empty store across the street; in this way, he created the Nuyorican Poets Cafe, a place where anyone could freely read his or her own work aloud.

Algarín owned the place, pouring in his own money to help keep it operating as a nucleus for Nuyoricans and their literature. For many new writers, particularly from the working class, the Nuyorican Poets Cafe became a favorite haunt, and its appeal rapidly extended to other communities. It was a writers' refuge, a place where work could be heard and a place to find food for spirit and body alike.

Algarín has also founded a publishing house (Nuyorican Press) and has cofounded another (Arte Público Press). He has translated into English the work of Chilean poet Pablo Neruda (*Canción de Gesta/A Song of Protest,* 1976) and choreographed *Body Bee Calling from the 21st Century,* a ballet of Algarín's thoughts about humanity after a nuclear war. In addition, Algarín has directed the Nuyorican Playwrights'/Actors' Workshop and has advised the Association of Hispanic Arts in New York City.

Further Reading

Mohr, Eugene V. *The Nuyorican Experience.* Westport, Conn.: Greenwood Press, 1982.

❦ Allende, Isabel (1942–) *writer*

Acclaimed Chilean novelist Isabel Allende has made her home in California. She is the most widely known member of the newer generations of Latin American writers who bear witness to their continent's history, which until recently was one of rigid, oppressive society and military dictatorship.

Allende was born on August 2, 1942, in Lima, Peru, where her father, a diplomat, held the rank of secretary at the Chilean embassy. He was a first cousin of Salvador Allende, the Chilean Socialist Party founder who was elected president of Chile in 1970 and died three years later during a right-wing coup

against his government. In the 1980s, when Isabel Allende first became famous, she was sometimes confused with her second cousin, the late president's daughter, also called Isabel Allende.

When her father abandoned them, Allende's mother formed a new family with another Chilean diplomat. Because of her stepfather's postings abroad, her youth was spent in Bolivia and in Lebanon. When civil war broke out in Lebanon and U.S. troops arrived in 1958, Allende's family was evacuated from that country with other diplomats' families for their own safety.

Allende worked as a secretary at an agency of the United Nations in Chile from 1959–65 before becoming a journalist and writer of children's literature. During the late 1960s and early 1970s, she hosted a television show of a mainly humorous nature, edited a juvenile magazine, and was on the staff of another journal—a women's magazine that pioneered feminism in Chile.

Allende was an early rebel against what she saw as prudish attitudes and outdated, unequal conditions in Chilean society. She remembers, however, that she was not directly interested in politics and considered the rising politician Salvador Allende as just another cousin within her large family.

When Salvador Allende was elected president of Chile in 1970, he appointed Isabel's stepfather ambassador to Argentina. In Argentina at that time, there were many political kidnappings. Isabel Allende's fears for her stepfather's safety moved her to write a play, her first, titled *El Embajador (The Ambassador),* about a diplomat who is taken captive by a group of guerrillas.

In 1973, after President Allende's left-wing government was toppled in a bloody uprising, a long period of military terror began in Chile. Isabel was outraged by the murder or forced suicide of the president. Shortly afterward, she cheered his memory in public at the funeral of the Chilean poet Pablo Neruda—a Nobel Prize winner in literature whom she had known personally. Her outspokenness at the funeral brought reprimands from her family for risking her safety in such a manner.

The targets of the new military government were not only people who were suspected of left-wing ideas, but also, among others, feminists. Isabel Allende and other staff members who were considered feminists were dismissed from the women's magazine.

She was also fired as editor of the children's magazine, because of a cover illustration ordered months before the military coup that depicted four gorillas. The cover was interpreted as a mockery of the four military members of the ruling government junta.

Only Allende's work on television was left undisrupted. She realized that it suited the junta to have a member of the Allende family appear in a lightweight TV show. It gave the impression that life was normal in Chile instead of its undergoing a wave of disappearances, torture, and murder. Allende resigned.

At the same time, she became increasingly involved in such clandestine activities as helping hunted people find asylum in foreign embassies, passing along information, and collecting food for the families of people who had been kidnapped by government forces, never to be seen again. She claims that initially she was not fully aware of the risks involved and that she never did it out of heroism but rather out of compassion, though she did possess a love of adventure.

But as the pressure rose, her fear increased, and in 1975 she left Chile for a life of exile. She and her husband and children lived in Venezuela for the next 13 years.

In 1982, at 40, Allende published her first novel, *La Casa de los Espíritus (The House of the Spirits)*, a fictionalized version of her own family history. It was followed two years later by another, *De Amor y de Sombra (Of Love and Shadows)*, about people involved in mass political murders, inspired by true events in Chile.

These books were immediate worldwide successes and were quickly made into motion pictures. Other works followed: the novel *Eva Luna* (1987) was considered "one of the year's best books" by the U.S. publication *Library Journal*, and *Cuentos de Eva Luna (Eva Luna's Stories)* was a popular selection of short narratives. Allende's works were translated into more than 25 languages, and her publishers called her the most widely read Latin American novelist ever.

On a trip to the United States in 1988, having divorced her first husband, Allende fell in love with a U.S. lawyer. They married and made their home in San Francisco. Soon after, Allende began to teach creative writing at the University of California. Although democracy has returned to Chile and Allende has visited there, she has elected to remain a resident of the United States.

In 1991, Allende's adult daughter Paula became gravely ill with a metabolic disease, porphyria. She soon fell into a coma, remaining in this condition for a year before dying. In 1994, Allende published a memoir, *Paula*, told through the harrowing story of her daughter's illness and death. Allende published *Aphrodite: A Memoir of the Senses* in 1998, and *Daughter of Fortune*, a historical novel about the California gold rush, in 1999.

Further Reading

Allende, Isabel. *Paula*. New York: HarperCollins, 1996.

Isabel Allende. Available online. URL: http://www.isabelallende.com. Downloaded October 10, 2000.

Shirey, Lynn. *Latin American Writers*. New York: Facts On File, 1997.

Unterburger, Amy L., and Jane L. Delgado, eds. *Who's Who Among Hispanic Americans*. Detroit: Gale Research, Inc., 1993.

Almendros, Néstor (1930–1992)
director of movie photography

It is unique that one of the most important Hispanics in Hollywood history is not an actor or actress but a technician—a director of photography. A director of photography is responsible for the cameras and lighting and thus greatly influences the way a movie "looks." "Néstor Almendros is one of the greatest directors of photography in the world," declared French director François Truffaut.

Néstor Almendros had a significant and highly respected career in the movie industry both in the United States and in France. He was crowned with the highest awards, winning the Oscar in the United States and the César in France. In later years, he was also known for condemning human-rights abuses in Castro's Cuba.

Néstor Almendros *(Cabrera Archive)*

Almendros (whose last name, in Spanish, means "almond trees") was born in 1930 in Barcelona, Spain. During the Spanish Civil War in the late 1930s, his father supported the Republicans—the losing antifascist side. Because of this, when the war ended and Franco came to power, Almendros's father had to leave the country. The rest of the family, including Néstor, followed him to Cuba in 1948.

Néstor Almendros went to the university in Havana and became so closely identified with Cuba that some sources wrongly report that he was born there.

As a result of his early family life, Almendros was left with a lifelong hatred of all strong-arm governments regardless of their ideology. Thus he would come to hate Castro's communist dictatorship in Cuba as fiercely as he had hated Franco's fascist one in Spain.

As a movie-mad young man, Almendros, together with other youths, founded Cuba's first film society. It was a place where they could show special artistic movies, old and new. He also began to dabble in directing short amateur films. But in 1952 Fulgencio Batista, a right-wing dictator, took over Cuba after ruling a puppet government since 1933. Soon Almendros, feeling oppressed under Batista's government, felt he had to leave.

In New York at City College, he studied moviemaking, and he continued his studies in Rome, Italy. When he graduated, he returned to the United States, taking a job at Vassar College as a Spanish teacher. He attributed getting the job to Vassar's knowledge that—with his background in film studies—he would be able to operate the audiovisual equipment in the then-new language laboratory.

With his earnings as a teacher, he bought a small 16-mm camera and began to make short films. In his autobiography, *A Man With a Camera,* Almendros cites New York as the place his movie career really began—in 1958, with his modest 16-mm work.

He did go to Hollywood for a few months, but the only work he could find was dishwashing and he noted what he later called "the almost insurmountable wall that surrounds American filmmaking."

In 1959, when Fidel Castro's revolution toppled Batista, Almendros enthusiastically returned to Cuba. There he found work in a movie production department created by the government. For this new job, he believed he owed thanks not only to his earlier connections with movies, but also to political history, having been an exile from Franco as well as from Batista. He also believed having his own 16-mm camera to work with helped.

Almendros made a number of professional 35-mm shorts in Cuba, frequently working as a cameraman, but after a time he began to feel disappointed. It seemed strange to him that a revolutionary government's production department demanded very traditional, Hollywood-like ways of photographing and lighting movies. He, on the other hand, wanted to make films in a more flexible, natural-looking style, like that of the French New Wave movement, then at its height. He tried to use this new style in a short movie he was working on but was forbidden to finish it.

He also felt condemned to make propaganda movies forever, as the production system had become highly bureaucratic and political. In addition, the continuing executions of enemies of the revolution shocked him. In 1961, Almendros undertook his third exile, this time from Castro.

He went to Paris. For three years, he hung around the fringes of the movie world without obtaining any work. Then, close to giving up, he got his chance. He was watching the shooting of a film when the cameraman quarreled with the director and quit on the spot. Almendros told them he was a cameraman, so they tried him for the rest of that day. When they saw his work, they let him stay on. One job led to another as he became increasingly renowned. His accomplishments in France led to his being asked to work on major movie productions in the United States. He called this his "second U.S. career."

Almendros's photography mastery was apparent in both his black-and-white and color work. In France, he was sought out by top directors, working with Truffaut on *The Wild Child* (1970) and *The Green Room* (1978), and with Eric Rohmer on *My Night at Maud's* (1969) and *Claire's Knee* (1971). He won the César award for his photography in Truffaut's *The Last Métro* (1980).

In the United States, he garnered Academy Award nominations for *Kramer vs. Kramer* and *The Blue Lagoon,* both in 1979. He won the Oscar in 1978 for *Days of Heaven,* a story of 19th-century farmers, rendered with unusual beauty. He continued as a director of photography in the 1980s, working on *Sophie's Choice* and *Places in the Heart,* among others.

He also campaigned against the Castro government's human-rights violations, particularly the violent persecution of homosexuals. Many intellectuals refused to recognize these abuses because of the Castro government's progress in other fields, such as health care and education.

Almendros did his campaigning through the medium he knew best: movies. In the 1980s, he directed documentaries on the subject, *Improper Conduct* and *Nobody Listened* (each one made in collaboration with an associate). These documentaries won interest, awards, and acclaim in their own right. He died in 1992.

Further Reading

Almendros, Néstor. *A Man with a Camera.* New York: Farrar, Straus & Giroux, 1984.

✏ Alomar, Roberto (1968–) *baseball player*

Roberto Alomar emerged in the 1990s as one of the most outstanding Hispanic baseball players at a time when Latino ballplayers were becoming ever more dominant in the United States. He came to be regarded as a controversial figure because of some aspects of his personality—but was also recognized as absolutely brilliant when playing at his best. A second baseman, Alomar is "so good it's frightening," declared Jackie Moore, the coach of the Cincinnati Reds.

His natural talent for the game turned out to be both an advantage and a disadvantage. The advantage is clear—thanks to his gifts, it is generally agreed that no list of the greatest second basemen of all time is complete without his name on it. But the disadvantage is that he had to convince others that he would not rely on his innate capacity alone in order to dazzle. He needed to show that he was also ready to train hard and cooperate with his fellow players to achieve genuine teamwork.

On February 5, 1968, Roberto was born in Salinas, Puerto Rico, to Sandy and María Alomar, who already had a two-year-old son, Sandy Jr., also destined to become a baseball player. Sandy Sr. himself was in the major leagues (he played for the Milwaukee Braves, New York Mets, California Angels, and Texas Rangers). His firstborn son did not think of baseball as his first career choice, and María did nothing to encourage her children to join the sport, being familiar with the difficulties it poses to those who wish to really stand out in it—not to mention how long it keeps them away from their wives as they go on the road.

Little Roberto, on the other hand, unlike his elder brother, never hesitated: baseball was his life. Roberto reached the minor leagues as a teenager, being signed by the San Diego Padres organization in 1985—and so were both Sandy Jr. and Sandy Sr., the latter as coach to his two up-and-coming children. Roberto immediately stood out more than his older sibling, batting .295, .346, and .316 as a switch-hitter in his first three years—including, in 1987, the hit that won the Texas League game for Wichita, the brothers' team in the league at that time. In 1988 both brothers were admitted to the major leagues, although the following year Sandy moved from the Padres to the Cleveland Indians.

Roberto Alomar established himself as a baseman specializing in a spectacular diving catch, including one in the 1993 World Series which is ranked with the most sensational in baseball history. By that time Alomar was playing with the Toronto Blue Jays, to which he had been traded in 1990, and which thanks to him reached the World Series for the first time, in 1992, and won it, which no non-U.S. team had ever done before.

Then, in 1993, when Alomar played in the All-Star Game for the fourth consecutive time and hit .480 in the World Series, he ensured that his team did

it again, making the Blue Jays only the second team ever to win the World Series two years in a row. (The New York Yankees won in 1977 and 1978.)

In 1995 Alomar switched to the Baltimore Orioles. In 1996, in a game against his old team, the Toronto Blue Jays, Alomar did something that would follow him for the rest of his career. In an argument with an umpire with whom he had seldom gotten along well in the past he disgustedly spat in the man's face, and was then thrown out of the game.

Contrition and amends afterward, and the umpire's acceptance of Alomar's apology, were not enough to erase the public memory of the episode. Also, even though in 1997 he helped the Orioles reach the American League Championship Series for the second consecutive year (during which he played against his brother), and in 1998 he was named Most-Valuable Player of the All-Star Game, he began to be increasingly criticized for an alleged lack of team spirit. It was charged that Alomar only played at his best when his teammates were also doing well, and lost his edge when his team did the same, instead of trying to rally it again.

But in 1999, when he switched to the Cleveland Indians—and thus found himself playing on the same team as his brother, Sandy—Alomar put in great performances that set career highs in on-base percentage, slugging percentage, runs, walks, homers (24), and RBI (120).

Further Reading
Paré, Michael A. *Sports Stars.* Detroit: UXL, 1998.

⁍ Alvarez, Everett, Jr. (1937–) *soldier*
Everett Alvarez Jr., a navy pilot, displayed exceptional endurance and mettle during eight-and-a-half years as a prisoner of war (POW) during the Vietnam War. He earned the Distinguished Flying Cross, two Purple Hearts, and two Legions of Merit. Afterward, he held high-ranking public-service jobs.

The son of working-class Mexican-American parents, Alvarez was born in Salinas, California, on December 23, 1937. He worked his way through high school and college, graduating from the

University of Santa Clara as an electrical engineer in 1960. He then joined the navy.

During Alvarez's jet fighter pilot training, the United States became increasingly involved in the war in Southeast Asia. In 1964, he piloted a fighter plane aboard the aircraft carrier *Constellation.* Just seven months after his marriage, he set off to destroy a North Vietnamese torpedo-boat base.

Some time earlier, the first U.S. POW taken by Communist forces in South Vietnam began the longest captivity in U.S. military history. Alvarez was shot down on his sortie. He was the second U.S. POW of the Vietnam War, the first pilot to be shot down, and the first POW captured in North Vietnam.

Alvarez remained in enemy hands for 3,103 days until 1973 when the United States pulled out of the war and some prisoners were released. Put through terrible conditions, Alvarez endured gallantly and was later praised for having put concern for others before concern for himself.

His wife waited for him for six years before getting a divorce and remarrying. Alvarez found it in him to understand and forgive her, and soon he too remarried.

He remained a navy pilot until 1980, continuing to be widely acclaimed for his exemplary strength of character as a prisoner of war. On his homecoming to Santa Clara, California, 100,000 people assembled for a parade in his honor.

His experiences led him to write two books, *Chained Eagle* and, as coauthor, *Code of Conduct.* He did not coast on his celebrity, however. He went back to school and earned a law degree from George Washington University.

After leaving the navy, he entered public service. He was appointed deputy director of the Peace Corps and then spent four years as deputy administrator of the U.S. Veterans Administration. Later, he served as vice president for government services at the Hospital Corporation of America. Then in 1987 he became president of a private company in Falls Church, Virginia.

That same year, Alvarez was one of the most enthusiastically received guests at a Library of Congress ceremony to honor Hispanic Americans in the armed forces. This was the first event of its kind to honor Hispanics specifically.

Further Reading

Alvarez, Everett Jr. *Chained Eagle.* New York: Donald I. Fine, 1991.

Alvarez, Everett Jr., and Samuel A. Schreiner. *Code of Conduct.* New York: Donald I. Fine, 1991.

Martínez, Al. *Rising Voices: Profiles of Hispano-American Lives.* New York: New American Library, 1974.

❦ Alvarez, Julia (1950–) *writer*

Julia Alvarez is an outstanding novelist and poet specializing in the depiction of the uprooted lives of Hispanic immigrants in the United States. In her work she makes use of her own experiences and of the sophisticated narrative devices of contemporary fiction.

(The Álvarezes in this book are not related.)

Her parents, both from the Dominican Republic, met in the United States, and Julia was born in New York City on March 27, 1950. Her mother's father was the Dominican cultural attaché at the United Nations in New York, so her mother's family was closely attuned to U.S. life. Her father, having been involved in agitation against the Dominican dictator Rafael Trujillo, had had to escape the country. But when Julia was only three weeks old, her father obtained a pardon and took his family back to the Dominican Republic, where she lived with her parents and three sisters (one older, two younger), until the age of 10. Life unfolded in her maternal grandparents' large family compound, and Julia found herself in a complex web of social relationships. Her family was respected in their community because they were rich and powerful. But within the family, her grandmother snobbishly harped on the fact that her son-in-law, Julia's father, was not as rich as the others were, and at the same time her cousins tended to stand in awe of Julia because she had been born in the United States. She was repeatedly asked to tell others what she "remembered" about the United States, and what she didn't know she made up: once, she told her cousins that snow comes in several colors.

By 1960, her father had become deeply involved in new plots against Trujillo. He was tipped off that he was about to be arrested, and once again fled the country with his wife and daughters in tow.

Thus, at the age of 10 Julia found herself back in the United States—and with a painful contrast between her expectations and reality. "When we landed in New York City," she wrote later, "we became spics who spoke English with an accent." More than the shock of finding herself squeezed with her family into a small apartment—after her affluent lifestyle in the Dominican Republic—the discriminatory taunts at school caused her the most pain.

Her liberation came with the discovery of writing, as a result of school assignments. Her own feelings and experiences, and those of her family, supplied the subject matter; the act of putting it all on paper helped her break out of her shell—and the English language provided the medium. "That was where I landed when we left the Dominican Republic," she has stated, "not in the United States but in the English language."

After studying at Connecticut College (and walking away with its poetry award) she earned undergraduate and graduate degrees in literature and writing from Middlebury College in Vermont and Syracuse University in New York, respectively. Alvarez would eventually settle in Middlebury, but not before a long period of traveling.

The Kentucky Arts Commission gave her the post of traveling poet-in-residence and she became what she calls "a migrant poet," teaching and talking at local communities in Kentucky, Delaware, and North Carolina. Once, she recalled, people misunderstood the word "poetry" and "thought I had come to do something with poultry."

Alvarez then taught English and writing at universities in Massachusetts, Vermont, Washington, D.C., and Illinois, before finally growing roots in Middlebury. Along the way she picked up grants from the National Endowment for the Arts, the Ingram Merrill Foundation and the Phillips Andover Academy, a PEN Oakland/Josephine Miles Award for excellence in multicultural literature, a Third Woman Press Award for narrative, and a notable book designation from the American Library Association (for *How the Garcia Girls Lost Their Accents,* 1991).

Her first published books were works of poetry, including *The Housekeeping Book* (1982), *Homecoming* (1984) and the bilingual *The Other Side/El otro lado* (1995). Later she concentrated more on novels. She earned wide recognition and several awards for her first, *How the Garcia Girls Lost Their Accents,* about four sisters who have come to the United States from the Dominican Republic. Alvarez pieces together their lives through a series of stories in which time flows backward. The stories begin with the four sisters as culturally assimilated adults in the present, and follows them back to their infancy abroad. Echoing general praise, one reviewer found "an authenticity and sense of urgency seldom found elsewhere" in Alvarez's description of the immigrant experience.

Alvarez's next novel was *In the Time of the Butterflies* (1994), a fictionalized account of the real-life murder of three sisters, political opponents of Trujillo, on the dictator's orders in 1960. *Yo!* (1997) is another novel about four sisters, the second of whom, Yolanda, is a novelist; Yolanda's portrait is assembled through her separate descriptions by other people in her life. ("Yo" is an interjection in slangy English, is Yolanda's nickname, and also means "I" in Spanish).

Something to Declare (1998) is a set of 24 essays in which Alvarez describes herself, her past, and her personality, again as a way to take the reader into the world of the immigrant who can never feel entirely at home anywhere.

Further Reading

Contemporary Authors. Detroit: Gale Research, 1999.

Novas, Himilce. *The Hispanic Hundred.* New York: Citadel Press, 1995.

Telgen, Diane, and Jim Kamp. *Notable Hispanic American Women.* Detroit: Gale Research, 1998.

 **Álvarez, Luis Walter** (1911–1988)
scientist

Luis Alvarez was one of the United States' leading physicists. A wizard within this most complex field, he won the Nobel Prize in 1968. He also received the Collier Trophy, the Scott Medal, the Einstein Medal, and the National Medal of Science.

Though his specialty was elementary particles (the discovery and study of the components of atoms), he also worked in many other areas, such as the development of the atom bomb, the physics of eyesight, and radar landing systems for airplanes.

Luis Alvarez (not related to Everett ALVAREZ Jr.) was born in San Francisco, California, on June 13, 1911, the son and grandson of medical doctors. The family traveled extensively. His father's father had emigrated from Spain to Cuba, then went to the United States, and studied medicine in California. Initially, he practiced in a village in Hawaii, which at that time was still an independent kingdom.

His son Walter, Luis's father, also studied medicine in California and upon graduation practiced in a mining town in Mexico. Walter Alvarez later became a respected researcher at the prestigious Mayo Clinic in Minnesota. Upon retirement, he took up writing newspaper columns on medical matters and was known as "America's family doctor." Luis's mother, Harriet Smyth, was the daughter of Irish missionaries and had grown up in China.

By the age of four, Luis, according to his father, had already shown a fascination with machinery. The family at that time was living in San Francisco and took him to see the Pan-American Exposition of 1915. At the exposition, his father caught the first glimpses of Luis's future.

When the family moved to Rochester, Minnesota, Walter Alvarez began to work at the Mayo Clinic there.

Luis grew up watching his father's experiments on the workings of stomachs and intestines. He found the medical part of the tests totally uninteresting, but the measuring instruments and other hardware cast a spell on him. During his high school years, he spent the summers working for, and learning from, the Mayo Clinic's machinists, who worked on the clinic's instruments.

Alvarez went to the University of Chicago, first studying chemistry and then physics. He received his Ph.D. from there in 1936 and then became a professor (later, a professor emeritus) at the University of California at Berkeley.

At Berkeley, he accomplished a large portion of his life's work, mainly at the Lawrence Radiation Laboratory, one of the world's top physics research cen-

ters. But he also did research at the Massachusetts Institute of Technology and at the Los Alamos Scientific Laboratory in New Mexico, participating in the development of the atom bomb there during World War II.

Some physicists prefer to do only theoretical work, employing nothing more than pen and paper; others are happiest among gadgetry, conducting complicated and precise experimental work. Luis Alvarez belonged to the latter group. With his team, he invented and developed machines, called bubble chambers, to study atomic particles by tracking their paths through liquid hydrogen. Equally important, Alvarez and his team created still other machines to record and interpret the information revealed by the liquid hydrogen bubble chambers.

It was this work in particle physics that earned Alvarez his Nobel Prize. Yet, he generously credited his fellow technicians because he believed that the teamwork devoted to nuts-and-bolts details is essential in his line of research. He gently scorned the scientific reports of an earlier generation, which were, as he put it, "signed by a single physicist that ended with a paragraph saying, 'I wish to thank Mr. . . . , who built the apparatus and took much of the data.'"

While working on the Manhattan Project, which developed the atomic bomb during World War II, Alvarez witnessed the world's first atomic explosion in New Mexico.

He flew over the city of Hiroshima on an observation plane after the bomb had been used on a city for the first time. He wrote then, in a letter for his four-year-old son to read when he was older: "What regrets I have about being a party to killing and maiming thousands of Japanese civilians this morning are tempered with the hope that this terrible weapon we have created may bring the countries of the world together and prevent future wars."

Alfred Nobel thought that his invention of high explosives would have this effect, by making wars too terrible, but unfortunately it had just the opposite reaction. Alvarez wrote: "Our new destructive force is so many thousands of times worse that it may realize Nobel's dream."

Alvarez died in 1988.

Further Reading

Alvarez, Luis Walter. *Alvarez—Adventures of a Physicist.* New York: Basic Books, 1987.

Daintith, John, Sarah Mitchell, and Elizabeth Toothhill. *Biographical Encyclopedia of Scientists.* New York: Facts On File, 1981.

Oleksy, Walter. *Hispanic-American Scientists.* New York: Facts On File, 1998.

Weber, Robert L. *Pioneers of Science: Nobel Prize Winners in Physics.* New York: American Institute of Physics, 1980.

Alvarez de Pineda, Alonso

(unknown–1520) *explorer*

Alonso (or Alonzo) Alvarez de Pineda is credited by Europeans with the discovery of the Mississippi River. He also proved to Europe that Florida was not an island and that between it and Mexico there lay not a waterway to the Pacific Ocean but a continent.

No information is known about Alvarez de Pineda's birth or early life. His recorded passage through history lasted less than two years and ended abruptly in 1520 at the hands of Mexican Indians. They killed him and are believed to have eaten him. Yet, his exploration was crucial to completing the European understanding of the North American coast.

Alvarez de Pineda was a lieutenant to Francisco de Garay, who arrived in America with Christopher Columbus and became governor of Spanish-ruled Jamaica. In early 1519, Garay sent Alvarez de Pineda north from Jamaica with a fleet of either three or four ships and almost 300 men.

Alvarez de Pineda's task was to explore the span between Florida and Mexico. Florida had been discovered by Juan PONCE DE LEÓN six years earlier and was believed to be an island. Mexico was Ponce de León's other discovery, and Hernán Cortés was planning to conquer it.

Alvarez de Pineda was to search for a strait between Florida and Mexico that would lead to the Pacific, which had been discovered at the same time by Vasco Núñez de Balboa. Alvarez de Pineda was to see also what wealth could be obtained from the land.

His first discovery was that any wealth that might be there would be hard to find and obtain. In Florida, he made his first landfall, which foreshadowed his last: he and his men were fiercely attacked by the local Indians. They took to their ships again and sailed along the coast.

Their expedition proved that the coastline was continuous, and though Alvarez de Pineda and most of his men eventually perished, they produced a fairly accurate map of the Gulf of Mexico. Alvarez de Pineda thus demonstrated that he was not merely a plunderer but an observant geographer.

In mid-trip, on June 2, 1519, the expedition discovered the mouth of a huge river. This waterway poured so much water into the gulf that the landmass containing it had to be very substantial. Because the discovery was made on the day of a religious feast, that of the Holy Spirit, Alvarez de Pineda named it the Río del Espíritu Santo—River of the Holy Spirit. This name was later changed to the Indian name, the Mississippi, Father of Waters.

Alvarez de Pineda's expedition took place 20 years before that of Hernando DE SOTO, who is sometimes mistakenly considered the first European to see the Mississippi.

The end for Alvarez de Pineda came on the coast of Mexico in early 1520, near the place where the city of Tampico now stands. Although the Indians they encountered there are believed to have been initially friendly, the Spaniards were nonetheless routed in a battle with them. The historical record is unclear; Alvarez de Pineda may have been killed fighting, or he may have been taken prisoner, in which case he would likely have been sacrificed in ceremonies of ritual cannibalism. What is certain is that only 60 men from his group survived, escaping in the one ship that Indians did not burn.

Further Reading

Bohlander, Richard E., ed. *World Explorers and Discoverers.* New York: Macmillan, 1992.

Morison, Samuel Eliot. *The European Discovery of America.* Vol. 2, *The Southern Voyages.* New York: Oxford University Press, 1974.

Waldman, Carl, and Alan Wexler. *Who Was Who in World Exploration.* New York: Facts On File, 1992.

Alvariño de Leira, Ángeles (Ángeles Alvariño) (1916–   ) *scientist*

Angeles Alvariño de Leira, whose maiden name is Angeles Alvariño, is a renowned scientist who discovered numerous new species of animals in her field of study. Her academic brilliance came into evidence early, and her work has earned widespread recognition both in the United States and abroad.

Alvariño was born in the city of El Ferrol, Spain, on October 3, 1916. She graduated with top honors—summa cum laude—from the University of Santiago de Compostela in 1933, when she was 17.

Two doctoral degrees would follow, but before she received them, her working career was already in full swing. Other events intervened as well—the devastating civil war in her native Spain, her marriage, and her move to the United States. Nevertheless, she earned the two doctorates from the University of Madrid, in chemistry and sciences, in 1951 and 1967, respectively, the latter again summa cum laude. She moved back and forth between Spain and the United States.

Alvariño de Leira first came to the United States in 1957 and became a U.S. citizen nine years later. She was both a researcher and a professor at various institutions in Spain, including the Spanish Institute of Oceanography, and worked in oceanography and biology (particularly histology, the study of living tissues). Then Alvariño de Leira began her U.S. career (1958) at the Scripps Institute of Oceanography at the University of California in La Jolla.

La Jolla, with its National Marine Fisheries Service, and San Diego became the sites of most of her scientific work and teaching. She achieved the status of emeritus scientist at the fisheries center in 1987. She was also a visiting professor at universities in Mexico, Britain, Brazil, and Venezuela. She earned fellowships and research grants from the Fulbright program (1956–57), the National Science Foundation (1961–69), the British Council, the U.S. Navy, and UNESCO.

Alvariño de Leira has discovered 22 new marine species. She has also done major research in ocean dynamics and in the biological environment of fish spawning grounds. The numerous scientific organizations to which she belongs include the Hispano-American Association of Researchers on Marine Sciences.

Further Reading
Who's Who in America. New Providence, N.J.: Reed Reference, 1994.

Anaya, Rudolfo A. (Rudolfo Alfonso Anaya) (1937–   ) *writer*

Rudolfo A. Anaya was, for decades, the best-known Hispanic novelist in the United States. He had a small-town upbringing and has been a lifelong resident of New Mexico. But he has also traveled as far afield as China. He writes about individuals and communities far removed, geographically and mentally, from skyscrapers and big-city life. His characters gain inner strength when they listen to the voice of the land and its myths. This message has earned him bestseller status and numerous honors and awards.

Anaya was born on October 30, 1937, in the village of Pastura, New Mexico. He was raised in the town of Santa Rosa and attended high school in Albuquerque. A serious childhood accident injured his spine, forcing him to remain a long period in a hospital in the town of Truth or Consequences, New Mexico.

After beginning business studies, Anaya switched to literature, graduating in 1963 from the University of New Mexico in Albuquerque. He added a master's degree in 1968 and began to teach English in Albuquerque public schools.

His interest in counseling students led him to add a master's degree in guidance and counseling in 1972. He then worked as director of counseling at the University of Albuquerque for two years.

Returning to the University of New Mexico, he taught creative writing and English. He now heads that university's creative writing program.

His writing, which began in childhood, took shape in a powerful first novel, *Bless Me, Ultima* (1972), which remains his most widely read and praised work; it sold 200,000 copies and was the first novel in what Anaya called his New Mexico Trilogy, which continued with *Heart of Aztlán* (1976) and *Tortuga* (1979).

Aztlán is a mystical area in northern Mexico or the southwestern United States—the cradle of the Aztec Indians, according to myth. Anaya is interested in emphasizing the ancient roots of his native region. This area has been continuously inhabited for 10,000 years, first by Indians and more recently by Spanish-speaking and then English-speaking Europeans and their descendants.

In *Bless Me, Ultima,* a boy matures with the help of an elderly *curandera,* or folk-medicine healer, called Ultima—a name that means "the last one." In *The Heart of Aztlán,* a family has a hard time adjusting to its move from a village to Albuquerque, but the head of the family eventually finds his way again with the guidance of a blind poet, Crispín, whose role is similar to that of Ultima. In *Tortuga,* a boy in the hospital, encased in a plaster cast—a strongly autobiographical element—gains wisdom with the participation of a paralytic mute called Salomón.

Salomón, Ultima, and Crispín play roles similar to those of indigenous shamans, or medicine men. Shamans are believed to heal, in part, through the restoration of harmony and order, acting within a long flow of legend and myth. This is a role that Rudolfo Anaya also claims for himself and others like him, as storytellers for the community.

Other works by Anaya include *The Legend of La Llorona* (1984), *Lord of the Dawn: The Legend of Quetzalcoatl* (1987), *Albuquerque* (1992) and more recently, *Conversations With Rudolfo Anaya, Farolitos For Abuelo* (both 1998), *My Land Sings: Stories From the Rio Grande, Shaman Winter* (both 1999), and *An Elegy on the Death of César Chávez* (2000). He has written plays and has edited such anthologies as *Cuentos Chicanos* (*Chicano Stories,* 1980).

The list of Anaya's prizes and honors includes the President's National Salute to American Poets and Writers, Governor of New Mexico's Public Service Award, Governor's Award for Excellence and Achievement in Literature, Mesa Chicano Literary Award, National Endowment for the Arts Creative Writing Fellowship, Before Columbus Foundation's American Book Award, and W.K. Kellogg Foundation Fellowship.

Further Reading

Chávez, John R. *The Lost Land: The Chicano Image of the Southwest.* Albuquerque: University of New Mexico Press, 1984.

Dick, Bruce, and Silvio Sirias. *Conversations with Rudolfo Anaya.* Jackson: University Press of Mississippi, 1998.

Lomelí, Francisco A., and Carl L. Shirley, eds. *Dictionary of Literary Biography: Chicano Writers, First Series.* Detroit: Gale Research, Inc., 1989.

Trujillo-González, César A., ed. *Rudolfo A. Anaya: Focus on Criticism.* Wellesley Hills, Mass.: Massachusetts Bay Press, 1989.

✎ Anthony, Marc (Marco Antonio Muñiz)
(1968–) *singer*

Marc Anthony's "pure, radiant voice is like drawing the curtains back from a picture window and letting in the summer light," wrote *Time* magazine in 1999, calling him "one of the finest male vocalists recording today." Not to be outdone, the *New York Times* spoke of his "sweet, supple tenor (voice) with a touch of a sob . . . which never loses its gentleness even at full power. Sometimes he sustains a note to superhuman length, as if he's defying time and gravity." *Interview* magazine noted that he reminds many people of "a young Sinatra."

Marco Antonio Muñiz was born in New York City on September 16, 1968. His father, Puerto Rico–born like his mother, was a musician who played traditional Puerto Rican *jíbaro* music on a guitar. He taught his son music, but young Marco Antonio initially was less interested in "old-fashioned" Latin sounds than in such other influences as Air Supply, Billy Joel, and José FELICIANO. He started out singing in English, doing jingles from the age of 12 after a producer heard him and a sister singing a Disney theme. Doing background vocals led to club and dance music and on to lead singing gigs.

His first album, *When the Night Is Over* (1991), was in English. Then Marc Anthony did a cultural crossover—in the opposite direction from the one dreamed of by most Latino performers. He began to value his roots and switched to Spanish (a skill he needed to perfect) and to salsa music, which he had disdained as a child.

The results, his albums *Otra nota* (Another Note, 1992) and *Todo a su tiempo* (All in Due Course, 1995), tended to please the critics on the

Marc Anthony *(Courtesy of Sony Records)*

strength of his singing rather than on the nature of the arrangements. This was because Anthony refused to abide wholly by the traditions of the music, and tinged it with his own pop-romantic background. To those who told him he was "doing it all wrong," he replied that he was bringing his own style to the material.

The public loved it. *Todo a su tiempo* was the first salsa album to be certified gold and eventually went quadruple platinum. His album *Contra la corriente* (Against the Current, 1997) would smash into the *Billboard* Latin 50 chart in the number-one slot, where no other salsa album had ever been in its first week.

Marc Anthony obtained the *Billboard* award as Best New Artist of the Year in 1994. *Ride on the Rhythm,* a single from *When the Night Is Over,* reached the number-one slot on the *Billboard* dance chart. He was the first Latin singer to sell out Madison Square Garden. In 1999, he won a Grammy Award for best tropical Latin performance.

Also in 1999, he returned to English for his album *Marc Anthony,* which brought him mainstream attention in the United States.

Marc Anthony has also written songs of his own, including his early *Boy, I've Been Told,* which became a Top 40 success. He has appeared in a handful of movies, though not—initially, at least—in major productions or big hits.

He has modestly told one magazine interviewer that the only reason for being compared to Frank Sinatra is "being skinny and young and a singer who makes movies." Only half agreeing, another wrote that it was because "like [Sinatra], Anthony's giant voice astonishes as it booms from a baby-faced wisp of a guy who looks half his age and appears to need a good hearty meal."

Anthony appeared in a Broadway musical, *The Capeman* (1998), with music by Paul Simon, whose lead character appears both as a 16-year-old (played and sung by Marc Anthony, then aged 29) and as an older man (this part being taken over by Rubén BLADES). The show was not a box office success, but it added to Anthony's renown.

Marc Anthony makes a point of saluting the Puerto Rican flag in his live shows as a mark of pride in his heritage.

Further Reading

Contemporary Musicians. Detroit: Gale Research, 1997.
"Marc Anthony." Columbia Records. Available online.
    URL: http://www.marcanthonyonline.com. Downloaded October 10, 2000.

Aparicio, Luis (1934–) *baseball player*

A legendary shortstop, Luis Aparicio, a Venezuelan, made the infield between second and third base almost uniquely his own on U.S. baseball diamonds. His career spanned 17 years, from 1956 to 1973.

Luis Ernesto Montiel Aparicio was born on April 29, 1934, in the city of Maracaibo in Venezuela. In Venezuela, baseball is played everywhere—in playgrounds and vacant lots. It dominates in the way that soccer (*fútbol*) does in other South American countries.

With his talent, Aparicio made his way to professional baseball teams in the United States to become American League Rookie of the Year in 1956.

Aparicio was infielder for the Chicago White Sox, the team with which he is most closely associated. He played for the White Sox from 1956 to 1962 and again from 1968 to 1970. He fielded for the Baltimore Orioles from 1963 to 1967 and for the Boston Red Sox from 1971 to 1973.

His career, during which he stole a near-record 506 bases, never experienced a serious dip. He was All-Star Team shortstop in 1964, 1966, 1968, 1970, and 1972; he won the Gold Glove as best American League fielding shortstop in 1958 through 1962 and in 1964, 1966, 1968, and 1970.

Aparicio was inducted into the National Baseball Hall of Fame in 1984. The records he set for games, double plays, and assists, and his American League record for putouts, stood for decades.

Further Reading

Luis Aparicio Statistics. Baseball-Reference.com. Available online. URL: http://www.baseball-reference.com/a/aparilu01.shtml. Downloaded October 10, 2000.

Shatzkin, Mike, ed. *The Ballplayers.* New York: Arbor House, 1990.

❦ Apodaca, Jerry (1934–) *government official*

In 1974, Jerry Apodaca became the first Hispanic governor of the state of New Mexico in more than half a century. In addition to politics, he has also won recognition in education and sports.

The Apodaca family had lived in the town of Las Cruces, New Mexico, for more than 100 years by the time Jerry Apodaca was born there on October 3, 1934. A younger brother, Rudy, is a New Mexico state court of appeals judge.

Apodaca went to the University of New Mexico in Albuquerque, where he shone as a football halfback. With his degree in education, he began his career as a teacher of history and as a sports coach. Then, after three years, he went back to his hometown and launched a series of business ventures.

Six years later, he entered politics and was elected New Mexico state senator, serving from 1967 to 1974. He then decided to run for governor. In the meantime, he had been elected chairman of the Democratic caucus in the state senate and was later the state's chairman of the Democratic Party. He was also a delegate to the party's national convention in 1968.

In his race for the governorship, Apodaca benefited from a rising, nationwide tide of Hispanic affirmation. The civil rights movements of the 1960s led an increasing number of Hispanics to run for office, and they were beginning to be elected. The same year that Apodaca ran for governor, another Mexican American won a state governorship, Raúl Castro of Arizona (no connection to Raúl Castro, the armed forces minister of Cuba). But Apodaca also owed his election to his own strengths. A supporter of liberal causes, he won the backing of Hispanic activists and of labor unions, and he was an effective, forceful campaigner.

During his governorship, Apodaca showed particular interest in energy and education. Under his leadership, the state approved its biggest education budget ever. He received an award for Distinguished Service to Higher Education, as well as honorary doctorates from universities not only in New Mexico but also in Texas.

When the governors of western states set up an energy-policy agency, they chose Apodaca to be its chairman. He was also cochairman of the Democratic Party's national convention in 1976.

Under the constitution of New Mexico, Apodaca was not eligible to run for a second gubernatorial term, so when his term ended, President Jimmy Carter appointed him chairman of the President's Council on Physical Fitness and Sports.

In the early 1980s, Apodaca ran for the U.S. Senate and lost. By that time, he had returned to earlier interests and held leadership positions in a number of business and sports organizations, including the presidency of the Hispanic Association for Corporate Responsibility. He still participates in the state Democratic Party.

Further Reading

Meier, Matt S. *Mexican American Biographies.* Westport, Conn.: Greenwood Publishing Group, 1988.

Who's Who in American Politics. New Providence, N.J.: R.R. Bowker, 1992–93.

Archuleta, Diego (1814–1884) *soldier, government official*

Diego Archuleta played a significant historical role in a period that saw the signing of the Treaty of Guadalupe Hidalgo (1848). Under this treaty, approximately half of Mexico was gained by the United States.

Archuleta's checkered career still generates debate today because at different times he was on diverse sides of the same issues. In this way, his career reflects those turbulent times. In Archuleta's day, northern Mexicans were being asked to switch their allegiance to the United States, a situation complicated by overlapping conflicts that pitted Texas against New Mexico, rich landowners against poor settlers, and Indians against whites.

Archuleta was classified as a *rico,* one of the "wealthy people," in the New Mexico area of Mexico where his family had an established position and where he was born in 1814.

He was educated in the Mexican city of Durango. However, he was back home in 1841 when the Texas Republic sent an armed expedition into New Mexico, causing widespread alarm. The armed expedition eventually surrendered to Governor Manuel Armijo.

The area had been receiving increasing numbers of Anglo (English-speaking) settlers. Trade with the Anglos was also increasing. This whole part of Mexico lay on the border of the United States, a new power that was quickly expanding economically and politically. Because of its location, this part of Mexico had been disputed for years.

Inhabitants were divided about the matter. Some felt little allegiance to the faraway authorities in Mexico City, and prosperity seemed to lie with the United States. Others strongly opposed every form of Anglo encroachment into Mexican lands. Archuleta noted that, after the failed Texan incursion into New Mexico, smaller armed raids continued in succeeding years.

He first became a congressman for New Mexico and served in Mexico City from 1843 to 1845. Then he again returned to his home province. By this time, he had become a military officer with the rank of colonel and was second in command only to New Mexico Governor Armijo when war broke out between the United States and Mexico in 1846.

A U.S. military occupation of New Mexico, under Colonel Stephen Kearny, advanced almost unresisted all the way to the capital, Santa Fe. It was alleged, though not proven, that Governor Armijo was bribed to give up without a fight.

Colonel Archuleta soon became one of the leaders of a rebellion in Taos against the new rulers. Within two months of arrival, Kearny had announced that the United States intended to keep the province as a permanent possession. Nevertheless, the Mexican colonel's motives are in dispute. Some historians speak of patriotism; others say Archuleta acted out of resentment at not being given a post in the new U.S. administration.

The plotters in Taos intended to assassinate the new U.S. governor, Charles Bent, and throw all U.S. forces out of the territory, but individuals who were spying for Bent revealed the conspiracy, and some of the participants were arrested. Archuleta himself managed to escape to lands that were still in Mexican hands.

There is disagreement over whether Archuleta was an instigator of a second uprising in Taos against the U.S. takeover. Early in 1847, with the war between the United States and Mexico still in full swing, the resistance, formed mainly by Pueblo Indians and Mexican peasants, went on the attack. They killed and scalped Governor Bent.

It is clear that Archuleta was not present during this new rebellion, and so he avoided being one of those hanged afterwards because of their participation.

After the war ended, Archuleta returned to New Mexico, swearing allegiance to the United States of America and entering the service of the newly expanded country. He was elected to the territory's assembly and worked in that body before being appointed Indian agent to the Ute and Apache nations in 1857.

As an assembly member, Archuleta had not only joined the system, but he was also among those who shaped the system by drafting legislation.

During the U.S. Civil War, Archuleta became a member of the New Mexico militia, attaining the rank of brigadier general. He then received an appointment from President Abraham Lincoln and served a second stint as an Indian agent.

With the Civil War over, Archuleta was reelected to the territorial legislature and served for the remainder of his life. He died in 1884.

Further Reading

Acuña, Rodolfo. *Occupied America: A History of Chicanos.* 3rd edition. New York: HarperCollins, 1988.

Meier, Matt S., and Feliciano Ribera. *Mexican Americans/American Mexicans: From Conquistadors to Chicanos.* Revised edition. New York: Hill and Wang, 1993.

✄ Arnaz, Desi (Desiderio Alberto Arnaz y de Acha III) (1917–1986) *actor*

Desi Arnaz was one of the great popularizers of Latin music in the United States. For years, he and his wife, Lucille Ball, were highly popular TV comedians. Through television, Arnaz introduced U.S. mass audiences to a new, more positive image of Hispanics.

The actor Desiderio Alberto Arnaz y de Acha III was born on March 2, 1917, in Santiago, Cuba, where his father had been city mayor. When he was 16 years old, he and his mother fled a revolution in Cuba and came to the United States.

Arnaz arrived as the United States was experiencing a wave of interest in Latin dance music. At that time, most English-speaking U.S. citizens first came into contact with something Hispanic through music. First it was the tango from Argentina and then a long succession of easier-to-dance rhythms from the Caribbean and Brazil—mainly the rumba, the conga, the mambo, the samba, the cha-cha, the bossa nova, and salsa. In addition to these rhythms there were some Mexican hits. Latin American music would in time fuse with jazz and ultimately influence all U.S. pop music. During the 1930s, the predominant beat was the rumba.

After coming to the United States in 1933, Arnaz moved to Cleveland. There, he joined the band of one of the biggest names in the Latin dance business, Xavier CUGAT. He toured with Cugat, but within a few months, he left to form his own group in Miami Beach.

As a bandleader, Desi Arnaz was most closely identified with the conga, which many dancers found particularly infectious as well as simple. The music invited them to form long lines that snaked around the floor, kicking out a leg at every fourth step. Arnaz maintained that he was the person who first brought this Cuban dance to the United States during the New Year celebrations of 1938, picking the conga because the non-Hispanic members of his band were unable to handle more complex rhythms. Historians have proven that the conga had already appeared in the United States by that time. Nevertheless, Arnaz undoubtedly gave this dance wide popularity.

By 1939, when his band was appearing in a New York nightclub called La Conga, he was invited to act and sing on Broadway, in *Too Many Girls,* a musical play by the famous team of Richard Rodgers and Lorenz Hart.

In 1940 *Too Many Girls* was made into a movie with Arnaz in a leading role. In one big production number, he sang with columns of fire around him while girls danced beneath him. His costar in the film was Lucille Ball. They fell in love and married the same year.

In 1941, Arnaz was the sole Hispanic chosen by Hollywood to go to Mexico on a promotional friendship tour. Arnaz's fellow travelers were Clark Gable, Mickey Rooney, James Cagney, Robert Taylor, and other top stars in motion pictures. The trip was made because this was a crucial period in U.S. relations with Latin American countries. The United States was on a collision course with Nazi Germany and had increased its interest in the countries of the Western Hemisphere. Its aim was to try to keep the governments of those countries from siding with the Nazis.

U.S. industries, meanwhile—Hollywood's movie industry among them—wanted to increase their sales in Latin America because the war had made it impossible to sell in Europe.

Desi Arnaz, however, noticed that the visiting actors were not enthusiastically welcomed in Mexico where all this friendliness was seen as sudden and rather strange. Many Mexicans had been offended by Hollywood in 1934 during the filming in Mexico of a U.S. movie with a Mexican theme, *Viva Villa!*

In the United States, Arnaz's musical and film careers were to continue for decades. He became particularly associated with certain songs, like "Babalú" and "The Coffee Song (They've Got an Awful Lot of Coffee in Brazil)." He appeared in a number of movies, such as *Father Takes a Wife* (1941), *Bataan* (1943), *The Long, Long Trailer* (1954, with Lucille Ball), and—as late as 1982—*The Escape Artist.*

But it was in television that Desi Arnaz made his biggest mark. He was far from the most famous Hispanic in show business in the United States (ranking a long way behind such stars as Rita HAYWORTH or Anthony QUINN). Yet, through TV, Arnaz exerted one of the strongest influences ever by a Hispanic showman in the United States because, unlike many others who rose high in the business, it always remained clear to viewers that Arnaz was Hispanic.

In the 1950s, he costarred in the triumphant weekly comedy show *I Love Lucy.* In the show, he played the on-screen husband, Ricky Ricardo, of his off-screen wife, Lucille Ball. Arnaz's role as Ricky Ricardo became crucial to the development of the Hispanic image. In Ricardo, viewers saw the Hispanic as the ordinary fellow next door.

From the beginning of the movies, when Hispanics had been shown at all, they were relegated to one of a small number of categories—generally portrayed as dangerous or exotic or both. For males, the roles were mainly those of ardent and often somewhat sinister lovers; of submissive, downtrodden peasants; or of cruel, although usually also cowardly, bandits (the rural forefathers of today's Hispanic drug-runner roles).

In the 1910s, the movies openly called Mexicans "greasers," even in titles (*Tony the Greaser, The Greaser's Revenge*). Hispanic organizations maintain that, to this day, recognizably Hispanic screen characters tend to fall within a few repetitive types, most of them unfavorable. In *I Love Lucy,* however, Arnaz portrayed someone very different.

Ricky Ricardo was clearly a middle-class person, with the same middle-class values and interests as most of the show's spectators. Also, Desi Arnaz basi-

cally played straight man to Lucille Ball's nutty character. Although both were funny, in this comedy it was the Hispanic who was the more ordinary person of the two.

The show was produced by their own company, Desilu Productions, which became so economically powerful that it controlled the RKO movie studio that had given Desi Arnaz his first screen role and where Lucille Ball, too, had worked.

Arnaz was a charming performer—charm being probably his strongest overall asset as a showman. This charm managed to make audiences accept a thick Hispanic accent as a friendly trait, rather than as a symbol of something alien and disturbing.

Unfortunately, commentators are in agreement that one essential reason why Arnaz was able to achieve so much was that his skin was noticeably white. He was not swarthy like the usual Hispanic stereotypes, whether slick romantic aristocrats or stubbly-faced sons of the soil.

In 1960, Arnaz and Ball divorced, and Arnaz sold his share of Desilu Productions to his ex-wife, but he continued to appear before TV viewers in *I Love Lucy*'s many reruns. Desi Arnaz and Lucille Ball raised a show-business family: Their children, Lucie and Desi Jr., are both actors. Arnaz died in 1986.

Further Reading

Arnaz, Desi. *A Book.* New York: William Morrow, 1976.

Hadley-García, George. *Hispanic Hollywood—The Latins in Motion Pictures.* New York: Citadel Press, 1990.

Roberts, John Storm. *The Latin Tinge—The Impact of Latin American Music in the United States.* Tivoli, N.Y.: Original Music, 1985.

Woll, Allen L. *The Latin Image in American Film.* Los Angeles: UCLA Latin American Center Publications, 1980.

✑ Arrau, Claudio (1903–1991) *pianist*

The Chilean-born Claudio Arrau, who made the United States his home for the last half-century of his life, was one of the great pianists of the century. He was particularly revered in Germany and Austria for his mastery of the music of those countries' major composers, especially Ludwig van Beethoven. Arrau was also recognized for his love of freedom, breaking with Germany because of the Nazis and, decades later, with Chile because of the dictatorship of General Augusto Pinochet.

Arrau was born in the Chilean city of Chillán on February 6, 1903, a child prodigy whose mother was an amateur pianist and his first teacher. Arrau gave his first public recital in the Chilean capital, Santiago, at the age of five, playing the works of Mozart, Beethoven, and Chopin. By the age of seven, in 1910, he had been given a special scholarship by the Chilean government to study music in Germany. He remained there for 11 years.

During those years of study, he gave recitals not only in Germany but also in Britain and Scandinavia, and he appeared with such top orchestras as the Berlin Philharmonic. Before he turned 20, he had won the Liszt Prize twice. Later he would win the Grand Prix International des Artistes.

After his return to his native country in 1921, Arrau embarked on a series of international tours. He played in the United States for the first time in 1924, appearing with the Chicago Symphony and the Boston Symphony orchestras. That same year, he returned to Berlin, having been offered a teaching post at a conservatory there, though he would continue his public recitals.

Claudio Arrau was especially praised for his interpretations of the music of the 19th-century Romantic composers. His style combined great precision with lyrical enthusiasm. In Germany, he was nicknamed the King of the Pianists largely because of his performances and recordings of Beethoven, the composer who launched Romanticism in music.

Yet, Arrau also dazzled listeners when playing the works of earlier composers. Between 1935 and 1936, during a series of 12 concerts in the German capital, he played every one of the pieces composed for keyboard instruments by Baroque musician Johann Sebastian Bach. Also in 1936, in a series of five concerts in Berlin, he played all the keyboard music of composer Wolfgang Amadeus Mozart. Two years later, he played all the piano concertos and sonatas of

Beethoven at concerts in Mexico, repeating the cycle the following year in Chile and in Argentina.

By then, the Nazi regime had hardened in Germany. Arrau left the country and settled in the United States in 1941. Musicians like Arrau tend to spend most of their time traveling around the world. Even when he was in his 80s, Arrau still gave about 80 concerts a year all over the globe. Nevertheless, he regarded New York as his home.

In 1978, in disgust at the right-wing military dictatorship governing Chile, he gave up his Chilean citizenship and became a U.S. citizen the next year. In 1984, after a 17-year absence, Arrau made a triumphant return to Chile to perform recitals there. He was one of his native country's national heroes and had won the Chilean National Arts prize in 1983.

In the 1960s, Arrau made milestone recordings of the Beethoven piano sonatas. He also headed historical research into the first versions of these pieces. He died in 1991 during a trip to Austria.

Further Reading

Horowitz, Joseph. *Arrau on Music and Performance.* Mineola, N.Y.: Dover, 1999.

———. *Conversations with Arrau.* New York: Limelight Editions, 1982.

Arroyo, Martina (1936–) *opera singer* Martina Arroyo is one of the United States' most outstanding sopranos. Her singing has been praised not only for its beauty but for its versatility, as Arroyo finds herself equally at home in Italian opera, in the German operatic repertory, and in modern works.

The daughter of a Spanish-born Puerto Rican immigrant father and an African-American mother from South Carolina, Arroyo was born in New York City on February 2, 1936. She grew up in the Harlem area and is a graduate of Hunter College.

Arroyo sang in church choirs, and soon her voice, though still untrained, attracted attention. She studied singing while still in college. An agent who heard her was so sure that she would become a great success that he offered to represent her almost for free until that success came. However, before

Martina Arroyo *(Cabrera Archive)*

being able to make singing opera a full-time career, she first worked as a high school teacher and as a social worker.

Arroyo first made her mark in 1958 when she debuted at New York's Carnegie Hall, singing in a contemporary opera, Pizzetti's *Murder in the Cathedral.* The following year, she sang for the first time at the Metropolitan Opera in the role of the unseen Celestial Voice in Giuseppe Verdi's *Don Carlos.*

She then turned to secondary roles in operas by Richard Wagner, followed by a European tour during which she sang in opera houses in Austria, Germany, and Switzerland. Arroyo also appeared as a soloist with orchestras in the United States, including the New York Philharmonic.

Arroyo's big break came in 1965 when the Metropolitan Opera asked her to substitute, at very short notice, for Swedish soprano Birgit Nilsson

in Verdi's *Aida.* Her performance was hailed as a triumph.

Now most operatic roles were hers for the choosing, and Martina Arroyo sang many of them. She appeared to enthusiastic applause in the world's major opera houses, including Milan's La Scala, the Paris Opera, London's Covent Garden, the Vienna State Opera, the Rome Opera, the Munich and Berlin operas and Buenos Aires's Teatro Colón. She has also recorded arias and complete operas.

The contemporary German composer Karlheinz Stockhausen chose Arroyo for the world premiere of his cantata *Momenten* (1962), a work for 13 musicians, four choirs, and a soprano. Arroyo has also presented distinguished interpretations of other modern works.

In 1985, Arroyo became a visiting artist at Louisiana State University. Since 1994 she has taught at the school of music at Indiana University.

Further Reading

Martínez, Al. *Rising Voices: Profiles of Hispanic-American Lives.* New York: New American Library, 1974.

Ayala, Francisco (1934–) *scientist*

Regarded as one of the foremost researchers and thinkers in the field of evolutionary genetics, Francisco Ayala was born in Madrid, Spain, on March 12, 1934. After studying at two Spanish universities—Madrid (B.S., 1955) and Salamanca (S.T.L., 1960)—he decided to continue his graduate education in the United States. He moved to the United States in 1961 and acquired his M.A. in 1963 and Ph.D. (in genetics) in 1964 at New York's Columbia University. Ayala became a U.S. citizen in 1971.

Ayala has devoted his life to finding out more about evolution and how it works from the molecular level upward. One way to understand the breadth of his contributions is to observe their range of subject matter, from the exact role of adaptation in the evolution of fruit flies, through cloning at both DNA level and in the reproduction of disease-carrying microbes (research that is crucial in the development of vaccines), to the influence of environmental factors on natural selection.

Francisco Ayala *(Carl Cox Photography, Rockville, MD)*

Another way to assess the scope of his work is to consider that it has involved three kinds of approaches that are often kept separate and handled by different people: experiment, theory, and the examination of ethical and philosophical aspects—which are of supreme importance in the field of genetics at a time when humans are learning to modify what nature does.

Ayala began his career as a research associate in genetics at the Rockefeller Institute and then became a professor of biology and genetics, first at Providence College, later at Rockefeller University, afterward at the University of California at Davis, and finally at the University of California at Irvine.

He has also been a Fulbright and Guggenheim fellow, a member of the executive committee of the Scientific Advisory Board of the Environmental Protection Agency, associate editor of *Biology & Philosophy* and *Molecular Evolution and Paleobiology,* and president of the Society for the Study of Evolution. Furthermore, he has held diverse other posts in such organizations as the National Science Foundation, National Research Council, and National Academy of Science.

His brilliance and dedication have not gone unrecognized: Ayala has won the Medal of the College of France, the W. E. Key Award from the American Genetics Association, the Scientific Freedom and Responsibility Award from the American Association for the Advancement of Science (in 1987; he became president of the association in 1994), honorary doctorates from universities in Spain and in Greece, and foreign memberships in the Academies of Science of Spain, Russia, and Mexico.

The list of Ayala's books, written in collaboration with other researchers, includes *Evolution* (1977), *Evolving: The Theory and Practice of Organic Evolution* (1979), and *Modern Genetics* (1984).

Further Reading

American Men and Women of Science. New York: R.R. Bowker, 1999.
"Biography: Dr. Francisco Ayala." Counterbalance Foundation. Available online. URL: http://counterbalance.org/bio/ayala-body.html. Downloaded October 12, 2000.
McMurray, Emily J. *Notable Twentieth-Century Scientists.* Detroit: Gale Research, 1995.

Baca, Elfego (1865–1945) *frontiersman*
Elfego Baca became a frontier legend by the time he was 19, thanks to an armed showdown in Frisco, New Mexico. He became a special hero to Mexican Americans in that shootout by demonstrating that one Mexican American could face and beat 80 Texan cowhands. His exploits became the subject of a Walt Disney television miniseries.

Baca was born into a modest household in central New Mexico in 1865, just as the Civil War ended, and grew up in the turbulent Wild West period that followed. His father became marshall of the town of Socorro, though not before spending some years with his family in Topeka, Kansas, when Elfego was a child.

In 1884, at the age of 19, Elfego Baca decided to run for sheriff in his home territory. In the town of Frisco, he found that a number of cowhands from Texas were drinking too heavily and engaging in the murderous—and racist—game of taking potshots at Mexicans. Baca appointed himself deputy and promptly arrested one of the shooters. A fight erupted, and Baca shot one of the Texans.

The next day, approximately 80 of the cowhands came after Baca, guns blazing. Baca answered their volleys from inside a hut. A siege followed that lasted a day and a half and involved the firing of more than 4,000 bullets. Baca survived the fusillade unscratched, in part because the floor of the hut lay a few inches below the ground around it. But the young Mexican-American "deputy" did not spend the 36 hours simply lying flat on the floor. He shot 12 of the attacking cowhands, killing four. Finally an actual deputy sheriff who knew Baca arrived and promised him a fair trial if he gave himself up. Baca surrendered to the deputy and was taken to Albuquerque for trial. He won an acquittal.

Due, probably, to Baca's race, the gunfight in Frisco never attained the epic status of such other Wild West showdowns as that in which Wyatt Earp and his allies faced the Clanton gang in Tombstone, Arizona, three years earlier. Baca's Frisco siege could even be interpreted as a kind of small El Alamo in reverse, despite all the participants being American born.

Though Baca's showdown never earned mythic proportions within the U.S. mainstream, it did give him sufficient celebrity to boost his candidacy in many elections in his home territory and, later, home state.

But Baca was not content to coast along on celebrity or even with holding a long succession of public offices. Instead he decided to study law while holding office. By 1894, he was a working attorney in Socorro, New Mexico. He later obtained a license to represent cases before the Supreme Court in Washington, though it was an option he never exercised. He was, at various times until the end of World War II, sheriff and mayor of Socorro, county clerk and district attorney, and at one point even superintendent of schools in the county.

Baca did not win all the elections he ran in, however. In 1912, for example, when New Mexico achieved statehood and he was living in Albuquerque, he was defeated in a bid to become state congressman for the Republican Party.

Baca also took an interest in Mexican politics. In 1913, he served as a representative of the Mexican government in New Mexico at a time when the dictator Victoriano Huerta controlled Mexico. Huerta would be arrested in the United States after being thrown out of office in 1914, but Baca continued to work as his agent until Huerta died in 1916.

In the 1930s, Baca worked for the U.S. politician Bronson Cutting. Baca carried out political investigations for Cutting—a job that led him to work as a detective afterwards—and even published a weekly paper in Spanish, *La Opinión Pública,* in the liberal politician's favor. But Baca outlived this political patron, too; Cutting died in 1935.

In this period, Baca himself was several times considered as a candidate for the job of governor of New Mexico. In 1944, at 79, he made one last run for public office, seeking the Democratic nomination for district attorney. He lost. The following year, he died.

In 1958, the Walt Disney film production company produced a television miniseries to celebrate Baca's adventures as a lawman. It was entitled *The Nine Lives of Elfego Baca* (with Robert Loggia playing the title role). In other countries, it was shown in condensed form as a feature movie. Unlike the few other Hispanic good guys on television, such as the characters played by Edward James OLMOS in *Miami Vice* and Erik Estrada in *CHiPS,* this one was based on a real-life hero.

Further Reading
Ball, Larry. *Elfego Baca in Life and Legend.* El Paso: Texas Western Press, 1992.

Meier, Matt S. *Mexican American Biographies.* Westport, Conn.: Greenwood Publishing Group, 1988.
Meier, Matt S., and Feliciano Ribera. *Mexican Americans/American Mexicans, from Conquistadors to Chicanos.* New York: Hill and Wang, 1993.

Baca, Judith (1946–) *artist, activist*
Judith Baca is a major leader of Los Angeles's great muralist movement and has coupled her artistic talent with a lifelong devotion to social causes to bring the races together and guide inner-city youths away from antisocial attitudes. (She is not related to Elfego BACA.)

Despite the fact that Baca prefers painting on walls rather than on paper or canvas, she obtained formal training as an artist at California State University in Northridge, earning an art degree in 1969. She went on to become a full professor of art at the University of California at Irvine.

Judith Francisca Baca was born in south central Los Angeles on September 20, 1946, to a Chicana mother. Her father, a musician, was not at home, yet Judith lived a well-adjusted early childhood in a household headed by her grandmother.

Things changed for the worse after her mother married another man when Judith was six years old and moved out of the neighborhood and away from the little girl's beloved grandmother. To this loss was added the fact that at school she was made very aware of her failings in handling the English language. As sometimes happens, a teacher inadvertently launched her toward her lifetime career, by letting her paint by herself while the class continued. Through this experience, Baca discovered her calling.

After Catholic high school came college and her art degree, and then a return to the same high school, this time as a teacher. Baca almost immediately launched herself into her dual interests—mural art and the bridging of racial divides. She organized the painting of a school wall by a multicultural group of students.

Her first public project—on a city wall in Los Angeles's Hollenbeck Park—followed a similar procedure. But by then she was working with a more diverse group of youths, including members of street gangs. This came about because of a change of jobs: she was dismissed from employment at the high school, along with 17 other teachers—including 10 nuns—for taking part in peace marches directed against U.S. participation in the Vietnam War.

Baca's next employment was at the Central Affairs division of the Los Angeles city government, which set her to work as a roving art teacher. The city approved of her initiative in channeling the artistic impulses of inner-city teenagers away from graffiti and car decorations toward more serious, and demanding, art forms. It was also impressed by her results in handling even "hard-case" youths. When the kids were working together to paint a mural, differences of race, turf rivalries, etc., faded. Judith Baca was Los Angeles's pioneer in bringing diverse young people together to paint murals.

Baca then decided that she wanted to learn more about mural painting and traveled to the one of the world's greatest sources for this art form: Mexico. There she studied at first hand the work of the "Three Greats" of muralism, Diego Rivera, José Clemente Orozco, and David Alfaro Siqueiros.

Fired with even greater enthusiasm than before, Baca on her return created the Citywide Mural Project, which was responsible for hundreds of artworks, including the monumental *Great Wall,* a history of the Los Angeles area since prehistoric times. Emphasizing the diversity of races participating in that history, it stretched half a mile along the sides of a drainage canal.

Baca later developed an idea to combine the salient feature of mural art—its great size—with the great advantage of smaller works: their mobility. Her next great project (1987), *World Wall,* subtitled *A Vision of the Future Without Fear,* was painted on movable panels. This enabled it even to be transported abroad, where foreign artists were provided an opportunity to paint additional panels of their own.

Baca founded the Social and Public Art Resource Center (SPARC) in Venice, California, in 1976 to advance her community work and artistic agenda.

Baca was one of the established artists participating, alongside younger artists, in the vast International Chicana, Chicano Art Exhibition held in San Diego in 1999.

Further Reading

Nagel, Rob, and Sharon Rose, eds. *Hispanic American Biography.* New York: International Thomson Publishers, 1995.
Telgen, Diane, and Jim Kamp. *Notable Hispanic American Women.* Detroit: Gale Research, 1993.

❧ Badillo, Herman (1929–)
government official

Herman Badillo was the first Puerto Rican to become a voting member of Congress. He was, for a number of years, the highest-ranking Puerto Rican politician in the mainland United States.

Badillo was born on August 21, 1929, in the town of Caguas, Puerto Rico. An epidemic of tuberculosis killed his father when Herman was five; his mother died, also of tuberculosis, when he was nine. Two years later, he was sent to live with other family members in New York, where he quickly stood out with high grades at school.

With jobs like dishwasher and bowling-alley attendant, Badillo financed his education at City College in New York. He received his degree from City College business school, graduating magna cum laude. This enabled him to obtain employment as an accountant while he continued studying at night, this time at Brooklyn Law School. He was valedictorian of his class and graduated from law school cum laude.

The young lawyer entered politics in 1960 to work for the presidential campaign of Democrat John F. Kennedy. Although Badillo was not well known, in 1961 he ran for the position of state assembly district leader. Because Badillo's campaign was so strong, he lost the election by the thinnest of margins (just 75 votes). Badillo may have lost the election, but it was because of this race that New York Mayor Robert Wagner noticed Badillo. The mayor appointed him deputy commissioner of the New York Department of Real Estate. This was soon followed by a higher appointment, the first of that rank to be given to a Puerto Rican: commissioner of the Department of Housing Relocation. In 1965, Badillo became borough president of the Bronx.

Badillo was thus participating in, and helping to lead, the gradual acquisition in the 1960s of some political power by Puerto Ricans, who had begun to migrate in large numbers to the mainland United States (particularly New York) after World War II. These immigrants were accustomed to an island society where people's skins came in all hues, and color made little difference. In the United States they met with a degree of racism and discrimination that shocked them all and discouraged many. Even those among them who happened to have light skin faced bias because of their accent.

Though citizens of the United States, Puerto Ricans felt the weight of prejudice. A memorable phrase of Badillo's summed it up: Puerto Ricans, he said, were "strangers in their own land." Yet, the civil rights movement and the sheer power of numbers—in 1970, there were more than 800,000 Puerto Ricans in New York City—ensured that they could no longer be swept entirely under the rug.

In 1969, Badillo ran for mayor of New York, and although he lost his bid to obtain the Democratic nomination, his electoral showing was regarded as a good one. When he campaigned for the U.S. House of Representatives the following year, he received 85 percent of his district's vote. That sent Badillo to Washington, with the power to vote in the House of Representatives. This was crucial because, under Puerto Rico's commonwealth arrangement with the United States, its people have a resident commissioner in Congress, but the commissioner is allowed no vote. Badillo's election to Congress allowed him to represent his constituency in New York.

Badillo was no shy freshman when he entered Congress. He complained when appointed to work on a committee that he considered too unimportant and won appointment to a better one. He had influential backing in his protest: *The New York Times* said his original posting was "an insulting waste of Badillo's talents."

Herman Badillo served four terms in Congress from 1970 to 1978. He then returned to New York City to serve as deputy mayor for management and policy. His congressional work emphasized minority rights, bilingual education, struggles in favor of the poor, and other liberal causes. In 1972, concerned over abuses in United States jails, he wrote and published *A Bill of No Rights: Attica and the American Prison System.*

A number of critics, however, charged that Badillo did not do enough—that his performance as deputy mayor had not matched his promise to the people of New York, much less his own expectations. In essence, he was faulted for being very ambitious and sure of his own worth.

These traits, however, are shared by many if not all politicians. Few politicians manage to change the world or to leave lasting impressions. Some analysts concluded that Badillo's critics were holding him to a different standard. Certainly, if anyone expected the first Puerto Rican to reach Badillo's level of political office to conform to some caricature of a Hispanic—bowing thankfully and apologetically while holding a big sombrero in his hands—he did not meet this person in the proud Herman Badillo.

Badillo is also a man of principle. In 1979, New York rejected a major redevelopment project in the South Bronx, a heavily Puerto Rican neighborhood that is one of the most depressed areas in the United States. Badillo, who in his post as deputy mayor was responsible for redevelopment projects, charged that Manhattan was being given preference over other boroughs of the city such as the Bronx and that the middle class was being favored over the poorer classes. Disgusted by such injustices, Badillo resigned from the city government job and went back to private practice as a lawyer.

In the mid-1980s, Badillo was appointed chairman of the New York State Mortgage Agency. He followed this with a bid for comptroller of New York State in 1986, which he lost at state level but in which he collected 61 percent of the vote in New York City itself. Badillo was appointed chairperson of the board of trustees of City University of New York in 1999.

Further Reading

Allyn, Paul. *The Picture Life of Herman Badillo.* New York: Watts, 1972.

Martínez, Al. *Rising Voices: Profiles of Hispano-American Lives.* New York: New American Library, 1974.

Rodríguez, Clara E. *Puerto Ricans—Born in the USA.* Boulder, Colo.: Westview Press, 1991.

Báez, Joan (Joan Chandos Báez)

(1941–) *singer, activist*

Joan Báez possesses two important gifts: a beautiful and exceptionally pure singing voice and an unyielding conscience and concern for social issues. Because of these attributes, in the 1960s she became an icon for millions of idealistic youths of her generation. She has, since then, tirelessly kept up both her work in favor of a variety of causes as well as her hugely successful musical career, which has yielded her eight gold albums and a gold single.

Joan Chandos Báez is Mexican American on her father's side (Dr. Albert Báez, a physicist, was born in Mexico) and British American on the side of her mother, a drama teacher. She was born on January 9, 1941, in Staten Island, New York.

Because of her parents' intellectual pursuits, Báez grew up in a succession of university cities from Massachusetts to California. She was a member of her high school choir in Palo Alto, California. Her soprano voice, which has been described as "ethereal," quickly singled her out as a soloist. By the age of 18, she was a professional singer, bowing in front of a cheering audience at the 1959 Newport (Rhode Island) Folk Festival.

Joan Báez came by her social concerns while still in school, through a variety of influences. She witnessed racism, she listened to folk songs that often dealt with the plight of the poor and the dispossessed, and she feared, as many did during the 1950s, that a nuclear war was coming. To the young and impressionable Joan Báez, it seemed inevitable that worse debacles would follow in the decades to come.

Báez sang in a natural, unaffected way, often barefoot on stage. The distinctively limpid quality of her voice wowed listeners, but people soon came to realize that there was more to Joan Báez than a singer of folk songs and ballads. She became known for her permanent and deep commitment to liberal causes.

The news magazine *Time* featured her on its cover in 1962 because of her activities in human rights, in particular her struggle to desegregate college campuses in the southern United States. The singer was married (1968–73) to a former student leader, David Harris.

Báez founded two organizations to support her favorite causes: in 1965, the Institute for the Study of Nonviolence; in 1979, the Humanitas International Human Rights Committee. In addition, she was part of the advisory board of the London-based Amnesty International human rights organization; she also participated in the founding of Amnesty West Coast, a branch of Amnesty International with headquarters in California.

One of the many political and human-rights problems that interested Báez was the plight of the (mainly Hispanic) farmworkers of California. These farmhands were overworked, underpaid, and unprotected until they organized with the help of such leaders as César CHÁVEZ, for whom Báez raised funds.

Her work in favor of racial equality, the hungry, and the oppressed both in the United States and overseas included two main activities: participating in marches and demonstrations—for example with the African American leader Martin Luther King Jr.—and singing at concerts to benefit various causes.

In the 1960s and early 1970s, Báez tirelessly opposed the Vietnam War, a conflict that divided the United States like few others. Báez supported North Vietnam, the U.S.'s enemy in the Vietnam War, when she saw it as a small country fighting some of the most powerful nations in the world. But she was also unafraid to attack its authoritarian government and did so in an "Open Letter to the Socialist Republic of Vietnam," after the north won the war. When thousands of "boat people" (refugees) fled Communist Vietnam, she lobbied successfully to have the United States Navy help in rescuing them.

In 1969, she was one of the main performers at the Woodstock music festival in New York State, an event that achieved almost mythical status among young people at the time.

Her activism earned her the respect and admiration of people with liberal inclinations. It also gained her the enmity of conservatives. For example, the highly conservative cartoonist Al Capp (Alfred Caplin) drew a character called "Joanie Phoanie" for his comic strip *Li'l Abner.* It was a stinging caricature of Joan Báez, but the singer would prove that she clearly was not a phony by her devotion to fighting cases of oppression in communist countries. This was an answer to conservative accusations that liberals were blind to such evils and attacked injustice only in capitalist countries.

In an autobiography, she described her "stronger and stronger aversion to the ideologies of both the far right and the far left and . . . deeper sense of rage and sorrow over the suffering they continue to produce all over the world."

Right-wing military dictatorships prevented her from singing in Argentina, Chile, and Brazil. So did the communist government of the Soviet Union, where she traveled to meet with such dissidents as Andrei Sakharov, Nobel Peace Prize winner.

Another proof of the sincerity of her commitment was that she continued her activism even after the Vietnam War ended. The late 1970s, the 1980s, and beyond seemed to be a period in which many people abandoned earlier ideals and turned only to making money and looking after their own lives. Báez herself put it this way: it was a time when people believed that "you just jog, eat enough of the right yogurt, and everything is going to be all right."

Báez did not indulge in such self-centeredness. In the 1970s, she traveled to North Vietnam at the height of the U.S. bombardment of the country. In the 1980s, she toured Israel and the Palestinian territories it was occupying. In the 1990s, she went to war-ravaged Bosnia-Herzegovina in Europe, always trying to contribute to peace.

To the numerous awards she earned for her music, Báez in 1979 added the American Civil Liberties Union's Earl Warren Award for her work for human-rights causes. In 2000, she received the Lifetime Achievement Award from the British Folk Awards organization.

Further Reading

Báez, Joan. *And a Voice to Sing With: A Memoir.* New York: Summit Books, 1986.
———. *Daybreak.* Garden City, N.Y.: Dial Press, 1968.
Garza, Hedda. *Joan Báez.* Chicago: Children's Press, 1991.
Romero, Maritza. *Joan Báez: Folksinger for Peace.* New York: PowerKids Press, 1997.
Swanekamp, Joan. *Diamonds & Rust: A Biography and Discography of Joan Báez.* Ann Arbor, Mich.: Pierian Press, 1980.
Telgen, Diane, and Jim Kamp, eds. *Notable Hispanic American Women.* Detroit: Gale Research, Inc., 1993.

❧ Baird, Lourdes G. (Lourdes Gillespie)
(1935–   ) *judge*

Ecuadoran-born Lourdes Baird is one of the most widely respected jurists in the United States. She can proudly point to the fact that she was nominated as U.S. attorney general in California's Central District by U.S. Senator Pete Wilson, a Republican, and President George H.W. Bush, also a Republican, although she is a Democrat—and there were three other very good candidates for the post, all of whom were Republicans.

Lourdes Baird *(Courtesy of Lourdes G. Baird)*

California's Central District is the biggest federal judicial district in the United States. It is also one that routinely faces some of the most sensitive cases in U.S. law, for example the case of Rodney King, a black motorist viciously beaten by white police officers after his arrest. Baird led the prosecution of the policemen for violation of King's civil rights after they had been acquitted of the beating, a prosecution that obtained two convictions.

In 1992, two years after her appointment as U.S. attorney in California's Central District, Baird became a federal judge in the district.

Moving fast has been a hallmark of Baird's career, because she launched into it relatively late in life. Lourdes was born in Ecuador's capital, Quito, on May 12, 1935, to James Gillespie and Josefina Delgado. When she was only one, she moved with her family to California.

After Catholic school came marriage at age 21 to a businessman, William Baird, whose name she kept even after their divorce 19 years later. Lourdes received the kind of traditional upbringing that leads women to see marriage and motherhood as their only career options, and so she concentrated on being a housewife and mother for the first 11 years after her wedding. But after the youngest of her three children was in school, Baird felt the urge to go to college, initially as a part-timer—and one who had misgivings, born of the fact that she was older than most other students. Yet Baird and studies, and particularly the law, soon proved to be an excellent match.

She graduated with highest honors from the University of California at Los Angeles (UCLA) in 1973, with a bachelor's degree in sociology, then three years later graduated with honors from the UCLA law school, after which she breezed through the California bar examination.

Her first job was as assistant U.S. attorney in Los Angeles. In the early 1980s she spent some years in private practice, but public service beckoned again. She became a municipal court judge, and she also began to teach law at Loyola University in Los Angeles.

Baird's reputation as both fair and tough was quickly established. In 1990, when Senator (and, at that time, gubernatorial candidate) Wilson put forward her nomination for the job of attorney general in the district, she won the loud endorsement of the *Los Angeles Times*. "Baird for U.S. Attorney? Of Course" was the headline of the newspaper's editorial dedicated to endorsing her for the post. "Baird," it stated, "is widely praised in legal circles for her judgement, fairness, administrative skills, her sense of humor and her ability to relate to a wide variety of individuals and groups."

In her work as a prosecutor and as a judge, Baird clearly sees the problem of drugs as the root of many of the ills besetting the United States. In specific cases, she is fully in favor of the death penalty.

Lourdes Baird is a member of the Mexican-American Bar Association, the Hispanic National Bar Association, the California Women Lawyers Association, the National Association of Women Judges, and the Latino Judges Association. She has been president of the UCLA School of Law Alumni Association.

In 1991 the UCLA School of Law named her Alumnus of the Year, and in the same year she was named Woman of Promise by the Hispanic Women's Council. Three years later she received the Silver Achievement Award for the professions from the YWCA.

Further Reading

Telgen, Diane, and Jim Kamp, eds. *Notable Hispanic American Women.* Detroit: Gale Research, 1998.

✍ Bañuelos, Romana Acosta (1925–)
businesswoman

Romana Bañuelos is a highly successful and respected self-made business owner and banker. She is also the first Hispanic to be appointed treasurer of the United States. Her biography would be a classic rags-to-riches story, except that Bañuelos had two extra hurdles to overcome on her way to success. In addition to being born into poverty, she was a member of a minority race and a woman within that minority.

Bañuelos was born on March 20, 1925, in the town of Miami, Arizona, whose main activity was mining copper. Her Mexican parents were living in the United States without proper residence papers, no severe problem in the 1920s, but in the 1930s, when the United States was suffering from the Great Depression and high unemployment, a very oppressive situation. In the case of Bañuelos's parents, this pressure took the shape of hard-selling recommendations by Arizona government officials to return to Mexico where they would allegedly find better job opportunities.

At the age of eight, Bañuelos thus found herself working alongside her parents on a tiny farm in the Mexican state of Sonora. Later, she would call this move by her family the best thing that could have happened to her. She said it allowed her to grow up in Mexico without experiencing any prejudice and to learn to be proud of her heritage.

She was 16 when she wed for the first time. The marriage lasted two years, during which time she moved back to the United States and lived in El Paso, Texas. But after her divorce, she decided to try her fortune in the city of Los Angeles. She arrived there at 19 with two children and with 36 cents in her purse.

A quarter of a century later, in 1969, she was named Businesswoman of the Year in Los Angeles. Ten years after that, her company, Ramona's (not Romana's) Mexican Food Products, Inc. had reached annual sales of $12 million and employed 400 people.

It was not an easy road for Romana Bañuelos, but it was a classic one: work hard, save a little, invest in a tiny business, keep on working hard, expand, work a lot more. Starting out with jobs in a laundry and as a dishwasher and an income of one dollar a day, it took five years for Bañuelos to save the $400 with which she went into business with an aunt. During these years, she also remarried.

The aunt took out a loan and joined Bañuelos in buying tortilla-making equipment. Bañuelos rose at two in the morning each day to start work at her small enterprise before going back home to wake up her children and send them off to school. After that, it was back to work.

To be an independent businesswoman in the 1950s, Romana Bañuelos had to overcome the expectations and outright prejudice that restricted women to being housewives and nothing else. This prejudice was particularly strong within communities with strong traditions like those of the Hispanics. But though raised in a traditional community Bañue-

los was not one to conform to the stereotypes of women by deferring to men and leaving money matters to them.

This did not mean that she forgot her roots—quite the opposite. Determined to help other small businesspeople in the Hispanic community and seeing how difficult they found it to obtain bank credits, she decided, in 1965, to found a bank.

When her Pan-American National Bank started to hand out small loans, it did not even have an office; it had to operate from a trailer. As president and chairman of the board of directors, Bañuelos turned it into an organization with assets of millions of dollars. She also gave scholarships to Chicano students through the Ramona's Mexican Food Products, Inc. Scholarship Foundation.

Bañuelos was awarded an honorary doctorate in business administration by the City University of Los Angeles and was named by the American Bicentennial Research Institute as one of the United States' valuable resources.

In the early 1970s, the Republican Party strove to lure Hispanics away from their previously massive preference for the rival Democratic Party. Republican strategy included prominent appointments in government to some Hispanics; Republican President Richard Nixon turned to Romana Bañuelos for the post of treasurer of the United States, a post which she held from 1971 until 1974. She was the first Mexican American (and only the sixth woman) ever to have her signature on U.S. money bills.

Further Reading

Acuña, Rodolfo. *Occupied America: A History of Chicanos.* New York: HarperCollins, 1988.
Martínez, Al. *Rising Voices: Profiles of Hispano-American Lives.* New York: New American Library, 1974.
Telgen, Diane, and Jim Kamp, eds. *Notable Hispanic American Women.* Detroit: Gale Research, Inc., 1993.

❦ **Banderas, Antonio** (José Antonio Domínguez Banderas) (1960–) *actor*
Spanish actor Antonio Banderas took Hollywood by storm in the 1990s and in short order established

himself as one of the most visible stars in U.S. show business. Despite the brevity of his career in the United States to date, he thus provides a perfect example of the outstanding Hispanic or person of Hispanic ancestry who spends a crucial part of his or her career in the United States.

Banderas was born on August 10, 1960, in the city of Málaga, Spain. His father was a police officer. Antonio was bitten early by the acting bug: he claims that it happened while watching the nude acting in a Spanish version of *Hair,* when he was 14. That's when, he has recalled, he turned "professional"—by acting on village streets. He supplemented five years of this street schooling by four years of more traditional training at Málaga's School of Dramatic Art.

By age 19 Banderas had arrived in the capital, Madrid, virtually penniless. One year later he acted on stage for the first time; the year after that, he took part in his first movie, and his career became unstoppable.

That first film, *Laberinto de pasiones* (Labyrinth of Passion), was made by Spain's most celebrated director of recent decades, Pedro Almodóvar. Banderas's participation in it, and in four others of Almodóvar's bizarre and often darkly comic works—*Matador* (Bullfighter), *La ley del deseo* (The Law of Desire), *Mujeres al borde de un ataque de nervios* (Women on the Verge of a Nervous Breakdown), an Oscar nominee, and *¡Atame!* (Tie Me Up! Tie Me Down!)—was one of the reasons for his celebrity. (Another was his good looks, which have earned him raves all through the years.)

In addition to his movies for Almodóvar, Banderas, a tireless worker, has acted in films by numerous other Spanish directors, including some of the top, internationally known names in that country's movie industry, such as Carlos Saura and Fernando Trueba.

Banderas arrived in Hollywood in 1992 to make the movie *The Mambo Kings,* based on the novel by Oscar HIJUELOS, *The Mambo Kings Play Songs of Love.* To get him one of the two lead roles, his agent lied to the producer, telling him Banderas spoke English. The agent later explained that he knew just looking at Banderas would be enough to win him the part, and the actor played it by learn-ing the English sounds by heart (meanwhile beginning proper English lessons).

Thereafter Banderas became a full-fledged U.S. star. He was hailed as "the sexiest man alive," by the actor Billy Crystal during an Oscar presentation ceremony. Producer Elizabeth Avellan said that "watching him up close, literally, my socks fell down." *People* magazine listed him in their annual feature, "The 50 Most Beautiful People in the World." Director Richard Donner said "he comes into our lives like Valentino in the 20s"—and also that "he's the personification of male musk."

Newsweek magazine objected to the allusions to Rudolph Valentino and "all the screen Latin lover comparisons—to César ROMERO, Fernando LAMAS, Gilbert ROLAND" as "off the mark and out of date" because "they were peacocks whose martinet machismo now seems anachronistic. Banderas is more leonine and internal: he may ooze sexuality, but he holds something sly in reserve."

Banderas' fame was also heightened by a much-followed romance with the U.S. actress Melanie Griffith, who gave up her husband, the actor Don Johnson, for him, while Banderas gave up his wife, Ana Leza, a Spanish actress, for her. They had a daughter, Stella del Carmen Banderas Griffith, in 1996.

Being a major celebrity did not keep Banderas from continuing his intense work schedule, which resulted in a large number of movies. Some critics indeed warned that he made too many and that his career was threatened by overexposure. Among the U.S. films he has made are *Philadelphia, Of Love and Shadows; Interview with the Vampire,* in which some say he stole scenes from costars Tom Cruise and Brad Pitt; *Desperado; Evita,* in which he sang his role as the revolutionary Che Guevara; and *The Mask of Zorro,* for the title role of which he was chosen ahead of Andy GARCIA.

In late 1999 Banderas presented his first film as director, *Crazy in Alabama,* starring his wife Melanie Griffith.

Banderas won a Golden Apple Award in 1995 and was nominated for Golden Globe awards in 1996 and 1999 for his role in, respectively, *Evita* and *The Mask of Zorro.*

Further Reading

Birk, Rosemary, and Eufronsina Stasnya. "Antonio Banderas: More Than Just the Ultimate Lover." Available online. URL: http://www.antonioban-derasfans.com. Downloaded October 10, 2000.

Contemporary Theatre, Film, and Television. Detroit: Gale Research, 1999.

International Dictionary of Films and Filmmakers. Detroit: St. James Press, 1997.

Tardiff, Joseph C., and Mpho Mabunda, eds. *Dictionary of Hispanic Biography.* Detroit: Gale Research, 1996.

✤ Benavídez, Roy P. (Roy Pérez Benavídez) (1935–) *soldier*

Roy P. Benavídez, a Green Beret sergeant, successfully carried out an amazing rescue operation in Cambodia despite sustaining numerous serious wounds. He was one of the most decorated soldiers of the Vietnam War. His awards for valor include the Congressional Medal of Honor. There is even a museum to celebrate his feat— the Roy P. Benavídez Airborne Museum.

Roy P. Benavídez was born in Cuero, Texas, on May 8, 1935, joined the United States Army's elite Special Forces, or Green Berets, as a teenager in 1952, and retired in 1976. His last eight years of service were chiefly spent recovering from the wounds suffered in the mission that put him into the military history books. When he was discharged, he was still almost wholly disabled.

The soldiers Benavídez rescued on May 2, 1968, were Special Forces fighters. They were pinned down by enemy fire during a highly secret mission inside Cambodia, just 30 miles from the border of Vietnam. The North Vietnamese force against them not only cut down the surrounded 12-man U.S. team, but also made access to rescue them almost impossible for U.S. helicopters.

Benavídez was a staff sergeant on the Loc Ninh radio team that received the squad's desperate calls for help. Aboard a helicopter returning from Cambodia after an unsuccessful rescue attempt was a wounded door gunner who died in Benavídez's arms. Benavídez then decided to go to the aid of the surrounded men himself and clambered into the next helicopter.

But when the chopper neared the attack site, the fighting was so intense that the pilot was unable to land. The pilot veered off to a nearby area where Benavídez jumped to the jungle floor. The helicopter pilot took off planning to return when the sergeant radioed him.

There were 75 yards to cover between Benavídez's drop-off and the surrounded Special Forces. However, the one-man rescue attempt almost ended the moment it began: Benavídez was caught by enemy fire as soon as he began his sprint. He was hit repeatedly in the legs and face, but each time he fell, he pulled himself up and continued ahead.

Eight of the 12-member squad were alive when Benavídez got to their perimeter, all of them wounded. Benavídez recovered secret documents and photographic equipment from the slain leader's body and detonated a smoke grenade to guide the helicopter to them.

The "Huey" chopper managed to land but could not get the U.S. soldiers out. Caught in the North Vietnamese fusillade, it burst into flame. Benavídez was hit again, this time in the back. Still, he reached the burning Huey and extricated two crewmen.

Six of the originally besieged men were alive at this point; with the two crewmen, Benavídez again had eight men to evacuate. He radioed for another helicopter, and organized the defense from that point on. He also gave himself and the wounded soldiers injections of morphine.

Another shot hit him, this time in the leg. More helicopters approached and were felled by enemy fire. It was more than seven hours before a Huey was able to land.

Welling blood, Benavídez started to load the other wounded onto the chopper. The North Vietnamese were now charging the aircraft bodily: one of them smashed a rifle butt into the back of Benavídez's head. The enemy soldier who had hit him next tried to bayonet him; Benavídez saw the movement as he turned around and seized the bayonet in the air. He sliced his hand open as he did so, but in the same movement he managed to kill the attacking soldier with a blade of his own. Then he resumed piling people into the helicopter. Two more North Vietnamese ran toward him; Benavídez shot them with a rifle he had grabbed.

By this time, he was literally holding his own intestines to keep them inside his body. This was his state when the helicopter evacuated him along with the other eight, plus a number of U.S. dead. As the doctors at the base in Vietnam separated the dead from the living, they counted Benavídez among the dead. Paralyzed and without strength even to moan, Benavídez spat at a medic as the only proof of life he could muster to avoid being stuffed into a body bag.

The list of medals later showered on this Hispanic hero included the Distinguished Service Cross, Purple Heart with four Oak Leaf Clusters, Defense Meritorious Service Medal, Army Commendation Medal, Army Achievement Medal, Good Conduct Medal with five loops, Army Occupation Medal, National Defense Service Medal with Oak Leaf Cluster, Armed Forces Expeditionary Medal, Vietnam Service Medal with four campaign stars, United Nations Service Medal, Republic of Vietnam Campaign Medal, Presidential Unit Citation with two Oak Leaf Clusters, Meritorious Unit Commendation, Republic of Vietnam Cross of Gallantry with Palm Unit Citation, and Republic of Vietnam Civil Action Citation with Palm.

Finally, in 1981, after corroboration of his actions had been laboriously obtained from the people he had saved, Roy Benavídez was awarded the Congressional Medal of Honor. He was the last surviving soldier of the war to receive the award. His inner drive did not stop with celebrity: After recovering from his wounds, he began to attend college. In the same year that the president of the United States pinned the Medal of Honor on him, at age 46, Benavídez also earned his B.A. degree.

Further Reading

Benavídez, Roy, et al. *Medal of Honor: A Vietnam Warrior's Story.* Washington, D.C.: Brassey's, 1995.

Benavídez, Roy, and Oscar Griffin. *The Three Wars of Roy Benavídez.* San Antonio, Tex.: Corona Publishing Co., 1986.

✎ Blades, Rubén (1948–) *singer, actor*

Panamanian-born Rubén Blades has established himself in the United States as an attractive, award-winning musician and actor. At the same time, he has involved his energetic, diverse personality in politics and law.

Blades (whose last name is properly pronounced not as BLAIDS but as BLAH-des) was born in Panama City on July 16, 1948. He graduated from the University of Panama as a lawyer and political scientist in 1974. That same year, he began his career as a professional musician and actor. However, he also worked as an attorney, both for the National Bank of Panama and for a recording company.

In the late 1970s, Blades went to the United States to continue his studies. He received his master's degree in international law from Harvard and is a member of the Harvard Law School Association; the American Society of Composers, Authors, and Publishers; the Screen Actors Guild; and a political party in Panama that he founded in 1991.

Blades made a name for himself in the United States as a leading composer and performer of the passionate dance music known as salsa. He also performs music in many other styles, from ballads to rock. He has received three Grammy Awards from the National Academy of Recording Arts and Sciences, the most recent in 2000, and has earned a large number of gold records.

Initially recording only in Spanish, in 1988 he cut his first English-language LP, *Nothing But the Truth,* and began to reach a wider audience. Many Latino performers in the United States want to "cross over" from their own, Spanish-speaking community into the general, English-speaking market. This is the subject of *Crossover Dreams,* a 1984 movie in which Blades starred, and that he also cowrote.

Blades has also acted in *Critical Condition* and *The Milagro Beanfield War* (in the 1980s) and *Mo' Better Blues, The Two Jakes,* and *From the Heart* (in the 1990s). He received a National Cable award for best actor (1990) and an Emmy award nomination (1991) for work in television. Recent movies starring Blades include *Chinese Box* (1997); *Cradle Will Rock* (1999), in which he played the Mexican muralist Diego Rivera; and *All the Pretty Horses* (2000).

Though praised as an affable and convincing performer, he considers acting a way to subsidize his musical career. He has refused many roles that he called "those junky-dope-addict-drug-dealer characters that only serve to reinforce negative stereotypes people already have about my culture. Those characters may exist, but I know the majority of Latins work and contribute to this country's cultural and economic welfare."

Blades has maintained a constant interest in social issues and works in support of causes that could lead toward what he has described as "a society that will be more integrated and fair, where character will be the most important thing, where hearts don't require visas."

Elections were held in Panama in 1994 to normalize the political situation following an invasion by U.S. troops to capture a military president accused of drug running. Blades ran for president of his country; his platform emphasized his commitment to social-welfare goals. Defeated in the polls, he returned to his career in the United States.

Further Reading

Cruz, Bárbara. *Rubén Blades: Salsa Singer and Social Activist.* Springfield, N.J.: Enslow, 1997.

Marton, Betty A. *Rubén Blades.* New York: Chelsea House, 1992.

Unterburger, Amy, ed. *Who's Who Among Hispanic Americans.* Detroit: Gale Research, Inc., 1992–93.

꙾   **Bocca, Julio** (Julio Adrián Bocca)
   (1967–   ) *ballet dancer*

Julio Bocca is a principal dancer at the American Ballet Theater. Since the late 1980s, he has been acclaimed as one of the world's top male ballet stars.

Born in Argentina in a working-class suburb of the capital, Buenos Aires, on March 6, 1967, Bocca began to study dance at the age of four under the tutelage of his mother, who gave classical dancing lessons in the back of her parents' home as well as at the National School of Dance of Argentina. Bocca's father was a bus driver. He refused to marry Bocca's mother or to recognize his son. He died when Bocca was six.

At age seven, the fledgling dancer entered the Advanced Art Institute, run by Argentina's main

Julio Bocca *(Cabrera Archive)*

venue for ballet dancing, the Teatro Colón. In 1982, he began his international career: At 15, he was contracted as principal dancer by ballet companies in Venezuela and Brazil and also continued dancing on the Colón's stage in Buenos Aires.

Bocca's total commitment to ballet forced him to cease his formal education after the seventh grade. Stardom beckoned in 1985 when Bocca participated in the Moscow International, the world's most prestigious ballet competition. He won the gold medal in his category. The following year, he was offered a contract as principal dancer at the American Ballet Theater. Since then, the New York company has been Julio Bocca's home base. While living in the United States, Bocca has even developed a love for country music.

"Dancer of the Year," *The New York Times* proclaimed Bocca in 1987. The newspaper's critic, Clive Barnes, drew comparisons between him and Rudolf Nureyev, one of the great dancers of this century. Barnes also declared Bocca to be the sole dancer of his stature in the world at the time. Critics worldwide praise Bocca for a combination of flawless technique and acting flair: "Julio Bocca's knees have been sculpted by Michelangelo," wrote the French newspaper *Le Figaro.*

Partnered with the world's leading ballerinas, Bocca has performed as guest dancer on all major international stages from the Americas to Asia. These include appearances with every one of the great ballet companies, including Moscow's Bolshoi, Leningrad's Kirov, London's Royal Ballet, Paris's Opéra, Milan's La Scala, and Madrid's La Zarzuela.

He has danced the classics of ballet as well as many modern works, a number of which have been created especially for him.

While continuing as principal in New York and in his many international appearances, Bocca in 1990 also founded his own company, Ballet Argentino. Argentine ballerina Eleonora Cassano has been his principal dancing partner in this company. He has danced many benefit performances around the world, including Crusaids in New York and the Telethon in St. Petersburg. In 2000, Bocca expanded his career into Broadway musicals, appearing in *Fosse.*

Bocca has been showered with awards from the world of ballet. In France in 1990, he was declared one of the Personalities of the Year, alongside Mother Teresa of Calcutta.

Further Reading

"Julio Bocca." American Ballet Theatre. Available online. URL: http://www.abt.org/dancers/bocca. html. Downloaded October 10, 2000.

Bocca, Julio, with Rodolfo Braceli. *Bocca: Yo, Príncipe y Mendigo (Bocca: I, Prince and Pauper).* Buenos Aires: Editorial Atlantida, 1995.

Unterburger, Amy, ed. *Who's Who Among Hispanic Americans.* Detroit: Gale Research, Inc., 1992–93.

✺   **Botero, Fernando** (1932–) *artist*

Fernando Botero, a Colombian-born artist who lived and worked in New York City for much of his career, is one of the most famous and best-selling Hispanic artists ever. He created one of the most instantly recognizable styles of any 20th-century painter or sculptor: Botero specializes in portraying bloated figures. Even the cats and dogs that appear in his works are immensely fat, and when he depicts a still life, he manages to make objects that are spherical to start with, such as a grapefruit, appear obese.

These figures do not seem to be ill at ease with their appearance—rather, they look lost in their individual thoughts and are often interpreted as a critique of smugness in society.

The future artist was born on April 19, 1932, in Medellín, Colombia. The grandson of an unsuccessful gold prospector and the son of a small-time merchant father and seamstress mother, he loved painting from an early but not precocious age. He painted his first serious work, a watercolor, at 12.

Botero was already 17 when he discovered one of his greatest idols, Pablo Picasso. He wrote an essay in defense of the Spanish artist that was passionate enough to end in his expulsion from his Roman Catholic school, where Picasso was viewed as someone who deforms God's work.

Two years later, Botero won a national prize for painting in Colombia. This earned him enough money to travel to Europe to study art and to view its masterworks firsthand. Technically very skilled with his brushwork, he managed to make a living in Spain by selling copies of the great paintings in the Prado Museum in Madrid. He was greatly influenced by the Spanish masters Velázquez and Goya, whose work was displayed at the museum. Nevertheless, he felt an even greater affinity with the Italian Old Masters

Fernando Botero *(Cabrera Archive)*

he studied in Florence. After Spain and Italy, he continued his studies in France.

As a professional painter, Botero set up headquarters in New York, although, with increasing fame and income, he later added homes in France, Monaco, and Italy, as well as in Colombia. His initial impact on his adoptive city was assured in the 1960s when New York's Museum of Modern Art hung his painting that depicted the Mona Lisa at the age of 12—a roly-poly satire of Leonardo da Vinci's masterpiece. At the same time, the Metropolitan Museum of Art was staging a special show of Leonardo's work.

Botero lost his small son in a car crash in Spain in 1974. He channeled part of his grief into painting a series of eight portraits of the boy, which he donated to a museum in his hometown. Another son, also called Fernando, later became Colombia's youngest senator ever and then defense minister.

Botero's works are exhibited in museums and galleries around the world. One of his paintings was sold at auction in 1992 for $1.5 million. This sale set the price range for his major works from then on.

In the 1970s, Botero began to sculpt, turning out huge three-dimensional versions of his fat figures, their chubby shape emphasized by the relative smallness of their extremities and other features. In 1992, the city of Paris set up an open-air exhibit of these sculptures along the Avenue Champs Elysées—one of the city's major cultural events of that year. The following year, the same was done along Park Avenue in New York City.

In 2000, Botero made a massive donation of 79 of his works to Medellín to help improve the image of his violence-torn native city. Medellín used the donation to open a museum dedicated to him, called Botero City. He also replaced one large sculpture, *The Bird,* which had been destroyed there in a bomb explosion in 1995 that killed 22 people.

Further Reading

Botero, Fernando. *Paintings and Drawings.* New York: te Neues, 1992.
Restany, Pierre. *Botero.* New York: Abrams, 1984.
Rivero, Mario. *Botero.* Bogotá, Colombia: Plaza & Janes, 1973.

 Bouchard, Hipólito (1780–1837)
soldier

During the struggle for independence by Spain's American colonies, Hipólito Bouchard brought the fight to the California coast, then a part of Mexico and ruled by Spain. For five days in 1818, his banner—the flag of the already independent Argentina—flew over the Californian capital, Monterey.

Bouchard led a highly adventurous life and died as violently as he lived. A native of France, he was awarded Argentine citizenship in 1813 by the government of that then new country, in thanks for helping Argentina in its fight for independence.

Born on January 15, 1780, Bouchard as a child worked for his father, a cork manufacturer. When his father died and was replaced by a heartless stepfather, Bouchard ran off and joined the French navy.

During Napoleon's conquest of Egypt, Bouchard distinguished himself in combat off the island of Malta. He appears to have been a quarrelsome person, difficult to work with and even harder to serve under. Yet, he was employed by several countries' governments in succession, because he could be relied on to rush to the front line in any battle.

In the early 1800s, he left the French navy to study navigation in the United States. From there, he went to what was to become Argentina, arriving before its rebellion against Spanish rule in 1810.

The next year Bouchard became second in command of Argentina's first naval squadron. As such, he participated in a battle against Spanish vessels, which the Argentines lost. A subsequent court-martial not only absolved Bouchard of blame but also praised him for his "bravery, zeal, and activity." Further, it declared that the combat would have been won if the squadron had attacked when Bouchard said it should.

He was later engaged in another naval skirmish, this one successful. But when a temporary cessation of hostilities was signed, the naval squadron was disbanded.

Bouchard then decided to continue fighting for Argentina's independence on land, specifically in a cavalry grenadiers squadron. This squadron was formed by José de San Martín, who would go on to become the general who threw off Spanish rule in Argentina, Chile, and Peru.

As lieutenant of this cavalry, Bouchard took part in the new unit's first battle, in 1813 at San Lorenzo in Argentina. It was Bouchard who killed the royalist forces' standard-bearer and captured the enemy flag.

Bouchard was made a captain in San Martín's army in northern Argentina, but when the force became bogged down in political quarrels, Bouchard resigned and went back to sea.

Lacking a navy of its own at the time, Argentina in 1815 began to commission privateers to wage war employing armed ships owned by private individuals. Privateers fought for a country under a government contract that entitled them to share the spoils of war. The system had been employed by the United States against Great Britain in the War of 1812, and many of the privateers first commissioned by Argentina were U.S. sailors. While the victims of privateers' attacks usually considered their attackers to be pirates, most countries employed them when proper navies were not available. Argentina began to use privateers against Spain under rules for their engagement issued by the king in Madrid in 1801. Commanding a corvette, Bouchard participated in a four-ship privateering expedition in the Pacific Ocean, headed by Guillermo (William) Brown, an Irishman, later regarded as the founder of Argentina's navy. Bouchard and Brown would often quarrel.

Off the coast of Peru in 1816, they captured a Spanish frigate, the *Consecuencia*. Refitted and renamed *La Argentina,* this vessel was armed with some 40 guns. Bouchard used it to terrorize the garrisons of the California coast during a new, one-ship privateering mission that set sail from Buenos Aires in 1817 and that he alone commanded. But before getting to California Bouchard first circumnavigated the globe. His mission was to attack Spanish vessels and possessions and, where possible, to further the cause of independence among those territories still under Spanish rule.

At first, the entire venture seemed doomed. There was a mutiny on board even before Bouchard set sail, triggered by a punishment meted out to a sailor. One man hurled an axe at Bouchard, who ducked. His second in command killed the mutineer with a sword.

Once at sea, while crossing the Atlantic and rounding the southern tip of Africa, there was a shipboard fire, but it was put out. In Madagascar, the ship came upon three British cargo ships and one French vessel that were loading slaves. Argentina had decreed emancipation in 1813. Bouchard took over the ships and freed the slaves, prompting diplomatic protests by Britain and France in Argentina.

Scurvy killed more than 40 of his 200 crew members. Next, Bouchard's ship was attacked by five boatloads of Malay pirates, but Bouchard and his crew defeated and captured them.

On board one of the pirate boats, Bouchard found evidence that they had slaughtered every crew member of a Portuguese ship after it had surrendered to them. Learning this, Bouchard put all the pirates, save a few who were very young, on board their mastless craft and shot it to the bottom of the sea.

In early 1818, he reached the Philippines, a Spanish possession, and spent two months there attacking enemy shipping.

Hawaii, an independent kingdom, was the next stop. Bouchard talked King Kamehameha I into recognizing Argentina's independence from Spain. He also discovered an Argentine corvette—another privateering vessel whose crew had mutinied and escaped to remote Hawaii for safety. Bouchard recovered the corvette and rounded up the mutineers who were hiding on various islands. He executed the ringleaders and flogged the rest. Then he set sail for California with both ships.

News of the approach of "the black frigate" (*La Argentina*) and "the small frigate" (the corvette) preceded them. The governor of California ordered the town's defenses reinforced and then left Monterey for inland. Rebellion against Spain in Mexico had been almost stamped out by 1818. In remote California, it had never taken root.

As Bouchard approached, the guns of the Monterey presidio (fort) outshot and obtained the surrender of the corvette, but the town did not have boats with which to transfer these new prisoners to land. During the night, while the fort's garrison was celebrating the apparent victory, Bouchard, in his frigate's boats, recovered the uninjured sailors from the corvette.

In the morning of November 24, 1818, he landed with his men. They overwhelmed the royalist foot soldiers and mounted militia who tried to stop them. They then scaled the fort's walls from the rear and overran it and the town.

Bouchard remained in control of the capital until November 29. He then decided to continue his travels, first spiking the fort's guns and burning the fort and then burning the property of the Spanish garrison, while sparing that of the local population.

The privateers then ransacked a coastal ranch, El Refugio, which had been evacuated before their arrival. Bouchard targeted it because its owners were known to have cracked down hard on locals sympathetic to the independence movement.

Next, he arrived outside Santa Barbara. It was one of the biggest of a number of missions set up by Spain along the California coast for religious and military purposes. After negotiations, he exchanged the one prisoner he was carrying for three of his own men who had been captured when they strayed off El Refugio. He sailed on and attacked and conquered San Juan Capistrano, leaving immediately after destroying Spanish armament and property, before Spanish reinforcements arrived.

The remainder of operations took place further south of what is now United States land. Bouchard harassed towns and shipping along the coast and, in southern Mexico, made contact with local anti-Spanish revolutionaries led by Vicente Guerrero. The Argentine naval expedition was unable to join forces with the local independence fighters because the latter lacked control of any port.

Bouchard ended the voyage in Chile, which had been freed of Spanish rule by General San Martín and was Argentina's ally. The head of the Chilean navy, Scotsman Thomas Cochrane, nevertheless jailed Bouchard for piracy and impounded his ships. It is believed that Cochrane was after the Spanish loot that Bouchard was bringing from Monterey, for an Argentine-Chilean naval campaign that was being prepared to free Peru from the Spaniards.

Bouchard was acquitted of piracy and the ships—minus armament and cargo—were returned to him. The sailor promptly reenlisted with his old commander, San Martín, and his ships were used to transport troops to Peru.

After the successful campaign, Bouchard entered the Peruvian navy. He won praise for valor in an attack against the port of El Callao in 1824.

Bouchard retired five years later to two farms that were given to him by the Peruvian government in payment for services rendered. The slaves on the farms were his own, and Bouchard did not free them as he had done with the slaves of the English and French traders in Madagascar. In 1837, he was killed in a slave uprising on one of the farms.

Further Reading

Breschini, Gary S. "Hipólito (Hypolite) Bouchard and the Pirate Raid of 1818." Monterey County Historical Society, 1999. Available online. URL: http://users.dedot.com/mchs/bouchard.html. Downloaded October 10, 2000.

Del Rey, Lester. *A Pirate Flag for Monterey—The Story of the Sack of Monterey.* Philadelphia, Pa.: Winston, 1952.

Gregory, Kristiana. *The Stowaway: A Tale of California Pirates.* New York: Scholastic, 1995.

Bujones, Fernando (1955–) *ballet dancer*

Widely regarded as the best U.S.–born dancer of classical ballet ever, Fernando Bujones was born in Miami on March 9, 1955. His parents, both Cubans, soon divorced, and his mother, a dancer, returned with him to Cuba when he was five.

He was a very thin child. This led his mother to enroll him in Cuba's prestigious Alicia Alonso Ballet Academy in order to develop his appetite and physique. The artistic results were quickly found to be spectacular.

When, at age 10, he returned to the United States with his mother, he was immediately accepted to the School of American Ballet with a full scholarship. The school was run by the New York City Ballet, a company headed by the famed choreographer George Balanchine.

At 15, Bujones was described by *The New York Times*'s influential critic Clive Barnes as the owner of "perfect feet," of "a style that is unmistakable," and of "the authority of a born classicist." Balanchine offered Bujones a position in the New York City Ballet; instead, Bujones chose to enter the American Ballet Theatre (ABT) in 1972.

In 1973, ABT made Bujones, who was acknowledged as the boy wonder among male dancers in the United States, a soloist. It was also the year he danced with Dame Margot Fonteyn in *Les Sylphides;* at age 18, he was the youngest dancer ever to be partnered with the great female star.

The next year, 1974, ABT promoted him again, to principal dancer. He also danced for the first time in Europe, where he was greeted with raves. In the highly regarded dance competition in Varna, Bulgaria, at age 19, he chose to compete as a senior (ages 20 to 28) and won the gold medal. Critics wrote about his "extraordinary extension and elevation" and his "virtuoso technique."

However, Bujones in his own opinion and that of ballet observers was to become the victim of bad timing: That same year, 1974, the cultural world was electrified when dance superstar Mikhail Baryshnikov defected from the Soviet Union and arrived in the United States. Bujones was eclipsed. He declared in print that "Baryshnikov has the publicity, but I have the talent!"

Bujones remained in the shadow of Baryshnikov. Nevertheless, he had an active career as a ballet star in the United States and abroad, having been principal guest artist of the Boston Ballet and associate artistic director of the Rio de Janeiro Opera House.

He has been a guest artist at many prestigious ballet institutions around the world, including the Joffrey Ballet, the British Royal Ballet, Canada's National Ballet, the Royal Swedish Ballet, the Deutsche Opera Ballet, the Royal Danish Ballet, the Rome Opera Ballet, and the Paris Opera. In the 1990s, he worked as artistic director of diverse ballet companies in the United States, Mexico, Brazil, and Spain. In 2000, he was appointed artistic adviser and choreographer in residence by the Southern Ballet Theatre in Orlando, Florida. Along with his numerous ballet awards, the city of Boston proclaimed a Bujones Day in 1991.

Bujones is married to Marcia Kubitschek, the daughter of Juscelino Kubitschek, the former president of Brazil and builder of its capital, Brasilia.

Further Reading

Philip, Richard, and Mary Whitney. *Danseur: The Male in Ballet.* New York: McGraw-Hill, 1977.

C

 **Cabeza de Vaca, Alvar Núñez** See
NÚÑEZ CABEZA DE VACA, Alvar

 **Cabrera, Lydia** (1900–1991) *writer*
Lydia Cabrera was Cuba's most outstanding woman
of letters and a pioneering researcher and popularizer
of the island's black cultural heritage. She maintained
her stature through more than 30 years of residence
and work in the United States and authored almost
two dozen books.

Cabrera was born in Havana on May 20, 1900,
into a household where intellectuals met to talk about
literary and artistic matters. The gatherings were
presided over by her father, a leading Cuban lawyer.

As she grew up, her early interests were art and
aspects of popular culture in Cuba. She combined
these interests by creating pictures of Cuban life. She
pursued her artwork at an art academy without her father's knowledge, however, because in those days
"proper" young Cuban ladies were expected to be
homebodies.

Cabrera was able to become more independent
after her father died. In 1927, she went to France to
study and graduated in 1930 from the Louvre Museum art school in Paris.

At that time, Negro themes had acquired great
favor in the bubbly artistic and literary world of the
French capital. This led Lydia Cabrera to find her true
calling. As a child she had been told many tales by
the Afro-Cuban servants in her family home. She remembered these stories and decided to set them down
on paper.

Her writing was informative, accurate, and very
entertaining. Her stories found immediate acceptance
and were brought out by one of France's top publishing houses, Gallimard. Thus, her first book came out
initially in a French translation, under the title *Con-
tes Negres de Cuba* (1936).

Two years later, she returned to Cuba, concerned
by the badly deteriorating political situation and the
threat of war in Europe. In 1940, those *Black Stories
from Cuba* came out in Cuba in their original language, as *Cuentos Negros de Cuba*.

Cabrera began to record the traditions, lore,
and sayings of Cuban blacks systematically. She is
credited not only with crisscrossing the entire country in search of material, but also with having spoken to virtually every single Afro-Cuban in the
capital.

Her work is acknowledged for having great eth-
nological value in addition to charming presentation.

She always treated her subjects with genuine interest and respect, never patronizing them.

Her works include *El Monte: Notas Sobre las Religiones, la Magia, las Supersticiones y el Folklore de los Negros Criollos y del Pueblo de Cuba* (*The Interior: Notes on the Religions, Magic, Superstitions and Folklore of Cuban-born Blacks and of the People of Cuba,* 1954) and *Refranes de Negros Viejos* (*Old Blacks' Proverbs,* 1955).

Cabrera compiled a dictionary of the Yoruba language of West Africa as remembered by Cuban blacks who continued to use the language of their ancestors. She carried out further research into secret religious societies of African origin.

The writer remained in Cuba during the dictatorship of Fulgencio Batista, but in 1960, after the arrival of the Castro regime, she left the country for the United States. She also spent time in Spain.

In the United States, after a lengthy period of coming to terms with her exile, Cabrera continued to write. Works of this period include *Francisco y Francisca: Chascarrillos de Negros Viejos* (*Francisco and Francisca: Old Blacks' Picaresque Anecdotes,* 1976).

She died in 1991.

Further Reading

Kanellos, Nicolás, ed. *Biographical Dictionary of Hispanic Literature in the United States.* Westport, Conn.: Greenwood Press, 1989.

Telgen, Diane, and Jim Kamp, eds. *Notable Hispanic American Women.* Detroit: Gale Research, Inc., 1993.

❧ **Canseco, José** (1964–) *baseball player*

José Canseco has been hailed as one of the most extraordinary baseball players of recent decades. He has shown that even when making wild boasts he must be taken seriously—in 1988 he said he would hit 40 home runs and steal 40 bases in one year (being unaware that nobody had ever done such a thing before), and he went ahead and did it. In fact he surpassed it, achieving 42 home runs as well as stealing the 40 bases. Additionally, he has repeatedly bounced back from serious injuries that seemed to herald the end of his career, but could not keep him from returning as strong as ever.

José Canseco was born in a suburb of Havana, Cuba, on July 2, 1964; his identical twin, Osvaldo ("Ozzie"), also became a baseball player. Their father was a well-to-do local executive for the Esso (later Exxon) oil company of the United States. He lost his job, house, and car in Cuba's communist revolution but was allowed to emigrate with his family when the twins were one year old.

Canseco grew up in the Miami area. Baseball did not interest him until the age of 12, and he initially showed little of his future dazzle; he was signed by the Oakland Athletics in 1982 almost as an afterthought. At 17, presumably at the end of his growing years, he was one inch short of six feet tall and weighed 165 pounds. Three punishing years later, during which he underwent relentless weight training, he had gained four inches and 67 pounds. This led to accusations that he had taken forbidden steroid drugs. Canseco hotly denied ever taking any drugs at all, saying that he did not even smoke.

Canseco was Minor League Player of the Year in 1985. Then came the majors; in 1986 he was American League Rookie of the Year, and he began to hit colossal 400-foot-plus and even 500-foot-plus balls that his fans recall with awe. One time he hit and left a mark on the center field TV camera over 400 feet away. Another time he landed a ball in the Toronto Skydome's fifth deck, a distance of 540 feet. Other memorable events include the occasion he achieved a home run with a broken bat and the time an unlucky third baseman who put his mitt in the way of one of Canseco's hits was knocked over backward.

But off the field, Canseco frequently found himself in trouble. He was arrested for speeding—driving 125 miles per hour—on the East Coast (he says he acted as if his Jaguar were a new toy, but that he has matured since then) and for gun possession on the West Coast (he says he had received anonymous threats). And he underwent a period of noticeable depression in the early 1990s after his divorce from his wife, a former Miss Miami.

Additionally, he was, especially at first, uncomfortable in the public limelight and sometimes bordered on rudeness in the face of the constant media attention. He argues that he was stared at "like the gorilla at the zoo"—and also felt "typecast as the dumb Latino," with sportswriters being "surprised I could talk."

A gentler side of his personality emerges from his philanthropic work, which shows that even if he resents being hemmed in by adults, he always has a soft spot for children. One of his favorite charities is the Make-A-Wish Foundation, which seeks to fulfill the wishes of children dying of disease. He flew 10 tons of toys to the children in a refugee camp on the U.S. military base in Guantánamo, Cuba.

On the sports field, Canseco helped take the Oakland Athletics to the World Series for three years in a row (1988–90), and in 1990 he was given a new five-year contract for $23.5 million, more than anyone else had ever earned in baseball. Two years later the Athletics amazed everyone—Canseco particularly—by trading him to the Texas Rangers (for three players).

More recently, Canseco has played for the Boston Red Sox, Oakland Athletics, and the Toronto Blue Jays. In 1999, playing for the Tampa Bay Devil Rays after signing on for three years on a $9 million contract, Canseco, typically, suffered from an injury— one that required back surgery—and, also typically, was near the top in his league in home runs (34) despite the time lost. In 2000, Canseco was picked up on waivers by the New York Yankees from the Devil Rays.

Further Reading

Aaseng, Nathan. *José Canseco: Baseball's 40-40 Man.* Minneapolis: Lerner Publications, 1989.

"ESPN.com: Jose Canseco Profile & Scouting Report." ESPN Internet Ventures. Available online. URL: http://www.espn.go.com/mlb/profiles/profile/3730.html. Downloaded October 10, 2000.

Sullivan, George. *Sluggers: Twenty-Seven of Baseball's Greatest.* New York: Atheneum/Maxwell Macmillan, 1991.

Carey, Mariah (1970–) *singer*

Mariah Carey was the undoubted female pop singing sensation of the 1990s. By the time she was 30 years

Mariah Carey *(Courtesy of Sony Records)*

old, she had sold 120 million albums, comparable in absolute terms to the figures amassed by the singing superstars Madonna and Whitney Houston—but, unlike them, achieving this within one decade. She has had more number-one hit songs (15, by late 2000), than any other female singer in history. Among males, only the Beatles (with 20) and Elvis Presley (18) have had more top hits. And in terms of the total number of weeks that her songs remained in the top slot, by 1999 she had topped the Beatles themselves. In the 1999 Billboard awards, Carey was honored as Artist of the Decade. In 2000 she and Michael Jackson were named the Best-Selling Artists of the Millennium at the World Music Awards in Monaco.

The reason for this overwhelming sales performance is clear: an amazing voice that ranges over five to seven octaves. "Mariah Carey," wrote a *New York Post* reviewer "is capable of hitting notes so high only dogs and dolphins can truly appreciate them." Indeed, some critics have charged her with showing off too much in this regard and welcomed changes in her style in the later 1990s under which she placed less emphasis on fireworks at the top of the scale.

Carey is also a songwriter. In this regard, her efforts have left many commentators less enraptured, as being too mushy or unoriginal, but they have clearly not dented her popularity. Of 14 number-one hits, she wrote or cowrote 13. She also works on the production side of her records, and at the end of the 1990s was making stabs at a movie acting career. She appeared in *The Bachelor* in 1999, and filmed *All That Glitters* in 2000.

Mariah Carey was born in New York City on March 27, 1970, the product of an interracial marriage destroyed by other people's bigotry. Her father, an aeronautical engineer, is a black Hispanic from Venezuela, her mother an Irish American whose family virtually disowned her because of her marriage. Neighbors proved to be equally racist but more violent: they poisoned the couple's dogs and set fire to their cars, and the stress eventually led to a divorce when Mariah was three years old.

Life was difficult for the girl while growing up because of a scarcity of money compounded by rejection from children at school, black and white, who also thought race was important and disliked Mariah's ambiguous appearance in this respect. (She is so light-skinned that at the start of her career, uninformed critics accused her of being a "white girl trying to sing black.") But she was fortunate in that her mother, an opera singer and coach, quickly discovered that Mariah sang with perfect pitch. Without pushing her daughter toward a singing career, Mariah's mother taught, encouraged her, and gave her confidence.

As soon as Mariah finished high school in Long Island, she moved to Manhattan, sharing an apartment with other would-be singers and working such jobs as waitress and hat-check attendant. Her main activity, however, from her own point of view, was taking demo tapes of her singing to one record company after another.

She did not get immediate attention, but she did obtain gigs as a backup vocalist for other singers. One of them, Brenda Starr, befriended her and helped her distribute her demo tapes. She took Carey to a fateful party in 1988 where she met Tommy Mottola, president of CBS (later Sony Music Entertainment), and as Starr was offering one of the tapes to another executive, Mottola grabbed it.

Mottola played the tape in his car as he left the party—and immediately turned around and dashed back to look for Carey. She had already left, but Mottola tracked her down and soon gave her a contract and organized her first album and its marketing.

Two years in the making, that record, *Mariah Carey,* was a smash success. It earned Carey two Grammy Awards (Best New Artist, Best Female Pop Vocalist) in 1990—the first in a long list of prizes over the following years, including Soul Train and Billboard awards. In one decade, Carey released nine albums, ending with *Rainbow* in 1999. In 2000, she received an Award of Achievement for her "rare and distinguished accomplishments" at the American Music Awards. Late in 2000, Carey released *Merry Christmas,* an album of Christmas carols and pop standards with a holiday theme.

Mottola and Carey were married in 1993 in a wedding that reportedly cost half a million dollars. The marriage ended four years later, and after that Carey began a romance with the Mexican hit singer Luis Miguel.

Carey has repeatedly taken time to work with disadvantaged children through the Police Athletic League and donated money from her hit singles to charitable causes.

Further Reading

"Mariah Carey—Rainbow." Columbia Records. Available online. URL: http://www.mcarey.com. Downloaded October 10, 2000.

Meier, Matt. *Notable Latino Americans.* Westport, Conn.: Greenwood Press, 1977.

Nickson, Chris. *Mariah Carey: Her Story.* New York: St. Martin's 1995.

———. *Mariah Carey Revisited: Her Story (The Unauthorized Biography).* New York: St. Martin's, 1998.

Carr, Vikki (Florencia Bisenta de Casillas Martínez Cardona) (1940–) *singer*

Vikki Carr is one of the most successful Hispanic performing and recording artists in the United States. She sings in both English and Spanish. She also has countless fans in Latin America, in Europe, and even in Australia and Japan.

Carr is also extremely active in philanthropic causes, particularly for Mexican-American charities, earning much recognition for her charitable work.

In her early days as a singer, she called herself Carlita. She soon simplified and Anglicized her stage name to Vikki Carr. Despite the name change, she makes a point of reminding audiences of her Hispanic full name, Florencia Bisenta de Casillas Martínez Cardona.

She was born on July 19, 1940, in El Paso, Texas. Her father was a construction engineer, and money was scarce. There were six other children besides young Vikki. She later recalled that flour mixed with water often replaced milk at the family table.

Her father instilled in her a pride in their Mexican-American ancestry. This pride helped the little girl when the family moved to a San Gabriel Valley town near Los Angeles. There, she was punished at school for her faulty English.

Music was also important in Carr's home. Little Florencia sang the hymn "Adeste Fidelis" in a Christmas play at the age of four, sang with amateur bands during her high school years, and first sang professionally at age 18 with a cross-cultural outfit called Pepe Callahan's Mexican-Irish Band at a nightclub in Palm Springs.

Vikki Carr's strong voice and talent for carrying a song gained quick recognition. Her first recording contract came in 1961. She went on such a successful tour of Australia that it led to television appearances on the Ray Anthony series back in the United States.

Television became a strong base for Carr's career. She appeared on shows with Dean Martin, Carol Burnett, the Smothers Brothers, Jackie Gleason, Red Skelton, and Bob Hope; on the *Tonight Show,* both with Johnny Carson and as a guest host; and on six special shows on British television.

Carr played all the top nightclubs in Los Angeles, Lake Tahoe, Reno, Las Vegas, Hawaii, Atlantic City, and New York; toured military bases in Vietnam with the comedian Danny Kaye; and sang at concert halls in Europe, Mexico, and Central America—all to standing-room-only audiences.

In 1967, she did a Royal Command Performance in London for Queen Elizabeth II. She sang at the White House for Presidents Richard Nixon, Gerald Ford, Ronald Reagan, and George H. W. Bush; at the inauguration of the Kennedy Music Center in Washington, D.C; and at the dedication of the Nixon Library in California.

Carr's first big hit in the United States was the song *It Must Be Him,* already a hit in Britain. Since then, she has recorded more than 50 LPs; 17 of them became gold records.

In 1972, she recorded her first Spanish-language LP, *Vikki Carr en Español.* It would be followed by many others, extending her popularity beyond the United States to Hispanic audiences in many Latin American countries. Two of these records, *Simplemente Mujer* and *Cosas del Amor,* won the U.S. music industry's top honor, the Grammy award.

In 1999, Carr launched *Vikki Carr: Memorias Memories,* a recording of songs included in a PBS performance program celebrating Latin America and its influence on U.S. pop music in the 1940s and 1950s.

Of her English-language albums, two, *It Must Be Him* and *With Pen in Hand,* have won Grammy nominations. Other honors have included the Entertainer of the Year award of the American Guild of Variety Artists and Mexico's Visiting Entertainer of the Year award.

Carr has sung in such musicals as *The Unsinkable Molly Brown* and *South Pacific,* giving performances in several cities and on Broadway.

She was married and divorced twice and has lost two children. A person of seemingly limitless energy, the five-foot-two-inch tall singer has thrown herself into her career and into humanitarian work. She sings for any charity benefit that comes to her notice, but makes a special point of helping Chicano causes.

Her particular field of interest has been education. She did not go to college, and she has said that the young people she helps to get an education take the place of her own children, whom she never got to raise.

Annually she raises money for a school in an impoverished Mexican-American neighborhood. In 1970, she founded her own philanthropic institution, the Vikki Carr Scholarship Foundation. It has helped finance the college education of hundreds of students. Carr does not merely provide money. She personally takes part in the final stages of selecting candidates for the scholarships. Two universities have given her honorary degrees as a token of thanks.

She was declared Woman of the Year by the *Los Angeles Times* in 1970 and by the League of United Latin American Citizens (LULAC) in 1983. She was also named Hispanic Woman of the Year and Woman of the World, a distinction conferred by the International Orphans Fund. She won the Founder of Hope award from the City of Hope, the Golden Eagle award for her work from the Nosotros Hispanic organization, and the For God and Youth award.

Carr runs her own corporation, Vi-Car Enterprises, to handle her career. "For business I'm very American, but my heart is totally Latin," she told an interviewer.

Further Reading

Martínez, Al. *Rising Voices: Profiles of Hispano-American Lives.* New York: New American Library, 1974.

Meier, Matt S. *Mexican American Biographies.* Westport, Conn.: Greenwood Publishing Group, 1988.

Telgen, Diane, and Jim Kemp, eds. *Notable Hispanic American Women.* Detroit: Gale Research, Inc., 1993.

❧ Carrasco, Barbara (1955–) *artist*

Barbara Carrasco is one of the best-known mural artists in the city of Los Angeles. She and her peers create vast, impressive works with Mexican-American themes. She is also recognized for her small-scale work, earning praise for a combination of excellent drawing skills, sharp wit, and social commitment. This latter trait has made her a tireless battler for Chicano causes.

Born in 1955, Carrasco was raised in a working-class area of Los Angeles and went to Roman Catholic grade school. The experience marked her strongly: her early ideals were offended when she perceived that "white students were treated better" by the nuns who ran the school.

She also found herself caught in the middle. She had "white" features and because of this and the general climate of racial tensions, some other Mexican-American children discriminated against *her* as a "gringa," or Anglo.

Carrasco has never forgotten these childhood experiences. In the 1980s, she mounted an exhibit entitled *The 13 Stations of the Double Cross* at a Los Angeles museum. The images recalled what she called "the guilt trips and the indoctrination" of a Catholic education. The "double-cross" reference in the title is characteristic of the word games she likes to play in connection with her works of art.

Carrasco studied painting, sculpture, and graphic arts at UCLA and holds B.A. and M.F.A. degrees from that university. Her public murals in Los Angeles remain her best-known work. The year she graduated from college, 1978, she participated in the creation of one of the most famous of the murals—*Zoot Suit,* at the Aquarius Theater in Hollywood.

She also committed herself to the cause of the United Farm Workers Union, which battled for Mexican-American workers' rights. Carrasco created artwork for the crusade. Her mother protested: "You are closer to Dolores HUERTA (one of the United Farm Workers' leaders) than to your own mother."

During this time, Carrasco was also working for the Chicano improvements-and-rights drive that participants called El Movimiento (The Movement). Before long, the electronic billboard at Times Square in New York City displayed Carrasco's drawings of farmworkers and the effects of pesticides.

Carrasco also found she had an extra battle on her hands. This one was within El Movimiento itself and, more specifically, among the muralists. It was the battle for women's equality and against machismo in Chicano ranks.

In 1983, a Los Angeles city agency commissioned Carrasco to paint a mural for the 1984 Olympic Games, to be held in Los Angeles. But when the agency saw what Carrasco had painted, they ordered her to redo it. Called *LA History—A Mexican Perspective,* the mural was a series of 51 scenes woven into the long hair of a "Queen of the Angels." The scenes included violent episodes of racism, such as the mass lynchings of Chinese workers at the end of the 1800s and the internment of Japanese Americans in concentration camps during World War II. The city argued that the scenes would distress Asian visitors during the Olympics. Carrasco rejected the demands for changes. She felt caught in a replay of a 1932 incident when Los Angeles had also played host to the Olympics. That time Los Angeles had invited the great Mexican muralist David Alfaro Siqueiros to execute a work. But because Siqueiros had expressed his feelings about the political and economic relationship between the United States and Mexico by painting an American eagle attacking a crucified Mexican peasant, the city immediately destroyed the mural. Before the 1984 Olympics, Los Angeles destroyed murals that the city considered politically offensive; these murals were created by the Chicano artists Robert Chávez and John Valadez.

But Carrasco had taken the precaution of painting her 16-foot-by-80-foot mural on a series of movable wooden panels. Because of her foresight, she was able to save the mural from the city. She gave it to United Farm Workers leader César CHÁVEZ to safeguard, declaring him "the only person I trust." The mural remains with the union.

The fight against censorship assured Barbara Carrasco's celebrity—the *Los Angeles Times* wrote about her "stormy temperament and iron will."

In 1984, she was invited by a Boston organization, Children Are the Future, to travel with a delegation to Armenia, then part of the Soviet Union. There, she would paint a mural on the Armenian capital's Children's Museum. In 1986, as part of a Chicano delegation to Nicaragua, she worked on a mural for a youth organization in that country.

Carrasco has also earned tributes for the small, precise drawings she executed with ballpoint pen on clay-coated paper. Especially valued were the series *Here Lies/Hear Lies* and another called *RIP*, which illustrated not only the idea of "Rest in Peace" but also concepts such as "Rest in Poverty," "Rest in Plenty," and "Rest in Politics." She drew sarcastic portraits of individuals such as *Our Judge, Our Preacher, Our Artist,* and *Our Journalist,* standing in upright coffins.

Carrasco's illustrations, while completely modern in appearance, have been repeatedly compared in intention to the fantastic, moralistic work of the Flemish painter Hieronymus Bosch at the end of the Middle Ages.

Carrasco's work was included in 1990 in a traveling exhibition called *Chicano Art: Resistance and Affirmation, 1965–1985,* created to make this art known across the United States. She participated in 1999 in the Maestras Atelier, an all-female silkscreen workshop described as "a remarkable event" by the University of California at Berkeley. Carrasco participated with a print portrait of Dolores Huerta whom she called "one of my role models as well as a dear friend."

Further Reading

Shorris, Earl. *Latinos: A Biography of the People.* New York: Avon Books, 1992.

❧ **Carrera, Barbara** (1951–) *actress*
Hollywood movie roles requiring beautiful, slightly exotic-looking female stars are Carrera's strong suit.

Carrera (whose last name means "career" or "race" in Spanish) was born on December 31, 1951, in Managua, Nicaragua. Her mother is Nicaraguan; her father, an American employee of the U.S. embassy in Managua. Her parents separated when Carrera was 10. From the age of 11, she received a convent education both in the United States (in Tennessee) and in Europe.

While on vacation in New York at the age of 16, she was window-shopping on Fifth Avenue when a fashion designer saw her and suggested she become a model. Initially, her almond eyes and strongly defined cheekbones caused model agencies to turn her down, calling her "too exotic." Nevertheless, by the following year, she had signed her first modeling contract and went on to become one of the world's best-paid fashion models, appearing in such top magazines as *Harper's Bazaar* and *Vogue.*

In 1970, she moved to Paris and later enrolled at the Sorbonne to study painting. But she was soon "discovered" by filmmakers while modeling in a fashion show in Cannes, France, site of one of the world's major film festivals.

This "discovery" led to supporting and leading roles in movies including *The Island of Dr. Moreau*

Barbara Carrera with Sean Connery in a production still photo for the film *Never Say Never Again* (Cabrera Archive)

(1977), *Never Say Never Again* (1983), and *Burnin' Love* (1987). More recently, her movie credits include *Love Is All There Is* (1996), *Waking Up Horton* and *Illusion Infinity* (both in 1998), and *Alec to the Rescue* (1999).

Carrera has also worked in television, appearing in productions ranging from the TV movie *Masada* (1981, playing a Jewish martyr and the love interest of a Roman general portrayed by Peter O'Toole) to the *Dallas* series.

Also an artist, Carrera has exhibited her oil paintings in the United States and in Europe.

Further Reading

Oshana, Maryann. *Women of Color—A Filmography of Minority and Third World Women.* New York: Garland Publishing, Inc., 1985.

Unterburger, Amy, and Jane Delgado, eds. *Who's Who Among Hispanic Americans.* Detroit: Gale Research, Inc., 1993.

 ### Carrillo, Leo (Leopoldo Carrillo)
(1881–1961) *actor*

Leo Carrillo, whose full name was Leopoldo Carrillo, had a long acting career with three distinct phases. He first played loathsome Mexican outlaws, then a comedy character, and finally the lovable assistant to television's Cisco Kid, battler for justice.

Carrillo (whose name means "cheek" or "jowl" in Spanish) was born in Los Angeles on August 6, 1881, into a family of long-established Hispanic settlers, or "Californios."

As a teenager, Carrillo showed a particular gift for drawing. He was also a champion swimmer, and he worked on the railroad in order to pay for art studies in San Francisco. After school, he was a cartoonist for the daily *San Francisco Examiner.*

However, Carrillo soon turned to acting, first as a vaudeville comedian, where he employed his gift for languages—he spoke Chinese, Japanese, and Italian in addition to Spanish and English—and second as a mimic of people's behavior.

After vaudeville, he appeared as an actor in the mainstream theatrical plays of the 1920s. He enjoyed a two-year run on Broadway playing a role in *Lombardi, Ltd.*

Because his way with language was an essential ingredient of his appeal as an actor, Carrillo waited until the late 1920s when the movies incorporated sound before he worked in that medium. In films, he played some lead roles but was mainly known for a long succession of secondary, character roles.

Many were unsavory. Hollywood had a long history of portraying Mexicans according to the vilest stereotypes. For many years, the movie industry openly used the word *greaser* as another way of saying *Mexican.* It did this even if the Mexican character was a "noble" type (that is, one on the side of the Anglos), as in *Tony the Greaser* (1911). Carrillo would play some of the worst of Hollywood's Mexican ruffians, notably in *Girl of the Rio* (1932). Mexico and a number of other Latin American governments complained officially about American movie portrayals of Latin characters, including Carrillo's.

However, he also managed to land many roles, mostly comic, as an amiable sidekick of the leading man in the 1930s and 1940s. After the movies came television, where he made his principal mark as Pancho, the Cisco Kid's jokey partner. This character was shaped after Don Quixote's squire, Sancho Panza.

Carrillo was such an enthusiast of early California history and of the state's attractions that he wrote a book on the subject. He was also appointed California beaches and parks commissioner and the Californian goodwill ambassador to the world. He liked to take part in Californian parades and appear at rodeos, riding his favorite palomino horse. Carrillo died in 1961.

Further Reading

Blackwell, Earl. *Celebrity Register.* Towson, Md.: Times Publishing Group, 1986.
Leo Carrillo. Available online. URL: http://www.westerns.com/stars/leo_carrillo. Downloaded October 10, 2000.
Meier, Matt S. *Mexican American Biographies.* Westport, Conn.: Greenwood Publishing Group, 1988.

❧ Carter, Lynda (Lynda Córdoba Carter)

(ca. July 24, 1951–   ) *actress*

Lynda Carter made her mark as television's Wonder Woman.

Carter was born on July 24—probably 1951, although the exact year remains a secret—in Phoenix, Arizona, to an English father and Mexican mother. While still in high school in Phoenix, Carter entered show business as a nightclub singer and dancer. She performed in her home state and then toured the country. At the same time, she went to college at Arizona State University in the city of Tempe.

Carter won the Miss World–USA crown in 1973, and from beauty pageants she went on to television. She remains best known for her title role in the *Wonder Woman* series, which aired from 1976 to 1979. Carter also starred in other series, such as *Partners in Crime,* and in TV movies. In *Rita Hayworth:*

The Love Goddess (1983), she reenacted the life of another Hispanic-American actress, Rita HAYWORTH (née Margarita Cansino).

Additionally, she sang and danced in TV specials and on nightclub stages in Las Vegas and elsewhere. She was named the Hispanic Women's Council's Hispanic Woman of the Year in 1983. The International Bachelors Association named her one of the Ten Most Exciting Women in the World.

Lynda Carter was contracted as a beauty and fashion director by a cosmetics company. The company's sales tripled 18 months after she began to appear in its advertisements and to act as product development and marketing consultant. She also heads her own television production company. Carter's recent television work has included *Someone to Love Me* (1998) and *Execution of Justice, Family Blessings,* and *Mercy* (all in 1999).

Carter is married to one of the best-known lawyers in Washington, D.C., Robert Altman. Altman was acquitted in 1993 of the first charges to come to trial in the notorious fraud case known as the BCCI banking scandal.

Further Reading

Blackwell, Earl. *Celebrity Register.* Towson, Md.: Times Publishing Group, 1986.
Meier, Matt S. *Mexican American Biographies.* Westport, Conn.: Greenwood Publishing Group, 1988.

❧ Casals, Pablo (1876–1973) *cellist*

Pablo Casals is universally regarded as one of the greatest concert performers of the 20th century. His mastery of the cello garnered him international renown throughout his long career. He also helped to transform Puerto Rico into a world-class center of classical music.

Puerto Rican on his mother's side, Casals was born in Vendrell, a town in Catalonia, Spain, on December 29, 1876. He was the Paris Opera's principal cellist by 1895 and a cello soloist in Paris and London in 1898. In 1905, Casals, violinist Jacques Thibaud, and pianist Alfred Cortot formed a concert trio.

Known primarily for his performances of the music of Johann Sebastian Bach, Casals greatly raised the prestige of his chosen instrument. He demonstrated to musicians everywhere that it is possible to be singled out as a major performer without playing one of the flashier instruments such as the piano or the violin.

Casals was praised not only for the virtuosity of his technique, but also for the way he absorbed and transmitted a great understanding of the musical qualities of the pieces he played. He became the undisputed standard by which all the cellists who followed were compared.

He was also a person with strong convictions about social equality. He believed that workers could and would enjoy classical music just as wealthier people did, if only it were brought to them. In 1919, he founded an ensemble for that purpose. He called it the Pau Casals Orchestra (using the spelling of his name in the Catalan language), and served as conductor.

Casals fiercely opposed the right-wing dictatorship of Generalissimo Francisco Franco, who had come to power following the Spanish Civil War (1936–39). After 1939, Casals never set foot in Spain again.

He first settled in France in order to be as close to his own country as possible without actually returning. He lived in Prades, a town in the Pyrenees mountains. In 1956 he decided to move to his mother's home country, and until his death in 1973 he resided in Puerto Rico.

In Prades, Casals had started a music festival, an annual celebration of great classical music. With his departure, the Casals Festival relocated to Puerto Rico.

Casals's stature in the music world ensured that the festival in Puerto Rico would attract great performers. Casals thus transformed Puerto Rico from a classical-music backwater into an important venue. Since his death in 1973, the Casals Festival has continued to be held in his honor.

Further Reading

Baldock, Robert. *Pablo Casals.* Boston: Northeastern University Press, 1993.

Forsee, Aylsea. *Pablo Casals: Cellist for Freedom.* New York: T.Y. Crowell, 1965.

Garza, Hedda. *Pablo Casals.* New York: Chelsea House, 1993.

Kirk, H. L. *Pablo Casals.* New York: Holt, Rinehart, and Winston, 1974.

Littlehales, Lillian. *Pablo Casals.* Westport, Conn.: Greenwood Press, 1970.

Taper, Bernard. *Cellist in Exile.* New York: McGraw-Hill, 1962.

Casals, Rosemary (1948–) *tennis player*

Rosemary Casals is one of the major names in the history of women's tennis, both as a singles player and particularly in doubles. She was also one of the key rebels who modernized professional tennis, making it what it is today.

Casals (who is not related to the musician Pablo CASALS) was born in San Francisco on September 16, 1948. Her parents, who had come to the United States from El Salvador, were so poor that they were unable to raise Rosemary and her sister Victoria. Instead, the girls were brought up in the household of a great-uncle, a small businessman.

This great-uncle was also a sportsman, having been a member of El Salvador's national soccer team. He helped the sisters start in tennis and especially encouraged Rosemary when she quickly demonstrated a talent for the game. He remained the only tennis coach of her career.

At age 13, Casals won her first championship. From the outset, Casals showed herself to be a go-getting, competitive participant in the sport, both on and off the court. She overcame a variety of hurdles and never avoided conflict. At the time, tennis was still perceived as a game for wealthy white people, and Casals was often snubbed for being, by comparison, penniless, as well as Hispanic.

"I felt stigmatized because we were poor," she recalled later. On the court, she also had to compensate for her height. Being only five foot two was a disadvantage.

Casals became a leader in the struggle to make tennis more democratic, less starchy, and more businesslike. She broke with the rule that dictated players could wear only white. Initially, this tradition was so strong that players could be physically barred from the courts for wearing other colors—unless they were as tenacious as Casals.

More important, she was in the forefront of two decisive battles. One of these was fought alongside male tennis players, and the other against them.

The first battle involved professionalizing the sport. This meant allowing players to be paid for winning and thus earn a living from the game. Without this decision, tennis would have remained an amateur sport whose players earned their money at something else, largely restricting the game to the rich.

The second battle was to make women's prize money approach the amounts paid to male players. It proved an even tougher struggle than the first. At first, women players had to organize their own tournaments, having been suspended from the Tennis Association, which governed the game. This suspension resulted from their demand that women's prize money be one-third that of men's. But by the end, Casals and fellow rebels achieved some considerable gains.

In her career, Casals has won almost 100 tournaments. Playing singles, she has triumphed against some of the top names in the game, including Margaret Court and Billie Jean King. But she was especially noted for her doubles game. With Billie Jean King, she formed a doubles team that won the U.S. Open twice and Wimbledon five times. The Tennis Association named her the top doubles player nine times.

Casals also had considerable success playing mixed doubles. She became an organizer of new tournaments for mixed doubles and, later, for senior (older) players. She and King won a senior women's doubles tournament in 1990.

After retiring from the tour, Casals launched an agency for tennis players and a television productions corporation.

Further Reading

Jacobs, Linda. *Rosemary Casals—The Rebel Rosebud.* St. Paul, Minn.: EMC Corporation, 1975.

Thacher, Alida. *Raising a Racket: Rosie Casals.* Milwaukee, Wis.: Raintree, 1976.

 Castañeda, Carlos (Carlos César Arana Castañeda) (1925–1998) *New Age guru, hoaxer*

Carlos Castañeda perpetrated one of the most masterly scientific deceits of modern times, often compared to the Piltdown Man hoax, in which an early human species was deduced from the "discovery" in 1912 of "ancient" bones that turned out to be the artfully doctored remains of a contemporary ape. Yet his sole real satisfaction appears to have been proving to himself that he could get his tall tales believed. He could have brought his message—about finding new ways for looking at oneself and at the world—in a straightforward manner. Even his detractors and skeptics admitted he was extremely gifted, and he would have found a ready market in those receptive days. Instead, he chose to cloak the message in an elaborate fabrication about a guru (spiritual teacher) called Don Juan, who, it emerged, was imaginary.

Nonetheless, Castañeda proved genuinely satisfying to throngs of seekers of the occult and of alternative lifestyles. He was one of the most famous of all the gurus who arose in (or flocked to) Western countries in the 1960s, an era when many millions of people sought inspiration or refuge in nontraditional answers to life's questions and problems.

Unlike many other such gurus, however, Castañeda (not related to Carlos E. CASTAÑEDA) fled from fame—he would not even allow his photograph to be taken—and from any other fortune than the royalties derived from his many best-selling books.

His father's name was César Arana and his mother's Susana Castañeda, so that his own, according to custom in many Latin American countries, was Carlos Arana Castañeda, or, in shortened form, Carlos Arana. He appears to have delighted in inventing stories about himself, and in covering up his tracks, from early days on. Although he was born in Cajamarca, Peru, on December 25, 1925, he claimed to have been born in São Paulo, Brazil, in 1931. Obscurely unhappy relationships with his parents have been advanced as a reason for much of Castañeda's adult behavior. When his mother died when he was 24, he locked himself up and fasted for three days, then abruptly left home. He also began using his mother's last name rather than his father's. Over the course of his life he appears to have abandoned two wives and two children, one of them twice—once in infancy and once after being reunited, and being forgiven by her, years later.

In 1951 he arrived in the United States, where he became a citizen in 1959. He wrote to a cousin—whom he referred to as his sister—that he had been discharged from the U.S. Army after some injury, but he never actually served in the army.

Castañeda studied creative writing at Los Angeles City College, then graduated with a degree in anthropology from the University of California at Los Angeles (UCLA). He later obtained a graduate degree, and his master's thesis was published in 1968 as his first book, *The Teachings of Don Juan: A Yaqui Way of Knowledge*.

In this book, Castañeda described his apprenticeship with Don Juan, a Yaqui Indian sorcerer in northern Mexico, who taught him about the search for an alternative reality. One of the techniques used was to eat mind-altering mushrooms.

The book's popularity was such that many disciples, and also doubters, traveled through the areas mentioned by Castañeda, trying to find Don Juan themselves. Nobody ever did, but Castañeda himself met with him many times more, leading to a total of 10 books. The third in the series, *Journey to Ixtlán: The Lessons of Don Juan* (1972), was accepted by UCLA as Castañeda's Ph.D. thesis (1973).

Although some critics pointed to contradictions within the books, and also found sources in other books from which Castañeda appeared to have copied many sections with only minor alterations, UCLA continued to defend its bestowal of his degrees. Alluding to the fact that Castañeda claimed that the magic taught by Don Juan included being able to turn people into animals, one writer, Kathryn Lindskoog, stated in the book *Fakes, Frauds, and Other Malarkey* that Castañeda's "only real sorcery was turning the University of California into an ass."

But UCLA was not alone in defending Castañeda. The *New York Times* declared that "We are incredibly fortunate to have Carlos Castañeda's books. . . . One can't exaggerate the significance of what he has done." *Life* magazine said that "Cas-

tañeda's sanity . . . compels us to believe that Don Juan is one of the most extraordinary figures in anthropological literature, a Neolithic sage." And the *Chicago Tribune* noted that "It's impossible to view the world in quite the same way after reading him . . . If Castañeda is correct, there is another world, a sometimes beautiful and sometimes frightening world, right before our eyes."

In keeping with Castañeda's reclusive ways, his death in 1998 was not revealed until two months after the event.

Further Reading

"Carlos Castañeda's Magical Passes." Cleargreen Incorporated. Available online. URL: http://www.castaneda.org. Downloaded October 12, 2000.

De Mille, Richard. *Castañeda's Journey: The Power and the Allegory.* Santa Barbara, Calif.: Capra Press, 1976.

De Mille, Richard, ed. *The Don Juan Papers: Further Castañeda Controversies.* Belmont, Calif.: Wadsworth, 1990.

Noel, Daniel C., ed. *Seeing Castañeda: Reaction to the "Don Juan" Writings of Carlos Castañeda.* New York: Putnam, 1976.

Novas, Himilce. *The Hispanic 100.* New York: Citadel Press, 1995.

❧ Castañeda, Carlos E. (Carlos Eduardo Castañeda) (1896–1958) *historian*

Carlos Eduardo Castañeda, a specialist in Texan studies at the University of Texas, was one of the most highly respected historians in the United States. He also worked to improve the working conditions of Mexican Americans at a time when they were the object of highly discriminatory practices.

Castañeda was born on November 11, 1896, in Ciudad Camargo in the Mexican state of Chihuahua, not far from the U.S. border. That he became an educator was not a total surprise as his father was also a teacher and had studied in the United States.

In 1908, when the political situation was becoming exceedingly tense in Mexico, the Castañedas immigrated to the United States, settling in Brownsville, Texas.

At school, Castañeda's intellect was apparent. He was his class valedictorian—this despite the fact that by that time he had already been orphaned. He was also the only Mexican American to complete the course of Brownsville High School in that era.

He studied next at the University of Texas in 1917. This was made possible when Castañeda won a scholarship. But when the United States entered World War I that same year, he enlisted in the army.

He spent the war years as a shooting instructor, and when they ended, he went back to the university. But he had to drop out when his scholarship money ran out.

Undeterred, he labored as an oil worker until he could earn enough to return to school. In 1921, he graduated Phi Beta Kappa with a B.A. degree in history.

Castañeda taught school to finance further studies and two years later earned his master's degree. This led to an appointment as associate professor at the College of William and Mary in Virginia. His appointment was to the Spanish Department, not the History Department. Castañeda's passions were, and remained, Texas and history. As soon as he could—in 1927—he went back to the University of Texas, working as a librarian. Five years later, he received his Ph.D. It was not until 1939, however, that he became a professor in the university's history department.

Castañeda also began to publish the first of his dozen books on historical subjects with *The Mexican Side of the Texas Revolution* (1928). The book reflected Castañeda's interest in correcting traditional views of Texan history. That book was followed by a study and republication, with his annotations, of a *History of Texas,* which dated from the Spanish colonial period. This book resulted from his Ph.D work.

The Knights of Columbus, a Roman Catholic organization, turned to Castañeda to write a history of Catholicism in his state. He worked on it from 1936 to 1950; the book, *Our Catholic Heritage in Texas,* ran to six volumes. It was to remain the cornerstone of his reputation. Over the course of his career, he would receive a large number of awards and honors, both from U.S. institutions and from others abroad. These included Latin American countries and Spain, whose government conferred the Order of Isabella the Catholic on him.

Castañeda also held various editorial positions on American historical journal staffs.

Concerned not only with the facts of history but with the welfare of his fellow Mexican Americans, Castañeda became a special assistant to the Fair Employment Practices Committee (FEPC). This organization was set up in 1941 by the Roosevelt administration as an instrument to fight discrimination. The FEPC's aim was to aid victimized workers from all racial minorities at a time when the best jobs were reserved for whites. In 1930, among Hispanic-American workers, for example, fully 85 percent held unskilled jobs. They found they would not be promoted, even if they had the skills for better jobs.

World War II gave the federal government a tool for remedying discrimination, at least in some industries, and at this time, the government was actually interested in doing something about discrimination. To gain a federal contract to manufacture weapons or other items related to the war effort, corporations were required to avoid racial discrimination in hiring. The FEPC monitored corporations for compliance.

Through his work with the FEPC, Castañeda was particularly instrumental in improving racial equality in the oil industry in Texas. He died in 1958.

Further Reading
Castañeda, Carlos E. *Our Catholic Heritage in Texas, 1519–1936.* Irvine, Calif.: Reprint Services Corp., 1993.
Directory of American Scholars. New Providence, N.J.: R.R. Bowker, 1957.
Meier, Matt S. *Mexican American Biographies.* Westport, Conn.: Greenwood Publishing Group, 1988.

Cavazos, Lauro F. (Lauro Fred Cavazos Jr.) (1927–) *government official*

After winning many awards in various fields, Lauro F. Cavazos became secretary of education from 1988 to 1990. This appointment made him the first Hispanic American to be a cabinet member.

Cavazos, a sixth-generation Texan, was born on January 4, 1927, on the huge King Ranch, where his father worked. He received a B.A. and an M.A. degree in zoology in 1949 and 1952, respectively, at Texas Technological University. In 1980, he was to become president of the university and of its Health Sciences Center. He was the first Hispanic and the first Texas Tech graduate to hold those posts.

Cavazos obtained a Ph.D. in physiology at Iowa State University in 1954. He mainly taught anatomy at Texas Tech and later became professor of anatomy at the Medical College of Virginia and then at Tufts University in Massachusetts. At Tufts, he was appointed dean of the School of Medicine.

He is the author of a large number of articles on medical subjects and the coauthor of two handbooks on human anatomy dissection.

An authority in his field, Cavazos became a member of such organizations as the American Association of Anatomists, Endocrine Society and Histochemical Society, American Association for the Advancement of Science, Pan American Association of Anatomy, and World Health Organization. Diverse medical journals have had Cavazos among their editors.

When, in August 1988, President Ronald Reagan appointed Cavazos to head the United States Department of Education, Reagan called his new cabinet member a leader in helping minorities gain educational opportunities.

Cavazos had explained, in a speech to Texas school administrators two years earlier, his commitment: "We will never really succeed in having the kind of world we want unless our children are educated. . . . While it is important to be prepared to defend the nation militarily, it is important also to be prepared intellectually to provide quality education for every child."

Cavazos pointed out that Hispanics, who at that time had a 45 percent dropout rate, were becoming an increasingly larger percentage of students in United States public school systems —"and getting them to stay in school is going to be difficult."

Thanks in great measure to Cavazos's influence, the President's Council on Educational Excellence for Hispanic Americans was created to stimulate scholarship among Latino youths. Cavazos's performance as secretary of education was criticized by some, but Cavazos was reappointed by the next president, George H. W. Bush.

Both Reagan and Bush picked Cavazos for the job despite the fact that he was a Democrat. Bush's Republican White House chief of staff, John Sununu, however, forced Cavazos to tender his resignation in 1990.

The League of United Latin American Citizens (LULAC) honored Cavazos with the title of Hispanic Educator of the Year (1983) and with a Hispanic Hall of Fame Award four years later. Among his honors are a Medal of Honor from the University of California, the President's Medal Award for Distinguished Achievement from City College of New York, the Medal of Merit from the Pan American University, and the Distinguished Service Medal from the Uniformed Service University for the Health Sciences.

Hispanic Business magazine named him one of 100 influential Hispanics in 1987.

Further Reading

Meier, Matt S. *Mexican American Biographies*. Westport, Conn.: Greenwood Publishing Group, 1988.

Chacón, Rafael (José Rafael Sotero Chacón) (1833–1925) *soldier, pioneer*

Rafael Chacón participated in many of the most significant events in New Mexico history in the 19th century—a tumultuous period in a key state in the southwestern United States—distinguishing himself as a man of courage, probity, and honor. His most important and lasting contribution, however, was to have chronicled it all. In so doing, he not only provided a wealth of historical detail, which fleshed out or corrected other, more "official" records, but also provided a unique Hispanic perspective of these events, many of which would otherwise only be recorded from the Anglo perspective.

In particular, he supplied detailed accounts of incidents demonstrating a strong and widespread anti-Hispanic prejudice by the English-speaking settlers who flocked into the previously Mexican territory.

This was something that he was well positioned to perceive, especially in the U.S. Army, to which he gave his best efforts. Yet at the same time it came naturally to him to make common cause with the Anglos against the Indians who had been the original inhabitants of the area. Chacón's life has considerable parallels with that of Manuel CHAVES.

One commentator wrote, "No knight of the Middle Ages had a life filled with more danger and adventure."

When Chacón was born on April 22, 1833, his native Santa Fe was situated in the Mexican territory of Nuevo México. His family traced its lineage, proudly but somewhat tenuously, to two local rulers in the previous century.

Although he repeatedly turned to the peaceful work of farming during his long life, violent events kept disrupting it, beginning when he was one year old and his mother's father was killed in battle with the Apache. When he was four years old, he was made to watch the executions that followed a local rebellion.

His father, a prosperous government official, pulled him out of one school after the child suffered a bad beating by the master. At the age of 11, he entered a military college in Chihuahua, Mexico, where he was robbed by other cadets. Two years later, Mexico was at war with the United States, and despite his age, Chacón was enrolled—along with his father—in the unsuccessful combat against the invading U.S. Army.

Chacón thereafter loyally served the new country in which he found himself. At age 22 he was a sergeant, serving under the command of the celebrated Indian agent Kit Carson, involved in fighting against the Apache—as his grandfather had done—and Ute Indians. Next came a period as farmer, tradesman, and justice of the peace. When the Civil War began, Chacón found himself in uniform again.

After assembling a mainly Hispanic volunteer company of the Union army, Chacón participated in the Battle of Valverde during New Mexico's brief and successful resistance against Confederate troops from Texas. Later, while the war still continued, he fought against the Navajo during a drive to resettle them on reservations. Later still, he was made commander of Fort Stanton—making him one of few Hispanics who reached the rank of major, and this despite the fact that his command of English was poor—and it was the Mescalero Apaches' turn to face him in battle.

Chacón also acted as escort for the first U.S. officials who traveled through the area on the way to Arizona, which had been sliced out of New Mexican territory.

After his last stint in a lengthy series of perilous military activities, Chacón served in the New Mexico legislature. After that, still only 33 years old, in 1866 Chacón, who had married 11 years earlier, began a new life as a farmer in Colorado.

In the early years of the 20th century, Chacón set about recording his life in his native tongue, Spanish—a job that took him six years. By then he was already recognized as an important source on New Mexican history. However, he never saw his book in print. It was not published until 1986, when it was released in an edition that included other biographical materials. Its appearance brought back to life a (by then) very remote era in which Hispanics found themselves on the fulcrum of a turning point in U.S. history.

Further Reading

Meketa, Jacqueline Dorgan, ed. *Legacy of Honor—The Life of Rafel Chacón, a Nineteenth-Century New Mexican.* Albuquerque: University of New Mexico Press, 1986.

Novas, Himilce. *The Hispanic 100.* New York: Citadel, 1995.

Chang-Díaz, Franklin (1950–)
astronaut

A Costa Rican who studied in the United States and made his home there, Franklin Ramón Chang-Díaz is a scientist who has worked in the most complex areas of physics, including the development of nuclear fusion reactors. He also became, in 1986, the first Hispanic American in space.

Although he was the first Hispanic American to become an astronaut, Chang-Díaz was not the first Hispanic in space. In 1980, Arnaldo Tamayo-Méndez, a Cuban Air Force pilot, flew on a Russian *Soyuz* mission, as a guest of what was then the Soviet Union. Also, the U.S. space program invited a Mexican scientist, Rodolfo Neri Vela, aboard a shuttle flight in 1985.

Chang-Díaz was born in the Costa Rican capital, San José, on April 5, 1950. When he was seven years old, the Soviet Union launched *Sputnik I.* This fired the imagination of the little Central American boy, making him a lifelong space enthusiast.

Though millions of others around the world were awed by the event, Chang-Díaz did something with his excitement: While still a schoolboy, he wrote a query about becoming an astronaut and sent it to the United States' National Aeronautics and Space Administration (NASA). He addressed it directly to the head of U.S. space research, who was then the German-born rocket engineer Wernher von Braun. Chang-Díaz received an answer: von Braun wrote to him and suggested that the best road to outer space passed through studying science in the United States. Chang-Díaz took his advice. He traveled to Connecticut, where he had relatives, and finished high school in Hartford. Then he went to the University of Connecticut, graduating as a mechanical engineer in 1973. At the Massachusetts Institute of Technology (MIT) four years later, he received a Ph.D. in applied plasma physics.

Although his first field of study was nuclear particles—high-energy physics research—Chang-Díaz began to study the possibility of building nuclear fusion reactors. Fusion reactors would follow a different principle than existing reactors, which operate through nuclear fission. Even after NASA chose him in 1980 as an astronaut, he continued to be a visiting professor at MIT's Plasma Fusion Center.

For NASA, Chang-Díaz has, among other jobs, worked on new methods of propelling rockets. He also developed shuttle avionics (control and other devices) and led the Cape Kennedy "Cape Crusaders" astronaut ground-support team. He also was a founder of an Astronaut Science Support Group, in 1988, and served as its first chief.

Twenty-nine years after *Sputnik I,* Chang-Díaz flew into Earth orbit on the *Columbia* shuttle. From *Columbia,* Chang-Díaz addressed Latin Americans and Hispanic Americans in Spanish. It was the last shuttle flight before the ill-fated *Challenger* launch.

Franklin Chang-Díaz *(NASA)*

Chang-Díaz orbited again in 1989 on the *Atlantis,* which released a probe, *Galileo,* to explore the planet Jupiter.

He flew into space again in 1992, 1994, 1996, and 1998, totaling almost 1,300 hours in orbit in his six forays beyond Earth. As of 2000, Chang-Díaz was director of the Advanced Space Propulsion Laboratory at the Johnson Space Center in Houston.

Further Reading

Cassutt, Michael. *Who's Who in Space.* New York: Macmillan Publishing Co, 1993.

❦ **Chaves, Manuel** (1818–1889) *soldier*

Manuel Antonio Chaves led the successful raid on the supply train of the Confederate forces who invaded New Mexico during the Civil War. Through this action at the Battle of Glorieta Pass ("the Gettysburg of the West") he, in effect, put an end to a drive by the South toward gold-rich California.

The family of Manuel Chaves arrived in what would become New Mexico as far back as 1598. They were among the settlers led by Juan de Oñate, who set out from Mexico (at that time called New Spain) to carve out a new province among the Pueblo Indians to the north. Chaves was a nephew of Manuel Armijo, the governor of Nuevo México who fought off encroachments by neighboring Texas.

Chaves was born in 1818 in Nuevo México, a territory that was ruled by the Mexican government. After a childhood spent ranching, he soon found himself embroiled in the political troubles and fighting that followed Mexico's independence. He was a combative person who earned the nickname "Little Lion"—*El Leoncito*. In 1839, Governor Armijo made threats against his nephew's life over a political disagreement, and Chaves escaped to St. Louis, Missouri.

He was back in New Mexico two years later, this time to fight *with* Armijo against a Texan expedition advancing on Santa Fe.

When the United States invaded and took over Nuevo México in 1846, Chaves switched sides again. In the short time between two outbreaks of Mexican resistance that erupted in the Taos area, he sided with the first rebellion; was arrested, tried, and acquitted; and opposed the second.

With the end of the Mexican–U.S. war Chaves returned to the work he had known as a child—ranching, but his life was not peaceful for long. Although he traded with Indians in his area who had submitted to white rule, he decided to fight against the tribes further afield still resisting, mainly the Apache, Navajo, and Ute.

He was well acquainted with the terrain and became a highly regarded scout for military expeditions against Indians. He was also given military rank by the U.S. Army. In 1861, as a lieutenant colonel, he commanded an outpost against the Navajo, Fort Fauntleroy.

The following year, the Civil War came to New Mexico. A Confederate force from New Mexico's traditional rival, Texas, entered the territory and conquered Albuquerque and Santa Fe. Its ultimate goal was Colorado and then California. The key battle

with Union forces, formed mainly by volunteers from New Mexico and Colorado, came at Glorieta Pass, on March 26–28, 1862.

Manuel Chaves guided the Northern troops to flank the Confederates at the pass. It was a narrow passage—part of the Santa Fe Trail beginning in Independence, Missouri. At Glorieta, the Confederate army would not have the advantage of a professional deployment against the Union volunteer force.

The first battle saw hard fighting. The day ended with a small Southern pullback, but only to await soon-to-arrive reinforcements. However, on March 28, as fighting began again, Chaves staged a raid on the enemy's supply train.

Because they were sheltered by a 200-foot cliff, the Confederates were only guarding their supplies lightly. Leading a few hundred men, Chaves negotiated the hilly terrain and appeared atop the cliff directly above the unsuspecting Southern soldiers. Chaves and his volunteers utterly overwhelmed the Confederates by suddenly dropping down on them by using ropes. Chaves then ordered the entire stock of supplies and wagons destroyed.

Having lost his supply train and recognizing that this could leave his men to die of hunger and thirst in the arid land, Confederate General Henry Hopkins Sibley decided to withdraw. New Mexico and, behind it, California were free from any Southern threat for the remainder of the war.

After the conflict ended, Chaves went back to his farms, although he remained a lifelong commander in the territorial militia. He suffered from wounds acquired in his campaigning years, but that never stopped him from hard work on his ranchland in the Indian frontier areas.

The clash at Glorieta Pass was incomparably smaller than Gettysburg the following year. But New Mexico historians compare the two because Glorieta was decisive in ending a Confederate invasion campaign, westward in New Mexico and northward in Pennsylvania.

Hispanics fought on both sides in the Civil War, and Chaves's role was, in a way, a mirror image of that of Santos Benavides of Texas. Benavides, who was mayor of Laredo, put together a Hispanic cavalry regiment that held off a Union thrust into Texas. The Union never attacked Texas again by land.

Chaves died in 1889.

Further Reading

Simmons, Marc. *The Little Lion of the Southwest.* Chicago: Swallow Press, 1973.

Twitchell, Ralph E. *The History of the Military Occupation of the Territory of New Mexico.* New York: Arno Press, 1976.

✎ Chávez, César (1927–1993) *labor activist*

César Chávez organized the first successful major labor action against the employers of California's exploited migrant farmworkers—most of them Mexican Americans. He then expanded his work to meet the needs and aspirations of the Hispanic-American community in general and to liberal and civil rights causes for all minorities. Through his work, he became one of the best-known Hispanic leaders in the United States and was hailed far and wide almost as a lay saint of the oppressed.

Because of his choice of nonviolent means, including fasts, to achieve his goals, Chávez has been compared to India's Mahatma Gandhi. His major talents as a leader were his ability to inspire his supporters, to make his cause widely known, and, especially, to enlist the support of liberal-minded people everywhere.

Chávez was born on March 31, 1927, in Yuma, Arizona. His family owned and worked a plot of poor-quality land, but they lost even this land during the Great Depression of the 1930s. The Chávezes then had to join the armies of rootless farmhands who followed the crops on the West Coast.

From the age of 10, Chávez worked hard in the fields. He also earned some extra pennies by collecting and selling cigarette wrappers. He never went past the seventh grade; yet, by the time he left, he had been to more than 30 schools up and down California because his family was endlessly on the move, following the crops.

In the 1930s, dust bowl conditions in many farm areas and the desperate economic situation forced thousands upon thousands of United States families to become migrant farmworkers. But over time, Anglo-Saxon migrants—like the "Okies" (Oklahomans) immortalized in John Steinbeck's *The Grapes of Wrath*—in many cases were able to move on to better jobs.

However, the farmhands with darker skins, including Mexican Americans like the Chávez family, faced an additional hurdle that kept them largely tied to migrant life: racism. Throughout his life, César Chávez would be haunted by the childhood memory of being refused service at a hamburger stall. The attendant waved him and his brother away with a laughing comment, "Goddamn dumb Mex!" He also remembered being shooed away from seats reserved for Anglos in movie theaters.

Chávez served in the navy during World War II and then returned to work in the Californian fruit and vegetable fields. In 1950, he lived in a neighborhood of San José that was so bad that it was called *Sal Si Puedes* ("Get Out If You Can"). At that time he was contacted by a worker for the CSO (Community Service Organization), a group created by Saul Alinsky, a pioneer in community organization in the United States.

At first, Chávez was not interested in holding the meeting—he thought, "It's probably just another university student studying the barrio [Hispanic neighborhood]." But the CSO worker had a different idea in mind: to invite Chávez and his wife to join the CSO as volunteers and to register Hispanics to vote.

Working for the CSO, Chávez quickly demonstrated his talent for convincing people. He signed up more than 4,000 new voters within two months, while continuing to work in the fields during the day.

At the same time, he began to suggest to his fellow farmhands that they form a union to fight against the miserable working conditions. When his employer found out about this, he immediately fired Chávez. Chávez then went to work for the CSO as a staff member. By 1958, he was CSO general director for California and Arizona.

He never forgot the idea of setting up a union. His determination to do so only increased over time. In those days, Mexican-American migrants earned little more than five dollars a day and had to spend an average of 15 hours at backbreaking labor to collect that amount. They lived in ramshackle huts or other temporary and poor housing. They enjoyed little or no legal or health protection. Farmwork is the occupation with the highest representation of Hispanics among all job categories in the United States (more than 20 percent).

The wretched conditions persisted as late as 1960 because the farmhands, unlike many other workers, had been unable to form unions to confront their employers with collective force. Chávez knew that this inability to form unions was because he and his fellow laborers had to follow the harvests. Never able to stay long in the same place, the workers found it hard to organize.

Another difficulty in creating unions was the landowners' ability to supplement or replace the Hispanic-American migrants with unlimited Mexican workers (called *braceros,* after their arms, or *brazos*). Owners trucked the workers in and out of the United States as needed.

In 1962, Chávez decided it was the time to act. He asked the CSO to back him in trying to organize a union. Both he and the other CSO activists knew that, since 1903, Mexican-American and Asian farmworkers in California had made many attempts to organize. They had also tried to strike for better pay and working conditions. The landowners had defeated every attempt, even resorting to physical violence against the workers.

This knowledge did not stop Chávez from wanting to try again, but it did stop the CSO, so Chávez quit.

With his savings of $1,200, he founded the National Farm Workers Association (NFWA)—which later became the United Farm Workers of America (UFW)—and began to recruit members. To do so, he had to resist brutal pressure not only from the employers but also from other sources as well.

His opposition included the Teamsters Union. The Teamsters tried to take over the operation, but Chávez mistrusted the huge union's motives. He wanted to keep the union a grassroots organization whose members would feel closely involved.

In 1965, the union staged its first strike. Chávez was unsure the union was really prepared

for it (the NFWA's strike fund amounted to less than $100). Still, the strike was necessary in order to support Filipino grape pickers who had begun a work stoppage near Chávez's headquarters in Delano, California.

Chávez's flair for organization and promotion and the help of assistants like the NFWA's courageous vice president, Dolores HUERTA, eventually turned this strike into the migrant farmworkers' first big victory. But it was only after five more years of harsh struggle that the growers finally agreed to recognize the union and to give the farmhands contracts that guaranteed improved conditions.

In 1968 Chávez launched a nationwide grape boycott, asking consumers everywhere to simply stop eating grapes until the workers who picked the fruit were paid decent wages, and were given acceptable working and living conditions. He succeeded in making millions of people aware of the plight of the migrant workers, and willing to support the boycott enthusiastically. The refusal to buy California grapes even spread to Europe.

Chávez viewed the struggle—which he and his followers called La Causa, "the cause"—as more than a labor dispute: It was a statement of the equal worth of Hispanics as human beings. Chávez would, in time, extend his movement to deal with other abuses and inequities in U.S. society. He was a forceful supporter of the civil rights movement and became a hero to the dispossessed everywhere.

Another tactic that Chávez employed was hunger strikes. Refusing all food was an effective way to publicize La Causa, but it also endangered his health. Robert F. Kennedy, then a United States senator, and his wife, Ethel, came to see the fasting Chávez less than three months before Kennedy was assassinated in 1968. This presidential candidate was the main standard-bearer of liberal causes at that time and said, "I come here as an American citizen to honor César Chávez." Chávez, he declared, was one of the heroic figures of our time.

The *Los Angeles Times* took a 1984 poll that showed Chávez to be "the Latino most admired by other Latinos." The *Village Voice,* in New York, described Chávez as a "symbol of the emerging Hispanic culture."

A popular song, *El Corrido de César Chávez,* written in the union leader's honor, proclaimed: *No pedimos limosna;/sólo un pago más decente/les exige César Chávez/para ayudar a la gente* ("We're not asking for alms;/Only better wages/Are demanded by César Chávez/To help the people").

By the time of his death in 1993 Chávez had had much success: Migrant farmworkers were now able to join unions, and they were engaged, like other groups, in the endless struggle to seek new improvements and to overcome new challenges.

Chávez at times was accused of running his union too closely, making too many decisions himself. Yet after his death, the union showed he had left it able to carry on its work without him.

Chávez also led the fight to ensure that farmworkers voted through secret ballots in union elections: At his prodding, this measure—a protection against abuses by union leaders—was made into law in California in 1975.

Further Reading

Day, Mark. *Forty Acres: César Chávez and the Farm Workers.* New York: Praeger, 1971.

Faivre, Lynn. *Chávez: One New Answer.* New York: Praeger, 1970.

Griswold del Castillo, Richard, and Richard García. *César Chávez: A Triumph of Spirit.* Norman: University of Oklahoma Press, 1995.

Levy, Jacques E. *César Chávez: Autobiography of La Causa.* New York: W.W. Norton & Co., 1974.

Matthiessen, Peter. *Sal Si Puedes: César Chávez and the New American Revolution.* New York: Random House, 1969.

Pitrone, Jean. *Chávez: Man of the Migrants.* New York: Pyramid Communications, 1972.

Taylor, Ronald B. *Chávez and the Farmworker.* Boston: Beacon Press, 1975.

❧ Chávez, Dennis (Dionisio Chávez)

(1888–1962) *government official*

Dennis Chávez became the first Hispanic elected to the United States Senate and was, for many years, the highest-ranking Hispanic in the federal government. In that position, he tirelessly worked for the advancement of the Latino community in the United States.

In 1988, the president of the United States declared Dennis Chávez Day on the centennial of Chávez's birth. The proclamation stated that Chávez "sought the well-being of every American and displayed lasting concern for those in need. Dennis Chávez truly exemplified the dedication of the public servant and won distinction in the service of New Mexico and of his nation; to this day, his life and career symbolize the countless achievements of Hispanic Americans and demonstrate the opportunity America offers."

Dennis Chávez (no relation to labor leader César CHÁVEZ) provided a classic example of the individual who advances a cause from within the system.

Born on April 8, 1888, in a hamlet near Albuquerque, New Mexico, he went to grade school in Albuquerque, where his family had moved when he was seven. But money was so scarce that he had to leave school and work as a delivery boy to help the family finances. Yet, though his formal education was interrupted when he was in the eighth grade, Chávez found a way to keep learning: after work, he would go to the public library and devour books on his favorite subjects, history and biography.

Chávez's go-getting zeal, self-acquired erudition, and knowledge of Spanish all proved helpful in gaining high office in later life. In 1916 Chávez became Spanish interpreter for the politician Andrieus Jones. Jones, a Democrat, ran for the U.S. Senate in New Mexico. The territory had become a state in 1912; this event fired the young Chávez's interest in politics.

Jones won the election and took Chávez to Washington with him. There, despite his lack of formal education, Chávez was given the position of Senate clerk. He also passed a special entrance examination to the Georgetown University Law School. So in 1920, only four years after landing the job as Spanish interpreter in Albuquerque, Chávez had his law degree from Georgetown.

Chávez returned to his home state to practice law, but though his practice did well, he decided to switch to politics as a Democrat. In 1923–24 he was a member of the New Mexico state legislature. By

1930, he was back in Washington, this time as a U.S. Congressman, a post to which he was then re-elected.

In 1934 he ran for the Senate, facing, as he had in his campaign for Congress, an incumbent Republican. But this time the incumbent, Bronson Cutting, won by a margin of only 1,261 votes. Chávez suspected that Cutting's victory had involved voter fraud. The issue was about to be investigated by the Senate when Cutting died in an airplane crash.

The governor of New Mexico then decided that Chávez should hold Cutting's seat until the next elections. In those elections in 1936, Chávez won. He would serve in the Senate until his death in 1962, achieving wide respect and praise for his work there.

As a senator, Dennis Chávez played an important role in the establishment of the Fair Employment Practices Committee (FEPC). Through this organization, the federal government pressured companies to end job discrimination against Mexican Americans during World War II. He also supported education, seeing it as a road for advancement for Mexican Americans.

In Washington, he was a great asset to the state of New Mexico. As chairman of the Senate Committee on Public Works, Chávez was able to channel federal assistance toward land improvement and flood control projects in the state. For the nation as a whole, he backed liberal causes, including President Franklin Roosevelt's New Deal, which helped pull the United States out of the Great Depression in the 1930s.

However, Chávez was not an automatic supporter of Democratic Party positions. He was an independent thinker and voter and was never afraid to take a position against a majority trend. He was more liberal than many of his constituents—most of the Mexican Americans in his state were Republicans—but he was willing to risk losing their votes.

When World War II started, he thought it was in the best interests of the United States to keep totally out of the conflict—and it did not bother him to oppose President Roosevelt's position on this matter. Later, Chávez was one of the few who publicly opposed the right-wing "witch-hunts" launched by Senator Joseph McCarthy.

Further Reading

Acuña, Rodolfo. *Occupied America: A History of Chicanos.* New York: HarperCollins, 1988.

Hall of Fame Essays. *Dennis Chávez.* Albuquerque: Historical Society of New Mexico, 1963.

Meier, Matt S. *Mexican American Biographies.* Westport, Conn.: Greenwood Publishing Group, 1988.

Chávez, Linda (1947–) *government official*

As director of public liaison and deputy assistant to the president, Linda Chávez was the highest-ranking woman in the White House during the Reagan administration. She was nominated, but withdrew, as George W. Bush's secretary of labor. She has stood out as an articulate spokesperson for conservative positions, particularly the assimilation of the Hispanic community in the United States.

Linda Chávez is unrelated to union leader César CHÁVEZ or to the politician Dennis CHÁVEZ, a fellow New Mexican. As a conservative, she is on the opposite side of the political spectrum from them. She backs right-wing causes with the full knowledge that this defies most people's expectations. Hispanic leaders, it is often assumed, will be liberal rather than conservative, save for the leaders of the Cuban exile community. In an interview with the *Washington Post,* Chávez commented: "I guess I'm just stubborn. I do go against the grain. . . . I've never run away from being Hispanic. [But] It doesn't mean I have to endorse the whole [Hispanic] agenda."

However, Chávez refuses to be taken for granted by conservatives either. She prefers to evaluate each issue independently, deciding to take the position she believes is right.

She has switched from the Democratic to the Republican Party and has worked for organizations of varying ideologies. In all of them, she has bristled when she considered that she might be valued mainly because it was good for the organization's image to have a Hispanic and a woman on board. For example, in 1987 she took the job of president of U.S. English but held it for only a year. This organization works to have English adopted as the official language of the

United States. The organization opposes the bilingual approach preferred by those who want to preserve Spanish alongside English. Chávez quit after having concluded that there was "anti-Hispanic and anti-Catholic" prejudice within the organization.

Chávez was born on June 17, 1947, in Albuquerque. The name *Linda* means "pretty" in Spanish. She is a descendant of a New Mexico pioneer family that had lived in the state for more than three centuries.

Chávez makes a distinction between *Hispanos* (not *Hispanics*) or Spanish Americans—like herself—and Mexican Americans. The difference, she explains, is that Mexican Americans also include Native Americans among their ancestors.

The Chávezes moved to Denver, Colorado, when Linda was nine years old. In 1970, she graduated from the University of Colorado in Boulder with a B.A. degree in English literature. She continued her education at the University of California at Los Angeles (UCLA) and at the University of Maryland in College Park.

Linda Chávez participated in demonstrations against racial segregation while in high school. At the University of Colorado she instructed Mexican-American students in remedial courses. At UCLA, she taught a course in Chicano literature, but she did so under protest because she felt that she was given the job solely because she was Hispanic. She also argued that there was not enough Chicano literature in existence to justify a full course of study.

In both teaching positions, Chávez came up against situations that ran counter to her values. Mexican-American students with lower academic skills than their Anglo counterparts asked that lower standards be applied to them because of their underprivileged backgrounds. Many also expected their courses to be more debate than study. But Chávez believed that special quotas, preferential treatment, and other affirmative action would only work against minorities, rather than in their favor. It was only through especially hard work, she held, that they could make progress. This was a conservative position that she would extend to all areas of life. It formed the cornerstone of her philosophy as a writer on public issues.

Tensions with her students made it impossible for her to continue teaching: after she gave failing grades to students who had not finished their required reading, she received threats against her family, and her house was vandalized.

Chávez quit classroom teaching, but not education. After working in Washington on the staff of the House Subcommittee on Civil and Constitutional Rights of the Judiciary Committee, she was employed by the National Education Association and later by the American Federation of Teachers (AFT). In 1988, she became chairperson of the National Commission on Migrant Education.

At the AFT, after a term as assistant director of legislation beginning in 1975, she was editor (1977–83) of the federation's award-winning quarterly publication, *American Educator.* She was also a consultant on education for the Department of Health, Education, and Welfare.

Under President Jimmy Carter, in 1977 she worked as consultant to the President's Reorganization Project at the Office of Management and Budget.

Meanwhile Chávez wrote articles with right-wing viewpoints in *American Education.* When Carter left office and conservative Ronald Reagan took over, she found herself in demand. In 1983 she was appointed staff director (and first woman member) of the U.S. Commission on Civil Rights and used that position to help turn the commission away from its affirmative-action policies. This was in line with her belief that the best way to help minorities is to treat them like everybody else, a polemical stand that led to her next post, in 1985, as director of the White House Office of Public Liaison.

However, Chávez was soon disappointed by the job, realizing how little influence on policy making she could exercise by working from within the White House. She resigned and in 1986 ran for senator from Maryland, where she was then living.

By demonstrating, on television, that she was better informed about current affairs than the other candidates, she won the Republican nomination. But in an unusual two-woman Senate race, Chávez lost a bitterly fought election against her Democratic rival, Barbara Mikulski. Because of her work with the U.S.

English organization, she became a senior fellow at the Manhattan Institute for Policy Research.

Her views have been published under the title *Out of the Barrio: Toward a New Politics of Hispanic Assimilation* (1991); she airs these views in frequent magazine and newspaper articles and television appearances. Chávez argues in her book that Hispanics are doing well, statistically, in the process of joining the mainstream of U.S. society, if one excludes Puerto Ricans and recent arrivals.

In 2001, Chávez was appointed to the cabinet by the new president, George W. Bush, as secretary of labor. However, Chávez withdrew her name from consideration following allegations that she had employed an illegal alien.

Further Reading

Chávez, Linda. *Out of the Barrio: Toward a New Politics of Hispanic Assimilation.* New York: Basic Books, 1991.

Telgen, Diane, and Jim Kamp, eds. *Notable Hispanic American Women.* Detroit: Gale Research, Inc., 1993.

☙ Christian, Linda (1923–) *actress*

Linda Christian had a minor career as a screen actress but a major one as a Hispanic celebrity, due to her many romances with film stars, playboys, and millionaires, which were breathlessly reported by the media. Her name was linked to those of two of the biggest male heartthrobs of Hollywood's golden era: She was discovered by Errol Flynn and married to Tyrone Power.

Her mother was Mexican (of Spanish, French, and German ancestry) and her father Dutch. Blanca Rosa Welter (whose first names mean "white rose" in Spanish) was born in Tampico, Mexico, on November 13, 1923. Her father worked in the oil business and frequently had to move his family from one country to another. Thus she was raised in Mexico, Venezuela, South Africa, the Netherlands, Switzerland, Italy, and what was at the time British-ruled Palestine. Living in all these countries, she learned to speak Spanish, English, Dutch, German, Italian, and French. These linguistic abilities led her to get a job, at the age of 18,

with the British wartime censorship office in Palestine. She inspected German and Italian correspondence during World War II.

Then, after returning to Mexico, she began to study medicine, but her studies were interrupted when she was seen by actor Errol Flynn, who convinced her—and her mother—that her beauty assured her a future in Hollywood. Flynn is also credited with having invented the stage name of Linda Christian for her.

Her film career did begin in Hollywood but in later decades tended more toward European productions. Her movies include *Holiday in Mexico, Tarzan and the Mermaids,* and *Slaves of Babylon* in the 1940s and 1950s; *The VIPs* and *The Beauty Jungle* in the 1960s; and one film in the 1980s, *Restless Love.*

When Linda Christian married Tyrone Power in Italy in 1948, it was billed as "the wedding of the century" (one of several so regarded in their time). She was later also married to the British actor Edmund Purdom. In addition, she dated a long succession of wealthy luminaries, including Prince Aly Khan, one of the most famous playboys of the mid-20th century.

Further Reading

Christian, Linda. *Linda: My Own Story.* New York: Crown, 1962.

Parla, Paul, and Charles P. Mitchell. "Linda Christian." Available online. URL: http://www.filmsofthe-goldenage.com/1998/october98/christianlind.html. Downloaded October 10, 2000.

Telgen, Diane, and Jim Kamp, eds. *Notable Hispanic American Women.* Detroit: Gale Research, Inc., 1993.

☙ Cisneros, Henry (Henry Gabriel Cisneros) (1947–) *government official*

Henry Cisneros established a reputation as one of the most outstanding young Hispanic politicians of the 1970s and 1980s. In 1992, President Bill Clinton appointed him secretary of housing and urban development (HUD), in recognition of his expertise on cities.

Texan Henry Gabriel Cisneros was born in San Antonio on June 11, 1947. In that city, ninth largest in the United States, he made a nationwide reputation as a four-time mayor who won a series of landslide elections. It was no disadvantage to Cisneros's career that San Antonio has a large Chicano population, but there had not been a Mexican-American mayor there since the 1840s.

One strand of Cisneros's family came from pioneer New Mexico stock, long established in the region: On his mother's side, he is descended from Mexicans who came to the United States early in this century to escape the Mexican Revolution. His father was a colonel in the army reserve at Fort Sam Houston; Cisneros himself joined the Reserve Officers Training Corps (ROTC) during his university days in the 1960s. This was a time of rising opposition to the Vietnam War and, consequently, to any military presence within universities. Thus, joining the ROTC was a move with political implications, and it was not the last time Cisneros was seen as avoiding radical positions.

In his field of special interest, city government, his emphasis has been on strengthening the urban middle class. Because of this, he has sometimes been accused of abandoning the urban poor. His position, however, has been that it is essential for the very survival of the cities to consolidate the trade, the technology, and the institutions that sustain the middle and professional classes. He argues that this will be advantageous to the poor in the long run and will aid their upward mobility to the middle class.

This also necessitates belief in a "trickle-down" theory: that wealth trickles down from wealthier people to poorer ones. Holding this belief caused Cisneros, a Democrat, to be well regarded by Republicans during the Reagan administration. Cisneros has been called "a conservative liberal" and "one of Reagan's favorite Democrats."

After receiving his B.A. degree in city management from Texas Agricultural and Mechanical University in 1968, he earned a master's degree in urban planning two years later from the same university. He added a second master's, in public administration, from Harvard University in 1973 and a Ph.D. from George Washington University two years after that. Later, his achievements in government would also earn him numerous honorary doctorates.

While studying, he became assistant to the city manager of the town of Bryan, Texas, then assistant director of the San Antonio Model Cities Program, and finally assistant to the executive vice president of the National League of Cities, in Washington, D.C.

In 1971–72, he worked as assistant to the Secretary of Health, Education, and Welfare as a White House Fellow. He was 24 and the youngest person ever to be given such a fellowship.

Cisneros went back to San Antonio after receiving his Ph.D. In 1974, he was an assistant professor at the University of Texas. In 1975 he ran for office for the first time and was elected at age 27 a member of the city council.

Quickly recognized as a politician with charisma and a lot to offer, he was overwhelmingly elected mayor of San Antonio in 1981, receiving 62 percent of the votes. After that, the electorate brought him back three more times by margins as high as 94 percent of ballots cast. Clearly, he appealed to much more than the Chicano vote. The San Antonio Chamber of Commerce pronounced him to be "perhaps the best thing that has happened to this city since it was founded."

He was chosen by U.S. Jaycees in 1982 as one of the Ten Outstanding Young Men of America, received the American Institute of Public Service's Jefferson Award, was chosen president of the Texas Municipal League, elected a vice president and then president of the National League of Cities, and later received that organization's President's Award (1989), as well as the American Institute of Planners' Distinguished Leadership Award. Cisneros also began to be considered as a possible candidate for the Senate, for state governor, or even for vice president of the United States.

President Reagan appointed Cisneros to the National Bipartisan Commission on Central America in 1983. In this capacity, Cisneros published an opinion that differed with the commission's majority report. He called for serious negotiations with the leftist government of Nicaragua, before the United States ran the risk of jumping into another situation similar to Vietnam. Later, he was a member of the Bilateral Commission on the Future of U.S.–Mexican Relations.

The Republican White House called on him again, this time in 1987 to assist in briefing Mikhail Gorbachev, then the leader of the Soviet Union, at a U.S.-Soviet summit meeting.

In 1988, Cisneros announced he would not run for mayor again and turned to private life as chairman of the board of the Cisneros Asset Management Co. This decision was seen as a major setback to the progress of Hispanic politicians. At least three things led to his move. Cisneros, a married man, received some bad press about his relationship with another woman, though polls showed that this would not have lost him the support of San Antonio's voters. Second, he wanted to spend more time with his youngest son, who had been born with serious heart and stomach ailments. Finally, he spoke of the sheer economic hardship of holding public office: The mayor's job paid him only $50 a week.

The financial situation, Cisneros pointed out, had two consequences. First, there was awkwardness in having to interact constantly, as mayor, with bankers and wealthy professionals while needing to make ends meet with his wife's earnings and a second job of his own as a university professor. Second, Cisneros charged that low salaries for elected officials, especially in Texas, constituted a form of systematic discrimination against Hispanic contenders. He pointed out that relatively fewer Hispanics than Anglos were wealthy enough to run without caring about the level of income.

In private life, Cisneros not only formed and led his own company, but he also became a board member of the Rockefeller Foundation, chairperson of the National Civic League, and deputy chairperson of the Federal Reserve Bank of Dallas.

In 1992, he was campaign adviser to Democratic presidential candidate Bill Clinton. When Clinton won the White House, he appointed Henry Cisneros secretary of HUD. In that office, Cisneros launched a plan to fight the high incidence of crime and drugs in public housing estates by gradually moving the residents to other neighborhoods. Cisneros served until 1997, when he went back to private enterprise as president of the Univisión television network in Los Angeles.

In 1999, the case concerning his extramarital relationship, which had been one of the reasons for his return to private life 11 years earlier, came to a culmination. Cisneros pleaded guilty to one misdemeanor charge related to the truth of statements that he had made to the FBI, about money he had paid to the woman in question, and was sentenced to pay a fine.

The following year, Cisneros launched a venture called American CityVista to develop affordable residential communities in the central areas of diverse cities.

In 2001, President Clinton gave Cisneros a pardon at the end of his presidency.

Further Reading

Cisneros, Henry G. *Interwoven Destinies: Cities and the Nation.* New York: Norton, 1993.

Gillies, John. *Señor Alcalde: A Biography of Henry Cisneros.* Minneapolis, Minn.: Dillon Press, 1988.

Roberts, Maurice. *Henry Cisneros, Mexican-American Mayor.* Chicago: Children's Press, 1986.

❧ **Cisneros, Sandra** (1954–) *writer*

Although her output of poems and short stories has not been abundant, Sandra Cisneros quickly won recognition as an outstanding Chicana writer. Some of her works found their way onto many universities' required-reading lists while she was still in her 30s.

Her Mexican father had been traveling through the United States when he fell in love with her mother in Chicago and settled there. They had six boys in addition to Sandra, who was born on December 20, 1954. (Sandra Cisneros is not related to the Texan politician Henry CISNEROS.)

The Cisneroses were able to afford a number of trips to Mexico with their children to visit her father's family. In Chicago, however, they had to live in a succession of low-income neighborhoods. Stability came when Sandra was 11 years old and her parents managed to buy a small house in a Puerto Rican area of town.

Meanwhile Sandra, encouraged by her mother, became a voracious reader from a very early age. Almost as quickly she began to write poetry. Nevertheless, she would remain lacking in self-assurance as a writer. This lasted until years later after some of her work was published. She finally found her confidence when she won a book contract with a top publishing company, Random House.

Cisneros had a formal literary education, earning a B.A. degree in English from Loyola University in Chicago in 1976 and a master's degree from the University of Iowa's Writers' Workshop two years later.

She has taught creative writing in Chicago at the Latino Youth Alternative High School and at California State University. She has also been involved in educational administrative work.

Cisneros wrote in English; she used Spanish only in conversations with her father. Initially, she did not consider herself part of the world of Chicano and Chicana writers. But she did turn to the Hispanic ghettoes where she grew up for subject matter.

Encouraged when one of her poems was chosen to appear in public buses in Chicago, she did many public readings of her poems, and some of them were published in literary magazines.

Her first collection of poems was published in San Jose, California, in 1980, under the title *Bad Boys*. In 1983 her collection of stories, *The House on Mango Street,* brought her celebrity. This book was published by Arte Público Press, a Houston publishing house that has given exposure to many Hispanic writers. Cisneros, however, became involved in an argument with the publishing company over literary rights. The conflict was unfortunate except that, as writer Earl Shorris pointed out, it was "a good sign for Latino literature, proof that there is something worth fighting over and that a Latina is willing to fight."

A feminist perspective is one of the hallmarks of Cisneros's writing. Her point of view is one of a woman who is proud of her Hispanic heritage, yet who is also conscious of, and willing to fight against, the secondary position that is all too often given to women within Hispanic culture. "I am one who leaves the table like a man, without putting back the chair or picking up the plate," says the narrator of *The House on Mango Street.* The book was hailed for its vivid portrayal of life in a Hispanic neighborhood, although sometimes also criticized for reinforcing Latino stereotypes.

In 1985 this book earned Cisneros a Before Columbus Foundation American Book Award. Other honors followed, including a National Endowment for the Arts (NEA) fellowship in fiction. She was

artist in residence for one season at a foundation in France, and used her NEA grant for European travel.

One magazine described her as the creator of "a unique feminist voice that is at once frank, saucy, realistic, audacious—and always loud." She has called herself, more simply, a "macha hell on wheels."

My Wicked, Wicked Ways, based on poems written for her master's thesis, was published by Third Woman Press in 1987. With *Woman Hollering Creek and Other Stories* (1991), published by Random House, she broke through to mainstream publishing. Her next collection of poems, *Loose Woman,* was published in 1994 by Knopf.

Further Reading

Lomelí, Francisco A., and Carl R. Shirley, eds. *Dictionary of Literary Biographies: Chicano Writers, First Series.* Detroit: Gale Research, Inc., 1989.

Sobek, Herrera, and Helena Viramontes, eds. *Chicana Creativity and Criticism: Charting New Frontiers in American Literature.* Houston: Arte Público Press, 1988.

✎ Clemente, Roberto (1934–1972)
baseball player

A virtual national hero in Puerto Rico, Roberto Walker Clemente is included among the greatest players in baseball history. There were three days of official mourning in Puerto Rico when his life was cut short by an airplane crash. His death in 1972 was also mourned all over the United States. The fatal crash came while he was en route to deliver earthquake relief to Nicaragua—supplies that he himself had gathered for the survivors of a huge quake.

He was born in Carolina, Puerto Rico, on August 18, 1934. The son of an impoverished sugarcane cutter, Clemente was a proud man who refused to adopt any English form of his first name, Roberto. Also, he never turned his back on his humble origins. While a star outfielder for the Pittsburgh Pirates from 1955 until his death, every winter he returned to Puerto Rico to work with the island's youth and to plan a sports center for children.

Clemente experienced constant back pain as a result of an injury suffered in a 1954 car crash. To this, he added a number of injuries during his baseball career, but he never allowed pain to diminish his performance. He was a perfectionist who agonized over the possibility that he might be doing less than his very best. That, he considered, would be like stealing money from the people who paid to see him play.

Clemente was renowned both as a right fielder with a strong throwing arm and as a batter who could handle just about anything thrown at him. He was only the 11th person in baseball history to achieve 3,000 hits, with a lifetime average of .317. He had 240 home runs to his credit when he died at 38 years of age. National League batting champion four times (in 1961, 1964, 1965, and 1967), Clemente was the league's Most Valuable Player in 1966 and led the league in assists five times—a major league record; earned a dozen Gold Gloves, and was included in All-Star teams 14 times; and was credited with helping the Pittsburgh Pirates to win the World Series twice, in 1960 and in the year before his death.

Managua, the Nicaraguan capital, was devastated by an earthquake in 1972. Clemente was flying supplies to the stricken neighboring countryside in a cargo plane when it crashed after taking off from the airport in San Juan on the last day of the year.

For Clemente, the Baseball Hall of Fame bypassed its rule of waiting five years after a player's last game: He was inducted at the first opportunity, in August 1973. The United States Post Office, with the authorization of Congress, issued a stamp in Clemente's honor in 1984.

Further Reading

Kanellos, Nicolás. *The Hispanic-American Almanac.* Detroit: Gale Research, Inc., 1993.

Martínez, Al. *Rising Voices—Profiles of Hispano-American Lives.* New York: New American Library, 1974.

Schulte Marketing.com. "Official Roberto Clemente Website." Available online. URL: http://www. robertoclemente21.com. Downloaded October 10, 2000.

Shatzkin, Mike, ed. *The Ballplayers.* New York: Arbor House, 1990.

✒ Coca, Imogene (Imogene Fernández y Coca) (1908–2001) *actress*

A hilarious comedian, Imogene Coca performed for most of the century. She hit the top of her career in the 1950s on television in *Your Show of Shows,* partnered with comedian Sid Caesar.

Coca was born on November 18, 1908, in Philadelphia. She is of Spanish ancestry on her father's side and Irish on her mother's.

Both her parents were in show business. Her father, Joseph Fernández y Coca, conducted Philadelphia's Chestnut Street Opera House. Her mother, Sadie Brady, was an actress and dancer in vaudeville who had run away from home to join a magic show. Imogene also left home, at the age of 15, attracted by the possibility of a stage career in New York. In Imogene's case, this move took place with her parents' encouragement and blessing.

A year earlier, they had given her the choice between high school and professional stage studies. The choice was an obvious one for the budding performer, who had studied piano from age five, voice from six, and dance from seven. Imogene had been performing child roles, songs, and dances ever since.

Coca never let her small size (112 pounds, five feet, three inches tall) stand in the way of her career. Her strongest asset was an enthusiasm that easily infected and charmed audiences.

In New York, she performed in nightclubs and obtained roles in plays and in vaudeville shows. She first made her mark in 1934 in a stage show called *New Faces* that included a funny, sham striptease that she invented during rehearsals. The producer enjoyed it so much that it was made a permanent part of the production.

One of her partners in *New Faces* was actor Henry Fonda; however, for Imogene Coca the partnership that struck gold was formed years later after World War II in the new medium, television. She was chosen to play alongside Sid Caesar in an NBC comedy series.

Broadcast live on Saturday nights for 90 minutes the show was launched as the *Admiral Broadway Revue* in 1949. It was renamed *Your Show of Shows* the following year. In content it was a collection of separate sketches and numbers. This made it, in effect, the television continuation of vaudeville, which by that time was defunct.

Caesar and Coca played so well together that they helped transform the show into a major success. It also helped that behind Caesar and Coca were such writers as Neil Simon, Mel Brooks, and Woody Allen and beside them was such talent as Carl Reiner, all of whom became famous comedians and writers and, in some cases, directors.

Regarded as one of the shows that made those years a golden period of U.S. television comedy, *Your Show of Shows* ran until 1954. Coca received a best-actress Emmy nomination and was chosen "Tops in TV" in a media survey.

Neither Coca's career nor Caesar's returned to this peak after the end of their Saturday night revue. Their specialty on television became guest appearances, though there were also additional series, TV movies, and other ventures. Imogene Coca also continued to act in dozens of plays, including Broadway's musical *On the Twentieth Century* (1978), as well as a handful of movies. Her last film was *Nothing Lasts Forever* in 1985.

Some commentators were led to think that she, at least, did last forever, when she teamed up with Sid Caesar in 1990 for a 40th-anniversary celebration of *Your Show of Shows*. The show, staged at Michael's Pub in New York, was so favorably received that they repeated it in Chicago and California.

Imogene Coca died June 2, 2001.

Further Reading

Brown, Les. *Les Brown's Encyclopedia of Television.* New York: Zoetrope, 1982.

Telgen, Diane, and Jim Kamp, eds. *Notable Hispanic American Women.* Detroit: Gale Research, Inc., 1993.

❧ Colmenares, Margarita (Margarita Hortensia Colmenares) (1957–) *engineer*

Margarita Colmenares excels in engineering and has earned many honors in the process. At the same time, she works unceasingly to promote the study of engineering and of the sciences among Hispanic students. She also assists in the development of the Hispanic community in more general ways.

In 1989, Colmenares became the first woman to head the Society of Hispanic Professional Engineers; she was also the first woman—Hispanic or otherwise—to occupy most of the posts she has held as a working engineer—for example, she was the first Hispanic engineer to become a member of the White House Fellowship program. Colmenares achieved this through a combination of brains and hard work.

While keeping busy with all these activities, Colmenares (whose last name means "apiaries," or honeybee colonies, in Spanish) has also found time to seriously pursue an interest in Mexican folk dancing. She performed with, codirected, and taught the Ballet Folklórico de Stanford University, in 1979–80, during her student days, and later danced with another California group, Los Lupeños.

Colmenares was born on July 20, 1957, in Sacramento to working-class parents who had come to California from Oaxaca, Mexico. The pattern of her hardworking, activist later life was already established in high school. She held part-time jobs in the evenings and launched and led a Hispanic student organization at her religious school.

Afterward she enrolled at California State University, in her hometown, to study business. Instead, after some exposure to engineering, she fell in love with the field. It was then that she began to discover the inadequacies of science education in the United States, which she would later lobby hard to improve.

If her school had prepared her for a working life at all, it was only for office jobs. But Colmenares was not discouraged to discover that her ignorance of science and mathematics prevented her from studying engineering immediately. She remedied it by going to junior college and used this catching-up period to her advantage.

When she did find herself ready, she was able to enroll at Stanford University: she not only had earned the grades, but she had also won five scholarships. In her spare time, she had gained practical experience with a job related to engineering—inspecting waterworks for the California government.

Colmenares graduated from Stanford as a civil engineer in 1981. By that time, she had already been associated with an oil company, Chevron USA, in a student work program. Chevron then snapped her up with a job offer. What followed was a rapid succession of successful projects, recognition, and promotions. In 1989, proud of her achievements, the company was pleased to lend her for a year, with salary, to the Society of Hispanic Professional Engineers (SHPE). A steady succession of posts with that organization led her to become the SHPE national president.

Then, in 1991–92, Chevron loaned her to the White House, where she was a Fellow within a program to expose a small number of outstanding individuals to government in action. Colmenares chose to work with the Department of Education. Here, as in other activities she has undertaken, she sought to study how to help the Hispanic community and especially how to train Hispanics for positions of leadership. In the late 1990s, Colmenares worked as director of the Office of Corporate Liaison at the U.S. Department of Education.

Colmenares has been honored with *Hispanic Engineer* magazine's Community Service Award, the SHPE Hispanic Role Model of the Year award, and inclusion among both *Hispanic* magazine's Outstanding Hispanic Women of the Year (1989) and *Hispanic Business* magazine's 100 Most Influential Hispanics in the Country (1990 and 1992). She has also been an official of such organizations as the Hispanic Women's Network of Texas and the Cultural Arts Council of Houston.

Further Reading

Telgen, Diane, and Jim Kamp, eds. *Notable Hispanic American Women.* Detroit: Gale Research, Inc., 1993.

Unterburger, Amy, and Jane Delgado, eds. *Who's Who Among Hispanic Americans.* Detroit: Gale Research, Inc., 1992–93.

❧ **Colón, Jesús** (1901–1974) *writer, activist*

Jesús Colón's acute observations of race and class divisions in the United States made him a pioneer of Puerto Rican literature in the English language. Only one collection of his writings, dating from the 1940s and 1950s, was published in book form, in 1961. He was a triply isolated figure as a writer because he was a Puerto Rican on the U.S. mainland, because he was black, and, particularly, because he was associated with the U.S. Communist Party. Nevertheless, his one book is regarded as an essential reference point for the Nuyorican literature that followed and a major work in its own right.

Colón was born in 1901 in the town of Cayey, on the island of Puerto Rico, the son of a baker. *Colón* is the Spanish rendering of *Columbus.* As a child, hanging around a cigar factory near his home, he listened to the workers talk and to the paid readers at the factory, whose words they worked by, in the days before radio. In this way, he started to hear about socialist thinking and to develop keen ideas of his own about what was right and what was wrong in society.

In 1917, as a teenager, Colón went to New York, stowing away on a ship bound for Brooklyn. The big city turned out to be far from paradise for a laborer. In Puerto Rico, he had already observed that many wealthy people, far from trying to help those who were less fortunate, mistreated and despised them. On the U.S. mainland, he also found something that Puerto Rico had not prepared him for: racial prejudice. Further, he discovered that for a Puerto Rican with African ancestors, being Puerto Rican mattered less in the eyes of bigots than being black. He learned about restaurants that would serve light-skinned Puerto Ricans but not dark-skinned ones.

On one occasion, he was mailed an employment offer as a writer on the strength of some articles he had submitted. When he turned up for work, however, one look at him was enough to get him sent away: "We thought you were white," was the simple explanation.

Even while continuing to earn a living as a manual worker, Colón embarked on busy and ambitious writing ventures. He wrote newspaper articles, attempted to launch a Spanish-language newspaper of his own, and translated poetry from English into Spanish. Also, he managed to start and run a publishing house, Editorial Hispánica.

His main output, however, was as a columnist for *The Daily Worker,* which was published by the Communist Party of the United States. While his writing could never stray from the party's official doctrine, on any given issue, Colón showed over and over that his thinking was inspired, not so much by any political theory, as by events and attitudes that he saw and observations that he made. His articles, collected in the book *A Puerto Rican in New York and Other Sketches,* are a source of autobiographical information on Colón as much as they are small parables summarizing his views on the issues.

Colón was a Hispanic community activist and a supporter of independence for Puerto Rico. He also campaigned for office twice: for senator in 1952 and for New York City comptroller in 1969. Running for the American Labor Party on the first occasion, and for the Communist Party on the second, he lost both times. He died in 1974.

Further Reading

Colón, Jesús. *A Puerto Rican in New York and Other Sketches.* New York: International Publishers, 1982.

Kanellos, Nicolás, ed. *Biographical Dictionary of Hispanic Literature in the United States.* Westport, Conn.: Greenwood Press, 1989.

Mohr, Eugene V. *The Nuyorican Experience: Literature of the Puerto Rican Minority.* Westport, Conn.: Greenwood Press, 1982.

✎ Colón, Miriam (1945–) *theatrical producer*

Miriam Colón is recognized as one of the main driving forces behind Hispanic theatrical activities in New York. She is the founder and artistic director of that city's Puerto Rican Traveling Theater and works to promote the Hispanic community's artistic development. Winner of numerous achievement awards, she also writes plays and performs on stage, on television, and in movies.

Miriam Colón (not related to her fellow Puerto Rican, the writer Jesús COLÓN) was born in 1945 in the city of Ponce, Puerto Rico, to a working-class family. Attracted to acting while still very young, she was given permission to pursue that calling with one condition: that she not get home too late. This became impossible to live up to when she moved to New York and continued her acting career.

Colón studied at the University of Puerto Rico in Río Piedras, the Erwin Piscator Dramatic Workshop and Technical Institute in New York City—which she attended on a scholarship—and New York's Actors Studio, where she was the first Puerto Rican student.

As an actress, Miriam Colón appeared in such plays as *The Innkeepers* (1956), *Matty and the Moron and the Madonna* (1965), and *Julius Caesar* (1979); on television almost 300 times; and has acted in a number of motion pictures. Marlon Brando chose the young performer for a role in the film he produced and directed in 1961, *One-Eyed Jacks.* She also appeared with him in *The Appaloosa* five years later. Other titles in her movie career include *The Possession of Joel Delaney* (1972), *Scarface* (1983) and more recently, *Gloria* (1999) and *All the Pretty Horses* (2000).

However, her founding in 1966 of the Puerto Rican Traveling Theater Company/El Teatro Rodante Puertorriqueño is considered the most lasting and significant contribution made by Colón to the arts and to the community. She has been its artistic director and guiding light ever since.

The company is housed in its own small theater—a converted firehouse in Manhattan—and for each play it presents, it alternates performances in English and in Spanish. Each summer, Colón takes the Traveling Theater's plays to the community, setting up street performances in every one of New York's boroughs as well as on tour: It has visited Spain, Mexico, and Colombia, as well as Puerto Rico.

Colón has often arranged to have the company perform works written by its own playwrighting unit, seeking out, in the founder-director's words, "writers who will present our (the Hispanic community's) problems and aspirations from their point of view." These include plays by Colón herself. The Puerto Rican Traveling Theater also helps to nurture acting talent, providing an annual program of free acting classes.

Colón is also a cofounder of a Spanish-language-only theater group, the Nuevo Círculo Dramático (New Drama Circle). She was awarded the White House Hispanic Heritage Award in 1990 and was a member of both New York's Council of the Arts for more than a decade and the Expansion Arts Panel of the National Endowment for the Arts.

The Mayor's Award of Honor for the Arts and Culture (1982) and an Athena Award from the New York Commission on the Status of Women (1985) were given to Colón, and the University of the State of New York and Montclair State College in New Jersey have honored her, as have the Puerto Rican Legal Defense and Education Fund and the National Council of Christians and Jews.

Further Reading

Telgen, Diane, and Jim Kamp, eds. *Notable Hispanic American Women.* Detroit: Gale Research, Inc., 1993.

❧ **Cordero, Ángel, Jr.** (1942–) *jockey*

Angel Cordero Jr. is one of the most successful jockeys in horse racing history, having accumulated 7,076 wins and purse earnings that totaled $165 million before retiring. The son of a jockey and trainer, Cordero was born in Santurce, Puerto Rico, on November 8, 1942. He began his professional career on the island in 1960.

Two years later, he resettled in New York, but not before reaching the top of the winners' list at the El Comandante racetrack in Puerto Rico with 124 wins. He achieved this figure despite having been suspended for a total of five months during the period he rode there.

He was already establishing a reputation both as an aggressive rider whom other jockeys sometimes accused of cutting into their paths and as the jockey to bet on: this jockey, if he did not arrive in first place (as he so often did), was likely to be second and therefore still deliver prize money.

If Cordero (whose last name means "lamb" in Spanish) was a tough opponent for other jockeys, he was gentle with the horses he rode. He used his whip sparingly. He also kept his head so low it was barely visible above the horse's, and he studied each racetrack and each mount to work out how to get the most out of them.

At the Saratoga racetrack in the United States, Cordero was the top jockey for 11 consecutive years.

He won the Kentucky Derby in 1974, 1976, and 1985; the Preakness Stakes in 1980 and 1984; and the Belmont Stakes in 1976 and 1991.

He retired in 1992 at 50, a very late age for a jockey, and returned to Puerto Rico to work as a horse trainer and jockey's agent. His victory at Belmont the year before showed that he remained formidable to the end of his career.

Cordero was awarded the George Wolf Award and three different Jockey of the Year awards in the early 1980s.

Further Reading

Blackwell, Earl. *Celebrity Register.* Towson, Md.: Times Publishing Group, 1986.

❧ **Coronado, Francisco Vázquez de**

See VÁZQUEZ DE CORONADO, Francisco.

❧ **Cortina, Juan Nepomuceno**

(1824–1892) *frontiersman*

Juan Nepomuceno Cortina was one of the most famous of the Hispanic "social bandits." After the annexation of part of Mexico by the United States, these so-called bandits took up arms to fight against the many cases of mistreatment of Mexican Americans by the new Anglo overlords.

Cortina was a Texan counterpart to California's bandit JOAQUÍN MURIETA. He is an ambiguous figure—possibly a hero of the oppressed like Robin Hood, possibly a cattle rustler, and possibly both. He certainly was representative of a troubled, lawless period on the new U.S.–Mexican border.

Juan Cortina (whose name means "curtain" in Spanish) was born on May 16, 1824, the son of the mayor of Camargo, Mexico. His family owned land on both sides of the Río Grande. His father's family was located in Tamaulipas state in the area of Camargo where Cortina was born; his mother's family in Texas near the area of Brownsville, which was still part of Mexico at the time.

Cortina was raised first on the south side of the river and then, after his father's death, on the north side. Thus, he found himself in Texas when the U.S.

Army, under General Zachary Taylor, attacked in 1846. Cortina took part in the Mexican resistance fighting.

When Mexico lost the war with the United States, however, Cortina appears to have accepted the political outcome. He even worked for the U.S. Army for a time in the Quartermaster Corps. Then he went back to cattle ranching on his Texas lands and later entered local politics as a Democrat, working among the Mexican-American population.

Cortina does not seem to have accepted the social consequences of the Mexican–U.S. war. The former Mexicans, who were now Mexican Americans, began to be systematically pushed out of their land holdings by a variety of methods, and they saw themselves treated with contempt by the Anglo settlers who were arriving in increasing numbers.

Cortina's life remained peaceful, however, until one day in July 1859 when, while having coffee at a barroom in Brownsville, he saw a Texas marshal arrest one of the Mexican cowboys (*vaqueros*) who had worked on his mother's ranch. As Cortina watched, the marshal brutally and needlessly pistol-whipped the man he was arresting. Cortina shouted to the lawman to "take it easy." The marshal, with a curse, turned on Cortina, still with the gun in his hand. Cortina then drew his own gun and fired. The bullet hit the marshal in the shoulder, and Juan Nepomuceno Cortina had entered the ranks of outlaws.

Years later, after he had become a legend, a political song in his honor, "El Corrido de Juan Cortina," announced, in English translation, that "That famed General Cortina [Cortina had become a general in the Mexican army]/Is quite sovereign and free/The honor due him is greater/For he saved a Mexican's life."

Now Cortina had to save his own life. He fled across the river to Mexico because he did not believe he would get a fair trial in an Anglo court. On the south bank of the Río Grande, he found many others who were angry over Anglo abuses. As someone who had actually faced up to Anglo force with force of his own, they turned to him as a leader.

On September 28, 1859, he began what became many years of guerrilla warfare in the border area, before, during, and after the U.S. Civil War. At the head of a force numbering approximately 100, Cortina attacked and briefly held Brownsville, where he killed three Anglos who were notorious for abuses against Mexican Americans. His actions, then and later, seemed to waver between attempts to avenge cases of mistreatment of Mexicans and bids to provoke Mexicans to throw off Anglo rule. He raised the Mexican flag over Brownsville.

In one proclamation, he reported that "the voice of revelation whispers to me that to me is entrusted the work of breaking the chains of your [Mexicans'] slavery." The Anglos certainly saw him not only as a bandit, but also as a leader of a political insurrection attempt.

After the raid on Brownsville, three different forces were sent to fight Cortina's men. They all failed, one after the other, thus adding to Cortina's fame. They were Texas militiamen, Mexican soldiers from Tamaulipas state who were invited by the Anglos to come and seize the bandit, and a contingent of Texas Rangers.

Then, in December 1859, the U.S. cavalry arrived, commanded by Colonel Robert E. Lee, who was fresh from suppressing John Brown's antislavery uprising in Virginia. Cortina and his men galloped back to Mexico, with Lee giving chase. Cortina would return, making forays into Texas whenever circumstances allowed.

In the meantime, he entered Mexican political and military life. He fought for Benito Juárez's patriots against the French intervention in Mexico, became a brigadier general in the Mexican army, and served as governor of Tamaulipas state where he was born.

As the Civil War raged in the United States, Cortina's position was one of opposition to the Confederacy. This brought him further enmity from Confederate Texas during the war. Later, though, it led to an attempt to get Texas to award Cortina a pardon, after the South had lost. But the pardon was never offered, and Cortina's raids across the border continued. Texas Rangers crossed the border in pursuit several times, without success.

In the 1870s Cortina was investigated by both the U.S. and Mexican governments. A committee of the United States Congress ruled that he was guilty of banditry. The Mexican position was more ambiguous and varied over the years as the political situation changed.

One investigation concluded that Cortina was mainly the victim of false evidence produced by political enemies in the United States. On another occasion he was arrested for cattle theft, but because of his popularity, he was quickly released. After having sided with an uprising led by another Mexican general, he was arrested again and sentenced to be shot. However, this sentence was commuted to restriction to Mexico City. He was allowed only one trip back to Tamaulipas, in 1890, to see his family. Still, when he died two years later, he was given full military honors.

"El Corrido de Juan Cortina" adds:

"The Americans made merry,
They got drunk in the saloons,
Out of joy over the death
Of the famed General Cortina."

Further Reading

Goldfinch, C. W., and José T. Canales. *Juan N. Cortina: Two Interpretations.* New York: Arno Press, 1974.

Woodman, Lyman. *Cortina, Rogue of the Rio Grande.* San Antonio, Tex.: Naylor Co., 1950.

❧ **Cortines, Ramón** (1932–) *educator*

Ramón Cortines has demonstrated a unique flair for solving knotty problems in the area of education, earning widespread respect for his skill and resourcefulness. He was the person New York City turned to when faced with an especially serious situation in its school community. He has explained that he achieves results by getting people to acquire a personal interest in seeing reforms carried out: "To make change stick, you've got to involve people who are going to do the changing. It's that simple."

Also, despite strongly holding to his ideals—even if it meant losing his job—when important principles were at stake, he was not a man to simply impose his will. "I don't believe," he said on another occasion, "there is one way to reform. I want there to be debate. We can learn from each other."

Ramón Cortines was born in San Antonio, Texas, on July 22, 1932. His Mexican-American mother, who was unwed, put him up for adoption. His adoptive parents—the father was also Hispanic, the mother British—had strong cultural interests, and communicated them to their new son. The future educator grew up in California and attended Pasadena College, where he shone brightly enough to be listed in the *Who's Who Among Students in American Universities and Colleges.* However, that was toward the end of the Korean War, and Cortines was drafted into the army in 1953, putting his studies on hold for two years. Not so his involvement in education, because his aptitude was quickly recognized in the armed forces, and he was assigned to train the newer recruits.

In 1956, a year after his discharge, he graduated with a B.A. degree to which he later added two master's degrees—in school administration (1964) and adult learning (1966). From 1966 to 1968 he worked at a Covina, California, high school as director of student activities.

Cortines found his real calling—superintending entire school districts—in 1972, when he obtained the post of superintendent of schools in Pasadena. In 1984 he shifted to San Jose, in 1986 to San Francisco, and in 1993, after one year in other positions—including leader of a presidential transition team for the newly elected Bill Clinton—to New York City.

All these were difficult assignments, and he achieved vast successes in each. In both Pasadena and San Jose, Cortines was involved in the implementation of school desegregation procedures; in Pasadena, the antidesegregation school board disliked his policies and fired him in 1978, although after the next elections, the following year, he was returned to the superintendency.

In San Jose, San Francisco, and New York, money was a huge problem. The San Jose school system, in fact, had just declared itself bankrupt. Cortines demonstrated a great flair both for making savings that did not undercut the quality of education, and for fund-raising. One favorite fund-raising technique was the "Principal for a Day" program, in which leading businessmen and women and other personalities were invited to involve themselves in schooling issues for one day—and to earn thanks and publicity for any money they were therefore motivated to donate.

The New York City school system was an especially hard nut to crack, for in addition to the usual problems seen at the time, including school violence, there was the huge size of the district (close to 1 million students) and such issues as a serious health scare over asbestos in school buildings. A New York City schools chancellor, Cortines instituted helpful programs to bring fast relief to the issues.

Even when engaged in major struggles over funding for the school systems, Cortines was noted for not only maintaining but also raising teaching quality and reducing dropout rates.

But the question of funding did finally terminate his position in New York City. Cortines resigned as chancellor in 1995 because he considered it impossible, without sacrificing quality, to implement cuts demanded by the city's mayor, Rudolph Giuliani.

Cortines became a senior adviser to the U.S. Secretary of Education Richard Riley, as well as holding posts concerned with educational reform at Stanford University and at Brown University's Annenberg Institute.

In 2000, Cortines served as interim administrator of the Los Angeles Unified School District, the second largest in the United States, with the task of reorganizing and streamlining it.

Further Reading

Novas, Himilce. *The Hispanic 100.* New York: Citadel Press, 1995.

Tardiff, Joseph C., and Mpho Mbunda, eds. *Dictionary of Hispanic Biography.* Detroit: Gale Research, 1996.

Linda Cristal *(Cabrera Archive)*

❦ Cristal, Linda (Victoria Moya) (1935–)
actress

Linda Cristal received a singular honor while appearing in a TV series called *The High Chaparral:* She played the role of a Hispanic woman who is powerful and cool, not working class and fiery. In so doing, she created an unusual role model for Hispanic women. She points out that she received thank-you letters from Spanish-speaking fans "from at least 16 nations."

She was born as Victoria Moya in Buenos Aires, Argentina, in 1935. Cristal's father was a journalist. She was told later that he earned the enmity of a powerful sect by writing a series of articles exposing it. She also heard that, in an attempt to silence him, another girl was kidnapped and murdered in the belief that she was María Victoria. Her parents left the country for safety's sake, but soon afterward committed suicide. "At least that is what was said; it was a very confusing episode," she would recall. Moya was 13.

Sent to Mexico to join aunts who were nuns in that country, she was discovered at age 16 by film people who offered her roles in the Mexican movie industry. One of them praised the sheen of her skin, which he compared to crystal. This gave rise to her stage name, Linda Cristal.

After five years in Mexican movies, she saw a chance for a Hollywood career. She read in a newspaper that U.S. producers had arrived in search of new Latin beauty along the lines of the stars Dolores DEL RÍO or María Félix. These producers were looking for someone who spoke English. Cristal did not, but she auditioned anyway, promising them that she would quickly learn the language. She landed a seven-year contract, which was followed later by others.

Settling in California, Cristal acted in dozens of movies, mainly westerns and action stories, including *The Alamo* (1960) with John Wayne and *Mr. Majestyk* (1974) with Charles Bronson. She studied acting with celebrated teachers, Lee Strasberg and Eric Morris. However, she was hampered, in part, by a Hispanic accent. She was disappointed at not being offered a wider range of roles, including the chance to play women of various nationalities.

Linda Cristal's major career break came when she was given the part of a cattle rancher in the television western series *The High Chaparral,* which aired from 1967 to 1970. The part turned out to be one of the strongest female Hispanic roles in the medium's history.

The series also provided an important boost for another Hispanic actor, Henry Darrow. Darrow enjoyed two advantages over Cristal in the U.S. entertainment industry: Having been born in New York, he had no Spanish accent, and he had changed his name from what it was originally, Enrique Delgado.

In addition to acting, Cristal has also participated in movie production.

Further Reading

Hadley-García, George. *Hispanic Hollywood: The Latins in Motion Pictures.* Secaucus, N.J.: Citadel Press, 1990.

❧ Cruz, Celia (ca. 1924–) *singer*

Celia Cruz is hailed as "the queen of salsa." A vibrant, tireless performer, she has won over several generations of listeners with her catchy Afro-Cuban rhythms.

Cruz was born in Havana, Cuba, on October 21. She has always refused to reveal the exact year of her birth but it may have been 1924. Other estimates range from as late as 1929 to as early as 1916. In any case, in the late 1990s, whether she was in her 70s or her early 80s, Celia Cruz continued to be a human dynamo, celebrated for public performances as electrifying and infectious as their music.

It is said that when as a girl she sang lullabies to smaller children in the household, her voice would draw the neighbors to come in to listen.

She originally intended to be a teacher. It was a career choice her family approved, much preferring it to that of a stage singer. But the talent and power of her voice eventually convinced both her and the family that her future lay with vocalizing. Her parents insisted, however, that she be chaperoned by older women in the family at all her performances.

In the 1940s, she began to sing on Cuban radio programs, and having decided to abandon any thought of being a schoolteacher, she studied at Havana's Conservatory of Music from 1947 to 1950.

In 1950, she was hired as lead singer for the island's top dance band, La Sonora Matancera. She soon made her first recordings.

Celia Cruz stayed with La Sonora Matancera until 1965, but not in Cuba: The band and Cruz left the island soon after Fidel Castro toppled the government of the dictator Fulgencio Batista. After a short period in Mexico, the band settled in the United States. "Castro never forgave me," says the singer. He refused to allow her to enter Cuba even to see her parents at the end of their lives.

Cruz found the beginning of her United States career difficult. Different strands of Latin music had been immensely popular in the United States for decades, but the early 1960s happened to be an exception because rock'n'roll ruled in those years. In time, though, Hispanic beats made a comeback in the United States, thanks in part to Cruz's work with the mix of rhythms given the name salsa.

Celia Cruz *(Cabrera Archive)*

In 1966 Cruz joined the orchestra of Tito PUENTE, with whom she has performed many hundreds of times. She has also worked with other bands—in 1982, she even had a reunion with La Sonora Matancera.

She has recorded scores of albums; in early 1995 she released her 74th, *Irrepetible (Unrepeatable)*. She has collected Grammys and other musical awards, made successful international tours, and been honored at special concerts, including sold-out performances at Madison Square Garden in New York on her birthdays. In 1973 she sang a role in *Hommy—A Latin Opera,* by Larry Harlow, in Carnegie Hall. As a performer she is known for her gaudy costumes as well as her musical skills, which include the art of improvisation.

Among her many best-selling albums are *Grandes Exitos de Celia Cruz (Celia Cruz's Big Hits), La Incomparable Celia (The Incomparable Celia), Feliz Encuentro (Happy Reunion),* and *Celia and Johnny,* recorded with bandleader Johnny Pacheco.

Cruz has been called "one of the world's great singers" by *The New York Times*. Various specialized publications have named her the best female vocalist in the United States on a number of years. The Na-

tional Ethnic Coalition of Organizations gave her the Ellis Island Medal of Honor (Mayor's Liberty Award) in 1986. In 1995 she received the National Medal for the Arts.

Further Reading

Telgen, Diane, and Jim Kamp, eds. *Notable Hispanic American Women.* Detroit: Gale Research, Inc., 1993.

❧ Cugat, Xavier (Francisco de Asís Javier Cugat Mingall de Brue y Deulofeo)
(1900–1990) *bandleader*

Xavier Cugat, "the rumba king," perhaps more than anyone else gave Caribbean rhythms a mass popular appeal in the United States, thus helping Hispanic music become incorporated into U.S. mainstream life in a major way.

Other musicians, like Don Azpiazú, brought Latin (and particularly Cuban) cadences to U.S. dancers and listeners in a purer, more authentic manner. But it was Cugat and his followers who best knew how to arrange and simplify this music just enough to make it more accessible to the U.S. public without unduly distorting its essence. Cugat also knew how to present it with the precise mix of flashy exoticism and sophistication that appealed to U.S. taste between the world wars.

Cugat was born in the city of Gerona, Spain, on January 1, 1900, with the full name of Francisco de Asís Javier Cugat Mingall de Brue y Deulofeo. He spent his first few years in the city of Barcelona, but the family moved to Cuba before he was five. Cugat, who sometimes gave contradictory accounts of his early years, said his father had been given 24 hours to leave Spain, but the young man never found out why.

In Havana, Cugat was given a miniature fiddle by a neighbor who was a violin maker. With this toy, Cugat quickly demonstrated musical talent. By the time he was seven or eight, he was playing in cafés; by age 11, he was first violin for the National Theater symphony orchestra.

He also played the violin to accompany silent pictures in a movie theater as part of a trio. The pianist was Moisés Simons, who in 1924 would compose

El Manicero (The Peanut Vendor), destined to become the best-known Cuban tune in the United States.

Within a few years, Cugat had become a violin soloist, emigrated to the United States (the date of arrival is variously recorded as 1915 or 1921), studied violin in New York, Berlin, and Paris, and played for famed tenor Enrico Caruso on a world tour. In New York, Cugat was less than successful at first. Caruso had promised to find work for him but died before he could do so. Cugat did work playing both classical music and in a dance band, but he also recalled having to sleep in Central Park several times. Eventually, he gave up the violin. He did so, he said, "because I would never play like Sarasate" (Spanish violin prodigy Pablo de Sarasate).

Cugat moved to California and became a cartoonist for the *Los Angeles Times,* using a talent Caruso (who was himself handy with a caricature) had nurtured. One of those rumored to have enjoyed Cugat's drawing skill was actor Rudolph Valentino, who supposedly befriended Cugat and encouraged him to organize a dance orchestra (originally for tango music). The flaw in this story is that Cugat began to work for the newspaper in 1927 and formed the band in 1928, while Valentino died in 1926.

Cugie, as he became known, was now on his way to fame in nightclub appearances. His band played first at a Los Angeles club, then at the well-known Coconut Grove, and later at the Waldorf Astoria in New York.

The 1930s were a decade of rumba mania in the United States, and Cugat was in the forefront in the popularization of it and other Afro-Cuban rhythms.

Celebrated pop composers vied to have him play and record their tunes. They included Cole Porter with "Begin the Beguine" and the Cuban master Ernesto Lecuona with "Para Vigo Me Voy" ("I am leaving for Vigo," better known in English as "Say Sí Sí").

In addition to decades of success as a bandleader, in the 1930s and 1940s Xavier Cugat often played himself in movie musicals such as *Go West Young Man, You Were Never Lovelier, Holiday in Mexico,* and *Neptune's Daughter,* starring Mae West, Carmen MIRANDA, Rita HAYWORTH, and Esther Williams, respectively.

Cugat is credited with the invention of a percussion instrument, the congat, a cross between bongo and conga drums. He also claimed credit for bringing Dean Martin and Jerry Lewis together on television as a comedy duo. He was an uncle, and for a time the employer, of actress-dancer Margo (Marie Marguerite Guadalupe Teresa Estela Bolado Castilla y O'Donnell). Cugat's orchestras featured young female singers whom Cugat usually ended up marrying, even when in his 70s: Cugat married in succession Rita Montaner, Carmen Castillo, Lorraine Allen, Abbe Lane, and Charo (Charo Baeza). After a series of heart attacks and strokes over the years, he died in 1990.

Further Reading

Cugat, Xavier. *The Rumba Is My Life.* New York: Didier, 1949.

Roberts, John Storm. *The Latin Tinge: The Impact of Latin American Music on the United States.* Tivoli, N.Y.: Original Music, 1985.

D

☙ Dallmeier, Francisco (Francisco Gómez-Dallmeier) (1953–)
scientist

A noted biologist, Francisco Dallmeier is at the forefront of scientific efforts to study—and help maintain—the planet's large diversity of plant and animal life. He has not only carried out major projects to protect this biodiversity, especially in tropical forests, but has also developed advanced methodologies for such work. These, in turn, have been of use to other researchers and conservationists in different parts of the world.

Science has been in Dallmeier's family for generations. One great-grandfather, Adolph Ernst, was a naturalist who immigrated to Venezuela from Germany before the rise of the Nazis there. Dallmeier's father, also named Francisco, managed a cancer research institute in Caracas, the Venezuelan capital.

Francisco Gómez-Dallmeier was born in Caracas on February 15, 1953. He developed a fascination with plants and animals at an early age—by his own account, at age three. He became a Boy Scout because it gave him an opportunity to go camping and be closer to nature than was possible in a big city like Caracas.

By age 14, his drive and talent for the study of biology was unstoppable. He became a volunteer worker at the LaSalle Museum, a natural history museum in Caracas, and only four years later, he was made curator of mammals for that institution. Two years after that, at the age of 20, he had risen to the post of museum director.

Not only was he the youngest person in the world to hold such a post, but he was still officially an undergraduate student. He also did research for the Institute of Tropical Zoology run by the Central University of Venezuela, doing fieldwork in the country's southern jungles, studying and mapping the wildlife with such techniques as placing bands on migrating birds to study their travels.

The two strands of Dallmeier's work were already present. Alongside his drive to gain biological knowledge for the thrill of knowledge in itself, he labored to maintain the ecology he was studying, participating in environmental protection programs run by two visiting Polish scientists.

Dallmeier graduated with a degree in biology from Venezuela's Central University in 1977. At that point he left the LaSalle Museum and went to work for a private Venezuelan environmental engineering firm, as well as for a U.S. company that was preparing

Francisco Dallmeier *(Photo by Julian Dallmeier)*

Venezuela's first study of a power plant's impact on the environment.

For his graduate studies, undertaken following four years of this practical work, Dallmeier chose to come to the United States, where he selected a school that was particularly strong in the field of wildlife management, Colorado State University in Fort Collins, Colorado. There, he obtained a master's degree in 1984 and a doctorate two years later. He remained in the United States—save for fieldwork in wilderness areas of other countries—becoming a United States citizen in 1988.

Dallmeier continued his career at the Smithsonian Institution (SI) in Washington, DC, heading the SI Man and the Biosphere program, dedicated to protecting biological diversity. This work, later renamed the Smithsonian Institution Monitoring and Assess-

ment of Biodiversity Program, was jointly undertaken with UNESCO, the United Nations Educational, Scientific and Cultural Organization.

Like other conservationists, Dallmeier realized that in order to prevent the disappearance of countless animal and plant species through the encroachment of farming into areas previously devoted to wildlife, it was not enough to simply ban the expansion of farmlands. Such a ban simply could not be enforced, as human population increased. What was needed was to find ways in which farming could be expanded while causing the minimum possible damage to the environment. Such sustainable development has been one of Dallmeier's main concerns.

In his effort to study the tropical forests he is trying to protect, Dallmeier and his team of colleagues established a system of intensive monitoring of specific plots of forest over a length of time, with standardized procedures so that work in one area can be compared with that of all the others, using the latest computerized technology. He also created the Smithsonian international training program in biodiversity monitoring and the Smithsonian Environmental Leadership program.

Dallmeier is the author of *Biology, Conservation and Management of Waterfowl in Venezuela* (1990) and of scores of other reports and coedited *Forest Biodiversity Research, Monitoring, and Modeling* (1997).

Further Reading

McMurray, Emily J., ed. *Notable Twentieth Century Scientists.* Detroit: Gale Research, 1995.

Oleksy, Walter. *Hispanic-American Scientists.* New York: Facts On File, 1998.

❦ de la Garza, Eligio "Kika" (1927–)
government official

Texan "Kika" de la Garza, a long-term chairman of the House Committee on Agriculture, was one of the most prominent Hispanic members of Congress and a staunch representative of southern conservatism.

Different de la Garza families (the name means "of the heron" in Spanish) are found in many parts of Texas; Eligio, nicknamed Kika, was born on

September 22, 1927, in the town of Mercedes to a family that traces its ancestry in the area almost 300 years.

De la Garza studied at Edinburg Junior College and at St. Mary's University in San Antonio. He graduated from law school in 1952, though his studies were interrupted by two separate stints in the armed forces. He was a 17-year-old volunteer in the navy in the last years of World War II and an army artillery officer during the Korean War.

In 1952, the same year he came home from Korea and began to practice law, he ran for the state legislature in Texas as a Democrat and won. His six terms in the Texas House of Representatives from 1953 to 1964 ended when he set his sights on Congress. His election was seen as a milestone for the Mexican Americans of Texas. He began to represent his district in the U.S. House of Representatives in 1965.

As a member of the Democratic Party's right wing, he was accused by liberals of funneling as much as 95 percent of federal funds received by his Texas district to Anglos, particularly Anglo business interests, despite the fact that Chicanos form 75 percent of the district's population. He voted against civil rights measures designed to help Chicanos, opposed the more militant Mexican-American leaders, such as Reies López TIJERINA and José Angel GUTIÉRREZ, and was in turn opposed by the Political Association of Spanish Speaking Organizations. Nevertheless, he enjoyed the support of the voters in his district, who demonstrated this by returning him to office repeatedly, until his retirement in 1997.

In addition to his participation in the Congressional Hispanic Caucus, de la Garza was a member of such organizations as the League of United Latin American Citizens (LULAC), Council of State Governments, American Legion, Catholic War Veterans, and the Border Development Committee. He was a member and later chairman of the United States-Mexico Interparliamentary Group since the year he arrived in Washington. In 1979 he was given the Order of the Aztec Eagle, the highest award that Mexico confers on foreigners. Other honors bestowed on him include the title of Mr. South Texas (1989), the St. Mary's University Law School Outstanding Alumnus Award, honorary degrees from universities in Maryland, Missouri, and South Korea, and a Lifetime Achievement Award from the Volcani Center in Israel.

Further Reading

Acuña, Rodolfo. *Occupied America: A History of Chicanos.* New York: HarperCollins, 1988.

Eligio "Kika" de la Garza II. Library of Congress. Available online. URL: http://lcweb.loc.gov/rr/hispanic/congress/delagarza.html

The Ralph Nader Congress Project. *Eligio de la Garza, Democratic Representative from Texas.* Washington, D.C.: Grossman Publishers, 1972.

Eligio "Kika" de la Garza *(Congressional Hispanic Caucus)*

de la Garza, Emilio, Jr. (1949–1970)
soldier

Emilio de la Garza Jr., a marine lance corporal in the Vietnam War, sacrificed his life to save two comrades.

De la Garza (not related to Congressman Eligio DE LA GARZA) was born in East Chicago, Indiana, on June 23, 1949.

In April 1970, as a lance corporal in Company E, 2nd Battalion, 1st Marines, 1st Marine Division, he found himself near Da Nang in South Vietnam. The commander of de la Garza's platoon took him and one other marine on a nighttime operation in search of two enemy soldiers who had been seen escaping after an ambush.

De la Garza soon discovered one of them, hiding in a small pond. The three U.S. servicemen grappled with him and were trying to haul him out when de la Garza realized that, in the struggle, their quarry had managed to pull the pin from a grenade. The 20-year-old marine immediately put his own body between the grenade and his comrades. He only had time to shout a warning before the grenade exploded, killing both him and the enemy soldier; the two men he had shielded were safe.

In a posthumous award of the Congressional Medal of Honor, his citation read: "By his prompt and decisive action, and his great personal valor in the face of almost certain death, L/Cpl. de la Garza upheld and further enhanced the finest traditions of the Marine Corps and the U.S. Naval Service."

Further Reading

The Committee on Veterans' Affairs. United States Senate. *Medal of Honor Recipients 1863–1978.* Washington, D.C.: U.S. Government Printing Office, 1979.

✎   **de la Hoya, Oscar** (1973–) *boxer*

Gifted with dazzling speed—and with the kind of good looks that have brought many women who were previously uninterested in boxing flocking to the ringside—Oscar de la Hoya emerged as indisputably one of the most outstanding fighters of the 1990s. He is also an active antidrug, antiviolence speaker at schools and community centers, strongly interested in keeping youths from falling into those dangers. Intensely proud of his heritage, he has made a point of waving U.S. and Mexican flags, one in each hand, after boxing victories.

De la Hoya's parents immigrated to the Unites States from Mexico, and Oscar was born in Los Angeles on February 4, 1973. Both his grandfather and

father boxed—his father at the professional level—as did his uncles, cousins, and older brother, so Oscar gravitated toward boxing naturally. At the age of six he had miniature gloves put on his hands and faced his first opponent, another child from the neighborhood, at a local gym. De la Hoya straightaway knocked him out.

This may have been medically dangerous for the other child but pointed the direction to Oscar's future. During his school years he assembled an extensive collection of amateur boxing titles, including the National Junior Boxing Championship, Golden Gloves, Goodwill Games, and U.S. National Championships, in diverse weight categories as he grew older and bigger (he eventually became five feet, 10 inches tall). He was so busy boxing, in fact, that he missed his high school graduation prom in 1991. That night, he was defeating a two-time world champion from Cuba.

In 1990 his mother, who had followed his career enthusiastically, died of cancer with a last wish for her son—that he win a gold medal in the 1992 Olympics, to be held in Barcelona, Spain. Oscar de la Hoya charged ahead and did just that. He was the only boxer to win a gold medal for the United States in those games.

The Olympic gold medal was the culmination of de la Hoya's amateur career, during which he won 225 fights, lost only 5, and achieved 153 knockouts. He had already been declared USA Boxing's 1991 Boxer of the Year. After Barcelona, he would become known as boxing's "Golden Boy."

De la Hoya then turned professional, launching a relentless series of ring victories that won him a devoted following even beyond the circles of habitual boxing fans. *Ring* magazine flatly pronounced him the best boxer in the world, pound for pound – and he became the second-best-paid athlete in the world, topped only by basketball's Michael Jordan.

In 1994 he was World Boxing Organization junior lightweight champion and afterward lightweight champion; in 1995, International Boxing Federation lightweight champion (the first Mexican American to reach that rank); in 1996, World Boxing Council (WBC) junior welterweight champion; and in 1997, WBC welterweight champion.

De la Hoya set himself a hugely ambitious goal: to win seven world championships, in succeeding classes, and retire by the age of 30. In addition to athletics, he mentioned dreams of becoming an architect, and he helped design his own house. However, he was also attracted to the idea of acting in movies, and made the most of the many advertising sponsorships he was offered. "De la Hoya is a Madison Avenue [advertising industry headquarters] dream," said *Los Angeles Magazine.*

The fighter retained the welterweight championship through several defenses in 1997 and 1998. Then, in 1999, he finally lost the title. It was his only defeat in 32 professional bouts, 25 of which he won by a knockout. In 2000, he won his first fight after losing the championship—and shortly thereafter recovered the title, when the new holder switched categories and left it vacant. In mid-2000 De la Hoya lost the title again, then took on a position promoting a national talent search for new Latino entertainers.

The Oscar de la Hoya Foundation channels money he donates to promote young athletes including the payment of educational scholarships for the talented.

Further Reading

Kawakami, Tim. *Golden Boy: The Fame, Money, and Mystery of Oscar de la Hoya.* Kansas City, Mo.: Andrews-McMeel, 1999.

Taylor, Robert. *Oscar de la Hoya: Boxing's Boy Wonder.* Rourke, 1993.

de la Renta, Oscar (1932–) *fashion designer*

One of the foremost high-fashion designers in the United States, Oscar de la Renta is also the only U.S. designer ever to have been invited to head a top French fashion house.

De la Renta was born in the Dominican capital, Santo Domingo, on July 22, 1932. Following his early interest in art, he studied at the University of Santo Domingo and then completed his studies at Spain's Academia de San Fernando in Madrid.

His original idea was to become a painter—specifically, an abstract painter; nevertheless, he discovered an interest in something extremely concrete, clothing design. He showed some of his sketches to the wife of John Lodge, U.S. ambassador to Spain, who was so impressed that she asked him to design her daughter's debutante dress. *Life* magazine printed a photograph of the debutante in de la Renta's gown on its cover; with this, the designer was securely ensconced both in his career and in the circles of the rich and famous—he designed their dresses and became one of their number.

Among the world's fashion-conscious, wealthy women who also appreciated his good looks and courtly charm, he was soon referred to simply as Oscar.

First, he entered the couture (high-fashion) house of designer Balenciaga in Spain; then, in 1961, he went to Paris as assistant to designer Antonio del Castillo at the Lanvin-Castillo fashion establishment. In 1963 de la Renta came to the United States. He became a U.S. citizen in 1971.

As a new New Yorker, he initially worked for other designers, first with Elizabeth Arden and then Jane Derby. After 1965, when Derby retired, he worked for himself.

He was married to Françoise de Langlade from 1967 until her death in 1983. Former editor in chief of *Vogue* magazine's French edition, her connections were invaluable for the rising fashion designer. One of his clients, a member of the wealthy Rothschild family, called de Langlade "Oscar's grey eminence"—the real power behind de la Renta. In 1989, he married a metals-fortune heiress, Annette Reed.

De la Renta works in both high-fashion and ready-to-wear clothing but is especially known for his evening wear. At first, he favored ruffles and frills, as well as bold colors; later, he developed a more stylized look, yet one that always remained easy to wear despite some spectacular touches.

He and a business partner also established a wide and profitable empire of franchises, licensing the use of the designer's name for a range of such quality products as perfume and jewelry.

Hispanic accents are often found in de la Renta's designs, something that he has attributed to the influence of his teacher Balenciaga. This Spanish master was the creator, he says, of "the most beautiful folkloric clothes ever made."

He is a member of the boards of the Metropolitan Opera and of Carnegie Hall, and his wife Annette Reed is vice chairman of the Metropolitan Museum of Art's board.

De la Renta has carried out philanthropic work. He opened La Casa del Niño, a center for aiding destitute children, in his native country in 1982. In addition to Dominican awards, he received the Jack Dempsey Award for Humanitarianism in 1988. With his first wife, he adopted a child who had been found abandoned in Santo Domingo.

Oscar de la Renta has collected many fashion industry honors, including the Coty Award (twice), being named to the Coty Hall of Fame, the Neiman-Marcus Award, the Fragrance Foundation Award, and the Council of Fashion Designers of America Lifetime Achievement Award in 1990. The fashion designer was chosen to appear on TV in a 1993 update of *The Flintstones*. In this mix of cartoon and live action, he created a wedding gown for Fred and Wilma Flintstone's daughter, Pebbles.

His ultimate honor was an invitation by Pierre Balmain's great fashion house in Paris to succeed its deceased creator as chief designer. Never before had French fashion looked to the United States to fill such a post. De la Renta presented his first Balmain collection in Paris in 1993 to instant acclaim.

At the same time, he continues to run his U.S. fashion enterprises, telling an interviewer, "If a tycoon can run several companies, so can I."

Further Reading

Blackwell, Earl. *Celebrity Register.* Towson, Md.: Time Publishing Group, 1986.

O'Hara, Georgina. *The Encyclopedia of Fashion.* New York: Abrams, 1986.

del Río, Dolores (Lolita Dolores Martínez Asúnsolo López Negrete)
(1905–1983)   *actress*

Dolores del Río was one of the most glamorous Hollywood stars of the 1920s, 1930s, and early 1940s. Her legendary beauty allowed her to survive the passage from silent movies to talkies. It was a beauty still admired in films made in the 1970s.

Del Río was a great star in a period of American film history when Hispanics had a chance to be regarded as highly romantic figures. Male or female, they could be seen as possessing an excitingly exotic allure if they had a regal bearing and pearly white skin, thus escaping typecasting as swarthy bandits and peasant girls.

She realized that this began to change around the 1940s when Latino minorities began to be much more visible in U.S. society: "It was," she declared in a 1979 interview, "as if reality had cut in on the glamour with which we [i.e., those like herself, Ramón NOVARRO, and Antonio MORENO] had always been associated."

This put an end to what she had hoped would be a road of increasing acceptance. "I was very popular for roles of all kinds, not just the stereotypical Latin spitfire. At the time, I thought that (other) Latin actresses, who had so far been ignored in favor of Europeans like [Greta] Garbo and [Marlene] Dietrich, would become more and more popular until they

Dolores del Río   *(Cabrera Archive)*

were routinely accepted and integrated into the Hollywood system. It never happened."

Born Lolita Dolores Martínez Asúnsolo López Negrete on August 3, 1905, in Durango, Mexico, Del Río's family had to flee the city in 1909 when the guerrilla leader Pancho Villa attacked during an uprising against the Mexican dictator Porfirio Díaz. Otherwise, her upbringing was uneventful. Her family had a high social standing, though her mother had Indian blood. Her father is believed to have been a bank president. Dolores received a convent education and at the age of 15 married a rich socialite, Jaime Martínez del Río. When she began to act, she used the second half of her husband's surname (*del Río* means "of the river" in Spanish).

Her induction into the movies came when a Hollywood director and producer, Edwin Carewe, passed through town. He met the Martínez del Ríos socially. Carewe told her husband, "Your wife could be a female Valentino" (comparing her to the great star of the time, Rudolph Valentino). It was then considered unseemly for a Mexican woman of del Río's social standing to become an actress, but her husband allowed himself to be talked into it, and she went to the United States.

Dolores del Río appeared first in a part in Carewe's movie *Joanna* (1925). This was followed by other films such as *The Whole Town's Talking* and *The Loves of Carmen*. In *Ramona* (1928), one of her most famous roles, she played an Indian maiden in old California.

Her career was well on its way, but she met two major obstacles. The first was that her husband did not like being regarded as "Mr. Dolores del Río"; they were soon divorced. The second problem was that her glossy beauty tended to stun her acquaintances. This impeded the development of normal relationships, which her lively nature would have preferred. One fan magazine, *Photoplay,* put it this way in 1934: "It was heartbreaking for her to discover that most people, following an introduction, backed off and looked at her as though she were the sacred ceiling of the Sistine Chapel."

Her movies continued with *Girl of the Río* (1932) and *Flying Down to Río* (1933). The "coincidences" with the star's name did no harm, but the insulting portrayal of Hispanics in *Girl of the Río* led to its being banned in several Latin American countries.

For *Bird of Paradise* (1932), in which she played a Polynesian, it is said that the producer David O. Selznick simply insisted on two surefire inspirations. "I don't care what story you use," he told the team, "as long as we call it *Bird of Paradise* and del Río jumps into a flaming volcano at the finish." She did.

In 1930 she married celebrated movie art director Cedric Gibbons. They split up in 1941. She was also courted by director Orson Welles, who directed her in *Journey into Fear* (1942).

The next year, however, del Río took a hiatus from the Hollywood career that had made her one of the most famous Hispanic names ever in the United States. At one point, she was one of the 10 biggest movie box-office attractions in the country.

No one has ever fully established why she returned to Mexico. It was said that she was dissatisfied with the mainly exotic roles she was given to play; yet, she repeatedly emphasized that she had been given a wide range of roles. In Mexico, Dolores del Río also had an intense movie career, playing in such films as *María Candelaria (Portrait of María)* (1943), one of the most significant in that country's history. She also acted for U.S. director John Ford in a film he shot in Mexico, *The Fugitive* (1947). As a result, she befriended Ford and prided herself in being one of the last people he asked to see when he was dying in 1973.

In the late 1950s del Río began another career in Mexico, as a stage actress. In the same decade, she considered offers to return to Hollywood, but with the United States going through a communist-hunting period, a visa request to film *Broken Lance* in 1954 was delayed because she had been in contact with communists in the Mexican movie industry. Also, she had given aid to people who had fled from Spain, which was then under the right-wing dictatorship of Generalissimo Francisco Franco.

She reassured the United States that she had never been a communist and that "I love America and regard it as my very own." She received the visa, but by that time the role had been given to the actress Katy JURADO. Eventually, she played actor-singer Elvis Presley's mother in *Flaming Star* (1960) in the

United States and then Omar Sharif's mother in an Italian movie, *More Than a Miracle* (1967). She did another U.S. movie, for John Ford in 1964, *Cheyenne Autumn,* and made appearances on U.S. television.

In her last role, Dolores del Río acted in the U.S.–Mexican coproduction *The Children of Sánchez* (1978), a film with the most valuable social content of her career. This was a study of a poor Mexican family and also involved other Mexican-born U.S. actors such as Anthony QUINN and Katy Jurado.

Offscreen, she was the founder and hardworking head of *Estancia Infantil,* a care center for actresses' children in Mexico.

Del Río died in 1983 in California. There is no connection between the actress and the Del Río Manifesto of 1969. This was a reaffirmation of Chicano cultural identity and protest against discrimination, made by such Mexican American youth leaders as José Angel GUTIÉRREZ. The manifesto was named after the place where it was issued, San Felipe del Río in Texas.

Further Reading

Hadley-García, George. *Hispanic Hollywood: The Latins in Motion Pictures.* Secaucus, N.J.: Citadel Press, 1990.

Oshana, Maryann. *Women of Color: A Filmography of Minority and Third World Women.* New York: Garland Publishing, Inc., 1985.

Woll, Allen L. *The Latin Image in American Film.* Los Angeles: UCLA Latin American Center Publications, 1980.

✣ de Soto, Hernando (ca. 1496–1542)
explorer

In 1539–42, Hernando de Soto led a major expedition through what is now the southern United States. Its goal was booty, its methods brutal, its monetary results nil, and its leader a fatality during it. But it did map a large territory and left a valuable record of the Native American societies it met.

De Soto is sometimes regarded as the first European to have seen the Mississippi River, although another Spaniard, Alonso ALVAREZ DE PINEDA, had already crossed its mouth two decades earlier. In any case, de Soto's voyage retains a large place in both the history and the imagination of the United States. Four hundred years after it took place, its path—more than 4,000 miles of it—was retraced by a U.S. government expedition. De Soto's landing in Florida is reenacted annually. A line of car models was even named after him.

The date of Hernando de Soto's birth has been placed sometime between 1496 and 1501. A member of the minor nobility, he was born in the town of Jérez de los Caballeros, in the region of Badajoz, Spain. This was also the birthplace of the discoverer of the Pacific Ocean, Vasco Núñez de Balboa, who was de Soto's brother-in-law.

De Soto campaigned first in Central America, then in South America, and finally in North America. He arrived in the Americas very young, in 1514, serving the governor of Panama. He took part in several expeditions exploring and conquering different parts of Central America and was described as "one of the best lancers that have come to the New World. . . . When he entered into battle he made way for ten of his men to follow."

In the early 1530s, Peru became de Soto's next goal. He held the rank of captain while taking part in Francisco Pizarro's conquest of the Inca empire. By then, he had made enough money to personally contribute four ships, 100 men, and 25 horses to Pizarro's expedition. de Soto reached the Inca heartland in the Andes Mountains ahead of Pizarro, crossing the Amazon River watershed. He was the first to meet Atahualpa, the Inca king. Atahualpa had impressed de Soto, and de Soto taught Atahualpa to play chess. While he opposed Atahualpa's execution by Pizarro, de Soto was not opposed to mistreating Native Americans in general, as he was to prove later in North America. Pizarro sent de Soto off on an expedition and killed Atahualpa before his captain's return.

Peru made de Soto rich. In 1536 he was back in Spain, where the king made him a marquis, but it seemed that he wanted to be another Hernán Cortés or Pizarro. After Mexico, which had fallen to Cortés, and Peru, which had been grabbed by Pizarro, could he not find himself another empire to subdue?

Hopefully, it would be as grand as that of the Aztec and especially as rich with gold as that of the

Inca. He decided to explore the largely uncharted lands north of Cuba, where, it was reported, there were wealthy cities to be found.

De Soto secured the title of governor of Cuba and was promised the governorship of the lands he conquered. He then mounted a nine-ship expedition. He and his 600 soldiers sailed from Spain in 1538. After a year in Cuba, he landed in Florida in May 1539. On the Florida leg of the trip, de Soto retraced the steps of another expedition led by Pánfilo de NARVÁEZ, which had covered that stretch in 1528.

He thus came across Juan Ortiz, a member of Narváez's party, who had been captured by Indians. Ortiz had been ordered killed by the Indian chief. His execution was prevented by the chief's daughter, who had fallen in love with him. Ortiz's adventure took place almost a century before that of Captain Smith and Pocahontas. Ortiz had been kept captive for 11 years and had learned the Indian languages of the area. Now he joined the campaign of his rescuer, de Soto, proving highly useful as an interpreter. But the enterprise was ultimately fatal for Ortiz, as he was killed in a battle with other Indians.

The expedition marched through parts of what are now Florida, Georgia, both Carolinas, Tennessee, Alabama, Mississippi, Arkansas, and Louisiana. At one site on the Savannah River in Georgia, the local Indian chief, a woman known as the Lady of Cofitachequi, invited de Soto into her village and made him a present of freshwater pearls.

But there was no gold or silver to be had in these territories. De Soto used terror tactics to seek information about riches: He took his benefactor, the Lady of Cofitachequi, prisoner in an extortion maneuver.

The Native Americans who fell into his hands repeatedly told him about great wealth somewhere else, to make him chase off in another direction. This misinformation accounted for the zigzag character of his path.

De Soto and his men were the first Europeans to cross the Appalachian range, in early 1540. They came to the Mississippi River in May 1541 and built barges to cross it. They may have reached as far west as Oklahoma before turning south again. De Soto fell ill with a violent fever in May 1542 and died, near the site of Natchez. Fearful of attack by local Indians

if it became known that de Soto was dead, the Spaniards weighted down his body and disposed of it in the Mississippi River.

The expedition, now under de Soto's lieutenant, Luis de Moscoso, decided to head back to Mexico. First, they turned west and marched into Texas, but they gave up this overland route because it seemed to go on forever. The men retraced their steps back to the Mississippi and built seven rough vessels. They now numbered slightly more than 300, or about half the original force. This was a relatively low rate of loss for a campaign like theirs. The remaining men floated down the Mississippi and the coast of the Gulf to Mexico.

Further Reading

The United States DeSoto Expedition Final Report. Washington, D.C.: Smithsonian Institution Press, 1985.

Chrisma, Abbott. *Hernando de Soto.* Milwaukee, WI: Raintree Publications, 1989.

Duncan, David Ewing. *Hernando de Soto: A Savage Quest in the Americas.* New York: Crown Publishers, 1995.

Galloway, Patricia, ed. *The Hernando de Soto Expedition.* Lincoln: University of Nebraska Press, 1997.

Leonardo, Bob M.C. "The Floridians: Conquistadors." Available online. URL: http://www.floridahistory.org/floridians/conquis.htm. Downloaded October 10, 2000.

Sakurai, Gai. *Hernando de Soto.* Danbury, Conn.: Franklin Watts, 2001.

Whitman, Sylvia. *Hernando de Soto and the Explorers of the American South.* New York: Chelsea House Publishers, 1991.

Díaz, Cameron (1972–) *actress*

Cameron Díaz's extremely fast rise in the movie business may be a result of her blonde good looks coupled with a personality that, on and off the screen, is fresh, intuitive, and unassuming. Without a stereotypical "Latina look," from the outset she landed mainstream, nonethnic roles. She came to films without any formal drama training, and in fact was refused as a pupil by an acting coach who declared, "Don't let this woman anywhere near an acting class. She is a rare natural."

Born in San Diego, California, on August 30, 1972, Cameron Díaz is Cuban-American on her father's side, as well as Native American, German, and English on her mother's side. Her father worked as an oil company foreman and her mother as an export agent.

Growing up as a tomboy with a taste for heavy metal rock, Díaz reports that she broke her nose accidentally three times and did not consider herself especially pretty. She kept two snakes, three dogs, three cats, and five birds, and dreamed of becoming a zoologist.

Her discovery, the "break" that countless young people hope for, happened at a party in Hollywood that she attended when she was 16 years old. She was spotted by a photographer who told her she had the makings of a model and who left her his card, with instructions that her parents should telephone him.

There was no slow rise through the ranks for Cameron Díaz. Within a week she was under contract as a model and almost immediately landed magazine covers and high-paying jobs involving travel abroad, from Mexico to Morocco and beyond. Her parents agreed with only one condition—that she not give up high school, but only postpone her studies until her working commitments allowed her to continue.

For the most part, Díaz handled her new lifestyle with assurance and maturity. Despite her immediate success, Díaz had not reached "supermodel" status by the time she switched to acting. She considers this an asset, since, she maintains, there is a prejudice against models who become actresses, the assumption being that they cannot act. Yet, she says, "modeling is like acting—it's just that you tell a story in one image."

Díaz turned down her first acting offer because it involved nudity. A better opportunity presented itself when she auditioned for a small part in *The Mask,* a 1994 comedy. Again, she had instant acceptance that went beyond her expectations. Instead of the role she had been seeking, she was given the female lead, star Jim Carrey's love interest—although the producers made her wear a padded bra to round out the lissome figure that had served her well as a model.

The Mask was a hit and made Díaz a well-known actress at the age of 22. She followed this success with a number of independent films in which she acted alongside established stars such as Harvey Keitel and Keanu Reeves.

The young actress was in another large-scale success with *My Best Friend's Wedding* (1997), in which the third-billed Díaz earned good reviews despite the starring presence of Julia Roberts. The following year, Díaz starred in the top-earning comedy *There's Something About Mary.*

Other titles in her career include *Being John Malkovich* and *Any Given Sunday* in 1999. In 2000, she costarred with Drew Barrymore and Lucy Liu in a film version of *Charlie's Angels.*

Cameron Díaz was proclaimed ShoWest Female Star of Tomorrow in 1996, received the Blockbuster Entertainment Award for favorite supporting actress in a comedy in 1997, and was named "The 'It' Girl of 1998" by *Entertainment Weekly.* In 2000, she won an ALMA Award for her role in *Any Given Sunday* and was nominated for an American Comedy Award for her role in *Being John Malkovich,* among numerous other awards and nominations.

Further Reading

Tony Tang Productions. "Best of Cameron Díaz." Available online. URL: http://cameron-diaz.com. Downloaded October 10, 2000.

Telgen, Diane, and Jim Kamp, eds. *Notable Hispanic American Women.* Detroit: Gale Research, Inc., 1998.

꧁ Díaz-Balart, Lincoln (1954–)
politician

Congressman Lincoln Díaz-Balart has helped shape some of the most crucial U.S. legislation on U.S.–Cuban relations and immigration. Two major achievements are the Helms-Burton law and the Nicaraguan Adjustment and Central American Relief Act (NACARA). NACARA—which allowed hundreds of thousands of illegal immigrants, who had arrived in the United States before a specific date, to acquire legal, permanent residence—is in fact informally known as "the Díaz-Balart law."

Díaz-Balart's life and career are in many ways typical of those of many Cuban Americans who have devoted themselves wholeheartedly to the fight against Fidel Castro's rule. The main difference is that he showed the talent to go further than many. Indeed, getting ahead in politics ran in the family. Lincoln Díaz-Balart was born in Havana on August 13, 1954. His grandfather and father had both been congressmen in Cuba, and his father reached the post of president of the Cuban Senate when the island was governed by the right-wing dictator Fulgencio Batista. In 1959 Fidel Castro ousted Batista and created a left-wing dictatorship. The Díaz-Balart family immigrated to the United States the same year.

Lincoln Díaz-Balart (who is not related to Cameron DÍAZ) had a cosmopolitan education. After grade school in Miami he attended high school at the American School in Madrid, Spain. He showed his political leanings early, as president of his high school student government. (He would also become president of the student government in college.) He received a B.A. degree in 1976 in international relations at the New College of the University of South Florida in Sarasota, then was off to Europe again, where he received a diploma in British politics from Cambridge University in England. In 1979 he obtained a law degree from Case Western Reserve University in Cleveland, Ohio.

Díaz-Balart showed a desire to help the underprivileged from the beginning of his career, when he gave free legal services to those unable to pay legal fees under the Legal Services of Greater Miami program. He also worked for a law firm and was assistant state attorney in Miami.

Originally a Democrat, Díaz-Balart reached the presidency of the Florida Young Democrats. But when he ran for the Florida legislature as a Democrat, he failed: his area's Cuban-immigrant population was heavily Republican. Plus, Díaz-Balart was frustrated by what he saw as weak Democratic anticommunist policies in the Caribbean then; as a result, he switched to the Republican Party.

In 1986 he was elected to the state House of Representatives by the largest margin ever. He served two terms in the House and was named "best in

Lincoln Díaz-Balart *(Courtesy of Lincoln Díaz-Balart)*

debate" in his first term of office. Then he moved on to the state Senate, where again he was reelected.

Despite the change to the more conservative of the two main U.S. parties, Díaz-Balart voted for the liberal position on services for the poor and for farmworkers, among other issues. He also championed redistricting in the Miami area to better reflect the Cuban-American population. A new district was created, and in 1992 its voters sent him to the U.S. House of Representatives in Washington.

There, as a member of the House Foreign Affairs Committee, he immediately plunged into the anti-Castro fray, seeking to tighten the U.S. embargo against Cuba, and even trying to get the entire United Nations to join the embargo. Díaz-Balart's other key interests were U.S. national security and strong relations with Israel.

Upon reelection (unopposed) in 1994, Díaz-Balart was appointed to the Rules Committee, which has the unique power to decide what legislation will be debated on the House floor. Voters in Florida continued to send him to the House in succeeding elections—in 1998, by 75 percent of the ballots cast.

The legislation known as Helms-Burton, aimed at tightening the squeeze on Castro, was to a considerable extent written by Díaz-Balart. NACARA is mainly Díaz-Balart's work, as the law's nickname testifies. The congressman's record also shows he led the successful effort to restore benefits that had been cut to legal immigrants.

In 2000, Díaz-Balart was again reelected to the House of Representatives.

Further Reading

U.S. House of Representatives. "Lincoln Díaz-Balart." Available online. URL: http://www.house.gov/diaz-balart. Downloaded October 10, 2000.

Meier, Matt S. *Notable Latin Americans.* Westport, Conn.: Greenwood Press, 1997.

❦ Domingo, Plácido (1941–) *opera singer, orchestra conductor*

The career of tenor Plácido Domingo can be described by a string of superlatives. Recognized as one of the "three supertenors" of his age, alongside Luciano Pavarotti and José Carreras, he easily outdistanced them in both quantity and variety of work undertaken, all of it to great acclaim.

A big dynamo of a man, he has striven all his life to spread his love for singing (especially opera, but many other kinds of music too) to audiences of all kinds and in all places. He has been enormously successful, not only in helping to introduce grand opera to millions, but also acquainting further millions with the power and resonance of an operatic voice as applied to everything from tango to country ballads.

He has done so much that for decades he has been criticized for jeopardizing his voice through overwork, something that many feared would shorten his singing career. The great Swedish soprano Birgit Nilsson declared, "God must have been in excellent spirit the day he created Plácido. He has everything needed for one of the greatest careers ever seen: an incredibly beautiful voice, great intelligence, an unbelievable musicality and acting ability, wonderful looks, a great heart, and he's a dear, dear colleague. He

is almost the perfect linguist—but, alas, he has not yet learned how to say 'no' in any language."

Apparently unconcerned, Domingo just kept on singing, in excellent form, although he added conducting to his other, main activity, not only because he loves it, but also because he saw it as a way to continue working in music after his singing days were over. Also, he told those who warned him about abusing his voice that he intended to continue singing "until the mid-1990s." But in 1999 he sang in the opening of the year's season at the Metropolitan Opera of New York—his 18th season opening—with no end in sight. In fact, Domingo's 18 openings broke the previous record of 17 openings at the Met set by the legendary Enrico Caruso, and which many had thought would stand forever.

Plácido Domingo (whose name in Spanish can be translated as "peaceful Sunday") was born in Madrid, Spain, on January 21, 1941. His parents were singers and producers of zarzuela—Spanish operetta. When he was a boy the family moved to Mexico City. He studied piano, easily reaching concert quality, then switched to singing—initially as a baritone before being advised to change to the higher tenor register.

He first sang opera professionally in Mexico, then briefly with the Dallas Civic Opera, then for more than two years with the Israel National Opera Company. While in Israel he added Hebrew to the several other languages in which he is fluent. His facility with languages is complemented by his memory, which allows him to quickly learn entire operas by heart and add them permanently to his mental repertory.

Domingo returned to the United States in 1965 and since then has made it the center of his opera life (although, living the constantly traveling life of a top musician, he has houses in New York, Los Angeles, Spain, Mexico, England, Austria, and Monaco). He sang first in New York with the New York City Opera; since 1968 he has been the virtual "house tenor" at the Metropolitan Opera. He is arguably its most representative artistic personality of recent decades other than house conductor James Levine.

In addition, in the 1980s Domingo became artistic consultant to the Los Angeles Music Center; in

1996, artistic director of the Washington (D.C.) Opera—the first Hispanic to hold that post in a major U.S. opera company—and in 2000, artistic director of the Los Angeles Opera. Also in 2000 Domingo was included in the annual list of honors conferred by the Kennedy Center for the Performing Arts.

In great demand around the world, he was invited to sing the title part in *Othello*—one of his most acclaimed roles—at the 100th anniversary of Europe's most famous opera house, the Teatro alla Scala in Milan, Italy, in 1987.

Because of his commanding presence and his capacity not just to sing but to act what he is singing, both with his body and with his voice, Domingo was the tenor of choice for movie versions of operas, including, most notably, *La Traviata* (1983) and *Carmen* (1984).

His colossally successful "Three Tenors" concerts with Carreras and Pavarotti, at unconventional venues such as soccer stadiums, have been watched by up to 800 million people around the world. The 1990 concert was also made into the best-selling classical record in history.

To a shelfload of Emmy and Grammy Awards Domingo has added Mexico's highest honor, the Order of the Aztec Eagle. It was given to him for his efforts on behalf of the victims of the 1985 earthquake that ravaged Mexico City, and killed several members of his family. Domingo devoted one full year to singing benefit concerts to raise money for the reconstruction work.

Domingo has sung more than 100 different operas and recorded about 80, plus numerous albums of other types of song.

Further Reading

Domingo, Plácido. *My First Forty Years.* New York: Alfred A. Knopf, 1983.

Goodnough, David. *Plácido Domingo: Opera Superstar.* Springfield, N.J.: Enslow Publishers, 1997.

Lewis, Marcia. *The Private Lives of the Three Tenors: Behind the Scenes with Plácido Domingo, Luciano Pavarotti, and Jose Carreras.* Secaucus, N.J.: Carol Publishing Group, 1996.

Plácido Domingo. Available online. URL: http://www.Placidodomingo.com. Downloaded October 10, 2000.

Schnauber, Cornelius. *Plácido Domingo.* Boston: Northeastern University Press, 1997.

Snowman, Daniel. *The World of Plácido Domingo.* New York: McGraw-Hill, 1985.

Stefoff, Rebecca. *Plácido Domingo.* New York: Chelsea House, 1992.

E

Escalante, Jaime (1930–) *educator*

Jaime Escalante is a teacher with a special gift for inspiring children from poor barrios (Latino neighborhoods) to excel in mathematics. This gift has won him nationwide recognition—a movie was even made about his life—and he has changed the lives of the large number of youths in whom he has instilled self-esteem.

Escalante was born on December 31, 1930, to a middle-class family in La Paz, the capital of Bolivia. He graduated from San Andrés University in La Paz and taught math and science at two high schools and at the military academy (Colegio Militar) in his home country, winning respect for his talent as an educator.

Nevertheless, in 1964 he and his wife decided to immigrate to the United States in search of greater stability than could be provided by Bolivia at that time. Escalante (whose name can be translated as "the climber") was not seeking easy money or to shirk hard work and difficult challenges. Rather, he is someone who actively seeks out hard work and challenges.

Escalante wanted to teach school in his new country, but was initially turned down because his English was deemed not good enough and because his Bolivian teaching credentials were not recognized in the United States. He decided to acquire the skills he needed. While working as a busboy, then as a cook, and later as a technician at an electronics company, he studied at Pasadena City College. He then went to California State University in Los Angeles, from which he graduated with a B.S. degree in mathematics. By 1974, Escalante was ready to teach.

His years of working at humble jobs had taught him street language. He would later use this to get through to students from impoverished neighborhoods. He could have had his pick of jobs, any number of which would have paid more than teaching school, but he did not abandon his original goal. Escalante deliberately chose to work in East Los Angeles at Garfield High School, knowing that in a Chicano barrio his work would be hard, but that there he could do the most good.

When the film *Stand and Deliver* was later made about his accomplishments, the advertisements described "A new troublemaker [who had] hit Garfield High. . . . He was tough. He was wild. He was willing to fight. He was the new math teacher."

Escalante found, as he had expected, that Garfield's students had grown up in difficult circumstances, leaving them surly and uninterested. His students discovered that Escalante would not give up. He also demonstrated a knack for uncovering their pride as well as their curiosity. He reminded them that the

Maya of Mexico and Central America, whose blood many of them carried, had been among the great mathematicians of antiquity. He demonstrated this by explaining the complex and accurate calendar system they had developed.

Escalante not only got the students to pass their basic math courses, but he also launched something more advanced—a calculus class. To do this, Escalante had to overcome much opposition. For example, many school officials thought that calculus was too demanding for underprivileged students.

In 1982, setting his pupils' sights ever higher, he had them take a nationwide examination, the advanced-placement calculus test. This test is so tough that just 2 percent of the pupils in U.S. high schools even try it. All of Escalante's students passed.

That was not the end of it, though. The results were so astonishing that it was thought there must have been a mistake, or, worse, cheating. So the students took a new test and got even better grades.

This story was a featured part of the 1988 film *Stand and Deliver*, which was directed and cowritten by the Cuban-born Ramón Menéndez. He was inspired to create it by an article about Escalante in the *Los Angeles Times*. Escalante was played by Edward James OLMOS; the cast also included Hispanic actors Lou Diamond Phillips and Andy GARCÍA. A math teacher was an unlikely movie hero, but the film was successful with critics and audiences alike. *Newsweek* called it "more exciting than *La Bamba*," alluding to Lou Diamond Phillips's previous hit.

Escalante discovered that he had become a celebrity. More gratifying still, as the years passed, increasing numbers of his barrio students succeeded in passing the difficult advanced-placement calculus test and went on to college with scholarship offers.

Recognized as one of the best teachers in the United States by his peers and as "an authentic American hero" by the media, Escalante was given the chance to bring his enthusiasm for mathematics to bigger audiences on television. He was featured on a PBS television program, *Futures*, and also became an education consultant. Yet throughout it all, he continues to do what he likes best—teaching. In 1991, he left Garfield High School to teach at Hiram Johnson High School in Sacramento.

Escalante has been honored by institutions not only in the United States but also abroad. They include the White House Hispanic Heritage Award (1989), the Hispanic Engineer National Chairman's Award (1989), and the American Institute for Public Service's Jefferson Award (1990). Despite the accolades, Escalante is most pleased by the student scholarship funds that have been created in his honor.

Further Reading

Matthews, Jay. *Escalante: The Best Teacher in America.* New York: Henry Holt, 1988.

Estefan, Gloria (Gloria Fajardo)
(1958–) *singer*

Gloria Estefan belongs to the small number of Hispanic singers who have completely crossed over to mainstream success in the United States and the world.

Gloria Fajardo was born in Havana, Cuba, in 1958. Estefan is her married name. Her later anti-Castro political stance was a family inheritance: her soldier father, José Manuel Fajardo, was a bodyguard of right-wing Cuban dictator Fulgencio Batista. The Fajardos had to flee Cuba when Batista was toppled by Fidel Castro in 1959. In 1961, Estefan's father was one of the Cuban exiles who took part in the Bay of Pigs invasion. The invasion failed and Fajardo was taken prisoner. Freed through an agreement between Cuba and the United States, he later fought in the Vietnam War as a member of the U.S. Army.

In Vietnam, Fajardo was one of the many U.S. servicemen who were exposed to Agent Orange. This powerful chemical was used to kill vegetation so as to remove the enemy's cover. His exposure to Agent Orange is believed to be the reason that he developed the paralyzing nerve disease multiple sclerosis in 1968. His daughter Gloria cared for him for eight years. He then required permanent hospitalization and later died. Throughout this period, Gloria's mother worked during the day and studied at night.

Gloria began to sing at home in those years as an emotional release. She also began to have recurrent fears that she would somehow become paralyzed herself. Years later, these fears almost came true as the result of an accident.

Gloria Fajardo attended the University of Miami and in 1978 received a B.A. degree in psychology. She never worked as a psychologist, however, because three years earlier she had joined a band called the Miami Latin Boys. Its leader, Emilio Estefan, invited her to be its lead vocalist. The group then changed its name to the Miami Sound Machine. The same year she graduated, Gloria married Emilio Estefan.

The Miami Sound Machine originally performed songs in Spanish only. Their strongly Latin sound made their first recordings major hits in Spanish-speaking countries. In 1986, with the band's first albums in English, *Eyes of Innocence* and *Primitive Love,* the crossover began.

Gloria Estefan recalls that, when they first played what became one of their biggest hit songs, "Conga," a producer complained that it was "too Latin for the Americans and too American for the Latins." Her answer, she says, was "Well, thank you, because that's exactly what we are!" No less than 1,250,000 albums featuring "Conga" were sold, and it was credited with establishing a "Miami sound"—an unabashed mix of styles and influences.

She has named singers as diverse as Celia CRUZ and Barbra Streisand as influences. Gloria Estefan's fame gradually became greater than that of the band. She still works with the Miami Sound Machine but also has a solo career as a singer and songwriter. Either way, success has been great, and not only in the United States. In Britain, Gloria Estefan and the Miami Sound Machine gave nine sold-out performances at the Wembley Arena.

The Estefans live in a house made of coral rock, on expensive Star Island close to Miami. The grounds feature 150 different types of palm trees.

In March 1990, while on tour in snowbound Pennsylvania, the band's bus was rammed by one truck and slammed into another. Emilio had minor injuries, and their son Nayib broke a shoulder bone, but Gloria suffered serious injury, having broken her back. Doctors initially believed that she would spend the rest of her life in a wheelchair. Yet she worked so hard at her recovery that by early 1991 she was not only on her feet but was launching a world tour. The tour was to promote the album *Into the Light.* It expressed her feelings as she emerged from the darkness of her accident.

Her recovery is considered total, except, she says, that when she leans back, she can feel the studs of two metal rods that were implanted to support her spine. Her injuries also made a second pregnancy difficult; Gloria Estefan had to undergo medical therapy to be able to bear another child and turned down an offer of $2 million for a single concert in Japan so as not to endanger the treatment. The treatment was successful, however, and a sister for Nayib was born in 1994.

Billboard magazine named Gloria Estefan Best New Pop Artist in 1986. A Grammy winner, she also received the American Music Award in 1989, and in 1990 was Crossover Artist of the Year in the Lo Nuestro ("our thing") Latin Music Awards.

Emilio Estefan left the Miami Sound Machine as a performer to become its manager and a record producer. He became president of a Sony Records company division. In 1994 he created a critically acclaimed and heavily Latin soundtrack for the movie *The Specialist.* He also made his film debut in that movie as a piano player.

In 1992, in the aftermath of Hurricane Andrew, which ravaged Florida, Gloria and Emilio Estefan set up a food-assistance organization. Their Hurricane Relief Food raised $3.8 million through a benefit concert. Other participants in the concert included Julio IGLESIAS—another Hispanic singer who resides in Miami and was almost paralyzed in a road crash—Jon SECADA, and Paul Simon.

The Estefans were the driving force in 1994 behind a prayer vigil at Miami's Orange Bowl stadium held to support refugees from Fidel Castro's Cuba. Forty thousand people participated in the event. But Gloria prefers to keep politics and religion out of her song lyrics. She likes to sing, she has said, about the things that draw people together, rather than those they quarrel over. In 1996, Estefan had a lead singing role at the closing ceremonies of the Olympic Games held in Atlanta, and was featured on the cover of *Time.*

In 1999, Estefan made her acting debut in *Music of the Heart.* She received an Award of Merit, and was honored with a musical tribute at the American Music Awards ceremony in 2000. That year, she released *Alma Caribeña,* a Spanish-language album.

Further Reading

Catalano, Grace. *Gloria Estefan.* New York: St. Martin's Press, 1991.

Gourse, Leslie. *Gloria Estefan: Pop Sensation.* Danbury, Conn.: Franklin Watts, 2000.

Stefoff, Rebecca. *Gloria Estefan.* New York: Chelsea House, 1991.

Emilio Estévez *(Cabrera Archive)*

✌ Estévez, Emilio (1962–) *actor*

Emilio Estévez stands out among a group of Hispanic actors who began to succeed in Hollywood in the 1980s. He has joined the still small number of performers who have gained recognition while retaining their Latino names.

Commentators often note two advantages that have helped Estévez within the still discriminatory U.S. motion picture industry despite his Hispanic name: He has blond hair and blue eyes, and he had an undeniable head start because he is the son of established actor Martin SHEEN. He has chosen to use Sheen's real surname, Estévez. His best-known brother is also an actor—the dark-haired, dark-eyed Charlie SHEEN.

Estévez was born in New York City on May 12, 1962. He made a mark playing teenagers in such films as *Tex* (1982), *The Outsiders* (1983), *Repo Man* (1984), and *The Breakfast Club, That Was Then . . . This Is Now,* and *St. Elmo's Fire* (all three in 1985).

In 1985, *New York* magazine did a cover story on a group of rising young actors it called Hollywood's Brat Pack. The article described Estévez as "the unofficial president" and "perhaps the smartest" of this group. He was also called "the unofficial treasurer" because "Estévez usually picks up the check." The article also noted that he was the one all the others would call their best friend.

The pack included Estévez, Sean Penn, Tom Cruise, Molly Ringwald, Ally Sheedy, and Judd Nelson. They were given the name of Brat Pack because they were personal friends who tended to appear together in movie after movie. This evoked the earlier "Rat Pack" of Frank Sinatra, Dean Martin, Sammy Davis Jr., and Peter Lawford. They were also linked by the fact that none had taken acting lessons or attended college. Estévez and several others went from Santa Monica High School straight into their careers.

Early on, Estévez demonstrated an interest in scriptwriting and directing in addition to acting. He scripted *That Was Then . . . This Is Now* and wrote and directed *Wisdom* (1987) and *Men at Work* (1990). In both of these movies, he also acted, and he costarred with his brother Charlie Sheen in *Men at Work.* Many critics faulted these efforts, but that did not affect his standing with the public.

Estévez was generally credited with a superior performance as Billy the Kid in *Young Guns* (1988). The film was followed by *Young Guns II.* In *Stakeout* (1987), for the first time, he played a grown man, beginning his transition to adult roles. Estévez directed as well as acted in the movie *Rated X* (2000).

In addition to his many films, Estévez has also acted on stage and television. His career in these mediums began at age 18, before his first movies. For TV, he made a rare appearance with his father in *Nightbreaker* in which he played Martin Sheen's character as a younger person. His recent television work has included *The Bang Bang Club* (1998), which he directed; *Dollar For the Dead* (1998); and *Late Last Night, Killer's Head,* and *Sand* (all in 1999).

Estévez was married to singer Paula Abdul from 1992 to 1994. He has two children.

Further Reading

Elkinton, Amy. "Presenting . . . Emilio Estévez." Available online. URL: http://home.pacifier.com/~amye. Downloaded October 10, 2000.

Hadley-García, George. *Hispanic Hollywood: The Latins in Motion Pictures.* Secaucus, N.J.: Citadel Press, 1990.

Press, Skip. *Charlie Sheen, Emilio Estévez & Martin Sheen.* Parsippany, N.J.: Crestwood House, 1996.

Riley, Lee, and David Shumacher. *The Sheens.* New York: St. Martin's Press, 1989.

Farragut, David (James Farragut)
(1801–1870) *soldier*

David Farragut was the first person ever to be given the rank of admiral of the U.S. Navy and is one of the most revered figures in United States naval history. A Union hero of the Civil War, having captured New Orleans and the forts that defended Mobile, Alabama, he is credited with the immortal rallying cry, during the battle of Mobile Bay, "Damn the torpedoes! Full speed ahead!"

The admiral's family, a military one, originally spelled its last name *Ferragut,* from the Latin word for "iron," and was long associated with Spain's Balearic Islands, Majorca and Minorca. In the 13th century, Pedro Ferragut was a trusted lieutenant of King James I, the Conqueror, of Aragon, who retook Majorca from the Arabs in 1229. The admiral's father, Jorge Farragut or Ferragut, was born on Minorca during one of two periods in the 1700s when, as a result of seesawing European wars, the island was held by Britain.

In 1776, the elder Farragut immigrated to North America and fought against the British during the American Revolution. As a lieutenant in the navy of South Carolina, he saw action at Savannah and Charleston. Later his son, while still a boy, would also hate Britain before and during the War of 1812.

James Glasgow Farragut was born on July 5, 1801, at Campbell's Station, near Knoxville, Tennessee. His mother was a native North Carolinian. Although James was born and spent his early years on what was then the U.S. frontier—first in Tennessee and then in the Territory of Orleans (Louisiana)—he learned his father's native language. He still spoke Spanish more than 60 years later when, as a retired and honored admiral, he made ceremonial visits to European seaports and conversed with Queen Isabella II of Spain.

"I am proud that your ancestors came from my kingdom," the queen said to him.

James's older brother, William, entered the navy before him—yet another in this Hispanic family to serve the United States.

James's own road to the sea was unusual. One day, when he was seven, his father, fishing on Lake Pontchartrain, rescued an elderly man who was fishing on another boat and collapsed because of the heat. Day after day, the sick man, David Porter, like his rescuer a naval officer in the Revolutionary War, failed to improve enough to be moved to his own house. The Farragut family looked after him at their home until he died. At the same time, James's mother died of yellow fever. They were both buried on the same day. Porter's son, also called David, was a navy commander and later a captain who would become famous leading the first U.S. naval ventures in the Pacific.

David Porter Jr. was grateful for the way the Farraguts had nursed his father. Because of this, he offered, in light of Mrs. Farragut's death, to adopt one of her sons and give him a naval officer's upbringing if both the father and the boy accepted. James's father agreed. James's brother, William, was already a midshipman (ensign), and so it was James who took the opportunity.

James Farragut changed his name to David in honor of his adoptive father. David Porter later had a son, David Dixon Porter, who likewise entered the navy. David Dixon would eventually serve under the command of his foster brother, David Farragut. He also became an admiral of the navy, the second after Farragut.

David Farragut was first taken by his new father to school in Washington. On their way to school, on a side stop in Havana, the boy and his elders were indignant to hear tales of Britain's interference with United States ships. At that time, Britain was stopping U.S. vessels to remove British-born sailors on board. These men were then forced to fight for the British navy in its wars with France.

This British practice—known as impressment—along with trade interference soon led to war between the United States and Britain. It was a time when young boys were sent to war in specific roles. David Farragut, made a midshipman at age nine, traveled on board Porter's ship and saw combat in the War of 1812.

In 1823, as a young officer, he commanded a naval force dispatched to the West Indies to flush out pirates. Decades later, he took part in the war against Mexico. Most of his life, however, Farragut served in peacetime. It was only when he was already 60 years old that circumstances revealed his talent as a fighter and leader. A captain since 1855, Farragut unhesitatingly left his home in Norfolk, Virginia, when the Civil War broke out and offered to serve the Union cause. As a Southerner, he wasn't fully trusted at first, but the Union was never to regret giving him a command.

Farragut's first great victory took place in April 1862 when he took New Orleans. The port city was vital to the Confederacy. Farragut, at the head of a 17-ship fleet, was sent to capture it. His instructions were to proceed cautiously. First, he was to bombard and try to destroy the forts protecting the mouth of the Mississippi. Instead, Farragut did something simpler and more courageous. He dashed past the forts during the night, as cannons roared. Because of his ability to pass through fire, he was given the nickname "Old Salamander." The forts and the city, which was the commercial capital of the South, were cut off from one another and surrendered to him.

Farragut next proceeded upriver, past other powerful Confederate batteries in Port Hudson. He did so without orders, reaching Vicksburg. Unable to coordinate with land forces, he could not take that city, but he managed to cut it off from supplies from points further south. In doing so, he laid the groundwork for General Ulysses S. Grant to obtain the surrender of Vicksburg and Port Hudson in 1863.

The Mississippi River was now wholly in Union hands. This sliced the Confederacy in two. President Abraham Lincoln declared that "The Father of Waters again goes unvexed to the sea" and promoted Farragut to rear admiral.

In August 1864, Farragut initiated his final and most famous campaign, a move to blockade Mobile, on the Gulf of Mexico. Mobile was defended by a number of forts and by one of the new ironclad vessels, the *Tennessee*. It was also protected by hundreds of what were then known as torpedoes, now called mines. These were floating gunpowder bombs that were rigged to explode when struck by any ship.

Farragut's fleet included armored vessels called monitors and some all-wooden ships, including his own, the *Hartford*. He climbed the rigging of his flagship, had himself tied into place by a quartermaster, and ordered the advance into Mobile Bay. The monitors took the lead, while the wooden ships followed behind in two columns.

Farragut was not reckless. He was known for studying a situation carefully and employing good tactical and strategic analysis before acting. In this case, he decided that many of the torpedoes, the casings of which were wooden barrels, would have been in the water so long that the gunpowder inside was most likely damp and useless. He also believed that once a course of action had been determined, it had to be pursued boldly, without any hesitation.

Many of the torpedoes did thud harmlessly against his ships, but not all. A mine exploded and sank one of the armored craft at the front, the *Tecumseh*. Other vessels then stopped or wavered. In an instant, his advance began to disintegrate. It was then that Farragut shouted the famous, defiant order, which was in full: "Damn the torpedoes! Captain Drayton, go ahead! Jouett, full speed!"

Farragut swung his own wooden ship ahead of the others and led the way, and the rest rallied behind him. The Confederate ironclad was captured; the forts were isolated and forced to surrender. From that day, Mobile was cut off from the Confederacy.

There are four different ranks of admiral: rear admiral, vice admiral, admiral, and, at the top, fleet admiral or admiral of the navy, also known as full admiral. This post, never before filled in the U.S. Navy, was given to Farragut in 1866. He also received an extremely high-paying job offer to become a company director and was asked if he would accept being nominated for president. He turned both offers down, saying that he knew nothing about either business or politics. Had he accepted the second offer, he might have become the United States' first, and only, Hispanic president to date. He died in 1870.

Further Reading

Duffy, James P. *Lincoln's Admiral: The Civil War Campaigns of David Farragut.* New York: Wiley, 1997.
Mahan, Captain A. T. *Admiral Farragut.* New York: Greenwood Press, 1968.

❧ Feliciano, José (1945–) *singer*

Blind since birth, José Feliciano overcame a daunting handicap to achieve international stardom as a performer. A major crossover artist and skilled at pleasing both Hispanic and mainstream U.S. audiences, he became the first singer to win Grammy awards in two languages. Feliciano has collected more than 45 gold and platinum records and sold almost 100 million records. In addition to pop music, he plays and composes classical as well as jazz and folk music.

Feliciano was born on September 10, 1945, in Lares, Puerto Rico. He moved to New York with his family at the age of five. Very early, music became his way to transcend his blindness. It was his most important way of communicating with the world he could not see. Largely self-taught, the child began by tapping a cookie can; then he played a second-hand accordion; later, at the age of nine, Feliciano began to play the guitar.

In love with classical music as a teenager his early ambition was to be "the best classical (guitar) player in the world. . . . I wanted to be like [Andrés] Segovia." He later thought of this as "a dumb goal when you're a kid." However, he recognized that part of what kept him from seriously pursuing that goal was being refused admission at the prestigious Juilliard school of music. He believes that in the early 1960s, unlike the piano or violin, the guitar was not considered a serious instrument. Nevertheless, he took private classical guitar lessons.

By the age of 11, Feliciano was skilled enough to play in public to enthusiastic applause. In 1962, at 17, he began to appear in Greenwich Village clubs and cafés. Two years later, he recorded his first single, "Everybody Do the Click," followed by his first (and bilingual) album, *The Voice and Guitar of José Feliciano.* With these records, he began to receive increasing recognition.

His album, *Feliciano!,* which included his recording of "Light My Fire," extended his celebrity nationwide. It was the first of his LPs to sell a million copies, and "Light My Fire" won him his first Grammy Award (1968) from the National Academy of Recording Arts and Sciences. Six years later, he won his first Grammy for a record in Spanish. All told, Feliciano has won six Grammys. He has toured internationally, playing to stadium audiences of up to 100,000 people.

The year 1968 brought trouble. His rendition of "The Star-Spangled Banner" at a World Series game in Detroit brought angry reaction from many. He sang the anthem in his own special way, tinged with the blues. Some praised his interpretation, but for years, many radio stations refused to play his records.

Slowly, however, he regained their approval. By 1984, however his patriotism was no longer in doubt: He was asked to participate in a special Statue of Liberty celebration.

Guitar Player Magazine named him Best Folk Guitarist in 1973; he was Best Pop Guitarist each year from 1973 through 1977. As a classical guitarist, he has performed with major orchestras around the world. Feliciano has made more than 100 television appearances. He had his own half-hour weekly TV program in Spanish, *Feliciano.*

One of his compositions, "Feliz Navidad" ("Merry Christmas") has become a Yuletide staple. In 1987, his name was added to those on Hollywood Boulevard, and a performing arts scholarship in his honor was established in East Harlem, New York City.

Feliciano received his latest Grammy nominations for *Americano* in 1997 and *Señor Bolero* in 1998. The singer signed a new contract in 2000 for English-language records.

For his entry in *Who's Who in America,* Feliciano included the following message: "The greatest tragedy for many so-called handicapped people is that they let others convince them that there are limits to what they can accomplish. It's just not so."

Further Reading

Feliciano Enterprises Inc. "José Feliciano." Available online. URL: http://josefeliciano.com. Downloaded October 11, 2000.

Martínez, Al. *Rising Voices: Profiles of Hispano-American Lives.* New York: New American Library, 1974.

Fernández, Mary Joe (María José Fernández) (1971–) *tennis player*

Mary Joe Fernández shone in the 1990s as one of the brightest new stars in women's tennis. She had earned millions of dollars in prize money and commercial endorsements, while just barely out of her teens.

Born in 1971 in the Dominican Republic, with the first names María José, she became known as Mary Joe after her family emigrated to the United States. She was then six months old.

In Miami, where the Fernándezes settled, she began to play tennis at the age of three and began formal lessons at five. Hers was a classic example of the tennis natural: She played in amateur competitions, accelerating through the age groupings. As soon as she reached the minimum age for one group, she would quickly defeat almost everybody else in the group, including the older players. She'd then graduate to the next age group, and repeat the procedure.

When Fernández began to play against professionals, she could no longer maintain the same proportion of wins. At 13, still playing as an amateur, she played in a professional tournament for the first time, winning the first round by defeating a player who was 33 but losing the second.

At 14, she made her first appearance at Wimbledon, England's mecca of tennis, and was defeated in straight sets: Her opponent was Chris Evert Lloyd.

Fernández went professional in 1986 but was not a full-time professional on the tennis circuit until she finished high school. This she did in 1989, graduating from Carrolton School of the Sacred Heart in Coconut Grove, Florida, with honors, a straight-A student. She could have earned much more money if she had become a full-time tennis professional earlier, but it was her own decision not to. It was a show of maturity: To have played professional tennis full time would have interrupted her education as well as her early social life, and, as she pointed out, she valued both of these.

Guided by the coaches Ion Tiriac and Tom Gullikson, Fernández participated in a restricted number of tournaments during her high school years. In 1990, she began to play full time and in Tokyo won her first professional championship, placing her fourth in the world among women tennis players. In 1991, for the first time, she made a million dollars in one year, including endorsement money. In 1992 she partnered with Gigi Fernandez (no relation) to win the Olympic gold medal in the women's doubles competition. In 1997, Fernández won her seventh singles title at the German Open. In 1999 she retired, though some expressed doubts that this move was final. By early 2000, her career prize money had reached nearly 5 million dollars.

Further Reading

Telgen, Diane, and Jim Kamp, eds. *Notable Hispanic American Women.* Detroit: Gale Research, Inc., 1993.

❧ Fernández Cavada, Federico

(unknown–1871) *soldier*

Federico Fernández Cavada (birthdate unknown) distinguished himself during the U.S. Civil War as one of the intrepid soldiers who scouted enemy troop movements from the air. A Cuban who had come to the United States and joined the Union army as an engineer, Captain Fernández Cavada, like a small number of others on both the Union and Confederate sides, took flight in hot-air balloons. With a sketch pad in hand, they observed and recorded information that was invisible to those on the ground.

An artist, as well, Fernández Cavada also painted full battle scenes on the basis of his aerial sightings. These paintings include *The Battle of Fredericksburg,* preserved in Philadelphia by the Historical Society of Pennsylvania.

In 1863, after the battle of Chancellorsville, balloon observations gave the Union Army of the Potomac its first information that the Confederate General Robert E. Lee had started to move northward. He was heading toward Pennsylvania, to initiate the Gettysburg campaign. But while Gettysburg ended in victory for the North, it proved disastrous for Fernández Cavada. He was taken prisoner by Rebel forces, who carried him away with them during their retreat and put him into prison in Richmond.

Conditions in Richmond's Libby Prison were vile. After regaining his freedom, Fernández Cavada wrote *Libby Life,* an account of his imprisonment.

The United States later appointed Fernández Cavada as U.S. consul to his native Cuba, at the time, still a colony of Spain. When an unsuccessful insurrection that became known as the Ten Years' War began in 1868, Fernández Cavada joined the cause of Cuban independence. As an experienced soldier, he was named commander in chief of the rebels. In 1871, three years into the revolt, Fernández Cavada was captured while taking risks to help a sick friend. This time, however, his captors sentenced him to death. "Good-bye, Cuba, forever!" were his last words as he faced the firing squad.

❧ Ferrer, José (José Vicente Ferrer Cintrón) (1912–1992) *actor*

José Ferrer was a widely respected stage and movie actor. Helen Hayes, considered by some to have been the "First Lady of the American Theater," called him the greatest actor since John Barrymore, whom many considered the greatest of the century.

Ferrer was the first Hispanic actor to win an Oscar. He was the only actor of his time who entirely escaped being typecast—made to play exclusively "Latin lover" and/or ethnic roles—despite retaining his Hispanic given name. It would be decades before Emilio ESTÉVEZ achieved the same feat in the 1980s.

Born on January 8, 1912, in Santurce, San Juan, Puerto Rico, José Vicente Ferrer Cintrón was the only son in a well-off household. His father was a

José Ferrer *(Cabrera Archive)*

prominent lawyer, and his mother came from a landowning family.

First taken to New York when he was still small, Ferrer recalled that he always felt totally at home in both cultures: "I spent my early years," he said, "going to school one year in New York, one year in Puerto Rico, so I became profoundly American and never ceased to be Hispanic. When I go to San Juan, I am going home; when I come to New York, I am going home. I think that's true of a great many Puerto Rican actors, and possibly Mexican actors as well."

Ferrer first turned to architecture. He completed undergraduate studies at Princeton's school of architecture, though he never obtained the license to practice.

He did, however, earn some money as a draftsman in his early days "to supplement my meager theatrical income." Among the fellow students of architecture he got to know at Princeton were the future movie actor James Stewart and the future movie director Joshua Logan.

Ferrer began to act in his university days. His strong stage presence naturally led him to Broadway in 1935.

Ferrer never suffered job discrimination as a Hispanic. He was never rejected for a role in favor of a nonminority actor, and he had a very clear idea why he escaped this obstacle. He believed it was a question of timing, recognizing that discrimination did become a real problem for other players in later years: "I've never been discriminated against because I began to be successful (in the New York theater) long before World War II, which was the period of the influx of Hispanics into New York and the time prejudice against Hispanics in jobs began in the East."

As for movies, he found that Hollywood did not hold his Hispanic name against him, as happened to many others, because he had already made it on Broadway: "I never made a film until 1947, by which time I was well-established in the theater."

At no time had José Ferrer contemplated adopting an Anglo-sounding name to make his career easier. He recognized the advantages of a name change: "Henry Darrow, in fact, has said on more than one occasion that while he was Enrique Delgado he had trouble finding a job, and as soon as he became Henry Darrow that problem vanished." Ferrer said, "I just

would feel very strange if I changed my name. Every person has his or her own standards and I would not like to comment about the Rita HAYWORTHs and the Henry Darrows of this world because I feel that if they thought it was the right thing to do, why not? I have no prejudice against it, it's just something that I don't think I could do."

The early and enduring hallmark of Ferrer's career on stage—he not only acted but also directed and produced—was his versatility. He shone in comedy in *Charley's Aunt* in 1940, and he was well received in 1942 as the villain Iago in a production of *Othello* opposite African-American singer and actor Paul Robeson. In his lifetime, Ferrer won five Tony awards.

Ferrer sang in musicals such as *Man of La Mancha* and even in opera, participating in regional productions from Beverly Hills to Brooklyn. He also conducted a Dallas production of a Mozart opera.

One of José Ferrer's most celebrated parts on Broadway was the title role in *Cyrano de Bergerac,* which he first performed in 1946. *Cyrano* remained for decades a virtual trademark of Ferrer's. He would play the character of Cyrano—the big-nosed, lovestruck, bragging, fine-talking swordsman—over and over in the theater. In 1950, he won an Oscar for the film version. He also played Cyrano on television, and almost 30 years after his debut in the role, he directed the play in England.

Cyrano de Bergerac, the motion picture, was Ferrer's fourth movie. In his first, *Joan of Arc,* he played the Dauphin of France opposite Ingrid Bergman's maid of Orleans. This role won him an Oscar nomination in 1948.

Another celebrated Ferrer role was also based on a real-life French figure, the painter Henri de Toulouse-Lautrec. The movie, *Moulin Rouge* (1953), won Ferrer a third Oscar nomination.

Toulouse-Lautrec suffered from a form of dwarfism and his legs had been crippled by two accidents in his youth; thus he was very short. To play the part, Ferrer had to walk on his knees the whole time.

A smaller, also memorable role was that of a Turkish officer in *Lawrence of Arabia* (1962). However, he expressed distaste for the part because of its sadistic nature.

Ferrer's own ethical and artistic preferences are apparent in *I Accuse!,* a movie he directed in 1958. It is regarded as the best among the several films he directed. Here, he cast himself as French army captain Alfred Dreyfus, a Jewish officer falsely accused of treason in a case that rocked French society in the 1890s, exposing anti-Semitism.

In his later years, José Ferrer did, to a certain extent, become typecast, not as a Hispanic but as a person of power. In that period, he said, "I'm invariably cast as somebody who wears dark suits and a vest, who runs a bank or is a prominent lawyer or a very successful doctor; with only a few exceptions, I'm someone who is sort of in the upper register of financial success and speaks English with an educated accent." Ferrer blamed television for this ("it's almost impossible to avoid typecasting on television"). But part of the reason, too, was his own success in giving every performance a characteristic air of authority. This stereotyping spilled over from television into movie roles. He played a pompous Nazi in *Ship of Fools* in the 1960s and a pedantic professor in Woody Allen's *A Midsummer Night's Sex Comedy* in the 1980s.

Ferrer was married several times, once to actress Uta Hagen and three times to singer-actress Rosemary Clooney. Ferrer and Clooney's son Miguel is also a stage, screen, and television actor whose movie appearances include *Star Trek III: The Search for Spock* and *Robocop*. His television performances include *Twin Peaks*.

For years, José Ferrer was the official English-language spokesman for the island of Puerto Rico. He always kept his roots in mind, sometimes using them in humor. On one occasion, he broke several plates in a restaurant while doing an impersonation of the actor Douglas Fairbanks Sr. He explained: "I'm Latin, remember; the juices flow strongly." He died in 1992.

Further Reading

Katz, Ephraim. *The Film Encyclopedia.* New York: Perigee Books, 1979.

❧ Ferrer, Mel (Melchior Gaston Ferrer)

(1917–) *actor*

Mel Ferrer has had a long career in Hollywood and later in foreign films. He was the former husband of actress Audrey Hepburn.

Mel Ferrer as King Arthur in the film *Knights of the Round Table* (Cabrera Archive)

Born on August 25, 1917, in New Jersey to a Cuban father and Anglo mother, Melchior Gaston Ferrer is not related to the Puerto Rican actor José FERRER, though like him, he was never typecast in Hispanic roles. Having the first name *Mel* helped him to avoid this.

Mel Ferrer began his professional career in 1938 as a chorus dancer in Broadway musicals. His career was soon interrupted by a polio attack. In the 1940s, he directed movies and began to act in film in 1949 in *Lost Boundaries.*

From 1954 to 1968 he was married to Audrey Hepburn. They appeared together in *War and Peace* (1956) and also on stage and television. Ferrer directed her in *Green Mansions* (1959) and produced another of her films, *Wait Until Dark* (1967). His single greatest achievement in film, however, was *Lili* (1953), in which he played a moody puppeteer, opposite actress-dancer Leslie Caron.

Other movies in which he starred include *Scaramouche* (1952), *Knights of the Round Table* (1954), and *El Greco* (1964), which he also coproduced and for which he wrote the music. On television, he appeared on *Falcon Crest* in the early 1980s and in *Stories From My Childhood* in 1998.

Further Reading

Katz, Ephraim. *The Film Encyclopedia.* New York: Perigee Books, 1979.

✒ Flores, Patrick (Patricio Fernández Flores) (1929–) *prelate, community activist*

Patrick Flores, archbishop of San Antonio, Texas, became in 1970 the first Mexican American to become a Roman Catholic bishop (one other Hispanic had become a bishop in 1936). Nine years later, he became the first Hispanic archbishop.

In addition to his pastoral work, Flores (whose last name means "flowers" in Spanish) has always

Patrick Flores *(Courtesy of Patrick Flores)*

labored tirelessly in favor of the rights and welfare of Hispanics and of immigrants in general, an undertaking that led him to befriend such renowned activists as César CHÁVEZ.

The seventh of nine children in a sharecropping family, Patricio Flores was born in Ganado, Texas, on July 26, 1929. He managed to get an education despite also working hard in the fields with his parents and siblings, going to school in Ganado, Houston, and Galveston. He eventually got his high school diploma in Galveston—with top grades but at the age of 20, and with the support of the bishop of Galveston, who had seen in him a youth of great potential.

Flores went to seminary in La Porte and Houston, and was ordained a priest in 1956. To make religious activities more attractive and meaningful to his impoverished and often illiterate parishioners, he used the Spanish language in his services—well before the Second Vatican Council instituted such use. He also incorporated Mexican mariachi music in his masses, becoming known, in later years, as "the mariachi bishop."

At the same time, his commitment to providing practical help to the poor was evident from the outset. During the grape strike led by César Chávez in California in the mid-1960s, when many poor laborers were tempted to go there and earn money by replacing the strikers, Flores forcefully explained to them how doing so would undermine the strike and ultimately hurt all farmworkers.

As a consequence of his social activism, when Flores was made an auxiliary bishop of San Antonio in 1970, such legendary community leaders as Chávez and José Angel GUTIÉRREZ participated in the ceremony.

In 1978 Flores was appointed bishop of El Paso, but did not stay there long—the very next year he became archbishop of San Antonio.

Flores founded or helped found numerous community organizations. They include Priests Associated for Religious, Educational and Social Rights or, in the original Spanish, Padres Asociados Para Derechos Religiosos, Educativos y Sociales—PADRES—for which he served as national chairman; the Mexican-American Cultural Center in San Antonio, to raise money for which he recorded an album called *The*

Singing Bishop; Communities Organized for Public Service, or COPS; the National Hispanic Scholarship Fund, the Office of Catholic Services for Immigrants, and the Telethon Navideño, or Christmas Telethon.

In addition, Flores has headed the Christian Family Movement, the Bishops' Committee for the Spanish Speaking, the Texas Advisory Committee to the U.S. Civil Rights Commission and the U.S. Bishops' Committee on the Church in Latin America.

In 1983, four U.S. bishops took part in a synod in Rome, and Patrick Flores was one of them. In 1986, just one bishop from the United States was asked to participate in a conference in Cuba on relations between church and government there: that bishop was Flores.

Archbishop Flores has won numerous awards, and not only from Catholic organizations: he is a recipient of the American Jewish Committee's Human Relations Award. Winner of three honorary doctorates, Flores also earned a Hispanic Heritage award for leadership in 1986, a Distinguished Churchman Award in 1995 and a Salute to Education award, also in 1995. The Medal of Freedom (Ellis Island Medal of Honor) was conferred on him in 1986.

In 2000, a man claiming to be wielding a hand grenade took Flores hostage in his office in a bid to force authorities to solve a passport problem he faced. He freed the 70-year-old archbishop nine hours later.

Further Reading

"Focus: Archbishop Patrick Flores." San Antonio Express-News. Available online. URL: http://www.mysa.com/mysanantonio/entertainment/cityguide/religion /religion4.shtml. Downloaded October 10, 2000.

McMurtry, Martin. *Mariachi Bishop: The Life Story of Patrick Flores.* San Antonio, Tex.: Corona Publishing, 1985.

❦ **Flores, Tom** (Thomas Raymond Flores)
(1937–) *football coach*

A former football star, Tom Flores later had a noted career as a coach, leading the Oakland and Los Angeles Raiders to two triumphs in the Super Bowl. He is the author of the book *Coaching Football* and coauthor, with Bob O'Connor, of *Football: The Violent Chess Match: A Fan's Guide.*

Flores (not related to Archbishop Patrick FLORES) was born in Fresno, California, on March 21, 1937, the son of field-workers. His father, Tomás, had immigrated to the United States to escape the strife that accompanied the revolution in his native Mexico.

As a child, Tom, too, worked in the fields. He went to school in Sanger, California, where today the high school's football field, where he once played, bears his name.

Sports—mainly football, but also baseball—were his major interest when he moved on to college. He studied at Fresno City College, where he made Honorable Mention Junior College All-American, and at the College of the Pacific in Stockton, California, where in his last year he was fourth-ranked in the United States in total offense on the football field. By the time he received a B.A. degree in education in 1958, he was a veteran of All-American teams.

His beginnings in professional play were inauspicious, owing to trouble with an old shoulder injury. After unsuccessful bids with the Calgary Stampeders and Washington Redskins, he bided his time with a coaching job at Fresno High School—little imagining that one day he would be better remembered as a coach than as a player.

In 1960, things changed. He was signed on as quarterback by the Oakland Raiders—and went on to lead the American Football League (AFL) in passing efficiency (252 passing attempts and 136 completions, a percentage of 54).

In a 10-season playing career, Flores served with the Raiders in 1960 and 1961 and again from 1963 to 1966 (illness forced him to skip 1962), then with the Buffalo Bills in 1967 and 1968, and finally the Kansas City Chiefs in 1969 and 1970. His best moment came in 1963, when in a game against the Houston Oilers he passed for six touchdowns.

He was also quarterback in the AFL All-Star Game in 1966. On his retirement four years later he could look back on a career record (topped by only one other player) for the lowest number of interceptions thrown: 192 in 1,715 attempts.

Flores began his coaching career as an assistant with the Buffalo Bills for one year and with the Oakland Raiders for seven (1972–78), then became the Raiders' head coach for nine more years (1979–87). That was the period during which the Raiders moved to Los Angeles (1981), Flores was Coach of the Year (1982), and the Raiders won the Super Bowl twice.

In their victory in 1981, against the Philadelphia Eagles, they did so as a wild-card team—the first time such a team won the Super Bowl. Their 1983 win was achieved with the most lopsided score ever, 38-9, against the Washington Redskins. Flores was even given an award by the city of Los Angeles in recognition of what he had done to improve the image of the city.

The following years were disappointing, but when Flores and the Los Angeles Raiders parted ways in 1987 he had posted an 83-53 record in the regular seasons and 8-3 in the playoffs and Super Bowls.

In 1989 Flores became president and general manager of the Seattle Seahawks. In 1992, after searching for a head coach for his team, he took the job himself. He was again doing what he liked best, but the Seahawks, partly because of a succession of injuries, did badly. They ended in last place in the AFC West for the three years that Flores was coach (1992–94), and his record with this team was 14-33. Flores's three-year contract had renewal options for the following two years, but they were not exercised, leading to Flores's retirement after the 1994 season.

Further Reading

Flores, Tom. *Coaching Football.* Indianapolis, Ind.: Masters Press, 1993.

Novas, Himilce. *The Hispanic 100.* New York: Citadel Press, 1995.

G

Ernesto Galarza acted as a major force in the effort to improve the conditions of western farmworkers (most of them Mexicans or Chicanos). He laid groundwork that later helped other labor leaders, including the successful struggle of César CHÁVEZ.

Galarza was highly educated. One of the first Mexican Americans to earn a Ph.D., he tirelessly promoted improvements in the education of Hispanic Americans while himself contributing to Chicano literature.

Galarza was born in 1905 in a small village in Mexico called Jalcocotán, near the town of Tepic in Nayarit state. The Mexican Revolution uprooted his family. After a long period of travel, they arrived in California, via Arizona.

He had already shown signs of his special aptitude for learning, despite the stop-and-go nature of his education, which took place in several locations in Mexico. Once in California, he made the most of school in Sacramento, even though he was soon orphaned.

His teenage years found him juggling work and school. Nevertheless, he graduated high school with such good grades that he won a scholarship to go to college in Los Angeles.

During one high school vacation, he took a job as a farm laborer. That summer, many workers fell ill. Galarza and others believed that the reason was contaminated water at the camp where he and the others had to live. Galarza found a lawyer to demand that the water supply be investigated. The lawyer advised him, "Tell the people in the camp to organize. Only by organizing will they ever have decent places to live."

Galarza graduated from Los Angeles' Occidental College with a degree in history. He received his master's degree in history from Stanford University in 1929. He then went to work as a schoolteacher in New York and in 1946 completed his Ph.D. studies in education from Columbia University, graduating Phi Beta Kappa. After teaching and codirecting at a progressive elementary school, Galarza worked in the late 1930s as a researcher for the Foreign Policy Association and for the Pan American Union. He was involved in the areas of Latin American affairs and education.

In the early 1940s Galarza returned to labor issues, heading the Division of Labor and Social Information at the Pan American Union. The work was interesting, but he realized that he wanted to participate personally in organizing farmworkers. One of the periodic efforts to unionize farmworkers was being launched at that time—the National Agricultural Workers Union (NAWU). So in 1947, after completing his Ph.D. in New York, Galarza returned to California and joined NAWU as field organizer and research director in San Jose.

He worked for the union throughout the 1950s and became its vice president, playing an active role in the improvement of farmworkers' living and working conditions. He helped lead the union in a strike that lasted from 1947 to 1950, but the union lost because employers were still too powerful.

Galarza continued to work for the rights of farm laborers for the remainder of his life, although by the 1960s he branched out into other interests as well. He became a professor of sociology and education at San José State University and at the University of Notre Dame, as well as guest lecturer at other institutions. He wrote and edited articles and books, including key texts on the history of farm labor, such as *Merchants of Labor: The Mexican Bracero Story* (1964). In two of his works, *Spiders in the House and Workers in the Field* (1970) and *Farm Workers and Agri-Business in California 1947–1960* (1977), he included examples taken from his own life. His memoir of his early years, *Barrio Boy,* is considered a major literary narrative on Hispanic-American life.

Galarza was active in civil-rights matters, in particular Mexican-American causes. He often acted as a consultant for organizations ranging from the U.S. House of Representatives' Committee on Education and Labor to the Ford Foundation and the Bolivian government.

An issue in which Galarza took a particular interest was the *bracero* farm-labor system. Under this program, the United States temporarily brought in Mexicans to work U.S. farm fields. As Galarza and others pointed out, this kept U.S. workers badly paid. It also kept them in weak bargaining positions because farm owners could rely on the imported workers who were willing to work for less. It did not really help the Mexicans either because they collected $3 for each 10-hour day and had to pay back $1.75 for paltry meals. Finally, once the harvest was over, the *braceros* were trucked back to Mexico to a point just across the border and simply left there.

For years, Galarza campaigned against this cruel system. It was finally ended in 1964. He achieved a significant personal victory when an attempt was made to reintroduce the system in the 1970s. Mexico, under pressure from strong U.S. farm-owning interests, was on the verge of agreeing to restart it. At the last moment, opponents of the *bracero* system convinced Mexican President Luis Echeverría to meet with Galarza, who persuaded Echeverría to back out of the proposal.

Galarza was also a strong proponent of bilingual education. He wrote a number of prose and poetry texts in Spanish for use in teaching, including *La Mula No Nació Arisca (The Mule Wasn't Born Unmanageable)* and *Rimas Tontas (Silly Rhymes)*. He died in 1984.

Further Reading

Acuña, Rodolfo. *Occupied America: A History of Chicanos.* New York: HarperCollins, 1988.

Chabran, Richard. "Activism and Intellectual Struggle in the Life of Ernesto Galarza." Available online. URL:http://www.chass.ucr.edu/csbsr/gala.htm. Downloaded October 10, 2000.

Galarza, Ernesto. *Barrio Boy.* Notre Dame, Ind.: University of Notre Dame Press, 1971.

Meier, Matt S. *Mexican American Biographies.* Westport, Conn.: Greenwood Publishing Group, 1988.

Gálvez, Bernardo de   (1746–1786)
government official

During the American Revolution, Bernardo de Gálvez was the unofficial Spanish protector of the American colonists, keeping them safe from military danger from the south.

He gave the revolutionaries invaluable material assistance, kept the Mississippi River supply line open to the colonists west of the Appalachians, and kept the British from posing any threat from the Gulf of Mexico. The city of Galveston, Texas, is named for him.

Gálvez's father and uncle were also involved in government roles in New Spain (Mexico). At that time, this Spanish colony extended from Central

America to the Mississippi on the east and California on the west. Gálvez's uncle, José de Gálvez, arrived in New Spain in 1765 as *visitador general* (inspector general) and was responsible for extending European rule north from Lower California into what is now the U.S. state of California. Considered the most powerful official in Spain after the king, Charles III, José de Gálvez sent the expedition that settled San Diego and Monterey and first explored the San Francisco area.

Bernardo de Gálvez was born in 1746 in a town near Málaga, Spain. At the age of 19, in 1765, he traveled with José de Gálvez to Mexico. By this time, he had already served as officer in the Spanish army for three years, demonstrating his courage and adventurous spirit.

However, Bernardo de Gálvez did not settle in the Americas until taking over the governorship of Louisiana. He fought for Spain in Europe and in northern Africa, as well as on New Spain's uncharted northern reaches. He arrived in Louisiana as its new ruler in January 1777, a young but seasoned war veteran.

Gálvez succeeded another Spanish governor of Louisiana, Luis de Unzaga, who had already begun to provide the Revolutionary armies with desperately needed gunpowder. Gálvez expanded this assistance, using Unzaga's reasoning. They both believed that although Spain was technically neutral in the war between Britain and its colonies, it would be best for New Spain if the British presence on the North American continent was weakened.

Eventually, however, the new nation Gálvez helped would pose a greater threat to the Spanish territories in North America (and later against Mexico) than the British ever were. Gálvez died young, but he still lived to see the beginning of this process.

The first thing Gálvez did as governor of Louisiana was continue Unzaga's secret supplying of the colonists. This had to be done without British knowledge because the activity violated Spain's neutrality.

Gálvez sent supplies up the Mississippi to the more isolated colonists. When colonists' ships openly docked to pick up supplies in New Orleans, Gálvez made a point of confiscating them while the British watched. But he then secretly freed them. At the same time, he made it difficult for the British to use New Orleans.

He also obtained loans from Spain for the colonists and readied himself to join the war. The British were catching on to his aid to the colonists. An attack seemed inevitable, but before it came, Spain declared war on Britain in 1779. It was Gálvez who attacked first, moving against British positions along the Gulf of Mexico in what were then known as West Florida and East Florida. These Florida territories had been held by Spain long before the British arrived. Only in the previous decade had they been relinquished to Britain after the French and Indian Wars.

Had these British outposts been left alone, they might have been used as staging posts for attacks on the patriots, either from the Mississippi or by sea from the Gulf of Mexico. In a relentless campaign, Gálvez conquered them one by one.

Marching upland in 1779, he took Fort Bute, then Baton Rouge, and then Natchez. Next, he formed a fleet and took Mobile in 1780. In 1781 after sailing to Cuba to obtain reinforcements, he conquered Pensacola.

As Gálvez took Florida, the Spanish prevailed against a British offensive on the then-Spanish city of St. Louis. This victory was followed by a Spanish counterattack in the direction of the Great Lakes. Together these Spanish campaigns covered the patriots' backs as they fought the British, and Gálvez had put West and East Florida back under Spain's control.

Gálvez did not stop fighting when Britain and the new United States made peace. He took his sea war to the Caribbean, conquering a British base in the Bahamas, and was preparing to attack Jamaica when orders to cease finally came from Europe, where an end to the British-Spanish war had been signed.

Gálvez returned to Louisiana, where he devised a way to obtain plentiful food supplies. He organized cattle drives from Texas, which was also a Spanish territory. The cattle drives brought conflict with the Comanche. This was a full century before the U.S. cowhand era.

Gálvez's most farsighted move was to encourage English-speaking colonists to immigrate to Louisiana, though this violated his orders from Spain. He did not demand that the colonists convert to Catholicism, only that they become citizens of Spain. He realized that, in the long run, his province needed to be more populated and that only then would it be able to hold its own against the fast-rising population of the growing United States. There is no way Gálvez could have stemmed the tide, but he saw the future clearly and did as much as he could.

In 1777, his soldiers set up a European settlement on an island off the coast of Texas. Called Gálvez, it later became known as Galveston.

For his exploits in war against Britain, Gálvez was made a count. In early 1785, he was appointed captain-general of Cuba and, a few months later, viceroy of New Spain, the post previously held by his father. Though his role in New Spain was cut short, lasting less than 18 months, he was known as a popular and enterprising ruler who introduced economic reforms and ordered roads built.

A deadly fever killed Bernardo de Gálvez in 1786. By that time, the United States was already laying claim to the West and East Florida territories that Gálvez had recovered. The United States argued that their territory extended further south into Spanish-held land.

Further Reading

Cabán, Pedro, et al. *The Latino Experience in U.S. History.* Paramus, N.J.: Globe Fearon, 1994.
Varona, Frank de. *Barnardo de Gálvez.* Milwaukee, Wis.: Raintree Publications, 1990.

❧ **Gamboa, Harry, Jr.** (1951–) *artist*

Harry Gamboa Jr. is a leader of the Chicano art scene. He combines satirical artistic and literary gifts with skills as an organizer that he developed as a student activist.

He is one of the founders of a pioneering performance art group, Asco. The word means "nausea," "disgust," or "revulsion"—feelings that the group gleefully generated at first. In time, though, Gamboa's work won recognition and honors from the artistic establishment, from the National Endowment for the Arts to the Ford Foundation.

Gamboa was born on November 1, 1951, in Los Angeles. His father had been christened Enrique at birth in Mexico but was told by his schoolteachers, on arrival in the United States as a youth, that *Enrique*

was not acceptable in the United States—that he had to call himself *Henry.* But his mother was incapable of pronouncing *Henry.* She said it like *Herry,* which in time turned into *Harry.* Harry Gamboa Jr. thus was named for his father.

A generation after his father, Harry Jr. continued to find attitudes of discrimination in U.S. schools. In the 1950s, if children could not speak English properly because of their immigrant background, they were punished. Some were actually forced to wear a dunce cap. Slow learners were also ridiculed. Gamboa has said that he is "sure I was one of the last students in public education to have a dunce cap put on, with a little lapel pin which said *Spanish.*"

In high school, his grade point average was 1.1. This was in the late 1960s, when rebellions of many kinds were occurring in several parts of the world. Los Angeles was one of those places. Harry Gamboa Jr. became an activist, spontaneously leading a student strike in 1968 at Garfield High School in East Los Angeles. This was the same school Jaime ESCALANTE would later make famous with his teaching successes.

Gamboa came into contact with other, politically more radical leaders. He learned much from them and wound up being included on a Senate roster of subversives. This classified him with such militant leaders as Angela Davis and Eldridge Cleaver.

Gamboa actually had become a subversive, but in the field of art. He formed a group in 1971 with three others. He had met them as teenagers when they were intellectual, mocking, and self-mocking fancy dressers known as the Jetters. They were Patssi Valdez, Willie Herrón, and a third known as Gronk, the most erudite of the group. His full name was Glugio Gronk Nicandro. His middle name means "to fly" in the language of a Brazilian Indian tribe. His mother had found the word in *National Geographic* magazine and chose it as a name for him.

Gamboa and these three called their group *Asco* after seeing how people reacted to their work. At a time when the Chicano mural-painting movement was blooming, they started out with a street performance as a "living mural," wearing costumes parodying the Stations of the Cross. Thus they were making a joke at the expense of both the murals and religion.

What Gamboa contributed to Asco, he later declared, "was organizational skill, how to reach out to people. I had worked with the propaganda arm of the (Chicano) movement and had become aware of how to tie art to social issues and make it socially relevant."

That same year or by other accounts in 1972, he and the others went to the Los Angeles County Museum of Art and asked to see Chicano paintings. The museum had none, and they were told that "there are no Chicanos doing any art." The foursome decided to turn the museum itself into a piece of Chicano conceptual art, and Gamboa, Gronk, and Herrón all signed it, with spray paint, at the museum entrances.

The first two publicized exhibitions of Chicano art in the United States had, in fact, been held in 1970 in California and in Texas. The Los Angeles County Museum of Art's first exhibit of Chicano art did not occur until 1974 when it exhibited the work of the group known as Los Four: Frank Romero, Carlos Almaraz, Beto de la Rocha, and Gilbert Luján.

Los Four created traditional Mexican-American art that incorporated recognizable elements of rural Mexico. Asco's art, on the other hand, was entirely urban and contemporary. What Asco created, a critic said, was a mix of "videos, performances, plays, poems, graphics, fashions, manifestos (etc.) [that] leave an impression that is both frightening and hilarious."

While the other members of Asco went in diverse artistic directions, Gamboa concentrated specifically on photography and playwrighting.

His plays *Shadow Solo* (1983) and *Jetter's Jinx* (1985) received particular notice. In 1974, he was given a fellowship to photograph Chicano life by the Mexican American Legal Defense and Educational Fund (MALDEF), and in 1989, a playwrighting commission by the Ford Foundation. The National Endowment for the Arts gave him artist fellowships in 1980 and 1987. The J. Paul Getty Trust Fund for the Visual Arts did the same in 1990. Gamboa wrote and produced a series of "conceptual dramas" in the late 1990s including *Frame of Relevance, Reedooss,* and *N/either Here N/or T/here.* He also won a fellowship from the Gluck Foundation in 1998–99 and the Flintridge Foundation Visual Arts Award in 2000.

Gamboa's fellow artists and writers have benefited from both his encouragement and his efforts to see that their work gains more recognition. He and Gronk were among the founders of Los Angeles Contemporary Exhibitions (LACE), a nonprofit group run by the participating artists themselves. Gamboa became the companion and collaborator of the artist Barbara CARRASCO.

Further Reading

Noriega, Chon A., ed. *Urban Exile: Collected Writing of Harry Gamboa, Jr.* Minneapolis: University of Minnesota Press, 1998.

Shorris, Earl. *Latinos: A Biography of the People.* New York: Avon Books, 1992.

✥ García, Andy (Andrés Arturo Garci-Menéndez) (1956–   ) *actor*

Andy García emerged in the 1980s as one of the brightest stars in a group of new Hispanic actors.

Born Andrés Arturo Garci-Menéndez in the city of Havana in 1956, his parents brought him to the United States when he was five years old. "I love Cubans and have pride in my heritage," he once declared, "but I cannot go there until the Castro regime is gone. It would not be a smart thing to visit there now."

Raised in Florida, he began to perform in local theaters, but after settling in Los Angeles in 1978, he worked sporadically in television while hauling furniture and waiting on tables to pay bills. His TV credits included *Hill Street Blues* and *For Love and Honor.* These television roles led him into movies.

Since his early TV appearances playing drug pushers and other assorted villains, García has seen an expansion in the range of roles he is offered. His first films, though, still found him mostly playing either cops (as in *The Untouchables* [1987], *Black Rain* [1989], and *Internal Affairs* [1990]) or robbers (notably in *The Godfather Part III* [1990]). He won both Golden Globe and Oscar nominations as best supporting actor for his role as a rising Mafia figure in *The Godfather Part III.* He was a coauthor of the screenplay for *Internal Affairs.*

Other film appearances include roles in *The Mean Season* and *Stand and Deliver* in the 1980s and *Hero* and *When a Man Loves a Woman* in the 1990s.

Andy García *(Cabrera Archive)*

García also appeared in *Hoodlum* (1992), as the gangster Lucky Luciano; *The Disappearance of García Lorca* (1997); *Desperate Measures* (1998); *Just the Ticket* (1999), which he also produced; and the TV movie *Swing Vote* (1999).

Simplifying his last name from *Garci-Menéndez* to *García* was a straightforward step for him. So was using *Andy* instead of *Andrés*. However, he refused to change his name entirely: "When I first came to Hollywood, I was asked several times to change my name to something less Latin," García recalled. "As a young man I didn't know what to think. But I did not choose to lose my identity."

García points out that he has no objection to playing Latino roles; yet he prefers not to be viewed only as an Hispanic actor. He feels he is a performer, not a representative of the Hispanic community: "No one asks Dustin Hoffman, 'How do you feel representing the Jewish community in Hollywood?'" He has also said, "I didn't take Hispanic Acting 101. I studied Shakespeare."

Further Reading
"Andy García Fan Site." Available online. URL: http://www.konary.com/andy. Downloaded October 10, 2000.

Katz, Ephraim. *The Film Encyclopedia.* New York: Perigee, 1993.

 **García, Héctor Pérez** (1914–1996)
activist

Héctor Pérez García founded one Hispanic-American organization, the American GI Forum (AGIF), and cofounded another, the Political Association of Spanish Speaking Organizations (PASSO). He was a leader in several others as well. Noted for his efforts on behalf of war veterans, García served for two years in the army in World War II. A longtime civil rights activist, he received the highest decoration the United States awards to a civilian, the Medal of Freedom, in 1984.

García was born in the town of Llera in the Mexican state of Tamaulipas on January 17, 1914. His parents brought him to the United States as a youth. He attended the University of Texas in Austin, receiving his B.A. degree in 1936. He then went to medical school, graduating in 1940.

García joined the army in 1942, following two years as an intern in Nebraska. He served in various locations in Europe both in the Engineer Corps and the Medical Corps. He was awarded the Bronze Star plus six Battle Stars.

After the war, García worked as a doctor in Corpus Christi, Texas. He grew increasingly angry as he repeatedly witnessed discrimination against Hispanic-American veterans. These veterans found that when they had a grievance, existing organizations such as the American Legion paid no attention. In response to this, in 1948, Dr. García founded AGIF to work for the rights of Hispanic veterans.

When Félix LONGORIA, a Mexican American who died a war hero in the Pacific, was refused burial services in a town in Texas, his fellow Hispanics were outraged. As a result, within a year and a half, more than 100 AGIF chapters had sprung up throughout the United States. It became one of the country's most important Hispanic civil rights organizations in the 1950s, with more than 20,000 members.

In 1960, García was one of the founders of PASSO and was elected its first president. He also took an active part in the work of the League of United Latin American Citizens (LULAC).

García joined the Democratic Party's National Committee. When John F. Kennedy ran for president, García helped him get Hispanic votes through "Viva Kennedy" clubs, of which he was national coordinator.

Inclined toward the more conservative wing of the Democratic Party, García was a backer of Lyndon Johnson following Kennedy's assassination. Johnson appointed him alternate U.S. ambassador to the United Nations in 1964. Johnson also made García the first Chicano member of the United States Commission on Civil Rights in 1968.

Other organizations in which he worked were the Advisory Committee to the Veterans Administration and the Catholic Council for Spanish Speaking People in the Southwest. Through all these organizations, he strove to improve the rights and the dignity of the Hispanic minority.

In addition to the Medal of Freedom, Héctor García received the National Council of La Raza's Maclovio Barraza Award (1990), the Texas Conference of Negro Organizations' Outstanding Democracy Forward Award, and Panama's Order of Vasco Núñez de Balboa. Other organizations ranging from the American Cancer Society to the U.S. Marine Corps have also honored him. He died in 1996.

Further Reading

American GI Forum. "Dr. Hector Perez Garcia." Available online. URL: http://www.neta.com/~1stbooks/forum0.htm. Downloaded October 10, 2000.

Meier, Matt S. *Mexican American Biographies.* Westport, Conn.: Greenwood Publishing Group, 1988.

❧ Garcia, Jerry (Jerome John Garcia)
(1942–1995) *rock musician*

Guitarist and composer Jerry Garcia was the informal leader of the Grateful Dead, one of the most popular and longest-lived of the rock bands that emerged during—and that helped to define—the rebellious 1960s. As such, he was a much revered figure of the counterculture that flourished in those years.

Jerry Garcia (none of the Garcias in this book are related) was born in San Francisco on August 1, 1942. His father, an immigrant from Spain, was a jazz musician and bartender, whose love of music was so strong that he named his son after the composer Jerome Kern.

Jerry's infancy was marked by calamity. When he was four years old, helping his older brother Clifford chop wood, Clifford accidentally sliced off half of the middle finger of Jerry's right hand. The next year, Jerry saw his father accidentally slip and drown while fishing.

Despite his missing finger, at his mother's insistence Jerry took years of piano lessons—which he did not enjoy. When he was 15, however, he found his musical calling with the discovery of rock 'n' roll. His mother gave him an accordion for his birthday, but he convinced her to swap it for an electric guitar, which he taught himself to play.

At school, which he disliked, he was soon marked as a troublemaker. At age 17 he dropped out and enlisted in the U.S. Army, but as he proved to be a misfit, his military career was ended by mutual agreement before a year had passed.

If nothing else, his brief period of military service exposed him to different types of music, including blues and folk. He also experimented with the banjo and acoustic guitar. The sound of the future Grateful Dead was to be marked by a fusion of rock with those and other diverse forms of music.

Garcia befriended other budding musicians in the Palo Alto area, where he worked in a music store, and they began to play at coffeehouses and clubs. In 1964 they formed a group called Mother McCree's Uptown Jug Champions. In 1965 they reorganized as the Warlocks, and in 1966, became known as the Grateful Dead.

They also moved to San Francisco, where the countercultural movement was born. Opposed to what adherents saw as the stuffiness, greed, and power-madness of mainstream U.S. society, it culminated in the famous "summer of love" of 1967. The Grateful Dead performed, among other venues, at two milestone concerts of the era, the Monterey Pop Festival of 1967 and Woodstock (in Bethel, New York) in 1969.

Garcia had begun taking drugs while in school. Now he delved into every available form of narcotic drug, including participation in government-sponsored tests of the hallucinogenic LSD. Drugs, and sporadic attempts to shake the habit, were to remain a constant factor in his life—he became informally known as Captain Trips. Drugs would ruin his health, leading to a five-day diabetic coma in 1986 (when he emerged from it, he had to take lessons to relearn to play the guitar) and to his death of a heart attack at age 53, in 1995.

But for now, the Grateful Dead had become an enormously successful, crowd-pleasing act whose unassuming, easygoing personality reflected Garcia's own. The band acquired a cult following of thousands of enthusiasts known as Deadheads.

The Grateful Dead's appeal was mainly based on live performances emphasizing improvisation, rather than exact reproductions of their albums. Their most successful albums, in fact, were live rather than studio recordings. Over the passing years, the Dead amassed the biggest total earnings from concerts of any group in rock music history.

Jerry Garcia was recognized as the spiritual head of the band, although he also occasionally worked solo or with other artists such as Bob Dylan; Crosby, Stills, Nash and Young; and jazzman Ornette Coleman. He is also considered one of the leading figures of the counterculture in general.

His death was publicly mourned by many thousands, and the president of the United States, Bill Clinton, called Garcia a genius. The Grateful Dead, which had weathered the earlier deaths of other members, disbanded after Garcia's.

Further Reading

Greenfield, Robert. *Dark Star: An Oral Biography of Jerry Garcia.* New York: Morrow, 1996.

Grushkin, Paul, Cynthia Barret, and Jonas Grushkin. *The Official Book of the Deadheads.* New York: Morrow, 1983.

Hake, Gordon. "In Memorian: Jerome John Garcia." Available online. URL: http://www.hake.com/gordon/garcia.html. Downloaded October 10, 2000.

Jackson, Blair. *Garcia: An American Life.* New York: Viking, 1999.

———. *Grateful Dead: The Music Never Stopped.* New York: Delilah Books, 1983.

Piccoli, Sean. *The Grateful Dead.* Philadelphia: Chelsea House, 1997.

Troy, Sandy. *Captain Trips: A Biography of Jerry Garcia.* New York: Thunder's Mouth Press, 1994.

García, Macario (1920–1972) *soldier*

Macario García single-handedly destroyed two enemy machine-gun emplacements during World War II, despite being wounded before he began the mission.

Since the Congressional Medal of Honor was created during the Civil War, almost 40 Hispanic Americans have received this medal, the highest award for military valor. In World War II, more Hispanics earned it than did members of any other ethnic group. Macario García joined their number on a hill in Germany.

García was born in Mexico in a hamlet called Villa del Castaño on January 20, 1920. After immigrating to the United States, he joined the army in Sugarland, Texas.

He attained the rank of sergeant and was an acting squad leader of Company B, 22nd Infantry. In this capacity on November 27, 1944, near a small German town called Grosshau, he and his men were pinned down by intense machine-gun fire. The enemy had the advantage of prepared defensive positions while the U.S. soldiers had to move uphill to fight and could find very little cover.

The German machine gunners continuously fired and artillery and mortar barrages pounded the hillside. García was wounded, but he refused to be evacuated. Instead, as his Medal of Honor citation noted, he decided on his own initiative to crawl forward alone until he reached a position near an enemy emplacement.

"Hurling grenades, he boldly assaulted the position, destroyed the gun, and with his rifle killed three of the enemy who attempted to escape," his citation reads. "When he rejoined his company, a second machine gun opened fire and again the intrepid soldier went forward, utterly disregarding his own safety.

"He stormed the position and destroyed the gun, killed three more Germans, and captured four prisoners. He fought on with his unit until the objective was taken, and only then did he permit himself to be removed for medical care."

The tribute by the Congress of the United States ended by describing Macario García's actions as "inspiring, courageous conduct" and "conspicuous heroism."

Later in a significant instance of racism in the United States, García was refused a cup of coffee in an eating establishment in Richmond, California. As a Chicano who dared enter the place, García was threatened by an Anglo with a baseball bat, and left.

Macario was killed in a car accident in 1972. A school in Houston is named after him.

Further Reading

Committee on Veterans' Affairs, U.S. Senate. *Medal of Honor Recipients 1863–1978.* Washington, D.C.: U.S. Government Printing Office, 1979.

❧ Gavin, John (John Anthony Golenor)

(1928–   ) *actor, government official*

John Gavin is a former Hollywood actor who drew attention by making the unusual, though not unprecedented, transition to U.S. ambassador.

Born John Anthony Golenor on April 8, 1928, in Los Angeles, he later took Gavin, the maiden name of his maternal grandmother, the mother of his Mexican mother, Delia Pablos. The Pablos family were ranch owners in the Mexican state of Sonora.

Gavin graduated from Stanford University in 1951 with a B.A. degree in political science and economics. He then joined the U.S. Navy and served for four years during the Korean War as an intelligence officer stationed on board a ship in Korean waters. He was later assigned to duty in Panama, where he specialized in Latin American affairs.

In 1955 he left the navy and became an actor. He played supporting or leading roles in such movies as *Imitation of Life* (1959), *Psycho* (1960), *Spartacus* (also 1960), *Romanoff and Juliet* (1961), *Thoroughly Modern Millie* (1967), and *The Madwoman of Chaillot* (1969). He was also president of the Screen Actors Guild (SAG) from 1971 to 1973. Gavin also worked on both television and Broadway.

During this time, Gavin maintained an active interest in Latin America, both from a political standpoint and as a businessman. He served as special adviser to the secretary general of the Organization of American States. He also worked to further the Alliance for Progress, a development program created by President John F. Kennedy.

As his politics became more conservative, Gavin began to work for the campaigns of Ronald Reagan, first for governor of California and later for president. In 1981, Reagan, also a former actor and a former president of SAG, decided to follow the example of former President Richard Nixon, who had appointed former actress Shirley Temple Black as United States envoy to the United Nations and later to Ghana. Reagan named Gavin ambassador to Mexico. The choice did not prove fortunate for relations between the United States and Mexico. Mexicans protested over what they saw as open interference by Gavin in internal Mexican affairs. This included giving public support to an opposition political party. Gavin resigned in 1986.

Returning to private life, Gavin maintained strong business ties with Latin America. He has served as vice president of the Atlantic Richfield Co. and president of Univisa and Gamma Services Co. and later of Gamma International.

Further Reading

Katz, Ephraim. *The Film Encyclopedia.* New York: Perigee Books, 1994.

❧ Goizueta, Roberto (Roberto Críspulo Goizueta) (1931–1997) *businessperson*

Roberto C. Goizueta was, for decades, the greatest success story of any Hispanic in the American business world. An immigrant from Cuba, he rose to be chairman of the board and chief executive officer (CEO) of one of the biggest and best-known companies in the world: Coca-Cola.

Born in Havana on November 18, 1931, in his rise up the corporate ladder Roberto C. Goizueta chose to remain publicly known as *Roberto* and not as *Robert* or *Bob* or other Anglicized versions of his name.

Goizueta came to the United States at the age of 18. He enrolled at Yale University and graduated in 1953 with a B.S. degree in chemical engineering. Joining the Coca-Cola Company in 1964 as assistant to the vice president for research and development, in two years Goizueta (whose surname is of Basque origin) was vice president of engineering; eight years after that, senior vice president; one year later, executive vice president.

By then it was 1975. After four years, he was appointed vice chairman; the next year, president and CEO, and the year after that—1981—chairman of the board, while remaining CEO. In 1996 his net worth was listed as 574 million dollars.

Hispanic community boosters have frequently singled out Goizueta as an example of how far Hispanics can rise in U.S. business, but some civil-rights activists have pointed out that Goizueta was the only high-ranking Hispanic in corporations of such size and influence. The next most prominent Hispanic businessmen are presidents of much smaller companies, heads of family firms, and the like.

Goizueta also sat on the board of directors of the Ford Motor Company and Eastman Kodak. He was a trustee of the Woodruff Arts Center and of Emory University. A board member of Boys Club of America, his commitment to community service earned him such honors as the Herbert Hoover Humanitarian Award in 1984, the Ellis Island Medal of Honor in 1986, the American Assembly's Service to Democracy Award (private sector) in 1990, and, in 1991, the National Equal Justice Award of the NAACP Legal Defense and Educational Fund.

He died in 1997.

Further Reading

Greising, David. *I'd Like the World to Buy a Coke: The Life and Leadership of Roberto Goizueta.* New York: Wiley, 1998.

☙ **Goldemberg, Isaac** (1945–) *writer*
Isaac Goldemberg is recognized as one of the United States' most significant Hispanic authors who writes in Spanish. He is also a leader of Latino literary circles in New York—an organizer and activist who urges his peers not to abandon the use of the Spanish language.

The product of a complex mix, or clash, of races and religions, reinforced by jarring shifts in his early life, Goldemberg turned his background into his sub-

ject matter. In doing so, he explored questions of who, precisely, is Hispanic and who, exactly, is Jewish.

Through his work and his life, this U.S.–Peruvian writer proves that it is self-defeating to attempt any strict, watertight definitions, particularly if based on such considerations as blood and religious beliefs. Goldemberg demonstrates that being Hispanic or being Jewish—he is both—is ultimately a question of *feeling* Hispanic or *feeling* Jewish and/or of being seen as Hispanic or Jewish by others.

Goldemberg was born on November 15, 1945, in a small Peruvian town called Chepén. His maternal grandmother was of partly Spanish and partly Quechuan Indian ancestry. His maternal grandfather was part Italian, part Basque, and part English. Goldemberg's father was a Jew from Russia.

The situation was made more complicated for the boy by the fact that his mother and father did not live together: His mother lived with her large, strict, Catholic family in the little town, while his father lived in the capital, Lima.

First, Isaac lived in Chepén in its strongly Roman Catholic environment. In a clearly autobiographical novel that Goldemberg wrote as an adult, *La Vida a Plazos de Don Jacobo Lerner* (published in translation as *The Fragmented Life of Don Jacobo Lerner*) there is a boy character called Efraín. Efraín lives in a very Catholic family and one day finds out that he is Jewish—but he does not know what that is. The novel was reissued in 1999 and was called "luscious" by the *Austin Chronicle.*

When he was eight years old, Isaac was taken to Lima to live with his father. Put into a Jewish school, he found that he had suddenly been shifted from a Catholic to a Jewish world, as well as from a sleepy town to a bustling city.

Goldemberg then went to a high school military academy, where anti-Semitism was a fact of life for the few Jewish students like himself.

Next he was bounced back into the Jewish world, living on a kibbutz, or cooperative, in Israel. He spent a year and a half in Israel, then a year in Spain, and finally a brief period in Peru before he immigrated to New York in 1965. Once in New York he tried to come to terms with the crosscurrents in his upbringing through writing.

Goldemberg is fluent in English. With a collaborator, he translated his book of poems *Hombre De Paso (Just Passing Through)* into English to publish it in a bilingual edition. As a matter of principle, however, he insisted on the value of immigrant writers maintaining their native language. He practiced what he preached and encouraged his peers to do so at annual Hispanic-American book fairs, which he organized, and by codirecting an Instituto de Escritores Latinoamericanos (Latin American Writers' Institute).

Goldemberg taught at New York University in the department of Spanish and Portuguese. From 1987 to 1988, he was writer-in-residence for the New York State Council of the Arts at the Ollantay Center for the Arts.

Further Reading

Goldemberg, Isaac. *The Fragmented Life of Don Jacobo Lerner.* New York: Persea Books, 1976.
———. *Hombre De Paso/Just Passing Through.* Hanover, N.H.: Point of Contact and Ediciones del Norte, 1981.
———. *Play by Play.* New York: Persea Books, 1985.
Kanellos, Nicolás, ed. *Biographical Dictionary of Hispanic Literature in the United States.* Westport, Conn.: Greenwood Press, 1989.

⚭   **Gómez, Edward** (1932–1951) *soldier*

In September 1951, Edward Gómez, clutching a live enemy grenade in his hand, ended his young life in a ditch in Korea to save his comrades in arms.

Gómez was born on August 10, 1932, in Omaha, Nebraska. He joined the marines as the Korean War was starting. One month after his 19th birthday, Gómez participated in the fateful assault on what was simply called Hill 749. When the day was over, Hill 749 was secured thanks, in part, to Gómez's bravery. The United States rewarded him, posthumously, with the Congressional Medal of Honor.

The citation spoke of Private First Class Edward Gómez's "conspicuous gallantry and intrepidity at the risk of his life above and beyond the call of duty while serving as an ammunition bearer in Company E (2nd Battalion, 1st Marines, 1st Marine Division)."

Boldly advancing with his squad in support of a group of riflemen who were assaulting a series of strongly fortified hostile positions, "Pfc. Gómez," read the citation, "consistently exposed himself to the withering barrage to keep his machine gun supplied with ammunition."

With a counterattack expected at any moment, the squad searched for a new spot to set up the machine gun. Gómez found an abandoned trench to use. At that moment, an enemy grenade dropped to the ground at a spot midway between where he was and the current position of the gun and the marines firing it.

Gómez gave warning and picked up the grenade.

"Determined to save his comrades," the United States government citation reads, "he unhesitatingly chose to sacrifice himself and, diving into the ditch with the deadly missile, absorbed the shattering violence of the explosion in his body. By his stouthearted courage, incomparable valor, and decisive spirit of self-sacrifice, Pfc. Gómez [. . .] sustained and enhanced the finest traditions of the U.S. naval service."

His superiors credited Gómez's selfless example with inspiring the other men to undertake new and heroic efforts to repel the enemy counterattack, despite being outnumbered, and to win Hill 749.

Further Reading

The Committee on Veterans' Affairs, United States Senate. *Medal of Honor Recipients 1863–1978.* Washington, D.C.: U.S. Government Printing Office, 1979.

⚭   **Gómez-Peña, Guillermo** (1950–)
artist

An immigrant from Mexico, Guillermo Gómez-Peña stands out among the artists who, in recent decades, have sought to break down barriers between various mediums. These artists merge these varied mediums into an "experience."

Gómez-Peña is an articulate writer and observer. He writes in many different forms, and his essays and other works have helped to define and explain Latino art for other communities.

Gómez-Peña was born in 1950 in Mexico City. As an adult he settled in San Diego, California, but retained strong links with his native country, where his writings are published as frequently as they are in his adoptive land. The bilingual and bicultural nature of contemporary Hispanic art is an aspect he has frequently emphasized.

His interdisciplinary art centers on performances in front of an audience. Gómez-Peña's performance art was included in a documentary film about the more recent immigrants to the United States—Louis Malle's *God's Country* (1985).

Gómez-Peña's performance and collaborative art—he likes to work with other artists, from both sides of the U.S.–Mexican border—includes an element of improvisation. However, his work is grounded not in intuition but in scholarship.

He studied Spanish literature and linguistics at the Universidad Ibero-Americana and at the Universidad Nacional Autónoma de Mexico (UNAM), where he was known as a student activist. In the United States in 1979, he earned BFA and MFA degrees in art from the California Institute of the Arts. In 1997, Gómez-Peña's book, *The New World Border,* received the American Book Award.

Gómez-Peña cofounded a performance art group, Poyesis Genética, in 1981. The following year, the group toured Europe and then settled in San Diego. That city's reputation as a border meeting place of cultures was an important attraction for Gómez-Peña. Watching the interaction between the United States and Mexico, Gómez-Peña asked, with acid humor, in the text of one of his film performances, directed by Louis Malle:

> But what if suddenly the continent turned
>   upside down?
> What if the U.S. was Mexico?
> What if 200,000 Anglo-Saxicans
> Were to cross the border each month
> To work as gardeners, waiters,
> 3rd chair musicians, movie extras,
> Bouncers, babysitters, chauffeurs,
> Syndicated cartoons, featherweight boxers,
> fruit pickers & anonymous poets?
> What if they were called Waspanos,
> Waspitos, Wasperos or Waspbacks?
> What if literature was life, eh?
> What if yo were you
> & tú fueras I, mister?

A point he has repeatedly made in articles and interviews is the continuity of modern Hispanic-American art with previous trends in the long history of Latin American art and culture. As Hispanic culture has spread across the United States and even into Canada in recent decades, Latino art can now be considered to extend all the way up and down the Americas. It thus forms, Gómez-Peña says, "a new artistic continent."

❧ Gonzales, Richard Alonzo "Pancho"
(1928–1995) *tennis player*

One of the greatest tennis players of all time, Richard Alonzo "Pancho" Gonzales also became one of the most popular ever. He has been compared to the baseball legend George Herman "Babe" Ruth in the enthusiasm he kindled among his fans.

Pancho Gonzales was a natural tennis phenomenon who learned to play virtually on his own. He remained a leader in the sport until he retired, by then in his 40s, in 1971.

Born in Los Angeles on May 9, 1928, Gonzales's parents were immigrants from Mexico who earned little money. His father was a carpenter and movie-set painter; his mother, a seamstress. After Pancho, they had six more children.

Pancho's being a self-taught tennis player was thus a matter of necessity. He received a tennis racket as a Christmas present when he was 12, but there was no money for lessons. Consequently, he hung about the public tennis courts and learned on his own. His game improved, but his attendance and his grades at school plummeted.

He won his first tournament while a student in junior high school, becoming the top-ranked junior tennis player in southern California, but his parents did not permit him to participate in any further competitions until his grades at school improved.

The strategy did not work. In 1944, at age 16, the strong-willed, moody Gonzales dropped out of high school altogether, and a year later, he joined the U.S. Navy and served until 1947. At the end of military service, Gonzales was discharged, married, and went into tennis full time. Because of his lack of formal training, his style of play was unorthodox, but he won matches. In rapid succession, he won six top amateur championships, five in singles—on grass, clay, and indoor courts—and one in doubles. In 1949, he also helped lead the United States to victory over Australia in the international Davis Cup.

That year he turned professional, and for more than a decade he was the dominant figure on the tennis stage. He won the U.S. Open seven times in a row, from 1953 through 1959, and then again in 1961. Among his other victories were the World Professional Championship at Wembley, England, in 1966, and the Tournament of Champions in Las Vegas in 1969, against the then leading player, Arthur Ashe.

Pancho Gonzales, who could always be counted on to provide an interesting show, came to be regarded as the grand old man of tennis. He retired several times but kept returning to the sport until his final good-bye to the professional circuit in 1971. That last year, he won the Pacific Southwest tournament.

After his final retirement, the self-taught Gonzales devoted himself to teaching others. He had already coached the U.S. Davis Cup Team in 1968, the same year he was elected to the National Lawn Tennis Hall of Fame in Newport, Rhode Island. His activities after retirement also included playing in exhibition tennis and in senior players' tournaments and coaching in Las Vegas and at his own Pancho Gonzales Tennis Ranch in Malibu, California. He died in 1995.

Further Reading

America USA. "PG." Available online. URL: http://www.neta.com/~1stbooks/PG-.htm. Downloaded October 10, 2000.

Anderson, Dave. *The Return of a Champion: Pancho Gonzales' Golden Year 1964.* Englewood Cliffs, N.J.: Prentice-Hall, 1973.

Frayne, Trent. *Famous Tennis Players.* New York: Dodd, Mead & Co., 1977.

✎ Gonzales, Rodolfo "Corky" (1928–)
activist, writer

Rodolfo "Corky" Gonzales was one of the principal leaders of the Hispanic-American civil rights movement that began in the second half of the 1960s. With the publication of his book-length poem *Yo Soy Joaquín/I Am Joaquín* in 1967, he personally helped launch a heightened form of Mexican American consciousness, often called the Chicano movement.

The activism of Gonzales and other leaders of that time, such as Reies López TIJERINA, differed from that of such previous organizations as the American GI Forum (AGIF, created in 1948) and the League of United Latin American Citizens (LULAC, formed in 1928). These groups had sought to integrate Hispanics fully into U.S. society. They even avoided such words as *Mexican* in their names.

Gonzalez and the other new activists would have had less success without the groundwork laid by the Hispanic-American activists who had come before. They were also indebted to the African-American civil rights movement. But the new Hispanic leaders felt that Mexican Americans—who increasingly called themselves Chicanos—and other Hispanic Americans should not try to assimilate into the mainstream in the United States. On the contrary, they said, Chicanos should be aware and proud of their heritage and maintain it. They believed that Chicanos had to resolve the contradictions posed by their triple cultural heritage (Indian, Spanish, and Anglo) without abandoning any of the three.

Gonzales's *Yo Soy Joaquín,* hundreds of thousands of copies of which were printed, proved to be the ideal instrument for teaching Chicanos about their past. It told them that they were not alone in feeling confused about their identity, and it helped raise their self-esteem.

Corky Gonzales (not related to Pancho GONZALES) was the son of migrant farmworkers. Born in a Mexican *barrio* in Denver, Colorado, on June 18, 1928, he was picking beets in the fields by the age of 10. He later switched to work in a slaughterhouse. In the meantime, his schooling continued.

Gonzale's next career, which he began in 1947, was boxing. A featherweight, he was a Golden Gloves (amateur) champion and then turned professional. The National Boxing Association ranked him third as a contender for the world title in his weight class. Of the 75 bouts he fought, he won 65. Decades later, he returned to boxing as a trainer.

Gonzales was also a longtime religious activist within the Presbyterian Church.

In the mid-1950s he left boxing and went into various businesses. He ran a bar, was a bail bondsman, and launched a car insurance company. Overall, his business career was successful. He also entered politics and became Denver Democratic Party district captain. He was the first Mexican American to hold this party post. He was also the coordinator of the Viva Kennedy clubs in the state of Colorado during the 1960 presidential elections and led President Lyndon Johnson's War on Poverty program in Denver from 1965 to 1966. The program ended abruptly in 1966 with charges that Gonzales was showing too much favor to Hispanics in the War on Poverty. He quit the Democratic Party to devote himself fully to his own efforts on behalf of the Mexican-American community.

In 1963, Gonzales launched his first organization, Los Voluntarios (The Volunteers). One of its main activities was protesting against cases of police brutality, which, Chicanos charged, was almost routinely suffered by Chicano suspects.

He transformed Los Voluntarios in 1966 into an organization with a wider scope in community affairs, renamed Crusade for Justice. The approach that he continued to develop was to seek the participation not only of youthful activists but of their entire families.

The next year, *I Am Joaquín* was released. This was Gonzales's only published literary work, although he is known to have also written two plays, *The Revolutionist* and *A Cross for Maclovio*. Yet, the impact of this one poem was so big that it turned him into a major Chicano literary figure. *I Am Joaquín* was reproduced in bilingual editions, staged in play form, and made into a movie by a Chicano troupe, Luis VALDEZ's Teatro Campesino.

Some commentators said that its literary merits were less than its value as an inspiration for countless Chicanos. Others have praised it as literature too, noting an expert marriage of its structure to its subject matter.

A long epic of Mexican and Chicano experience, *I Am Joaquín* moves back and forth in time. Its hero, Joaquín, identifies with many different characters over the centuries, both the oppressors and the oppressed. He witnesses many events and circumstances, including war heroics by the Aztec, the defense of

Mexico City in 1847 by boy cadets who died fighting rather than surrender to the invading U.S. Army, and the rattling conditions in a modern Chicano urban ghetto. Gonzales is believed to have been inspired to write the poem by the figure of Joaquín MURIETA, a Californian bandit-hero from the gold-rush period.

In 1968, Gonzales took part, with the Crusade for Justice, in a Poor People's march on Washington, D.C. There, he launched a series of demands called the "Plan of the Barrio," among which was that ancient land rights be given back to Chicanos.

In Denver, Gonzales set up a Crusade headquarters in an old church complex. He included a theater, a school—from which many future Chicano activists arose—a cultural center, a bookstore, a nursery, a curio shop, a gym, and a newspaper.

Organizing or participating in many marches and demonstrations, he was arrested in one violent episode but was acquitted when it was proven in court that the violence had been started by the police.

Gonzales also launched Chicano youth conferences, the first of which, in 1969, issued a statement called *El Plan Espiritual de Aztlán* (The Spiritual Plan of Aztlán). Here he developed the idea of identifying Aztlán—a mythical original land of the Aztecs—as a spiritual homeland in the U.S. Southwest for Chicanos.

In 1970, he participated in the launching of the La Raza Unida Party (RUP or LRUP), the Party of the United Race, which was set up in different states to fight for Chicanos' rights on a political level. In 1972, in El Paso, Texas, LRUP held its first national convention. The convention boiled down to a confrontation between Gonzales and another leader, José Angel GUTIÉRREZ. Gonzales wanted LRUP to participate in elections as a third party, opposing both Republicans and Democrats. Gutiérrez adopted a less radical position, asking LRUP to run its candidates within the two-party system. He won. For Gonzales, this began a period of continued activism in civil rights and other causes but with less satisfaction and fewer results. Like other leaders, he discovered that the heady era of militancy during the 1960s was over.

Gonzales suffered serious injuries in a car crash in 1987.

Further Reading

Bruce-Nova, Juan D. *Chicano Poetry: A Response in Chaos.* Austin: University of Texas Press, 1982.

Castro, Tony. *Chicano Power: The Emergence of Mexican America.* New York: Saturday Review Press, 1974.

Lomelí, Francisco A., and Carl R. Shirley, eds. *Dictionary of Literary Biography: Chicano Writers—First Series.* Detroit: Gale Research, Inc., 1989.

Marín, Christine. *A Spokesman for the Mexican American Movement: Rodolfo "Corky" Gonzales and the Fight for Chicano Liberation.* San Francisco: R and E Research Associates, 1977.

❧ González, Alfredo (1946–1968) *soldier*

Alfredo González was one of four U.S. soldiers to earn the Congressional Medal of Honor through selflessness and courage during the bitter fight to retake the Vietnamese city of Hue. This occurred after Hue had been captured by communist forces during North Vietnam's Tet Offensive. Two of the four medals were awarded posthumously. González's was one of them.

González was born in Edinburg, Texas, on May 23, 1946. In January 1968, as a 21-year-old marine sergeant, he commanded the 3rd Platoon, Company A, 1st Battalion, 1st Marines, 1st Marine Division. In the course of five continuous days of combat that ended with his death, he became leader of the whole company.

González's Alpha Company was rushed by truck to Hue on the morning of January 31, as soon as the city—an old Vietnamese imperial capital—came under extremely heavy enemy attack. The battle began immediately. Heavy sniper fire engaged them while still on the road south of the city. González is credited with clearing the snipers by "aggressively maneuvering" his platoon and directing its fire until the area had been secured.

The company then crossed a river to enter the city. Riding on tanks, they were met by strong fire. A rocket-propelled grenade smashed the lead tank, wounding several marines who fell to the ground. Seeing them lying on the road exposed to enemy fire, González immediately jumped down from his tank and, in the words of his Medal of Honor citation,

"with complete disregard for his safety" braved the enemy's fire. He lifted one of the marines up and—ignoring fragmentation wounds he sustained—carried the marine to shelter.

A fortified machine-gun bunker kept the marines from advancing further. González led his platoon to the protection of a dike, which bordered a rice paddy alongside the road. Once again exposing himself to the relentless fire that pounded the area, he ran to the enemy bunker and leveled it with hand grenades.

On the same day, the company commander sustained a wound that required him to be pulled out of the battle. Sergeant González was now in command of the fighting, which continued street by street, day after day.

González sustained a new and serious wound in combat on the fourth day of the battle, February 3. He could have been evacuated for medical treatment, but he refused to leave while the battle for Hue continued.

The end came for him the next day, February 4, 1968. A concentrated attack by enemy rockets and automatic weapons began to kill and wound more and more of his men. Again González charged forward alone, running along the street and picking up a light antitank assault weapon dropped by a dead comrade. He used it to hit one of the enemy emplacements. These antitank weapons fired only one shot each, so González ran ahead and picked up another one and then another. Single-handedly, González destroyed one of the rocket positions of the enemy and silenced most of the small-arms fire—but he was killed by a machine-gun blast.

In its citation, the Medal of Honor committee commended the fallen soldier for his "heroism, courage, and dynamic leadership."

In 1996, a guided missile cruiser was given the name *Sergeant Alfredo González*—the first time a vessel of the U.S. Navy has borne the name of a Hispanic marine.

Further Reading

The Committee on Veterans' Affairs, United States Senate. *Medal of Honor Recipients 1863–1978.* Washington, D.C.: U.S. Government Printing Office, 1979.

The editors of Boston Publishing Company. *Above and Beyond: A History of the Medal of Honor from The Civil War to Vietnam.* Boston: Boston Publishing Company, 1985.

Gonzalez, Celedonio (1923–) *writer*

With his four novels and one collection of short stories written over the course of two decades, Celedonio González is one of the foremost authors on Cuban-American life. A native of small-town Cuba, he was transplanted to the urban United States by political events. Born in La Esperanza (the name means "hope") on September 9, 1923, González grew up with ideals of a fairer society. These ideals were to be repeatedly disappointed in practice.

As a young man, he opposed the right-wing military dictatorship of Fulgencio Batista, and he welcomed Fidel Castro when he threw out Batista in 1959. Yet, he quickly joined the ranks of those who opposed Castro when Cuba's new leader established his communist government. Arrested on charges of conspiring against the Fidel Castro government, González spent two months in prison in 1960. Freed, he and his family left Cuba to go to the United States. In the United States González lived in Miami, then in Chicago, and finally again in Miami.

Like many Cubans who came to the United States in those years, González realized that his new country was not what he had imagined it would be. He found that it could be very hard on outsiders and on those who did not succeed quickly.

While holding a long succession of small but tiresome jobs, González began to write about the lives and often-dashed hopes of Cuban Americans. Through dogged persistence, he managed in 1971 to get a novel published, *Los Primos (The Cousins).* He described the book as "a mirror of Cuban life in Miami in the early sixties." His Cuban-American readers have generally found their image in his works accurate.

Los Primos was followed by a story collection, *La Soledad es una Amiga que Vendrá (Loneliness Is a Friend Who Will Come,* 1971) and the novels *Los Cuatro Embajadores (The Four Ambassadors,* 1973), *El Espesor del Pellejo de un Gato Ya Cadáver (The Thick-*ness of the Skin of a Cat Which Is Already Dead, 1978) and *Que Veinte Años No Es Nada (That Twenty Years Are Nothing,* 1987). He published *Fontainebleau Park* in 1998. Cuban Americans consider González to be *el cronista de la diáspora*—the chronicler of the Cuban diaspora, or exile.

Celedonio González worked for the anti-Castro Radio Martí as a writer and for the newspaper *Diario Las Américas* as a columnist. He has received Ciudad de Oviedo (Spain) and Voice of America awards for his writing.

Further Reading

Kanellos, Nicolás, ed. *Biographical Dictionary of Hispanic Literature in the United States.* Westport, Conn.: Greenwood Press, 1989.

Gonzalez, Henry B. (Henry Barbosa Gonzalez) (1916–2000) *government official*

The first Mexican American to be elected in Texas to the House of Representatives, Henry B. González championed a number of laws to improve the condition of minorities in U.S. society.

Congressman González was frequently seen as an example of the Hispanic leaders who rose to prominence in the years after World War II. This group often bucked the authority of earlier Hispanic organizations, which they considered too tame and entrenched. Nevertheless, this generation of leaders achieved advances by working within the existing political system.

González's generation tended to oppose the more militant Hispanic leaders who emerged during the mid-1960s. The younger generation often criticized the system itself. González and the politicians of his generation stuck to the middle ground, claiming that the new, loud, and sometimes violent activists scared away moderate supporters. Thus, they argued, the militants might do more harm than good.

Henry Barbosa (Barbosa was his mother's maiden name) González's parents were mine owners in Durango, Mexico. They immigrated to the United States as refugees from political disorders in their home country. Henry was born on May 3, 1916, in San Antonio, Texas, and obtained most of his education in that city, save for a period when he studied civil engineering at the University of Texas in Austin. He graduated from St. Mary's University School of Law in San Antonio in 1943.

González served in both army and navy intelligence during World War II, censoring civilian cables and radio. Before entering politics, González worked, among other jobs, in a translations company owned by his father, in the county probation service, and in the city's housing authority.

González lost his first political race—a 1950 attempt to enter the city council—by a small number of votes. He tried again in 1953, and this time, having put together his own grassroots support, independent of established Hispanic organizations, he won. A San Antonio councilman from 1953 to 1956, he immediately established his liberal credentials when he authored a proposal to put an end to segregation in San Antonio's public facilities; it was approved as a city ordinance. In 1955–56, he acted as temporary mayor of San Antonio.

In 1956 he won the election for state senator by fewer than 300 votes. For 110 years—virtually the entire time since Texas joined the United States in 1845—no Mexican American had been a Texas state senator, despite the state's large Mexican-American population.

In the state senate, González, a Democrat, crusaded for minority rights and against all forms of racism. He never advocated the cause of Hispanics alone, but always that of all minorities together. Later, he would regard any proposals worded solely in pro-Hispanic terms as reverse racism. In 1974, he voted against extending the Voting Rights Act to Mexican Americans.

In 1958, he was defeated in the race for state governor. Two years later, he campaigned for John F. Kennedy's presidential candidacy, as he would later for other Democratic presidential candidates.

González won in 1961 in a special election for a Texas congressional seat and went to Washington. Again, it was a first; Texans had not elected a Mexican American to Congress before. Texas voters reelected González continuously; in 1991, he celebrated his 30th year as a congressman, and he headed the powerful House Banking Committee. He started a new term in office in 1995 but did not stand for reelection in 1998, and retired from Congress.

Among his most important achievements in the U.S. House of Representatives was his contribution in 1964 to ending the *bracero* program, a system used by big farm owners that exploited both U.S. and Mexican farmworkers.

González also proposed or supported both civil rights measures to end discrimination as well as laws supporting human rights, education, and decent wages. His objection to specifically Hispanic legislation and activism led to his being called a rightist in later years, despite the fact that in his early days he had been called a leftist. Nevertheless, in 1975 he helped found the National Association of Latino Elected and Appointed Officials (NALEO), an organization that has lobbied to have more Hispanics hired in government posts.

González died in 2000.

Further Reading

Martínez, Al. *Rising Voices: Profiles of Hispano-American Lives.* New York: New American Library, 1974.

The Ralph Nader Congress Project. *Henry Gonzalez, Democratic Representative from Texas.* Washington, D.C.: Grossman Publishers, 1972.

Rodríguez, Eugene. *Henry B. Gonzalez: A Political Profile.* New York: Arno Press, 1976.

Sloane, Todd. *González of Texas: A Congressman for the People.* Evanston, Ill.: John Gordon Burke Publisher, 1996.

Gormé, Eydie (1932–) *singer*

Eydie Gormé achieved celebrity singing in both English and Spanish both before and after her marriage to singer Steve Lawrence. Gormé and Lawrence combined their talents on records, in nightclubs and concert halls, and on television and radio. Her recordings with the Spanish-language Trío Los Panchos won her a large following in Latin America.

Gormé's Hispanic roots derive from her Sephardic Jewish heritage. Sephardic Jews lived in the Iberian peninsula during the Middle Ages and were strongly influenced by their surroundings. This influence included adopting a language, called

Ladino, which is similar to the Spanish of that time. They also helped shape Spanish culture. Thrown out of Spain, many moved to Turkey. Eydie Gormé's parents came from that country. Eydie was born in the Bronx on August 16, 1932.

One student of Hispanic culture, Earl Shorris, wrote that in Gormé's "long, very slightly nasal notes, one can hear overtones of the Moorish or ancient Hebrew ancestors of Spanish flamenco. Curiously, the sound of Spain is less evident when she sings in Spanish."

As a teenager, Gormé sang on Spanish-language radio stations in New York. At the same time, she sang in English for several pop music bands, including those of Tommy Tucker, Tex Benecke, and Ray Eberle.

She began to find herself in increasing demand to make singing appearances on radio and TV, as well as in nightclubs. A major club, the Copacabana, presented her in her own show in 1956.

Three years earlier, when television launched *The Steve Allen Show* and then turned it into the first version of the *Tonight Show,* the producers signed Eydie Gormé as one of a permanent corps of singers and actors who were all early in their careers. It was here that she met Andy Williams, Don Knotts, and Steve Lawrence. She and Lawrence married in 1957.

Gormé went on to a career of both solo and joint appearances and recordings with her husband. They also appeared together in a 1968 Broadway show, *Golden Rainbow.* In 1960 they won a Grammy for their record, "We Got Us." In 1966, one of Gormé's solo recordings, "If He Walked Into My Life" also won a Grammy.

Gormé and Lawrence were known for TV specials devoted to their singing tributes to such great U.S. songwriters as Irving Berlin, the Gershwin brothers, and Cole Porter. Each of these three specials won awards: The first won seven Emmys, the second, two. Often performing in Atlantic City casino shows, Gormé and Lawrence were inducted into the casino industry's Gaming Hall of Fame in 1999.

Singing in Spanish proved a way for Gormé to extend her celebrity from the United States to Spanish-speaking countries. In these recordings, she was accompanied by the popular Los Panchos trio.

Further Reading

Blackwell, Earl. *Celebrity Register.* Towson, Md.: Times Publishing Group, 1986.

❧ Gutiérrez, José Angel (1944–)
activist

A leading figure in the Hispanic civil rights activism boom that began in the mid-1960s, José Angel Gutiérrez was also considered one of the most polemical because of the wild, incendiary phrases he used in his speeches. When it came to actions rather than words, however, he was practical rather than radical.

Gutiérrez was born on October 25, 1944, in Crystal City, Texas. His family remained well off while his father, a doctor, was alive. After his death, however, the family was reduced to farm labor. This happened when José Angel Gutiérrez was 12 years old. The boy nevertheless managed to continue his schooling. His later skills as a public speaker and as an organizer began to develop in this early period. In high school, Gutiérrez was elected student-body president and was the best debater in the school.

During the almost 40 years of his education, Gutiérrez divided his studies between two fields: political science and law. In 1966 he earned a B.A. degree in political science from Texas Arts and Industries (A&I) University in Kingsville. Then he began to study law at the University of Houston. He later transferred to St. Mary's University in San Antonio and received his master's degree in political science in 1968. He earned his Ph.D. degree in political science from the University of Texas in Austin in 1976 and in 1988 added a doctorate in law from the University of Houston.

Gutiérrez's activism began when he was an undergraduate at Texas A&I: he and other students worked for the improvement not only of learning conditions, but also of the Hispanic community in general. It wasn't until some years later, in 1967, that the group was formally founded as the Mexican American Youth Organization (MAYO), with Gutiérrez as president. From the start, Gutiérrez had a reputation as a fiery radical. When in 1968 the Ford Foundation awarded MAYO $8,000 to aid its community work, the foundation was criticized by more conservative Hispanics for making the donation.

In 1969, Gutiérrez taped a Chicano protest statement to the window of the courthouse in San Felipe Del Río, Texas. It became known as the Del Río Manifesto. This act was the highlight of a demonstration that Chicanos held in that town to call attention to a number of issues from development assistance to police brutality.

Later that year, Gutiérrez went back to Crystal City to put his thinking into practice. He believed that the way to achieve real improvements was to obtain political power. Even where Chicanos were in a majority, like Crystal City, they were often dominated and exploited because an Anglo minority held power. To combat this state of affairs, Gutiérrez founded a political organization of the Chicanos' own in 1970 called the La Raza Unida (The United People) Party (LRUP). It soon expanded to other states.

La Raza Unida immediately won representation in the city council and on the school board. It wasn't a major breakthrough in terms of numbers because Crystal City, despite its name, is a town of no more than 8,500 people. Still, it proved significant for Chicanos as a psychological milestone.

Gutiérrez regarded participation on the school board as especially important because, in his view, education was being used as a tool to keep Chicanos down. Chicano students were not allowed to use Spanish in school. Many Mexican Americans spoke Spanish better than they spoke English. Because they were unable to speak Spanish in school, they dropped out in large numbers. Without enough education, they were unable to compete. Chicanos were even barred from many extracurricular activities.

Gutiérrez was elected to the school board and was soon its chairman. He saw to it that school policies were quickly changed to eliminate discrimination and to allow bilingual approaches. In public statements, Gutiérrez declared his goals in extreme terms. He said, "We are going to move to do away with the injustices to the Chicano, and if the gringo doesn't get out of our way, we will stampede over him." He also said, "Kill the gringo." He meant this figuratively. Nevertheless, the slogan was roundly condemned, not only by Anglos but by many Chicanos.

In 1972, the La Raza Unida Party held a national convention in El Paso, Texas. Despite his rhetoric, Gutiérrez held a moderate position on what should be done next. Rodolfo "Corky" GONZALES of Colorado demanded that LRUP become a true third party. Gutiérrez, instead, held that its members would achieve greater success if they fought for their ideals from inside the existing Democratic and Republican parties. The moderate course was finally adopted.

In 1974 Gutiérrez was elected a county judge in Texas. The following year, he accepted an official invitation from Fidel Castro to visit Cuba, a decision that met with more criticism. His work as a judge was marked by feuding with the legal establishment, where Anglos were in a strong majority. In 1981, he resigned to work as a college professor, but he continued to be active in Mexican-American organizations, such as the Oregon Council for Hispanic Advancement in 1985. He did research on Hispanic community history, uncovering evidence that the FBI had spied on Mexican-American organizations in the 1940s and 1950s.

He also published works such as *A Gringo Manual on How to Handle Mexicans* (1972) and *A War of Words* (1984). *Hispanic Business* magazine named him one of the 100 most influential Hispanics in the United States in 1991.

After obtaining his law degree, Gutiérrez began a legal practice in Dallas. In 1990, Gutiérrez again became a judge, handling administrative law in Dallas. However, Gutiérrez did not abandon activism. In 1996 he coordinated the United States' first Hispanic March for Justice with nationwide reach—an event that mobilized 100,000 Hispanic demonstrators in the nation's capital.

Further Reading

García, Ignacio. *United We Win: The Rise and Fall of La Raza Unida Party.* Tucson, Ariz.: MASRC, University of Arizona, 1989.

Hammerback, John, et al. *A War of Words: Chicano Protest in the 1960s and 1970s.* Westport, Conn.: Greenwood Publishing Group, 1985.

Martínez, Al. *Rising Voices: Profiles of Hispano-American Lives.* New York: New American Library, 1974.

Stocky, John. *Chicano Revolt in a Texas Town.* Notre Dame, Ind.: University of Notre Dame Press, 1974.

Gutiérrez, Sidney (Sidney McNeill Gutiérrez) (1951–) *astronaut*

As pilot of a *Columbia* space-shuttle mission in 1991, Sidney Gutiérrez participated in one of NASA's most ambitious life-sciences experiments in outer space.

Sidney Gutiérrez (not related to political activist José Angel GUTIÉRREZ) was born on June 27, 1951, in Albuquerque, New Mexico. After completing school in his hometown, Gutiérrez joined the U.S. Air Force. He graduated from the Air Force Academy at Colorado Springs in 1973 with a degree in aeronautical engineering. He also became a master parachutist and a member of the U.S. national championship team, with more than 550 parachute jumps to his credit.

Gutiérrez became an air force pilot in 1975 after studying at Laughlin Air Force Base in Texas. He stayed there as an instructor for two years, and took postgraduate courses in management. In 1977 he received his master's degree in management from Webster College in St. Louis, Missouri.

Gutiérrez then served as an F-15 pilot at the Hollomon Air Force Base in his home state. In 1981, he moved to Edwards Air Force Base in California to attend the Air Force Test Pilot School there. He tested F-16 jets and added to his already wide range of piloting experience by flying dozens of different types of aircraft.

The National Aeronautics and Space Administration (NASA) chose Gutiérrez as a potential astronaut in 1984. After qualifying as a space shuttle pilot the following year, he worked in a range of jobs for the agency from testing the computer software used on space flights to assisting in launches from the Kennedy Space Center in Florida. Gutiérrez also worked at NASA headquarters investigating the 1986 *Challenger* disaster.

In 1989 Gutiérrez was appointed pilot of the *Columbia* shuttle for the Spacelab Life Sciences mission two years later. In the course of a nine-day mission, Gutiérrez and the six other crew members

Sidney Gutiérrez *(NASA)*

successfully employed the Spacelab module, a fully equipped scientific laboratory, to carry out a series of experiments on the effects of space flight.

As test subjects, the astronauts used jellyfish and rats, but they themselves were the main test subjects. NASA had not attempted such wide-ranging life-sciences experimentation in space since 1974.

Gutiérrez returned to outer space in 1994 aboard the shuttle *Endeavour,* logging 270 hours in space in addition to the 218 of his first mission. Later that year he retired from NASA to work for Sandia National Laboratories.

Further Reading

Cassutt, Michael. *Who's Who in Space.* New York: Macmillan Publishing Co., 1993.

Hayek, Salma (1968–) *actress*

Once named by *People* magazine as one of the 50 most beautiful people in the world, Salma Hayek is hailed by the Hispanic community in the United States as the first Mexican actress to obtain leading roles in Hollywood since Dolores DEL RÍO half a century earlier. No overnight success, Hayek had already established a solid position in the Mexican entertainment industry, when she decided in 1991 that she would henceforward seek her career in the U.S. movie industry. After initial disappointments, she achieved U.S. success.

The daughter of a Mexican mother and a Lebanese immigrant father, Salma Hayek was born in Coatzacoalcos, in the state of Veracruz, Mexico, on September 26, 1968. From her earliest years, she was expected to grow up as a beauty; her grandmother repeatedly shaved her head and plucked her eyebrows in the belief that this would strengthen hair growth.

Her father was a successful businessman who was able to send Salma to a Catholic boarding school in Louisiana. However, the nuns did not see eye to eye with her on the question of her sense of humor, objecting to such stunts as her stealing into their rooms to set their clocks back. The result was that after two years her parents were asked to take her back.

Hayek also lived for a period with a relative in Houston, after quickly completing high school in Mexico thanks to a nimble mind for studies. She has recalled that these early sojourns in the United States led her to believe that she spoke enough English for a career in the United States. She was to discover, however, that this was not the case, and that she would require intensive schooling in the language.

Although she set out to study international relations and drama at Mexico City's Universidad Iberoamericana, her ambition was to be a television and movie actress. Against her family's wishes, she dropped out of college to pursue her dream.

Her looks ensured that her success in Mexican soap operas was a speedy one. However, she also won respect for her acting ability, obtaining a Mexican TV award as best actress for her title role in the soap *Teresa* in 1989. But her sights were set across the Rio Grande, and on the big screen. Without waiting to obtain any jobs, and leaving behind throngs of disappointed Mexican admirers, she moved to Los Angeles.

There was to be no fast start for her in Hollywood. Instead, for three years Hayek did the usual progression from rejections to bit appearances to a speaking part—just one line—in a film. During this time, she returned to Mexico for one good movie role in *El callejón de los milagros* (Midaq Alley, 1995) which led to a nomination for the Mexican version of the Oscar, called the Ariel.

Hollywood was then preparing a big sequel, entitled *Desperado,* to a Mexican movie (reportedly made for only $7,000) that had been a great success, *El mariachi* (1992). It was to be directed by the same person who made the earlier movie, Robert Rodríguez, but it was to have a large budget and a top cast headed by Antonio BANDERAS. Rodríguez had agreed to make the sequel on the condition that 80 percent of the team be Hispanic. When he saw Hayek on a United States talk show, he decided that she must have the main female role in the movie.

Banderas and Hayek then earned a joint nomination for an MTV Movie Award in the Best Kiss category. Later, however, when she acted in a movie with Laurence Fishburne, she said that he had "the best lips." Fishburne returned an even more valuable compliment, saying that Hayek has the perfect comedy timing of a Lucille Ball.

Desperado (released in 1995) was Hayek's big break. From it flowed major roles in other United States movies, including *From Dusk Till Dawn, Fools Rush In, Dogma,* and *The Wild, Wild West.*

Hayek says she does not mind playing Latina stereotypes, although she may not be condemned to that kind of role alone—in the movie *Breaking Up* (1997) her character was not originally conceived as Hispanic. However, she has said that she would like "to be able to change the image of Latin people in United States society." In her view, as she said on another occasion, "Latinos are not treated as first-class citizens here. And in the entertainment industry they're perceived as the help."

In 2000, Hayek appeared in *Timecode* and *Chain of Fools.* In 2001, she began filming the title role of *Frida Kahlo.*

Further Reading
Ducal, Patricia. *Salma Hayek.* New York: St. Martin's, 1999.
Salma.com. Available online. URL: http://www.salma.com. Downloaded October 10, 2000.

Telgen, Diane, and Jim Kamp, eds. *Notable Hispanic American Women.* Detroit: Gale Research, Inc., 1998.

Hayworth, Rita (Margarita Carmen Cansino) (1918–1987) *actress*

Hollywood coined the phrase "love goddess" for Rita Hayworth. She was one of the world's most famous and most glamorous actresses of the 1940s. She thus replaced the great 1930s star Jean Harlow and foreshadowed Marilyn Monroe in the 1950s.

For Hispanic Americans, as for many others, the surest way to achieve truly massive fame has not been to become politicians or soldiers, but movie actors, pop singers, or sports figures. Among Hispanic-American movie stars, none, with the possible exception of Anthony QUINN, has become more of a household name than Rita Hayworth.

Hayworth was also a gifted dancer whom Fred Astaire declared to be his favorite dancing partner. Astaire, the top male dancer in movie musicals, formed

Rita Hayworth in *Gilda* (Cabrera Archive)

a better-known partnership with Ginger Rogers but reserved his highest praise for Rita Hayworth. (The two women were related by marriage; one of Hayworth's uncles married one of Rogers's aunts.)

Among her other gifts, Astaire admired Rita Hayworth's professionalism. "She learned steps faster than anyone I've ever known," he stated. "I'd show her a routine before lunch. She'd be back right after lunch and have it down to perfection. She apparently figured it out in her mind while she was eating."

Margarita Carmen Cansino was born in Brooklyn, New York, on October 17, 1918. Both her Spanish father and her Irish-American mother were dancers, and Margarita began to learn to dance at the age of six. Her immigrant father could trace many generations of Spanish dancers among his ancestors and ran an act called The Dancing Cansinos. Her mother, who belonged to a long-established U.S. family, had been a member of the Ziegfeld Follies cast.

By the age of 13, Margarita Cansino was on stage, performing Spanish dances with her father. They first danced together publicly in Los Angeles, then in Tijuana, Mexico, next in Santa Monica (on a gambling ship at anchor in the harbor), and finally in Agua Caliente, Mexico. There she was discovered by a Hollywood producer and put under contract by the Fox Film Corporation. In 1935, at age 17, she began to appear in small movie roles with the name Rita (a shortened form of *Margarita*) Cansino in such films as *Under the Pampas Moon, Charlie Chan in Egypt,* and *Trouble in Texas.*

Next, she was set to play the title role in *Ramona* (1936), a remake of a silent movie that had starred Dolores DEL RÍO. But the studio decided instead to give this plum part to a more seasoned actress, Loretta Young. It was the biggest disappointment in Rita's professional career, one she never got over. This frustration may also have helped shape her personality, which was in sharp contrast to her film image. While immensely attractive on camera, in person she was shy, quiet, and unassertive. She was also unhappy most of the time, due to the contrast between the starlike behavior expected of her and her real feelings. At the height of her fame, an article reported that, on an average day, she spent 11 percent of her time crying.

Fox not only changed its mind regarding who should play the lead in *Ramona;* it also declined to renew Rita Cansino's contract. Next, her career was taken over by a promoter, Edward Judson, whom she married in 1937. She was 18, he was 40. He secured a contract for her with Columbia Pictures, and between Judson and Columbia's boss, Harry Cohn, Rita was made over.

Judson and Cohn eliminated everything Hispanic about her. They raised her hairline through electrolysis. Her father had dyed her brown hair black to make her look more Latin; Judson and Cohn dyed it varying shades of strawberry blonde and red.

Finally, Cohn rejected the name *Cansino.* "It sounds too Mexican," was his objection. Judson suggested Rita's mother's Irish maiden name, which was written *Haworth* and pronounced *Hayworth.* Cohn agreed, as long as it was written the way it was said, and *Hayworth* she became.

Her first big role, after many small parts, was in *Only Angels Have Wings* (1939) with Cary Grant. Then came *Blood and Sand* (1941) with Tyrone Power and two movies with Fred Astaire, *You'll Never Get Rich* (1941) and *You Were Never Lovelier* (1942). Rita Hayworth was a star.

Soldiers in World War II had her photograph as their second-favorite pinup, after Betty Grable. She was on the covers of *Time* and *Life* magazines a number of times. Soldiers pasted one photo of her, one of *Life*'s covers that was copied endlessly, on an atom bomb that was tested in the Pacific.

In 1943, Hayworth divorced Judson and had a romance with actor Victor Mature. That same year, she began a five-year marriage with director-actor Orson Welles, a union many called "Beauty and the Brains."

The actress danced with Gene Kelly in *Cover Girl* (1944) and in 1946 played her most famous role, *Gilda,* with Glenn Ford. One of its scenes became especially celebrated in movie history: In it, Hayworth slowly, teasingly removes a long black glove as she dances and sings (her voice was dubbed) a song written for the movie, "Put the Blame on Mame."

Two years later, the actress appeared in *The Loves of Carmen* and *The Lady From Shanghai.* She filmed the latter for Orson Welles, but their marriage was already over. No star outshone her, and she was being paid a quarter of the profits of each of her movies. This was something that superstar Greta Garbo herself did not achieve.

Later in 1948, on a trip to Europe, she was introduced to one of the best-known, wealthiest playboys in the world, Aly Khan. He was a prince of the Ismaili sect of the Muslim religion; this sect is led by hereditary leaders. Rita Hayworth and Aly Khan then fell in love, which was treated as major news around the world and also resulted in moral outrage because Aly Khan was already married to somebody else. He divorced, and in 1949 he and Hayworth married.

She was the first Hollywood actress to marry a prince. Earlier, she had also been courted by the shah (king) of Persia. The degree of excitement the event generated among fans was such that the newlyweds' honeymoon trip to Africa was turned into a documentary movie, *Champagne Safari.* At the wedding, her first initial, spelled out in flowers, was *M:* Privately, she still considered herself Margarita Cansino.

The marriage lasted two years. Aly Khan, with lack of chivalry, called her "boring." She herself said that her husbands had fallen "in love with Gilda"—the alluring image she projected on screen—and then realized that what they got was simply "me." She would marry two more times.

In the 1950s, Hayworth's career had passed its peak. In *Pal Joey* (1957) with Frank Sinatra, she played a glamorous but maturing woman; the main romantic role was played by a newer star, Kim Novak. She was still to play two roles that were among the most rewarding of her career: one in *Separate Tables* (1958) with David Niven and the other in *They Came to Cordura* (1959) with Gary Cooper. She made her last movie in 1972.

In the early 1970s, she also tried to work on stage but was unsuccessful because she had trouble remembering her lines.

Her memory, appearance, and health deteriorated quickly in the years that followed. She was said to be suffering from alcoholism. Only in the 1980s was it learned that she was actually a victim of Alzheimer's disease, which totally incapacitated her in her last years. She remained in the care of her daughter, Princess Yasmin Aga Khan, until her death in 1987.

The movie *The Barefoot Contessa,* filmed with Ava Gardner (1954), is considered to be inspired loosely by Hayworth's life. A biographical television movie appeared in 1983, *Rita Hayworth: The Love Goddess,* starring Lynda CARTER.

Further Reading

Edmonds, Mark. "Rita Hayworth." Available online. URL: http://www.mmje.demon.co.uk/hayworth. htm. Downloaded October 10, 2000.

Kobal, John. *Rita Hayworth.* New York: Norton, 1978.

Leaming, Barbara. *If This Was Happiness: A Biography of Rita Hayworth.* New York: Viking, 1989.

Morella, Joe, and Edward Z. Epstein. *Rita: The Life of Rita Hayworth.* New York: Simon and Schuster, 1983.

✎ Hernández, Antonia (1948–)
activist

Antonia Hernández has devoted her entire professional career to promoting the civil rights of Hispanic Americans. As member and later president and general counsel of the Mexican American Legal Defense and Education Fund (MALDEF), she has launched and pursued many legal battles against discrimination and other evils. She has concentrated particularly on the areas of immigration, voting rights, and education.

Hernández was born on May 30, 1948, in the city of Torreón, Coahuila state, Mexico. Her parents brought her to live in the United States when she was eight. By that time, she had already acquired a strong sense of her Hispanic heritage—"centuries of rich civilization," as she put it. This belief helped her survive difficult times as an impoverished immigrant. It also helped shape her decision to devote her life to improving the lot of Hispanic Americans, many of whom she saw being treated as second-class citizens.

Family life in her East Los Angeles barrio was tight knit, although money was always in very short supply. Her father was a gardener and odd-job man, and both her mother and Antonia herself—the oldest of six children—became occasional odd-job women, too.

Antonia Hernández's family ties were so strong that she later chose to go to law school in Los Angeles rather than at the most prestigious schools in the country in order to stay close to her family. Later still, it took a great amount of cajoling before she would take a job in Washington, D.C.

In elementary school, Hernández was made to study entirely in English despite her lack of familiarity with the language. This was known as the "sink-or-swim system." Years later, she fought hard for children to be allowed to learn with bilingual methods.

Hernández originally intended to become an educator: She graduated from UCLA in 1971 and two years later received a teaching certificate from the school of education at the same university. However, she switched to law school, determining that bad laws were keeping minorities back. She believed these laws needed to be changed before education could successfully put minorities on an equal footing with the majority.

In 1974, Hernández earned a law degree at UCLA and immediately took jobs in which she defended the rights of Hispanics. Initially, she worked for the East Los Angeles Center for Law and Justice and then for the Legal Aid Foundation of Lincoln Heights as director. The call from Washington came in 1978, and she finally accepted a post on the staff of the Judiciary Committee of the United States Senate. Here, she expanded her work to immigration and human-rights issues of all types.

When the chairman of the Judiciary Committee, Senator Ted Kennedy, ran for the Democratic Party's nomination for president in 1980, Hernández worked for his campaign. On a leave of absence from the committee, she served as the campaign's coordinator in the Southwest.

A field of particular interest to the lawyer was ensuring fair voting practices for minorities. She knew that specific sectors of the population were being robbed of their rightful electoral strength because the borders of their voting districts were being defined in an unequal way or through other dishonest practices. Hernández has been highly active in correcting such wrongs through lawsuits.

In 1981 Hernández went to work for MALDEF, first in Washington and later back home in Los Angeles. Joining the organization as a lawyer, she rose to vice president in two years and to president and general counsel in two more.

Los Angeles invited her in 1992 to take a leading post in a community effort called Rebuild LA. She also helps to administrate such organizations as the National Hispanic Leadership Conference and the Latino Museum of History, Art, and Culture.

To assure the rights of immigrants, Hernández proudly fought against the Simpson-Mazzoli Bill, an immigration measure that was regarded as discriminatory against Hispanics. The proposal did not succeed.

Further Reading

Telgen, Diane, and Jim Kamp, eds. *Notable Hispanic American Women.* Detroit: Gale Research, Inc., 1998.

Hernández, Rafael (1892–1965)
composer

Rafael Hernández used music to become one of the prime shapers of the Puerto Rican character of the El Barrio area of New York City. (*El Barrio,* meaning "the neighborhood," is East Harlem in Manhattan). He composed popular tunes—most notably "Lamento Borincano"—that express Puerto Ricans' memories and longing for the idyllic rural past they were forced to abandon for economic reasons. (None of the Hernándezes in this book are related.)

Hernández was born on October 24, 1892, in the port of Aguadilla, Puerto Rico. His musical education was a lifelong process, beginning when he was a child in his hometown and continuing in the U.S. Army during World War I. Late in his life, he became interested in classical music.

After his wartime service, Hernández settled in New York. His presence there in the 1920s helped it become a musical center of the Puerto Rican migration to the mainland. With his sister, he set up Almacenes Hernández, the city's first Hispanic music store. He is also credited with forming its first professional music band with an authentic Hispanic character.

Sitting on the sidewalk outside his store in 1929, Hernández composed "Lamento Borincano" (*borincano, borinqueño,* and *boricua* are words that refer to Puerto Rico). It was a nostalgic tune that quickly became, and remains, one of the acknowledged classics among Latino melodies. It has sometimes been described as almost an anthem for Puerto Ricans.

Hernández's music was successful from the outset. He alternated between New York and Puerto Rico, went on tour in several Latin American countries, and led a succession of music combos, including the Victoria string quartet, which won particular acclaim.

Financial security, however, long eluded him. In the late 1930s and early 1940s, he decided to live and work in Mexico, where he also studied at a conservatory. When he returned to Puerto Rico in 1947, he was given a hero's welcome, complete with a street parade in which he stood in an open car with top island officials alongside him.

Other popular tunes by Hernández are "El Cumbanchero" (The Merrymaker), "Capullito de Alelí" (Wallflower Bud), "Tabú," and "Preciosa" (Precious). He also composed the music for a zarzuela, or Spanish operetta, *Cofresí* (1949).

In the 1950s, Hernández conducted a pop orchestra, the Sinfonietta, at a Puerto Rican radio station, WIPR. He found financial stability there as the station's musical adviser.

Inclining increasingly toward more serious music, Hernández, who was black, composed a number of piano works with African-derived ingredients. These include "Ebano" (Ebony) and "Aristocracia Negra" (Negro Aristocracy).

Rafael Hernández died in San Juan in 1965. He was the subject of a movie filmed by Hispanic producers in the following year, *El Jibarito Rafael (The Peasant Lad Rafael)*.

Further Reading

La Gran Enciclopedia de Puerto Rico. Madrid: Ediciones R, 1976.

❧ **Hernández Cruz, Víctor** (1949–)
writer

Regarded as perhaps the most outstanding Nuyorican poet, Víctor Hernández Cruz very successfully blended his Puerto Rican heritage with his English-language perceptions of the mainland. In so doing, he created a style that appeals to the mainstream, while remaining faithful to his true, bicultural nature.

Hernández Cruz was born in a small Puerto Rican town, Aguas Buenas ("Good Waters"), on February 6, 1949. He moved to New York with his family at the age of five. Nevertheless the influence of Puerto Rico remains clear and strong in both the subject matter and the sound of his poetry, which he began to write while still in school. A strong sense of rhythm, of music, is the backbone of his work, which he terms "Afro-Latin." His work is expertly bilingual as well as richly experimental.

Hernández Cruz has sometimes been classified as a jazz poet. This accounts in part for the praise his texts have received from Allen Ginsberg, a top poet of the U.S. literary movement known as Beat or Beatnik. One of the traits that defined the Beat writers was their love of jazz.

Recognition, if not fame or fortune, soon came to Hernández Cruz. His poems were published in leading journals such as *Ramparts, Evergreen Review,* and the *New York Review of Books*. Two of his poetry collections, *Snaps: Poems* (1969) and *Mainland* (1973), were published by Random House.

In 1976, his book *Tropicalization* received a grant from the Creative Artists Public Service Program. *By Lingual Wholes* (1982)—whose title demonstrates his love of wordplay—received grants from the National Endowment for the Arts and the California Arts Council National.

Life magazine in 1981 listed Víctor Hernández Cruz as one of the most distinguished young poets in the United States. Nevertheless, poetry has not provided him with a living. While continuing to write, he moved to San Francisco in 1973 and began to work as a postal employee. In 1989, he moved back to Puerto Rico. Recent works include *Panoramas* (1997).

Hernández Cruz is a founding member of the Before Columbus Foundation.

Further Reading

Babín, María Teresa, and Stan Steiner, eds. *Borinquen: An Anthology of Puerto Rican Literature*. New York: Vintage Books, 1974.

Kanellos, Nicolás, ed. *Biographical Dictionary of Hispanic Literature in the United States.* Westport, Conn.: Greenwood Press, 1989.

✑ Herrera, Carolina (María Carolina Josefina Pacanins) (1939–) *fashion designer*

A highly regarded member of the small circle of top fashion designers in the United States, Carolina Herrera entered the profession relatively late but established her reputation quickly in a field generally dominated by men.

A longtime resident of New York, Carolina Pacanins (María Carolina Josefina Pacanins) was born in Caracas, Venezuela, in 1939. She married Reinaldo de Herrera in 1969. Two years later, she appeared on the International Best-Dressed List. Thereafter, she remained a regular fixture on this list. The fashion magazine *Elle* named her one of the Ten Most Elegant Women in the World.

The clothes she wore to achieve her well-dressed look began to include items that she herself designed and made. Well connected socially, Herrera increasingly found that her acquaintances among the rich and famous encouraged her to sell her designs. Therefore, in 1981, she accepted the challenge and launched her first line of clothes, a ready-to-wear collection.

Capitalizing quickly on success, her House of Herrera expanded to other clothing areas. She has been particularly associated with sleek, graceful day wear and tasteful evening wear. Avoiding the gaudy, Herrera emphasizes well-cut, elegant and yet comfortable garments made of fine fabrics. There is a decided preference for white, black, and yellow in her color choices.

Her list of clients grew to include many of the top names in U.S. social circles. Herrera designed the bridal gown for the wedding of Caroline Kennedy, daughter of the late president John F. Kennedy.

Jasmine-based Carolina Herrera Perfumes and Carolina Herrera Costume Jewelry are other enterprises she has launched, as well as a Herrera for Men line.

In 1987, she became the third recipient of the MODA Award for Top Hispanic Designer, after Oscar DE LA RENTA and ADOLFO. In accepting the

Carolina Herrera *(Cabrera Archive)*

prize in Washington, D.C., Herrera declared that "This award is very special to me because of my Hispanic heritage. Hispanic women have always had an incredible sense of style and elegance. Hispanics have had an influence in fashion since the fifteenth century. Let's not forget that the greatest of all designers, Cristóbal Balenciaga, was from Spain."

In addition to expressing pride in her roots, she has often found a source of inspiration in 17th- and 18th-century Spanish clothing. Her designs find acceptance among fashionable and well-heeled people of all cultures, for as Herrera has declared, "taste is universal."

Further Reading

"Carolina Herrera." Firstview.com. Available online. URL: http://firstview.com/designerlist/Carolina-Herrera.html. Downloaded October 11, 2000.

✑ Herrera, Paloma (1975–) *ballerina*

Paloma Herrera has enjoyed a meteoric, highly regarded rise in the world of classical ballet, being appointed principal dancer of the American Ballet Theatre (ABT) at the age of 19—the youngest ever in the 50-year history of the distinguished New York ballet company. Within the span of a few years she has collected a dazzling profusion of praise. "To have seen eighteen-year-old Paloma Herrera in Balanchine's *Theme and Variations* . . . was to be in the presence of a near miracle. So fresh, so precise, so buoyant. . . . Here was a prodigy at work," said *Dance Magazine* of her early career. In 1999, a *Dance Magazine* a reader survey chose her as one of the 10 greatest ballerinas of the 20th century. At the same time, CNN and *Time* pronounced her to be one of the "Leaders of the New Millennium."

Like ABT male principal dancer Julio BOCCA, Herrera hails from Argentina. (None of the three Herreras in this book are related.) Paloma (the name means "dove" in Spanish) was born in the Argentine capital, Buenos Aires, on December 21, 1975. Her father was a prominent lawyer and her mother a professor of literature turned decorator. The family was

Paloma Herrera in *Don Quixote* (Photo by Nancy Ellison)

cultured, but was by no means particularly ballet-oriented.

Still, at age seven Paloma suddenly, and most firmly, decided that she wanted to be a ballerina. She pestered her parents until they provided her with dancing shoes, a tutu, and a ballet teacher—and never looked back. The rigorous training demanded by a life in classical ballet—sometimes involving 12 hours a day of practice—was never a hardship, always a delight, and Herrera communicates her pleasure in what she is doing to her audiences.

Herrera's natural ability was immediately obvious to her teachers. At eight she was accepted by Argentina's top ballet school, that of the Colón opera house, and she went on to win awards in Buenos Aires and in Lima, Peru. She made her parents take her very early every morning to the Colón, while it was still closed—because she loved to see the ornate doors open.

At age 11 she studied at the Minsk Ballet School in what was then the Soviet Union. At age 14, in 1990, she was a finalist in the important International Ballet Competition in Varna, Bulgaria. Her performance there caused her to be taken under the wing of the great ballerina Natalia Makarova, who organized her enrollment in English National Ballet classes.

After that, in 1991, she was "scouted" by the School of American Ballet in New York. There, although recognized for her talent, she found that she had to learn to move with a new freedom, after her training in the more formalized, Russian-based tradition ("she was 15, dancing 35," said one teacher).

Her adaptation was lightning fast, however. After only six months she was selected to play the female lead in the school's annual workshop performance.

Two days later, she auditioned for the American Ballet Theatre and was offered a contract. She signed the contract on what she called "the happiest day of my life." Then the 15-year-old dashed over to the telephone to inform her nonplussed parents in Argentina that her stay in New York—originally planned for only six months—was now for keeps.

After joining the ABT corps de ballet in 1991, Herrera was named a soloist in 1993 and became principal dancer in 1995. The appointment, said *Dance View* magazine, was "no surprise to anyone who has been awed by her phenomenal abilities."

Not only has she taken up residence in New York, but in a sense she became a symbol of the city: when *The New York Times Magazine* in 1994 devoted a special issue to the question of "What's New York the capital of now?" its choice for the cover was a photo of Paloma Herrera doing a spectacular backward high kick on a New York street.

Soon Herrera had danced all the major female roles in ballet at the main centers for this activity in the United States and in other countries from Canada and Britain to France and Russia. *Time* praised her "Miraculously delicate musicianship."

Further Reading

American Ballet Theatre. "Paloma Herrera." Available online. URL: http://abt.org/dancers/herrera. html. Downloaded October 10, 2000.

Ellison, Nancy. *Romeo and Juliet: The Love Story in Dance.* New York: Universe Publishing, 1998.

Kaye, Elizabeth. *American Ballet Theatre—A 24-Year Retrospective.* Kansas City: Andrews McMeel, 1999.

Schatz, Howard. *Passion and Line.* New York: Graphics Press, 1997.

✎ **Herrera, Silvestre** (ca. 1925–1945)
soldier

Silvestre Herrera, an army private in World War II, continued fighting even after both his feet were blown off by a land mine. His courage enabled his squad to capture an enemy position. Herrera survived to receive the Congressional Medal of Honor.

A native of El Paso, Texas, Herrera (no relation to Carolina HERRERA) found his place in the honor rolls of his country's military history toward the end of the war, in March 1945. The location was near Mertzwiller in France.

Herrera actually carried out two separate acts of heroism in a row. In the advance toward Germany with Company E, 142nd Infantry, 36th Infantry Division, Private First Class Herrera was pinned down,

along with the rest of his platoon, on a woodland road. Nazi machine gunners were raking the area. The rest of the U.S. soldiers maintained cover while Herrera rose and, in the words of the Medal of Honor citation, "made a one-man frontal assault on a strongpoint." Herrera single-handedly took the position, capturing eight enemy soldiers in the process.

The platoon was then able to move forward again, only to meet a second, similar enemy stronghold. This time, the ground between the U.S. soldiers and the Nazi machine gunners was littered with land mines, some of which exploded from the impact of bullets while others remained intact.

Once again, Herrera rose alone and went on the offensive, oblivious to the risk. He was able to advance but then tripped a land mine, and it exploded. Herrera was flung to the ground, his legs now mangled stumps. Yet, the private kept on shooting. It was not wild firing; ignoring the gruesome pain, the horror of the maiming, and the blood that kept flowing out of him, Herrera "pinned down the enemy with accurate rifle fire while a friendly squad captured the enemy gun by skirting the minefield and rushing in from the flank."

A second position had been wrested from the enemy, thanks to Herrera. Only after it fell could the blood-soaked soldier receive medical assistance.

Six months later, in awarding him the United State.'s highest decoration for battlefield distinction, the government commended Herrera for his "magnificent courage, extraordinary heroism, and willing self-sacrifice."

Further Reading

The Committee on Veterans' Affairs, United States Senate. *Medal of Honor Recipients 1863–1978.* Washington, D.C.: U.S. Government Printing Office, 1979.

✎ **Hidalgo, Edward** (1912–1995)
government official

A successful lawyer in private practice, Edward Hidalgo was appointed assistant secretary and later secretary of the U.S. Navy. By holding this position, he showed that Hispanics could reach the top echelons of the U.S. armed forces—not only within their military ranks, but also in civilian positions. He also worked to boost Hispanic-American enrollment in the navy.

Hidalgo was born in Mexico on October 12, 1912. He changed his name from Eduardo to Edward after arriving in the United States. He became a U.S. citizen, studied law, and made his career in the United States, although he obtained an additional law degree in Mexico.

After graduating magna cum laude from Holy Cross College in Washington, D.C., in 1933, Hidalgo obtained a doctorate from the Columbia Law School in New York in 1936. He added his Mexican law degree almost a quarter of a century later, in 1959. He then founded and was a partner in a law firm in Mexico City.

Hidalgo saw wartime service in the United States Navy as a lieutenant, beginning in 1942. After leaving the service in 1946, Hidalgo practiced law in a succession of firms, including one company's Paris office from 1966 to 1972. In 1972, he was appointed to a government post in the United States as special assistant and later federal counsel to the United States Information Agency. He worked as congressional liaison for the agency until 1976.

Hidalgo also maintained a connection with the armed forces. He took part in a special group, called the Eberstadt Committee, which studied questions related to the unification of military services. He was awarded a commendation ribbon from the navy for this work.

In addition, he served as special assistant to two secretaries of the navy. In 1977 the Department of the Navy appointed him assistant secretary. Hidalgo's performance in that office led to his promotion to secretary in 1979. He served until 1981, when he returned to private law practice.

Hidalgo's role in attracting Hispanic Americans to the navy was recognized at a 1987 Washington special ceremony to honor Hispanics in the U.S. armed services. The period of his connection with the navy was one in which Hispanic participation in the service increased markedly. There were only five Hispanic cadets at the U.S. Naval Academy in

1976; a decade later the number had risen to more than 200.

Hidalgo (whose name originally meant a member of the minor nobility in Spain) received a knighthood from the government of Sweden in 1963. In 1980, while he was secretary of the navy, the Mexican government decorated him with the Aztec Eagle Award.

He died in 1995.

Further Reading

Meier, Matt. S. *Mexican American Biographies.* Westport, Conn.: Greenwood Publishing Group, 1988.

Unterburger, Amy L., and Jane L. Delgado, eds. *Who's Who Among Hispanic Americans.* Detroit: Gale Research, Inc., 1993.

Hijuelos, Oscar (1951–) *writer*

A vivid chronicler of the Cuban immigrant experience in the United States in the 1940s and early 1950s, Oscar Hijuelos is the second Hispanic American to have won the Pulitzer Prize; the first was William Carlos WILLIAMS.

Hijuelos's working-class parents emigrated from Cuba to the United States in the 1940s. Their son Oscar was born in New York City on August 24, 1951.

Unlike many other authors who are first- or second-generation immigrants, Hijuelos obtained a solid academic grounding in creative writing. He graduated from City College of New York in 1975 with a B.A. degree in English and obtained a master's degree in English and writing from the same institution the following year. After working at the TDI Winston Network, he began to teach in 1989 at Hofstra University in Long Island.

Because of his education, Hijuelos has fit into mainstream literary circles to a degree matched by few other Latino writers. As he began to write short stories and then the novels that established his reputation, he began to collect major awards and fellowships. These include the Ingram Merrill Award for fiction in 1982, a National Endowment for the Arts Fellowship in 1985, an American Institute of Arts and Letters Rome Prize, also in 1985, and a Guggenheim Fellowship in 1990. He was also a finalist in 1989 in both the National Book Critics Circle Award and the National Book Foundation's National Book Award.

Hijuelos (whose name, in Spanish, can be translated as "young offspring") published his first novel in 1983, *Our House in the Last World.* His second, in 1989, *The Mambo Kings Play Songs of Love,* was treated as a major literary event. It was given top billing in the catalogue of one of the most prestigious U.S. publishing houses, Simon & Schuster, and a launch the size of which had never before been provided to a work by a Hispanic-American writer. Both works have been criticized for coming close to stereotyping their characters. Their portrayal of macho attitudes and alcoholism has been both condemned as a negative image of the society shown and praised as a mature evaluation of real social flaws. There is, however, general agreement on the skill and intensity of Hijuelos's writing.

The Mambo Kings Play Songs of Love covered terrain that mainstream English-language fiction had not yet explored, capturing a particular moment in time when mambo music and the personality of Desi ARNAZ had America enthralled. The book won the Pulitzer Prize for fiction in 1990 and was turned into a movie, *The Mambo Kings,* in 1992.

More recently, Hijuelos published *Empress of the Splendid Season* in 1999.

Further Reading

Carlson, Lori, ed. *Cool Salsa: Bilingual Poems on Growing Up Latino in the United States.* New York: Ballantine, 1995.

Hijuelos, Oscar. *Empress of the Splendid Season.* New York: HarperCollins, 1999.

Riley, C. *Contemporary Literary Criticism.* Detroit: Gale Group, 1973–

✎ Hinojosa-Smith, Rolando (1929–   )
writer

One of the most widely read and admired Chicano writers, Rolando Hinojosa-Smith has often been compared to William Faulkner, the novelist who invented and peopled a place, Yoknapatawpha County, Mississippi, as a setting for his narratives about the Old South. Similarly, Hinojosa-Smith created Belken County in southern Texas. His books have painted a rich portrait of the lower Río Grande valley, where Mexican and U.S. cultures overlap.

His work goes far beyond regional description, however. By detailing Belken County with love, concern, and skill, Hinojosa-Smith has made it universal.

Belken County is the site of the equally fictional Klail City. All of the author's works, including poems and even a detective story, are meant to be seen as forming part of one vast literary canvas entitled the Klail City Death Trip Series.

Born in the town of Mercedes, Texas, on January 21, 1929, Hinojosa-Smith emphasizes his bicultural roots by use of a hyphen to join the surname of his father, Manuel Hinojosa, with that of his Anglo mother, Carrie Smith. (Sometimes, however, his name is published as simply Hinojosa).

The Hinojosas trace their history in the Río Grande valley area to 1749. The Smiths, originally from Illinois, arrived after the Civil War and became bilingual, too. Hinojosa-Smith writes alternately in Spanish and English. Some of his books are published first in one language and then republished in the other.

At the age of 15, while in high school in Mercedes, Hinojosa-Smith published some writings in a literary magazine, *Creative Bits,* but did not publish again for almost 30 years.

He enlisted in the army at age 17 and then began university studies. He was called back into active service as a second lieutenant during the Korean War. Following his war years, he returned to his studies and worked in a variety of jobs, including high school teacher, before he became a university teacher and administrator.

Hinojosa-Smith obtained a B.A. degree in 1953 from the University of Texas in Austin, an M.A. from the New Mexico Highlands University in Las Vegas 10 years later, and a Ph.D. from the University of Illinois in Urbana in 1969. His career as an educator took him to Trinity University in San Antonio, Texas;

Texas A&I University in Kingsville; the University of Minnesota in Minneapolis; and the University of Texas.

Hinojosa-Smith had been writing continuously, but he did not publish his first novel until 1973: *Estampas del Valle y Otras Obras/Sketches of the Valley and Other Works*. Here, he began to weave his tapestry about the lives of ordinary Mexican Americans and Anglos in the Río Grande area. It won a Chicano literature prize, the Quinto Sol Award. Its English edition was published in a revised form as *The Valley* in 1983.

Hinojosa-Smith's second novel also received immediate recognition, winning Cuba's widely respected Casa de las Américas (House of the Americas) award. It was published in Cuba in 1976 as *Klail City y Sus Alrededores (Klail City and Its Surroundings)* and in a U.S. Spanish-language edition the following year as *Generaciones y Semblanzas (Generations and Portrayals)*. It came out in English in 1987 as *Klail City: A Novel*.

Hinojosa-Smith's Korean War experiences formed the background for his next work, a book of poems, *Korean Love Songs from Klail City Death Trip* (1980). The following year he took up fiction again in *Mi Querido Rafa*, translated as *Dear Rafe* in 1985. He followed with *Rites and Witnesses* (1982), *Partners in Crime: A Rafe Buenrostro Mystery* (1985), *Claros Varones de Belken/Fair Gentlemen of Belken County* (1986), and *Becky and Her Friends* in 1989.

Hinojosa-Smith has also written short stories, articles, and scholarly pieces on Chicano literature, including coauthorship of a biography of his colleague Tomás RIVERA.

He is director of the Texas Center for Writers, is a fellow of the Hispanic Society and of the Society of Spanish and Spanish-American Studies, and has been chairman of the Modern Language Association's Commission on Literature.

Further Reading

Bruce-Novoa, Juan. *Chicano Authors: Inquiry by Interview*. Austin: University of Texas Press, 1980.

Lee, Joyce Glover. *Rolando Hinojosa and the American Dream*. Denton: University of North Texas Press, 1997.

Lomelí Francisco, and Carl Shirley, eds. *Chicano Writers, First Series*. Detroit: Gale Research, Inc., 1989.

Saldívar, José David. *The Rolando Hinojosa Reader: Essays Historical and Critical*. Houston: Arte Público Press, 1984.

∾ Huerta, Dolores (Dolores Fernández)
(1930–) *activist*

A founder of the Farm Workers Association (which became the United Farm Workers, UFW), Dolores Huerta was the right hand of its leader, César CHÁVEZ. As the first vice president of that trailblazing union, she quickly emerged as a powerful leader and a skilled organizer and negotiator. A battler for social justice and human rights, she gave women of all heritages a new role model.

The feminist magazine *Ms.* called Huerta "the La Pasionaria of the farm workers," comparing her to another Dolores—the fiery, legendary leader on the Republican side in the Spanish Civil War, Dolores "La Pasionaria" Ibarruri.

Huerta appears in Chicano murals and ballads. Her life's work has earned her shelves of awards: she was the first Hispanic American to be inducted into the United States Women's Hall of Fame. In the 1990s, she continued to campaign for causes such as immigrants' rights and the elimination of dangerous pesticides that compromise the health of farmworkers and their families.

Dolores Fernández was born on April 10, 1930, in Dawson, New Mexico, a mining town where her father was a coal miner as well as migrant farmworker during the beet-picking season. Though her parents separated, she learned from both of them. Her father became a labor activist and New Mexico state representative, whose uncompromising nature quickly caused his political career to be cut short. Her mother, who took her to live in Stockton, California, was an enterprising, determined woman who encouraged her children to be active and to aim high.

Working and saving, Huerta's mother eventually managed to buy a small, working-class hotel. Huerta and her brothers helped their mother run it. Her mother sometimes let poor farmworkers' families stay at the hotel for free.

After high school, Dolores Fernández entered Stockton College, held diverse jobs, married and divorced early, graduated, and became a schoolteacher. However, after a time she gave this up to seek a more immediate way to help her community. "I realized one day that as a teacher I couldn't do anything for the kids who came to school barefoot and hungry," she would say later.

In 1952, she accepted an invitation to work for a grassroots activist group, the Community Service Organization (CSO). It was while working for the CSO that she first met César Chávez and also her second husband, Ventura Huerta. (She would keep his name even after they divorced.)

Later still, Huerta started a third family with Chávez's brother Richard. She had a total of 11 children. Until her children were grown, she had to face the hard struggles that bind women who have both active careers and families to raise.

For the CSO, Dolores Huerta, a gifted, inspiring speaker, performed a wide array of services, including voter registration drives and lobbying in the state capital of Sacramento. But she became increasingly interested in doing something to help farm laborers: they had been unable to form unions and were among the most exploited workers in the country. When César Chávez left the CSO to devote himself to trying to organize the farmworkers, Huerta soon followed. She joined in the founding of the union, a milestone in both labor and Chicano history, and when the union went on strike it benefited from her expertise and sheer drive as Chávez's chief lieutenant. The name *Huerta* means "orchard" in Spanish, but because of some similarity with the Spanish word for "strike," namely *huelga,* Dolores Huerta came to be nicknamed *Dolores Huelga.*

Huerta has been a driving force behind all UFW activity throughout the years, including its political lobbying through the Citizenship Participation Day Department. She has carried on the union's work after Chávez's death.

In 1988, while demonstrating in San Francisco, she was clubbed by the police, suffering six broken ribs and a ruptured spleen. Her spleen had to be removed. The attack was proven to have been unprovoked, and the government was forced pay her a record amount in compensation. In addition, the San Francisco Police Department was forced to take steps to prevent the use of unnecessary force by its officers.

Huerta's activism remained unabated. In 1998, she was named one of *Ms.* magazine's three Women of the Year and was proclaimed one of the "100 Most Important Women of the 20th Century" by the *Ladies Home Journal.* She was a founding board member of the Majority Foundation, a feminist organization. As such, she participated in 2000 in a symposium, "Stopping Sweatshop Slavery and Servitude" in Baltimore.

Further Reading

"Dolores Huerta: The UFW's Grand Lady of Steel." Lared Latina. Available online. URL: http://www.inconnect.com/~rvazquez/huerta.html. Downloaded October 10, 2000.

Levy, Jacques E. *César Chavez: Autobiography of La Causa.* New York: W.W. Norton & Co., 1974.

Matthiessen, Peter. *Sal Si Puedes: César Chávez and the New American Revolution.* New York: Random House, 1969.

Meister, Dick, and Anne Loftis. *A Long Time Coming: The Struggle to Unionize America's Farm Workers.* New York: Macmillan, 1977.

Perez, Frank. *Dolores Huerta.* Orlando, Fla.: Raintree Steck-Vaughn, 1995.

Taylor, Ronald B. *Chávez and the Farmworker.* Boston: Beacon Press, 1975.

Iglesias, Enrique (1975–) *singer, lyricist*

With just his first four albums, Enrique Iglesias has sold 18 million copies and collected hundreds of platinum and gold testimonials to his sales power around the world. He also drives female audiences wild in the tradition of his father, Julio IGLESIAS. When the actor Will Smith chose Enrique to contribute to the soundtrack of his movie *The Wild, Wild West* (1998), it was because he had watched the audience at one of his concerts and, as he told an interviewer, "you've just never heard this kind of sustained screaming." Iglesias made a major impact on that movie soundtrack with his rendition of the song "Bailamos" (We Dance), his biggest hit, in a mix of English and Spanish.

Born in Madrid, Spain, on May 8, 1975, Enrique Iglesias has been based in Miami since the age of seven. Despite his father's example, becoming a singer was not his obvious career choice; he initially studied business management. But from there he turned first to modeling and thereafter to singing. A similar progression marked the trajectory of his older brother, Julio Iglesias Jr., born in Madrid on February 25, 1973, who wanted to be a football player but became a model and then a singer. Both have striven to adopt styles different from that of their famous, and famously suave, father—despite the unfailing support for their careers expressed by Julio Sr.

In Enrique's case, particularly, the difference has been to be grittier, not only in his voice but in his appearance, with stubble on his cheeks and casual clothes on his six foot, one inch frame.

Enrique Iglesias began writing lyrics—first in English, then in Spanish—as a teenager, in what he regarded as a form of intimate diary which he did not show to others. He still considers writing more of an accomplishment than singing.

When he began to sing, both his own songs and those of others, he likewise did it secretly, recording under the name Enrique Martínez. He did not tell his father about his first CD until it was finished. Enrique has repeatedly emphasized that this was not due to a family rift or even rivalry but to a desire to establish himself on his own. The main influence which he admits receiving from Julio Sr. is "a work ethic. He works very hard at his music and so do I." The *Los Angeles Times* reported in a review: "Displaying a vulnerability that his father Julio would never allow his fans to see, Iglesias presented himself as less of a superstar and more of a poet."

The young Iglesias also marks the difference between himself and other successful Hispanic singers of his own time. He is a great fan of Marc ANTHONY and Ricky MARTIN, he told an interviewer, "but they're tropical. I'm from Spain. I'm much more Mediterranean. . . . There's a difference between salsa and flamenco." And as he points out, "There just can't be one Latin guy doing pop."

When his first album, *Enrique Iglesias,* appeared in 1995, its success was immediate. It had sold 1 million copies in three months, and ultimately almost 6 million were sold. The first three albums, all sung in Spanish before Iglesias began to turn to English with the single "Bailamos," together topped the 13-million-copy mark.

Of 12 singles, 10 reached number one on the *Billboard* Latin song chart, and the other two came very close, making it to the number-two slot.

Iglesias's success—also seen in big-selling world tours and in a 1996 Grammy Award for best Latin pop performer, as well as other awards—was viewed as a long-term proposition by the music industry. This was demonstrated in 1999 with a six-album contract amounting to 40 million dollars, and by the sales of his fourth English-language album, *Enrique,* which quickly surpassed the 5-million-copy mark.

Further Reading

UNI/Interscope. "Enrique Iglesias." Available online. URL: http://www.enriqueig.com. Downloaded October 10, 2000.

❧ Iglesias, Julio (1944–) *singer*

A Spaniard who has made his home in Miami for almost 20 years, Julio Iglesias is arguably the most successful recording artist of all time. He wrote in his memoirs, *Entre El Cielo y El Infierno (Between Heaven and Hell):* "Sinatra has sold one quarter of the records I have." Iglesias has earned 2,600 platinum and gold records. He has sold more than 250 million albums.

Initially little known in the United States despite having established a huge following in other countries, Iglesias achieved the crossover to mainstream fame after he began to sing in English and recorded hit singles together with U.S. singing stars Diana Ross and Willie Nelson. He would later make a record with the singer he used as a measure of success—Frank Sinatra.

His worldwide earnings in 1994 totaled $13 million; he earned $15 million in 1993. Both years, he was the only Hispanic among the top 40 money earners in the entertainment industry.

Julio Iglesias, whose mother came from a Puerto Rican family, was born in Madrid, Spain, on September 23, 1944. As a youth, he was sent to religious schools and initially set out to be a lawyer before taking an entirely different direction toward becoming a professional soccer player.

Iglesias (the name in Spanish means "churches") was goalkeeper of the youth division of the front-ranking Real Madrid soccer team. He was singled out as a rising star after becoming—during practice—one of the few goalies ever to catch a penalty shot kicked by the Argentine ace Alfredo Di Stéfano.

But at the age of 19, while driving a car on a highway near Madrid, Iglesias took a curve too fast and crashed. The accident left him entirely paralyzed. It took his doctors a long time to discover the precise cause—a blood clot in his spine, invisible to X rays. After surgery, he made a slow, painful, but virtually complete recovery; a career in soccer, however, was now out of the question. Instead, Iglesias turned to songwriting and singing.

In 1968, he won first prize in Spain's Benidorm Song Festival, and his career as a crooner took off. Displaying matinee-idol good looks while delivering romantic songs in a satiny voice, he collected millions of fans around the world, filled stadiums on concert tours, broke sales records with his albums, and began to receive as many as 5,000 letters a week, including numerous marriage proposals.

Indian Creek, in Miami Beach, became his place of residence because of the sunny weather, the beauty of the place, the quick connections everywhere, and the Hispanic flavor around him. Another reason, he added, is that U.S. citizens "aren't offended if you ride in a Rolls; they don't scratch it with a knife when nobody's looking or spit on the windshield as happens in some places. They are delighted to see that you are a person who is on the crest of the wave."

Among Iglesias's top-selling albums are *Julio Iglesias* (1972), *De Niña a Mujer* (*From Girl to Woman,* 1981), *Momentos* (*Moments,* 1982), *Un Hombre Solo* (*A Man Alone,* 1987) and *Nonstop* (1988).

Further Reading

Anchor Marketing Inc. "The Official Julio Iglesias International Fan Club." Available online. URL: http://julioiglesiasfanclub.com. Downloaded October 11, 2000.

Daly, Marsha. *Julio Iglesias.* New York: St. Martin's Press, 1986.

J

Jiménez, José (José Francisco Jiménez) (1946–1969) *soldier*

Mexican-born José Jiménez, a lance corporal in the U.S. Marine Corps in the Vietnam War, sacrificed his life in a daring, solitary advance against North Vietnamese soldiers, for which he was posthumously awarded the Congressional Medal of Honor.

Jiménez was born in Mexico City on March 20, 1946. He came to the United States and joined the marines in Phoenix, Arizona. He was subsequently sent to Vietnam. He was only 23 years old on the day in 1969 when he died, demonstrating what his citation called "indomitable courage, aggressive fighting spirit, and unfaltering devotion to duty."

Jiménez's unit in Company K, 3rd Battalion, 7th Marines, 1st Marine Division, was sent against the enemy in Quang Nam province of South Vietnam. Advancing, it found itself under extremely heavy fire from regular North Vietnamese army troops. The latter had the advantage of attacking from entrenched and camouflaged positions. "L/Cpl. Jiménez reacted by seizing the initiative and plunging forward," according to his citation.

In his first rush, Jiménez killed several enemy soldiers, quieting the antiaircraft gun they had been fir-

ing. Immediately, the corporal continued his one-man advance.

"Shouting encouragement to his companions," Jiménez dodged, weaved, and jumped, coming within 10 feet of a trench where another group of enemy soldiers were maintaining steady streams of fire. He destroyed this emplacement as well.

Most of the surviving enemy soldiers in the area now aimed straight at him. Jiménez, however, resumed his progress, now at a rapid, relentless crawl. He was about to reach a point where he could have killed at least one more enemy soldier when he was finally hit by a deadly round of fire.

Further Reading

The Committee on Veterans' Affairs, United States Senate. *Medal of Honor Recipients 1863–1978.* Washington, D.C.: U.S. Government Printing Office, 1979.

Jiménez, Luis (Luis Alfonso Jiménez Jr.) (1940–) *artist*

Luis Jiménez Jr. has worked in a variety of artists' media, especially with modern materials. He has made his mark with large sculptures of colored fiberglass,

141

Luis Jiménez installing one of his sculptures, *Vaquero*
(*Luis Jiménez*)

The younger Jiménez learned the skills of the trade at his father's side. He helped make neon signs by the age of six, coming to understand and to share his father's fascination with the border between commercial crafts, even kitsch, and "high" or "real" art.

Jiménez Sr. yearned to poke through that shadowy border. Years later, Luis Jr., as a trained artist, toyed with the borderline from the other side, taking the strengths of each.

Jiménez graduated from the University of Texas in Austin in 1964 with a degree in fine arts. He received a fellowship from the National University of Mexico that same year. This was followed by other fellowships and awards from organizations ranging from the Francis J. Greenburger Foundation and Hassam Fund to the National Endowment for the Arts and the American Academy of Arts and Letters.

He lived in New York for a while but made his home in Hondo, New Mexico. Jiménez has exhibited his works at major sites, including the Long Beach Museum of Art in California, the Whitney Museum in New York City, the Denver Art Museum, and the Smithsonian Institution in Washington, D.C.

For the subject matter of his fiberglass spectaculars, Jiménez used such emblems of the frontier as a coyote and an Indian brave. *Sodbuster,* a figure with a big white beard, creating a cascade of earth as he advances with his hand-held plow, stands in Fargo, North Dakota. The city of Buffalo commissioned a sculpture of a steelworker in 1982.

The first touring retrospective of his career, a major exhibition of his fiberglass sculptures plus other works, was organized at the Tacoma Art Museum in 1998. Jiménez won the National Endowment for the Arts award in 1990 and 1997 and the Artist of the Year Award from the Art League of Texas in 1998.

One of Jiménez's sculptures, *Vaquero* (1977)—the first public commission he received, from the city of Houston—is his reminder to the United States that the cowhand was a Mexican invention. As he declared in an interview, "It was the Spaniards who brought the cows and the horses, and it was

meant for display in public spaces, and he is known for recasting well-known historical elements from the Southwest, the Old West, and other traditions and renewing them vibrantly for modern viewers.

Jiménez (not related to Vietnam War hero José JIMÉNEZ) was born in El Paso, Texas, on July 30, 1940. He comes from what he calls a minority within a minority, "Mexican Protestants, a very small group with a strong sense of community."

His future career was strongly influenced by the work of his father, a signmaker with a nationwide reputation for large-scale neon signs. Luis Jiménez Sr. was granted such unusual commissions as that for a concrete bear, made for a dry-cleaning establishment, and one for a huge horse's head with eyes that lit up, created for a drive-in movie theater.

Mexicans who became the cowboys (in Spanish, *vaqueros*). It wasn't John Wayne who was the original cowboy."

Further Reading

Unterburger, Amy L., and Jane L. Delgado, eds. *Who's Who Among Hispanic Americans.* Detroit: Gale Research, Inc., 1993.

Juliá, Raúl (Raúl Rafael Carlos Juliá Arcelay) (1940–1994) *actor*

Widely praised for his versatility, Raúl Juliá was regarded as José FERRER's heir as the most successful Hispanic actor on Broadway. He also became one of the busiest actors in Hollywood, sought after both for leading roles and character parts. In one count conducted between 1987 and 1989, Juliá, with eight movies and one TV movie, shared the top of the Hollywood list with Gene Hackman and Charlie SHEEN (also a Hispanic actor), who had each made nine movies in that same time span.

Raúl Rafael Carlos Juliá Arcelay was born in San Juan, Puerto Rico, on March 9, 1940. He was described as a shy child who bloomed when he played a surprisingly energetic devil in a first-grade school play. He obtained a B.A. degree in liberal arts from the University of Puerto Rico, but the law career his parents had envisioned did not attract him.

Acting had been his goal, he recalled later, ever since he saw Errol Flynn in *The Adventures of Robin Hood,* as a boy. He considered going to Italy to study acting there, but was instead talked into trying his luck in New York. He arrived there in 1964.

His first performance on the mainland was in a Spanish-language production of a Spanish classic, Pedro Calderón de la Barca's *La Vida es Sueño (Life Is a Dream).* The classics, particularly Shakespeare, were to remain a mainstay of Juliá's stage career; musicals were another.

After spending time in street theater performing in both English and Spanish, in 1966 Juliá began to be cast by producer Joseph Papp in roles in the New York Shakespeare Festival and in other works staged in New York. Juliá first appeared on Broadway in 1968. By the time of his first film ap-

pearance in 1971, Juliá was a recognized theatrical name. Papp said he always appeared "larger than life" on stage.

Juliá's career in the theater earned him four Tony award nominations: for *The Two Gentlemen of Verona* (1971), *Where's Charley?* (1974), *The Threepenny Opera* (1976, playing the character Mack the Knife), and *Nine* (1982). Other highlights of his stage work included *Hamlet, Arms and the Man,* and *Man of La Mancha.*

In films, he began with roles in *The Panic in Needle Park* (1971), *Been Down So Long It Looks Like Up to Me* (1971), *The Eyes of Laura Mars* (1978), and *One From the Heart* (1982). He hit the big time as an imprisoned Latin American revolutionary in *Kiss of the Spider Woman* in 1985. Other major roles for Juliá were in *Moon Over Parador* and *Tequila Sunrise* (both 1988), *Romero* and *Mack the Knife* (both 1989), and

Raúl Juliá *(Cabrera Archive)*

The Addams Family and *Addams Family Values* (1991 and 1993).

Juliá did comparatively little television work but did appear on *Sesame Street* in the 1971 season and played the title role in *The Richest Man in the World: The Story of Aristotle Onassis* in 1988. He played a Brazilian activist who is murdered in *The Burning Season* in 1994.

In 1982, *Current Biography* noted that Juliá's strength as a stage actor was "an uncommon ability to establish a conspiratorial bond with audiences," but this capacity to charm his audience worked against him when he played the villain Edmund in *King Lear.*

In the movie *Tempest* (1982), a modern version of Shakespeare's *The Tempest,* he played the Greek goatherd Kalibanos (a stand-in for Shakespeare's character, Caliban). One of the other characters pronounces him "attractive, in a Third World sort of way." This all but sums up how Juliá was viewed for much of his career.

Juliá was one of the first Hispanic actors to avoid entirely being typecast in Hispanic or other "exotic" roles, although he played his share of those. He managed to break out of the stereotype despite the fact that, unlike his fellow Puerto Rican actor José Ferrer, he retained a Hispanic accent.

Ferrer himself noted in an interview that Juliá "has done everything, played Englishmen and every other kind of nationality, and he speaks with a trace of an accent; but he's so successful and so good, that he seems to have been able to overcome that obstacle."

Juliá was active in the Hispanic Organization of Latin Actors (HOLA) and in philanthropic work through New York's Project Hunger. He died in 1994, following a stroke. The next year, he was awarded a posthumous Golden Globe award as best actor in a TV miniseries or telefilm for his 1994 work in *The Burning Season.*

Further Reading

Brainard, Nathan. "Raul Julia Biography." Available online. URL: http://www.geocities.com/Hollywood/Set/4596/bio.htm

Stefoff, Rebecca. *Raúl Juliá.* New York: Chelsea House Publishers, 1994.

 ## Jurado, Katy (María Cristina Jurado García) (1927–) *actress*

Katy Jurado has played a number of significant roles in Hollywood movies, most notably as Gary Cooper's Mexican girlfriend in *High Noon.* She has invested her characters with dignity, managing to do this even when those characters could have merely been Hispanic stereotypes.

María Cristina Jurado García was born in Guadalajara, Mexico, on January 16, 1927. She started out as an actress in Mexico's film industry in 1943. Even after she began to act in U.S. movies in the 1950s, she occasionally took roles in Mexican films, including *El Bruto* (1952), by the famed Spanish-born director Luis Buñuel.

Jurado's entry into the U.S. movie industry came by way of a 1951 English-language motion picture that Hollywood shot in Mexico, called *The Bullfighter and the Lady.* On the strength of her performance in that movie, she was invited to Hollywood by producer Stanley Kramer, who was preparing to shoot the western *High Noon* (1952), which proved to be the highlight of her career. Her performance as store-and-saloon owner Helen Ramírez was one of the most favorable portrayals of a Mexican ever in a U.S. film, and Jurado made the most of it.

The script followed a traditional theme in U.S. movies featuring Latinos: A Latino and an Anglo compete for a woman and the Anglo wins her in the end. Or, the Anglo who falls for a Latina never really wants to stay with her for life. Thus, in *High Noon,* Will Kane, the lawman played by Gary Cooper, used to be Helen Ramírez's lover, but he marries Amy, the Anglo beauty played by Grace Kelly.

Yet, despite this formula, Ramírez is shown to be the bravest and most dignified character in the cowardly town defended by Kane. Ramírez tells Kane's new bride how she should behave—she should back her husband instead of abandoning him in his hour of greatest need.

Hollywood regarded Jurado, as one studio put it, as "a dark-haired Mexican actress with pouting lips and flashing eyes." Still, the actress said in an interview that she considered the Mexican film industry was worse than the U.S. industry in offering her only stereotyped roles to play. "They always offered me

Katy Jurado with Karl Malden in *One-Eyed Jacks* *(Cabrera Archive)*

roles as a dangerous woman, with a smoking cigarette between her lips," she said. She believed, however, that "If you're good at your work and respect yourself, they'll respect you."

A description of Katy Jurado in her Hollywood heyday was provided by the Mexican-born U.S. actor Anthony QUINN: "She had everybody nuts with those eyes and that fiery-lady attitude. I was crazy about her. But she was so willful, so proud, so bellicose that nobody dared approach her. People expected her to be sweet like Dolores DEL RÍO or loony like Lupe VÉLEZ. But Katy was different: she was temperamental.

"And that was the kind of role in which the studios typecast her. It was her defense against the roles of docile Indian maidens which were being written in those days."

Jurado played her share of Indian women in movies, including roles in *Arrowhead* with Charlton Heston, *Broken Lance* with Spencer Tracy, and *Stay Away, Joe* with Elvis Presley. *Broken Lance* (1954) won her an Oscar nomination. (Many believed that she should have been awarded one for *High Noon,* for which she did win a Golden Globe nomination). But her diversity was also shown when she played a Hebrew woman in the movie *Barabbas* (1961).

Jurado's other film appearances include *The Man From Del Río, One-Eyed Jacks* (1961) with Marlon Brando, *Pat Garrett and Billy the Kid* (1973), *The Children of Sánchez* (1978), *Under the Volcano* (1984), *The Hi-Lo Country* (1998), and *El evangelio de las maravillas* (1998).

On television, she acted in *A.k.a. Pablo,* a comedy series with Hispanic characters. She also acted in the telefilm *Evita Perón.* Jurado likewise took part in stage productions on Broadway and elsewhere. In Mexico, she was made head of the film industry in the state of Morelos.

In the early 1960s, Katy Jurado married U.S. actor Ernest Borgnine; the union ended in divorce.

Further Reading

Hadley-García, George. *Hispanic Hollywood—The Latins in Motion Pictures.* Secaucus, N.J.: Citadel Press, 1990.

Oshana, Maryann. *Women of Color—A Filmography of Minority and Third World Women.* New York: Garland Publishing, Inc., 1985.

K

Kanellos, Nicolás (1945–) *literary historian and activist*

A major pioneering force to give Hispanic writers access to a readership, Nicolás Kanellos is a tireless activist in the field of gathering and disseminating information about Hispanic history and achievement in the United States. Himself an award-winning nonfiction writer, he founded and heads one of the most important Hispanic publishing houses in the United States, Arte Público Press in Houston.

Kanellos was born in New York City on January 31, 1945. He is Puerto Rican on his mother's side. He earned a B.A. degree from Fairleigh Dickinson University in New Jersey in 1966 and obtained an M.A. in 1968 and a Ph.D. in 1974, both from the University of Texas in Austin.

Kanellos began to teach at Indiana University Northwest in 1973, became professor of Hispanic and classical languages, and then in 1980 moved to the University of Houston, where he has remained.

In 1973, with Luis Dávila, Nicolás Kanellos founded a Hispanic literary journal in Gary, Indiana, *Revista Chicano-Riqueña (Chicano-Rican Review)*. This influential magazine was transformed in 1987 and renamed *The Americas Review*. In 1979, when he moved to Houston, he shifted the magazine's head-

quarters there. That same year, he founded Arte Público Press, which became associated with the University of Houston. Arte Público, where many important voices in Latino literature were first published, is the oldest U.S. Hispanic publishing house currently in existence; the first, Editorial Quinto Sol, went out of business in the 1970s.

Kanellos edited diverse anthologies of Hispanic works, such as *Hispanic Theater in the United States* (1984) and *Short Fiction by Hispanic Writers of the United States* (1992). He also wrote a monograph in 1990 entitled *A History of Hispanic Theater in the United States,* which earned him three book awards.

In 1992, with a Rockefeller Foundation grant, Nicolás Kanellos began a drive to collect every single piece of Hispanic literature produced in the United States from the earliest times to 1960. The undertaking was called Recovering the Hispanic Literary Heritage of the United States.

Although his main field of interest is Hispanic literature, Kanellos also deals with all other aspects of Hispanic life and culture. Along with Claudio Esteva-Fabregat, he is one of the general editors of another monumental project, this one sponsored in the 1990s by Spain's Institute of Ibero-American Cooperation: the four-volume *Handbook of Hispanic Cultures in*

Nicolás Kanellos *(Arte Público Press)*

the United States, published by Arte Público Press. Kanellos is likewise the author of two comprehensive one-volume reference works for a Detroit publishing house, *The Hispanic-American Almanac* (1993), and *Hispanic Firsts: 500 Years of Extraordinary Achievement* (1997).

In 1994, President Bill Clinton appointed Kanellos to the National Council on the Humanities. Among the awards Kanellos has collected are the Coordinating Council of Literary Magazines' Outstanding Editor Award in 1975, the White House Hispanic Heritage Award for Literature in 1988, the Before Columbus Foundation's American Book Award in 1989, the 1995 annual PREMIO award, the 1995 Annual Achievement in Publishing Award from the National Hispanic Academy of Media Arts and Sciences, and the 1996 Annual Hispanic Publication Award. He has also received fellowships from the Ford Foundation National Research Council, Eli Lilly Foundation, and National Endowment for the Humanities.

Further Reading

Kanellos, Nicolás, ed. *Hispanic American Almanac: A Reference Work on Hispanics in the United States.* 2nd ed. Detroit: Gale Group, 1997.

———. *Hispanic Firsts: 500 Years of Extraordinary Achievement.* Detroit: Gale, 1997.

———. *Hispanic Literary Companion.* Detroit: Visible Ink Press, 1996.

———. *Thirty Million Strong: Reclaiming the Hispanic Image in American Culture.* Golden, Colo.: Fulcrum, 1998.

Kanellos, Nicolás, and Helvetia Martell. *Hispanic Periodicals in the United States, Origins to 1960.* Houston, Tx.: Arte Público Press, 1999.

Lamas, Fernando (1915–1982) *actor*

Fernando Lamas played a dashing Latin in many Hollywood movies and TV shows.

Fernando Lamas was born on January 9, 1915, in Buenos Aires, Argentina. He first made his mark as a movie actor there in the 1940s.

During the heyday of the Hollywood contract system, Lamas was signed to the Metro-Goldwyn-Mayer studios. Among the movies he appeared in were *The Avengers* (1950), *Rich, Young and Pretty* (1951), *The Merry Widow* (1952), *The Girl Who Had Everything* (1953), *The Lost World* (1960), *The Magic Mountain* and *The Violent Ones* (both of which he directed), *Kill a Dragon* (1967), *100 Rifles* (1969), *Won Ton Ton, The Dog Who Saved Hollywood* (1976), and *The Cheap Detective* (1978).

After two marriages, Lamas married Hollywood actress Arlene Dahl in the late 1950s and then Esther Williams in 1967. Dahl and Lamas's son, Lorenzo, was born in Santa Monica, California, on January 20, 1958. (Lorenzo Lamas had a starring role in the television series *Falcon Crest*. He has made numerous TV appearances. His movie credits include *Grease* (1978), *Body Rock* (1984) and *Night Warrior*. He has his own film company, Blueline Productions. As a professional race car driver, Lorenzo Lamas won first place in the Toyota Grand Prix of Long Beach, California, in 1985.)

Fernando Lamas, who costarred on Broadway with Ethel Merman in the musical *Happy Hunting,* died in 1982.

Larrazolo, Octaviano (1859–1930) *government official*

Mexican-born Octaviano A. Larrazolo was one of the delegates who fought to ensure that the rights of Mexican Americans would be protected by the 1910 constitution of Santa Fe. Two years later, New Mexico joined the Union as the 47th state. Larrazolo became the state's third governor in 1918. He also briefly served as a U.S. senator for his state.

Larrazolo was born on December 7, 1859, the son of a rancher in the Mexican state of Chihuahua in the hamlet of Allende. In 1871, his family sent him to the U.S. territory of Arizona, where a friend of his parents was bishop. Because this bishop was also his first teacher in the United States, Larrazolo initially wanted to enter the priesthood. After finishing high school in Santa Fe, New Mexico, however, he became an educator instead. He was, first, a schoolteacher in Tucson, Arizona, and then a school principal in a town in Texas called San Elizario. In Arizona, in New Mexico, and in Texas, Larrazolo saw the inequity between the way most Mexican Americans lived and the way their Anglo peers lived. He became a lifelong defender of Mexican-American rights.

In 1884 he took the first in a series of posts as court clerk in El Paso, Texas, won both by appointment and by election. After studying law and becoming a lawyer in 1888, he was elected state attorney for a Texas district.

Larrazolo moved to New Mexico at the age of 35 to practice law and participate in politics. As a member of the Democratic Party, he took part in political races in 1900, 1906, and 1908 but lost every time. As a result, he decided that his own party was secretly undermining his efforts because he was not an Anglo. In 1911, he switched to the Republican Party, only to find, later on, that his views were not popular there either. Anglos in both parties objected to his continually raising the question of Hispanic rights and living conditions.

In 1910, the New Mexico constitutional convention was held in Santa Fe. Larrazolo attended as one of the recognized leaders among the Hispanics, who made up a third of the delegates. Over the objections of some of the others, the Hispanics obtained the inclusion of several articles guaranteeing the civil rights of *nuevomexicanos*—New Mexicans of Mexican descent.

They managed—on paper, at least—to bar all forms of discrimination, including separate teaching facilities. The Hispanics also tried to extend this to ban the separate schooling of blacks, but this was too far ahead of its time in 1910. The U.S. Congress, they were told, would never approve a state constitution containing such a clause.

An Anglo was the first governor of New Mexico in 1912. In 1916, in New Mexico's second gubernatorial race, Larrazolo supported a Hispanic, though his own Republican party had nominated another Anglo. The Hispanic won but soon died in office. In 1918, Larrazolo was nominated and then elected third governor of New Mexico.

Bilingual education was one of the causes he particularly backed while in office, and Larrazolo was generally acknowledged as a good, effective governor. However, the Republican Party did not nominate him

for future terms. He returned to his law practice, although he continued to work for some Republican campaigns.

Larrazolo was considered and then rejected for the appointment of governor of Puerto Rico. He was later defeated in an election for state supreme court justice.

However, in 1928 he ran successfully for the U.S. Senate, where, in addition to his work for the state of New Mexico as a whole, he continued his life's work in support of the rights of Latinos. After only two years in office, he died of a liver disease.

Further Reading

Córdova, Alfred C., and Charles B. Judah. *Octaviano Larrazolo: A Political Portrait.* Albuquerque: University of New Mexico, 1952.

❧ **Limón, José** (José Arcadio Limón)
(1908–1972) *ballet dancer*

Acknowledged as one of the giants of modern dance and especially praised for his intensity and grace, José Arcadio Limón (the last name means "lemon" in Spanish) was born in Culiacán, Sinaloa state, Mexico, in January 1908. He was brought to the United States in 1915 by his parents, who were escaping the turmoil that followed the Mexican Revolution of 1910. They settled in Los Angeles after an initial stay in Arizona. Limón inherited a taste for music and the arts from his parents; his father was a professional musician.

Initially, Limón was interested in a career as a painter and studied art first at the University of California at Los Angeles and later at the New York School of Design. However, he felt entirely out of touch with the art trends of the 1920s, so he gave up his plan of becoming an artist—with no idea what else to do.

In 1928, he had what, to him, was a revelation: he discovered modern dance through a performance of the dancer Harald Kreutzberg. Limón began to study dance with Doris Humphrey and first danced as a member of her company. He excelled to such a degree that, in later days, Humphrey went to work for *him*, becoming artistic director of the dance company Limón founded, José Limón and Dancers.

Almost from the outset, Limón choreographed as well as performed. He initially choreographed Broadway shows before switching to dance recitals in the late 1930s. In 1937, Vermont's Bennington School of Dance awarded him a fellowship in recognition of his choreographic work.

Military service in World War II interrupted his dance career for two years. After the war ended and he was discharged from the service, Limón began his most productive and acclaimed period. The U.S. Department of State sponsored many foreign tours by his company; as well, the Capezio Dance Award was conferred on him in 1965. He was hailed as one of the leaders in his field. Despite the accolades, financial security eluded him for many years.

The principal works Limón choreographed include *The Moor's Pavane* (1949, considered a masterpiece and still performed), *Missa Brevis, Danza de la Muerte, Danzas Mexicanas, The Story of Mankind,* and *La Malinche.* His Mexican heritage, of which he was always very proud, was evident in many of his dances, beginning with their Spanish titles.

Limón also went on frequent working visits to Mexico. Nevertheless, when he was offered the post of head of Mexico's National Academy of Dance, he elected to remain in the United States instead.

Limón mined current events for material for his dances. His *The Traitor* was inspired by the case of Julius and Ethel Rosenberg, the couple executed in the United States in 1953, having been convicted of passing nuclear secrets to the Soviet Union.

A longtime teacher at the prestigious Juilliard School of Music of New York, José Limón also taught at numerous other institutions, including the Connecticut College School of Dance.

Dance Magazine gave him its annual award in 1957. Wesleyan University in Connecticut conferred upon him an honorary doctorate in fine arts. The New York State Council on the Arts in 1964 appointed Limón artistic director of its project, the American Dance Theatre. He died in 1972.

Further Reading

Chujov, Anatole, and P. W. Manchester, eds. *The Dance Encyclopedia.* New York: Simon & Schuster, 1967.

Clarke, Mary, and David Vaughan. *The Encyclopedia of Dance and Ballet.* New York: G.P. Putnam's Sons, 1977.

Dunbar, June, ed. *José Limón: The Artist Re-Viewed.* Newark, N.J.: Harwood Academic Publishers, 2000.

Lewis, Daniel. *The Illustrated Dance Technique of José Limón.* Hightstown, N.J.: Princeton Book Co., 1999.

Limón, José. *José Limón: An Unfinished Memoir.* Middletown, Conn.: Wesleyan University Press, 1999.

Martínez, Al. *Rising Voices: Profiles of Hispano-American Lives.* New York: New American Library, 1974.

❧ Longoria, Félix (1926–1945) *soldier*

Félix Longoria was one of the many Hispanic Americans who gave their lives for their country during World War II. He is noted for becoming a victim of posthumous discrimination in an incident that triggered widespread anger and led people to organize to advance the civil rights of Hispanics.

Among the almost half-million Hispanics who fought in World War II, more would win the Medal of Honor than those of any other ethnic background. Hispanics also enlisted as volunteers in the armed forces in a higher proportion than others. But all this had little effect on the bigots who discriminated against Latinos. The Longoria case, though, made a difference.

Little is known about the life of Félix Longoria, who became such an important Hispanic symbol. A Mexican American, he was born in 1926 and raised in the Texas town of Three Rivers, south of San Antonio. He also married there.

In 1944, he was drafted into the army. The following year, Longoria was sent to the Philippines. The Japanese had occupied the islands since 1942 and were holding out against a U.S. drive to free the country. Longoria was killed in combat on the island of Luzon in 1945, near the end of the war.

Initially, like many of the war dead who were buried where they fell, Longoria received burial in the Philippines. In 1948, however, his body was sent back to his widow.

The trouble began there: There was only one mortician in Three Rivers, and he refused to make funeral arrangements for Longoria. War hero or not, this funeral parlor was not about to handle the burial of any "Mexican." This set off a furor. Across the country, newspapers devoted front-page stories to the Longoria case. The Good Neighbor Commission of Texas called the funeral parlor's decision discriminatory.

Most upset, of course, were Mexican Americans. In 1949, a *corrido*—a form of folk ballad usually referring to current events—was composed, called *Discrimination Against a Martyr*. This song about Longoria said, in part:

> The mortuary of his home town
> Denied him a funeral;
> That is discrimination arrived
> Against a poor human being.
> Not even in a cemetery
> Do they admit a Mexican.

Mexican-American war veterans held a major meeting in Corpus Christi, Texas, in 1948 to debate the Longoria affair and other cases of injustice against them. As a result, they created a new organization to spread the word and rally for their rights: the American GI Forum (AGIF), led by Dr. Héctor Pérez GARCÍA.

Dr. García worked hard on the Longoria case, and through AGIF the federal government was forced to act. One of the senators for Texas, Lyndon B. Johnson, later president of the United States, stepped in to obtain justice for Private Félix Longoria. Longoria was finally buried, with full honors, at the Arlington National Cemetery outside Washington, D.C.

Further Reading

American GI Forum. "Pvt. Felix Longoria." Available online. URL: http://www.agif.org/longoria.html. Downloaded October 10, 2000.

Castro, Tony. *Chicano Power: The Emergence of Mexican America*. New York: Saturday Review Press, 1974.

❦ **López, Baldomero** (1925–1950) *soldier*
Marine First Lieutenant Baldomero López gave his life during the Korean War to protect the lives of the men under his command.

López was born in Tampa, Florida, on August 23, 1925, and spent most of his brief life there. It was in Tampa, too, that he joined the U.S. Marine Corps.

The United States had gone to war in Korea, so López joined the ranks of military heroes near Seoul, the South Korean capital. He participated in the celebrated U.S. landing at Inchon. He hit the beach with the first assault waves on September 15, 1950, as a rifle platoon commander of Company A, 1st Battalion, 5th Marines, 1st Marine Division. Eliminating the enemy's beach defense positions was the first task at hand.

Deadly fire from a North Korean pillbox was keeping López and his men locked in place on the sand. López moved to reduce the fortification, although he knew that he was making himself a target for the enemy machine gunners.

He managed to come abreast of the pillbox and pull out a hand grenade. But as he began to hurl it into the pillbox, two enemy bullets struck him—one in the chest and the other in his throwing arm's shoulder. López was hurled backward, and the live grenade fell from his hand.

Despite the severity of his injuries, López made a second attempt to throw the grenade toward the enemy. He exerted extreme effort just to reach it, but, having done so, he found that he was unable to pick it up, much less throw it. As the seconds ticked away, López summoned the strength for one last move. He pulled the grenade toward him, tucking it under his own body, just before it exploded.

"He gallantly gave his life for his country," reads his posthumous Medal of Honor citation. "His exceptional courage, fortitude, and devotion to duty reflect the highest credit upon 1st Lt. López and the U.S. Naval Service."

Further Reading

The Committee on Veterans' Affairs, United States Senate. *Medal of Honor Recipients 1863–1978*. Washington, D.C.: U.S. Government Printing Office, 1979.

❦ **López, Jennifer** (1970–) *actress, singer*
Inspired by artists such as Cher, Barbra Streisand, Diana Ross, and Bette Midler, Jennifer López has

made it a goal to become the first Hispanic acting and singing superstar. "What," she asks, "is wrong with being ambitious?" Nothing, apparently, as the results show. She was the first Latina to be paid 1 million dollars to act in a movie (*Selena,* 1997); then she became the first to be paid 2 million (*Out of Sight,* 1998), and by 1999 she was being offered 5 million dollars per film.

Jennifer López was born in the Bronx, New York City, on July 24, 1970. Her grandparents were immigrants from Puerto Rico. Her father was an office worker who became a computer specialist, and her mother a kindergarten teacher. (None of the five Lópezes in this dictionary are related.)

As a child with dreams of making it big in show business, López says she found just one Latin role model: Rita MORENO, whom she would watch, over and over, in *West Side Story.*

After graduating from the same school where her mother worked, she attended only one semester at Baruch College in New York City before turning full time to preparing herself for a career in dance, hoping to get roles in musicals. She did obtain two parts, but as far off Broadway as possible: she toured Japan with a staging of *Synchronicity* and Europe with a production of *Golden Musicals of Broadway.* She also did some modeling.

In 1990 López managed to break into television, triumphing over 2,000 contestants to obtain a part as a dancer in a comedy series, *In Living Color,* choreographed by Rosie PÉREZ.

There followed roles in some TV pilots, a TV movie, and finally, in 1995, a part in a movie: *My Family (Mi Familia),* starring Jimmy SMITS and directed by Gregory NAVA. After that, one role led to another, including films with such stars as Jack Nicholson and Robin Williams and top directors such as Oliver Stone.

Also directed by Nava, *Selena,* the biography of the popular singer SELENA, who was murdered by a fan, made López a star in her own right, and earned her several acting awards and a Golden Globe award nomination. López felt an identification with the character she was playing. "Though I'm Puerto Rican from the Bronx and she [Selena] was a Mexican in Texas, we've both been treated the same way as minorities and as women," she declared.

In *Out of Sight* she was given the lead female role, that of a U.S. marshal, opposite George Clooney as a criminal. Most Hispanic actors seek (in most cases fruitlessly) to reach the point where they are considered for any role, not just to play Latino types, and the director of *Out of Sight,* Steven Soderbergh, noted that he did not choose López on ethnic grounds.

"I just thought she was the best actress for that part," he said. "She can do just about anything, and it's not often you find someone with that kind of range."

In 1999, López released her first compact disc. She called it *On the 6,* a reference to the subway line she used to take from her Bronx home to Manhattan, in the days before she entered the world of chauffeured limousines and her own Mercedes-Benz. The disc sold more than 2 million copies around the world. On one of its tracks she sings with Marc AN-THONY in Spanish.

In December 1999 Jennifer López was in the news when she was arrested with her then boyfriend, rap music tycoon Sean "Puffy" Combs, in an incident in which a gun was allegedly found in Combs's possession. Later, however, on examination of the evidence, charges against López were dropped.

In 2000, López starred in the movie *The Cell.*

Further Reading

Kioken Design, Inc. "Jennifer Lopez Online." Available online. URL: http://www.jenniferlopez.com. Downloaded October 10, 2000.

Telgen, Diane, and Jim Kamp, eds. *Notable Hispanic American Women.* Detroit: Gale Research, 1998.

✎ **López, José** (1920–1944) *soldier*

An army sergeant in World War II, José López single-handedly killed more than 100 German soldiers while protecting his company during a tactical withdrawal in Belgium, during the Allied drive toward Berlin. Awarded a Medal of Honor by the United States Congress for his deed, the citation stressed López's "gallantry and intrepidity."

José López was born about 1920 in Mission, Texas, and joined the army in the nearby city of

Brownsville. He served with Company K, 23rd Infantry, 2nd Infantry Division.

Near the town of Krinkelt in Belgium in December 1944, counterattacking German infantry, backed by tanks, not only stopped Company K in its tracks, but seemed on the verge of overpowering it from the left. While covering the company's right flank with heavy machine-gun fire, López realized the imminent danger and, acting on his own initiative, picked up the machine gun and carried it to the left flank. He was just in time to intercept an advancing party of 10 enemy soldiers, the first to be killed by him that day.

A German tank then began to shoot directly at the source of López's fire. His only protection was a hole barely deep enough for his legs. López simply ignored the tank and kept firing. Twenty-five more Nazis lost their lives to his steadfast machine gunning, but immediately afterward, a German artillery blast hit so close to López it left him "dazed and shaking." Still he realized that the brunt of the Nazi infantry attack had now shifted to the front, rather than from the left flank. He also saw that, in the face of this onslaught, Company K was in retreat.

López's only thought was to cover his men. Once more, he picked up the heavy machine gun and took it farther to the rear and to the right, seeking a new emplacement. Another explosion knocked him off his feet, but he picked himself up, placed the machine gun in firing position, and began to fire again.

López did not stop shooting until he saw Company K withdraw from the area. Then, while the Nazis fired at him wildly with small arms, he himself retreated, taking the machine gun with him. He would not leave it to the advancing enemy.

In the distance, López saw that some of the men from Company K were organizing a new line of defense. He immediately joined them with his machine gun. He fired from this new emplacement until he ran out of ammunition. Only then did he and the other soldiers retreat again toward the town of Krinkelt. When they reached it, López was still hauling the machine gun. His Medal of Honor citation described his feat as "seemingly suicidal." Noting the high number of enemy soldiers cut down in the course of his actions—"at least 100"—the citation

pronounced him "almost solely responsible for allowing Company K to avoid being enveloped, to withdraw successfully, and to give other forces coming up in support time to build up a line which repelled the enemy drive."

Further Reading

The Committee on Veterans' Affairs, United States Senate. *Medal of Honor Recipients 1863–1978.* Washington, D.C.: U.S. Government Printing Office, 1979.

⚬ López, Nancy (Nancy Marie López)
(1957–) *golfer*

Nancy López is regarded as quite possibly the best woman golfer of all time. With her dazzling succession of tournament wins, her record-breaking play, and her open, friendly nature, López has contributed more than anyone else to the increase in popularity of women's golf as a spectator sport. Her fans formed such an enthusiastic and committed group that they became known as "Nancy's Navy."

Nancy Marie López was born on January 6, 1957, in Torrance, California. She was raised in Roswell, New Mexico, where her father, Domingo López, had an auto body shop.

When Nancy López was about eight, a doctor recommended that her mother, Marina (née Griego), take up golfing for her health. Nancy's father learned the game, too, and both parents taught their daughter how to play. Her instructions were simple: "Just put the ball on the ground and . . . hit it into the hole down there." Nancy proceeded to do just that. At 11, she could beat either of her parents. In 1969, just 12, she launched what the editors of *Golf Magazine* called a "phenomenal" amateur career by winning the New Mexico Women's Amateur Tournament.

Her school in Roswell, Goddard High, had a golf team that up to then had been exclusively male, but it accepted Nancy López. She quickly led the team to the New Mexico state championship.

Her family backed her to the hilt. To protect her hands, her parents told her not to do any housework. They postponed buying a new house so that they could afford braces for her teeth because, as her father put it, "Nancy's gonna be a public figure."

López went to the University of Tulsa, Oklahoma, on a golfing scholarship, but quit after two years, having won the national collegiate golf championship. She then began her career as a professional golfer. As an amateur, she had won 10 titles in all, as well as placing second in the U.S. Women's Open championship in 1975.

López launched her pro career in 1978 by winning the Bent Tree Ladies Classic in Sarasota, Florida. She never looked back. She has great power in her drive, hitting as long as 240 yards. She combines this power with precise putting.

In 1978, the Ladies Professional Golf Association (LPGA) named her Rookie of the Year and Player of the Year and Female Athlete of the Year. She won five consecutive titles in 1978 and nine overall. It was a record number of wins. She also earned a record $190,000 that year. Her 275-stroke total for the 72-hole LPGA Championship that year was also a record.

The next year, López broke her own earnings record, winning $216,000 and soon became one of the first women golfers to accumulate earnings of more than $1 million. She won eight tournaments that year and was named Pro Golf Player of the Year. *Sports Illustrated* magazine called her winning streak "one of the most dominating sports performances in half a year."

Some golf commentators consider her best year to have been 1985: She won the LPGA Championship again, plus four other titles, was among the top 10 players in 21 events, and finished among the top 5 in 12 tournaments in a row. López became the first player to earn more than $400,000 in one year, and she set three records and was once more Player of the Year.

López had already accumulated her second million dollars in earnings by 1987, the year she was inducted into the LPGA Hall of Fame, an honor that requires 35 official tournament wins. Two years later in 1989, she was also inducted into the Professional Golf Association's (PGA's) World Golf Hall of Fame. She also won her third LPGA Championship that year.

López collected her 48th career title in 1997, doing less well thereafter, particularly because of a knee injury requiring surgery in 1999.

Nancy López is married to New York Mets third baseman Ray Knight. It is her second marriage.

She is the author of two books, *The Education of a Woman Golfer* (1979) and *Nancy López's The Complete Golfer* (1987).

A Baptist, López has said that she believes that the game of golf is "why God put me on this earth."

Further Reading

Ladies Professional Golf Association. "Player Biographies: Nancy López." Available online. URL: http://Lpga.com/tour/players/bios/Lopez.asp. Downloaded October 10, 2000.

López, Nancy. *The Education of a Woman Golfer.* New York: Simon & Schuster, 1979.

Phillips, Betty Lou. *The Picture Story of Nancy López.* New York: J. Messner, 1980.

✿ López, Trini (Trinidad López III)
(1937–) *singer*

His runaway success with songs that mix Mexican and Anglo musical elements has made Trini López a popular figure who helped create a period of renewed Hispanic influence on U.S. popular music. His recording of the song "If I Had a Hammer" sold well over 4.5 million copies.

Trinidad (the name means "Trinity") López III was born on May 15, 1937, in "Little Mexico," an impoverished neighborhood in Dallas, Texas. His father was a farm laborer. His mother also worked in the fields and took in laundry.

Originally from Guanajuato, in Mexico, López's parents had entered the United States illegally 10 years earlier by crossing the Río Grande. Trini López was their firstborn; five siblings followed.

In spite of the hard struggle for daily subsistence, López's father gave him a $12 guitar when he was 11 years old. It was his father's soundest investment ever. López learned some guitar from his father, and later, the talent he quickly displayed urged the family to find a way to pay for lessons with a guitar teacher. He began to sing Mexican songs at home and then formed a combo with four friends and expanded his repertory to include English-language songs. The group soon began to perform.

López's success was not spectacularly fast, but it was steady. Beginning in restaurants in their area, his combo went on to play in nightclubs and hotels in other parts of Dallas and then in other cities of the Southwest, venturing farther and farther away from home.

The big test came in 1960 when the group went to Los Angeles. Trini López passed the test, but the rest of the group failed—unlike López, they couldn't land a job. A Los Angeles nightspot called Ye Little Club hired him and featured him in its act, together with another performer, Joanie Sommers. His initial booking at the club was set to last two weeks, but he stayed there for a year. It was a hard decision for López, just 23 years old, to make. His loyalty to the group was strong, but his calling was even stronger. His next booking was at a better-known Hollywood nightclub, PJ's. There, in 1963, he caught the attention of Don Costa, then musical director of Reprise Records. Costa got the head of Reprise—Frank Sinatra—to listen to López. López's association with Reprise began during the three years in which it was headed by Sinatra. Sinatra quickly agreed to produce an LP of López's music, as well as to put him under exclusive contract. Following this, Trini López's ascent to celebrity became explosive. The LP, titled *Trini at PJ's,* sold more than 1 million copies. One of the singles from the album, "If I Had a Hammer," had already been a smash hit for Peter, Paul, and Mary in 1962. López's version became the top-selling single in 23 different countries.

After this success, López was able to form an 11-musician group of his own, which included his brother Jesse. The group toured domestically and internationally. He was well received everywhere he went: Audiences found him charming, and his Tex-Mex mixture of folk and pop, Anglo and Latino strands, proved infectious.

In the United States, rock and roll had kept the Hispanic beat on the sidelines for some years. López is credited with having helped push Hispanic rhythms back into the center of American pop music; when Latin rock emerged, López was regarded as one of its forerunners.

Another of López's top successes was "Lemon Tree" in 1965. Frank Sinatra had sold Reprise Records in 1963, the same year he signed López, but the new owners, Warner Brothers, kept releasing López's records, many of which went gold. In 1967 López was named Dallas Man of the Year.

The singer maintained a consistent performing and recording career, including many benefit performances for philanthropic causes. He also became a sharp businessman who handled his own investments. In 1991, Warner Brothers released the (slightly belated) album, *Trini López—25th Anniversary.* A *Trini López Dance Party* album was released in 1998. López signed a two-year deal with Sony International Records in 2000.

In addition to his many television appearances, López appeared in two Hollywood films, most notably as one of the misfit soldiers in *The Dirty Dozen* (1967). Its script followed Hollywood formula with regard to racially integrated platoons in war movies. The Hispanic in the group—López—was the most expendable. When the Dirty Dozen parachute into enemy territory, he is the first to die. He does not even reach the ground—he is caught by a tree and left dangling there.

Further Reading

López, Trini. "Trini Lopez Official Web Site." Available online. URL: http://www.trinilopez.com. Downloaded October 10, 2000.

Martínez, Al. *Rising Voices: Profiles of Hispano-American Lives.* New York: New American Library, 1974.

Meier, Matt S. *Mexican American Biographies.* Westport, Conn.: Greenwood Publishing Group, 1988.

Newlon, Clarke. *Famous Mexican Americans.* New York: Dodd, Mead, 1972.

Nite, Norm N. *Rock On.* New York: Harper & Row, 1982.

Roberts, John Storm. *The Latin Tinge: the Impact of Latin American Music on the United States.* Tivoli, N.Y.: Original Music, 1985.

Lorenzo, Frank (Francisco Anthony Lorenzo) (1940–) *businessperson*

Airline executive Frank Lorenzo has been one of the most controversial businessmen of recent decades. To some he is a champion of the free market and a company-saving wizard, but to others he is a merciless union-buster and company-wrecking fiend. *Time* magazine described him as "the flying ace in the new area of unregulated airline routes and prices." The *Wall Street Journal* quoted a banker as saying, "Frank Lorenzo is as smart as they come." *Fortune* magazine described him as "The new master of the skies." The unions, said an industry analyst, "view Lorenzo as Darth Vader." Others described him as "the most hated man in America." He, in turn, charged he was being made a scapegoat for changes that were inevitable in the industry.

The son of immigrants from Spain who operated a beauty parlor in New York, Frank Lorenzo was born in New York on May 19, 1940. To help pay his tuition at Columbia University—from which he graduated with a degree in economics in 1961, following this with a master's degree in business administration from Harvard in 1963—he worked as a part-time Macy's salesperson and as a Coca-Cola trucker.

After a few years of working for airlines, Lorenzo and a partner in 1966 formed their own airline consulting firm, later adding a jet leasing company. In those days, the airline industry was in a slump, so those endeavors did not prosper greatly; neither did Lorenzo's first attempt to obtain control or ownership of an airline of his own (in this case, Mohawk Airlines).

But in 1972 he got his chance. His firm was asked to study how to save another carrier, Texas International Airlines (TXI), then close to bankruptcy. Lorenzo arranged financial deals by which he and his associates obtained a significant stake in TXI, and he was elected its president. Through cost cutting and, especially, aggressive marketing, Lorenzo managed to turn the airline around.

In 1978 he entered negotiations with a carrier, National Airlines, thrice the size of his own line ("Lorenzo the Presumptuous," said *Forbes* magazine, in allusion to a 15th-century ruler of Florence, Lorenzo the Magnificent [de Medici]). TXI did not buy National, but in any event made $48 million when selling its stock in the airline.

At this time, the airline industry was full of talk of acquisitions. Lorenzo next entered discussions with TWA, which was much larger even than National, although no deal was reached. In the meantime he established a holding company called Texas Air, and a small shuttle airline called New York Air.

In 1981, in another bid for an existing carrier, he zeroed in on Continental Airlines. After a sharp legal and financial struggle—and the suicide of the previous Continental president—Lorenzo took over the airline.

Continental was losing $20 million a month. It was a classic example of a company with bloated labor costs, which Lorenzo promptly slashed. When the strikes came, rather than close the airline down, he started bankruptcy proceedings, fired everybody, took some people back at half their wages, and kept on going. Almost from the beginning of bankruptcy, Continental was profitable within its new structure.

In 1985 Lorenzo made another attempt to control TWA. He reached an agreement for its acquisition that was never completed because of share purchases made by another investor. Then he held talks with Frontier Airlines, without reaching an agreement.

But in 1987 he gained control of Eastern Airlines. It was the largest passenger airline outside the Soviet Union, but it had been riddled with labor and mechanical problems for years.

Also, in yet another acquisition, he bought People Express—and in so doing also obtained its subsidiary Frontier Airlines, on which no deal had been reached before. He merged them with Continental, thus creating one of the largest airlines in the United States, and setting up a major new aviation hub in Newark, New Jersey.

Meanwhile Lorenzo and the unions at Eastern were at war. The labor problems that began under previous administrations continued under Lorenzo, directly affecting airline performance. Lorenzo responded to the company's cash needs by selling off Eastern assets and explored the possibility of declaring it bankrupt as he had done with Continental.

When accused of being anti-union, he replied that what the workers really hated was the deregulation of the airline industry that had taken place in those years, and that he was just a handy symbol of the new situation. As evidence that he did not hate unions, he pointed to the fact that he had once been a member of the Teamsters Union during his truck driving days.

He finally declared Eastern's bankruptcy in 1989. However, instead of winning out as in the case of Continental, he found that this time, at the urging of the unions, the bankruptcy judge in 1990 replaced control by Lorenzo's Texas Air with that of a trustee designated by the judge himself. The company was by then so weakened it soon went out of business.

Lorenzo also sold his holdings in Continental. Shortly thereafter he founded a company in Houston to pursue other business ventures.

In 1993 he applied for a "fitness" certificate to start a new airline. With intense union lobbying, over 120 U.S. congressmen petitioned against it. Lorenzo also mentioned, as a factor in the issue, the inauguration of the pro-labor Clinton administration. He was unable to obtain the certificate.

In 1996, Lorenzo told an interviewer he had "no interest in running a carrier again." As a result, he explained, he started Savoy Capital, a small investment firm. He invested in Iberia, a Spanish airline, and Nations Air in the United States, as well as in regional gourmet food companies in the United States.

Further Reading

AvStop Magazine Online. Available online. URL: http://avstop.com/History/HistoryOfAirlines/ FrankLorenzo.html. Downloaded October 10, 2000.

Bernstein, Aaron. *Grounded: Frank Lorenzo and the Destruction of Eastern Airlines.* New York: Simon & Schuster, 1990.

Murphy, Michael. *The Airline That Pride Almost Bought.* New York: Franklin Watts, 1986.

Rowan, Roy. *Powerful People.* New York: Carroll and Graf, 1996.

Tardiff, Joseph C., and Mpho Mbunda, eds. *Dictionary of Hispanic Biography.* Detroit: Gale Research, 1996.

❧ Lozada, Carlos (1946–1967) *soldier*

Puerto Rican-born Carlos Lozada, a private in the Vietnam War, selflessly remained behind with his machine gun to protect his army comrades during a tactical withdrawal. In doing so, he sacrificed his life for theirs. A posthumous Medal of Honor was awarded him for "conspicuous gallantry and intrepidity in action at the risk of his life above and beyond the call of duty."

Lozada was born in the city of Caguas, Puerto Rico, on September 6, 1946. He later went to New York City, where he joined the United States Army.

In November 1967, two months after his 21st birthday, Private First Class Lozada, Company A, 2nd Battalion, 503rd Infantry, 173rd Airborne Brigade, found himself in the midst of the battle for Dak To in South Vietnam. This was one of the rare cases of full-scale combat during the Vietnam War, which was fought mainly in vicious smaller-scale encounters and skirmishes rather than large battles.

At Dak To, U.S. and South Vietnamese forces had to methodically dislodge North Vietnamese regular army troops who were entrenched atop what was known as Hill 875. The North Vietnamese units were retreating toward Cambodia, but they made a strong stand on the hill. It was here that Carlos Lozada's "heroic deed . . . served as an example and an inspiration to his comrades throughout the ensuing four-day battle."

Along with three other men, Lozada was to protect the rear of his company, which was advancing up the hill. He was the first to see an enemy company coming up behind them. Warning the others with a shout, he began to fire his M60 machine gun. His deadly precision resulted in 20 or more enemy deaths.

Still the enemy kept coming. At one point, Lozada saw that the M16 rifle carried by the leader of his four-man group had jammed. Lozada jumped up to protect him, firing from a standing position.

Company A was now in retreat; the North Vietnamese were advancing on them from three directions. Only if someone kept firing steadily could the enemy be stopped from cutting off and entirely demolishing the U.S. group as it withdrew. Lozada determined to be that someone, even though it was clearly a suicidal mission.

Shouting that he was staying behind to provide cover, Lozada maintained a necessary and accurate flow of fire that hindered the enemy's thrust until he received a deadly wound in the head. His buddies succeeded in pulling him away toward their re-grouped perimeter, but he died quickly thereafter.

"Pfc. Lozada's actions," declared the United States Congress, "are in the highest traditions of the U.S. Army and reflect great credit upon himself, his unit, and the U.S. Army."

Further Reading

The Committee on Veterans' Affairs, United States Senate. *Medal of Honor Recipients 1863–1978.* Washington, D.C.: U.S. Government Printing Office, 1979.

The Editors of the Boston Publishing Company. *Above and Beyond: A History of the Medal of Honor from the Civil War to Vietnam.* Boston: Boston Publishing Company, 1985.

Lucero-Schayes, Wendy (Wendy Lucero) (1963–   ) *Olympic diver*

Wendy Lucero-Schayes provides a good example of a person who perseveres in pursuit of a goal—in her case, participating in an Olympic athletic event—and who goes out of her way to help motivate others to reach for excellence. As an athlete, she was not fated to reach the topmost slots, but for her, as for so many other partici-pants, just having made it to the Olympics was satisfac-tion enough. Only very few people become Olympians, and Lucero-Schayes has become a role model as well as an eloquent communicator inspiring youths to emu-late her drive and ambition.

Wendy Lucero is a descendant of Spanish immi-grants on her father's side and is of Irish descent on her mother's. She has not been the victim of discrim-ination. However, her father, Don, an electrician, has recalled that he found employment more easily when people looked at his name and imagined that—rather than Hispanic—he was Italian, a national origin that tends to obtain a higher acceptance in the United States.

Born in Denver, Colorado, on June 26, 1963, Wendy was interested in sports from childhood and found ready support from her family. Also, in a sister who is two years older, she found somebody to be constantly in competition with. And yet, she was not sufficiently driven—not by herself, and not by her parents—to start early enough in two sports that she considered later: gymnastics and ice-skating.

Usually, Olympic athletes excel in one certain sport, which creates in them the desire to reach the Olympics. In Lucero's case it happened the other way around: by the age of nine she had a burning ambi-tion to become an Olympic contestant, and with that in mind she went about choosing a sport in which it might happen.

Lucero discovered that by the time she set her aim on gymnastics at around the age of 10, she was al-ready "too old," being at an overwhelming disadvan-tage with respect to other children who had started to train even earlier. Ice-skating, her second love, con-ceived at the age of 14, was another activity that de-mands a very early start. Thus, although she devoted four years to it, she eventually decided she could never become competitive in it at the level of perfection that she sought. Another consideration was that the expert training required to reach the very top in ice-skating was too expensive.

Diving, on the other hand, was less costly. In fact it could even be made to provide a source of financial assistance: thanks to the prowess she soon began to exhibit on the diving board, once she settled on that sport, Lucero enjoyed a full athletic scholarship at the University of Nebraska.

On the other hand, she had no intention of being "just an athlete" who neglects her studies, and proved it by earning the title of Academic All-Ameri-can. Her lifelong interest in addition to sports has been broadcasting and related fields. In 1986, she graduated with a B.S. degree in television sales and management and began to take jobs as a sports event production assistant, sportscaster, and talk show host.

Springboard diving meanwhile remained at the center of her life, and as she began to collect prizes at different events in the United States, participation in the Olympics began to seem feasible. However, it only happened after a change in coaches, when she found a new trainer to replace one whom she felt was too negative about her chances of success.

Lucero made it to the Olympic Games in 1988—the year the event was held in Seoul, South Korea—and placed sixth.

The years that followed were her best in the sport. Altogether, in her diving career Lucero-Schayes collected nine U.S. national titles and three U.S. Olympic Festival medals; she was U.S. Female Diving Athlete of the Year in 1990 and 1991. She also married basketball player Dan Schayes around this time.

By the approach of the 1992 Olympics, however, she had the bad luck to contract an intestinal infection that seriously interfered with her training, and she failed to make the U.S. team that traveled to the games in Barcelona, Spain.

A person of strong optimism and commitment, Lucero-Schayes has made a career in television broadcasting and has used her speaking skills in seeking to motivate young people, many of them Hispanic, to set good goals and work toward them with their full dedication.

Lucero-Schayes has also been a spokesperson for the American Cancer Society.

Further Reading

Telgen, Diane, and Jim Kamp, eds. *Notable Hispanic American Women.* Detroit: Gale Research, 1998.

✑ Luján, Manuel, Jr. (1928–   )
government official

A longtime member of the United States House of Representatives, Manuel Luján Jr. was appointed secretary of the interior under President George Bush. He was the first Hispanic American to fill that post and only the second, after Lauro CAVAZOS, to achieve cabinet rank in Washington.

Luján was born on May 12, 1928, in the town of San Ildefonso, New Mexico. He received his early education there before going on to St. Mary's College, in California. He later returned to his home state and received his B.A. degree from the College of Santa Fe in 1950.

After graduation, Luján entered the family business—a major insurance firm in the area. He then went into politics, a field in which the Lujáns were already prominent: Manuel Luján Sr. was a former mayor of the state capital, Santa Fe, and had been a candidate for U.S. congressman and state governor.

His son's initial step was not auspicious. As a Republican, Luján sought a seat on the New Mexican senate in 1964 but lost to the Democratic candidate. In 1968, however, he was successful in a bid to become a U.S. congressman and then was reelected many times, remaining in Washington from 1969 to 1989. For the most part, he won reelection by wide margins, although he also had a narrow victory in 1980.

Despite a major health problem in 1986 which required triple-bypass surgery, the voters kept bringing him back. Luján's 20-year congressional stint was the longest ever by a Republican from his state. He also served as a vice chairman of the New Mexico state Republican Party.

In Congress, Luján served on the Committee on Interior and Insular Affairs and on the Committee on Science, Space, and Technology. It was because of his interest in these areas as well as his conservative positions that he was considered for the post of head of the Department of the Interior by Republican president Ronald Reagan, in 1981. He was passed over by Reagan in favor of James Watt. But Reagan's successor and former vice president George Bush appointed Luján to be his secretary of the interior in 1989.

Over the years, Manuel Luján's positions have generally supported allowing businesses to develop natural resources, particularly energy resources. He has therefore been applauded by proponents of such development. At the same time, his positions have been criticized by environmentalists: Luján was in favor of relaxing the rules on strip mining. He backed turning over a greater share of federal land to logging and mining companies and supported nuclear energy.

At the Department of the Interior, however, he held that a fair balance could be achieved between development and conservation. He was involved in several environmental projects from California to Florida while still maintaining his aggressive pro-development stance.

Following his return from Washington, Luján dedicated himself to work as a business consultant, board member, and lobbyist.

Further Reading

Kanellos, Nicolás. *The Hispanic-American Almanac.* Detroit: Gale Research, Inc., 1993.

Meier, Matt S. *Mexican American Biographies.* Westport, Conn.: Greenwood Publishing Group, 1988.

Machito (Frank Raúl Grillo)

(ca. 1912–1984) *bandleader*

Machito's musical group, the Afro-Cubans, has been called "the greatest Latin band ever, no ifs, ands, or buts." Together with his musical director—the arranger and trumpeter Mario Bauzá (who was also his brother-in-law)—Machito pioneered in the fusion of Hispanic and jazz elements during the early 1940s and is considered a forerunner of both Latin jazz (in particular of the "Cubop" Latin-and-bebop movement) and salsa.

Many of the biggest names performed with Machito, from Latino bandleader Tito PUENTE and singer Celia CRUZ to jazzmen Charlie "Bird" Parker, Dizzy Gillespie, Cannonball Adderley, Stan Getz, Dexter Gordon, and Buddy Rich. One of Celia Cruz's most celebrated concerts was a special tribute to Machito in 1988.

Although his heyday was in the 1940s, Machito continued to perform influentially and successfully until his death in 1984. In fact, he was working with his band in London when he died of a stroke in April 1984.

Frank Raúl Grillo (the last name means "cricket" in Spanish) is believed to have been born on February 16, 1912, in Havana, Cuba. However, the historical record is contradictory, and some sources date his birth at 1908. One version has it that he was actually born in Tampa, Florida, despite having been raised in Havana.

Grillo acquired the nickname Machito, the diminutive of *macho,* as an infant. He was his parents' first son; they already had three daughters.

In Cuba, Machito worked as a maracas player and singer and remained in secondary positions. This changed when he came to New York in 1937 with a Cuban band, La Estrella Habanera (The Havana Star). Among the other groups he performed with in the United States was that of famed bandleader Xavier CUGAT.

In 1940, he formed his own combo, the Afro-Cubans. Their impact on the U.S. music scene was both relatively fast and very long-lasting. It was recognized that their sound remained more authentically Cuban than that of Cugat and other popular performers—even as it incorporated elements of U.S. swing music.

While Bauzá is credited with shaping much of the band's ultimate sound, it was Machito who had the idea of uniting a Cuban rhythm section with a front line of saxophones and trumpets. He had thought of this before Bauzá, who had been musical director for Chick Webb's swing band, joined the Afro-Cubans.

The Afro-Cubans played at various nightclubs in New York, notably at La Conga and, later, the Palladium. Machito himself always considered his combo to be "strictly a dance orchestra."

In 1943, during World War II, Machito served in the U.S. Army, was injured, and was then discharged, all within six months. In the meantime, the Afro-Cubans were led by Machito's sister Graciela, the group's lead singer.

After the war, jazz underwent one of the biggest revolutions in its history, with the arrival of the cerebral, cool, small-band sounds of bebop. Machito and Bauzá embraced the change enthusiastically, as their arrangements demonstrated. This led Machito to play and record with such leaders of the jazz new wave as Parker and Gillespie. Jazzman Stan Kenton named a tune "Machito" in 1947.

In almost half a century of music making, Machito recorded 75 albums. He won a Grammy Award for *Machito and His Salsa Big Band 1982.* After he split with Bauzá in the mid-1970s, his son Mario Grillo became his musical director. Other noted recordings include *Afro-Cubop, The Afro-Cuban Suite* and *Machito at the Crescendo.*

In 1987, Machito was the subject of an affectionate and flattering TV documentary, *Machito: A Latin Jazz Legacy.* Calling it "a memorable document about the joy and pain of being a serious musician," *The New York Times* noted that it showed Machito as a modest person who had lived in the Bronx and always remained approachable.

Further Reading

Clarke, Donald, ed. *The Penguin Encyclopedia of Popular Music.* New York: Viking, 1989.

Kernfeld, Barry, ed. *The New Grove Dictionary of Jazz.* London: Macmillan Press Ltd., 1988.

Roberts, John Storm. *The Latin Tinge: The Impact of Latin American Music on the United States.* Tivoli, N.Y.: Original Music, 1985.

✎ Marín, Richard Anthony "Cheech"

(1946–   ) *comedian*

"Cheech" Marín formed an extremely successful comedy team with Tommy Chong during the 1970s and early 1980s. After the team split up, Marín expanded on the social-commentary aspect of his humor, making particular references to the situation of Hispanics in United States society.

In 1994, one example of Marín's sarcastic wit was picked up by his friend, TV personality Geraldo RIVERA, who quoted it on TV. The joke made reference to the many charges of discrimination against Hispanics and other minorities in television employment. While Hispanics in the mid-1990s made up almost 10 percent of the U.S. population, their participation in TV programming was only 1 percent and was actually seen to be dropping over time. Said Marín, "For years Hispanics have been complaining of not getting on TV enough. Last year they had the most incredible coverage! It was the Menéndez brothers." (The brothers Lyle and Erik Menéndez of California were charged with shot-gunning their wealthy parents to death, and their trial was the object of rapt attention in the media.)

Cheech Marín was born on July 13, 1946, in Los Angeles. He graduated from California State University in Northridge.

Interested in an acting career, the future comedian then cofounded a stage improvisational group called City Works in Vancouver, Canada, where he first worked with the actor Tommy Chong. In 1970, they formed the comedy duo Cheech and Chong. In all their joint work, Marín not only acted but helped write their material. Appearing at clubs not only throughout the United States in such locations as the Kennedy Center in Washington and Carnegie Hall in New York, but also in Canada, Australia, and Europe, Cheech and Chong had a runaway success with a brand of lowbrow humor, often involving jokes about drug use.

The pair recorded their comedy routines and found additional legions of fans through their albums: The first, *Cheech and Chong,* became a gold record; their second, called *Big Bambu,* was voted the top comedy record of 1972; the third, which had a Spanish-language title—*Los Cochinos (The Pigs)*—won a Grammy Award for best comedy record of 1973.

While continuing to make albums, Cheech and Chong took their gags and sketches into the movies in 1978 with *Up in Smoke.* The film disgusted the critics, who called it brainless, but it earned more than $100 million, more than any other film that year.

They then did variations on the formula in a number of other films in the following years, including *Cheech and Chong's Next Movie, It Came from Hollywood, Yellow Beard, Still Smokin',* and *Cheech and Chong's The Corsican Brothers.*

When Chong went his separate way in 1985, Marín continued in such movies as *After Hours* (1985) and *Rude Awakening* (1988). He also made cameo appearances in films, including *Ghostbusters II* (1989). In 1999, he was cast along with actor Don Johnson in the TV dramatic series *Nash Bridges.* His other recent movie work has included *Paulie* (1998), *The Venice Project* (1999), and *Picking Up the Pieces* (2000). Marín won the 1999 National Council of La Raza/Kraft Foods ALMA Community Service Award for his Hispanic community work.

Because of his gift for mimicking voices, Marín has been in demand as a voice actor in animated movies. He supplied the voice of a frenzied chihuahua dog, Tito, in the Disney company's *Oliver & Company,* and did the character Stump in *Ferngully: The Last Rainforest.* In 1994, he did the voice of Banzai, one of three wicked but dumb hyenas in Disney's *The Lion King;* Whoopi Goldberg and Jim Cummings provided the voices of the other two.

In 1987, Marín created a video parody of the Bruce Springsteen hit, "Born in the USA" called *Born in East LA.* (East Los Angeles is a heavily Chicano neighborhood.) He then turned the video into a movie, directing, writing, and starring in it.

Noting that the feature film version of *Born in East LA* was made for little more than $5 million and earned more than $17 million, Marín advocated making more Hispanic movies. He noted, "In a business where only three out of 10 films show a profit, Hispanic films return more on the dollar than their mainstream counterparts."

Marín has also worked on television, acting in situation comedies such as *The Golden Palace* and starring in a 1994 TV movie, *The Cisco Kid.*

Further Reading

Katz, Ephraim. *The Film Encyclopedia.* New York: Perigee Books, 1994.

The Netshow Company. "Nash Bridges Cast." Available online. URL: http://nashbridges.com/cast/cheech1.html. Downloaded October 10, 2000.

Marisol (Marisol Escobar) (1930–)
artist

In the 1960s, Marisol became fashionable as a portrait sculptor, usually working in wood and with doll-like or blocklike shapes. Her work is owned by major museums and private collectors around the world. For her career as a professional artist, Marisol chose to drop her last name, Escobar. Although both her parents were born in Venezuela, Marisol was born in Paris on May 22, 1930. Her parents were wealthy and traveled frequently. They raised her in France, Venezuela, and the United States.

Marisol, who showed an early interest in an artistic career, attended the École des Beaux-Arts, a highly regarded Parisian school for the arts. She graduated in 1949.

By that time, a major shift had taken place in the art world. For hundreds of years, its center of attention worldwide had been Paris, but following World War II, the center moved to New York, and so did Marisol.

In 1950, Marisol began to study art in New York City at the Art Students' League and then at the New School for Social Research and the Hans Hoffman School. In later years, she would be associated with the Moore College of Art, Science, and Industry in Philadelphia and with the Rhode Island School of Design in Providence.

Of her teachers, Hans Hoffman was one of the most celebrated, but his art—Hoffman was an abstract expressionist—left little mark on her.

At the Art Students' League, Marisol came into contact with artists of her own generation, such as Robert Rauschenberg and Jasper Johns. They were to become leaders of a new movement that flourished in the late 1950s and 1960s. Called pop art, it worked with objects and images from everyday life and popular culture. Marisol was regarded as being part of the pop art scene.

However, her work also revealed her Latin American roots. She thus expanded the scope of pop art by including elements of the popular and folk culture of Latin America in her work. She also brought in American Indian elements. In particular, the wood sculptures, in which she soon specialized, had echoes of "primitive" art and mythology.

Marisol had her first one-woman show in 1958. By the early 1960s, she had begun to find favor among the rich and famous. From President Lyndon B. Johnson to patrons of the arts and Hollywood stars, many asked to have their portraits done in her original and often humorous style. She frequently rendered their faces separately. Then she attached or stamped these facial portraits onto the simple geometric shapes that represented the bodies, with clothing painted or marked on.

She also began to make versions, in her own sculptural style, of some of the most famous paintings in world history. Particularly notable was her 1984 impression of Leonardo da Vinci's *The Last Supper.*

This practice was defended by *New York* magazine, which praised Marisol's "gentle audacity." The article argued that rather than showing disrespect for the works she thus transformed, Marisol was exhibiting her "deep affection" for them.

In addition to a large number of solo exhibitions over the years, Marisol has been invited to participate in such major group shows as "Painting of a Decade" at the Tate Gallery in London in 1964, "Art of the USA 1670–1966" at the Whitney Museum of American Art in New York City in 1966, and "American Sculpture of the Sixties" at the Los Angeles Museum of Modern Art in 1967.

In addition, there have been many others, including shows at the National Portrait Gallery in Washington, D.C., and the Rose Art Museum in Waltham, Massachusetts, and museums in Italy, France, and the Netherlands.

Museums that have Marisol sculptures in their permanent collections include the Whitney, the Museum of Modern Art and the Metropolitan Museum in New York, the Art Institute of Chicago, the Hakone Open Air Museum in Tokyo, and the Wallraf-Richartz Museum in Cologne, Germany.

A work by Marisol was chosen for permanent public installation at the Battery Park promenade in New York City: the American Merchant Mariner's Memorial.

Further Reading

Blackwell, Earl. *Celebrity Register.* Towson, Md.: Times Publishing Group, 1986.

Maillard, Robert, ed. *New Dictionary of Modern Sculpture.* New York: Tudor Publishing Co., 1971.

✍ Martin, Ricky (Enrique Martín Morales)
(1971–) *singer*

Ricky Martin rode a wave of popularity of Latin music that swept the United States in the late 1990s. But he was trying to build a lasting career that would continue even after the fad had passed. Generally regarded as the most powerful luminary among a group of Hispanic performers who shot to great heights in that period (among them Marc ANTHONY, Enrique IGLESIAS and Jennifer LÓPEZ), Martin was celebrated by his fans as having the best-moving pelvis since Elvis Presley's. Among the impressive commercial milestones he set were the biggest sales of any hit single in the entire history of Columbia Records—with the song that virtually defined him, "Livin' la vida loca" (Livin' the Crazy Life). But even before he became "the hottest pop star in the world," in the words of *New York* magazine in 1999, Martín was a member of the all-boys pop group Menudo. The five school-age Puerto Rican singers who made up Menudo generated so much enthusiasm and so much money in the early 1980s that they attracted an unusual amount of mainstream attention.

Born on December 24, 1971, in the Puerto Rican capital, San Juan, Enrique was the son of psychologist Enrique Martín Sr. and accountant Nereida Morales (Ricky changed the pronunciation of his last name, by dropping the accent mark on the letter "i," after going into show business).

His parents separated when he was two years old, in part because of disagreements over Enrique Jr.'s nascent career—he started out as an infant model for baby food labels. Ricky was estranged from his father for a decade after Enrique Sr. told him he had to choose between him and his mother.

Ricky Martin *(Courtesy of Sony Records)*

Ricky continued to be an advertising model as a child, took singing lessons, then auditioned for Menudo at age 10, only to be rejected for being too young. A second attempt had the same result, but on the third try, at 12, the minimum age for the group, he was accepted. Martin served with the group for five years, finding that the strenuous life of concerts, constant travel, hard practice, studies, and media glare provided good training for individual stardom later on.

Upon parting company with Menudo and completing high school Martin spent a fruitless year, from a career viewpoint, in New York City, then decided to try his luck in Mexico, where he found work in soap operas. Back in the United States as of 1994, he obtained a role in the TV series *General Hospital,* then landed a part on Broadway in the musical *Les Misérables.*

But it was his phenomenally successful recording career, initially in Spanish, that shot Martin to prominence. He obtained a recording contract with Sony in 1990, and has released four albums which have collectively sold over 15 million copies and made Martin famous from Puerto Rico to Israel to Australia. When he sang "La copa de la vida" (The Cup of Life) at the 1998 World Cup soccer championship, he had a ready-made, enthusiastic audience of 2 billion people.

The mainstream United States suddenly took notice of him when he sang during the 1999 Grammy Awards ceremony, during which he collected the prize for best Latin pop album. His infectiously enthusiastic performance shook the industry as much as the audience—the singer Madonna instantly pronounced herself his fan—and announced the establishment of a major star, one who clearly wanted his listeners to have as much fun as he was having.

The result was his first English-language CD, *Ricky Martin* (1999), which sold 4 million copies in a month and soon topped 6 million.

Behind his careful image as a cute poster boy, Martin is strongly concerned with improving the perception—and realities—of Puerto Rico. The fact that "people think . . . that we ride donkeys to school—that must change," he has declared. He is willing to take a monetary loss to back up his principles: he rejected a role in a project to remake *West Side Story,* in which he would have starred with Jennifer López, because he considers that it demeans the image of Puerto Ricans.

Martin took the occasion of a visit to the White House in February 2000 to state his concern over an issue of importance to his native commonwealth, the U.S. Navy's use of the island of Vieques as a bombing range.

He has also sung with the "supertenor," Luciano Pavarotti, in a benefit for the victims of the war in Kosovo, Yugoslavia.

Further Reading

Furman, Elina. *Ricky Martin: The Captivating Story of the Sexy Singing Sensation.* New York: St. Martin's, 1999.

Krulk, Nancy. *Ricky Martin: Rockin' the House!* New York: Pocket Books, 1999.

Marrero, Letisha. *Ricky Martin, Livin' la Vida Loca.* New York: Harper Entertainment, 1999.

Roberts, John Storm. *The Latin Tinge: The Impact of Latin American Music on the United States.* Tivoli, N.Y.: Original Music, 1985.

Sony Music Entertainment Inc. "Ricky Martin." Available online. URL: http://www.ricky-martin.com. Downloaded October 10, 2000.

Sparks, Kristin. *Ricky Martin: Livin' the Crazy Life.* Boulevard, 1999.

Tracy, Kathleen. *Ricky Martin: Red-Hot and On the Rise.* Zebra, 1999.

Martínez, Antonio José (1793–1867)
prelate, activist

Father Antonio José Martínez played a significant role in the history of New Mexico. Known simply as "the priest of Taos," he was a steadfast defender of the rights of Mexican Americans and of the poor in general. In order to keep working in their favor, Martínez endured excommunication, the expulsion from his church.

Martínez also had an interesting political career. He was a member of the legislature when Nuevo Mexico was still part of Mexico and was a strong opponent of the United States takeover of the area. Then he became a member of the legislature of the territory under U.S. administration and was the assembly's first president.

His work among Mexican Americans made him one of the most beloved historical figures of many New Mexicans, but others saw Martínez as highly controversial. One of his posthumous critics was Willa Cather, a United States writer with strongly conservative views who tended to regard Mexicans as people who needed to be tamed. Cather used Father Martínez as the archvillain in a historical novel about New Mexico, *Death Comes for the Archbishop* (1927).

Martínez was born in Abiquiu, a hamlet in northern Nuevo Mexico, on January 7, 1793. In 1805, the family resettled in the nearby town of Taos. The Martínezes were a long-established and influential *nuevomexicano* clan. Although he was a Roman Catholic, the priesthood was not his first career choice; he married at the age of 19, yet he did not remain a family man for long. His wife died in childbirth, and the daughter she bore died as a little girl.

It was then that the grief-stricken Martínez decided to become a priest. He entered a seminary in the Mexican city of Durango in 1817, exhibited brilliance in his studies, and was ordained in 1822. By the following year he was back in his home area, filled with the liberal ideas then circulating through Mexico, a country that had just achieved its independence from Spain. Martínez served as a priest first in the town of Tomé, then in Abiquiu, the town where he was born, and finally, beginning in 1826, in Taos, where he had grown up. He helped transform Taos into a local center of learning, determined to help the people of the area to improve their lives. First, he established a school and then a seminary and a college. It attracted many of the brightest youths of Nuevo Mexico. The result was that the majority of the next generation of outstanding individuals in the territory studied with Father Martínez.

The priest also studied law, with the same dedication and capacity with which he had earlier studied religion. He then entered politics, believing that politics provided an additional road for working for the benefit of his people. In the 1830s, he was one of the most significant figures in the legislature of Nuevo Mexico. He was also elected, as alternate deputy, to the federal Congress in the nation's capital, Mexico City.

Martínez's speeches in opposition to the creation of new taxes are believed by some historians to have been the direct cause of an uprising in 1837. In this action, the people of the town of Chimayó attacked the province's capital, Santa Fe, and killed the governor. The rebellion was then quashed.

Martínez decided to do something about the scarcity of reading materials for his students in Taos. In 1834, the first printing press was brought to that area, later the U.S. Southwest. The printing press was used in Santa Fe for the publication of Nuevo Mexico's first newspaper, *El Crepúsculo de la Libertad (The Twilight of Freedom)*. In 1838, Martínez bought the press, had it transported to Taos, and became a publisher of both religious and lay materials. If suitable texts were not available for printing, he wrote them himself.

Meanwhile, Martínez recognized the threat of encroachment into Nuevo Mexico by the nearby

United States. He repeatedly alerted *nuevomexicanos* that, one way or another, the United States, which was pushing at its frontiers, was certain to try to take over the territory.

Some sectors of Nuevo Mexican society welcomed the possibility; they saw no reason to feel loyal to the government in Mexico City and thought they might profit from a change of nationality. Others were strongly opposed; Martínez was their chief spokesman.

One of the things that worried Martínez was the Anglo settlers' slaughter of huge numbers of bison; most particularly, he spoke against what had become an increasing trend in the region—making large land grants to U.S. settlers.

He was even more strongly opposed to the actual invasion of Nuevo Mexico by the U.S. Army in 1846 at the beginning of the war between the United States and Mexico. In consequence, when acts of resistance against the invaders surfaced in the Taos area, he was suspected of being behind them. A plot for violent action was discovered, and suppressed, by the U.S. authorities in late 1846. It was succeeded by an actual uprising in early 1847 in which the governor sent by the United States was killed and scalped. The United States then retaliated, reimposing its rule with large-scale slaughter.

Martínez, however, escaped punishment. No evidence was found of his alleged involvement. It appears that, in fact, he very quickly realized the new situation was permanent, and he had to adapt. After New Mexico was organized into a U.S. territory in 1850, he served in the new assembly that was formed, becoming its first president.

In the 1850s, Martínez continued to be as influential in the affairs of New Mexico as he had earlier been when it was still Nuevo Mexico. However, the priest of Taos now had a new battle on his hands, this one on the religious front. The United States not only took over Nuevo Mexico as a political entity; the Catholic church in the area was also integrated into the U.S. Catholic church. In 1851, Martínez was assigned a new religious leader, Jean-Baptiste Lamy, a Frenchman who came as vicar general and was soon raised to bishop. Lamy considered himself to be on a mission to civilize a backward population. Of "our Mexican population," he wrote, "very few of them will be able to follow modern progress. They cannot be compared to the Americans in the way of intellectual liveliness, ordinary skills, and industry." This racist attitude was, by itself, sure to cause friction with the pastor in Taos, a longtime champion of his people. It was compounded by a clash of views on the collection of "tithes and first fruits"—in effect, taxes to be paid by each church's parishioners to their priests for the church's upkeep and works.

Bishop Lamy embarked on a drive to expand the activities of the church, in particular, its role in public education. He justified this by arguing that it managed to keep education in the territory in Catholic hands, withholding it from the hands of Protestants.

Father Martínez was a supporter of the separation of church and state and so advocated keeping public education out of religious hands altogether, whether Protestant, Catholic, or any other denomination.

Lamy, furthermore, in order to raise the money for the building of new churches and schools, demanded that everybody be made to pay tithes. He ordered his priests to refuse to give the sacraments to those who did not pay. Martínez held that tithes had to be voluntary, both as a matter of principle and because many of his parishioners were very poor.

The resulting clash lasted years. It became a mix of racial, political, and religious confrontations between different sectors of the population.

Lamy first suspended Martínez as a priest and then excommunicated him. Martínez decided to ignore this and continued to act as pastor to the poor in Taos until his death in 1867. Although he lacked all church authorization, the people, who loved and respected him for his life's work, continued to view him as their priest.

Willa Cather's *Death Comes for the Archbishop* cast Lamy (renamed Latour in the novel) as the hero who tames a wild area and symbolically manages to build a cathedral there. To do this, he must first overcome all the backward forces that are opposed to his authority. This is how the author and others viewed Martínez for defending the rights of Hispanic, Indian, and mixed-blood people.

Further Reading

Acuña. Rodolfo. *Occupied America: A History of Chicano.* New York: HarperCollins, 1988.

Mares, E. A., et al. *Padres Martínez: New Perspectives From Taos.* Taos, N. Mex.: Millicent Rogers Museum, 1988.

Meier, Matt S. *Mexican American Biographies.* Westport, Conn.: Greenwood Publishing Group, 1988.

❧   Martínez, Benito (1931–1952) *soldier*

As a corporal in the U.S. Army during the Korean War, Benito Martínez mounted a night-long, single-handed, suicidal resistance against a strong enemy attack. The United States, in awarding him a posthumous Congressional Medal of Honor, officially called his courage "incredible."

Benito Martínez was born in Fort Hancock, Texas, on March 21, 1931. (None of the Martínezes in this book are related.) It was also in Fort Hancock that he joined the army. In 1952, at the age of 21, Martínez thus found himself as a machine-gunner with Company A, 27th Infantry Regiment, 25th Infantry Division, near Satae-ri in Korea.

The Korean War pitted the United States, South Korea, and other countries, fighting under the United Nations banner, against North Korea and China. For Corporal Martínez in September 1952, it boiled down to his buddies in a line behind him, the enemy lines ahead, and himself at a forward listening post in between.

At first, his post was part of a wider defensive perimeter, but most of the perimeter had to be abandoned in the face of a major enemy attack. While most of the soldiers on the perimeter fell back to the main line, Martínez chose to stay where he was. From there, he could protect their withdrawal with machine-gun fire.

"In a daring defense," reads the Medal of Honor citation, "he raked the attacking troops with crippling fire, inflicting numerous casualties."

On several occasions, the U.S. forces contacted Martínez by field telephone and offered to mount an operation to bring him out. Each time, the corporal refused, arguing that the risk to the rescuers would be too great. Finally, though, the enemy rushed forward with such force that he retreated on his own, but only a short distance. He immediately took up a new position.

Now, however, the machine gun was out of his reach. He had only his rifle and a pistol. Still, he kept up a defense that lasted six more hours through most of the night. Day was just about to break when he made phone contact with his comrades. The hostile forces, he reported, were coming straight at him. It was the final communication from Benito Martínez.

"His magnificent stand," the official record states, "enabled friendly elements to reorganize, attack, and regain the key terrain. Corporal Martínez's incredible valor and supreme sacrifice reflect lasting glory upon himself and are in keeping with the honored traditions of the military service."

Further Reading

The Committee on Veterans' Affairs, United States Senate. *Medal of Honor Recipients 1863–1978.* Washington, D.C.: U.S. Government Printing Office, 1979.

❧   Martínez, Bob (Robert Martínez)
(1934–) *government official*

Bob Martínez was the first Hispanic mayor of the city of Tampa and later the first Hispanic governor of Florida. Noted for his energetic antidrug policies as well as for his strong actions in favor of the environment, he then served in the U.S. capital as director of the Office of National Drug Control Policy, or "drug czar."

On December 15, 1934, Martínez was born in Tampa, a city with a small Hispanic population. Both his father, a waiter, and mother, a garment worker, were the offspring of Spaniards who had left their poverty-hit region in the north of the country and immigrated to the United States, where they found work manufacturing cigars.

An only son, whose hard-working parents mostly had to leave him in the care of his grandmother, Martínez was nonetheless able to go to college, graduating in 1957 from the University of Tampa as a social sciences teacher. In 1964 he earned a master's degree in labor and industrial relations from the University of Illinois. He went back to teaching but soon he put his new knowledge to use when he became head of the local teachers' union. He proved to be a forceful union leader who was unafraid to lead an illegal strike in favor of teachers' rights statewide.

Some 10 years later, Martínez made his first bid for political office. Martínez, a Democrat, failed to become mayor of Tampa in 1974, although he placed a respectable third among nine candidates. The following year he switched careers to run a family restaurant in the city. This new line of work brought him into contact with many local political and business leaders. (During this time, the state governor invited him to work on a water management board.) In 1978, he again ran for mayor, enjoying their support, and won.

Voters found Bob Martínez to be an efficient mayor who turned the city's fortunes around at a time when Tampa was in poor administrative condition. He did this by unhesitatingly ditching his earlier pro-union position and cracking down on city unions. The money he saved was put into infrastructure projects. In this way, in the course of his tenure (Martínez was reelected in 1982) Tampa began to be held up as an example of what could be done to improve smaller cities around the country.

During this time, Martínez switched to the Republican Party, and found favor among national leaders of the party, including then-president Ronald Reagan. In 1984 and 1988, Martínez spoke at the party's national conventions.

In 1986 he was elected governor of the state of Florida, to a great extent on the basis of promises not to raise taxes. But one of his first projects as governor was to establish a service tax. The move backfired badly, had to be abandoned, and his administration was off to a bad start. But his concern as governor for a traditionally liberal cause, the environment, led him to set up a land protection scheme, Preservation 2000, that earned him a Conservationist of the Year award.

In other respects he acted as a staunch conservative, beginning to stand out in the fight against narcotics, with an approach that put greater emphasis on prosecution and on building more jails than on educating people away from drug consumption. He called out the National Guard in the fight against smuggling, opposed abortion and sex education, and cracked down on obscenity and brutality in pop song lyrics.

Martínez lost his gubernatorial reelection bid in 1990 to a Democratic senator, Lawton Chiles, despite campaign support from the family of then-President George H. W. Bush, but his antidrug credentials quickly came in handy when President Bush appointed him "drug czar." In this capacity Martínez stressed education, and he had the satisfaction of seeing drug-use levels descend among young people. His period in office was controversial, however, with regard to administrative practices–Martínez was charged with being imperious and disorganized.

Martínez held that post from 1991 until the end of Bush's term in 1993. He thereupon returned to private business with his own marketing firm in Tampa.

Further Reading

Division of Historical Resources. "(Robert) Bob Martínez, Portrait and Biography." Available online. URL: http://dhr.dos.state.fl.us/governors/martinez.html. Downloaded October 10, 2000.

Tardiff, Joseph C., and Mpho Mabunda, eds. *Dictionary of Hispanic Biography*. Detroit: Gale Research, 1996.

U.S. Senate Committee on the Judiciary. *Mr. Robert Martínez to be Director of National Drug Control Policy*. Washington, D.C.: U.S. Government Printing Office, 1991.

Martínez, Joe P. (ca. 1922–1943)
soldier

Joe P. Martínez daringly played a key role in the reconquest of one of the few U.S. territories actually captured by the Japanese during World War II—Attu Island in Alaska's Aleutian archipelago. Although only a private, he provided inspiration to others through the bravery he exhibited at the cost of his life. Distinguished with a posthumous Medal of Honor by the United States Congress, Martínez is remembered by the U.S. military for "conspicuous gallantry and intrepidity above and beyond the call of duty."

Born around 1922, Joe Martínez was a native of Taos, New Mexico, who joined the army in Ault, Colorado. He was then shipped to Attu with Company K, 32nd Infantry, 7th Infantry Division. Attu, a cold, remote place, had been seized by the Japanese, along with two other Aleutian Islands, because of its strategic position between Asia and America.

In 1943, the United States had to wage a 19-day battle to displace enemy forces once they had entrenched themselves in the snowy mountain fastnesses on the island. Day after day, the U.S. troops repeatedly failed to conquer one commanding mountain pass held by the enemy. At this decisive moment, it was Private Joe Martínez who led the victorious advance.

To advance, in this case, meant to climb a steep and craggy slope while it was being raked by machine-gun, rifle, and mortar fire from hostile forces above. Under these conditions, a new drive by a reinforced battalion of U.S. soldiers became bogged down. Martínez, armed with a Browning automatic rifle and hand grenades, decided to act on his own.

Standing up and shouting, he began to climb again, stopping only here and there to yell to the others soldiers to follow. Some of them did, and later others also followed. But in the meantime, Martínez reached one Japanese position and put it out of action with his hand grenades and rifle.

His charge had only begun, however, and the terrain ahead was even more dangerous. The mountain pass was still 150 feet higher, and every step of the way was exposed to fire from the enemy posted behind rocks on the sides and behind snow trenches straight ahead.

"Despite these obstacles, and knowing of their existence," reads his medal citation, "Pvt. Martínez again led the troops on and up, personally silencing several trenches with (automatic-rifle) fire and ultimately reaching the pass itself. Here, just below the knifelike rim of the pass, Pvt. Martínez encountered a final enemy-occupied trench, and as he was engaged in firing into it he was mortally wounded."

Thanks to his leadership, the pass was conquered. For the Japanese, the loss of this position led to the crumbling of their hold on the island.

Further Reading

The Committee on Veterans' Affairs, United States Senate. *Medal of Honor Recipients 1863–1978*. Washington, D.C.: U.S. Government Printing Office, 1979.

Martínez, Vilma S. (Vilma Socorro Martínez) (1943–) *activist*

As president and general counsel of the Mexican American Legal Defense and Educational Fund (MALDEF), Vilma S. Martínez fought and won many battles in favor of voting rights and other important causes of Mexican Americans. By dynamically championing the rights of Hispanics—not only in MALDEF but also in many other organizations— Martínez became a leading figure and spokesperson in the community.

Martínez was born in San Antonio, Texas, on October 17, 1943. A first child, she was followed by four siblings. Her father was a carpenter. Early in life, she saw and began to hate the discrimination and patronizing attitudes faced by Hispanics. She saw her parents endure them, and she was forced to endure them herself. In an Anglo culture where the word *Mexican* was considered virtually offensive, teachers who wanted to be nice to her called her *Spanish* instead. By so doing, they demonstrated their belief that to be Mexican was to be inferior. They thus insulted her, managing to achieve what they wanted to avoid.

Martínez was a bright pupil and was an officer of the National Honor Society. Nevertheless, when she was given high school counseling, she was told that a university education was out of reach for a Mexican-American girl.

Vilma Martínez resisted. She decided that she would not only become a lawyer, but also that she would use the knowledge and skills she acquired in order to improve the civil rights and status of her fellow Hispanics. She went to the University of Texas in Austin, financing her studies with jobs at the university and a partial scholarship. She obtained a B.A. degree in less than three years, graduating in 1964.

Martínez followed the suggestion of a professor and continued her studies in New York to get away from the Texas surroundings she found so biased. Armed with another scholarship, she went to Columbia University Law School in 1964, graduating in 1967 and passing the New York bar exam the following year. She also passed California's bar exam in 1975.

Martínez immediately sought a job in civil rights: she found it with the National Association for the Advancement of Colored People's (NAACP's) Legal Defense and Education Fund as a staff attorney involved in general civil rights lawsuits. Quickly, she was immersed in a field that became her specialty— labor cases that involved minority workers against employment discrimination.

Throughout her career, Martínez has judged a case on its merits: she is just as ready to defend a company against charges of discrimination if she believes the defense to be justified. She has done this even when it meant facing accusations of selling out, that she had changed from the side of minority workers to the side of the businesses that employ them.

After three years with the NAACP, Martínez worked for two years for the New York State Division of Human Rights, again with an emphasis on employment-discrimination law. Then she continued to work in that field for a New York law firm and also joined MALDEF's board of directors. At that time, when she and another female lawyer were made directors of the Mexican-American organization, they were the first women to hold board positions.

Martínez so impressed MALDEF that in 1973, before her 30th birthday, she was named president and general counsel. The new, dual-function job prompted her move from New York to California.

At the helm of MALDEF, Martínez was successful in two different ways: advancing the civil rights of Hispanics and giving the organization she headed a better structure and more solid finances. Through lawsuits, she strengthened the Hispanic right to vote, the right to a bilingual education, and the right to free public education for children without proper immigration papers.

After almost a decade with MALDEF, Martínez joined a prestigious California law firm as a partner.

She would later rejoin MALDEF as a director. She also accepted an invitation to join the board of directors of a large corporation, Anheuser-Busch, Inc. Since then, other institutions, ranging from a bank to several universities, have also asked her to form part of diverse leadership bodies.

Both during her MALDEF years and since, Martínez has contributed her work to a large list of organizations and commissions, often without charge, and she has also lectured at many universities and other institutions. A member and also chairperson of the University of California Board of Regents, she was as well one of President Jimmy Carter's advisers on the selection of ambassadors.

She has also advised the United States Census Bureau and helped obtain the inclusion of the category "Hispanics" in U.S. censuses. The census is crucial to the mapping of electoral districts. Thus Martínez found in it another way to help ensure that Hispanics received the maximum benefit from their right to vote. "Chicana with a Backbone of Steel" was the headline that *Quest* magazine gave to an article about her.

Recognition has come to Vilma Martínez in the form of the American Institute for Public Service's Jefferson Award in 1976, Rockefeller Foundation's John D. Rockefeller III Youth Award in 1977, Columbia University Law School's Medals of Excellence in 1978 and 1992, MALDEF's Valerie Kantor Award for Extraordinary Achievement in 1982, the Mexican American Bar Association's Lex Award in 1983, and the University of Texas Distinguished Alumnus Award in 1988. Martínez acted as chair of a blue-chip study group assembled to draw up a report, titled *Mexico Transforming,* on Mexico before their presidential elections in 2000.

Further Reading

Codye, Corrin. *Vilma Martínez.* Milwaukee, Wis.: Raintree Publishers, 1990.

Meier, Matt S. *Mexican American Biographies.* Westport, Conn.: Greenwood Publishing Group, 1988.

Telgen, Diane, and Jim Kamp, eds. *Notable Hispanic American Women.* Detroit: Gale Research, Inc., 1993.

❧ Mas Canosa, Jorge (1939–1997)

activist

A leader of the community of exiled Cubans in Florida, Jorge Mas Canosa was recognized as the most powerful anti-Castro activist in the United States. He lobbied tirelessly, and successfully, in Washington in favor of legislation tightening the U.S. embargo and other steps taken against the communist government in Cuba. Although never holding any political office himself—he was a businessman in the telecommunications field—he influenced politics through the sway he exerted over Cuban Americans' votes. He was able to deliver votes to politicians who voted in favor of anti-Castro laws, and to deny votes to those who opposed such measures. An article in the *Wall Street Journal* summed it up like this: "When Mas Canosa says 'Jump,' politicians lace up their sneakers."

Mas Canosa was surrounded by controversy because of a readiness to bully opponents, leading to charges that he was, in his own sphere, as dictatorial as his archenemy Fidel Castro was in his. A bumper sticker seen in Miami proclaimed "*Fidel y Mas Canosa, la misma cosa*"—the message, which rhymes in Spanish, being that "Fidel and Mas Canosa are the same thing."

The son of a Cuban army veterinarian, Jorge Mas Canosa was born in Santiago, Cuba, on September 21, 1939. In his youth he opposed first the right-wing dictator Fulgencio Batista and then Castro. He was initially arrested at age 14 for speaking out against Batista in a radio program, after which his family sent him to the United States to cool off.

Mas Canosa attended junior college in North Carolina. When Castro ousted Batista, he went back to Cuba but quickly became disenchanted with the new government—and, as outspoken as ever, was arrested by Castro's police. Briefly jailed, he then immigrated to the United States for good, at age 21. However, he did not become a U.S. citizen until 1982.

In 1961 Mas Canosa volunteered for the exile task force that the U.S. government, through the CIA, was organizing for an invasion of Cuba. The force landed in the Bay of Pigs area of the island and was roundly defeated. The ship Mas Canosa was on remained at sea during the fighting, and he was thus able to return safely to the United States. There, he served in the army before going back to civilian life.

After a period holding such jobs as dishwasher, milkman, and shoe salesman, Mas Canosa went to work for a phone services subcontractor company. With a 50,000-dollar bank loan, in 1961 he bought the firm, and over the decades developed it into a telecommunications business worth almost half a billion dollars.

During all this time his constant concern was finding ways to unseat Fidel Castro in Cuba. At first he toyed with diverse military options; then, when these were seen to be impracticable, gradually decided that the work had to be done in the political field. He became the biggest Hispanic contributor to the Republican Party in the United States, seeking the support of conservative politicians for Cuba-contention policies.

Jorge Mas Canosa *(Courtesy of the Cuban American National Foundation)*

In 1980 Mas Canosa founded the Cuban American National Foundation (CANF) to help Ronald Reagan become president of the United States. CANF, however, quickly turned into a specifically anti-Castro organization, the biggest in the country, and Mas Canosa's personal power base. In time CANF was seen as the springboard from which Mas Canosa hoped to jump to the presidency of Cuba if and when Castro was overthrown.

Mas Canosa was credited for almost single-handedly preventing the United States from establishing normal diplomatic relations with Cuba during the administration of President Jimmy Carter. All U.S. presidents up to and including Bill Clinton consulted him on Cuban affairs.

Among the initiatives Mas Canosa successfully promoted was the creation of Radio Martí in 1985 and of TV Martí in 1990. These networks broadcast to Cuba, countering the information available from the Castro-controlled media with the exiles' and the U.S. government's own views.

As the person who ran the U.S. agency in charge of Radio and TV Martí, Mas Canosa was investigated on charges of mismanagement and abuse of the broadcasting stations for his own political purposes. The charges were found to be true, but the investigation itself was accused of being politically inspired by Mas Canosa's enemies.

Mas Canosa died in 1997 of complications from lung cancer.

Further Reading

Mas Canosa, Jorge, et al. *Cuba in Crisis: Proceedings of a Conference Sponsored by the CANF.* Miami: CANF, 1993.

Meier, Matt S. *Notable Latin Americans.* Westport, Conn.: Greenwood Press, 1997.

Tardiff, Joseph C., and Mpho Mabunda, eds. *Dictionary of Hispanic Biography.* Detroit: Gale Research, 1996.

Mata, Eduardo (1942–1995)
conductor

A Mexican who made his home in the United States from 1977 until his death, Eduardo Mata was widely recognized as the person who turned the Dallas Symphony into a world-class orchestra. Earlier, he was credited with single-handedly leading a resurgence of interest in classical music in Mexico.

Mata was born in Mexico City on September 5, 1942. Quickly cognizant that his destiny centered on classical music, he studied at the National Conservatory of Music from 1954 to 1963, in addition to receiving private tutoring.

By the age of 15, he was conducting full-scale orchestras in public performances, and in 1964, Mata attended conducting seminars at Tanglewood in Lenox, Massachusetts.

In early life, Mata composed music, including five symphonies, chamber music, and a ballet, *Débora* (1963). Gradually, however, as his career as a conductor blossomed, he gave up composing and at 21 was given his first permanent conducting job with the Mexican Ballet Company. The next year, 1964, he led the Guadalajara Symphony Orchestra.

Eduardo Mata became conductor and musical director of the Philharmonic Orchestra of the National Autonomous University in Mexico's capital (1966–75). During these years, thanks to his enthusiasm and the brilliance of his work, many Mexicans became interested in classical music.

In 1969, he gained a foothold in the United States, accepting an invitation to become principal conductor and musical adviser of the Phoenix Symphony Orchestra in Arizona, a position he held until 1978. He was fully immersed in the hectic life of an international musician, rushing from city to city and country to country for performance after performance, plus making dozens of recordings. Two of his records earned Grammy Award nominations.

In addition to his work in Mexico City and Phoenix, he also directed music festivals and made appearances with other orchestras as a guest conductor. His reputation extended from North America, growing throughout the world. Over the years, he conducted orchestras from Minnesota to Berlin, and from Venezuela to New Zealand. Regarded as one of the principal conductors of his generation, Mata went on tours with, among others, the Cleveland Orchestra, the London Symphony, and the Rotterdam Philharmonic. Principal guest conductor of the

Pittsburgh Symphony and artistic adviser to the Mexico City National Opera, he also worked closely with the National Arts Center in Ottawa.

In 1977, Mata became musical director and conductor of the Dallas Symphony Orchestra. He adopted the city as his headquarters and stayed until 1993.

Mexicans had often been looked down on in Texas as allegedly inferior in cultural matters. Thus, it was most unusual for a Texan city to choose a Mexican to head its symphony. It proved to be a wise move. The Dallas Symphony had been regarded as an orchestra of merely regional importance.

Mata polished its sound, working until it became acknowledged as one of the major orchestras internationally. He also assisted in the acoustic design of the Morton H. Meyerson Symphony Center in Dallas. It opened in 1989, taking its place as one of the world's major concert halls. In 1993, when he retired as its principal conductor, the Dallas Symphony named him its first-ever "conductor emeritus for life."

Eduardo Mata died two years later while piloting his own plane on a trip within Mexico. The aircraft crashed shortly after takeoff from an airport near the capital. His wife, who was traveling with him, was also killed. At the time of his death, Mata had begun to make an ambitious series of records of top symphonic works by the composers of Latin America.

In 1991 Mata received the White House Hispanic Heritage Award for Performing Arts/Music. He also received many honors in Mexico, including (1984) life membership in the National College (an award reserved for the nation's top intellectuals and artists), the Golden Lyre Award (1974), the Elías Sourasky Prize in the Arts (1975), and the Mozart Medal (1991).

Further Reading

Kanellos, Nicolás. *The Hispanic-American Almanac.* Detroit: Gale Research, Inc., 1993.

Slonimsky, Nicolas. *Baker's Biographical Dictionary of Musicians.* New York: Schirmer Books, 1994.

Medina, Harold (Harold Raymond Medina) (1888–1990) *judge*

A highly respected jurist, Harold Medina was a great champion of the First Amendment who helped establish directions in important areas of U.S. law. He was known to be happiest when presented with cases of the most extreme complexity on which he could bring his formidable legal mind to bear. In an unusually long life and career Medina successively achieved renown as a law professor, as a trial lawyer, as a judge who presided over one of the most famous trials in its time, and finally as the oldest federal judge in the United States, who was still at work at the age of 92.

The rather flamboyant Medina was described by William O. Douglas, a U.S. Supreme Court justice and former student of Medina's—as "bright, able, and a ham actor" both at the university lectern and at the trial bench. At the same time he was a notable erudite in literature who read the Greek and Latin classics in their original languages.

Harold Medina was born in Brooklyn, New York, on February 16, 1888. His businessman father had come to the United States at the age of 12 to escape warfare in the Yucatán area of Mexico; on his mother's side he was descended from the early Dutch settlers of what are now New York and New Jersey. Medina's brilliance was evident from his student days at Princeton University and then Columbia Law School, from which he graduated in 1909 and 1912, respectively. He earned a Phi Beta Kappa key and emerged at the top of his law class. He passed the New York bar examination even before graduating. He then developed a course to prepare others for the bar exam that was so successful he could have retired and lived for the rest of his life on the money earned by that course alone. But that was not his intention. He taught law at Columbia for more than 30 years.

The young lawyer was very shaken in 1915 when a trial client of his committed suicide, apparently because Medina had put in a poor presentation in court. Thereafter he became an appeals lawyer instead and did not participate in trials again until more than 15 years later. But then he distinguished himself at such trial work, as he had previously done in appeals procedures.

It was thanks to Medina that Fiorello La Guardia won a 1932 court case that allowed him to run for the post of mayor of New York City, where La Guardia became one of the most famous holders of that office ever. Ten years later, during World War II, successfully defending a man who had apparently committed treason in his relations with two Nazi spies, Medina convinced the Supreme Court to establish tougher requirements for demonstrating treason.

Medina was appointed federal judge in 1947. In 1951 he became an appellate court judge, in 1958 he was named senior judge, and he retired in 1980, 68 years after starting out as a lawyer.

In addition to teaching, practicing, and ruling on the law, Medina wrote many books on the subject. Two of his works, *Judge Medina Speaks Out* (1954) and *Anatomy of Freedom* (1959) can be regarded as his political testament, his affirmation of the value he placed on the fundamentals of the rule of law, particularly the First Amendment to the U.S. Constitution.

The most celebrated case that Medina tried in court took place in 1949, when 11 leaders of the U.S. Communist Party were convicted of trying to overthrow the government by force. The nine-month-long trial was famous not only because of the nature of the charges but also because of the abuse the defense heaped on Medina in the hopes of forcing the declaration of a mistrial. Medina refused to fall for the ploy, presiding over the trial with such dignity that he was nicknamed "Judge Patience." After the trial, he punished the offending defense lawyers.

Because all 11 defendants were found guilty, and because of the summary way Medina dealt with the disruptive lawyers afterward, anti-Communists—and conservatives in general—praised him highly. On the other hand, in this trial Medina established a principle (later upheld by the Supreme Court) that a distinction must be made between advocating the violent overthrow of a government with specific intent to see it carried out, and advocating it only in general, abstract terms, which would not be enough to convict a defendant. This distinction was Medina's liberal-minded extension of the application of his favorite principle, free speech.

Medina also helped define the scope of antitrust legislation in a banking case that expanded the types of financial activities banks would thereafter be allowed to carry out in the United States. Showered with scores of awards including 25 honorary university degrees, Medina was a trustee emeritus of both Princeton and Columbia Universities.

He died in 1990, at age 102.

Further Reading

Hawthorne, Daniel. *Judge Medina: A Biography.* New York: W. Funk, 1952.

Meier, Matt S. *Notable Latino Americans.* Westport, Conn.: Greenwood Press, 1997.

Meléndez, Bill (José Cuauhtémoc Meléndez) (1916–) *cartoon animator*

Animator of all the feature movies and TV specials based on Charles M. Schulz's *Peanuts* comic strip, as well as many other acclaimed productions, Bill Meléndez is a successful businessman as well as a prizewinning artist. He founded his own animation company, Bill Meléndez Productions, and has employed as many as 50 animators or more at its Los Angeles headquarters. The studio's branch in London employs about the same number.

Born José Cuauhtémoc Meléndez on November 15, 1916, in the town of Hermosillo, Sonora state, Mexico, he was given his middle name in honor of the last Aztec king: Cuautémoc, the successor of his uncle Moctezuma (Montezuma) and of Moctezuma's brother Cuitláhuac, was tortured and later strangled by the Spaniards. He is a national hero in Mexico.

Bill Meléndez *(Bill Meléndez Productions)*

José's father, Ramón Meléndez, was a general in the Mexican civil wars who, according to his son, "was always on the wrong side, and he was so loyal nobody could get him to switch, the way so many others were doing. He'd rather fight. But he usually was off hiding in the hills somewhere." The general's wife took her family across the border to the United States.

"We never knew we were poor until we came to the United States," her son would later recall.

In his new country, José Cuauhtémoc became "Bill." He also grew into a large (six-foot-plus), strong man with a full mustache, whose impressive physical presence was invariably commented upon by the people who met him.

Meléndez's schooling began in Douglas, Arizona. At 11 years of age, because his English was poor, he was initially placed in kindergarten.

Gifted with an ability to draw, the boy's early ambition was to be a cartoonist. He studied at Los Angeles Polytechnic High, then at Los Angeles City College, and finally at Chouinard Art Institute.

At first, all the places where he applied for work as a cartoonist turned him down. Before he finally found work in his chosen field, Meléndez had to work in a lumber yard. However, once he landed his first drawing job, his career reads like an abbreviated history of U.S. movie animation.

That first job was with the Walt Disney studios. It was 1938, and Meléndez was only 22. He joined the company as an assistant animator, perfecting his skills and working on the animation of Donald Duck and Mickey Mouse shorts, as well as the feature-length classics *Fantasia* and *Pinocchio* (both 1940), *Dumbo* (1941), and *Bambi* (1942).

By the time *Bambi* was released, Meléndez was no longer with Disney. After three years with Disney, Meléndez switched to another company, but his new employer, Leon Schlesinger Productions, was bought by Warner Bros. For seven years, Meléndez worked there on the animation of such characters as Bugs Bunny, Porky Pig, and Daffy Duck.

In 1948, Meléndez left Warner Bros. for United Productions of America (UPA), which strove to provide the direct opposite of Disney's very naturalistic drawing style. There, Meléndez helped animate one of UPA's favorite characters, Gerald McBoing Boing, who first appeared in 1950.

After UPA, Meléndez drew animated cartoons for TV commercials. He is credited with having directed more than 1,000 of these even before he established Bill Meléndez Productions in 1964. He also amassed shelfloads of prizes for his TV advertising work at competitive festivals, both in the United States and in Europe. When the American TV Commercial Festival was held in New York in 1960 and gave prizes to the 20 best commercials, it was almost a clean sweep—all but two of the top 20 had been directed by Meléndez.

He thus established himself as "the (animation) industry's most distinguished Latino," as the New York *Daily News* called him when it devoted a cover story of its magazine to Meléndez in 1989.

Meléndez's association with Charlie Brown, Snoopy, Lucy, Linus, and the rest of the *Peanuts* gang began before he founded his own animation company. An advertising agency had the idea of using the *Peanuts* characters in ads to sell the Ford Motor Co.'s Falcon cars. The agency asked Meléndez to draw the commercials if the comic strip's creator, Charles M. Schulz, could be persuaded to accept the idea. His creations had never before been used to advertise products. Meléndez visited and won Schulz over with his career credentials and his obvious feeling for the characters. The commercials were broadcast in 1957 and were greatly liked, particularly by Schulz. The voices were supplied by actual children, save for Snoopy's which was provided by Meléndez himself. Later he animated these characters in commercials for other products, again with great success.

In 1965 a producer approached Schulz with an idea for a TV special. Schulz agreed on the condition that Meléndez do the animation. The half-hour special, *A Charlie Brown Christmas,* won Meléndez an Emmy Award as well as a Peabody Award. A string of Peanuts specials followed over the years, including *It's the Great Pumpkin, Charlie Brown* (1966) and *Play It Again, Charlie Brown* (1971), which, taken together, collected another four Emmys, another Peabody, and Oscar and Grammy nominations as well. In addition, a weekly TV series was aired on Saturday mornings, and four full-length movies—*A Boy Named Charlie Brown*

(1969), *Snoopy, Come Home* (1972), *Race for Your Life, Charlie Brown* (1977), and *Bon Voyage, Charlie Brown (And Don't Come Back)* (1980) were made. Meléndez's products are often rebroadcast on television and some have also been issued on videotape.

Bill Meléndez also worked on many other productions, winning yet another Emmy for animating the Cathy character created by cartoonist Cathy Guisewite. Based on drawings by the British cartoonist Ronald Searle, Meléndez animated, at his studio in England, an homage to Gilbert and Sullivan operettas, titled *Dick Deadeye, or Duty Done*. Other TV works include *Yes, Virginia, There is a Santa Claus* (1974) and *The Lion, the Witch, and the Wardrobe* (1979).

Both the Los Angeles Art Directors' Club and the New York Art Directors' Club have awarded Meléndez their medals three times. He won the *Journal of Commercial Art* awards twice and the Communications Art Award of Excellence.

Meléndez has taught movie cartooning at the University of Southern California and in courses run by the Screen Cartoonists Guild. Over and over, he has visited predominantly Chicano schools to try to inspire the students to excel. It can only be done through hard work, he has always told the schoolchildren: "Don't be lazy!" For those who dream of following his personal career: "Learn to draw!"

Further Reading

Shorris, Earl. *Latinos: A Biography of the People.* New York: Avon Books, 1992.

Solomon, Charles. *The History of Animation: Enchanted Drawings.* New York: Knopf, 1989.

The Cartoon Factory, Inc. "Bill Melendez Biography." Available online. URL:http://www.cartoon-factory.com/melendez_bio.htm. Downloaded October 10, 2000.

✤ **Mendoza, Lydia** (1916–) *singer*

Celebrated for decades as *La alondra de la frontera,* or Lark of the (Mexican–U.S.) Border, Lydia Mendoza was the first recording star of the popular songs of the Texas frontier area. She was later recognized as an authority on that type of folk music. When President Bill Clinton conferred the Medal of Arts and National Humanities Medal on Mendoza in 1999, he noted that she and other recipients of the award have, each in her or his own way, "defined who we are and what we are as a nation."

Mendoza was born in Houston, Texas, in 1916, the daughter of immigrants from Mexico. In her childhood she was not sent to school because her father thought girls did not need to be educated; nor did she learn English. Until she was 11 years old, the family shuttled frequently between the United States and Mexico, where her father was a railroad mechanic and brewery worker. The only education Lydia got was lessons from her mother at home. Nor did she learn to read music, even though her family was musical, but she did learn to play 12-string guitar and the mandolin and to sing. In music, her grandmother was her main teacher.

When Mendoza's father became ill and was forced to leave the Mexican railroad job, the family started to play and sing music in the streets and restaurants of Texas border towns. A small breakthrough occurred in 1928 when the family was contracted by a San Antonio phonograph company to record 20 songs. These were among the very first recordings of the popular music of the region.

For two years after that the Mendozas tried to make a go of it in Michigan, but success was made even more difficult by the Great Depression. They returned to Texas, where they continued to play and pass the hat in public. These were times of great economic difficulties for the family group—made worse when from time to time some establishment refused to let them in because they were "nonwhite."

In addition to singing with her family, the teenage Lydia now also sang alone. She entered and won a radio singing contest, marking the beginning of a radio and recording career in which she became well known and acquired the "Lark" nickname. In particular, one of her songs, "Mal hombre" (Evil Man), became a hit as far afield as South America.

In 1935 Mendoza married her first husband (after his death in 1961 she remarried—both her husbands were shoemakers). Her career was put on hold during World War II but bloomed anew afterward. She not only performed Tejano and many other types of Latin and southwestern music live but made numerous recordings, including many of songs she wrote herself.

By about 1970 Mendoza had become something of an institution. A serious interest in folk music of the various regions of the United States had grown, and after so many years of being a local phenomenon, she found herself being invited to play and record her art for such organizations as the Library of Congress and the Smithsonian Institution. The *New York Times* praised her "strong, clear mezzo-soprano" register and "tempestuous" vocal style. In 1977, Lydia Mendoza played at President Jimmy Carter's inauguration. In 1982 she received a National Endowment for the Arts National Heritage Fellowship. Two years later she was inducted into the Tejano Music Hall of Fame, in 1985 into the Texas Women's Hall of Fame, and in 1991 into the Conjunto Music Hall of Fame.

Further Reading

Griffith, S. J., et al. *Ethnic Recordings in America: A Neglected Heritage.* Washington, D.C.: American Folklife Center, Library of Congress, 1982.

Mendoza, Lydia, with Chris Strachwitz and James Nicopulos. *Lydia Mendoza: A Family Autobiography.* Houston, Tex.: Arte Público Press, 1993.

National Association of Latino Arts and Culture. "El Aviso—Lydia Mendoza, 'La Cancionera de los Pobres.'" Available online. URL: http://www.nalac.org/mendoza.html. Downloaded October 10, 2000.

⧬ Menéndez, Bob (Robert Menéndez)

(1954–) *government official*

A congressman known for working with equal energy for issues of interest to the Latino community, to his own constituency in New Jersey, and to the United States in general, Bob Menéndez in 1999 was elected vice chair of the Democratic Caucus in the U.S. House of Representatives—the fourth-ranking Democrat in the House. He was the first Hispanic elected to such a position of leadership in either party in congressional history. When the voters sent him back to Congress for the fourth consecutive term in 1998, they did so by a vote of 83 percent.

Robert Menéndez *(Courtesy Office of Robert Menéndez)*

He is not known to be descended from Pedro MENÉNDEZ DE AVILÉS.

Bob Menéndez was born on January 1, 1954, in New York City, to which his family had emigrated from Cuba. When Bob was a child, the Menéndezes moved to Union City, New Jersey.

Interested in a law career, he obtained a B.A. degree from St. Peter's College in Jersey City, New Jersey, in 1976, and he went on to graduate from Rutgers Law School in Newark in 1979. The following year he was admitted to the bar in New Jersey and entered private practice. He dealt with a variety of cases including criminal, family, and real property law, and quickly gained recognition. In 1981, a year after starting out in the profession, he received a Community Service award from the Gran Logia del Norte lodge and an Outstanding Service award from the Hispanic Law Enforcement organization, and the following year he was given an Outstanding Community Service award by *Actualidades* magazine.

Community service had long been a hallmark of Menéndez's career. In the 1970s, while still an undergraduate, he served with Union City's elected board of education—which he had himself helped create. In 1982 he founded and became president of the Alliance civic organization, and in following years was a member of the Governor's Hispanic Advisory Committee in Trenton, New Jersey, and of the Governor's Ethnic Advisory Committee in Washington, D.C.

Union City elected Menéndez as New Jersey's first Hispanic mayor in 1986. While continuing to serve as mayor, the next year he also entered the New Jersey legislature, first in the assembly and then in the state senate. Again, he was the first Hispanic to serve in the latter.

In 1993 Menéndez first went to Washington as a congressman for New Jersey. With an emphasis on the areas of transportation, economic development, education, and human rights worldwide, he stood out as an activist legislator. Vice President Al Gore noted in 1999 that "Congressman Bob Menéndez has never been one to stand back and let things happen."

The Kiwanis Club conferred its Man of the Year award on him in 1994. Four years later, he won the Ellis Island Medal of Honor for his work on behalf of human rights, an area of concern that was not born during his years in Washington: Menéndez had already sponsored a milestone bias crime law during his service in the New Jersey State Senate.

Environmental and health issues have been another area of achievement for Menéndez, who was placed on the 1998 Honor Roll of the bipartisan League of Conservation Voters "for his consistent efforts on behalf of conservation and public health initiatives."

In the security area, one of the most successful efforts he has participated in for his New Jersey district has been the placing of almost 800 policemen on its streets through the COPS (Community Oriented Policing Services) program. In the field of education, he participated in the drive to fund the hiring of 100,000 additional teachers around the United States.

In 2000, Menéndez was reelected as a congressman for New Jersey.

Further Reading

U.S. House of Representatives. "Congressman Robert Menendez, 13th District, New Jersey." Available online. URL: http://menendez.house.gov. Downloaded October 10, 2000.

Menéndez de Avilés, Pedro
(1519–1574) *conqueror*

In 1565, Pedro Menéndez de Avilés founded the oldest continuously inhabited European town in U.S. territory—St. Augustine in Florida.

An expert sailor and fighter who was as ruthless as he was fearless, Menéndez de Avilés put a permanent stop to any French attempts to colonize Florida. In fact, he put a halt to all serious French forays for more than a century into what was to become U.S. territory. When the French did reconnoiter again in 1674, they did so along the Mississippi, marching down from the Great Lakes—not along the coast that Menéndez de Avilés had secured.

A member of the nobility in the region of Asturias in Spain, Menéndez de Avilés was born in the city of Avilés on February 15, 1519. He was an adventurer from early on: at the age of 14 he ran away to sea. He returned after two years but went to sea again though he had just been forced to agree to a marriage; his bride-to-be was only 10, and before they could actually marry, he once again left for sea.

During his first outings, as a cabin boy aboard a Spanish vessel, Menéndez de Avilés participated in battles against French privateers (warships sent to sea not by governments, but by private individuals) that hovered around Spanish shores and sea lanes.

Spain and Portugal had beaten other European powers to new worlds, and their expeditions first ventured far down the coast of Africa and west to the "Indies." The English, the French, and the Dutch then helped themselves to the riches of these lands without going to the trouble of initial discovery and conquest. These other countries sought to take what Spain had settled, or, more simply, they waited for Spanish conquistadores to plunder those lands thoroughly and then, inaugurating a golden age of piracy, they in turn plundered the loot-laden ships on their way back to Europe.

Menéndez de Avilés first made a name for himself fighting to protect Spanish vessels from such attacks. He rose to the rank of captain general of the Indies fleet. Around 1560, he organized the shipments of silver from America to Spain into a system that actually rendered them safe from everything but the weather. Instead of each ship making the voyage separately as they had before, they now traveled in convoys that were too large (about 30 cargo vessels) and too well protected by Spanish warships to be attacked by pirates.

The captain general, however, was not above smuggling for his own benefit on the way back to the Caribbean. Many officials were engaged in the same trade, but Menéndez de Avilés, with his impetuous ways, had made too many enemies to avoid intrigues and betrayal. In 1563, King Philip II of Spain threw him into jail in the city of Seville. But two years later, Philip needed Menéndez de Avilés to eradicate a French presence that had been detected in Florida. For this, the king appointed him governor and captain general of Florida and promised to make him a marquis afterward.

In addition to driving the French out, Menéndez de Avilés was to establish permanent Spanish settlements. From Juan PONCE DE LEÓN in 1513 onward, the Spaniards had not only been the first to explore the area, but they had also been the first to try to set up a permanent colony in what was later the United States. This was Lucas Vázquez de Ayllón's fort of San Miguel de Guadalupe, founded in 1526 in what is now South Carolina. That settlement, however, proved short-lived.

Now, Menéndez de Avilés learned, the French were trying to set up forts that would be handy bases for attacks on Spanish shipping. The first, Charlesfort in South Carolina, failed the same year of its founding, 1562. But the French soon followed it with Fort Caroline in what is now Florida.

Within a few months of being released from prison, Menéndez de Avilés left Spain with a fleet in July of 1565. In August, he landed in a bay not far from Fort Caroline and founded the fort of San Agustín de la Florida—now St. Augustine. In September, he attacked Fort Caroline and slaughtered most of the adult male inhabitants. He followed this with a massacre of French castaways on a nearby island.

Menéndez de Avilés acted with a mixture, typical of his time, of religious, political, and economic motives. The political reason held that the French, in Spain's view, were trespassing on Spanish territory. The Spanish and Portuguese convinced the pope to divide the New World between their two nations. The economic reason stated that the French bases were a threat to Spanish shipping. To add religious fuel to this, these particular Frenchmen were Huguenots— French Protestants. The Huguenots were also persecuted in France, notably during the Saint Bartholomew's Day Massacre, seven years after Menéndez de Avilés's brutal deeds in Florida.

Conquistador Menéndez de Avilés had the bodies of his victims hung from trees with signs saying that they had been executed not for being Frenchmen but for being heretics. He spared some who were Roman Catholics and the few others who consented to convert to Catholicism.

Menéndez de Avilés spent the next two years founding other forts on the coast and struggling, with little success, to obtain aid for the new settlements from the Spanish authorities in the Caribbean. He finally returned to Spain and sought help from the king directly. In 1568 he was named governor of Cuba as well as Florida. But Menéndez de Avilés didn't have much time to use his new post to send reinforcements to Florida. The king found a new assignment for him, this time in Europe. Philip II put him in charge of organizing a fleet for an invasion of England. It was a long-term project, and what Menéndez de Avilés began finally grew into Spain's "Invincible Armada." However, he never saw the great defeat suffered by the armada in 1588: Menéndez de Avilés died long before, in 1574.

Further Reading

Lyon, Eugene. *The Enterprise of Florida.* Gainesville: University Presses of Florida, 1976.

Thompson, Kathleen. *Pedro Menéndez de Avilés.* Milwaukee, Wis.: Raintree Publishers, 1990.

❧ Migenes-Johnson, Julia (1945–)
opera singer

Julia Migenes-Johnson emerged in the 1980s as one of the best and most distinctive sopranos of her time. She shone particularly in the title role of the opera *Carmen,* singing opposite Plácido DOMINGO, one of the world's greatest tenors.

Of Puerto Rican, Greek, and Irish ancestry, Migenes-Johnson was born on March 13, 1945, in New York City. She has been on stage virtually all her life, beginning at age three as one of the children who are seen in the opera *Madama Butterfly.* She was in the musical *South Pacific* when she was six.

Migenes-Johnson went to a special school for children working in the performing arts, the Moser Academy. She then continued at the High School of Music and Art, training as a singer and dancer, and then at Juilliard, a music conservatory in New York City. While in high school, she took part in a Young People's Concert led by the conductor Leonard Bernstein. She then began to sing in Broadway musicals, including *Fiddler on the Roof* and *West Side Story.*

Soon, her strong soprano voice within a little figure led Migenes-Johnson to specialize in opera, though she occasionally performed in other disciplines. She first sang for the New York City Opera in 1965 in the opera *The Saint of Bleecker Street.* She then decided to expand her operatic training through study in Europe. She trained in Vienna, Austria, and Cologne, Germany, and performed with the Volksoper company in the Austrian capital.

In 1978 she was back in the limelight in the United States, singing the role of Musetta in *La Bohème* at the San Francisco Opera. The next year she performed for the first time at New York's Metropolitan Opera, singing the role of Jenny in *The Rise and Fall of the City of Mahagonny.*

She was now an international star, acclaimed both in Europe and in the United States. Although critics remarked on her powerful and very individual singing voice, they also made particular note of her talent as an actress. She never merely stood on stage and sang her lines but clearly felt their meaning and transmitted it to the audience. As a result, she received the ultimate praise for a soprano: that of being compared to the late singer Maria Callas. Callas, too, was

as famous for her tempestuous acting style as for her voice. Among those who made the comparison to Callas was critic Clive Barnes of the *New York Post.*

Because of her mix of singing and acting talent, Migenes-Johnson was selected to play the title role in a 1984 film of *Carmen,* directed for the screen by Francesco Rosi. The lead male role was sung by Plácido Domingo.

Because the role of Carmen is written for a mezzo-soprano, a lower voice, Migenes-Johnson practiced for a full year to bring down the register of her own voice rather than simply sing the part in a higher key. She also took special Spanish dancing lessons. The result was highly regarded both as opera and as movie entertainment. Migenes-Johnson received best actress nominations for this role in Italy and in France.

In her original soprano vocal register, Migenes-Johnson has also had successes in many 20th-century operas that are considered difficult to sing, such as *Lulu* and *Salome.*

In 1985 she was the subject of a profile on television's *60 Minutes* program.

Further Reading
Blackwell, Earl. *Celebrity Register.* Towson, Md.: Times Publishing Group, 1986.
Slonimsky, Nicolas. *Baker's Biographical Dictionary of Musicians.* New York: Schirmer Books, 1994.

❧ Miranda, Carmen (Maria do Carmo Miranda da Cunha) (1909–1955) *actress*

Carmen Miranda was one of the most famous Latino figures, male or female, ever.

In 1945, at the height of her career, Miranda was Hollywood's best-paid actress. In movie after movie, she played a character who was instantly recognizable and has remained so, even decades after her death. That character was a caricature, a mishmash of exaggerated Latin American ingredients, usually topped by an outrageous hat or turban piled high with tropical fruit. As played by Carmen Miranda, however, this caricature was a friendly, good-natured one. She transformed herself into a cheerful parody of Latina women in general. The United States saw her as the ultimate Hispanic female.

Despite her enduring fame, Miranda's career in the United States was closely linked to a given political situation in the Americas. Specifically, it was tied to a strategy devised by U.S. President Franklin Delano Roosevelt to deal with Latin America, called the Good Neighbor Policy. When the international situation changed, Carmen Miranda's star began to wane.

Maria do Carmo Miranda da Cunha was born in Portugal, on February 9, 1909, in a small locality called Marco de Canavezes near Lisbon. However, in the same year, when she was only three months old, her family moved to Rio de Janeiro, which was then the capital of Brazil.

The girl grew up feeling Brazilian, and Brazil in time came to regard her as a great national figure. Her early death was felt as a major loss for the country. When her career took her to the United States, she was hailed as "the Brazilian Bombshell." Yet, the screen character created for her, with her help, was not specifically Brazilian; it was a full Latin American and Caribbean composite.

Carmen Miranda with Groucho Marx *(Cabrera Archive)*

Educated in a convent school, she afterward found work as a hatmaker and model in a Rio de Janeiro department store. Her father was a barber, though Hollywood embroidered this, claiming him to be a wealthy fruit trader.

Marked by a very lively personality and a love for song, the young Miranda often sang during her work at the department store. This became her passport to a show-business career. She was overheard by a guitarist who, impressed by her voice, managed to get her out of the department store and onto a radio show. From there she moved to nightclub performances and then to motion pictures. Miranda made four movies in Brazil, beginning with *A Voz do Carnaval (The Voice of Carnival)* in 1933.

A U.S. theatrical producer, Lee Shubert, saw and heard her perform at a nightclub in the Brazilian capital. Correctly suspecting that she could be a sensation in the United States, he invited her to appear on Broadway. Carmen Miranda thus arrived in New York at the age of 30.

She first appeared in a 1939 Broadway musical called *The Streets of Paris*. She was described as "the biggest theatrical sensation of the year." She next appeared in a nightclub act at the Waldorf Astoria. Immediately, Hollywood beckoned, and she left for California, although she would later return to work on Broadway.

During the 1930s, President Franklin D. Roosevelt had inaugurated the Good Neighbor Policy to woo the allegiance of Latin American countries. The United States realized that some of those countries were in danger of succumbing to fascism, which was then on the rise in Europe.

Under the Good Neighbor Policy, the United States attempted to change its reputation in Latin American nations. Previously, Latin America had been either insulted, ignored, or actually invaded by the United States. Now, as the United States faced times of increasing tension and then war in Europe, there was a boom of U.S. interest in and respect for Latin America.

Hollywood aided the government in the Good Neighbor Policy. These were the years when Walt Disney created movies with Latino subjects such as *The Three Caballeros* and introduced Latino characters such as the Brazilian parrot José Carioca. Hollywood's adoption of Carmen Miranda fell clearly within this trend.

Starting with *Down Argentine Way* (1940), *That Night in Rio* (1941), and *Week-End in Havana* (1941), Miranda began to appear in a string of movie musicals. The best and most extravagant of them was *The Gang's All Here* (1943), in which she performed a song created especially for her, *The Lady in the Tutti-Frutti Hat.*

As the titles of these films indicate, their alleged locations varied from one end of Latin America to the other. In actual fact, however, they were set in an indefinite tropical never-never land where Carmen Miranda could bubble over with her infectious enthusiasm and show off her jokey costumes. She said she herself invented her huge platform shoes, to disguise her height—only five feet two inches.

The Miranda character, basically repeated in movie after movie, was a spoof of Latino elements, exaggerated as far as they could go. Yet, Carmen Miranda was so famous that there were numerous attempts to parody the parody. No sooner had she made her presence known in the musical *The Streets of Paris,* singing the song *South American Way,* than the comedienne Imogene COCA, appearing in a show called *The Straw Hat Revue,* lampooned her and sang *Soused American Way* (*soused* meaning "drunk").

After 1945, the political situation changed, and the career of Carmen Miranda, as well as that of other Latinos in U.S. show business, changed with it. In her case, the change was quite abrupt.

In Europe, Germany and Italy had been defeated, and the new enemy was the communist Soviet Union. The United States considered it unlikely that any of the Latin American governments of the time might be tempted by communism. Thus the United States largely reverted to a lack of interest in Latin America.

Also, a large-scale migration of Puerto Ricans to New York began after World War II. When many people in the United States thought about Hispanics, they no longer saw them as something exotic and far away, save for Mexicans, but as an actual presence. The immigrants created new challenges. The Carmen Miranda character became essentially old-fashioned.

Miranda was offered smaller roles in smaller movies. After 1946, she made only four more films, including *A Date With Judy* (1948) and *Scared Stiff* (1953); in the latter, she was parodied by the comic actor Jerry Lewis.

An extremely hard worker, she was very disappointed and upset by her new situation. In 1955, she appeared in a television production headed by the comedian Jimmy Durante, pouring all her energy into this show. Then, following the performance, at age 46, she died of a heart attack.

In later decades, a character in TV commercials, Chiquita Banana, was created with Carmen Miranda as an inspiration. But, at a time when people were becoming more sensitive about racial stereotypes, there were increasing protests, and the Chiquita Banana commercials were eventually withdrawn from television.

Nevertheless, Miranda herself continues to be remembered with affection. Even as late as the 1990s it was possible to assemble enough Carmen Miranda imitators to hold a special parade in her honor in New York City.

Further Reading

Montero-Gil, Martha. *Brazilian Bombshell: The Biography of Carmen Miranda.* New York: Donald I. Fine, 1989.

Oshana, Maryann. *Women of Color: A Filmography of Minority and Third World Women.* New York: Garland Publishing, 1985.

Woll, Allen L. *The Latin Image in American Film.* Los Angeles: UCLA Latin American Center Publications, 1980.

✤ Miró, Esteban Rodríguez

(1744–1795) *government official*

As Spanish governor of Louisiana, Esteban Rodríguez Miró encouraged settlement by English-speaking colonists from the new neighboring country, the United States of America.

A native of Catalonia in Spain, born in 1744, Miró was a career soldier. Before being sent to America, he had already fought against Portugal, at the age of 18.

In the viceroyalty of New Spain (Mexico), Miró served under Bernardo de GÁLVEZ, governor of Louisiana. This was the Spanish province in closest proximity to the British area of North America.

When the 13 colonies fought for their independence, Spain was their ally. Gálvez, with Miró as his senior assistant, kept the British in the Gulf of Mexico tied down by attacking and conquering cities in British-held West Florida. In this campaign, Miró rose to the rank of colonel and was later appointed to succeed Gálvez as the acting governor of Louisiana (1782).

His years in office, like those of his predecessor, were marked by the problem of relations with the English speakers to the east. These Anglos were becoming increasingly powerful and were rapidly increasing in number.

As part of his efforts to deal with the pressures on his borders, Miró also negotiated with the Native Americans in the area. In 1784, he signed an agreement with the Creek Nation, entitled "Articles of Agreement, Trade, and Peace."

In the same year, by order of the Spanish king, the use of the port of New Orleans and transit along the lower Mississippi River were barred to U.S. colonists and traders. Spain was attempting to enforce the same policy it had always tried to apply in trade with the Americas. This policy, ever since the continent's discovery, had been to give a monopoly to Spanish ships. What triggered this new crackdown was the rising number of U.S. colonists, a large enough number to threaten to swamp the Spanish-speaking territories. Indeed, they would do so in the following century. Governor Miró, however, chose to be very lax in implementing the trade restrictions ordered by the Spanish capital, Madrid.

Miró, who in 1785 was promoted from acting to full governor, had a different idea of what needed to be done to stem the Anglo tide. He believed that interfering with shipping and with trade only made the Anglos furious and might even lead to war. Like the previous governor, Gálvez, Miró believed that the best barrier was a human one—the presence of many colonists flying the Spanish flag.

The governor lobbied the king on behalf of his ideas and, in 1788, obtained an order that partly reopened Mississippi River shipping to foreigners and, in addition, offered free land to settlers in the Spanish province. When Miró took office, in 1782, there were 20,000 inhabitants in Louisiana. Ten years later there were 45,000.

Miró ended his term of office in 1791. His governorship was regarded as progressive: He was tireless in reconstruction efforts after a devastating fire in New Orleans in 1788, and he kept the Spanish Inquisition from setting up office in Louisiana.

His military career also advanced. He was made brigadier general in 1789 and field marshal after his return to Spain, where he died in 1795. In Madrid, he was accused of having enriched himself, while governor, through illegal trade in tobacco with the United States. He was acquitted of the charges.

Further Reading
Malone, Dumas, ed. *Dictionary of American Biography.* New York: Charles Scribner's Sons, 1934.

❦ Mohr, Nicholasa (Nicholasa Golpe)
(1935–   ) *writer*

One of the most successful Hispanic-American authors, Nicholasa Mohr has won wide recognition and many awards for her heartfelt portrayals of Puerto Rican life on the U.S. mainland. She writes in English, and most of her books have been published by major, mainstream publishing houses. She has also earned high praise as an illustrator.

Nicholasa Golpe was born on November 1, 1935, in New York City, the last, and the only girl, of seven children. Both of her parents were born on the island of Puerto Rico, as were the first four of her brothers. The family arrived in New York eight years before Nicholasa's birth.

The family's life, as the future author was growing up in the city's Spanish Harlem neighborhood, was one of hard work and little money. The girl inherited storytelling skills from her mother, also called Nicholasa, although in her mother's case the talent was expressed orally rather than in writing.

Because of her gift for drawing, Nicholasa's first vocation was not literature but graphic arts. Between 1953 and 1969, she studied successively at the Art

Nicholasa Mohr *(Arte Público Press)*

Students League of New York, the Brooklyn Museum Art School, and the Pratt Center for Contemporary Printmaking. To finance her studies, she did English/Spanish translations and worked as a waitress and in an office. During her student years, Nicholasa was married.

Years later, after the death of her husband, Irwin Mohr, and with her own two sons grown, she was able to live off her writings. However, she could have just as easily made her living as a graphic artist, having been successful in that profession in her early work life.

In the early 1970s, however, Mohr began to channel more and more of her creativity into writing. Although she was a New York City Schools artist-in-residence in 1973–74 and taught art in New Jersey

before that and later in New Hampshire, she was also writer-in-residence in 1972 at the MacDowell Colony. She returned there twice more.

In 1973, her first book, *Nilda,* a fictionalized autobiography, was published and immediately established her reputation as an important writer. It also showed her talent as a graphic artist because Mohr both illustrated the book and designed its cover. The cover was honored by the Society of Illustrators' Citation of Merit. The book, which describes the maturing years of Nilda, a Puerto Rican girl in New York, received the *School Library Journal* Best Book Award, the Jane Addams Peace Association's Children's Book Award, and *The New York Times* Outstanding Book Award for Juvenile Fiction.

The New York Times declared that among books depicting what it is like to grow up being both poor and a member of a minority, "few have come up to *Nilda* in describing the crushing humiliations of poverty and in peeling off the ethnic wrappings so we can see the human child underneath."

Because *Nilda* was written for young readers and was a success, Mohr has had to fight against being typecast as a writer exclusively for that age group. After that first novel, she has published works for both adults and children, including collections of short stories and short novels, full-length novels, and essays on Puerto Rican immigrant issues.

She has expressed a feminist viewpoint by depicting women who fight traditions that keep them restricted to the roles of wives and mothers. Mohr has been acknowledged for writing with great insight and tact about very sensitive subjects.

Two of her works, although written in English, include Spanish words in their titles to reflect Puerto Rican speech: *El Bronx Remembered* (1975) and *In Nueva York* (1977). The first of these two won another *New York Times* award and a second *School Library Journal* prize. The other won yet another *School Library Journal* award plus the American Library Association Best Book Award and the National Conference on Social Studies Notable Book Award.

Her other works include *Felita* (1979), *Rituals of Survival: A Woman's Portfolio* (1985), *Going Home* (1986) and *A Matter of Pride and Other Stories* (1997). Again and again, Mohr has demonstrated an underlying belief in the strength of a human will that is capable of overcoming problems of racism, poverty, and exploitation.

Further Reading

Contemporary Authors, New Revision Series. Detroit: Gale Research, Inc., 1981.

Hernández, Carmen Dolores. *Puerto Rican Voices in English: Interviews with Writers.* Westport, Conn.: Praeger, 1997.

Kanellos, Nicolás, ed. *Biographical Dictionary of Hispanic Literature in the United States.* Westport, Conn.: Greenwood Press, 1989.

Kurcinka, Josh, Megan Kral, Christie Mason. "Voices from the Gaps: Nicholasa Mohr." Available online. URL: http://voices.cla.umn.edu/Authors/NicholasaMohr.html. Downloaded October 10, 2000.

❦ **Molina, Gloria** (1948–) *government official*

An outspoken community activist, Gloria Molina has made a career out of being the first Hispanic, or the first woman, or both, in a succession of government jobs. She has been listed by *Time* magazine as "one of the nation's most prominent Hispanic politicians."

Molina has not, however, allowed this phenomenon to become an end in itself. Wholly committed to fighting for the rights of minority groups, in 1992 she passed up an opportunity to run for mayor of Los Angeles, which would have been a resounding new first for her, and where she was considered to stand a very good chance of winning. Instead, she stayed on in her job as a member of the Los Angeles County Board of Supervisors—out of fear that if she left a vacancy in the board, it would be filled by a conservative who might undo much of her work. She thus let her concern for the people she represents come ahead of her own political career.

Gloria Molina was born in the Los Angeles suburb of Montebello on May 31, 1948. Her father, though born in the United States, had grown up in Mexico, where his family originated. Entering the United States again to work as a *bracero* (a hired hand imported from Mexico), he and Gloria's mother arrived the year before Gloria's birth. After her came nine other children.

Growing up in Pico Rivera, California, Molina later went to Rio Hondo College in Whittier, East Los Angeles College, and California State University in Los Angeles, from which she graduated in 1970. She worked first as a legal assistant, then, starting in 1971, as a job counselor at the East Los Angeles Community Union.

Her dedication to helping her community, born amid the student activism of the 1960s, was quickly maturing. Molina worked with United Way of Los Angeles and the Latin American Law Enforcement Association, and in 1972 successfully petitioned the state of California that a Hispanic woman be included in the California Commission on the Status of Women.

The following year she became founding president of a Hispanic women's organization, Comisión Femenil de Los Angeles. The year after that she be-

Gloria Molina *(Courtesy of the Office of the Supervisor, First District, Los Angeles)*

came its national president and held that position for two years. She also became administrative assistant to a state assemblyman, and took time to help found local chapters of several organizations, including the National Association of Latino Elected and Appointed Officials (NALEO) and Hispanic American Democrats.

In 1977, President Jimmy Carter appointed Molina a regional director of the Department of Health and Human Services' Intergovernmental and Congressional Affairs office. She served in that capacity for three years. Then, in 1980, she became chief deputy to the speaker of the California State Assembly, and two years later thought she might make a run for the assembly herself. Her seniors told her she did not have the qualifications—and furthermore, she realized that they preferred not to have women in the assembly.

Her dander up, Molina discovered she had a talent for organizing a campaign through personal action among the voters, without the support of a party organization. She won that 1982 election, becoming the first Hispanic woman in the California Lower House. Along the way to reelection afterward, she was named Hispanic of the Year by *Caminos* magazine in 1983, Democrat of the Year, also in 1983, by the Mexican American Opportunity Foundation, and Woman of the Year by *Ms.* magazine in 1984.

One of the major struggles in which Molina played a leading role in those years was the popular crusade against the building of a prison in East Los Angeles.

In 1987 Molina ran for a seat on the Los Angeles City Council. She won by a handy margin despite a crowded field of opponents and entered the council as its first Hispanic member. There, she continued to work for her favorite community causes such as services for minorities, women, children, and the poor, and the fight against drugs.

Setting her sights higher, in 1990 she entered a race for the Los Angeles County Board of Supervisors, a powerful body with a bigger budget than those of most states. Her victory in 1991, after a runoff election, meant she was the first Hispanic on the board in over a century, and the first woman in its history.

As Jimmy Carter had done in 1977, 15 years later President Bill Clinton turned to Molina, in his case appointing her cochair of his national presidential campaign. No Hispanic woman had ever held a similar position. She remained, however, on the Los Angeles County Board of Supervisor.

Molina has long been known for being as combative as she is effective, unafraid to challenge the biggest bosses in any organization if she finds fault with it, and reluctant to compromise to achieve her goals. A survey among the community in 1991 revealed her to be the most admired Hispanic leader in the United States.

Further Reading

Hewett, Joan. *Getting Elected: The Diary of a Campaign.* New York: Lodestar Books, 1989.
LA County Online. "Supervisor Gloria Molina." Available online. URL: http://molina.co.la.ca.us. Downloaded October 10, 2000.
Tardiff, Joseph C., and Mpho Mabunda, eds. *Dictionary of Hispanic Biography.* Detroit: Gale Research, 1996.

✆ Molina, Mario (Mario José Molina)
(1943–) *scientist*

Mario Molina has garnered two of the highest achievements in science. He has won the most prestigious award in the world, the Nobel Prize. And he has, very concretely, helped "save the planet" with work he has done that led directly to the international adoption of policies to protect the global environment. Neither of these, however, was a goal that Molina had consciously set himself. It was scientific curiosity that led him, with another chemist, F. Sherwood Rowland, to investigate the effect of a class of chemicals—called chlorofluorocarbons—on the ozone in the upper atmosphere. Yet it was their research in this field that jointly steered them to those unexpected results.

Mario Molina (not related to Gloria MOLINA) was born in Mexico City on March 19, 1943, the son of a lawyer and diplomat. Although briefly tempted to become a musician, by age 11 Mario knew that his future lay in chemistry, the result of a fascination that

Mario Molina *(Courtesy of Mario Molina)*

began with his first toy chemistry set. After high school, Molina studied chemical engineering at the National Autonomous University of Mexico, from which he earned a B.S. in 1965. He then mastered, in 1967, at the University of Freiburg in Germany. After a year spent teaching at the university in Mexico, he came to the United States—where he thereafter made his career—to study physical chemistry at the University of California at Berkeley, from which he earned a Ph.D. in 1972.

By 1973, Molina had found his particular field of interest. That year, he associated with Sherwood at the University of California at Irvine to study the interaction between chemical pollution and atmospheric gases. They zeroed in on chlorofluorocarbons (or CFCs), which were known to be very useful to humans. They made refrigerators and air conditioners possible, and were the gases that propelled products inside the spray cans that had quickly become common over much of the earth. The result was that increasingly large amounts of these chemicals were seeping out into the atmosphere.

The effect of this was unknown, but by the following year Molina and Sherwood had found it out. They discovered that CFCs wreaked havoc with ozone, a special molecular form of oxygen. Ozone will act as a poison if one is exposed to it on the earth's surface, but in the upper atmosphere it forms a thin layer that protects life below from the destructive effects of the sun's ultraviolet radiation.

When the two chemists announced their results, which they perfected and expanded in later years, the news had profound effects. Governments, individuals, and organizations were alarmed, and industrial chemists were put to work to find other materials that could replace CFCs but would lack their harmful effects.

In 1987 the United Nations adopted a treaty leading to a gradual international ban on CFCs.

Molina continued research—with a team that, among others, included his wife Luisa Tan, also a chemist—and teaching. He moved to the California Institute of Technology in 1982, and to the Massachusetts Institute of Technology seven years later.

For his work in the chemistry of the atmosphere, Molina shared the Nobel Prize for Chemistry in 1995 with his colleague Rowland and Paul J. Crutzen. Numerous other high honors have come Molina's way. They include the Esselen Award, Tyler Ecology Award, Max Planck Award, Walker Prize, Hispanic Engineer National Achievement Award, UN Environmental Program Global 500 Award and NASA Medal for Exceptional Scientific Achievement.

Molina has been a member of the National Academy of Sciences since 1993. In 1994 he was invited by President Bill Clinton to join the President's Committee of Advisors on Science and Technology.

Among the many associations of which he is a member is the Society for the Advance of Chicano & Native American Scientists.

Further Reading

Massachusetts Institute of Technology. "Mario J. Molina Homepage." Available online. URL:

http://eaps.mit.edu/molina. Downloaded October 10, 2000.

McMurray, Emily J., ed. *Notable Twentieth-Century Scientists*. Detroit: Gale Research, 1995.

Olesky, Walter. *Hispanic-American Scientists*. New York: Facts On File, 1998.

Montalbán, Ricardo (1920–) *actor*

Ricardo Montalbán's career in films and on television is distinguished and lengthy. At the beginning of his career he was given mainly "Latin lover" parts, but he went on to lend extra gravity and dignity to a succession of supporting but still important "character" roles. He was also one of the founders and was the first president of Nosotros, a self-help organization for Hispanics in the movie and television industry.

Montalbán was born in Mexico City on November 25, 1920. His parents were Spaniards who had immigrated to Mexico in 1906. When Ricardo was five, the family moved from the Mexican capital to Torreón, a city where his father ran a dry-goods store. Montalbán grew up speaking Spanish with the characteristic lisping inflections of Spain. He was taunted by his fellow Mexican schoolboys for being a *gachupín*, a Spaniard, just as he would later face discrimination in the United States for being Mexican.

One of his older brothers, Carlos, became an actor before Ricardo did. Carlos Montalbán (1904–1991) appeared in such movies as *Flying Down to Rio* (1933), *The Harder They Fall* (1956), and Woody Allen's *Bananas* (1971), in which he played a Central American dictator.

When Ricardo finished high school in Mexico, Carlos was already a Hollywood actor, although Ricardo later became much better known than his older brother. Carlos took Ricardo to the United States to continue his education. Driving across Texas, they were kept out of a diner by a sign reading, "No dogs or Mexicans allowed." Later, on his first outing to a dance in Los Angeles, Ricardo and a friend were kept out of the ballroom for being Mexicans.

In his memoirs, Montalbán recalled having asked himself, "How could this happen in a city whose name was *Los Angeles,* which Mexicans had settled long before anyone else arrived, which had streets named *Alvarado, Sepulveda, Pico, Santa Monica, Figueroa?*"

Carlos later took Ricardo to New York where the younger brother obtained some parts in Broadway plays. The parts were small, but the stars with whom he appeared were major ones, such as Tallulah Bankhead. Bankhead threatened to have Ricardo Montalbán boiled in oil if the nervous new actor forgot his lines onstage, but he did not, and his career was launched.

He then had to return to Mexico because his mother had taken ill. Instead of going back to the United States afterward, he worked in the Mexican movie industry, where he had a successful four years, starting in 1942. When his career seemed settled in Mexico, he was "discovered" by Hollywood's MGM studio, which put him under contract. His first U.S. movie was *Fiesta* (1947) costarring Esther Williams and Mary Astor. In it, he danced with Ann Miller and Cyd Charisse.

Handsome and debonair, Montalbán did well in roles as a Latin romantic figure where his Hispanic accent was actually an asset. In later years, without ever

Ricardo Montalbán in the film *Star Trek II: The Wrath of Khan (Cabrera Archive)*

fully losing his accent, he managed to be accepted in a variety of roles. His accent was seen as just another trait of the characters he portrayed. Not infrequently, he was cast as a member of another race, as when he played a Japanese in *Sayonara* (1957).

However, he never, in his own words, got "the big dramatic role that is so important for an actor's career." That break might have been provided by the role of a trapeze artist in *The Story of Three Loves* (1953). But after casting Montalbán and training him on a trapeze for a month in preparation for the role, the studio changed its mind and instead gave the part to a bigger star, Kirk Douglas.

Films in which Montalbán did appear include *Neptune's Daughter* (1949), *Latin Lovers* (1953), *The Saracen Blade* (1954), *Cheyenne Autumn* (1964), *Sweet Charity* (1969), *Escape From the Planet of the Apes* (1971), *Star Trek II: The Wrath of Khan* (1982), and *The Naked Gun: From the Files of Police Squad* (1988).

Although he had ridden horses since childhood, Montalbán was thrown by a horse during the filming of a movie in 1950. He fell on his back, hitting a rock, injured his spine, has suffered constant pain, and has had a limp ever since. He has always been unwilling to risk taking painkillers that might be addictive.

Montalbán has worked on the stage in diverse productions over the years, both on Broadway (opposite Lena Horne in *Jamaica*) and on nationwide tours. Nevertheless, he gained his biggest exposure on television. He often appeared in *The Loretta Young Show*, weekly half-hour dramas that were first broadcast in the 1950s. The hostess and star was the sister of Montalbán's wife, Georgiana Young.

In 1978 Montalbán was awarded an Emmy for his performance in a TV miniseries, *How the West Was Won*. In that same year, he started out in perhaps his best-known series role, as Mr. Roarke, the island ruler of *Fantasy Island*. In the 1980s, he had a major part in the *Dynasty II: The Colbys* series.

One of Montalbán's most significant roles has been spokesperson and advocate of Hispanics in the entertainment industry. In 1971, he was one of the founders of Nosotros (which means "We"). Montalbán was chosen as the organization's first president so that his celebrity would open doors for the group.

Thanks to his name, Nosotros received a degree of attention from the media and from movie and TV industry leaders that it might otherwise not have.

Nosotros's method has been friendly, reasoned persuasion, not militant confrontation; this is in line with Montalbán's own personal style. The organization's main goals are to improve the image of Hispanics in movies and on television and to get more jobs for Hispanic actors and actresses. Its success over the years has been moderate.

In 1988 Montalbán was honored with the Mexican American Foundation's Golden Aztec Award.

In 1998 Montalbán appeared as himself in the TV program *Behind the Planet of the Apes* and was featured in an episode of *The Love Boat: The Next Wave*.

Further Reading
Meier, Matt S. *Mexican American Biographies*. Westport, Conn.: Greenwood Publishing Group, 1988.
Montalbán, Ricardo, with Bob Thomas. *Reflections: A Life in Two Worlds*. Garden City, N.Y.: Doubleday & Co., 1980.
Newlon, Clarke. *Famous Mexican Americans*. New York: Dodd, Mead & Co., 1972.

Montoya, Joseph M. (Joseph Manuel Montoya) (1915–1978) *government official*
Joseph M. Montoya went from a boy-wonder career in the New Mexican legislature to two decades in the U.S. Congress, where he made his mark as an influential and respected legislator. His particular fields of interest included consumer protection and the progress of the Hispanic community in the United States.

Montoya's family arrived in New Mexico from Spain in the 18th century. Joseph's father, Thomas, was sheriff of the state's Sandoval County, and it was there, in the village of Peña Blanca, that Joseph was born on September 24, 1915.

The boy went to high school in Bernalillo, New Mexico, graduating in 1931. He then went to college in Denver, Colorado. After college, he enrolled in Georgetown University Law School in the nation's capital. He graduated in 1938.

By that time, however, he already had a flourishing political career. In 1936, when he was 21 years old and was still in his second year at Georgetown, Sandoval County elected him to New Mexico's House of Representatives. He was the youngest state representative in New Mexico's history. In 1938, he was reelected and was chosen floor leader of the Democratic Party majority in the House, again the youngest person ever to hold that position. Montoya quickly followed this in 1940 by being elected to the New Mexico Senate, where he was the youngest state senator ever. He was then reelected repeatedly until he became lieutenant governor of the state. He held that post four times.

At the age of 42, in 1957, Montoya switched from state to national politics, winning election to the U.S. House of Representatives. This was followed by three reelections in a row, each garnering 60 percent or more of the votes.

The next logical step was the United States Senate. It came after the death of New Mexican Senator Dennis CHÁVEZ. Joseph M. Montoya was elected to replace him 1964 and handily reelected in 1970.

As a member of such important Senate committees as Appropriations and Public Works, Montoya was recognized as one of the Senate's key members. The only Mexican American in the Senate, he drafted legislation on bilingual education and other measures to benefit Hispanic Americans, including the establishment of the annual Hispanic Heritage week, and legislation to help minorities in general. He was also noted for advocating environmental and consumer-protection measures.

Montoya also stood out for his strong opposition to the Vietnam War. This was not, however, his only participation in international affairs. He was the U.S. representative at various inter-American conferences and was especially active in strengthening U.S. ties with Mexico.

With the emergence of radical forms of struggle for the civil rights of Hispanics, Montoya, always a moderate, began to be seen in some quarters as old-fashioned. He opposed civil disobedience, including such steps as the forcible takeover of federal lands by Chicano activists.

In 1976, a former astronaut who had newly entered politics, Harrison Schmitt, defeated Montoya in his bid for reelection to the Senate. It was only the second time that Montoya had ever lost an election; the other was a Democratic Party primary in 1950 in one of his runs for the state Congress.

Montoya developed cancer after his 1976 defeat and died two years later.

Joseph M. Montoya of New Mexico is not to be confused with Joseph Montoya of California, a member of that state's senate who was convicted on charges of extortion and racketeering, or with painter and poet José Montoya of New Mexico.

Further Reading

Martínez, Al. *Rising Voice: Profiles of Hispano-American Lives.* New York: New American Library, 1974.

Meier, Matt S. *Mexican American Biographies.* Westport, Conn.: Greenwood Publishing Group, 1988.

Moraga, Cherríe (1952–) *writer*

Cherríe Moraga is recognized as a pioneer in Chicana letters, not only writing with a new freedom in the mixing of literary forms—and of languages—but also opening up new areas of experience for women to write about. She is important both as an author and as a collector and editor of the writings of other minority women whom she, for the first time, gave a voice in print. She cofounded Kitchen Table/Women of Color Press for this purpose of encouraging the work of women who had previously been silent in terms of literary expression.

Moraga was born on September 25, 1952, in Whittier, California. Her mother, Elvira Moraga, was a Mexican American, while her father, Joseph Lawrence, was British Canadian. In her mother's family she found born narrators whose stories around the kitchen table she eagerly soaked up.

After going to college in Los Angeles (she graduated in 1974), Moraga initially settled into a career as a high school teacher. However, a writing course that she took at the Los Angeles Women's Building opened a new world for her, which she began to explore with increasing interest. In those same years Moraga publicly declared herself to be a lesbian, and she sought to bring this fact together with her budding writing career.

In 1977 she moved to San Francisco. There she continued to seek out and study links that she saw existing between the issues that interested her: feminism, lesbianism, racial divides, and the treatment of minorities. After earning a master's degree from San Francisco State University in 1980, in the early 1980s she lived in Boston and later New York, where she was exposed to the Puerto Rican strand of Hispanic culture. Later, she returned to California and its Chicano culture.

In her personal evolution, Moraga came to terms with the issue of her mother's brown skin (she herself had always been light-skinned enough to avoid racial discrimination). In her collection *Loving in the War Years: lo que nunca pasó por sus labios* (What Never Passed Her Lips, 1983), she explored what parallels might exist between the case of Malinche, the Indian lover of the Spanish conqueror Hernán Cortés, and that of her own "brown" mother and "white" father.

Meanwhile Moraga discovered that there were divides that needed to be bridged among the various minority groups she belonged to: white feminist writers might be prejudiced against those with darker skins, heterosexual Chicanos against gays and lesbians of the same ancestry, and so on. These were the subjects that Moraga addressed in her poems and essays and, later, in stage plays. She also actively worked to bring together the people in those disparate groups. Among other achievements, she helped establish the concept of "women of color" to link women from various different races which had previously been separated by mistrust and ignorance.

With two others, she founded Kitchen Table/Women of Color Press in 1981. In that year, with fellow writer Gloria Anzaldúa, she published *This Bridge Called My Back: Writings by Radical Women of Color.* This award-winning volume, which originated as Moraga's master's thesis, was widely seen as a watershed in the development of minority women's consciousness, and established Moraga as a reputed anthologist.

Moraga herself was a contributor to the book and to *Cuentos: Stories by Latinos* (1983). In 1986, she published a collection of her own poems and essays, *The Last Generation.* In later years she gave more emphasis to plays, such as *Giving Up the Ghost: Teatro in Two Acts* (1986), *Shadow of a Man* (1988) and *Heroes and Saints* (1992).

In 1995, Moraga's play *Circle in the Dirt,* based on oral histories of the small town of East Palo Alto, California, was produced, and in 1996, her play *Watsonville: Some Place Not Here* was produced as the inaugural production of the Brava Theater Center in San Francisco. In 1997 she published *Waiting in the Wings: Portrait of a Queer Motherhood.*

Always a seeker of links among the phenomena she feels deeply about, in both private and public life, Moraga believes that she has seen a correspondence between macho attitudes in U.S. society and U.S. government support, over many years, for right-wing dictators in Latin America.

Further Reading
Dictionary of Literary Biography. Detroit: Gale Research, 1989.
Novas, Himilce. *The Hispanic 100.* New York: Citadel Press, 1995.
Telgen, Diane, and Jim Kamp, eds. *Notable Hispanic American Women.* Detroit: Gale Research, 1998.
University of Illinois at Chicago. "Cherríe Moraga." Available online. URL: http://www.uic.edu/depts/quic/history/cherrie_moraga.html. Downloaded October 10, 2000.

Moreno, Antonio (Antonio Garrido Monteagudo y Moreno) (1887–1967) *actor*

Spanish-born Antonio Moreno is regarded as the first, and one of the greatest, of the Hispanic romantic stars in the early days of Hollywood. He was immortalized in an oft-quoted statement by British novelist Elinor Glyn, who was working in Hollywood in the 1920s. Glyn had become the "high priestess of allure" in the movie capital. It was Glyn who named the actress Clara Bow "the 'It' girl"—one of the best-known star nicknames of the period. "It" was a special quality that was hard to define but which included being glamorous, attractive, and charismatic. Glyn's full statement was that only four in Hollywood had "It": "Tony [Antonio] Moreno, Rex the Wild Stallion (an acting horse), the doorman at the Ambassador Hotel, and Clara Bow."

Moreno was born in Madrid on September 26, 1887, with the name Antonio Garrido Monteagudo y Moreno. He arrived in the United States, where he shortened his three surnames to Moreno, at the age of 14.

He began as a theater actor but in 1912 switched to motion pictures. There, like many other top stars of the silent-movie era, Moreno first acted for director D.W. Griffith.

Moreno's good looks propelled him to increasing levels of fame. His early days in the movie industry coincided with a period in which Latin actors, if they were very fair-skinned and aristocratic-looking, were considered romantically exotic. With Moreno heading the ranks, this trend was so strong that one Austrian Jewish actor changed his name from Jacob Krantz to Ricardo Cortez in order to take advantage of it.

Tony Moreno appeared in a large number of movies, among them *Two Daughters of Eve* (1912), *By Man's Law* (1913), *The Hidden Letters* (1914), *Rose of the South* (1916), the *Perils of Thunder Mountain* serial in 1919, *A Guilty Conscience* (1921), *The Spanish Dancer* (1923), *Her Husband's Secret* (1925), *Mare Nostrum* and *The Temptress* (1926), *Venus of Venice* and *It* (1927), *Romance of the Rio Grande* (1929), and *One Mad Kiss* (1930). Moreno's leading ladies included most of the principal female stars of the period, such as Greta Garbo, Pola Negri, Mary Pickford, Lillian Gish, and Gloria Swanson.

When soundtracks were added to the movies, Moreno was one of those who suffered during the transition. He retained a Spanish accent, which was not as welcome by audiences as had been dashing Latin looks. Also, with passing years, tastes had changed in the United States, and the "Latin lover" ideal began to be eclipsed. In addition, Moreno was entering middle age; as he grew older, his roles changed from leads to smaller parts.

In the early 1930s he spent a period in the Mexican movie industry, directing as well as acting. Moreno directed the first talking movie made in Mexico, *Santa* (1931). His later Hollywood pictures included *Rose of the Rio Grande* (1938), *Valley of the Sun* (1942), *Notorious* (1946), *Captain from Castile* (1947), *Mark of the Renegade* (1951), and *The Crea-*

Antonio Moreno *(Cabrera Archive)*

ture From the Black Lagoon (1954). Antonio Moreno's last role was in a classic Western, *The Searchers* (1956). In the 1950s, he also attempted to enter the Cuban movie industry, but Fidel Castro's revolution put an end to the venture.

Further Reading

Hadley-García, George. *Hispanic Hollywood: The Latins in Motion Pictures.* Secaucus, N.J.: Citadel Press, 1990.

Katz, Ephraim. *The Film Encyclopedia.* New York: Perigee Books, 1979.

Moreno, Luisa (1907–1992) *activist*

Luisa Moreno was a prominent, tireless fighter for labor and civil rights during the 1930s and 1940s from New York to California. She championed both Mexican Americans in particular and exploited laborers in general. In the 1950s she was expelled from the United States as a foreigner who was accused of being either a communist or a communist sympathizer.

Moreno was born in 1907 into a wealthy family in Guatemala. As an adult, she made no claim to her family wealth. When the time came, she went to work to support herself and the cause of the poor and mistreated. She died penniless in Guatemala. The exact circumstances and date of her death are unknown.

Her school years were spent first in her home country and then in the United States at a prestigious religious school for Catholic girls in Oakland, California.

In the 1920s, Moreno settled in Mexico City to work as a newspaper reporter. She married a Mexican and the couple moved to New York City in 1928 with their small daughter. Her husband was unable to find work in New York, so Moreno took a job as a seamstress in a dress factory. The event changed her life. She was so appalled at the sweatshop conditions in the garment industry that she decided to devote herself to the fight to improve them. She fought for labor rights not only in the garment sector but in all businesses where workers were being badly paid and abused.

Luisa Moreno would become a full-time labor organizer, first with the International Ladies' Garment Workers' Union and then for the American Federation of Labor (AFL). Beginning in 1937, she worked for the Congress of Industrial Organizations (CIO), a more radical organization than the AFL.

As an enthusiastic activist, Moreno helped organize cigarmakers in New York, Pennsylvania, and Florida and then moved into the heartland to try to unionize rural workers from Texas to Michigan. She was particularly active in a significant strike that broke out in 1938 among pecan shellers in Texas.

These workers were mainly Mexican Americans and Mexicans, prompting another career shift for Moreno. She increased her specific interest in the plight of Hispanic workers and decided to expand her work from labor rights to civil rights in general. Labor rights could not be protected, she realized, unless the workers were first protected as people, free from intimidation and violence.

In pursuit of these goals, Moreno sought strength in unity, and sought to bring together all associations working for Hispanics, not only for Mexican Americans but also for Puerto Ricans, Cuban Americans, and others. She thus became one of the principal founders, in Los Angeles in 1938, of El Congreso de los Pueblos de Habla Español—The Congress of Spanish-Speaking Peoples.

Although it helped in the struggle to achieve its goals, El Congreso had an active life of only a few years. From the start, it was the target of red-baiting—accusations of communism. But World War II principally led to the organization's end as social and economic conditions changed sharply. A large number of El Congreso's members went into the armed forces, and many efforts were redirected toward winning the war.

In the late 1930s and in the 1940s, Moreno was associated closely with a CIO affiliate, the United Cannery, Agricultural, Packing and Allied Workers of America (UCAPAWA). She began as the editor of the union's newspaper and became the first Hispanic woman to join its executive committee. She was UCAPAWA's international vice president, as well as vice president of the Los Angeles Industrial Council. In addition, she was chairperson of a committee against labor discrimination in California and vice president of the CIO in that state.

One of Moreno's causes was opposing the deportation of large numbers of Latinos from the United States. This began in the Great Depression years of the 1930s, when it was felt that they were "stealing" jobs in the United States. Those who were deported included many who were in the United States illegally and many others who were legal residents but had no papers to prove it. Among them were descendants of families who had been in the southwest long before the Anglos arrived.

In a speech on this subject in Washington, D.C., in 1940, Moreno pointed out that these workers, with or without legal papers, "have contributed their endurance, sacrifices, youth, and labor to the southwest. Indirectly, they have paid more taxes than all the stockholders of California's industrialized agriculture, the sugar companies, and the large cotton interests. . . ."

In the end, Moreno was herself deported. By the late 1940s, the focus of the deportation drive had shifted from economic reasons to political ones. It was never proven that Moreno had been a member of the Communist Party. However, her radical demands for social justice aroused suspicion, and she was deported as an undesirable alien.

Moreno settled in Mexico. She went to Cuba when General Fulgencio Batista's right-wing government was toppled and spent some years contributing to Fidel Castro's new government. She then returned to Mexico. Finally, with increasing age, ill health, and poverty, she returned to Guatemala, where on Novemeber 4, 1992, she died.

Further Reading

Meier, Matt S. *Mexican American Biographies.* Westport, Conn.: Greenwood Publishing Group, 1988.

Mirandé, Alfredo, and Evangelina Enriquez. *La Chicana: The Mexican-American Woman.* Chicago: University of Chicago Press, 1979.

Telgen, Diane, and Jim Kamp, eds. *Notable Hispanic American Women.* Detroit: Gale Research, Inc., 1993.

❧ Moreno, Rita (Rosa Dolores Alverio)

(1931–) *actress*

Rita Moreno was the first Hispanic actress to win an Oscar and more than three decades later remained the only one ever to have done so.

She had her biggest successes playing fiery Latinas. Nevertheless, she is noted in the entertainment industry for the determination with which she has fought to play diverse roles.

She is in the *Guinness Book of Records* as the only person ever to win the four major prizes in show business: the Oscar, the Grammy, the Tony, and the Emmy. She has two Emmys, in fact.

Moreno won her Academy Award as best supporting actress in 1962 for her performance in *West Side Story;* her Grammy in 1972 for her recording of *The Electric Company Album,* which compiled her singing for a children's educational TV series; her Tony in 1975 for her performance in *The Ritz.* Television conferred Emmys on her in 1977 and again in 1978 for appearances in *The Muppet Show* and *The Rockford Files,* respectively.

Rosa Dolores Alverio was born in Humacao, Puerto Rico, on December 11, 1931. When she was three years old, her mother went to New York, obtained a job as a seamstress, and earned enough money to bring Rosa to New York the following year. Rosa grew up speaking English without a Hispanic accent.

In later years, she would only use an accent when it was necessary for her roles as Hispanic firebrands or when poking fun at those roles. She said these parts mainly required her to "flare my nostrils and gnash my teeth" and say things like, "Yonkee peeg, you steal my people's gold."

Dancing lessons began when she was six. At seven, she performed onstage at a nightclub as a Spanish dancer; she would continue doing nightclub acts in the decades ahead. By 11 and technically a professional, she earned money doing an imitation of the actress and singer Carmen MIRANDA at a bar mitzvah party for a Jewish family.

Two years later she appeared on Broadway for the first time. She also did radio dramas and dubbed American movies into Spanish for Latin American markets.

At 14, pretty and talented, she was taken to Hollywood, where she appeared in a succession of films such as *A Medal for Benny* (1945), *So Young, So Bad* and *Pagan Love Song* (1950), *Latin Lovers* (1953), and *The Yellow Tomahawk* (1954). Slowly, the quality of the movies and the roles she was given improved: She appeared in *Singin' in the Rain* (1952) and then her breakthrough role as Tuptim in *The King and I* (1956).

West Side Story (1961) was, for Rita Moreno, a source of both great pride and great frustration. Her dynamic acting, dancing, and singing in the role of Anita, the heroine's brother's girlfriend, earned her an Oscar, but it also threatened to typecast her forever. Again and again, she was offered virtually the same role in other movies. It was, in effect, racial discrimination at the casting office. The experience caused her enough stress to require six years of psychiatric treatment in order to deal with what she called "my race problem." As she explained, "I spoke perfect English—but they gave the roles I wanted to Mitzi Gaynor and other non–Puerto Ricans." She

Rita Moreno dancing with George Chakiris in *West Side Story* *(Cabrera Archive)*

did not object to Hispanic parts, but she did insist on a wider choice of roles.

Stubbornly, she reacted by staying away from Hollywood for most of the 1960s. Instead, she did more Broadway work, appearing in such works as *The Sign in Sidney Brustein's Window* (1964–65), *Gantry* (1969), *Wally's Cafe* (1981), and a female version of *The Odd Couple* in 1985.

Rita Moreno did return to Hollywood in 1969. Marlon Brando (who had once been Moreno's lover and over whom she attempted suicide in Brando's living room) persuaded the producer of one of his movies, *The Night of the Following Day,* to give Moreno a role in it.

In the same year of her comeback, she appeared in two other films, *Popi* and *Marlowe.* Among the milestones in her film career since then have been *Carnal Knowledge* (1971), *The Four Seasons* (1981), and *Life in the Food Chain* (1991).

Moreno herself provided the inspiration for a play when, at a party, she gave a full-bodied imitation of Hollywood's image of the volcanic Latin woman. A playwright, Terrence McNally, saw her doing the hilarious caricature and decided, then and there, to create a play for her with such a character in it. The play was *The Ritz* (1975), and her performance as Googie Gómez won Moreno the Tony award. The next year, she starred in the movie version.

Rita Moreno's 1980s television work included a costarring role in the *9 to 5* series (1982–83).

The actress has worked within the entertainment industry to secure more jobs for Hispanics in the business. In 1988 she was given a New York Image Award for lifetime achievement from the Hispanic Academy of Media Arts and Sciences.

In the late 1990s, Moreno's movie appearances included *Slums of Beverly Hills* (1998), *Carlo's Wife* (1999), and *Blue Moon* (2000). Her TV work was highlighted by the cabke series, *Oz.*

Further Reading

Suntree, Susan. *Rita Moreno.* New York: Chelsea House, 1993.

✎ Muñoz Marín, Luis (1898–1980)
government official

Like his father, Luis MUÑOZ RIVERA, Luis Muñoz Marín played a crucial role in establishing the relationship between Puerto Rico and the United States. Together, they constitute a revered first family of Puerto Rican political history. Muñoz Marín obtained Puerto Rico commonwealth status in association with the United States. He was its long-term governor and transformed its economy through his "Operation Bootstrap" development plan.

Luis Muñoz Marín was born on February 18, 1898, in San Juan, Puerto Rico. He began his education on the island and then continued it in the United States, where his father was Puerto Rico's resident commissioner.

As a teenager with poetic inclinations, he wrote two books and was later to be nicknamed *El Vate*—The Bard. This literary bent was one of his inheritances from his father.

After his father's death, Muñoz Marín became secretary to the next resident commissioner of Puerto Rico. He then began to study law and later switched to journalism and worked for several publications in the United States.

Muñoz Marín returned to Puerto Rico and entered politics, initially as a member of the Socialist Party. In 1926, and again in 1932, he edited *La Democracia,* the first paper founded by his father.

In 1932, Muñoz Marín also helped found the Liberal Party, which nominated him to run for resident commissioner in the United States. He chose instead to remain in Puerto Rico and won an election as member of the local senate.

In the 1930s, he began to show an increasing interest in dealing with the widespread poverty in Puerto Rico and in 1936 opposed a U.S. senator's project to grant independence to Puerto Rico under conditions which, he felt, would leave its economic problems unsolved. However, he did want independence for the island. This led him to break with more conservative factions in the Liberal Party.

Muñoz Marín in 1938 formed the Popular Democratic Party, which came to dominate Puerto Rican politics in later years. In 1940, he was elected senator and president of the island senate. This was repeated four years later.

In the meantime, President Franklin Delano Roosevelt had appointed him to a commission to suggest a future political organization for Puerto Rico. Muñoz Marín began to sketch out the principles of commonwealth status for the island, now rejecting both independence and U.S. statehood.

In 1948, when the United States gave Puerto Rico the right to choose its own governor, Muñoz Marín was elected by a large margin. He became not only Puerto Rico's first self-chosen governor, but also its only one, winning reelection three times through 1964, when he chose not to run again.

The United States accepted Muñoz Marín's home-rule plan in 1950. In that year, both Muñoz Marín and U.S. President Harry Truman escaped unharmed from attempts on their lives by extreme supporters of Puerto Rican independence.

The island's new constitution, officially instituting the commonwealth, was enacted in 1952, and it was Muñoz Marín who first raised Puerto Rico's flag alongside that of the United States.

Under the Operation Bootstrap which he espoused, Puerto Rico was industrialized by offering U.S. companies incentives to invest in the island's economy. Per-capita income multiplied tenfold in three decades. In 1963, the United States awarded Muñoz Marín the Presidential Medal of Freedom.

After leaving the governorship, Muñoz Marín returned to the Puerto Rican senate. He sporadically participated in politics in his later years until ill health put an end to his career in 1976. He died in 1980.

Further Reading

Bernier-Grand, Carmen T. *Poet and Politician of Puerto Rico: Don Luis Muñoz Marín.* New York: Orchard Books, 1995.

Chrisman, Abbot. *Luis Muñoz Marín.* Milwaukee, Wis.: Raintree Press, 1989.

George, Linda, and Charles George. *Luis Muñoz Marín: Father of Modern Puerto Rico.* Danbury, Conn.: Children's Press, 1999.

Hett, Gunter. *Luis Muñoz Marín.* San Juan, P.R.: Star Press, 1964.

Mann, Peggy. *Luis Muñoz Marín.* New York: Coward-McCann & Geoghegan, 1976.

Norris, Marianna. *Father and Son for Freedom.* New York: Dodd, Mead, 1968.

❧ Muñoz Rivera, Luis (1859–1916)
government official

Luis Muñoz Rivera is the senior member of a political dynasty that proved crucial in Puerto Rico–U.S. relations. Muñoz Rivera struggled, through both journalism and political action, to obtain Puerto Rico's autonomy from Spain and later from the United States. He was also the island's resident commissioner in Washington, D.C.

Luis Muñoz Rivera was born on July 17, 1859, in the town of Barranquitas, Puerto Rico. Like his son Luis MUÑOZ MARÍN after him, he had a passion for literature; also like his son, he went through a succession of political alliances, including parties founded by each Muñoz in turn, always in pursuit of one goal: obtaining what he saw as best for Puerto Rico.

Under Spanish rule, Puerto Ricans found themselves torn among different options. These options were the same ones that continue to the present day, with regard to the United States rather than to Spain. With Spain, some Puerto Ricans called for immediate, total independence. Others believed that the best course for the island was a full merger with Spain. A third group sought some intermediate course.

Both Muñozes would change their minds as circumstances varied. However, both eventually settled for the practical, middle-ground solution.

Muñoz Rivera began to work in his family's businesses in his hometown before entering politics in 1883. He was a town councillor for the Liberal Reformist Party, helped found the Autonomist Party, and was elected a provincial deputy (legislator), but he was kept from taking office through political trickery by his opponents. Later in his career, he once fought a duel with an opposing politician.

In 1890, in the city of Ponce, he founded the newspaper *La Democracia,* one of the most influential in the island's history. He used its pages to champion the cause of freedom for Puerto Rico from its colonial overlord, Spain. Muñoz Rivera's strategy was to make ties with Spanish political parties that would give Puerto Rico autonomy if these parties reached power in Spain. In the mid-1890s, he spent three years in Spain following his marriage to Amalia Marín, the younger Luis's mother.

In 1897, the leader of the Spanish party with which Muñoz Rivera had allied was appointed to head the Spanish government. Under these circumstances—and under strong pressure from the United States—Spain granted home rule to Puerto Rico. Muñoz Rivera was appointed as a minister in the first autonomous government. When elections were held in March 1898, he became president of the first government to be elected by the islanders.

However, in April Spain and the United States went to war, and by October the island was under U.S. rule. Autonomy had ended. The first U.S. military governor of Puerto Rico included Muñoz Rivera in his working cabinet; the second, in 1899, did not.

In the years that followed Muñoz Rivera dedicated himself to campaigning against the system created by the United States under the Foraker Act to govern Puerto Rico. The act left control tightly in U.S. hands: Not only the governor, but the entire island senate was appointed by the United States.

Muñoz Rivera founded in 1900 another newspaper, *Diario de Puerto Rico,* to add to *La Democracia* as an organ of his views. The next year he founded yet another, in New York, *The Puerto Rico Herald.*

In 1904, he helped set up another political party, the Union for Puerto Rico, to fight for self-government under U.S. sovereignty. He won elective offices in succeeding years.

Muñoz Rivera was elected in 1910 and again four years later resident commissioner of the island in the U.S. capital and headed his crusade against the Foraker Act from there. However, illness struck him in 1916 and he returned to Puerto Rico.

He died there that year without seeing the enactment, in 1917, of the Jones Act, which was an improvement on Foraker. The governor of Puerto Rico was still appointed by Washington, but Puerto Ricans could elect the members of the island's senate. They also became U.S. citizens just in time to be drafted in World War I.

Further Reading

Méndez, Eugenio Fernández. *Luis Muñoz Rivera.* San Juan, P.R.: Biblioteca de Autores Puertorriquenos, 1982.

Norris, Marianna. *Father and Son for Freedom.* New York: Dodd, Mead, 1968.

Reynolds, Mack. *Puerto Rican Patriot.* New York: Crowell-Collier Press, 1969.

⤎ Murieta, Joaquín (unknown–1853)
frontiersman

Joaquín Murieta, who inspired the fictional characters of Zorro and the Cisco Kid, was an outlaw who terrorized Anglos at the time of the great California gold rush in order, it appears, to avenge equally brutal misdeeds that had been committed against him.

Up to 1848, when the hunt for gold started, California had been Mexican. Many Spanish speakers in California felt, during the following years, that they were being thrown out of their own lands and jobs by the English speakers who arrived in vast numbers. Rightly or wrongly, they saw Murieta as a kind of Californian Robin Hood.

After his death at the hands of a posse, his legend grew and was embroidered and twisted until it was almost unrecognizable. He is generally regarded as a "social bandit"—one who maintains that his deeds are not merely for plunder, but to right the grievances of a group of people who have been wronged.

However, there is disagreement about how valid his claim was, in part because the facts are so uncertain. Little is known for sure about the short life of the real Joaquín Murieta. This applies to the place and date of his birth and to his name, nor is it even certain that the person who was killed by the posse was truly who they thought he was. Murieta's surname is also found spelled as *Murrieta* and sometimes *Muriati*, although the latter is a highly unlikely Italian spelling. He was either a "Californio" (a native Californian from before the U.S. takeover) or came from Sonora, Mexico, or even, in some versions, from Santiago, Chile. His birth may have taken place in 1830 or, more likely, a few years later.

After gold was discovered in California, Murieta in 1849 became one of the prospectors who set up a claim in the area. However, in mining as in farming, the newly arrived Anglos often pushed the Spanish speakers out of business. The adoption in California in 1850 of a Foreign Miners Tax law gave this largely anti-Mexican policy a legal basis.

Accompanying the legal restriction, there was often physical violence. Murieta's story is the embodiment of this unsavory period. According to the accounts, Murieta's wife was raped, or possibly raped and killed, by Anglos who drove him from his mining claim in 1850 or the year after. He then sought to earn a living as a card player. He and a brother were accused of stealing a horse; the brother was hanged, and he was flogged. After this, he became the leader of a gang of bandits that preyed bloodily on Anglos.

The hills were beginning to fill with displaced Californios and Mexicans who had turned to violence. A deputy sheriff of Los Angeles, a Texan named Harry Love, tracked Murieta to one of his camps in 1852 and almost succeeded in capturing him. The following year, as banditry increased, Love was empowered by the California legislature to form a temporary group of rangers to hunt for all of the outlaws. The outlaw leaders were thought to all have the same first name and were known as "the five Joaquíns." In addition to Murieta, the most feared of all, there was supposed to have been a Joaquín Valenzuela, a Joaquín Carillo or Carrillo, a Joaquín Ocomorenia, and a Joaquín Botilleras or Botellier. In July 1853, the posse had a shootout with a group of Spanish speakers and killed two. One of them was determined to have been an outlaw known as Three-Fingered Jack García; the other, it was decided, was Joaquín Murieta. Love and his men cut off Murieta's head and García's three-fingered hand, preserved them in jars of alcohol, and collected the bounty they had been promised. The head was a great traveling attraction in California until the turn of the century. It was destroyed in the San Francisco earthquake of 1906.

The process of turning Joaquín Murieta into a legend began the year after his death, when the first book about him was written, packed with fantasy. Over time the legend has grown, developed, and changed. Murieta has been the source of numerous works of literature. The epic Chicano poem *I Am Joaquín* by Rodolfo "Corky" GONZALES is believed to have been inspired by Murieta. The great Chilean poet Pablo Neruda wrote a play called *Fulgor y Muerte de Joaquín Murieta (Shine and Death of Joaquín Murieta)*. Neruda was one of those who espoused the theory that the celebrated social bandit was of Chilean birth. A number of motion pictures have been made about Murieta, including *Robin Hood of El Dorado* (1936), *The Firebrand* (1962), and *Murieta* (1965), as well as the TV movie *The Desperate Mission* (1971) with Ricardo MONTALBÁN.

But Murieta also gained a new form of life—and many more film and TV renditions, in addition to great success in comic strips—under the guises of Zorro and of the Cisco Kid. These are imaginary characters who fight to redress wrongs. The inspiration for their creation has been traced back to the history of Murieta. As usually happens when a historical event or person is adopted as the basis of a legend or myth, enormous changes were introduced along the way, particularly in the case of Zorro. These changes to the myth generally reflect what the society needs to believe about itself. For the benefit of Zorro's mainly Anglo audience, the identity of his enemies has been turned on its head. Instead of reacting against Anglo usurpation and injustice as Murieta is believed to have done, the transformed hero battles corruption, oppression, and banditry among his own people, Hispanics.

Further Reading

Latta, Frank. *Joaquín Murieta and His Horse Gangs.* Santa Cruz, Calif.: Bear State Books, 1980.

Malakoff and Co. "Gold Rush Players: Joaquín Murieta." Available online. URL: http://malakoff.com/grpjomu.htm. Downloaded October 10, 2000.

Nadeau, Remi. *The Real Joaquín Murieta.* Corona del Mar, Calif.: Trans-Anglo Books, 1974.

Ridge, John Rollin. *The Life and Adventures of Joaquín Murieta, the Celebrated California Bandit.* 1854. Reprint, Norman: University of Oklahoma Press, 1955.

Narváez, Pánfilo (unknown–1528)

explorer

Pánfilo Narváez was one of the earliest European explorers of what later became the southeastern United States. His expedition, disastrously unsuccessful in itself, was the springboard for Alvar NÚÑEZ CABEZA DE VACA's amazing cross-continental trek.

The dates given for Narváez's birth range between 1450 and 1480. His place of birth is believed to have been the city of Valladolid in Castile, Spain, although it may have been the nearby town of Cuéllar.

Some sources refer to him as *Pánfilo de Narváez,* although it is unclear at what point he began to use the *de* in his name.

From his life's history, he appears to have been tough, resourceful, and cruel but also bumbling and unlucky. One historian, Samuel Eliot Morison, calls him flatly "the most incompetent of all who sailed for Spain in this era."

Narváez's first trip to America took him to Jamaica, one of the first territories invaded by Spain in the hemisphere. From there, he took part in the conquest of Cuba in the early 1510s.

In 1520, the Spanish governor of Cuba put him at the head of an expedition to Mexico to chase Hernán Cortés, who was in the process of conquering that country and was accused of acting in defiance of orders.

Narváez landed on the Mexican coast, and there Cortés quickly defeated him in battle. Narváez's men then changed sides and stayed on to fight for Cortés. Narváez also stayed but as Cortés's prisoner.

Upon his release, Narváez returned to Spain where, in 1526, he received a commission from the king to conquer and colonize the uncharted land known as Florida. The Spanish were motivated by reports, which were all to prove false, of rich cities in the interior of Florida.

The Narváez expedition arrived on the coast of Florida in 1528. Narváez landed with approximately 300 of those with him. His reputation as an exceptionally inept commander rests, to a large extent, on his next decision—to send his ships away to seek a better harbor. They planned to meet up again further ahead, but they never did. The ships would search along the coast for almost a year.

Cortés himself had made a comparable yet even more drastic decision when he landed in Mexico: he had his ships burned to force his soldiers to look forward to conquest alone, with no immediate possibility of retreat. If Cortés is praised for his boldness and Narváez criticized for his folly, it is mainly because

Cortés succeeded in Mexico, while Narváez failed in Florida.

Marching overland, Narváez made his progress more difficult by treating the Indians whom he encountered with extreme ferocity. This differed from Cortés's policy of forming alliances with some Indians in order to use them to fight against others.

Because of Narváez's unilateral attacks on Indians, during the months of arduous marching westward along the coast of the Gulf of Mexico, his troops and colonists were constantly sniped at by Indian archers.

After losing many men to Indian attacks, and unable to find his ships on the coast, Narváez decided that they would build their own boats and then attempt to return by sea to that part of Mexico already in Spanish hands. Although they had no tools other than knives and only one professional carpenter among them—who was not, however, a shipbuilder—they managed to put together five boats. They assembled a forge to improvise metal parts, sewed together their shirts for use as sails, made ropes from plant fibers and horsehair, and used their last horses for food. Then they set out in 1528, keeping close to the coast.

The distance, however, was much greater than Narváez had calculated. They also encountered storms that the boats could not withstand. Many men drowned; others, shipwrecked on shore—some as far west as Texas—perished from hunger or from further Indian attacks. Narváez's own boat was lost at sea. Of the entire expedition, only five persons are known to have survived and been found by Europeans again: One was a soldier called Ortiz, who was found by Hernando DE SOTO's expedition to Florida in 1539; the other four, led by Núñez Cabeza de Vaca, were chanced upon in 1536 along the Gulf of California, on the other side of the continent, by the members of a Spanish raid to enslave Indians.

Further Reading

Leonard, M. C. Bob. Available online. URL: http://floridahistory.org/floridians/conquis.htm.

Morison, Samuel Eliot. *The European Discovery of America.* Vol 2, The Southern Voyages, 1492–1616. New York: Oxford University Press, 1974.

❦ **Nava, Gregory** (1949–) *movie director*

On large and small productions, director and screenwriter Gregory Nava has demonstrated a distinctive feel for stories about the Hispanic immigrant experience in the United States. The movie that is generally regarded as his best, *El Norte* (The North, 1984), received a nomination for the Oscar for best original screenplay.

Born in San Diego, California, on April 10, 1949, Nava comes from a Mexican-Basque family living on both sides of the U.S.–Mexican border. While his part of the family has been in California since the 1880s, he has close relatives who live in Tijuana, Mexico. Thus he was intimately involved in a bicultural world from his earliest years.

Nava's first film work, a short made while studying at the UCLA Film School, was about the great Spanish poet Federico García Lorca. In 1976, he shot his first feature-length movie, a medieval story called *The Confessions of Amans,* in Spain, using costumes and materials left over from the making of the 1961 screen spectacular *El Cid.* The movie won the Best First Feature award at the Chicago Film Festival.

It was Nava's second feature, *El Norte,* that brought him widespread critical notice and praise. He made it with independent funding—that is, without monetary backing from the established movie studios—and with an independent frame of mind, demonstrated by the name itself: a Spanish title although it is definitely a U.S. production.

Among the particular traits of Nava's most personally felt works is the fact that, although he is basically a Hollywood moviemaker, they show their subject from the Latino immigrants' viewpoint. His achievement is put into focus by the realization that this is not the mainstream movie industry's usual procedure with comparable "nonwhite" material. Generally a narrative is chosen that sees the events not through the eyes of the most directly involved people, but through those of a Western observer. The latter is often a journalist, as in the film industry's key work on the Cambodian civil war, *The Killing Fields;* on the apartheid regime in South Africa, *Cry Freedom;* and on the Central American civil wars, *Salvador.*

The Central American civil wars provide the springboard for Nava's *El Norte*. It tells the story of a brother and sister, peasants from Guatemala, who flee massacres in their own land and illegally enter the United States, where they face enormous problems adapting to their new situation. Nava resisted pressure to cast Anglo actors in the leads, and used only Hispanic actors that reinforced the film's feeling of authenticity.

The movie was highly praised for its depth of understanding and its beautiful—and original—imagery. One scene stood out in particular. In it, a U.S. housewife attempts to explain the advanced controls of a washing machine to the newly arrived immigrant maid. She speaks kindly and with goodwill, but her grasp of their cultural differences is even poorer than the maid's comprehension of a complicated modern appliance. The episode is not only richly comic, but also a brilliant summary of the clash of cultures.

Another Nava movie that closely reflects his special interest in the life of Hispanic immigrants in the United States is *My Family* (Mi Familia, 1995), an ample fresco in which he chronicled several generations in the life of a family in East Los Angeles. For this project—which despite the title was inspired by episodes lived by many families he knew, not only his own—Nava attracted the backing of the major Hollywood producer Francis Ford Coppola. He was therefore able to cast many leading Latinos including Jimmy SMITS and Edward James OLMOS. In its first week, the film made more money than any other new release in the United States, demonstrating the power of the Hispanic market when presented with a product that interests it.

In 1997 Nava directed the movie version of the life of the Tejano singer SELENA. The motion picture, simply titled *Selena*, starred Jennifer LÓPEZ. Two years later, Nava again explored the immigrant experience, but this time from a documentary angle, in the 1999 TV movie *The 20th Century: In the Melting Pot*.

Further Reading

Tardiff, Joseph C., and Mpho Mabunda, eds. *Dictionary of Hispanic Biography*. Detroit: Gale Research, 1996.

 Novarro, Ramón (José Ramón Gil Samaniegos) (1899–1968) *actor*

One of the biggest stars of silent movies, Ramón Novarro was regarded as "the second Valentino," although his career was much more varied than the famous Italian-born actor's. Novarro was a second cousin of Dolores DEL RÍO, one of the great female stars of the period, although they did not meet until they were both working in Hollywood.

Novarro was born in Durango, Mexico, the same city del Río was born in, on February 6, 1899. The son of a dentist, José Ramón Gil Samaniegos had both Aztec and Spanish ancestors. The turmoil during the Mexican Revolution drove the family out of the country and to Los Angeles in 1914.

A fan of the movies from childhood, the young Samaniegos worked his way into show business, taking jobs as a professional tango dancer, a singing waiter, and a vaudeville performer. In 1917, he began to get roles as an extra in Hollywood.

Stardom was not immediate, although Samaniegos made important friends, among them the star Antonio MORENO. On one occasion, Moreno smuggled Samaniegos, hidden in his car, past the guard at the studio gate. The bit player was tested for bigger parts, and his career began to improve after 1921.

His first chance at an important role came when he auditioned for director Rex Ingram for the role of the villain, Rupert of Hentzau, in *The Prisoner of Zenda* (1922). Ingram told him that he was "just the opposite" of what he was looking for. What he wanted, Ingram told him, was someone "six foot two, blond, Teutonic." Samaniegos was Latin and dark. He was also short enough to have to wear lifts when he later worked with Greta Garbo.

He nevertheless impressed Ingram sufficiently to land the coveted role. After this, the director took charge of his career for a while. It was Ingram who changed Samaniego's name to Ramón Novarro. He also cast him in the lead in other movies, including *Where the Rainbow Ends* and *Scaramouche* (both 1923) and *The Arab* (1924).

The Arab was an unabashed attempt to copy *The Sheik*, a 1921 film that starred Rudolph Valentino. Valentino and Novarro were cast in the same type of

Ramón Novarro with Greta Garbo in *Mata Hari* *(Cabrera Archive)*

role—"Latin lovers," dark-haired romantic leading men with smoldering eyes.

In their careers both Novarro and Valentino played a wide variety of ethnic roles. They also became friends, though professionally Novarro always remained in Valentino's shadow. More than half a century later, in a European survey of the handsomest actors in motion picture history, Novarro was still second, after Valentino. They both came ahead of (in this order) Robert Taylor (born Spangler Brugh), Barry Norton (an Argentine-born Hollywood actor whose real name was Alfredo Birabén), Alain Delon of France, and Tony Curtis (born Bernard Schwartz).

In 1926, Novarro had the biggest role of his career: the lead in the most expensive spectacle Hollywood had made up to then, a $5-million silent version of *Ben-Hur*. Among other Novarro titles of

the 1920s were *The Student Prince* (1927) and *Forbidden Hours* (1928).

When the movies entered the sound era, Novarro's accent was not a barrier, and his talent as a singer proved an asset. He sang in several pictures, including *In Gay Madrid* (1930), but his most important film during this period was *Mata Hari* (1931) with Greta Garbo.

Nevertheless, his career began to decline. He received fewer and smaller roles. Part of the reason was that he had retained an old-fashioned acting style in the new, more realistic 1930s. He also refused to marry, despite the wishes of studio bosses, who in those days tried to run their actors' private lives. He also complained about parts that portrayed Hispanics in a bad light.

Novarro directed Spanish-language versions of some movies and also directed a film in Mexico in the 1940s. His last movie appearances were in *Crisis* (1950) and *Heller in Pink Tights* (1960). He had earned, and saved, enough money in his prime to last him for the rest of his life.

In 1968, he was brutally clubbed to death in his Los Angeles home. His murderers, two young brothers, were caught and convicted.

Further Reading

Ellenberger, Allan R. *Ramon Novarro: A Biography of the Silent Film Idol, 1899–1968.* Jefferson, N.C.: McFarland, 1999.

O'Brien, Stephen. "Ramon Novarro." www.mdle. com/ClassicFilms/Guest/rna.htm. Downloaded October 11, 2000.

Shipman, David. *The Great Movie Stars: The Golden Years.* New York: Hill and Wang, 1979.

Novello, Antonia (1944–) *physician, government official*

Antonia Novello is the first Hispanic—and the first woman—appointed surgeon general of the United States, the highest medical official in the country.

Born Antonia Coello in Fajardo, Puerto Rico, on August 23, 1944, she lived in pain from a congenital intestinal disorder that was not cured until she was 18. Out of her suffering was born the desire to help others by going into medicine.

The young woman is remembered as an exceptionally bright student at the University of Puerto Rico, from which she graduated with a B.S. in 1965 and a medical degree in 1970. That year, she married Joseph Novello, a child psychiatrist.

Antonia Novello's medical specialty is pediatrics, particularly the treatment of those with kidney diseases. She has also dedicated herself to treating children with AIDS, to the prevention of alcoholism among the young, and to other areas where medicine meets social issues.

She has won praise for the warmth she brings to her work, as well as for her medical skills and administrative abilities.

After spending her first years as a doctor at the University of Michigan Medical Center in Ann Arbor, she transferred to Georgetown University Hospital in Washington, D.C., in 1974. Four years later, she began an association with the National Institutes of Health (NIH). In 1982, she received a master's degree in public health, awarded by the Johns Hopkins School of Hygiene and Public Health in Baltimore.

Meanwhile she held a succession of posts at NIH and in 1986 became the deputy director of NIH's National Institute of Child Health and Human Development. She also has acted as a medical adviser to a U.S. congressional committee and was a professor of pediatrics at Georgetown University Hospital.

Her career peaked in 1990 when President George Bush appointed her surgeon general, the top public health and safety position in the United States. She made a special commitment to issues affecting children, women, and minorities.

In 1993, Novello was appointed United Nations International Children's Emergency Fund (UNICEF) Special Representative for Health and Nutrition. Three years later, she was back on the lectern as visiting professor at Johns Hopkins University. In 1999, Novello took the post of commissioner of health for the state of New York.

Novello has won many awards in the course of her career, including the University of Michigan Pediatrics Department's Intern of the Year Award (1971; she was the first woman to win this award), the first Women in Health Award of the Visiting Nurse Service of New York (1990), the National Puerto Rican Coalition's Life Achievement Award (1990), the Simón Bolívar National Award (1991), the Ronald McDonald Children's Charities Award for Medical Excellence (1995), and numerous honorary degrees from universities. In 1998, she was the winner of the Award for Leadership from the Hispanic Heritage Awards organization.

Further Reading

The Puerto Rico Herald. "Puerto Rico Profile: Antonia Novello." Available online. URL:http://www. puertorico-herald.org/issues/vol4n12/ProfileANovello-en.shtml. Downloaded October 10, 2000.

Telgen, Diane, and Jim Kamp, eds. *Notable Hispanic American Women.* Detroit: Gale Research, Inc. 1993.

Núñez Cabeza de Vaca, Alvar

(1490?–1559?) *explorer*

Alvar Núñez Cabeza de Vaca and three others under his command carried out an epic, involuntary, 6,000-mile voyage across what were to become the southern United States and northern Mexico. They were the first Europeans to cross the continent.

Along the way, Núñez Cabeza de Vaca attentively observed the Indian tribes that he encountered and learned many of their languages. Later, he wrote a book about his experiences that has provided historians with valuable information.

The tremendous hardships of this expedition, one of the great journeys in the history of world exploration, did not curb his quest for adventure. Some years later, he carried out another great overland trip, this time across the jungles of southern Brazil.

He was described as a big, strong, red-bearded man who had all the endurance of the other Spanish conquistadores, but none of the cruelty toward Indians and ruthlessness toward competitors that marked many of his peers.

Alvar Núñez Cabeza de Vaca was born around 1490 in the Spanish city of Jérez de la Frontera into a military family. His grandfather, Pedro de Vera, had conquered the Grand Canary Island for Spain. His mother was Teresa Cabeza de Vaca, whose surname he used with pride, preferring it to Vera. His mother's family's military lineage was even more celebrated. *Cabeza de Vaca* means "cow's head" and the name was bestowed on an ancestor who almost 300 years earlier had fought against the Muslims in Spain and had guided a Christian army to victory by marking a key mountain pass with the skull of a cow.

As a young man, Núñez Cabeza de Vaca helped administer the holdings of a duke in the port of Sanlúcar de Barrameda. Some of Spain's great maritime expeditions set off from that port, including the fleet of Ferdinand Magellan that completed the first circumnavigation of the globe.

In 1527, Núñez Cabeza de Vaca signed up for an expedition that was being assembled by Pánfilo NARVÁEZ. The mission was to conquer and settle Florida. Narváez gave him the title of treasurer and constable of the ill-fated enterprise.

Narváez and his men landed in Florida in 1528. Núñez Cabeza de Vaca argued against Narváez's decision to send the ships away and to meet up with them again later, but he was overruled. The overland expedition began to be decimated by hunger and by Indian arrows, and finding the ships again proved a futile search.

The men improvised their own boats and tried to travel around the Gulf of Mexico. They had to fight Indian attacks when putting ashore at various points and faced shipwreck out at sea in their flimsy craft. Núñez Cabeza de Vaca's boat capsized twice, with several men drowning each time.

In the end, he and about 60 other survivors of the original expedition's 300 made it by sea as far as some point on the coast of Texas by late 1528. After the winter, only 15 had survived hunger and disease, living among the natives of the area. These Indians barely subsisted as hunter-gatherers. Núñez Cabeza de Vaca and three others, the final known survivors of the expedition, became medicine men or faith healers among the Indians mainly by saying prayers over them. They were also used by the Indians as virtual slaves while they remained among them.

After years of this, in 1533, the four decided to continue their attempt to find Spanish settlements, this time on foot. Núñez Cabeza de Vaca's companions were two Spaniards and the black slave of one of them, Esteban, who had been born in Morocco. The four walked for the next three years, barefoot, without clothes, and constantly undernourished. "Twice a year, we cast our skins like serpents," Núñez Cabeza de Vaca wrote later. They did their faith healing along the way and were often accompanied by hundreds of Indians from one village, who announced their skills to the inhabitants of the next.

The precise route taken by the expedition is not known, but it is believed to have taken them across Texas, New Mexico, Arizona, and northern Mexico. Their initial overland route had gone through Florida and coastal Alabama, Mississippi, and Louisiana, where they crossed the mouth of the Mississippi River.

Núñez Cabeza de Vaca never encountered any Indians who were significantly better off than those along the coast. Nevertheless, he heard stories about some fabulously rich cities further north ("the seven cities of Cibola") and claimed later to have received some arrowheads made of emeralds. These claims later inspired other explorers to renew efforts in what is now the southwestern United States.

In 1536, they were stumbled upon, in what is now the north Mexican state of Sonora, by a group of Spaniards who were raiding Indian settlements to take slaves. This had been forbidden by the Spanish government—in favor of importing slaves from Africa—but the practice still continued. Núñez Cabeza de Vaca had a hard time convincing his rescuers not to enslave the Indians who followed his group at the time.

The explorers were hailed as heroes on their arrival, first in Mexico City and later back in Spain. Núñez Cabeza de Vaca published a book about his journey, *Shipwrecks,* in 1542. The two other Spaniards went back to Mexico and ended up wealthy. In 1539 Esteban, the Moroccan slave, was assigned to an advance party for an expedition to the Seven Cities of Cibola and was slaughtered by Pueblo Indians.

In 1540 Núñez Cabeza de Vaca was appointed *adelantado* (governor of a frontier area) to the River Plate in South America. The previous settlers in the area had retreated to Asunción, a town they had founded far upriver, in what is now Paraguay.

Núñez Cabeza de Vaca sent part of his expedition to Asunción by boat, but he himself traveled overland from what is now Santos, in Brazil. He discovered the large Iguazú waterfalls in the course of his explorations.

When he reached Asunción, he came to believe that it was badly ruled by the acting governor, Domingo Martínez de Irala. A religious, austere person, Núñez Cabeza de Vaca tried to redress the wrongs he found. The result was that Martínez de Irala rebelled in 1544, imprisoned him for a year, and then sent him back to Spain, charging that Núñez Cabeza de Vaca had mismanaged the affairs of government.

A Spanish court found him guilty and banished him to serve in Africa for eight years. Upon his return to Spain, however, he was still able to obtain a position as a judge in Sevile. He lived there for the remaining years of his life. He died around 1559.

In 1974, a direct descendant of his, Fernando Cabeza de Baca (a modern spelling of the name) of New Mexico, was appointed special assistant to President Gerald Ford, becoming the top-ranking Hispanic in the federal government at that time.

Further Reading

Syme, Ronald. *Cabeza de Vaca: The First Man to Cross America.* New York: William Morrow & Co., 1961.

Wild, Peter. *Alvar Núñez Cabeza de Vaca.* Boise: Idaho State University Press, 1991.

Obregón, Eugene (Eugene Arnold Obregón) (1930–1950) *soldier*

Eugene Obregón won a posthumous Medal of Honor from the United States Congress because of a simple but great act of courage: he gave his life for a wounded comrade.

Born in Los Angeles on November 12, 1930, Obregón joined the U.S. Marine Corps during the war in Korea.

A private first class in Company G, 3rd Battalion, 5th Marines, 1st Marine Division, Obregón acted as ammunition carrier for a machine-gun squad. A sudden attack in September 1950 by hostile forces found Obregón in a protected position, while other men in his company were exposed on a road. A marine who had been advancing near Obregón was hit by enemy fire and fell on the roadway.

The Medal of Honor citation, which praises Obregón for "conspicuous gallantry and intrepidity," notes that although "armed only with a pistol, he unhesitatingly dashed from his covered position to the side of the casualty. Firing his pistol with one hand as he ran, he grasped the comrade by the arm with his other hand and, despite the great peril to himself, dragged him to the side of the road."

Obregón was still in the line of fire as he began to apply first aid to the other man's wounds. Moments later, the enemy began an advance directly toward him.

Again, Obregón did not hesitate. He protected the fallen man with his own body. Then, grabbing the other man's carbine, he began to fire against the enemy attackers. His shots were described as "accurate and effective." Obregón continued to fire until he was hit and killed by an enemy machine gun. He was two months shy of his twentieth birthday.

"By his courageous fighting spirit," states his medal citation, "fortitude, and loyal devotion to duty, Private First Class Obregón enabled his fellow marines to rescue the wounded man and aided essentially in repelling the attack."

Further Reading

The Committee on Veterans' Affairs, United States Senate. *Medal of Honor Recipients 1863–1978.* Washington, D.C.: U.S. Government Printing Office, 1979.

Ocampo, Adriana (1955–) *scientist*

Adriana Ocampo is a noted planetary geologist who has been unraveling secrets far out in the solar system—and has helped point to the resolution of the riddle of the dinosaurs back on Earth. It was Ocampo who first linked a series of sinkholes aligned as part of a circle in Mexico's Yucatán peninsula with the tremendous impact of an asteroid that may have been the reason that the dinosaurs, along with many other species, quite suddenly died off some 65 million years ago.

A native of Colombia who spent her childhood in Argentina, Adriana Ocampo was born on January 5, 1955, in Barranquilla, on Colombia's Caribbean coast. Her mother is a schoolteacher from Argentina, her father an engineer, and education was of paramount importance in the household. The family moved to Buenos Aires, the Argentine capital, when Adriana was less than a year old, and then to Pasadena, California, when she was 15. There, as Adriana was finishing high school, she had an opportunity to pursue a dream to work at the National Aeronautics and Space Adminis-

Adriana Ocampo *(Courtesy of Adriana Ocampo)*

tration (NASA) Jet Propulsion Laboratory (JPL), which is located in that city.

Part-time jobs were available through a project that JPL and the California Institute of Technology (CalTech) have set up for high school students. It was a wonderful opportunity for Adriana, who had dreamed of a career in space exploration, preferring to look and wonder at the stars or to tinker with a chemistry set instead of playing with dolls or other toys. She was the kind of girl who wanted to take a course in car mechanics in high school at a time when such choices were ruled out because of sex discrimination, so she jumped at the chance to learn about space technology.

Ocampo worked full-time at JPL during her undergraduate years at California State University at Los Angeles. She graduated as a geologist in 1983. She would remain at JPL, working on space exploration until 1998, a full quarter-century after entering as a technical aide. In that year she was assigned to work for JPL at NASA headquarters in Washington, D.C.

In order to carry out studies at a distance on the geology of other bodies in the solar system—planets, satellites, and asteroids—Ocampo developed special expertise in the remote sensing of data. During the Viking mission to Mars in the 1980s, she collaborated in the creation of an atlas—the first ever—of Phobos, one of that planet's two moons.

In the late 1980s she began research in Mexico and Belize on the impact of the deadly asteroid that is thought to have ended the long reign of the dinosaurs on Earth. The theory of the asteroid crash as the cause of a dust cloud that killed them off—a theory based on the presence, in rocks from the time of their disappearance, of the element iridium which is more abundant on asteroids and comets than on Earth—had been put forward by the physicist Luis ALVAREZ and his son Walter, a geologist like Ocampo.

In the 1990s, Ocampo was in charge of spectrometers traveling on the Mars Observer mission to the red planet and on the Galileo mission to Jupiter and other celestial objects, as well as being appointed coinvestigator on the proposed Hermes mission to Mercury.

In 1997 Ocampo obtained a master's degree in geology from California State University at Northridge.

A former national vice president of the Society of Hispanic Professional Engineers, for a period of over five years, Ocampo has shown a special interest in developing education among Hispanic Americans and in developing scientific links between the United States and other countries, particularly in Latin America. Her transfer to NASA headquarters in Washington was to become a program executive managing NASA missions in space science with international collaboration.

Among the many honors Ocampo has collected are a Woman of the Year Award in Science from the Comisión Femenil organization (1992) and a science and technology prize from the Chicano Federation (1997).

Further Reading

Bailey, Martha. *American Women in Science, 1950 to the Present.* Santa Barbara, Calif.: ABC-CLIO, 1998.

JPL. "Profiles of Women at JPL: Adriana Ocampo." Available online. URL: http://www.jpl.nasa.gov/tours/women/ocampo.html. Downloaded October 11, 2000.

Oleksy, Walter. *Hispanic-American Scientists.* New York: Facts On File, 1998.

Ellen Ochoa *(NASA)*

❦ Ochoa, Ellen (1958–) *astronaut, scientist*

In 1990, Ellen Ochoa became the first Hispanic woman astronaut. By then, though still in her early 30s, she had also established a solid reputation as a research scientist, displaying talents in several fields. Her success made her a role model for Hispanics and for women. Conscious of this, she is a frequent public speaker, inspiring others, especially schoolchildren, to higher achievements.

Ochoa was born in Los Angeles on May 10, 1958, and grew up in La Mesa, California. She credits her mother, in particular, with teaching her the importance of studying hard to obtain the best possible education. In Ellen Ochoa's case, a strong dedication to her studies was complemented by prodigious natural talent that led her to do well at whatever she tried. Although she excelled particularly in math and science, her facility in other areas left her unsure about what to do after graduation.

The Stanford Symphony Orchestra gave her a student soloist award in 1973 as a flutist, and when she entered San Diego State University, she originally intended to major in music. Flute playing remained a passion of hers, but after a while she changed her major to business, then to journalism, and again to computer science. Finally, she settled on physics and graduated in that field in 1980.

From San Diego State, she went to Stanford University to study electrical engineering, receiving her master's degree in 1981 and her doctorate in 1985.

Immediately after graduation, Ochoa began to work at Sandia National Laboratories in Livermore, California, researching in the field of image processing. She specialized in the replacement of computer operations by optical processes to improve images. In the course of this work, she quickly took out two patents in optical processing.

By this time, she had determined to become an astronaut. In 1988, as a first step, she obtained a license as an airplane pilot. That same year, she joined the staff of a NASA research center in Mountain View, California. In short order, she became chief of the information sciences division, heading a team of 35 scientists and engineers. Together, her team worked to improve computer systems for use in aerospace. In 1989, she won the Hispanic Engineer National Achievement Award for Most Promising Engineer in Government.

NASA selected Ochoa as an astronaut candidate in 1990, the year the National Hispanic Quincentennial Commission gave her its Pride Award. By the following year, she was a trained space shuttle specialist.

Ochoa first flew into outer space in 1993 on the *Discovery* shuttle. The mission of this flight was to monitor changes in the gases of the Earth's middle atmosphere, as well as to deploy and retrieve a satellite for the study of the sun's atmosphere.

In 1994, she was payload commander on a flight of the *Atlantis* shuttle, whose aim was again related to the Earth's atmosphere: to chart its chemistry to understand the drop in the level of protective ozone gas. Ochoa handled the shuttle's robot arm to recapture a satellite used to measure the ozone layer.

Ochoa made a new foray into outer space in 1999, once again aboard *Discovery,* on a flight that performed the first docking with the International Space Station.

Further Reading

Cassutt, Michael. *Who's Who in Space.* New York: Macmillan, 1993.

St. John, Jetty. *Hispanic Scientists.* Mankato, Minn.: Capstone Press, 1996.

Telgen, Diane, and Jim Kamp, eds. *Notable Hispanic American Women.* Detroit: Gale Research, Inc., 1993.

꿈 **Ochoa, Severo** (1905–1993) *physician*
Spanish-born Severo Ochoa, who became a United States citizen in 1956, shared a Nobel Prize in medicine in 1959, given to him for his research into nucleic acids in the body's cells.

Ochoa (not related to scientist Ellen OCHOA of California) was born in Luarca, Spain, on September 24, 1905. He graduated with a B.A. degree from a college in the Spanish city of Málaga in 1921 and earned his medical degree from the University of Madrid in 1927.

A keen, lifelong interest in physiology and biochemistry led him to study, teach, and research in those fields in Spain, Germany, Britain, and, starting in 1941, the United States. From Washington University in St. Louis, Missouri, where he began his U.S. career, he moved to the School of Medicine at New York University (NYU). At NYU, in addition to his duties as a professor, he became chairman of the department of pharmacology in 1946 and chairman of the department of biochemistry in 1954. He held numerous concurrent positions at universities on several continents. In 1985, the year in which he turned 80, he took a position as professor of biology at the Autonomous University of Madrid.

Together with a colleague, in 1959 Ochoa won the world's highest award in his field, the Nobel Prize in Medicine and Physiology, for their discoveries of the mechanisms of the biological synthesis of nucleic acids. In further research on nucleic acids, he managed to grow viruses outside living cells.

A member of the U.S. National Academy of Science, among other professional organizations, Ochoa received honorary university degrees among numerous awards, which include the Neuberg Medal in Biochemistry (1951), New York University Medal (1960), Japan's Order of the Rising Sun second Class and Gold Medal (1967), Spain's Quevedo Gold Medal Award (1969), and the National Medal of Science (1979).

Further Reading

American Men and Women of Science, 1995–96. A Biographical Directory of Today's Leaders in Physical, Biological and Related Sciences. New Providence, N.J.: R.R. Bowker, 1992–93.

Sourkes, Theodore. *Nobel Prize Winners in Medicine and Physiology 1901–1965.* New York: Abelard-Schuman Ltd., 1967.

꿈 **Olmos, Edward James** (1947–) *actor*
A major movie and television actor, Edward James Olmos's work has been recognized with a variety of

awards and nominations. He is also a tireless campaigner for self-improvement, and against gang violence among youths coming from underprivileged backgrounds.

Time magazine made Olmos a symbol of Hispanic pride and achievement. In a July 1988 issue, the magazine devoted a special section to the increasing influence of Hispanic culture in the United States, choosing Olmos for the cover.

Olmos was born on February 24, 1947, in Los Angeles. His ancestors had been active in the Mexican Revolution. They owned and ran a prorevolution newspaper in Mexico City, and a great-uncle is credited with inventing the "Land and Liberty" slogan used by the revolutionaries.

After World War II, Edward's father and mother immigrated to the United States. They were forced to raise their children in a tough neighborhood in East Los Angeles. Later, his mother, by then divorced, moved her children to a better area in the suburbs.

As a child, Edward developed two interests, baseball and music, that helped keep him out of trouble and eventually led to his acting career. He founded a rock band called Eddie James and the Pacific Ocean.

He initially took acting lessons to improve his performance as a singer but finally concentrated on acting and theatrical work. He received an associate arts degree from East Los Angeles College and attended California State University.

At the start of his acting career, Olmos also delivered furniture to supplement his income. However, his fortunes gradually improved with his performance in *Zoot Suit* (1978), a play about an incident of anti-Hispanic hatred during World War II. This performance earned him the Los Angeles Drama Critics Circle Award and a Theater World Award as Most Outstanding New Performer. The play went to Broadway, and Olmos was nominated for a Tony award. He also acted in the movie version of *Zoot Suit* (1981).

After a role in the movie *Blade Runner* (1982), he appeared in the film *The Ballad of Gregorio Cortez* (1983), which was originally made for television. Like *Zoot Suit*, *The Ballad of Gregorio Cortez* dealt with a real-life Mexican American, who was wrongly accused of murder in 1901. Olmos believed strongly in the project and in the importance of its message. He not only starred in the movie but helped produce it, wrote some of the music, and devoted years of work to promoting its exhibition after the release.

Olmos's biggest career opportunity came in 1984 when he took a major role, that of Lieutenant Martin Castillo, in the TV series *Miami Vice*. He would not accept the role until he obtained complete control over the way the character was portrayed. Olmos won a Golden Globe and an Emmy Award for his performance.

In 1988, Olmos earned acclaim playing the inspiring math teacher, Jaime ESCALANTE, in *Stand and Deliver*. The part won him an Oscar nomination. In its cover story on Hispanics that year, *Time* magazine called him "not only possibly the best Hispanic American actor of his generation, but one of the best performers working today."

Four years later, he wrote, directed, and acted in *American Me*, a movie about a young gang member. A major concern for Olmos is to help Mexican Americans escape the trap of gang culture. In his spare time, he frequently speaks in schools, reformatories, and jails.

Among Edward James Olmos's other films are *Triumph of the Spirit* (1989), *Maria's Story* (1990), and *My Family* (1995). His TV appearances have ranged from *Kojak* and *Hill Street Blues* to *Hawaii Five-O*. In 1995, he won another Golden Globe award for his work in *The Burning Season*. More recently, Olmos acted in *The Wall* (1998), *The Wonderful Ice Cream Suit* (1999), and *Gossip* (2000). For television, he produced *Americanos: Latino Life in the United States* (1999), as well as appeared in *12 Angry Men* (1997) and *Bonnano: A Godfather's Story* (1999).

Further Reading

Carrillo, Louis. *Edward James Olmos*. Orlando, Fla.: Raintree/Steck-Vaughn, 1997.

Katz, Ephraim. *The Film Encyclopedia*. New York: Perigee Books, 1994.

Martinez, Elizabeth C. *Edward James Olmos: Mexican-American Actor*. Brookfield, Conn.: Millbrook Press, 1994.

❧   **Ortega, John** (1840–unknown) *soldier*
Spanish-born John Ortega distinguished himself in
action as a sailor on a United States Navy ship during
the Civil War. He was awarded a Medal of Honor by
the United States Congress in 1864.

Little is known about Ortega. His mention in
the annals of the Medal of Honor, like the others of
that time, is extremely brief. He was born in Spain in
1840 as Juan Ortega and emigrated to the United
States. In military records, his home state is listed as
Pennsylvania. His date of death is not recorded.

The citation for the Medal of Honor reads,
"Served as seaman on board the *USS Saratoga* during actions of that vessel on two occasions. Carrying
out his duties courageously during these actions,
Ortega conducted himself gallantly through both
periods."

The only other information known is that, in addition to receiving the military decoration, Ortega
was promoted from seaman to acting master's mate.

By exhibiting a valor capable of earning him the
highest award his adoptive nation could bestow, Ortega ensured that his record, though short, would remain a part of history.

Further Reading
The Committee on Veterans' Affairs, United States
    Senate. *Medal of Honor Recipients 1863–1978.*
    Washington, D.C.: U.S. Government Printing
    Office, 1979.

❧   **Ortega, Katherine D.** (Katherine
    Dávalos Ortega) (1934–   ) *business-*
    woman, government official
A highly successful accountant and banker, Katherine D. Ortega served as treasurer of the United States
from 1983 to 1989. She was the second Latina to
hold that post, after Romana BAÑUELOS.

The daughter of a blacksmith and coffeehouse
owner in rural New Mexico, Ortega (not known to be
descended from John ORTEGA) might have lived her
life as a schoolteacher in that state. Instead, an incident of anti-Hispanic racism launched her on a new
career that led to high national office and material re-
wards.

Ortega's family can be traced on her mother's side
to the 1880s in the state of Texas. Her ancestors then
moved from Texas to New Mexico. Her mother's
maiden name is Dávalos, which became Ortega's middle name. She was born—her parents' ninth child—
on July 16, 1934 and raised in the village of Tularosa,
New Mexico.

From her earliest school days, Katherine did well
in math and by the age of 10 was handling the cash
register at her parents' coffeehouse.

Before finishing high school in Alamogordo, she
was working in a bank; after high school, she continued to work at the bank for two years to finance her
college education. Ortega studied business and economics at Eastern New Mexico State University at
Portales and graduated with honors in 1957. Her
plans, at the time, were to teach typing and shorthand
to high school students, but her college business
school's chairman told her that, as a Hispanic, she
need not even apply for a job in that area. At that
time, Ortega decided to go into business for herself.
With one of her sisters she opened an accounting firm
in Alamogordo.

When she moved to California in 1967, she
continued working in the same field. Two years
later, she joined a large accounting firm in Los Angeles as a tax supervisor, where her capabilities did
not go unnoticed: In 1972 she was offered the position of vice president at the Pan American National Bank in Los Angeles. Three years later, she
became president as well as director of the Santa
Ana State Bank. Ortega was the first woman to become president of a commercial bank in the state
of California.

The strongly conservative Ortega was also active
in the Republican Party. This would lead to her government appointments in later years.

Ortega returned to New Mexico and to the fam-
ily-run accounting firm in 1979. In 1982, she was appointed to President Ronald Reagan's Presidential
Advisory Committee on Small and Minority Business
Ownership. Later that same year she became commissioner of the Copyright Royalty Tribunal.

In 1983, she was nominated and confirmed as
U.S. treasurer. President Reagan described her as
"symbolic of the values the Hispanic community

represents." She was the keynote speaker at the 1984 Republican Convention in Dallas, where Reagan was nominated for a second term in office.

Returning to private life after her six years as treasurer, she was invited to join the board of directors of a number of large corporations. In addition, she joined the advisory board of the National Park Service. She has also served as an alternate U.S. representative to the United Nations.

Ortega has won the Treasury Department's Alexander Hamilton Award for outstanding service (1989), the California Businesswoman's Achievement Award, the Damas de Comercio (Businesswomen) Outstanding Woman of the Year Award, and the Outstanding Alumni of the Year Award from her alma mater, Eastern New Mexico University, plus several honorary degrees.

Further Reading

Meier, Matt S. *Mexican American Biographies.* Westport, Conn.: Greenwood Publishing Group, 1988.

Telgen, Diane, and Jim Kamp, eds. *Notable Hispanic American Women.* Detroit: Gale Research, Inc., 1993.

❦ Ortiz-Del Valle, Sandra (Sandra Ortiz)

(1951–   ) *basketball referee*

The participation of women as referees in men's professional basketball was made possible by the pioneering work of Sandra Ortiz-Del Valle. This extended not only to the lesser leagues but also to the National Basketball Association (NBA) itself. Ironically, Ortiz-Del Valle was unable to enjoy such a post in the NBA herself, despite winning a $7.85 million discrimination lawsuit against the organization in 1998. She nevertheless won the struggle on behalf of women in general, because the NBA hired two other female referees—its first ever—on the eve of the trial, in an (unsuccessful) effort to convince the jury that it was not anti-women. In the same year, *The Sporting News* included Ortiz-Del Valle among the "100 most powerful people in sports." She was rated in 98th position and was one of only six women on the list.

Sandra Ortiz was born into a Puerto Rican family in New York City on April 23, 1951. Her father was an electrician, and her enterprising mother was the only Hispanic on the school board in her area, an otherwise almost wholly African-American part of Harlem.

After high school (where she developed a lifelong devotion to the sport of basketball) she studied at City College in New York and played center and forward on the college's basketball team. She received a B.Sc. degree in education in 1974, followed by a master's degree in administration and supervision in 1983.

Ortiz-Del Valle began refereeing youth basketball games in 1978. By 1984 she refereed for the Biddies League and the men's Pro-Am League. Five years later she was offered a refereeing job by the United States Basketball League (USBL), making her the first of her sex to referee men's professional basketball games. From 1992 to 1994, she refereed preseason scrimmages for the New Jersey Nets. However, Ortiz-Del Valle, a member of the International Professional Basketball Officials Association, had her eyes set on the foremost U.S. league: the NBA.

Ortiz-Del Valle had been recommended to the NBA by its own scouts, but the idea of taking her on as a referee was apparently rejected higher up in the organization. For eight years, Ortiz-Del Valle attempted to gain entry to the league's referee training program. She was given a variety of excuses: that she had not applied correctly, that she did not have enough experience, that she was not in good enough physical shape.

During all her years of progress in her work, Ortiz-Del Valle often encountered resistance from men unwilling to allow women into the profession, but always managed to overcome the hurdles in a stubborn but quiet way. The clash with the NBA could not be solved in that unsensational manner. However, when the case came to court, it was found that the NBA had hired 10 men with less experience than she had.

After a one-week-long trial, the jury found that the NBA had indeed discriminated against her, and awarded her $7 million in damages and $850,000 in other compensation. Ortiz-Del Valle was reported to sob and shake uncontrollably on hearing the court's decision.

A year later, in 1999, an appeals court judge reduced the award to a total of $350,000.

Originally, Ortiz-Del Valle had sued not only for monetary compensation but to force the NBA to include her in its roster of referees. However, in the aftermath of back injuries suffered in a car crash in 1997, she decided to abandon that part of the lawsuit.

Following her court victory, Ortiz-Del Valle returned to a job teaching—and coaching the boys' basketball team—at the High School for Humanities in New York.

Further Reading

Nagel, Rob, and Sharon Rose, eds. *Hispanic American Biography*. New York: UXL, 1995.

P

Pelli, César (1926–) architect

César Pelli is one of the most eminent architects in the United States, and the world. An emigrant from Argentina, he was dean of Yale University's School of Architecture and designed such landmarks as the World Financial Center in New York City and the world's tallest building, in Malaysia.

Pelli was born on October 12, 1926, in the provincial city of Tucumán, Argentina. He studied architecture at the university there, graduating cum laude in 1949. He then went to work for a governmental urban planning office in Tucumán.

In 1952, Pelli won a scholarship to pursue a master's degree in architecture from the University of Illinois in Champaign-Urbana. He went there for what he thought would be nine months. Instead, he remained in the United States.

First, he was offered a teaching job at the University of Illinois and then a position as associate at the firm of the famed architect Eero Saarinen, where he worked from 1954 to 1964 in both Michigan and Connecticut. He became a U.S. citizen in 1964.

After that, he spent four years and then nine years, respectively, at two other architecture companies in Los Angeles. At the same time, he was visiting professor of architecture at two universities in Argentina and two in the United States—Yale University in New Haven, Connecticut, and University of California at Los Angeles.

Known as a modest person, Pelli at age 50 believed his life would continue much as it had in previous decades. He was surprised when, in 1977, he was invited to become dean of Yale's School of Architecture. Because of this prestigious position, he began to receive commissions for major architectural works, both in the United States and abroad. His buildings were received with such praise that his work was more and more in demand.

The architect founded his own firm, César Pelli and Associates, in New Haven. That city remained his headquarters even after he concluded seven years as head of the School of Architecture there.

Pelli has been described as an architect who, without neglecting the insides of his buildings, is a specialist in their outer "skins." An often-cited example is his work on the Museum of Modern Art (MOMA) in New York City (1984), where he built the gallery expansion and residential tower. The tower is sheathed with colored glass in a variety of hues, which he subtly graded in order to better blend with the building's surroundings.

The 1980 edition of *Contemporary Architects* states that "more than anyone else in his generation, Pelli is an architect's architect." The World Financial Center and Winter Garden in New York was described by *Time* magazine as "a glistening gem on the tip of lower Manhattan."

Over the years, Pelli has collected many architecture awards. He has been named to the Top Ten List of Living American Architects. The American Institute of Architects, in particular, has awarded him numerous prizes, including its 1995 Gold Medal for life achievement. In that year, Pelli's firm employed 80 people, working on 10 projects around the world. These included the New Main Terminal at Washington National Airport and the twin Petronas Towers in the capital of Malaysia, Kuala Lumpur, which are seven meters (about 23 feet) higher than the previously tallest building in the world, the Sears Tower in Chicago.

Other notable buildings Pelli has designed include the Century City Medical Plaza and the Pacific Design Center in Los Angeles; the Pacific Center in Vancouver, Canada; the United States Embassy in Tokyo, Japan; Four-Leaf Towers, Four Oaks Towers, and Rice University's Herring Hall, all in Houston, Texas; the Norwest Center in Minneapolis, Minnesota; the Canary Wharf Tower in London, England; and Carnegie Hall Tower in New York City. In 2000, Pelli unveiled his design for a new athletics center at the University of Chicago—a design that the president of the university called "a triumph."

Further Reading

Matthews, Kevin, and Artifice, Inc. "Cesar Pelli." Available online. URL: http://www.greatbuildings.com/architects/Cesar_Pelli.html. Downloaded October 11, 2000.

Morgan, Anne Lee, and Colin Naylor, eds. *Contemporary Architects*. Chicago: St. James Press, 1987.

Pastier, John. *César Pelli*. New York: Whitney Library of Design, 1980.

———. *Monographs of Contemporary Architecture: César Pelli*. New York: Facts On File, 1989.

Pelli, César. *César Pelli: Buildings and Projects, 1965–1990*. New York: Rizzoli, 1990.

❧ **Peña, Elizabeth** (1959–) *actress*

Elizabeth Peña has had a busy career although her looks, quickly classifiable as Hispanic, have caused producers more than once to rule her out for certain roles. She has not allowed herself to become bitter because of typecasting in Latina roles, but has seen it as a challenge and an opportunity.

"There are certainly enough five-foot-seven blondes," she declared in an oft-quoted interview in *People* magazine.

At the same time she has refused to go along with too much stereotyping. One of her best-known roles was as a maid in *Down and Out in Beverly Hills* (1985). During the shooting of the movie, Peña convinced the director, Paul Mazursky, to make a significant change. In one sequence the homeowner, played by Bette Midler, was supposed to try to teach the maid to speak English. But Peña told the director, "This little girl is smart and slick. She knows English, believe me." The scene was altered so that it was she who was shown teaching Midler to speak Spanish instead.

Three years later, Peña also refused a major role in Robert Redford's movie *The Milagro Beanfield War* to avoid excessive typecasting as a Mexican.

The future actress was born in Elizabeth, New Jersey, on September 23, 1959, and her father and mother named her after her town of birth. Her parents, who had immigrated into the United States from Cuba, were in the theater business, her mother Estela as a producer and her father Mario as an actor, director, and writer.

When she was only four months old, the family went back to Cuba, where her parents held high hopes for the future because of the fall of the dictator Fulgencio Batista. But a poem written by Mario Peña was decreed by Fidel Castro's new government to be "anti-system" and landed him in jail, from which he was ejected to depart again for the United States. Estela and her two daughters, however, were not allowed to leave Cuba to rejoin him until 1968.

Although the Peñas returned to theatrical activities once they were back together and in New York City—where they founded the Latin American Theater Ensemble—Estela opposed her daughter Elizabeth's career choice: acting. She had seen from up close how hard a life it can be.

Elizabeth Peña, however, was already capable of the same unyielding resolve that was later to mark her pursuit of roles in movies. She could not be dissuaded from attending New York's prestigious High School for the Performing Arts, where she earned good grades but also experienced a major disappointment. She was barred from a part in the senior-year play, *Picnic,* because, essentially, she didn't look "American" enough for it.

After high school, and a number of courses in diverse acting specialties, Peña began to appear in small theatrical and movie roles, notably *El Super* (1979), *They All Laughed* (1981) and *Crossover Dreams* (1984), the latter alongside Rubén BLADES.

The following year, Peña left New York for Hollywood. She had $2,000 saved up, but no job and no agent. Hearing about the search for an actress to play the maid in *Down and Out in Beverly Hills*—a role that was also coveted by the Brazilian star Sonia Braga—she acted as her own agent, repeatedly sending her photo and pestering the production until she was given a chance to try out for it. The movie's male star, Richard Dreyfuss, then convinced Mazursky to give her the part.

The one problem she faced during the filming was that her English was "too good." She told an interviewer, "I had spent thousands of dollars learning to speak Eastern Standard English. Paul (Mazursky) kept on saying, 'You gotta make it more Latin.' So for three months, I pretended I was talking with a banana in my mouth."

Though occasionally appearing on stage again, Peña has consistently preferred movies and television. Among the works she has acted in are *La Bamba,* the biography of Ritchie VALENS (1987), *Jacob's Ladder* (1990), *Fair Game* and *The Invaders* (both 1995), *Lone Star* (1996), *The Second Civil War* (1997) and *Rush Hour* (1998). Her part in *Jacob's Ladder* had not been created as Hispanic, but was altered to fit her.

Peña has collected such critical appraisals as "warm," "sympathetic," and "versatile." She was described as "assertive and gutsy" in a *Washington Post* review of a TV show—*Shannon's Deal,* centering on a male lawyer—that the newspaper otherwise did not like. "Maybe the show should be about *her,*" the reviewer wrote.

In 1994, Peña herself created and directed a series of theatrical presentations in Hollywood, called *Celebrando la diferencia, a Latino Literature Series for Children,* to help make Hispanics proud of their heritage.

Peña received the U.S. Congress Congressional Award, the Hispanic Women's Council Woman of the Year Award and the Nosotros Golden Eagle Award, all in 1988.

Further Reading

Novas, Himilce. *The Hispanic 100.* New York: Citadel Press, 1995.

Tardiff, Joseph C., and Mpho Mabunda, eds. *Dictionary of Hispanic Biography.* Detroit: Gale Research, 1996.

❧ Peña, Federico (1947–) *government official*

Federico Peña became the first Hispanic to be elected mayor of a United States city without a major Hispanic population: Denver, Colorado. He spent eight years as mayor and was later named to the cabinet as President Bill Clinton's secretary of transportation. Although he has spent most of his political career in Colorado, Peña is a Texan. Members of his family can be found in the annals of Texas public life for 200 years. He is not related to Elizabeth PEÑA.

Born on March 15, 1947, in Laredo, he went to school in Brownsville, graduating with honors from St. Joseph's Academy. At the University of Texas in Austin, Peña earned a B.S. degree in 1969 and a J.D. degree in 1972.

A person with strong liberal convictions and a lifelong passion for politics, Peña entered the political arena while still in school, serving in various student government offices. As an adult, he worked to help elect Democratic Party candidates.

His first years as a lawyer demonstrated his commitment to helping the Hispanic community, the poor, and minorities in general. He spent them at a legal aid office in El Paso, Texas, and, after moving to Denver in 1972, at the Mexican American Legal Defense and Educational Fund (MALDEF) and then the Chicano Education Project. Later, he and his brother founded their own law firm, Peña and Peña. In 1979, Federico Peña ran successfully for the Colorado General Assembly. His talent was quickly recognized in the state legislature and within two years he was House Minority Speaker and had won the General Assembly's Outstanding House Democratic Legislator Award.

After only four years as a legislator, Peña had acquired enough of a reputation to campaign for and win the mayor's office in Denver. He was reelected in 1987. Peña's success in Denver brought him nationwide attention.

After his two terms in office, in 1992, Peña founded another private firm in Denver, Peña Investment Advisers Inc. However, he soon received President Clinton's call to Washington, D.C., as secretary of transportation.

In 1997 Clinton appointed Peña secretary of energy—the first Latino to hold that post.

Further Reading

Meier, Matt S. *Mexican American Biographies.* Westport, Conn.: Greenwood Publishing Group, 1988.

❧ **Pérez, Manuel, Jr.** (1923–) *soldier*

Manuel Pérez Jr. killed 18 Japanese soldiers while single-handedly assaulting and conquering a fortified enemy position in the Philippines during World War II. His heroism earned him the Congressional Medal of Honor.

Pérez was born in Oklahoma City on March 3, 1923. He later moved to Chicago, where he joined the U.S. Army. As a private first class, Pérez was sent to the Philippine Islands with Company A, 511th Parachute Infantry, 11th Airborne Division.

Japan had occupied the Philippines earlier in the war, and the U.S. forces were fighting to retake the country. In February 1945, on Luzon, the biggest island in the Philippines, Pérez participated in an attack on Japanese-held Fort William McKinley. The Japanese defended strongly.

One area leading to the fort was protected by a series of 12 fortified machine-gun nests known as pillboxes. Company A advanced with Pérez as lead scout and destroyed all but one of these pillboxes.

In these actions, Pérez was credited with killing five enemy soldiers with his rifle. With grenades he'd thrown into the nests, he also killed an undetermined number of others who are not included in the total of 18 mentioned in his citation.

One last pillbox now confronted the U.S. soldiers. Pérez decided, on his own initiative, to embark on a one-man attack mission. Edging closer by a roundabout route and shooting four enemy soldiers dead as he did so, he managed to get within grenade-throwing distance of the emplacement. He hurled a grenade in, and the Japanese gave up the position, trying to escape into a tunnel dug behind the pillbox. Pérez, however, succeeded in killing eight of the escaping soldiers, despite having to reload his rifle during shooting.

At this point, one of the Japanese infantrymen threw his rifle at Pérez, bayonet first. Pérez parried with his own rifle but lost his grip, and it fell out of his hands. Seeing the enemy soldier's gun closer to him than his own, he picked it up and used it to shoot another two men.

Pérez then charged forward, wielding the rifle like a club and killing three more soldiers. Finally, with one Japanese soldier left alive in the pillbox, Pérez rushed in and killed him with the bayonet.

The Medal of Honor citation praises Pérez for "neutralizing the position that held up the advance of his entire company," and it adds: "Through his courageous determination and heroic disregard of grave danger, Private First Class Pérez made possible the successful advance of his unit towards a valuable objective and provided a lasting inspiration for his comrades."

Further Reading

The Committee on Veterans' Affairs, United States Senate. *Medal of Honor Recipients 1863–1978.* Washington, D.C.: U.S. Government Printing Office, 1979.

❧ **Pérez, Rosie** (Rosa María Pérez)
(1964–) *actress, choreographer*

Without ever having taken acting lessons, Rosie Pérez has landed movie roles that were sought by better-known stars, and has earned an Oscar nomination. And although her features cause her to be immediately grouped in what are known as "ethnic" categories, she is one of the few Hispanic performers who in recent years have obtained roles originally designed for "mainstream" racial types. Pérez has managed to do this by conveying a bouncy, sassy personality and an air of street-level authenticity strong enough to override all other considerations. In 1992, *Newsweek* magazine dubbed her "Rosie the Riveting." She is also much in demand as a pop-music choreographer, again without the help of formal training in that area, and is a clever businesswoman who runs her diverse undertakings with a canny touch.

Pérez (not related to Manuel PÉREZ Jr.) was born on September 6, 1964. She is a native of Brooklyn, New York City, where she grew up in Bushwick, an area of Brooklyn nicknamed "Little Puerto Rico." Rosie was one of 10 children of Ismael Serrano, a seaman, and Lydia Pérez, formerly a singer in Puerto Rico. Money was scarce but, as the actress has recalled, there was comfort in the fact that everybody in the neighborhood was in the same situation. "I didn't know I had secondhand clothes, I just thought my mother had bad taste," she said.

Once having become a celebrity Pérez revealed that at the age of 12 she was put in a group home after slitting a woman's throat in unclear circumstances. One of her aunts can be given much credit for straightening out Rosie's life; she visited the girl every day with advice and encouragement, and upon leaving the group home Rosie went to live with her.

Her grades in school were good and Pérez decided that an education was what would improve her life. At that stage she wanted to put as much distance as possible between herself and her old neighborhood, and, interested in becoming a marine biologist, she enrolled in the University of California at Los Angeles, majoring in biochemistry.

However, she was "discovered"—and she herself discovered the depth of her talents in other fields—before graduating. Her home had been music-filled, and she had often watched her parents dance salsa. For Pérez, dancing was a self-taught passion and one she often indulged in in Los Angeles. A scout for a TV show saw her in a club and invited her to dance professionally, and that in turn led to choreography jobs.

Pérez has created choreography for individual singers like Bobby Brown and Diana Ross, for rap groups like Heavy D & the Boyz, for videos, and for the Fly Girls in the television program *In Living Color,* as well as managing a rhythm-and-blues group, Five AM. She obtained an Emmy nomination for her *In Living Color* choreography.

It was also while dancing at a cabaret that she got her start in acting. She was spotted at the club by the director and actor Spike Lee, who offered her a part in *Do the Right Thing* (1989). It was a typical Puerto Rican spitfire role, and Pérez made the most of it. Finding herself criticized by Hispanic groups for perpetuating the type, she defended herself by saying she was "not portraying something that's not really out there."

Nevertheless she has tried, where possible, to obtain parts in which "I'm not screaming at the top of my lungs" (*Vibe* magazine said her vocal range "starts at Betty Boop and ends somewhere around car alarm"). That meant, in her own words, "stealing the roles written for nonminorities," because as regards Hispanics, "we're not even in the running. There are no roles." In the comedy *White Men Can't Jump* (1992), with Woody Harrelson and Wesley Snipes, she was cast as Harrelson's girlfriend in a role that was intended for a white woman with an Ivy League background. For Pérez the role was rewritten for a former Brooklyn disco queen. And in the drama *Fearless* (1993), starring Jeff Bridges and Isabella Rossellini, she played a mother who loses her child in a plane crash—an originally Italian-American role that the stars Winona Ryder and Jodie Foster were both known to want. Her performance made her a best-supporting-actress nominee for the 1994 Academy Awards.

Other movies Pérez has acted in include *Perdita Durango* (1997), *The 24 Hour Woman* (1999) and *King of the Jungle* (2000). Pérez was the voice of Chel in DreamWorks' animated film *The Road to El Dorado* (2000).

Concerned over the issue of the U.S. Navy bombing range on the island of Vieques off the coast of Puerto Rico, Pérez was arrested in 2000 at a protest rally in New York.

Further Reading

Disney Enterprises, Inc. "Mr. Showbiz Celebrities: Rosie Perez Profile." Available online. URL: http://mrshowbiz.go.com/people/rosieperez/Index.html. Downloaded October 11, 2000.

Novas, Himilce. *The Hispanic 100.* New York: Citadel Press, 1995.

Telgen, Diane, and Jim Kamp, eds. *Notable Hispanic American Women.* Detroit: Gale Research, 1998.

❧ Piñero, Miguel (1946–1988) *writer*

A petty criminal who turned to writing and revealed a powerful, if unschooled, talent, Miguel Antonio Piñero wrote the play *Short Eyes,* which won wide acclaim and established him as one of the most significant Nuyorican (New York Puerto Rican) authors. Principally a playwright and poet, Piñero also wrote prose and worked as a scriptwriter for major television crime series.

Piñero was born on December 19, 1946, in Gurabo, Puerto Rico, but he grew up on New York's Lower East Side. Although the family came from Puerto Rico together, Miguel's father abandoned his wife and children soon afterward, leaving them to live in the streets for a time. In this tough environment, the boy became truant while still in grade school. He dropped out of junior high school and did not continue his education until he was in prison in later years.

As a street gang leader, Peña was first arrested at the age of 13. He progressed from shoplifting to taking and running drugs and on to armed robbery. The armed-robbery charge landed him in Sing Sing prison at the age of 24.

A prison theater program led Piñero to writing and also to acting, which he would afterward continue in tiny, walk-on roles both on television (*Miami Vice*) and in movies (*The Godfather* and *Fort Apache, The Bronx*).

Written while Piñero was in jail, *Short Eyes* was first performed at a New York church. It was then produced at Joseph Papp's Public Theater. *Short Eyes* is a hard-hitting play about guilt, prison violence, and especially the way people establish power relationships. Power would be Piñero's central subject throughout his working career.

Short Eyes won the New York Critics Circle Award for Best American Play of the 1973–74 season, an Obie Prize, and a Drama Desk Award. The play was published in 1975 and made into a movie two years later. Piñero wrote the screenplay and also played a role. It has been released both as *Short Eyes* and as *Slammer.*

Piñero published a collection of poems in 1980, *La Bodega Sold Dreams.* In 1982, he won a Guggenheim Fellowship. A three-play collection was published two years later titled *The Sun Always Shines for the Cool; Midnight Moon at the Greasy Spoon; Eulogy for a Small-Time Thief.* The collection *Outrageous One-Act Plays* followed in 1986. Most of his plays were produced.

For television, Piñero participated in writing for several series, including *Kojak, Baretta,* and *Miami Vice.*

His writing and the celebrity it brought him in literary circles kept Piñero from going back to crime, but he was unable to conquer his drug addiction and drinking problems. In 1988 he died of cirrhosis of the liver, a disease often associated with alcohol abuse.

Further Reading

Kanellos, Nicolás. *Biographical Dictionary of Hispanic Literature in the United States.* Westport, Conn.: Greenwood Press, 1989.

❧ Plunkett, Jim (James Plunkett) (1947–) *football player*

Despite being plagued by a succession of injuries, Jim Plunkett entered the record books as one of football history's great quarterbacks. Mexican American on his mother's side (and German and Irish on his father's), Plunkett from early on took the time to counsel Mexican-American youths, particularly about the importance of completing their education. At a crucial point in his career, he passed up a large amount of money in order to continue this work.

Both his parents, Carmen Blea and William Plunkett, were blind. They met at a school for the blind in Albuquerque, New Mexico. In the early 1940s, they left for California. James William Plunkett was born in San Jose on December 5, 1947. His father ran a newsstand, and as a child Jim delivered newspapers. Later, he worked as a gas-station attendant.

Always big for his age, Plunkett became an athlete in his school years. He took part in wrestling, track events, baseball, basketball, and, particularly, football. Under his leadership, the football team at James Lick High School was chosen All-League Team. Plunkett's performance led to football scholarship offers from universities, and in 1967, he chose Stanford University, which had the advantage of being close to home so that he could remain near his disabled parents.

Plunkett took his political science studies seriously and maintained a B average, but he was also a star on the football field. Thanks in large part to him, Stanford won the Rose Bowl, and Plunkett earned the Heisman Memorial Trophy as the best college football player in the country, the Maxwell Award, and several player-of-the-year and all-American awards. He was the first major college football player to top 7,000 offense yards, reaching 7,887.

In addition to broken bones on the field, Plunkett had to have a thyroid operation to remove a benign tumor. This delayed his studies and meant that he received offers to join professional football teams before earning his college degree.

Accepting one of these offers would have assured financial security for his mother (his father had since died). However, Plunkett realized that dropping out of college to turn professional would set a bad example for the high school students whom he had been counseling. Plunkett stayed in college, graduating in 1971.

As a pro, Plunkett played with the Boston Patriots (now the New England Patriots) from 1971 to 1976, the San Francisco 49ers from 1976 to 1978, and the Oakland Raiders (now the Los Angeles Raiders) from 1978 to 1988.

He began his career by being named Rookie of the Year but became bogged down in the years that followed by a string of serious injuries and conflicts with coaches.

In 1980, however, playing for the Raiders, Plunkett returned to top form and was voted Comeback Player of the Year. He led his team to victory in the Super Bowl in 1981 and was named Super Bowl Most Valuable Player. New injuries meant more setbacks, but by 1984 he was again able to take the Raiders to the Super Bowl and triumph.

In his overall career, Plunkett passed for a total of 25,882 yards, with 164 touchdowns, a completion rate of 2.5, and 1,237 rushing yards. After retiring from the game, Plunkett began a new career in 1990 as a radio sports announcer in Los Angeles.

Further Reading

Martínez, Al. *Rising Voices: Profiles of Hispanic-American Lives.* New York: New American Library, 1974.

Plunkett, Jim, with Dave Newhouse. *The Jim Plunkett Story: The Saga of a Man Who Came Back.* New York: Arbor House, 1981.

Porter, David L. *Biographical Dictionary of American Sports-Football.* Westport, Conn.: Greenwood Press, 1987.

Ponce de León, Juan (1460?–1521)
conquistador

Juan Ponce de León was the first European to land on what became the United States. He also first sighted Mexico and identified the Gulf Stream, the strong current in the Atlantic Ocean that became immensely important to navigation. What he did not discover was what he had set out to find, the legendary Fountain of Youth that would make the old young again.

Ponce de León also conquered Puerto Rico and founded its capital, San Juan. The island's second-biggest city, Ponce, is named after him.

The details of Ponce de León's early life are scarce and contradictory. He is likely to have been born in 1460 in the vicinity of the city of Valladolid, Spain. Like his ancestors before him, he fought in his youth against the Moors in Spain.

Ponce de León came to America with Christopher Columbus on Columbus's second trip to the New World in 1493. The first land the Spaniards settled in the Americas was the island of Hispaniola—today's Dominican Republic and Haiti. Ponce de León participated in the conquest of that island and in subjugating the Indians who originally inhabited it. He was made governor of one of its provinces.

In 1506, with 100 soldiers and permission to conquer the neighboring island of Puerto Rico, Ponce de León landed there and wrested it from its inhabitants. He was confirmed as governor of that territory by King Ferdinand of Spain. He then made himself rich by exploiting the island's wealth. He set up his capital in San Germán, then shifted it to Caparra, and finally moved it again, ordering the founding of San Juan.

The conquistador was now becoming involved in a power struggle with the family of Christopher Columbus. In 1511 the king took the governorship of Puerto Rico away from him and gave it to Columbus's son, Diego.

Ponce de León returned to Spain, and King Ferdinand gave him the right to explore further territories north of Cuba. Bartholomew Columbus, Christopher's brother, had asked for this expedition, but Ferdinand was careful not to give too much power to the Columbuses.

The lands that Ponce de León set out to explore were at that time believed to be only islands. What attracted Ponce de León to these lands was the belief that they contained the fabled Fountain of Youth whose water was thought to restore youth and vigor.

The explorer began his search with three ships, leaving harbor in Puerto Rico in early March 1513. A month later, on April 2, the crews spotted the land which Ponce de León named La Florida; the site was possibly near today's Daytona Beach. They were the first Europeans to see what was to become the territory of the United States. They landed on the following day.

Ponce de León then proceeded south, following the coast and discovering the Gulf Stream. At the tip of Florida, he turned northward again and scouted the western coast of the peninsula, which he still believed to be an island. His contacts with the Florida Indians convinced him that nobody there had ever come across a Fountain of Youth.

Reluctantly giving up the search there, Ponce de León and the expedition next crossed the Gulf of Mexico. At the end of June they found land that they initially believed to be Cuba. However, it turned out to be the mainland of Mexico—a part of the Yucatán peninsula, which Ponce de León also thought to be an island.

On their way back to Puerto Rico, two ships went one way and the third another so as to increase the possibility of coming across the land of the Fountain of Youth. Again disappointed, Ponce de León abandoned his quest. When he later returned to Florida, it was to colonize it, not to search for the fountain.

The explorer reported back to the king in Spain in 1514 and was named governor of the lands he had discovered. He did not, however, immediately return to them. He spent the following years in wars against Indians on Caribbean islands.

In 1521, he led a new expedition to Florida. The attempt to set up a permanent settlement there was to prove fatal for him as the local Seminole Indians gave him battle. Ponce de León received an arrow wound that became infected. Seriously ill, he was taken to Havana, Cuba, where he died in 1521.

Further Reading

Baker, Nina. *Juan Ponce de León.* New York: Knopf, 1957.

Blassingame, Wyatt. *Ponce de León.* Champaign, Ill.: Garrard Publishing Co., 1965.

Freeman, Bernardine. *Juan Ponce de León: First in the Land.* Boston: Houghton Mifflin, 1958.

Fuson, Robert H. *Juan Ponce de León and the Spanish Discovery of Puerto Rico and Florida.* Blacksburg, Va.: McDonald & Woodward, 2000.

Leonard, M.C. Bob. "Florida of the Conquistador." Available online. URL: http://www.floridahistory.org/floridians/conquis.htm. Downloaded October 11, 2000.

Principal, Victoria (1950–) *actress, fitness guru*

Victoria Principal has had several careers: as an actress in the *Dallas* television series, in which she acted for a decade; as a physical fitness enthusiast and writer of exercise and diet books; as a model; and as an agent.

Principal is of Hispanic descent on her father's side. The name *Principal,* in Spanish as in English, means "main" or "leading." Her father, Victor Principal, was a U.S. Air Force sergeant major. He and his family were posted at various bases over the years. She was born in Fukuoka, Japan, on January 3, 1950. As a child, Principal lived mainly on air force bases in Britain and the United States. After high school, while living in Florida, she attended Miami-Dade Community College.

Her original intention was to become a chiropractor. However, a pretty face and a lithe body quickly led to modeling jobs in New York and exposure in television commercials. Modeling led to a Hollywood career, beginning in 1972 with *The Life and Times of Judge Roy Bean,* in which she played a major part opposite Paul Newman.

However, she was less satisfied with the roles she was next offered. The motion pictures she appeared in included *Vigilante Force; Earthquake; I Will, I Will . . . For Now;* and *The Naked Ape.*

In 1975, Principal decided to give up acting and work instead as an agent. Thus, at the age of only 25, she was embarking on a third career, though she did appear on TV in the *Fantasy Island* series in 1977. She had success as an agent and might have remained in that career, but in 1978 she was offered a big role in the *Dallas* television series. Acting as her own agent, Principal negotiated a salary rumored to be $25,000 per episode. *Dallas* became a huge hit both in the United States and abroad, and her fame and income soared. Principal began to appear in a number of television movies and programs, including *Not Just Another Affair* (1982), *Blind Witness* (1989), and *Sparks* (1990).

After leaving *Dallas,* Principal formed Victoria Principal Productions and continued to work as an actress and producer.

Around 1980, the actress, who had always been active in many sports, became particularly interested in physical fitness. She researched and developed her own exercise program and in 1983 published a book on her exercise method, *The Body*

Principal. It did so well in bookstores that it was followed by *The Beauty Principal* in 1984 and *The Diet Principal* in 1987. She also created her own skin care line. Principal currently chairs Victory Over Violence, a nonprofit group dedicated to ending violence against women.

Further Reading

Inman, David. *The TV Encyclopedia.* New York: Perigee Books, 1991.

Scheuer, Steven H., ed. *Who's Who in Television and Cable.* New York: Facts On File, 1983.

Who's Who in Entertainment 1992–1993. 2nd ed. Wilmette, Ill.: R.R. Bowker, 1992.

✎ **Prinze, Freddie** (Freddie Karl Pruetzel)
(1954–1977) *actor, comedian*

Freddie Prinze was one of the most charismatic young comedians to emerge on television in the 1970s.

Prinze was born Freddie Karl Pruetzel on June 22, 1954. Born to a Puerto Rican mother and a Hungarian father, Prinze grew up in the Washington Heights district of Manhattan and attended the New York High School of the Performing Arts. Studying to become an actor or a dancer, Prinze discovered his ability to make classmates laugh through mimicry and ethnic humor. Prinze developed his comedic talent in the improvisation stages of the New York comedy circuit.

In 1972, Prinze made his first television appearance on *The Jack Parr Show,* and in 1973, he made a breakthrough appearance on *The Tonight Show* with Johnny Carson. Soon after, Prinze auditioned for the lead role on a comedy series to be produced by James Komack. Prinze won the role of a poor Mexican youth on the show *Chico and the Man.* The series debuted in September 1974 and became a hit, ranking close behind *All in the Family* and *Sanford & Son* in the ratings.

In 1975, Prinze married Kathy Cochran, and they had a son, Freddie Jr. Despite the success of his career and the addition to his family, the pressure of fame took its toll and Freddie began to become dependent on drugs. As his addiction escalated, Prinze missed tapings of *Chico and the Man* and Las Vegas stand-up performances. In 1976 his wife Kathy filed for divorce.

By 1977, Prinze's mental health began to suffer. On January 28, 1977, Prinze ended his life by consuming a large number of Quaaludes and alcohol and shooting himself in the head. For the young comedian, it seemed that living up to the public's expectations had become too much to handle.

Following in his father's career path into acting, Freddie Prinze Jr. has become a Hollywood star, appearing in the popular *I Know What You Did Last Summer* (1997) and its 1998 sequel, *I Still Know What You Did Last Summer; She's All That* (1998); and, in 2002, the live-action movie of the classic cartoon series *Scooby-Doo*.

Further Reading

Looking Goood. "Who Was Freddie Prinze?" Available online. URL: http://freespace.virginet.co. uk/laurence.horton/main.html. Downloaded March 1, 2001.

Sitcoms Online. "Chico and the Man Online." Available online. URL: http://www.sitcomsonline. com/chicoandtheman.html. Downloaded March 1, 2001.

✍ **Puente, Ernesto Anthony "Tito"**
(1923–2000) *bandleader*

One of the biggest names in big-band Latin music in the United States, Tito Puente was one of the creators of the mambo dance craze that swept the United States in the late 1940s. Almost a half-century later, after the Latin sound had evolved into salsa, he remained one of its leaders. Over the years, several musicians—including Puente—have been given the title King of the Mambo. Puente, however, reigned for decades as sovereign of so many Latin music waves that he became simply The King—El Rey.

Puente (whose name means "bridge" in Spanish) was born in New York to Puerto Rican parents on April 20, 1923. A formally trained musician, he studied at the prestigious Juilliard Conservatory and the New York School of Music.

In 1946, Puente joined the drum section of a major band led by a Cuban musician, pianist José Curbelo. It was the time when the mambo was being shaped by fusing its Cuban roots with a New York verve and drive, and Puente was a key participant in the process. The following year, he left Curbelo and launched his own band, which he called The Picadilly Boys.

As a bandleader, his personal contribution focused particularly on arrangements and percussion. His arrangements of mambo tunes are regarded as the most sophisticated in the business, and he was an acknowledged master of percussion instruments, especially the *timbales* (kettledrums), although he also played the saxophone and clarinet.

Puente worked in many kinds of dance and also jazz music, often backing such top Latin-sound singers as Santos Colón and Celia CRUZ. Jazz luminaries Lionel Hampton, Dizzy Gillespie, and Woody Herman all invited him to play with them. He appeared in Woody Allen's movie *Radio Days* (1987), as well as in *Armed and Dangerous* (1986). Puente recorded more than 100 albums, winning five of the recording industry's Grammy awards between 1978 and 2000, although many specialists consider that his best record was 1958's *Dance Mania*. In 1986, he was given the New York Music Award; four years later, his star was added to the Hollywood Walk of Fame. He died on May 31, 2000.

Further Reading

Loza, Steven. *Tito Puente and the Making of Latin Music.* Champaign: University of Illinois Press, 1999.

Roberts, John Storm. *The Latin Tinge: The Impact of Latin American Music on the United States.* Tivoli, N.Y.: Original Music, 1985.

Quinn, Anthony (Antonio Rodolfo Quinn Oaxaca) (1915–2001) *actor*

Among the finest actors in Hollywood, Anthony Quinn has been one of the most recognizable people in the world for many years. He starred in one of the most celebrated movies of all time, Italian director Federico Fellini's *La Strada* (1954), as well as many other notable productions. He is also a prizewinning painter and sculptor. His specialty in the movies has been to play manly, often gruff, types with a strong zest for living. He has displayed the same vital force in private life.

Quinn is of Mexican ancestry (mainly Indian rather than Spanish) on his mother's side, and Irish/Mexican on his father's. His rugged face has helped him portray a wide range of nationalities: for example, he was virtually accepted as an honorary Greek after his title role in *Zorba the Greek* (1964), which he also performed on the stage with great success.

Appropriately, in *The 25th Hour* (1967), he played a man whose features cause his background to be disputed by crazed Nazi researchers who define him as one race on one day and as a different one the next.

Quinn was born in Chihuahua, Mexico, on April 21, 1915. His mother, Manuela Oaxaca, told him

that she had been about 15 when she followed his father to war. Francisco Quinn, the son of an Irish railroad engineer who had married in Mexico, was about two years older than Manuela. They barely knew each other when Francisco asked her to be his *soldadera* (soldier's woman). The Mexican Revolution was under way, and Francisco had enlisted with the revolutionary leader Pancho Villa. In Mexico, women often accompanied their husbands to war, although they remained in the rear during actual battle. Manuela packed some things and went with Francisco. They were married by a priest on the train that was taking them to the front.

When Manuela became pregnant she was sent home by the army. After Anthony was born and Francisco returned to Chihuahua, Francisco's mother took her son away from his wife. Manuela, with the baby, followed him once more, this time to Ciudad Juárez/El Paso, Texas. Later, they moved to Los Angeles.

Anthony Quinn, a self-educated man who amassed a book collection of more than 5,000 volumes, was a high school dropout. He worked at many jobs from childhood, among them mattress maker, cement mixer, boxer, dress cutter, ditch digger, and electrician. His mother once told him that she had been afraid, at first, that he might "end up being just another Mexican fruit picker"; fruit picking was, indeed, another of his occupations before becoming an actor. Acting, however, would lead him to wealth and fame unimagined by his mother or himself.

Early on, as a Mexican American, he was fully aware of discrimination. It went beyond seeing "No Mexicans allowed" signs. One incident occurred in the 1940s when he was acting in a war movie being filmed at a marine base near Los Angeles. It was a time of strong anti-Mexican sentiment in some quarters. This had been set off by the "Sleepy Lagoon" case, a murder trial that was under way, in which a score of Mexican youths had been accused of murder. Some marines who were participating in the war movie with Quinn walked up to him and, to show that they considered him "one of the boys," invited him to go to Los Angeles with them "to beat up some Mexicans."

"I guess my name being Quinn, they never thought I was Mexican," the actor wrote in his memoir *The Original Sin*. The incident ended with Quinn in a fistfight with the marine ringleader.

In the 1920s, Quinn's father had worked in the movie industry, feeding trained animals, cranking hand-operated cameras, and doing other jobs. His son is reported on one occasion to have played a jungle child in a movie; however, the young man did not become an actor by this route; rather, as an adult, he found acting through the theater.

One obstacle was Quinn's speech impediment, which he overcame by surgery and subsequent speech therapy that involved holding a cork in his mouth while speaking.

He studied to be a theater actor and played the lead role in a Los Angeles production of the play *Clean Beds* opposite actress Mae West in 1936. Then came more plays and, in the same year, his first film parts.

In 1937, he appeared in *The Plainsman*, landing a role by pretending to be a Cheyenne Indian and claiming to speak the language. The producer-director was celebrated movie pioneer Cecil B. De Mille. Quinn met De Mille's daughter Katherine and married her that same year, 1937. De Mille disapproved strongly of the marriage and did nothing to help his son-in-law's career.

Quinn then proceeded to play many roles as an Indian, a bandit, and a native of assorted "exotic" countries. Portrayals of Mexicans were often unflattering, following the established Hollywood tradition. However in *The Ox-Bow Incident* (1943), Quinn got to play a Mexican—one of three accused men—who is braver, more skilled, and possibly even better educated than anyone else in the story.

Other movies in Quinn's early decades as an actor include *King of Alcatraz, Island of Lost Men,* and *Emergency Squad* in the 1930s and *They Died With Their Boots On, The Black Swan, Guadalcanal Diary, Irish Eyes Are Smiling,* and *Back to Bataan* in the 1940s.

Quinn also maintained his interest in stage acting. He appeared, unsuccessfully, on Broadway in 1947 but was then acclaimed on tour as the male lead in *A Streetcar Named Desire.*

He achieved real stardom—and won two Academy Awards—in the 1950s, first for *Viva Zapata!* (1952), in which he played the brother of Mexican revolutionary leader Emiliano Zapata, and second for *Lust for Life* (1956), in which he was the French painter Paul Gaugin.

In the same decade he was invited to appear in European films. He was Attila in an Italian-French production of the same name. Fellini gave him the leading role (of a carnival strongman) in *La Strada,* which won the Oscar for best foreign-language film in 1954.

Another highlight in Quinn's career was the artistically acclaimed *The Children of Sánchez* (1978), which also starred Dolores DEL RÍO. A U.S.–Mexican coproduction, it was based on a real-life study of a family in a Mexico City tenement.

Other major titles in his career have been *The Hunchback of Notre Dame* (as Quasimodo, 1956), *Wild Is the Wind* (1957), *The Black Orchid* (1958), *Last Train From Gun Hill* (1959), *The Guns of Navarone* and *Barabbas* (1961), *Requiem for a Heavyweight* and *Lawrence of Arabia* (1962), *The Visit* (1964), *Marco Polo* (1965, playing Kublai Khan), *The Shoes of the Fisherman* (1968, as a Russian pope), *The Secret of Santa Vittoria* (1969), *The Greek Tycoon* (1978), *The Last Action Hero* (1993), *Camino de Santiago* (1999), and *Oriundi* (1999, which he also produced).

All through his life, Quinn was active as a painter and sculptor. By the mid-1990s, he had had nine major exhibitions of his work. In 1989, he created an original lithograph at the request of the United Nations to commemorate the fortieth anniversary of the Universal Declaration of Human Rights.

The following year, he received a medal from France in recognition of his life achievement in art—becoming a French Commander of Arts and Letters. Quinn received a Hispanic Heritage Award in 2000.

Quinn had five children by Katherine De Mille, to whom he was married for more than 25 years; one drowned at the age of three in the swimming pool of the comedian W. C. Fields. He has three children with his second wife, Iolanda Addolori, an Italian film-industry worker whom he met while filming *Barabbas* and to whom he was married for 31 years. He fathered two more children when he was more than 75 years old. He married Kathy Benvin in 1997. His children Danielle, Francesco, and Valentina are also actors.

Anthony Quinn died June 3, 2001.

Further Reading

Amdur, Melissa. *Anthony Quinn.* New York: Chelsea House, 1993.

Classic Movies. "Welcome to the Golden Years." Available online. URL: http://www.Geocities.com/Hollywood/9766/quinn.html. Downloaded October 11, 2000.

Marill, Alvin H. *The Films of Anthony Quinn.* Secaucus, N.J.: Citadel Press, 1975.

Quinn, Anthony. *The Original Sin: A Self-Portrait.* Boston: Little, Brown, 1972.

Quinn, Anthony, with Daniel Paisner. *One Man Tango.* New York: HarperCollins, 1995.

Ramírez, Francisco P. (1835?–1890?)
journalist

Founder and director of the first Spanish-language newspaper in Los Angeles, Francisco P. Ramírez used it to crusade for the rights of Spanish speakers in the period after the United States takeover of California.

Ramírez was a Californio—a member of the community of Spanish-speaking settlers of California. When he was born, in about 1835, the region was still part of Mexico. Then came its annexation by the United States, followed immediately by its great boom during the gold rush.

These events caused wrenching changes in Californios' lives. They found that they had become a minority—one often despised and discriminated against—in what had been their land. Ramírez's journalistic work was a response to this situation and sought to correct it.

Much remains unknown about Ramírez's early days as well as his later years. His record comes into focus when he went to work for the Los Angeles *Star,* possibly when he was still a teenager. This English-language newspaper published a sheet in Spanish, under the title *La Estrella* (meaning "Star" in Spanish), and Ramírez was employed in the print shop as a typesetter and assistant.

However, the *Star,* despite publishing that Spanish-language supplement, betrayed strong prejudices against Californios and Mexicans. Because of this, Ramírez decided to start his own paper to guide and defend his people.

In 1855, when Ramírez was only about 20 years old, he left *La Estrella* and launched his journal, *El Clamor Público (The Public Outcry)* and published it as a weekly.

Ramírez's position strongly favored the assimilation of Mexican Americans into U.S. society. He saw it as their only chance to gain acceptance and to progress within an ever-growing Anglo majority. *El Clamor Público* counseled Mexican Americans to set aside "all bygone traditions, and become Americanized all over—in language, in manners, in customs and habits," while remembering their history and remaining proud of it.

At the same time, Ramírez strongly championed the rights of Spanish speakers at a time when many of the state's Mexicans and Californios were being forced off their lands, barred from gold mining, treated as inferiors, and sometimes physically persecuted and lynched. The newspaper not only chronicled the outrages but also tried to teach its readers how to improve their lot. One road that Ramírez advocated was increased participation in the political process; another was education. *El Clamor Público* came out in favor of more rights for blacks and for women, even advocating women's education.

Ramírez supported the Republican Party and was in turn supported by it. In 1859, after he made a bid to be elected as a Los Angeles assemblyman and was unsuccessful, he lost that backing and was forced to close his weekly. After a period working as a printer in Mexico, Ramírez returned to Los Angeles. He was appointed postmaster of the city in 1864 and then as official state translator in 1865.

Seven years later, he reappeared as editor of another weekly publication in Spanish, titled *La Crónica (The Chronicle),* but he held this position for only a short time. He died in about 1890.

Further Reading
Meier, Matt S. *Mexican American Biographies.* Westport, Conn.: Greenwood Publishing Group, 1988.

❧ Rebozo, Charles Gregory "Bebe"

(1912–1998) *businessman*
The close friendship of "Bebe" Rebozo, a wealthy banker, and United States President Richard Nixon made Rebozo an object of deep curiosity in the world of politics as Nixon faced increasing trouble during his presidency. However, Rebozo remained an enigmatic figure. Reporters never learned anything from him, except that he was truly loyal to his friend and would never reveal any of Nixon's confidences.

Charles Gregory Rebozo was born in Tampa, Florida, on November 17, 1912. He became a real estate executive and a banker, reaching the post of chairman and president of the Key Biscayne Bank of Florida in 1964.

Long active in business affairs and in those of the community at large, rather than specifically the Hispanic community, Rebozo was president of the Boys Clubs of Miami from 1956 to 1960 and is a recipient of the Man and Boy Award from the Boys Clubs of America. He was also president of the Key Biscayne Chamber of Commerce in 1976–77 and reached the top at the clubs he joined—president of

the Kiwanis Club and commodore of the Key Biscayne Yacht Club.

When Richard Nixon was president in the early 1970s, his friendship with Rebozo was discovered. In consequence, when Nixon was accused of serious crimes in office, Rebozo found himself very much in the national news. There were many attempts to interview and obtain information from him, all unsuccessful. One of the characteristics that Nixon valued in Rebozo and that led to his choice of Rebozo as confidant was precisely his ability to remain tight-lipped. Interest in Rebozo began to wane after Nixon resigned the presidency in 1974.

Further Reading
Who's Who in America. New Providence, N.J.: Reed Reference Publishing Co., 1995.

❧ Rivera, Chita (Dolores Conchita Figueroa del Rivero)

(1933–   ) *dancer*
Chita Rivera has been recognized as a leading, vital force in Broadway musicals since the 1950s. In addition, she has frequently performed in other media.

Music is an inherited passion of Rivera's. Her father—who, like her mother, was Puerto Rican—was a clarinet and saxophone player in the U.S. Navy Band. He died when Chita (a nickname derived from her middle name, Conchita) was seven.

Dolores Conchita Figueroa del Rivero was born in Washington, D.C., on January 23, 1933. She was trained as a classical ballet dancer. Her early dance lessons (along with singing and piano coaching) led in 1950 to a scholarship at the prestigious School of American Ballet in New York City. Rivera, who was in high school in Washington, was sent by her mother to live with relatives in the Bronx so that she could attend the school, which was led by choreographer George Balanchine.

In 1952, a year after Rivera's high school graduation, dancers were required for the touring company of the musical *Call Me Madam.* A friend of Rivera's at the ballet school went to the casting call to try her luck; Rivera went along with her and on the spur of the moment decided to audition too. The friend did not get a part in the play, but Rivera did.

Less than a year later, she was invited to appear on Broadway in *Guys and Dolls*. After that came, among others, *Can-Can, Seventh Heaven, Mr. Wonderful,* and, in 1957, her big break: the role of Anita, the girlfriend of the heroine's brother, in the musical *West Side Story*. In this part, Rivera won the first of many Tony Award nominations. Next, she signed to appear in *Bye Bye Birdie* and was then offered the chance to play Anita in the movie version of *West Side Story*. It would have meant a chance to begin a movie career, but Rivera remained faithful to her contract for *Bye Bye Birdie*. If she hadn't, she said, her word would have been worthless, "and besides, they gave the role (of Anita) to Rita MORENO, who is my friend. Between Rita and me, there has never been any envy or jealousy."

In the 1960s and 1970s, she appeared in leading or significant roles both on Broadway and on tour, in *The Threepenny Opera, Flower Drum Song, Born Yesterday, The Rose Tattoo, Kiss Me Kate,* and *Chicago*. In *Sweet Charity,* on tour, she played the title role. Then in 1969, the movie version was made and the part was given to the actress Shirley MacLaine; Rivera appeared in the movie as Charity's roommate.

In the 1980s, she shone in *Merlin, Jerry's Girls, The Mayflower Madam,* and once more in *Can-Can. The Rink* (1984) was a musical written especially for her in which she played singer-actress Liza Minnelli's mother. Her performance won a Tony Award.

One review of her performance in *The Rink,* in *Time* magazine, has been often quoted: "Packing 30 years of Broadway savvy into the frame of a vivacious teenager, the 51-year-old entertainer could by now sell a song to the deaf; she commands the audience like a lion tamer. . . . She eats costars for breakfast."

Although she broke her leg badly in a car accident in 1986, she came back to dance. In 1992, at the age of 59, she scored a triumph in the lead in the musical *Kiss of the Spider Woman*. In 1994, she reprised the role in a production of the play in Boston. One of her successors in its long run on Broadway was another Hispanic singer-actress, the Cuban-born, Venezuela-raised María Conchita Alonso. Rivera costarred with Ben Vereen in 1999 in a revival of the musical *Chicago,* which she had appeared in two decades earlier.

In addition to her career in the theater, Chita Rivera has been a busy and highly successful nightclub entertainer. Her nightclub act won the 1980 award of the National Academy of Concert and Cabaret Arts.

She has also appeared in a large number of television productions, including *The New Dick Van Dyke Show* (1973–74) and *Broadway Plays Washington: Kennedy Center Tonight* (1982).

Further Reading

Telgen, Diane, and Jim Kamp, eds. *Notable Hispanic Women.* Detroit: Gale Research, Inc., 1993.

❧ Rivera, Geraldo (Geraldo Miguel Rivera) (1943–) *TV journalist*

One of the best-known television personalities in the United States, Geraldo Rivera also has a record as an advocate of the civil rights of U.S. Hispanics and as a crusading journalist who has exposed social ills and who has been able, in some cases, to help correct them. He is the winner of more than 100 awards, including some of the most prestigious in the television industry—ten Emmys (three national and seven local) and a George Foster Peabody Award for Distinguished Achievement in Broadcast Journalism.

Geraldo Rivera was born in New York City on the 4th of July, 1943. His father, Cruz Allen Rivera, was Puerto Rican. His mother, Lillian Friedman, was Jewish, as is Geraldo. As a child, he learned Spanish while visiting his grandparents in Puerto Rico.

Rivera (none of the Riveras in this biographical dictionary are related) went to school in Brooklyn and then joined the merchant marine as a sailor. He worked at various occupations briefly in the U.S. Southwest before attending the University of Arizona, where he graduated with a B.S. degree in 1965. He received his J.D. degree from Brooklyn Law School in 1969, passed the New York Bar the following year, and did postgraduate work at the University of Pennsylvania before finally attending Columbia University's School of Journalism.

Active from his student days in the defense of the civil rights of Hispanics, other minorities, and the poor, Rivera was a spokesman and lawyer for a radical

Puerto Rican movement called the Young Lords and also recruited lawyers for the United Farm Workers, the union of migrant workers formed by labor leader César CHÁVEZ.

Rivera also helped found a major Puerto Rican civil rights organization, the Puerto Rican Legal Defense and Education Fund, and worked for neighborhood antipoverty law firms, Harlem Assertion of Rights, and Community Action for Legal Services.

In 1970, he accepted a job as a bilingual reporter for the WABC-TV channel in New York because Rivera had come to believe that as an investigative reporter he might be able to do more to help people than as an antipoverty lawyer. The quality of Rivera's work caused him to progress from local coverage to ABC's national television network. He worked for that network's *Eyewitness News, Good Morning, America,* and *20/20;* he also hosted *Entertainment Tonight* and *Good Night, America.*

Geraldo Rivera built a major reputation with a hard-hitting documentary, *Willowbrook* (1972). It exposed ghastly conditions at Staten Island's (New York) Willowbrook state school for the mentally retarded. As a direct consequence of Rivera's coverage, the governor of the state, Nelson Rockefeller, returned $20 million to Willowbrook's budget, which had been cut to save money.

Conditions at mental hospitals became one of Rivera's favorite causes, and in the succeeding decades, he did more than 50 follow-up reports to help modernize and humanize such institutions.

He also investigated such subjects as migrant workers (titling his report *Migrants: Dirt Cheap*) and the children of drug addicts (*The Littlest Junkie*). He declared: "I'm not in the business of making people cry. I'm in the business of change." Rivera has written on these issues as well, including a book about the Staten Island school, *Willowbrook—A Report on How It Is and Why It Doesn't Have to Be That Way,* published in New York by Random House in 1972.

The Associated Press (AP) praised him as a "special kind of individualist in a medium which too often breeds the plastic newsman." AP also named him Broadcaster of the Year three times. He received two Robert F. Kennedy journalism awards and two Columbia-DuPont awards.

Already a celebrity, Rivera became a household word as a talk show host with *Geraldo* in 1987, which he also produced. It was followed by *Now It Can Be Told,* in 1991. These shows made him a subject of controversy. He was attacked and ridiculed by critics who saw his programs as "tabloid journalism," pandering to a low level of audience interest. He defended himself by asking whether the fact that he is Puerto Rican means that he does not have the right to report on the same subjects others do. He has also pointed out that many of the follow-up reports on mental institutions have taken place on his talk show.

Rivera was likewise proud to have "the most integrated staff in the talk show business." He sees this as not only worthy in itself, but also a help to achieving more balanced coverage.

The *Geraldo* talk show ended in 1998 after 2,163 episodes. Rivera then returned more actively to the field of investigative journalism.

Further Reading

Martínez, Al. *Rising Voices: Profiles of Hispano-American Lives.* New York: New American Library, 1974.

Rivera, Geraldo, with Daniel Paisner. *Exposing Myself.* New York: Bantam, 1991.

❧ Rivera, Tomás (1935–1984) *writer, educator*

Tomás Rivera wrote one of the pathbreaking novels of Chicano literature, . . . *Y No Se lo Tragó la Tierra/* . . . And the Earth Did Not Part. A noted university administrator, he was also the first member of a minority to be appointed chancellor by the University of California.

Rivera came from a family of migrant farmworkers. His parents immigrated to the United States from Mexico. As a youth Rivera also worked as a migrant farmworker in various states every year. His literary goals were related to this experience: He sought to tell about the lives of the migrant workers and to extol the virtues and nobility he found among them.

Born in Crystal City, Texas, on December 22, 1935, Tomás Rivera's first language was Spanish. He went to school in his hometown and then to

Southwest Texas Junior College and Southwest Texas State University. He graduated in 1958 and received a master's degree in educational administration in 1964. Five years later, he earned a doctorate in romance languages and literature from the University of Oklahoma.

Rivera wrote only one complete novel; another remained unfinished at the time of his death. However, . . . *Y No Se lo Tragó la Tierra* is regarded as a milestone in the history of Mexican-American narrative because of its use of a modern structure and division into episodes. It was translated into English and first published in 1971 in a bilingual edition. In 1985, it received a second translation, by Rolando HINOJOSA-SMITH, and was republished as *This Migrant Earth*. The novel won a Quinto Sol National Chicano Literary Award. Though Rivera's reputation was solidly established by this one work, he also wrote a book of poetry, *Always and Other Poems* (1973), and a number of works of literary commentary.

Rivera began to work as a schoolteacher in Texas while still a university undergraduate. He then moved to teaching and administration at the university level. Eventually, he concentrated on administrative work and was widely praised for his talent and his responsiveness to the needs of his students. He began at Southwest Texas Junior College, continued at Sam Houston State University, and then administered at the University of Texas.

In 1979, Rivera was named chancellor of the University of California at Riverside. Not only was he the first minority chancellor, but also the youngest ever.

Rivera was also a member of the boards of the Fulbright scholarship program, of the Ford Foundation, of the Carnegie Foundation for the Advancement of Teaching, and of the National Chicano Council on Higher Education.

After his death of a heart attack in 1984 at the age of 48, the University of California at Riverside named its library after him.

Further Reading

Hinojosa-Smith, Rolando, Gary Keller, and Vernon E. Latin. *Tomás Rivera, 1935–1984: The Man and His Work.* Tempe, Ariz.: Bilingual/Editorial Bilingüe, 1988.

Lomelí, Francisco A., and Carl R. Shirley, eds. *Dictionary of Literary Biography: Chicano Writers, First Series.* Detroit: Gale Research, 1989.

Rodríguez, Juan "Chi Chi" (1935–)
golfer

One of the big names in golf, "Chi Chi" Rodríguez is noted for hitting the ball great distances despite his relatively small physical size. The editors of *Golf Magazine* have written that "Rodríguez has one of the best pairs of hands in the golf business—he is a consummate shotmaker and one of the few sand players who is mentioned in the same breath as Gary Player [a golfing superstar from South Africa]."

In addition to his power and skill, Rodríguez is known for his humor while playing and for his charitable work. He heads the Chi Chi Rodríguez Youth Foundation, a counseling and educational service for troubled, abused, and disadvantaged children with headquarters in Clearwater, Florida.

Juan Rodríguez was born in Bayamón, Puerto Rico, on October 23, 1935. His father was a plantation field worker, and the family lived in great poverty. The "Chi Chi" nickname was given to him because of a baseball player whom Juan greatly admired.

But it was in golf, not baseball, that he found his talent. While still in grade school, he earned money as a caddy, his introduction to the sport. Later, however, he also had to work as a shoeshine boy and to drop out of high school in the 11th grade because of a lack of money. The reason he loves children, Rodríguez has said, is that he never really had a childhood of his own.

It was for the money that he joined the army at 19, serving a two-year hitch. His mastery of golf would in time earn him well over $3 million. But his golf career, begun in 1960, developed somewhat slowly and unevenly. Measuring 5 feet, 7 inches tall and weighing 130 pounds, he found that most of his competitors towered over him; yet, he was able to awe spectators with 300-yard drives, and he delighted them with gags and jokes, which led to his being called the "Clown Prince" of golfers.

Among other victories, Rodríguez won eight events on the Professional Golfers' Association (PGA) tour: the Denver Open Tournament (1963), Lucky International Open and Western Open (in 1964, his best year), Texas Open (1967), Sahara Invitational (1968), Byron Nelson Golf Classic (1972), Greater Greensboro Open (1973), and Tallahassee Open (1979).

In 1985, at the age of 50, Chi Chi Rodríguez joined the ranks of senior players and began to accumulate a long list of tournament triumphs in this new category. He was, in 1987, the first golfer to top half a million dollars in prizes in one year as a senior.

Included among his wins since 1985 are the Senior Tournament Players Championship (1986), Silver Pages Classic (1987), Digital Seniors Classic (1988), and Las Vegas Senior Classic (1991). In 1997, he recorded 13 consecutive rounds of par or better. By century's end, Chi Chi had finished first on the Senior PGA Tour 22 times.

Further Reading

The editors of *Golf Magazine*. *Golf Magazine's Encyclopedia of Golf*. New York: HarperCollins, 1993.

Martínez, Al. *Rising Voices: Profiles of Hispano-American Lives*. New York: New American Library, 1974.

PGA Tour. "Chi Chi Rodríguez Bio, Stats, and Results." Available online. URL: http://pgatour.com/players/intro/2015.html. Downloaded October 11, 2000.

Matt Rodríguez   *(Courtesy of Matt Rodríguez)*

ꕥ Rodríguez, Matt L. Matthew Louis

Rodríguez (1936–   ) *police officer*

At the culmination of a 33-year career with the Chicago police department, Matt L. Rodríguez was its superintendent. He is the first Latino to have reached such a position in a city of that size. Other Hispanics in similar positions included: Philip Arreola, born in Mexico, was chief of police of Milwaukee, Wisconsin, and of Tacoma, Washington; Louis Cobarruviaz headed the police department in San Jose, California; Raúl Martínez took office as police chief of Miami in 2000.

Rodríguez's career has been that of a model policeman and citizen. A former altar boy, he entered the police force as a patrolman at age 23, worked his way through the ranks with solid achievement at each stage, and reached the highest post in the department. Throughout his life—when not lecturing on police work in places as far afield as China—he has lived in Chicago, married to the high school sweetheart whom he wed when he was 19 and she 17 years old, and participating in numerous professional, community, and charity organizations.

Matt Rodríguez (none of the Rodríguezes in this book is related) was born in Chicago on April 5, 1936, one of four offspring of a mixed marriage. His family is Mexican on his father's side and Polish on his mother's, and he learned Spanish and Polish alongside English. He went to both Polish and Mexican churches, and has acknowledged that growing up astride two worlds gave him a head start in dealing with a city known for diversity.

When already embarked on his lifelong career in the police, Rodríguez continued with his education. He obtained an A.A. degree in business administration, with high honors, from Wright College in 1973, then switched to public administration at Roosevelt University, where he earned a B.S. degree with honors two years later, and an M.P.A. (master of public administration) degree with honors the year after that. He then carried out postgraduate studies at Northwestern University in 1976 and 1977.

In 1980 he became an adjunct professor of criminal justice at the University of Illinois, a position he retained even after his retiring from the police department. Criminal justice and technological developments that help the police in their work—one of his special interests—have been the subjects of innumerable lectures and articles by Rodríguez over the years.

His progress in the Chicago police department meanwhile was methodical and covered virtually all aspects of police work. From patrolman he rose to sergeant in 1965, reached the rank of lieutenant in 1978, and in 1980 became one of the department's five deputy superintendents—the officials in charge of technical services, from fingerprinting to bomb deactivation.

After being twice considered for the job of superintendent in 1983 and 1987, Rodríguez was finally appointed to the top spot in 1992. During the selection process in 1987, he was endorsed—and a rally was even held in his support—by members of diverse Chicago-area minorities, including Latinos, Filipinos, and Chinese. Many saw this as proof of Rodríguez's effectiveness in bridging gulfs among various ethnic communities. Among the recognition Rodríguez has garnered over the course of his career have been awards from Jewish and Polish groups as well as from diverse strands of Hispanics.

In 1993, the Major City Chiefs Association chose Rodríguez as chairman. He has also been chairman of the Hispanic Institute of Law Enforcement as well as a committee member of the International Association of Chiefs of Police.

Rodríguez retired from the force in 1997 and later worked as an independent police management consultant.

Further Reading
Chicago Police Department. "Biography of Matt L. Rodríguez." Available online. URL: http://www. ci.chi.il.us/CommunityPolicing/Welcome/RodriguezBio.html. Downloaded October 11, 2000.

Morey, Janet Normura, and Wendy Dunn. *Famous Hispanic Americans.* New York: Cobblehill Books, 1996.

☞ **Rodríguez, Paul** (Pablo Leobordo Castro Rodríguez) (1955–) *comedian*

Paul Rodríguez established himself as a stand-up comedian viewing the Hispanic experience in the United States through a filter of humor—providing Latinos with a service similar to that performed by many African-American or Jewish comedians for their communities. In addition, Rodríguez is a very active television and movie actor and TV producer, as well as an occasional film director. He is also in the forefront of many philanthropic activities and frequently seeks out opportunities to counsel Hispanic youths about their future.

The future comedian was born in the city of Mazatlán, Mexico, on January 19, 1955. His family, which also included four elder siblings, moved to the west coast of the United States when Pablo—later "Paul," as changed by the unilateral decision of a judge processing his citizenship papers—was three years old. Following the crops, the Rodríguezes picked vegetables and fruit up and down the coast, until Pablo's father was injured in an accident and was forced to seek more sedentary work in Los Angeles.

Rodríguez, a high school dropout, became familiar with street gang life in deprived neighborhoods of the city. One day, his best friend was shot while standing near him. But a funny streak in Rodríguez, apparent since childhood, stood him in good stead: he found he could disarm an edgy situation with a wisecrack, rather than needing to tough it out. However, he realized he wanted something better in life. He did four years of service in the U.S. Air Force, rising to the rank of sergeant, seeing the world, and widening his interests.

Military service also allowed him, after hanging up his uniform in 1977, to go back to school with U.S. government help. Rodríguez earned an associate of arts degree at Long Beach City College, and, planning a law career, went on to California State University at Long Beach. He was sidetracked, however, by theater classes. His drama teacher discovered his comic talents and introduced him to the world of stand-up comedy.

Providing opening acts at live shows and concerts—in Spanish or English, according to who his listeners were—brought him to the attention of a TV producer, who was so impressed that he offered him a television show of his own.

The result was *a.k.a. Pablo* (1984), a sitcom in which Rodríguez relived his own life in fun. Although it only lasted six episodes, the entirely Hispanic show was a milestone in the presentation of Latino life on U.S. television. It also was criticized, however, for allegedly confirming Anglo viewers' unfavorable image of Hispanic life, because what Rodríguez highlighted, or even exaggerated for comic effect, Anglos might take as constant, everyday reality.

Rodríguez thereafter appeared in other TV series including *Trial and Error* (1988), *Grand Slam* (1990) and *Future Quest* (1994). He also hosted *The Newly-wed Game Starring Paul Rodríguez* (1988–89) as well as *El Show de Paul Rodríguez* (The Paul Rodríguez Show) for the Spanish-language Univisión network.

The television special has been Rodríguez's most active field, both as performer and as producer. He has been in scores of such shows, encompassing both his own work and that of other performers and groups. Some of the specials point to the comedian's serious concerns with social matters and his interest in helping people on the margins of society. Some of these specials are *Paul Rodríguez: Crossing Gang Lines* (1991); *Paul Rodríguez: Behind Bars* (also 1991); *Paul Rodríguez: Live in San Quentin* (1995).

He released a recording, *You're in America Now, Speak Spanish,* and directed and starred in a movie, *A Million to Juan* (1994), an adaptation of a Mark Twain story first filmed 40 years earlier starring Gregory Peck (*Man With a Million*) about a poor man with a million-dollar bill in his possession. Rodríguez transferred the situation, originally set in London and with pounds sterling rather than dollars, into a Hispanic environment. He described his version as "the only Latino movie that you'll see that's made in America that has no gangs, drugs or cursing in it."

He has also acted in other movies including *Born in East LA* (1987), *Made in America* (1993), *Mambo Café* (1999) and *G-Men From Hell* (2000).

The National Leukemia Telethon, hosted by Rodríguez, is one of numerous charities he supports.

Further Reading

Morey, Janet Normura, and Wendy Dunn. *Famous Hispanic Americans.* New York: Cobblehill Books, 1996.

Paul Rodriguez. Available online. URL: http://www.paulrodriguez.com. Downloaded October 11, 2000.

❧ Roland, Gilbert (Luis Antonio Dámaso Alonso) (1905–1994) *actor*

At the time of his death Gilbert Roland was the most durable of Hollywood's "Latin lover" actors. Without ever becoming as well known as an Antonio MORENO, Ramón NOVARRO, or Ricardo MONTALBÁN, he held his own as a handsome, romantic presence in movies for more than 60 years.

Roland was noted particularly for his leading role in the 1927 version of *Camille,* for 11 films playing the Cisco Kid, and for his parts in *The Bullfighter and the Lady* (1951) and *Cheyenne Autumn* (1964). In these last two, he played, as the titles hint, a bullfighter and an Indian. He also frequently appeared in television roles.

Another way in which he made his mark was by refusing all roles that, in his view, demeaned the image of Hispanics. If the Cisco Kid reads Shakespeare in one of his films, it is because Roland requested the scene.

Quietly and under his own initiative, he also lobbied congressmen for measures helpful to Mexican Americans, such as bilingual education. Luis Antonio Dámaso Alonso's parents arrived in Mexico from Spain. He was born in Ciudad Juárez on December 11, 1905, the son and grandson of bullfighters. He might have ended up as a toreador himself; his father groomed him from infancy for the job. But the Mexican Revolution changed that plan. In the face of a threatened attack by the revolutionary Pancho Villa, the Alonso family fled Ciudad

Juárez for the United States on the other side of the Río Grande.

There, the movies caught the boy in their spell, and at the age of 14, he made his way, penniless, to Hollywood. His idols at the time were actress Ruth Roland and actor John Gilbert. From their names, he fashioned his own. The new "Gilbert Roland" found jobs as an extra almost immediately. Thereafter, his climb was not a particularly fast one, and he seriously considered going back to Mexico or Spain and pursuing bullfighting. But his career was secured when he was cast in the lead in *Camille.* The star Norma Talmadge played the heroine in this silent movie, and Roland's performance alongside her won him praise and other major roles.

Gilbert Roland never lost his Hispanic accent; yet opinion is divided as to whether this affected his career. He participated in a number of European movies in the 1960s and 1970s without interrupting his Hollywood output.

Among the scores of movies Roland appeared in were *The Blonde Saint* (1926), *She Done Him Wrong* (1933), *Juárez* (1939), *The Sea Hawk* (1940), *South of Monterey* (1946), *Ten Tall Men* (1951), *The Bad and the Beautiful* (1952), *The Big Circus* (1959), *Deliver Us From Evil* (1975) and *Barbarosa* (1982). Other films of note include *Pirates of Monterey, Mark of the Renegade, Crisis, Beneath the 12-Mile Reef,* and *Islands in the Stream.* On television, he appeared in the *The Fugitive* and *The Alfred Hitchcock Hour.*

Roland was also a short story writer; one of his works won a contest run by the publication *Writer's Digest.*

With the United States at war, Roland became a U.S. citizen in 1942 and served in the U.S. Army Air Corps.

Gilbert Roland *(Cabrera Archive)*

The first of his two wives was the actress Constance Bennett. The second was Guillermina Contu.

He received the League of United Latin American Citizens Entertainment Favorite Award in 1969 and commendations from the California state legislature and the city of Los Angeles in the same year.

Further Reading

Martínez, Al. *Rising Voices: Profiles of Hispano-American Lives.* New York: New American Library, 1974.

Roland, Gilbert. *Wine of Yesterday.* n.p., n.d.

᪥ Romero, César (1907–1994) *actor*

A long-lasting presence in the entertainment world, César Romero started as a professional dancer, went on to act in scores of movies, and achieved his greatest renown as the Joker on television's *Batman* series.

In some ways, Romero's life and career resembled Gilbert ROLAND's: Both failed to reach real stardom but had very long and successful careers; both first hit their stride as "Latin lover" actors and later matured into character roles; both played the Cisco Kid on screen many times—Romero, who was just 14 months younger, played Cisco before Roland; both died in 1994.

Romero came from a Cuban family and was born in New York City on February 15, 1907. He counted José Martí, the Cuban poet and independence leader who died in battle 12 years before his birth, among his ancestors.

An urbane personality and smooth dancing skills led Romero to an early career in nightclub dance shows and in musicals. In the 1930s, this in turn took him to Hollywood. There, he was to exhibit the same charm in his social life for decades. He was celebrated as a lifelong bachelor who would never miss a party. One commentator wrote that Romero "would attend the opening of a napkin."

Romero's first appearance in a film about the Cisco Kid, dispenser of frontier justice, was in a supporting role in 1939. The same year, however, he was back as the Kid himself in another movie, *The Cisco Kid and the Lady.* He played the part half a dozen times.

César Romero in *Latitude Zero* *(Cabrera Archive)*

Other highlights in César Romero's movie career were *The Thin Man* (1934), *The Devil Is a Woman* (1935), *Wee Willie Winkie* (1937), *Tall, Dark and Handsome* (1941), *Springtime in the Rockies* (1942), *Captain From Castile* (1948), *Vera Cruz* (1954), *Around the World in 80 Days* (1956), *Donovan's Reef* (1963), *Skidoo* (1968), *The Proud and the Damned* (1972) and *Simple Justice* (1989). Romero also appeared in Broadway plays including *Dinner at Eight, The Social Register, My Three Angels,* and *Never Get Smart With an Angel.* Television gave Romero a wide audience, particularly in villain roles on *Batman,* beginning in 1968. He also appeared in *Falcon Crest* 20 years later. Other television work included *Chico and the Man* and *Passport to Danger.*

During World War II, Romero served as a chief bosun's mate in the U.S. Coast Guard.

Further Reading

Hadley-García, George. *Hispanic Hollywood: The Latins in Motion Pictures.* Secaucus, N.J.: Citadel Press, 1990.

Katz, Ephraim. *The Film Encyclopedia.* New York: HarperCollins, 1994.

✎ Ronstadt, Linda (Linda Marie Ronstadt)
(1946–) *singer*

Among the most popular and possibly the most versatile stars in pop music, Linda Ronstadt made five platinum albums in a row between 1974 and 1977 and has won nine Grammy Awards between 1975 and 2000. Her chief asset is her full, powerful voice, boldness, and a wide range of musical interests. The voice has been described as a "gorgeous wail" by *The New York Times* and as having "the richness and cutting edge of a muted trumpet" by *Newsweek* magazine.

The broadness of Ronstadt's musical tastes has led her to compile a repertory of country, rock, pop, folk (and various gradations of all of these), romantic ballads, Mexican pop and mariachi music, operetta, and more. She has sung music by modern classical composer Philip Glass and an off-Broadway, off-Lincoln Center, updated production of Puccini's opera *La Bohème* (1984). She credits her habit of listening to the recordings of the late opera singer Maria Callas as the most useful contribution to her singing.

Linda Marie Ronstadt was born in Tucson, Arizona, on July 15, 1946. Her father, a hardware store owner who was half Mexican and half German, exposed her to Mexican music throughout her childhood. Ronstadt found that her Mexican ancestry was most influential. When singing Mexican music, she explained, "I feel completely enchanted by [it], and I feel very connected to what I am." When she sang country-and-western music, the same applied, she said on another occasion. The Mexican sounds she grew up with were country—"It just doesn't happen to be this country."

As a child, Linda was in charge of the soprano parts in family sing-alongs; her remarkable vocal qualities were apparent from the start. After high school, she enrolled at the University of Arizona in her hometown, but the pull of a singing career was strong, and after some months she quit and left for Los Angeles.

There she set up a folk-rock group named Linda and the Stone Poneys. The group signed a recording contract that first year in California, 1964, when she was 18. In 1969, she began her solo career.

In 1973 she changed recording companies, switching to one specializing in country rock, and her first platinum album, *Heart Like a Wheel,* came the following year.

Though Ronstadt generally prefers the recording studio to live performance, she collected a devout following for her live appearances. She sang at the inauguration of President Jimmy Carter in 1977.

In 1981, she appeared as a singer-actress on Broadway in the British operetta, *The Pirates of Penzance.* Success was immediate, and she also starred in a movie version, in 1983.

That same year, she began to sing romantic ballads from the years before rock'n'roll. Her first album in this genre, recorded with band leader Nelson Riddle, was ironically titled *What's New.* It also achieved platinum sales and led to other such records. In 1986, she recorded an enthusiastically received album of country music with Dolly Parton and Emmylou Harris, *Trio.*

A Spanish-language album of Mexican songs, favorites of her father's, came the following year. *Canciones de Mi Padre (Songs of My Father)* created a whole new market for her, while also appealing to a large proportion of her earlier fans. The album led to a TV special and to a book, both under the same title. *Más Canciones (More Songs)* followed in 1991.

Other albums, in other styles, were interspersed with her Mexican-music ventures. *Feels Like Home* (1995) combined her various musical interests, despite having been initially planned as a country-only production like *Trio.*

Ronstadt was awarded the Dick Clark Productions American Music Award in 1978. Her collection of Grammy awards includes prizes for best female pop performance, best country performance, best Mexican American performance, and best pop vocal performance in a duo or group.

The singer has also been in the news for dating such famous people as Jerry Brown, then governor of California, movie director George Lucas, and comic actor Steve Martin. In the 1990s, still single, she adopted two children.

Further Reading
Amdur, Melissa. *Linda Ronstadt.* New York: Chelsea House, 1993.

Bego, Mark. *Linda Ronstadt: It's So Easy.* Austin, Tex.: Diamond Books, 1990.

Berman, Connie. *Linda Ronstadt.* Madrid, Spain: Jucar, 1985.

Partridge, Tony. "The Linda Ronstadt Homepage." Available online. URL: http://www.crosswinds. net/~ronstadt/index.html. Downloaded October 11, 2000.

✄ Ros-Lehtinen, Ileana (Ileana Ros)

(1952–) *government official*

The first Hispanic woman, and also the first Cuban American, to be elected to the United States Congress, Ileana Ros-Lehtinen used this position to become one of the strongest and most visible spokespersons against Cuban leader Fidel Castro. She has been described frequently as "the darling of the Cuban community."

The daughter of an accountant, Ileana Ros was born in Havana, Cuba, on July 15, 1952. When she was seven years old, Cuba's right-wing military dictatorship was overthrown by Fidel Castro. His government became openly communist, and the next year, 1960, her family fled to Miami, where Ros went to school and college. She received an A.A. degree from Miami Dade County Community College in 1972, a B.A. from Florida International University in 1975, and an M.S. in education from the same school in 1987. Ros continued her studies of education at the doctoral level at the University of Miami.

Her work as a teacher led her to found a school, Eastern Academy, in 1978 and to serve as its principal until 1988. However, the politician in her soon eclipsed the educator. She holds the strongly conservative views of her parents, Enrique and Amanda Ros, who were backers of the failed Bay of Pigs invasion that sought to remove Castro from power in Cuba in 1961. Her father was credited with helping guide his daughter's political career.

In 1982 Ros, a Republican, was elected to the Florida legislature; she was a representative until 1986 and a state senator from that year until 1989. She married her fellow legislator and later U.S. attorney in Miami, Dexter Lehtinen, and adopted the name Ros-Lehtinen.

Ileana Ros-Lehtinen *(Congressional Hispanic Caucus)*

She ran for the U.S. House of Representatives in 1989 to fill the vacancy left by the death of an incumbent congressman. No Cuban American had ever been elected to Congress, nor had any Latina of any national ancestry. Dade County, her district, had not sent a woman to Congress in a half-century. Although President George Bush helped in her campaign, the election was decided mainly along ethnic lines. Ros-Lehtinen's Democratic opponent was Jewish, and the race proved highly divisive for the area, which was at the time almost precisely 50 percent Hispanic. When she obtained 53 percent of the vote and her victory was announced, singer Celia CRUZ, who had strongly backed her, expressed in this way: *"¡Los cubanos han ganado!"* ("The Cubans have won!") However, Ros-Lehtinen quickly showed a capacity to heal campaign wounds and to expand her following. She had to face reelection the following year, and this time won with 60 percent of the vote.

In Washington, Ros-Lehtinen used membership on the House Foreign Affairs Committee to further her struggle to secure democracy in Cuba. She has ties to the main hardline anti-Castro organization in the United States, the Cuban-American National Foundation (CANF), founded by Jorge MAS CANOSA. In particular, in 1995 Ros-Lehtinen was one of the country's most vocal critics of President Bill Clinton's Cuban policies, which were designed to avoid more waves of Cuban refugees reaching the United States. Their effect, she said, was to relax U.S. pressure at a time when it should have been tightened.

In 2000, during the struggle between the United States and Cuba over custody of a six-year-old boy, Elián González, Ros-Lehtinen was one of a group of three legislators who offered to help Elián's father remain in the United States. The other members of Congress in the group were Lincoln DÍAZ-BALART and Bob MENÉNDEZ.

Also in 2000, Ros-Lehtinen was reelected to the U.S. House of Representatives.

Further Reading

Nodal, Elizabeth. "Office of Congresswoman Ileana Ros-Lehtinen." Available online. URL: http://www.house.gov/ros-lehtinen. Downloaded October 11, 2000.

Telgen, Diane, and Jim Kamp, eds. *Notable Hispanic American Women*. Detroit: Gale Research, Inc., 1993.

❧ Roybal, Edward R. (1916–)

government official

Edward R. Roybal is a father figure in Chicano politics. In 1949, he became the first Mexican American elected to the Los Angeles City Council since 1881. For the next decade and a half, he put his stamp on the area's politics as a champion of liberal causes.

In 1963 he began to serve as a member of Congress in Washington and was invariably reelected by big majorities. He distinguished himself in office there until his retirement 30 years later. Roybal has also founded a political dynasty: He is the father of

Lucille ROYBAL-ALLARD, another outstanding member of Congress from California.

Despite his close association with California, Roybal is not a native Californian. He was born in Albuquerque, New Mexico, on February 10, 1916. His family moved to Los Angeles when he was four.

When Roybal finished high school in the midst of the Great Depression of the 1930s, there was no chance of his entering college immediately. Instead, he worked with the Civilian Conservation Corps and as a clothes presser until he had saved enough to enter the University of California at Los Angeles. He then continued his studies at Southwestern University and Kaiser College, also in Los Angeles.

He had studied for a career in business administration. However, Roybal went to work for the California Tuberculosis Association in 1935 and became a health educator instead. In 1942, he was appointed director of health education for the Los Angeles County Tuberculosis and Health Association, maintaining that post until 1949, save for war service in 1944 and 1945. Educating people on health matters not only gave him the satisfaction of being useful to the community, it also increased his awareness of the needs of the poor, the disadvantaged, and the victims of discrimination. He made it his life's work to try to alleviate those needs.

Going into politics was the next step, but in 1947 Roybal lost his first attempt to run for city council.

Roybal next helped to create the Community Service Organization (CSO), which became a major Mexican-American institution. One of the CSO's activities was to encourage voting by Mexican Americans. With its help, two years after his first bid, Roybal won enough votes to join the city council.

A major test came the following year, 1950. It was a time of "witch hunts" against supposed communists, although communism was not outlawed in the United States. Anyone who opposed the witch hunters' methods—hearsay, pressure, blackmail—was himself liable to come under suspicion. Roybal, however, followed his conscience and voted against a proposal to set up a register of alleged subversives.

His position did not hurt his career. He was reelected several times to the city council, and in the words of one commentator (Rodolfo Acuña), "dominated the political history of Los Angeles Chicanos" in those years. Public-health matters were one of his main concerns, as they would later be in Washington.

In 1959 Roybal, a Democrat, was a cofounder of the Mexican American Political Association (MAPA), an organization designed to support worthy Chicano candidates, whether Republicans or Democrats.

Three years later, he won election for the first time to the United States House of Representatives. He remained in office until he retired in 1992 at 76. As a member of the House Appropriations Committee from 1971 to 1992, Roybal had considerable power.

Among other achievements in health, social, and economic areas, legislation proposed by Roybal led to the first federal bilingual education act. He also worked in favor of the rights of undocumented workers and managed to restore money that had been cut from programs for senior citizens.

Roybal obtained the creation of a cabinet Committee on Opportunities for Spanish-Speaking People. He pushed through truth-in-lending legislation to protect people who take out loans and advocated the privacy of credit information.

In addition to recognition from several universities, Roybal's work earned him an Excellence in Public Service Award from the American Academy of Pediatrics (1976) and the Joshua Award for his support of improved Jewish-Hispanic relations.

In the 1970s, Roybal continued to help set up Hispanic organizations: the National Association of Latino Elected and Appointed Officials and the Congressional Hispanic Caucus. Roybal was also a vice chairman of the Democratic National Committee.

In 1999, the Centers for Disease Control and Prevention in Atlanta, Georgia, honored Roybal with the Champion of Prevention Award, reserved for individuals who have made significant contributions to public health, and named its main campus the Edward R. Roybal Campus.

Further Reading

Acuña, Rodolfo. *Occupied America: A History of Chicanos.* New York: HarperCollins, 1988.

Martínez, Al. *Rising Voices: Profiles of Hispano-American Lives.* New York: New American Library, 1974.

Meier, Matt S., and Feliciano Rivera. *Dictionary of Mexican American History.* Westport, Conn.: Greenwood Press, 1981.

Roybal-Allard, Lucille (1941–)
government official

The first Mexican-American woman in the U.S. Congress, Lucille Roybal-Allard is the daughter of the distinguished former U.S. congressman Edward R. ROYBAL. She was born in Los Angeles on June 12, 1941, was educated in that city, and obtained a B.A. degree from California State University in 1961. She hyphenated her surname when she married her second husband, Edward Allard, a consultant.

Roybal-Allard has demonstrated that she shares her father's passion for social issues, but she adds a special commitment to women's rights. Like her father, she is a Democrat.

Along with other family members, she helped work on Edward Roybal's campaigns since infancy, beginning by stuffing envelopes. However, rather than be seen as an extension of her father, she initially resisted politics. Instead, she entered community service, working for the Alcoholism Council of East Los Angeles, the United Way, and as executive director of the National Association of Hispanic CPAs. In 1987 she finally switched to politics and was elected to the California State Assembly.

Roybal-Allard's years in the assembly were marked by a soft-spoken but tenacious—and effective—defense of East Los Angeles, a largely Hispanic area. Until then, East Los Angeles had been seen as having insignificant political power; consequently, it was proposed as the site of a prison and a toxic-waste incinerator that had been rejected by other towns and neighborhoods. In the long, hard struggle against these proposals, Roybal-Allard participated in the launching of Mothers of East LA (MELA), a strong local institution.

Lucille Roybal-Allard *(Congressional Hispanic Caucus)*

Her father retired from Congress in 1992, the year Roybal-Allard arrived in Washington. Her legislative work has earned much recognition, including the Honorary Award of the Los Angeles Commission on Assaults Against Women, the Sierra Club's California Environmental Achievement Award, the Asian Business Association Public Service Award, the President's Award of the Latin American Professional Women's Association, and County of Los Angeles President's Public Service Award.

In 2000, Roybal-Allard was reelected to the U.S. House of Representatives.

Further Reading

U.S. House of Representatives. "Congresswoman Lucille Roybal-Allard, Serving the 33rd District of California." Available online. URL: http://www.house.gov/roybal-allard. Downloaded October 11, 2000.

Telgen, Diane, and Jim Kamp, eds. *Notable Hispanic American Women.* Detroit: Gale Research, Inc., 1993.

✎ Rubio, Eurípides (1938–1966) *soldier*

A U.S. Army captain in the Vietnam War, Eurípides Rubio ignored his wounds, rallied his forces, and defied enemy fire in a battle-winning action that cost him his life. A posthumous Congressional Medal of Honor recognized his heroic and selfless contribution.

Rubio (which means "blond" in Spanish) was born in Ponce, Puerto Rico, on March 1, 1938. He joined the U.S. Army at Fort Buchanan on his native island.

Tay Ninh province in the Republic of Vietnam was where Rubio went "above and beyond the call of duty," in the characteristic phrase used in his medal's honor citation. In November 1966, Captain Rubio was serving as communications officer of the 1st Battalion, 28th Infantry, 1st Infantry Division when the battalion's defense perimeter was attacked by a larger enemy force. Rubio, who was in a comparatively safe position, left on his own initiative to join the fighting.

As he advanced, he received two serious wounds, but they did not deter him from his purpose. He sought to aid the besieged men by helping them regroup, passing ammunition, and attending to the wounded. When a company commander was hit in the fighting and had to be evacuated, Rubio took command. He continued to ignore his wounds and rallied his men. Struck for a third time by enemy fire, he still continued to assist in the care of the wounded.

Suddenly, he saw a U.S. smoke grenade lying in the wrong spot. These grenades were used to guide air attacks to hostile forces, but this one had fallen too close to the U.S. troops' position by mistake. Without hesitation, Rubio ran toward the grenade, with the intention of throwing it in the right direction, but enemy fire hit him for the fourth time, and he fell to his knees. Rising to his feet once more, Rubio managed to pick up the smoke grenade and continue his charge.

The Medal of Honor citation states that he "ran through the deadly hail of fire to within 20 meters of the enemy position and hurled the already smoking grenade into the midst of the enemy before he fell for the final time. Using the repositioned grenade as a marker, friendly air strikes were directed to destroy the hostile positions. Captain Rubio's singularly heroic act turned the tide of battle."

The citation further notes that the Puerto Rican hero's "extraordinary leadership and valor were a magnificent inspiration to his men."

Further Reading

The Committee on Veterans' Affairs, United States Senate. *Medal of Honor Recipients 1863–1978.* Washington, D.C.: U.S. Government Printing Office, 1979.

S

Salas, Floyd (1931–) *boxer, writer*

Floyd Salas was not only a boxer and boxing coach but also a highly praised author and teacher of creative writing.

Salas traces his ancestry in the United States to the 1500s on his mother's side and the 1600s on his father's. The family of his mother, Ana (Anita) Sánchez, arrived in New Mexico with the explorer Juan de Oñate at the end of the 16th century and later moved north to Colorado. The ancestors of his father, Edward Salas, first landed in Florida. In the 1800s, they traveled the Santa Fe Trail, also to Colorado. Floyd Francis Salas was born in Walsenburg, Colorado, on January 24, 1931. When he was eight, the family moved to California.

Salas (which means "rooms" or "auditoriums" in Spanish) grew up as a little brawler. As a youth, the death of his mother affected him deeply and heightened his hair-trigger temper. He was arrested for fighting five times within a year and a half. Finally, he was sentenced to prison for three months. The experience, in his case, proved a salutary one: thereafter, he channeled his aggression into boxing. What he experienced in jail became the seed of his first and most acclaimed published work, the prison novel *Tattoo the Wicked Cross*.

After studying at California College of Arts and Crafts and Oakland Junior College, Salas won a boxing scholarship in 1956 to the University of California at Berkeley, the first boxing scholarship ever awarded there. This led to work as a boxing coach in 1975 at Berkeley, and he became a member of the USA Amateur Boxing Federation. He also earned B.A. and M.A. degrees from San Francisco State University in 1963 and 1965, respectively.

Salas began to write. *Tattoo the Wicked Cross* would undergo many revisions, however, before first being published in 1967. His other works of prose and poetry include *What Now My Love* (1970) and *Lay My Body on the Line* (1978), as well as a memoir in 1992.

Salas's writing earned him many scholarships and fellowships beginning in 1958. He has been honored by the *Centro Mexicano de Escritores* (Mexican Writers' Center), sponsored by the Rockefeller Foundation; the National Endowment for the Arts; and the University of California. He received the San Francisco Foundation's Joseph Henry Jackson Fiction Award in 1964. More recently, Salas's *State of Emergency* won the 1997 PEN Oakland Literary Censorship Award.

Salas has taught creative writing since the 1960s at San Francisco State University, the University of

California at Berkeley, and Foothill College in Los Altos.

A keen participant in the radical movements which marked the San Francisco Bay area in the 1960s, Salas also became known for his outspoken polemics on social and political issues.

Further Reading

Lomelí, Francisco A., and Carl R. Shirley, eds. *Dictionary of Literary Biography: Chicano Writers—First Series.* Detroit: Gale Research, Inc., 1989.

Salas, Floyd. *Buffalo Nickel.* Houston: Arte Público Press, 1992.

Salazar, Alberto (1958–) *runner*

Cuban-born Alberto Salazar is regarded as the greatest long-distance runner in U.S. sports history. He won the most famous marathon races in the country, and returned from over a decade of illness and injuries—caused mainly by training too hard—to win an even longer race in South Africa in what has been described as the most fantastic comeback in any sport ever. Salazar has often emphasized that he runs with his heart, in reference both to his love for the sport and to his commitment to winning. Yet at the same time he is a deeply cerebral strategist who is sure to evaluate all factors in a race—including his own condition, that of his competitors, and the terrain. For example, the precision of his working methods is such that he could declare that if his training indicated he could run a given race in two hours and 10 minutes, he would go out and give it his best, but if he thought he might take two hours and 12 minutes, he would not even start out.

Alberto Salazar was born in Havana, Cuba, on August 7, 1958. The following year, after Fidel Castro's revolution, the family immigrated to the United States. Salazar is one of the huge number of Cubans who have enriched U.S. life thanks to their (or originally their parents') disagreement with the Cuban communist government.

As a boy, he grew up in Wayland, Massachusetts, where his parents settled after periods spent in Miami and in Manchester, Connecticut. Then he attended the University of Oregon, becoming an All-American athlete in track and cross-country racing. Running became the focus of his life, and in short order he set U.S. records for the 5,000-meter and the 10,000-meter race.

He also established a reputation as a big-talking upstart—he was quickly nicknamed "the Rookie" at the Greater Boston Track Club, where he trained—who seemed to be heading for humiliation as he set his sights on longer races. "I shall never be broken," he had written on a paper pasted on his wall in his university days—allowing another runner to overtake him was something he found unthinkable. However, Salazar was only stating what he fully intended to do because he knew what he was able to achieve. This led *Runner's World* magazine, in an article on Salazar, to bring up a saying of boxer Muhammad Ali's: "It's not bragging if you can do it."

To "do it," in a sport that makes enormous physical demands on its practitioners, Salazar was willing to race to the point of exhaustion and beyond. Twice he has collapsed at the end of a race, once so close to death that the Catholic last rites were administered to him.

In 1980 he entered his first marathon—a race of over 26 miles in length, run in honor of a soldier who in 490 B.C. ran that distance, from the plain of Marathon in Greece to Athens, to tell the Athenians of their army's victory over the Persians. For his debut in this most prestigious of all long-distance races, Salazar chose to enter the New York Marathon. He won it—in 2:09:41, a record for the New York marathon and indeed the fastest time for any first-time marathoner. Salazar shaved almost a minute and a half off his time in the following year's New York Marathon, setting a world record—which he had predicted before the race. In 1982 he won the Boston Marathon, setting another record (2:08:51) for that race, and the New York Marathon for the third time with a time of 2:09:29.

Salazar was acknowledged as the top long-distance runner in the world in those years. However, excessive training with little or no rest in between finally harmed his body's metabolism, as well as causing more ordinary muscular and tendon ailments. By 1983 his performance was down sharply. He had qualified for the Moscow Olympics in 1980, but never competed because the U.S. boycotted the competition. In 1984 he managed to qualify again, but emerged 15th in competition.

Long lean years ensued, during which Salazar tried not only diverse medicines and types of training but also made a religious pilgrimage to Medjugorje, Yugoslavia, where the Virgin Mary is said to appear. Finally, he recovered, thanks to doses of an antidepressant drug that was found to also heal some metabolic problems. In 1994 he astounded the sports world with a victory in the "ultramarathon" category—South Africa's almost 54-mile-long Comrades race.

The day after that race, he went for a four-mile run for relaxation, believed to be the first time a winner of Comrades did any running the following day.

In later years Salazar has worked as a coach and promoter of running events.

Further Reading

Amacher, Walt. "Alberto Salazar: The Marathon Legend Talks About His Life." On the Run. Available online. URL: http://www.ontherun.com/news/0264. Downloaded October 11, 2000.

Higdon, Hal. *Boston: A Century of Running.* Emmaus, Pa.: Rodale Press, 1983.

Hoban, Brom. "Marathon Man Alberto Salazar." Hispanic Magazine. Available online. URL: http://www.hisp.com/janfeb95/test.html. Downloaded October 11, 2000.

❧ **Salazar, Rubén** (1928–1970) *journalist*
The leading Hispanic journalist in the United States at the time of his death, Rubén Salazar was killed by a police tear gas canister in an incident that was never fully explained. This event became a milestone in the history of tense relations between the Los Angeles Chicano community and the authorities.

Salazar (not related to Alberto SALAZAR) was born in Ciudad Juárez, Mexico, on March 3, 1928. His family moved to El Paso, Texas, the following year, and he grew up there. In 1949, he became a U.S. citizen and in 1950 enlisted in the army and served two years. Following his discharge, he went back to his studies and in 1954 graduated from the University of Texas in El Paso with a B.A. degree.

Journalism attracted Salazar from the start; he went to work as a reporter for the El Paso *Herald-Post* while still a university undergraduate. He quickly demonstrated both his talent and his passion for bringing society's ills to light. His biggest coup in that period was to go undercover in El Paso's jail, getting himself arrested in order to report on jail conditions from the inside.

After graduating from college, Salazar moved to California to take a job at the Santa Rosa *Press Democrat.* In 1957, he went to work for the *San Francisco News,* from there to the Los Angeles *Herald-Express,* and finally the *Los Angeles Times* in 1959.

Salazar won awards for his articles about Hispanics in Los Angeles. In addition, the *Times* assigned him to a one-year stint as a war correspondent in Vietnam during the 1960s. He also spent three years at the newspaper's bureau in Mexico City, where he became the head of that office.

At the end of the 1960s and back in Los Angeles, Salazar began to write a weekly column for the *Times* on Chicano affairs. He also moved into television work, as news director at KMEX, a TV station broadcasting in Spanish. In both positions, Salazar maintained a steady barrage of criticism of the prejudice and discrimination that he saw Chicanos suffering: they were virtually second-class citizens in their own country. In particular, he denounced the Los Angeles police for rough treatment of Mexican Americans. Historical records from the period reveal that, in consequence, he received threats from police officers.

In August 1970, Chicanos held a large demonstration in Los Angeles against the Vietnam War. The event was organized by the National Chicano Moratorium Committee, an antiwar group. The Moratorium Committee's specific complaint was inequity in the military draft that resulted in a disproportionately large number of Mexican Americans fighting and suffering casualties in the war—almost twice their proportion in the population as a whole. Rubén Salazar was among the journalists who covered the protest meeting.

The demonstration was primarily peaceful. Nevertheless, the police, according to testimony afterward, used minor disturbances as an excuse to disrupt it and to make blanket arrests.

The actions of the police triggered panic and several deaths; one of these was Salazar's. He was sitting in a bar later that afternoon when the place was besieged by police searching for a man with a gun. As shown in photographs that were published in the papers, customers who tried to leave the bar were ordered back in by the police, who then fired a tear gas canister into the bar. This was described as unnecessary in reports and newspaper editorials about the event. The canister, which when fired can slam through walls, hit Salazar in the head. He died as a result. Although police were informed of this, they made no move to find him until two hours later.

The authorities decided not to prosecute anyone for the possibly unwarranted use of force that led to Salazar's death. The facts, therefore, were never established in a court of law.

The death of the crusading journalist became a rallying cry for Chicanos at a time when they were becoming more self-aware as a group. A park in a Mexican-American neighborhood in Los Angeles and a library in Santa Rosa have been given his name.

A Spanish-language folk song of the *corrido* type was composed in Salazar's honor, titled *El 29 de Agosto* (the date of his death in 1970). It describes how "misfortune befell a great man and good human being . . . a Mexican journalist of international fame . . . a spokesman for the community."

Further Reading

Acuña, Rodolfo. *Occupied America: A History of Chicanos.* New York; HarperCollins, 1988.

Martínez, Al. *Rising Voices: Profiles of Hispano-American Lives.* New York: New American Library, 1974.

Shorris, Earl. *Latinos: A Biography of the People.* New York: Avon Books, 1992.

Sánchez, Loretta (Loretta Sánchez Brixey) (1960–) *government official*

Loretta Sánchez is one of the first Mexican-American women to become a member of the U.S. House of Representatives. Unlike the first, Lucille ROYBAL-ALLARD, who reached Congress not only on her own merits but as part of a well-known political family, Sánchez battled her way into Congress as an unknown and speedily made a name for herself. Part of her quick renown was due to her feisty defense of minorities and the downtrodden. Another ingredient—an ironic one—was the unceasing attack on her by the congressman whom she had unseated in the election.

Sánchez was born in Lynwood, California, on January 7, 1960. Her parents, immigrants from Mexico, spoke only Spanish in the home. Loretta became one of the initial participants in the Head Start effort, established under President Lyndon Johnson in 1964 to help prepare "culturally deprived" children for school, particularly through help with their English. (Sánchez is the first Head Start graduate to become a member of the U.S. Congress.)

When Loretta was five years old the Sánchez family moved to the then mostly white city of Anaheim in Orange County, California. Loretta was raised there, lived most of her life in that community, and would eventually represent it in Congress. But when the Sánchezes first arrived, the immediate reaction of the neighbors was to move out because they were Mexican. Decades later one of these neighbors would resurface and apologize for the insult.

Like her six sisters and brothers, Loretta was made to study hard by her parents, who recognized the importance of education. She graduated in 1982 from Chapman University in her home county, with a B.A. degree in economics and the honor of having been chosen Student of the Year. Two years later she received an M.B.A. degree in finance from American University, in Washington, D.C.

As part of her work toward the M.B.A. degree Sánchez spent a year studying in Italy at the European Community's Market Management School in Rome. This was an indication of an internationally minded outlook she would display in Congress in the following decade, when as a member of the House, she was to mix interest in the welfare of her own constituency with trips to such destinations as Vietnam and Kosovo, Yugoslavia—places where the United States has fought wars.

Sánchez made a career in business, her specialty being municipal and other forms of finance. After a

Loretta Sánchez *(Courtesy of the Office of Representative Loretta Sánchez, U.S. House of Representatives)*

job as financial manager for the Orange County Transportation Agency she worked for two private firms and later launched a consultancy company of her own in Santa Ana. Her expertise in the raising and handling of funds for both government and private organizations, and in financial matters in general, was recognized when the California state government appointed her as an independent reviewer of the finances of the bankrupt Orange County. She found ways for the county to save hundreds of millions of dollars in financial costs. Such skills would come in handy later as a congresswoman, when she raised plentiful federal funding for projects in Orange County.

Sánchez was a member of the Republican Party, but in 1992 she became strongly disenchanted with what she perceived as a new antiminority swing in the party line. This made her become more politicized than she had previously been. Switching to the Democratic Party, she became more active in Hispanic and welfare causes, and gave preference again to her Hispanic maiden name instead of the married name, Brixey, that she had used since being wed to an Anglo securities trader, Stephen Brixey. Then she sought political office as a way to help her community and the disadvantaged in general.

Although resoundingly defeated in her first bid to become a city councilwoman, in 1996 Sánchez ran for the House of Representatives. Against all expectations, she defeated the incumbent congressman for the conservative Orange County, Robert Dornan. She achieved this through aggressive, grass-roots campaigning. However, she won by a margin of only 984 votes, and Dornan cried fraud, charging that illegal immigrants had somehow managed to vote for Sánchez.

After a year-long House investigation, the charges were dismissed. It was found that although some cases of fraud might have occurred, at most they added up to a few dozen in the county, not enough to overturn the election result. Dornan's attacks backfired badly, making Sánchez a celebrity and irritating minority voters who had been investigated as a result of the former congressman's accusations.

Sánchez distinguished herself as an activist congresswoman who flew back from Washington to her home district every weekend to meet her constituents, and who participated in 97% of all votes taken in the House. In the 1998 elections, when Dornan tried to regain his old seat, Sánchez won by a bigger margin than before—57 percent.

In 2000, Sánchez was again reelected to the U.S. House of Representatives.

Further Reading

U.S. House of Representatives. "Congresswoman Loretta Sánchez—Official Website of the 46th District." Available online. URL: http://www.house.gov/sanchez: Downloaded October 11, 2000.

Telgen, Diane, and Jim Kamp, eds. *Notable Hispanic American Women.* Detroit: Gale Research, Inc. 1998.

Santana, Carlos (1947–) *guitarist, singer*

Carlos Santana became nationally and internationally famous through his appearance at Woodstock in 1969. He is regarded as the founder of the "Latin rock" sound. He was also influential in the development of "Latin jazz."

Santana was born in Autlán de Navarro, Jalisco state, Mexico, on July 20, 1947. The family moved to San Francisco in 1962. Carlos's father, a violinist, played in groups that performed the Mexican music known as mariachi. As a child, Santana began to study the violin and the clarinet and, at 14, the guitar. His father was his first teacher. The next year, when the family moved to California, he discovered rhythm and blues, performed primarily by black musicians. For a time he moved wholly away from his Latin roots, and in 1966, the guitarist formed a bluesy rock group, the Santana Blues Band.

By 1969, however, he was bringing Latin sounds into rock. This fusion generated a whole new form of pop music, Latin rock. The Latin influence that he incorporated was not Mexican; it was an Afro-Caribbean sound that had developed in New York.

His group became known as the Santana Sextet or just Santana. *Santana* was also the name of the band's first album, released in 1969. That same year, he played a lengthy piece called *Soul Sacrifice* at the Woodstock festival in New York state. He had composed it especially for the festival.

Woodstock was a massive event and a defining one for a whole generation of youth. Santana's appearance proved to be one of the festival's resounding highlights, and his celebrity was assured. His group's first album *Santana* sold 2 million copies within a year.

In 1972, Santana came under the influence of Indian guru Sri Chinmoy. Among Sri Chinmoy's other followers were jazz musicians, and Santana, through his contact with them, began to explore another fusion of sounds. He then became one of the musical forces that launched Latin jazz. He has played with many of the big names in jazz and pop, including Herbie Hancock, José FELICIANO, and Aretha Franklin.

In 1976, Santana returned to Latin rock, but his string of innovative musical fusions had not ended. The following year, with the album *Festival,* he helped bring Brazilian influences into rock for a time.

Santana has recorded more than 30 albums and has made countless live appearances. He has toured internationally and in the 1980s appeared at Live Aid, a benefit concert that brought together some of the biggest names in rock. He won a Gold Medal Award in 1977 and a Grammy Award in 1989.

After three decades in the business, Santana in 1999 for the first time reached the top of the charts with his pop-rock album *Supernatural.* The smash success made him a star again at the age of 52—and led him to sweep the Grammy Awards in 2000, when he walked away with nine of the prizes. He followed that honor with a Latin Grammy Award. Also in 2000, he was honored with a Life Achievement Award by *Hispanic* magazine.

Further Reading

Leng, Simon. *Soul Sacrifice: The Santana Story.* London: Firefly, 2000.

Roberts, John Storm. *The Latin Tinge: The Impact of Latin American Music on the United States.* Tivoli, N.Y.: Original Music, 1985.

Santana Management. Available online. URL: http://www.santana.com. Downloaded October 11, 2000.

Shapiro, Marc. *Carlos Santana: Back on Top.* New York: St. Martin's, 2000.

Slonimsky, Nicolas. *Baker's Biographical Dictionary of Musicians.* New York: Schirmer Books, 1994.

Santayana, George (Jorge Ruiz de Santayana) (1863–1952) *philosopher*

One of the most important philosophers of the 20th century, George Santayana was also a distinguished writer. Though he did not begin to learn English until the age of nine, it became his primary language. His skillful, poetic use of English has been universally acclaimed, not only as found in his poems and other literary works, but also in his philosophical writings.

A Spaniard, Santayana grew up, studied, and worked in the United States, where he lived for 40 years. A renowned professor at Harvard University, he is credited with helping give the philosophy department there its "golden age."

Jorge Ruiz de Santayana was born in Madrid on December 16, 1863. His parents separated when he was a child, and his mother went to live in the United States to be with the family of a former, deceased husband who had been a U.S. businessman. In 1872, Jorge was sent to live with her in Boston. Although he was nine years old, he was put into kindergarten because he did not speak English.

The transition from being Jorge to being George proved hard for him. This is believed to be one of the reasons he developed the stance—in philosophy and in life—of being a detached observer, an outsider contemplating things with a skeptic's eye. He soon caught up academically and entered the Boston Latin School in 1874. At 18, he went to Harvard, and in 1886 he graduated summa cum laude with an A.B. degree.

Proficient in several languages—he later translated French and Italian poetry into English—Santayana followed Harvard with two years of graduate study in Germany. After another year at Harvard, he received his doctorate and in 1890 began to teach philosophy there. He remained there for 22 years.

His fellow professors were eminent philosophers who had earlier been his teachers, William James and Josiah Royce among them. James and Santayana had very different views of the world and did not get along well, although they did agree on Santayana's doctoral thesis (a study of the German philosopher Rudolf Lotze): James called it "the perfection of rottenness," while Santayana referred to it as "my dull thesis on Lotze." Despite their differences, James, Santayana, and Royce would turn Harvard into a beacon of philosophical thought by the end of the century.

Santayana's thinking is both subtle and diverse. One of his major fields of interest was the nature of human knowledge. Here, he stressed the importance of reason and yet concluded that a great part of knowledge is based on nothing more solid than what he called "animal faith."

He was also very interested in esthetics, and it was the subject of one of his major works, *The Sense of Beauty* (1896).

He summed up his philosophy in a huge treatise, *The Life of Reason.* Its five volumes were published

1905–06. In the decades that followed, he published *Skepticism and Animal Faith* (1923) and the four-volume *Realms of Being,* released between 1928 and 1940, among other works.

A man of letters, Santayana helped found the literary magazine *The Harvard Monthly* in 1885 and wrote many poems in an elegant, traditional style. He produced two important collections of poetry: *Sonnets and Other Verses* in 1894, which was revised and expanded two years later, and *A Hermit of Carmel and Other Poems* in 1901.

At Harvard, Santayana taught poet T.S. Eliot. Two modern poets, Robert Lowell and Wallace Stevens, wrote poems about and in homage to Santayana in the 1950s.

Santayana also wrote criticism, the subject matter of this work often overlapping with philosophical and especially religious concerns. Here, his books range from *Platonism in Italian Poets* (1896) and *Interpretations of Poetry and Religion* (1900) to *The Genteel Tradition at Bay* (1931). He also published a novel, *The Last Puritan* (1935), which was a candidate for the Pulitzer Prize in fiction but was passed over for the runaway success *Gone With the Wind.* Between 1944 and 1953, a three-part Santayana autobiography, *Persons and Places,* appeared.

Santayana remained at Harvard until 1912 and was widely praised for his qualities as a teacher as well as for his published work. In that year, however, his mother died, and he received an inheritance. It was enough money to enable him to pursue his meditations and writings without needing to teach, so he decided to leave Harvard. His decision astonished the academic world. Commenting on the reaction, one observer asked, ironically, "How could one leave Harvard and Boston by choice?" However, Santayana left not only the university and the city but also the country. His four decades in the United States, during which he had established his reputation, were over. He spent the remainder of his life in Europe, briefly in Spain at first, then in Britain, and finally, from 1924 until his death at the age of 88, in Italy.

Further Reading

Arnett, Willard E. *George Santayana.* New York: Washington Square Press, 1971.

Howgate, George W. *George Santayana*. New York: A.S. Barnes, 1961.

McCormick, John. *George Santayana*. New York: Knopf, 1987.

Munson, Thomas N. *The Essential Wisdom of George Santayana*. New York: Columbia University Press, 1962.

Santayana, George. *Persons and Places*. New York: Scribners, 1944, 1947, 1953.

Singer, Irving. *George Santayana, Literary Philosopher*. New Haven, Conn.: Yale University Press, 2000.

Stallknecht, Newton Phelps. *George Santayana*. Minneapolis: University of Minnesota Press, 1971.

Schifrin, Boris Claudio "Lalo"

(1932–) *composer*

One of the most sought-after composers in Hollywood, Lalo Schifrin has written more than 100 scores for movies and television. Some are regarded as classics, such as the theme music for the TV series *Mission: Impossible.* Noted for the wide range of his musical talent, he has conducted classical music at the world's finest concert halls; written pop songs that have been performed by such singers as Barbra Streisand, Tony Bennett, Carmen McRae, and Peggy Lee; and played piano with some of the world's top jazz musicians.

Schifrin was born in Buenos Aires, Argentina, on June 21, 1932. Given the names Boris Claudio, he became known by the nickname Lalo. Music ran in the family. His father, Luis Schifrin, was, for 35 years, concertmaster of the Buenos Aires Philharmonic Orchestra at the Colón concert hall and opera house. He nurtured his son's prodigious musical talent by having him taught by the best classical musicians in Argentina. However, as the young man grew older, he tended to prefer jazz music to the classics.

After finishing his schooling in Buenos Aires, Schifrin pursued his musical interests in Paris during the early 1950s, studying classical music with the modern composer Olivier Messiaen and spending his nights playing with jazzmen. The piano had become his chosen instrument. In 1955 he represented Argentina in the International Jazz Festival in Paris; back in his hometown, he became one of the luminaries of a local jazz upsurge and led his own group.

Bandleader Xavier CUGAT invited him to New York in 1958 as an arranger for his Latin combo. Schifrin took the offer and has made the United States his headquarters ever since. Jazz giant Dizzy Gillespie heard Schifrin play in Buenos Aires during a Latin American tour and invited him to join his band as pianist and composer. Schifrin's work with Gillespie brought him into contact with a jazz recording label that was a subsidiary of the MGM movie studio in Hollywood.

Having been an avid movie fan since infancy and seeing some favorite films more than a dozen times, Schifrin was particularly interested in movie scores. A classic historical epic by the Russian director Sergei Eisenstein, *Alexander Nevsky* (1938), was a particular influence. Its impressive score, written by the master composer Sergei Prokofiev, proved an inspiration for Schifrin.

He took the next step, asking MGM if it would let him try his hand at composing music for its movies; he had already done this for some films in Argentina and France. The studio agreed, and from 1964, Hollywood became his home.

Schifrin won Oscar nominations (to add to a collection of Grammy Awards) for his work on *Cool Hand Luke* (1967), *The Fox* (1968), *Voyage of the Damned* (1976), *The Amityville Horror* (1979), *The Competition* (1980), and *The Sting II* (1983).

Among the motion pictures Schifrin scored are *Bullitt, The Cincinnati Kid, Cool Hand Luke, Hell in the Pacific, THX-1138, The Eagle Has Landed, Brubaker, Caveman, Black Moon Rising,* and *Return to the River Kwai.*

He has also been closely associated with Clint Eastwood, scoring such films as *Coogan's Bluff* (1968), *The Beguiled* and *Dirty Harry* (both 1971), and *Magnum Force* (1973).

For television, he composed the themes for the *Starsky & Hutch, The Planet of the Apes,* and *Mannix* series, in addition to his most celebrated TV theme, *Mission: Impossible* (1966). He has also composed scores for many TV movies, miniseries, pilots, and documentaries, including *Princess Daisy, Rita Hayworth: Love Goddess, The World of Jacques Cousteau,* and *The Rise*

Lalo Schifrin *(Cabrera Archive)*

and Fall of the Third Reich, the score of which was independently performed as a cantata (1967).

In 1987 Schifrin was appointed musical director of the Paris Philharmonic Orchestra, achieving recognition for his continuing work in the field of classical music, though he continued his movie and TV work. Interested in developing new talent, he also became musical director of the Young Musicians Foundation Debut Orchestra in Los Angeles.

Schifrin received the Distinguished Artist Award from the Los Angeles Music Center in 1998. The following year, he was appointed music director of the Los Angeles Latin Jazz Institute/Festival.

Schifrin has led such orchestras as the Los Angeles Philharmonic, the Israel Philharmonic, and the New American Orchestra and has conducted at New York's Lincoln Center, Britain's Royal Festival Hall, and the Netherlands' Concertgebouw. His classical compositions, often commissioned by some of the world's top music ensembles, include *Canons For String Orchestra, Continuum for Harp, Capriccio for Clarinet and Strings, Tropics,* and *Invocations.* He has also been active in imaginative fusions, combining classical religious music with other musical forms, as in his *Jazz Mass, Rock Requiem,* and *Madrigals for the Space Age,* which has accompanying texts by science fiction writer Ray Bradbury.

Further Reading

Harrington, Sean. "Lalo Schifrin." Available online. URL: http://www.schifrin.com. Downloaded October 11, 2000.

Katz, Ephraim. *The Film Encyclopedia*. New York: Perigee Books, 1994.

❧ Secada, Jon (Juan Secada) (1961–)
songwriter, singer

Jon Secada has demonstrated a knack for shaping highly professional blends of diverse pop and rhythm-and-blues elements and turning them into big-selling romantic ballads—but he has also relied on the personal appeal that caused him, on his debut, to be dubbed a "new Julio IGLESIAS," while another magazine described him as one of the sexiest young men on the rock scene. Underneath a surface smoothness that has led some critics to accuse his work of a lack of distinctiveness lies the technical expertise of a trained jazz musician and voice teacher. He releases records in both English and Spanish versions with equal success.

Afro-Cuban Juan Secada, an only son, was born in Havana, Cuba, on October 4, 1961, to a black father and white mother who owned a coffee shop in the city. His father's sister, Moraima Secada, was a well-known singer of the type of Latin songs known as *boleros.* As an opponent of Fidel Castro's government, Juan's father, José, spent time in jail and in a work camp. In 1971 the family was allowed to emigrate and settled in Miami, where Juan's parents again went into the coffee-shop business. In the U.S. "Juan" was transformed into "Jon."

As a teenager Secada began to take an increasing interest in music and decided to make it his career. He received a bachelor's degree in music and a master's degree in jazz vocal performance from the University of Miami, and for six years taught singing at Miami-Dade Community College.

Secada next joined Gloria ESTEFAN's group, the Miami Sound Machine, as a backup singer and songwriter. He gained entrance to the group after a demonstration tape of his work was played for Emilio Estefan, Gloria's husband and partner, by friends of Secada's who had already become Sound Machine members. It was the beginning of a long and fruitful friendship in which Gloria Estefan, admiring Secada's talent, generously gave him opportunities to shine and to thus emerge as a star in his

own right, while Emilio masterminded his career. Gloria even sang backup lyrics for him in one of his earliest songs, something she had never done for another singer.

Secada's first album was released in 1992. Titled *Jon Secada* in English and *Otro día más sin verte* (Another Day Without Seeing You) in Spanish, it sold 6 million copies and won Secada a Grammy Award as Best Latin Pop Album.

The debut album was followed by others at an average rate of just under one a year, including *Heart, Soul & a Voice* (in Spanish, *Si te vas,* meaning If You Leave) in 1994, *Secada* in 1997 and *Greatest Hits (Grandes Exitos)* in 1999. They included many hit singles, which, like the albums, were often offered to his fans in English and Spanish versions.

"Secada can take a line like 'I promise to love you as if your heart were my own' and deliver it with unabashed conviction," wrote a reviewer in the *New York Times.*

"I feel like I'm a perfect example of the American dream," Secada exclaimed to *Entertainment Weekly* magazine, contemplating his success, which encompasses large international sales and world tours. By the end of 1999, Secada had sold more than 20 million albums.

In his continuing work as a songwriter, Secada has penned songs for Don Johnson, Pia Zadora, Luis Miguel, and Ricky MARTIN, among others. Secada was invited to sing alongside Frank Sinatra in the latter's album *Duets II.* He sang another duet entitled *If I Never Knew You* with the singer Shanice on the soundtrack of the Disney movie *Pocahontas.*

In 1995 Secada played a role in the musical *Grease* on Broadway.

Further Reading

Contemporary Musicians. Detroit: Gale Research, 1994.

Sony Music Entertainment. "Jon Secada." Available online. URL: http://www.jonsecada.com. Downloaded October 11, 2000.

Tardiff, Joseph C., and Mpho Mabunda, eds. *Dictionary of Hispanic Biography.* Detroit: Gale Research, 1996.

❧ Seguín, Juan N. (Juan Nepomuceno Seguín) (1806–1889?) *soldier*

Juan Nepomuceno Seguín was the military leader of the tejanos (Texans of Mexican ancestry) who sided with the cause of Texan independence. He fought in the two Alamo battles and is regarded as one of the heroes of the battle of San Jacinto, which finally secured independence for Texas. But his efforts were repaid with the mistrust of English-speaking Texans. He was finally forced to flee to Mexico. Seguín was the last Hispanic mayor of San Antonio until Henry CISNEROS in the 1980s. The Texan city of Seguin (spelled without an accent) is named after him.

Juan Seguín was born in 1806 in San Antonio. His family history included French ancestry. Erasmo Seguín, Juan's father, was a prominent and wealthy tejano who owned land in the San Antonio area (also referred to, at the time, as San Antonio de Béxar, San Fernando de Béxar, and just Béxar).

Erasmo and his son held the same political views on the situation in Texas at the time. Both believed that Texas was at a disadvantage by being a very remote outpost of Mexico. Juan went into politics at the age of 18, and despite his youth became mayor of San Antonio, a post he would hold again when Texas was an independent republic.

Before gaining independence, Texas was not a Mexican state but a part of the state of Coahuila. It was also receiving from the United States a large influx of settlers who soon outnumbered the tejanos. One of these Anglos was Stephen Austin, a friend of Erasmo Seguín. In 1833 Austin went to the capital, Mexico City, to petition for statehood for Texas, but he was unsuccessful. Worse, Mexican President General Antonio López de Santa Anna was becoming increasingly dictatorial, taking away local freedoms that had been awarded under an 1824 federalist constitution.

Thus, when Texas rebelled against Santa Anna's rule, the Seguíns did not see the conflict as one of native tejanos versus incoming Anglos. In their eyes, it was a conflict that united Texans—Mexican and Anglo—against a faraway, tyrannical government.

A gathering organized by Juan Seguín in San Antonio has been called the "first strictly revolutionary meeting in Texas." He recruited volunteers for Austin and took part in fighting at Concepción alongside one of the heroes of the Texan secession from Mexico, Jim Bowie.

Erasmo Seguín, for his part, was mistreated by the troops sent by Santa Anna to subdue what Mexico viewed as sedition in Texas. These troops, commanded by Santa Anna's brother-in-law, General Martín de Cós, took over San Antonio and entrenched themselves in the town's stronghold, an old mission building known as the Alamo.

Meanwhile, Erasmo Seguín placed all the resources of his farms at the disposal of the rebel movement. His assistance, consisting of food, horses, and mules, is considered to have been of major importance to the rebels.

Juan Seguín, who had been appointed a captain of the insurgent forces, fought under Austin's command during his siege of the Alamo in 1835—the first battle of the Alamo. Cós held out for 41 days before being forced to withdraw, and Seguín was at the side of rebel leader William B. Travis when he pursued the retreating federal army.

Then Santa Anna himself came to crush the revolt. This time the situation was reversed with the rebels defending the Alamo against the Mexican army. This second battle for the Alamo gave time to the main Texan army under Sam Houston to regroup and strengthen. In this second and more famous Alamo battle (1836), the defenders commanded by Travis included a number of tejanos, veterans of the earlier siege of the Alamo. The tejanos were led by Juan Nepomuceno Seguín. The Mexican army took the Alamo in 10 days, using frontal charges that would have been regarded as heroic had Mexico ultimately won.

Before Santa Anna's last assault, Travis sent Seguín and another tejano to slip through the siege lines and seek help, but no help was available for the defenders. They were all killed.

Houston then put Seguín in charge of protecting the rear of his retreating army. The tejano officer did this successfully at an encounter on the Brazos River near San Felipe, where he held back Santa Anna's advance. Seguín then rejoined Houston and fought with distinction in the battle of San Jacinto. During this battle fought a month after the Alamo, Santa Anna was taken prisoner.

Seguín, now a colonel, was appointed military commandant of San Antonio. He returned to the city where he organized the military funeral given to the heroes of the Alamo's defense. Seguín, who did not speak English, delivered his funeral oration in Spanish.

In 1838 and 1839, he served in the Texas Senate and in 1840 won another election, this time becoming mayor once again of San Antonio. His term in office was marked by increasing troubles with the incoming waves of Anglos. They tended to regard all Mexicans as enemies, regardless of their service in the Texan war of independence. Seguín defended tejanos as best he could from discrimination, bodily attacks, and dispossession. The "only crime" of these people, Seguín declared, "was that they owned large tracts of land and desirable property." Because of his defense of fellow tejanos, Seguín began to be accused of anti-Texan, pro-Mexican activities. In 1842, faced with threats on his life, he was forced to resign from office and flee.

He crossed the border and was promptly jailed in Nuevo Laredo. Santa Anna ordered that Seguín be sent to him, but the local military commander offered Seguín a deal instead: serve in the Mexican armed forces and avoid being sent to Mexico City as Santa Anna's prisoner. Seguín, seeing no alternative, accepted.

Even while in Mexico, Seguín continued to be concerned with political affairs in Texas. In 1845, he argued against Texas becoming a U.S. state. He believed that he had not fought to make Texas independent just to see it absorbed by the United States; the solution for Texas, he felt, was for Mexico to finally recognize Texas's independence.

When war broke out between the United States and Mexico, Seguín ironically found himself fighting for Mexico and for Santa Anna, who was again president.

In 1848, Mexico lost the war, and Texas became part of the United States. Seguín applied to the United States for permission to recross the Río Grande. He lived uneventfully in Texas through the Civil War period. In 1867 he returned to Nuevo Laredo and is believed to have resided there until his death in 1889 or 1890. A century later a television film was made about him, called *Seguín,* starring Edward James OLMOS.

Further Reading

Best, Hugh. *Debrett's Texas Peerage.* New York: Coward-McCann, 1983.

Meier, Matt S., and Feliciano Rivera. *Dictionary of Mexican American History.* Westport, Conn.: Greenwood Press, 1981.

Seguín, Juan N. *A Revolution Remembered: The Memoirs and Selected Correspondence of Juan N. Seguín.* Austin, Tex.: State House Press, 1991.

Selena (Selena Quintanilla Pérez)
(1971–1995) *singer*

Known as "the queen of Tejano music" and as "the Mexican-American Madonna," Selena put a relatively little known regional form of music, Tejano, on the music map of the United States. Although she was murdered at the age of 23, by then she had been performing for 14 years, and the outpouring of grief was so large it made other sectors of U.S. society—particularly business—more aware of the size and significance of the Hispanic community in their midst. The repercussion of her death is therefore credited as one of the direct sources of a Latino boom in the United States in the late 1990s, which led to the emergence of such superstars as Jennifer LÓPEZ, Marc ANTHONY, and Ricky MARTIN.

Selena Quintanilla Pérez, who would become famous under her first name alone, was born on April 16, 1971, in Lake Jackson, Texas. Her father, Abraham Quintanilla Jr., was a shipping clerk at a chemical factory, but had earlier been leader of a band that played a blend of Mexican music and rock'n'roll that would evolve into Tex-Mex music. Quintanilla encouraged the singing talent he quickly discovered in his daughter, and in 1980 went into business with it. He opened a restaurant in Lake Jackson where his three children performed under the name Selena y Los Dinos (Selena and the Boys). Selena sang and her two older siblings played drums and bass guitar. The little band began to prosper, and added more instrumentalists, but the restaurant failed. The Quintanillas then went on the road in Texas. Selena was forced to complete her schooling by correspondence.

As her renown expanded, Selena, who had grown up speaking only English, also had to learn to speak

Spanish. She had always sung in Spanish, but previously she had learned the lyrics phonetically. She always gave her name an English rather than Spanish pronunciation.

Selena began to draw increasingly larger crowds, and in 1984 she made her first recordings. In 1987, at age 15, she won the Tejano Music Award for female vocalist of the year—an honor she would walk away with every year thereafter until her death.

In her live performances, the sounds Selena sang were a mix of diverse musical forms that was expertly tailored to her diverse rural or city audiences, emphasizing country music, Latin, or other elements as the case might be. And despite the disapproval of her father-manager, a strict Jehovah's Witness, as Selena grew older she developed a sexy onstage presence, including revealing outfits, that triggered her comparison to the singer Madonna. Offstage, however, she led a quiet life, marrying her band's lead guitarist, Chris Pérez, in 1992.

With acceptance by a major recording company, EMI, in 1989, Selena came to national prominence. She drew record crowds—up to 61,000 people—when she performed at the Houston Astrodome. Her record *Amor prohibido* (Forbidden Love), released in 1994, sold a million copies around the world. Likewise in 1994, her work *Selena Live* earned her a Grammy Award for best Mexican-American album. She sang and appeared briefly in the 1995 movie *Don Juan DeMarco*.

Soon, EMI decided she was ripe for a crossover to English-language songs. On March 31, 1995, however, before her first English-language album could be released, Selena was shot dead in Corpus Christi, Texas. The murderer, who was subsequently sentenced to life in prison, was a woman who had founded and been president of a Selena fan club. She later ran Selena merchandising businesses, including the sale of clothes designed by the singer herself. Confronted by Selena, who suspected her of stealing money, she killed her with a gun that she claimed she had intended to use on herself. Selena's death stunned her legions of fans and resulted in greater fame than she had enjoyed while alive. Some fans even began to treat her as a type of lay saint in their prayers.

Selena's debut English-language album, *Dreaming of You*, released posthumously, entered the Billboard chart at the top after selling 330,000 copies in its first week (including 175,000 on the first day)—the second-best launching ever, topped only by Michael Jackson's *HIStory*. It eventually went triple platinum.

Selena's life became the subject of a 1997 movie, *Selena*, directed by Gregory NAVA, in which Jennifer LÓPEZ played her and Edward James OLMOS portrayed her father, and of a musical, *Selena Forever*, in 2000.

Further Reading

Arrarás, María Celeste. *Selena's Secret: The Revealing Story Behind her Tragic Death.* New York: Simon & Schuster, 1997.

Hernandez, Abel M. "Selena's Page." Available online. URL: http://www.ondanet.com/tejano/selena. html. Downloaded October 11, 2000.

Richmond, Clint. *Selena! The Phenomenal Life and Tragic Death of the Tejano Music Queen.* New York: Pocket Books, 1995.

☙ Serra, Junípero (1713–1784) *prelate, colonizer*

Fray (Friar) Junípero Serra, a Franciscan priest, founded missions up and down the coast of California. In doing so he helped establish a European presence in the region in a form that caught and has held the Californian imagination to this day. Father Serra has been called "the apostle of California" for his untiring missionary work. He is a candidate for sainthood and was beatified by Pope John Paul II in 1987.

Serra was born in Petra, on the Spanish island of Majorca, on November 24, 1713. He became a member of the Franciscan order in 1730 and was ordained eight years later.

Serra's place in history comes from his practical work—setting up missions in inhospitable territory. Serra was also a learned man in religious matters, who was at one time a professor of philosophy at a university on Majorca, but his calling was missionary work among the Indians of the New World. He arrived in

Veracruz, New Spain (Mexico) in 1749. He then walked from there to the Mexican capital. An insect bite during this journey caused an infection in his leg, and he was never again able to walk without pain. Serra was not a strong man, and he was small, just 5 feet, 2 inches tall, but he was known to be unstoppably energetic.

From 1750 to 1767, he worked in the existing network of missions in Mexico. Then, in 1768, politics changed things. First, the Jesuit order was expelled because it had become too strong for the Spanish king's comfort. The Franciscan order was sent to replace the Jesuits at their missions in Lower (Baja) California. This part of California was already under Mexican colonization. It would remain in Mexican hands even after the war with the United States in the following century.

The Franciscan Father Serra was initially put in charge of these Baja missions, but soon came new instructions giving Serra the chance to establish missions in new territories. These new orders were triggered by a political situation between Spain and Russia. From their bases on Alaskan islands, the Russians had begun to explore south along the western coast of North America.

Spain, alarmed by the Russian movements, decided to secure the territories to the north of its Mexican dominions. Serra was named to head the missionary part of the expedition. Gaspar de Portolá, governor of Baja California, headed the military command.

Spain had been aware of the coastline of Upper (Alta) California—what is now the U.S. state of California—for more than 120 years, but no serious colonizing had been attempted until Portolá and Serra set out in 1769. Serra and Portolá headed two parties. Serra's proceeded overland on mules. Portolá navigated ships up the coast. It took several months to make the trip up Lower California to what is now San Diego. Both parties suffered hunger and disease on the way, and the ships were hit by storms. One quarter of the expedition's 219 men died along the way, and another quarter deserted.

The hardships of the journey were typical of those Serra would face in the early years of his California mission work, but he was not deterred. After

founding a mission in San Diego in 1769, he moved north and founded one in Carmel-Monterey the next year. He gradually established missions in the territories between these first two, as well as some further north.

In addition to the original two, Serra would found seven other missions before his death in Monterey in 1784. They were San Antonio and San Gabriel, founded in 1771; San Luis Obispo, 1772; San Francisco and San Juan Capistrano, 1776; Santa Clara, 1777; and San Buenaventura, 1782.

The ultimate goal was a string of missions at a distance of no more than one or two days' travel from one another and joined by a "Royal Road"—*Camino Real*. Serra dearly wanted to establish more than his nine missions, but it was his successors who would continue his work, eventually more than doubling the number.

Serra did not attain this goal during his lifetime because of a number of obstacles: The missions were subsisting at near-starvation rations; the friars at the missions often quarreled with the military powers in the *presidios* (forts) set up nearby. In 1775 Serra took his mission's problems to Mexico City, but he returned to California largely empty-handed.

The Mexican government did not allow more missions to be established quickly because it did not have the resources to protect them against possible Indian attacks or to prevent the Indians inside the missions from escaping.

Serra, like virtually all Europeans, saw the missions as doing the beneficial, "civilizing" job of bringing agriculture to "backward" tribes. The tribes saw this as a total disruption of their hunter-gatherer lifestyles, one that actually kept them better fed than at the missions until the farming was properly underway. The food shortages were only part of the problem. The missionaries attempted to force the Indians to convert from their own beliefs to Catholicism. The Europeans also brought diseases and spoke a language that was foreign to the Indians.

Serra was played by actor Michael Rennie in the movie *Seven Cities of Gold* in 1955. Anthony QUINN played Portolá, and Rita MORENO had a role as an Indian maiden.

Further Reading

Bolton, May Ivy. *Father Junípero Serra.* New York: Messner, 1952.

Demarest, Donald. *The First Californian: The Story of Fray Junípero Serra.* New York: Hawthorn Books, 1963.

DeNevi, Don, and Noel Francis Moholy. *Junípero Serra.* New York: Harper & Row, 1985.

Dolan, Sean. *Junípero Serra.* New York: Chelsea House, 1991.

Englebert, Omer. *The Last of the Conquistadors, Junípero Serra, 1713–1784.* Westport, Conn.: Greenwood Press, 1956.

Gleiter, Jan. *Junípero Serra.* Milwaukee, Wis.: Raintree, 1989.

Serra Club of Bethlehem, Pennsylvania. "Blessed Junípero Serra, 1713–1784." Available online.

URL: http://www.catholic-church.org/serra-beth/serra-4.htm. Downloaded October 11, 2000.

The Sunset Editors. *The California Missions.* Menlo Park, Calif.: Lane Publishing Co., 1979.

Sheen, Charlie (Carlos Irwin Estévez)
(1965–) *actor*

One of the most sought-after young actors in motion pictures at the time, in 1994 Charlie Sheen added his handprints on Hollywood's Walk of Fame. Charlie is the brother of actor Emilio ESTÉVEZ.

Charlie Sheen was born Carlos Irwin Estévez on September 3, 1965, in New York City. After high school, he attended the University of Kansas, although he reportedly lost a chance at an athletic scholarship due to a poor attendance record at school.

Charlie Sheen in the movie *Platoon* (1986) *(Cabrera Archive)*

Despite his show-business family, his early ambition was to be a baseball player. He starred on his high school baseball team and went to a baseball camp every summer in Springfield, Missouri. He was scouted in his senior year and received an offer from the Dodgers to play shortstop. Nevertheless, the pull of an acting career eventually won out.

At nine he acted as an extra in a 1974 TV movie, *The Execution of Private Slovik,* in which his father, Martin SHEEN, had the lead role. Five years later, he again appeared as an extra in one of his father's pictures, *Apocalypse Now.* He credits his decision to go into acting to the excitement of having spent months on location in the Philippines during the filming, watching director Francis Ford Coppola in action.

Charlie and Martin Sheen have appeared together in several other movies: In the docudrama *Jack London's California* about the author of *Call of the Wild,* Charlie played London at age 18, and Martin played him at age 40. Another joint appearance was in *Wall Street* (1987), where they played father and son. Standouts among Charlie Sheen's other movies include *Red Dawn* (1984), *Platoon* (1986), *Young Guns* (1988), *Major League* (1989), *The Three Musketeers* (1993), and *Terminal Velocity* (1994).

In 1998 Charlie's father had to resort to requesting an arrest warrant to force him to go into a drug rehabilitation center. Sheen was put on a two-year probation for alcohol and drug offenses from which he was released early in 2000.

The younger Sheen's drug problems did not keep him away from work. He appeared in the *Sugar Hill* TV series in 1999 and in movies including *Money Talks* (1997), *No Code of Conduct* (1998), *A Letter from Death Row* (1998), *Free Money* (1998), *Being John Malkovich* (1999), and *Rated X* (2000). He also replaced the actor Michael J. Fox in the TV sitcom *Spin City.*

Further Reading

Riley, Lee, and David Schumacher. *The Sheens.* New York: St. Martin's Press, 1989.

Press, Skip. *Charlie Sheen, Emilio Estévez & Martin Sheen.* Parsippany, N.J.: Crestwood House, 1996.

Martin Sheen *(Cabrera Archive)*

Sheen, Martin (Ramón Estévez)
(1940–) *actor*

Martin Sheen ranks among the most distinguished actors in Hollywood. He has also made numerous TV-movie and theatrical appearances, and he is the center of a large acting family that includes his brother—who has acted both as Joseph Estévez and as Joe Phelan—and Martin's four children, Charlie SHEEN and Emilio, Ramón (Jr.), and Renée Estévez.

His two eldest sons, Emilio ESTÉVEZ and Charlie Sheen, have since the mid-1980s been what their father has proudly called "far and away bigger draws than I've ever been."

Ramón Estévez Sr., was born in Dayton, Ohio, on August 3, 1940. His father, Francisco Estévez, had immigrated to the United States from Spain, while his mother, Mary Ann Phelan, had emigrated from Ireland. The couple, living in impoverished circumstances, had 10 children.

As a child in Ohio, Ramón worked as a golf caddie and entertained the idea of becoming a professional golfer, but he began to act in high school. This changed his direction. At 18, a trip to New York, won as a talent show prize, allowed him to try his luck as an actor there.

Nevertheless, he wanted to show his father that he had at least tried to go to college. He took a college admissions test but failed on purpose.

He has said that he changed his name to Martin Sheen because he sought Hispanic parts and was told he didn't look Hispanic, so his agents couldn't find jobs for him. He did look Irish, so he took the name of a well-known Irish-American bishop, Fulton Sheen.

He has also expressed regret over the name change, which he used for work only; he never legally changed it. In 1981, when he accepted an award from Nosotros, an association of Hispanic actors, Sheen delivered his speech in Spanish and dedicated the Golden Eagle to "the man who called me Ramón, my father Francisco Estévez." Then he repeated the speech in English "for our gringo friends who don't understand Spanish."

Sheen supported himself in New York at odd jobs and started out in the experimental group, the Living Theater, where he also swept up to help pay his expenses. His debut, in 1959, came in the play *The Connection,* but he made his mark in 1964 on Broadway in the play *The Subject Was Roses.* He also played Hamlet in a rock version of the classic, and appeared in *Death of a Salesman* on Broadway. In 1986, he appeared in *The Normal Heart* in London.

Among the highlights of his film career are *The Incident* (1967, his first film), *The Subject Was Roses* (1968, the movie version of his stage success), *Badlands* (1973, which won him a best-actor award at the San Sebastián Film Festival in Spain), *The Cassandra Crossing* (1977), and *Apocalypse Now* (1979). He suffered a heart attack during the shooting of the latter. He also appeared in *Gandhi* (1982), *Firestarter* (1984), *Wall Street* (1987), *Judgment in Berlin* (1988), and *Cadence* (1990, which he directed).

He also acted in dozens of made-for-TV movies, including *The Execution of Private Slovik* (1974), *Shattered Spirits* (1986), and *Gettysburg* (1993). He played Robert Kennedy in *The Missiles of October* in 1974, President John F. Kennedy in *Kennedy* in 1983,

and narrated the movie *JFK* about the president's assassination, in 1991. He won an Emmy award in 1983 and a Golden Globe in 2001 for his role as a U.S. president on TV's *The West Wing.*

Sheen is known for active participation in many liberal causes, particularly nuclear disarmament. He has been arrested many times at protests. In 1994, he spoke out against controversial legislation in California that denies all but emergency services to illegal immigrants, who are mainly Hispanics.

Maintaining a busy schedule, Sheen appeared in movies, including *Monument Ave.* and *A Letter From DeathRow* in 1998; *Lost and Found, A Texas Funeral* and *Ninth Street* in 1999; and *O* in 2000.

On the small screen, he appeared in the TV movies *Hostile Waters* (1997) and *Voyage of Terror* (1998). He then had a great success in *The West Wing* (1999–).

Further Reading

Riley, Lee and David Schumacher. *The Sheens.* New York: St. Martin's Press, 1989.
Press, Skip. *Charlie Sheen, Emilio Estévez & Martin Sheen.* Parsippany, N.J.: Crestwood House, 1996.

❧ **Smits, Jimmy** (1955–) *actor*

Jimmy Smits has carved a solid name for himself with good parts in TV series as well as in a number of movies. His career goal, which he has to a considerable degree achieved, is to be considered not as an ethnic actor but as an actor, period. At the same time he has remained concerned with the image of Latinos presented by the entertainment media. "I am really irritated about the way Hispanics are treated on screen," he told an interviewer after securing the very positive role of an intense, attractive lawyer who just happens to be Hispanic, in the series *L.A. Law.* "I can only hope that that will change and that I am doing my part to affect that change."

Smits was born on July 9, 1955, in Brooklyn, New York, to a Puerto Rican mother and a father from the South American country of Dutch Guiana (now Suriname), who had both Dutch and South American Indian blood. Although his mother often talked to him in Spanish, the boy had little familiarity with the language when, at the age of 10, his family relocated in Puerto Rico for two years. He initially had a hard time adjusting to his new surroundings on the island, but he was later to credit the experience with strengthening his Hispanic roots.

Smits loved to act from an early age, and was always an active participant in school plays. After completing high school in New York, where his family had moved in the mid-1960s, his parents expected him to become a teacher, and he enrolled in Brooklyn College with that purpose, but once there he switched his major from education to theater. He graduated with a B.A. degree in theater in 1976. Then, rather than going straight to work, he determined to first obtain the best possible grounding in his craft. He obtained a scholarship to study at Cornell University and received a master of fine arts degree in theater in 1978. He has often spoken to groups of Hispanic children on the importance of getting an education.

Smits's first job after graduation was as a community organizer. Gradually, however, he became able to support himself and his family (he married the year after leaving university) with a diversity of small parts on stage and on television. Smits wanted to play all kinds of roles, high as well as low, and even acted in Shakespearean plays. But he soon found that, despite his Dutch last name, he ran the risk of being typecast in Hispanic roles, possibly because of a skin color that has been described as "caramel." His other option was exotic types in general—he had a tiny role as a Tibetan monk in the *All My Children* soap opera.

His first big assignment, though it lasted only about 20 minutes of TV time, was in the pilot episode of the *Miami Vice* series in 1984, playing star Don Johnson's first partner, who was quickly killed off.

The following year he auditioned for *L.A. Law*—twice. Auditions for the series were being held in New York and Los Angeles. He had done badly—or so he felt—in New York, so he flew to the other coast and tried again, this time successfully. The role of a hard-driven lawyer made him a star. He also found that people began to ask him for legal advice, and several bar associations, including the Alaska Trial Lawyers Association, even invited him to become a member.

He received an award from the Mexican national bar association in 1988 for improving the image of Hispanic lawyers.

Smits also discovered that he was seen as an example of a long-dormant species, the "Latin lover." In 1995 *People* magazine listed him among the "50 most beautiful people in the world."

Smits stayed with *L.A. Law* until 1991. In 1993 he got another choice role in a TV series, as a detective on *NYPD Blue*, where he remained until 1998. Among other television work, he appeared in the title role in a 1994 version of *The Cisco Kid*, as well as playing Solomon in *Solomon & Sheba* in 1995. For his *L.A. Law* work he earned four Emmy Award nominations and one Emmy (1990) plus one Golden Globe Award nomination; for *NYPD Blue* he obtained another Emmy nomination.

In movies, Smits got his first major role as a general in the Mexican Revolution—and Jane Fonda's love interest—in *Old Gringo* (1989). Among Smits's other films are Gregory NAVA's *Mi Familia, My Family* (1995), *Lesser Prophets* (1997), and *Price of Glory* (2000).

Further Reading

Internet City. "Jimmy Smits." Available online. URL: http://www.internetcity.com/jimmysmits. Downloaded October 11, 2000.

Parish, James, and Don Stanke. *Hollywood Baby Boomers.* New York: Garland Publishing, Inc., 1992.

Tardiff, Joseph C., and Mpho Mabunda, eds. *Dictionary of Hispanic Biography.* Detroit: Gale Research, 1996.

❦ **Sosa, Sammy** (1968–) *baseball player*

At a time of decaying interest in baseball among the U.S. population in general, aggravated by a bitter players' strike four years earlier, Sammy Sosa helped reinvigorate the sport. He did it with one other player, Mark McGwire, in a phenomenal 1998 season during which the two sluggers engaged in a record-shattering race for the most home runs. The race was good for baseball not only because of the dazzling numbers achieved but because of the spirit of friendly rivalry—

Sammy Sosa *(Steve Green photo courtesy of Chicago Cubs)*

in a word, sportsmanship—in which it unfolded. In handing him the Commissioner's Historic Achievement Award on a special "Sammy Sosa Day" celebration at Wrigley Field in Chicago, Commissioner of Baseball Allan "Bud" Selig told Sosa, "Your achievements are legendary, but more importantly you've handled yourself with a class and dignity that has been unparalleled."

Samuel Sosa was born on November 12, 1968, in Consulo, near the city of San Pedro de Macorís in the Dominican Republic, a country where he has become a national hero and has been named an honorary ambassador. He was one of seven brothers and sisters whose father, a farmer, died when Samuel was seven years old.

Years later, when asked about the "pressure" of the home-run contest against McGwire, Sosa said he felt it less as such than as a source of enjoyment. "Pressure," he said, "is shining shoes and washing cars to support my family in the Dominican Republic."

Although his first sporting interest was boxing, Sosa also played some baseball as a child, often in his bare feet, with no mitt (until he made one out of a milk carton) and a stick for a bat, plus a rolled-up sock for a ball. He was 14 before he wielded a real bat for the first time.

The next year, however, the Philadelphia Phillies were impressed enough by what their scouts told them that they put him on contract—only to have it voided because he was only 15 years old. One more year was enough: at the age of 16 he was given another contract, this time by the Texas Rangers, and Sosa landed in Florida (where the Texas Rangers have their rookie league affiliate), the following year, with no English but a big ambition to succeed.

He proved to be a player who thrived on challenge, shining the most when out to impress a new club, when his team is in contention for the pennant—or, later on, in his hand-to-hand duel with McGwire. His career always showed the existence of solid talent but featured some flashy initial spurts of achievement that were not maintained over time. Entering the major leagues in 1989, he made two hits against the New York Yankees on his first day, then slumped, was relegated to the minors again, and then traded by the Rangers to the Chicago White Sox.

With the White Sox, he had a good first season. He was the only player in the American League to reach double figures in doubles, triples, homers, and stolen bases. Unfortunately, he did not live up to that beginning the following year. The White Sox, too, sent him back to the minors and finally traded him in 1992, this time to the Chicago Cubs.

Looking back, Sosa acknowledged later what the critics, including some who called him "Sammy So-So," had been saying—that he had started out strong, but raw, and needed to become more of a team player. For the Cubs, Sosa delivered increasingly powerful performances, although he was sidelined for part of 1996 by injuries. He was named to the National League All-Star team in 1995, the year he also collected the Silver Slugger Award.

In 1997 Sosa entered the ranks of the highest-paid players with a $42.5 million, four-year contract. The following year he showed the world why he thought he was worth it.

A record for the highest number of home runs in one season—60—had been set by Babe Ruth in 1927. It had been broken only once, by Roger Maris in 1961. His record, 61, stood for 37 years. In 1998, as entranced baseball fans watched the figures relentlessly escalate, two men surpassed it and went far beyond: St. Louis Cardinals first baseman McGwire and Chicago Cubs outfielder Sosa. McGwire won the final count, with 70 homers. Sosa hit 66. When McGwire reached 62 and broke Maris's record in a game against Sosa's Cubs, Sosa went over and embraced him in the middle of the field.

Some observers complained that during the entire season, the media paid considerably more attention to McGwire than to Sosa. The latter was the first immigrant, the first Latino, and the first nonwhite (he is black) to hit 60 home runs in one season. But Sosa did not lack recognition entirely. When he hit his 62nd homer, fans gave him a six-minute standing ovation. In 1998, Sosa also became the National League's Most Valuable Player, having delivered his career-best batting average (.308) among other top statistics. And the Cubs reached the World Series playoffs.

The next year, Sosa set a record of his own when he became the first player ever to hit 60 home runs in two different seasons. Despite that lead, he was bested again by McGwire in the number of homers by year's end, with 65 against Sosa's total of 63.

Sosa is active in a number of charitable undertakings in the United States and in the Dominican Republic, including the Sammy Sosa Foundation and Sammy Claus, which provide support and gifts for underprivileged children, and Sammy Sundays, which gives tickets to baseball games to such children in Chicago.

Further Reading

Duncan, Patricia. *Sosa! Baseball's Home Run Hero.* New York: Simon and Schuster, 1998.

ESPN Internet Ventures. "Sammy Sosa." Available online. URL: http://espn.go.com/mlb/profiles/profile/4344.html. Downloaded October 11, 2000.

Gutman, Bill. *Sammy Sosa: A Biography.* New York: Pocket Books, 1998.

Muskat, Carrie. *Sammy Sosa: An Authorized Biography.* Childs, Md.: Mitchell Lane Publishers, 1999.

Schreiber, Lee. *Race for the Record: The Great Home Run Chase of 1998.* New York: HarperCollins, 1998.

✍ Soto, Gary (1952–) *writer*

Gary Soto is a prizewinning poet, essayist, and short story writer who among other accomplishments has given sharp, clear voice to the pain and dignity of impoverished Hispanic workers. Yet, in so doing, he has penned lines that address universal experiences, particularly the wonderment of childhood.

Soto was born in Fresno, California, on April 12, 1952. His grandparents were Mexican immigrants; his parents were farm laborers who did factory work when each year's picking season was over. When Gary was five years old, a roofing accident

Gary Soto *(Photo by Carolyn Soto)*

killed his father, Manuel. This loss reverberates in some of his poems, where there are allusions to the importance of living life fully every day.

Some years of manual labor, mainly as a gardener and car wash worker, left an indelible impression on Soto—particularly as regards the personality of his fellow workers, whom he would later evoke in his writing. Nobody in his household was a habitual reader. He entered Fresno City College to avoid being drafted for the Vietnam War and to escape a life in a factory. Originally, he set out to study geography, owing to a fascination with maps. But exposure to poetry opened a new world for him. He found he liked it so much that his grades skyrocketed. He switched to California State University and in 1974 graduated magna cum laude. Two years later Soto earned a master's degree from the University of California at Irvine and was recognized as Graduate Student of the Year in Humanities.

Following an extended journey to Mexico, he spent a semester as writer in residence at San Diego State University. In 1979 Soto began a career as a professor, first part time and later full time, at the University of California at Berkeley, complemented by other teaching positions at the University of Cincinnati in Ohio and at Wayne State University in Michigan. His poetry first appeared in print in 1974 and quickly found favor. In 1993 he gave up his university professorship and turned to writing full time.

While initially concentrating on poetry, Soto later also wrote fiction and essays, and later still became interested in writing for children and young adults. Race relations is another subject that has turned up in Soto's writings. He married a Japanese American, Carolyn Sadako Oda; they have a daughter called Mariko Heidi.

Soto's first collection of poems, *The Elements of San Joaquin* (1976), already established him both as a champion of the underprivileged—with emphasis on the overworked and underpaid Hispanic laborers of the U.S. West and Southwest, both in the fields and in violent urban surroundings—and as a skilled craftsman of language. "Soto's remembrances are as sharply defined and appealing as bright new coins," said one critic in later years, Alicia Fields of the *Bloomsbury Review.*

Other titles in Soto's output include *The Tale of Sunlight, Black Hair* and *Who Will Know Us?: New Poems; Living Up the Street: Narrative Recollections; Small Faces* and *Lesser Evils: Ten Quartets,* memoirs; *Baseball in April and Other Stories* and *Local News,* short stories, and *Too Many Tamales, Off and Running,* and *Petty Crimes,* children's and juvenile stories. *Novio Boy* (1997) and *Nerdlandia* (1999) are plays, the latter also the title of one of several short movies he has produced and directed.

Soto also is interested in helping other Mexican-American writers establish a reputation. To this end he edited a short story collection titled *Pieces of the Heart: New Chicano Fiction* (1993).

Among the many awards Soto has collected are the *Discovery/The Nation* award in 1975; International Poetry Forum award in 1976; Levinson award from *Poetry* magazine in 1984; American Book Award from the Before Columbus Foundation in 1985; National Book Award in 1995, and a Beatty Award from the California Library Association in 1996.

He also received fellowships from the Guggenheim Foundation (1979), the National Endowment for the Arts (1981 and 1991) and California Arts Council (1989).

Further Reading

Contemporary Authors. Detroit: Gale Research, 1999.

Nagel, Rob, and Sharon Rose, eds. *Hispanic American Biography.* New York: International Thomson Publishing, 1995.

Novas, Himilce. *The Hispanic 100.* New York: Citadel Press, 1995.

Riggs, Thomas, ed. *Contemporary Poets.* New York: St. James Press, 1996.

Soto & Friends. Available online. URL: http://www.garysoto.com. Downloaded October 11, 2000.

Tardiff, Joseph C., and Mpho Mabundo, eds. *Dictionary of Hispanic Biography.* Detroit: Gale Research, 1996.

❦ Suárez, Xavier L. (Xavier Louis Suárez)
(1949–) *government official*

Elected mayor of Miami in 1985, Xavier Louis Suárez was the first Cuban American to head the government of any large city in the United States.

Suárez was born in the province of Las Villas, Cuba, on May 21, 1949. In 1961, following the Castro takeover in Cuba, Suárez's parents left the island for the United States. He was 12 at the time.

The Suárezes settled in Washington, D.C. He went to school there and then continued his education at Villanova University in Villanova, Pennsylvania, where he studied engineering. In 1971, he graduated summa cum laude and first in his class, with a B.M.E. (bachelor of mechanical engineering) degree. Despite his aptitude for engineering, he next went to Harvard Law School and Harvard's John F. Kennedy School of Government. He obtained both his law and his master of public policy degrees in 1975.

Suárez then settled in Miami and went to work as an attorney. In the heavily Cuban district known as Little Havana, he was called "the people's lawyer," because of the large amount of legal work he did without charge for people unable to pay.

In 1985, Xavier Suárez ran successfully for mayor of what he described as the largest Spanish-speaking city in the United States. The people of Miami then reelected him to a succession of terms in office. Suárez ran as an independent candidate and thus was not affiliated with a political party.

Among his many activities, Suárez has taught law at Biscayne College, been chairman of the Miami Affirmative Action Commission, and been a board member of the Legal Services Corporation, appointed by the president of the United States. He has been chairman of the board of regents of Catholic University, a member of the nominating committee of the U.S. Conference of Mayors, and a member of the Governor's Task Force on Urban Growth Patterns. In 1994, he was one of the lawyers who filed suit against a then-new policy of returning illegal Cuban refugees to Cuba.

In 1997, Suárez won an election to regain the post of mayor of Miami but lost the job after a few months when a judge threw out the absentee ballots that had given him the winning margin, because of voter irregularities. He then organized a drive to demand a new election, but a court again ruled against him.

Telles, Raymond (1915–) *government official*

Raymond Telles became mayor of El Paso, Texas, in 1957. In the U.S. Southwest—an area with a large Mexican-American population—he was the first Chicano to become mayor of a big city since the previous century. In addition to this milestone, he has had distinguished military and diplomatic careers.

Telles was born in El Paso on September 5, 1915. He went to school there through college, attending the International Business College and Texas Western College (now the University of Texas at El Paso).

Entering government service as a Justice Department employee, he worked in accounting and administration, holding that job from 1934 to 1941.

When war broke out early the next year, he joined the air force as an enlisted man and worked his way up to major by the time he was discharged in 1947. With newfound self-confidence, Telles ran for county clerk in El Paso in 1948 and won. It was his first campaign. He was reelected in three subsequent elections but rejoined the air force during the Korean War, serving in 1951–52. This time he earned the rank of lieutenant colonel and a Bronze Star for bravery.

In 1957 he ran for mayor of El Paso. His opponent was an Anglo candidate, and it was a racially divisive campaign. El Paso's main business interests let it be clearly known that a Mexican American was not, in their view, qualified for the job. Telles brought out 90 percent of the Chicanos to vote. He also won Anglo votes, in part because of his war record, but also because his running mate, an Anglo, was a well-liked local radio and TV personality. Their ticket won. It was a turning point in Mexican-American political history.

Telles ran and governed as a conservative Democrat. His administration has been described as one of cautious reform. This won Telles the respect of the community, and in the next election, he ran unopposed.

In 1961, President John F. Kennedy appointed him ambassador to Costa Rica, where he served for six years. The appointment was in part due to service he had given Kennedy as a military aide. He had also been a military aide to two other presidents, Harry Truman and Dwight Eisenhower, during state visits to Mexico. The United States had also called on him to act as an aide to top Latin American officials visiting the United States.

President Lyndon Johnson turned to Telles to head the U.S. delegation of the joint United States-

Mexico Commission for Border Development and Friendship, and President Richard Nixon made him a member of the Equal Employment Opportunity Commission.

After his last stint in government office, Telles went to work as a business consultant.

In addition to a number of U.S. awards for public service, four Latin American countries—Brazil, Mexico, Nicaragua, and Peru—have given Telles decorations, and two Mexican presidents invited him to their inaugurations.

Further Reading

García, Mario T. *The Making of a Mexican American Mayor.* Austin, Tex.: Texas Western Press, 1998.
Meier, Matt S. *Mexican American Biographies.* Westport, Conn.: Greenwood Publishing Group, 1988.

☙ Thomas, John Peter "Piri" (1928–)
writer

Piri Thomas's novel *Down These Mean Streets* (1967) is one of the fundamental works of English-language Puerto Rican literature. A rehabilitated former convict and drug addict, Thomas turned his life's experiences into widely read and acclaimed books, and he has dedicated himself to helping others through prison and drug rehabilitation programs.

John Peter "Piri" Thomas was born in New York City on September 30, 1928. His parents had met and married in New York the previous year. Both had emigrated from Puerto Rico, though his father was originally from Cuba. After Thomas, there were six more children. The family lived in Spanish Harlem and considered themselves wholly Puerto Rican. In New York, Piri Thomas found that the deciding factor in human relations was skin color. The racism he experienced during the poverty of the Great Depression marked Thomas deeply. He even felt that he was experiencing discrimination within his own family. His father was much darker-skinned than his mother, and Piri was darker, like his father, while his siblings were lighter, like his mother. Thomas believed that his father preferred his "whiter" children.

In Thomas's literary work, these questions of racial and national identity and the confusions brought by the questions became central issues. A key scene in *Down These Mean Streets* comes when two Puerto Rican buddies are divided: One has to stand in a prison food line with the other "blacks," and the other with the "whites."

For Thomas, the issue became so crucial that when his family managed to move to a middle-class suburb—where they also encountered racism—he returned to his old neighborhood to live alone. He was 16 years old at the time and became attracted to street gang life.

He next visited the most diehard racist sections of the southern United States. Then he joined the merchant marine as a sailor. He continued to meet prejudice wherever he went.

After returning to New York in the late 1940s, Thomas became a heroin addict and drug dealer. He managed to quit his drug dependency but became a holdup man. In 1950, he was arrested, convicted, and sentenced to up to 15 years in prison. He served seven before being paroled. In jail, Thomas acquired a serious interest in writing. He briefly became a Black Muslim and then converted again after his release, becoming a Pentecostal Christian. As soon as he was released from prison, Thomas began counseling and rehabilitation activities, determined to help others from backgrounds like his.

His efforts to write an autobiographical novel attracted the attention of an editor, and in 1962 he obtained a foundation grant to complete the book. It was five more years before he finished it and saw it published by a major house as *Down These Mean Streets*. That same year, he also received a Lever Brothers community service award. Thomas's first novel had an electrifying effect in literary circles. It received the highest praise, except among some critics who feared that it might reinforce public stereotypes about marginal Puerto Rican existence.

Thomas found that he had become a public personality, a lecturer much in demand, and a spokesman on Puerto Rican affairs. A television documentary on Spanish Harlem which he cowrote and narrated, was titled *The World of Piri Thomas.* Other books based on his life followed: *Savior, Savior Hold My Hand* (1972), *Seven Long Times* (1974), and *Stories from El Barrio* (1978). Thomas also began to write essays and articles as well as plays that have been performed but not published. He also writes poetry, which he performs but does not publish.

He became interested in filmmaking and is now vice president of Third World Cinema Productions. He is also a trustee of the American Film Institute and of the Community Film Workshop Council.

Further Reading

Kanellos, Nicolás, ed. *Biographical Dictionary of Hispanic Literature in the United States.* Westport Conn.: Greenwood Press, 1989.

The Official Piri Thomas Website. Available online. URL: http://www.cheverote.com/piri.html. Downloaded October 11, 2000.

Tijerina, Reies López (1926–)
activist

Reies López Tijerina was one of the most militant and magnetic of the Latino leaders of the 1960s and 1970s, a period when the push for Hispanics' rights reached a peak. In that campaign, Tijerina earned the nickname of El Tigre—The Tiger. El Tigre scorned the idea of nonviolent protest, the style employed by farmworkers' leader César CHÁVEZ and others. Instead, Tijerina took his confrontations as far as he could. On one occasion, this led to a prison term of two years.

Tijerina was born on September 21, 1926, near Falls City, Texas, on the farmland where his parents were working as migrant harvesters. The life he knew as a child was one of backbreaking work and harsh exploitation, made worse by the widespread poverty of the Great Depression. He obtained what schooling he could, attending a score of different schools.

Reies inherited a strong religious bent from his mother. At the age of 17, he converted to a Protestant denomination called the Assembly of God. The following year, he enrolled in the group's Bible school in Ysleta, Texas, where he studied for three years.

Tijerina spent a decade as a traveling preacher in heavily Mexican-American areas along the frontier between the United States and Mexico. Gradually, confronted by the poverty and discrimination he saw wherever he went, these issues came to affect him more than religious ones. In 1950, he argued with the Assembly of God ministers, and the sect took away his credentials as a minister. Undeterred, Tijerina continued preaching for some time, though he was not attached to any church.

In 1955, he founded a small Mexican-American cooperative based on utopian ideals near Eloy, Arizona. He called it Valle de la Paz (Valley of Peace). The surrounding English-speaking communities harassed it endlessly, and the experiment failed after two years.

Tijerina developed a growing interest in the question of historical land grants in what is now the U.S. southwest. In the days when the area had been in the hands of Spain and later of Mexico, many tracts of land had been granted to the inhabitants, only to be lost after the United States took over the region. This loss of ancestral land, he concluded, lay at the root of Mexican Americans' woes and had to be reversed. Tijerina went to Mexico and stayed from 1958 to 1959 to delve into land-grant histories. The next year, he went to New Mexico to continue his research there. He also began to attract followers with his theories. In 1963, he set up an organization to pursue the matter, Alianza Federal de Mercedes (Federal Alliance of Land Grants). Later, its name was changed to Alianza Federal de Pueblos Libres (Federal Alliance of Free Towns).

Tijerina and his *aliancistas* (members of the alliance, who within a few years numbered 20,000) failed to interest the Mexican government, the U.S. government, or U.S. courts in their claims. In 1966, Tijerina took direct action instead. With 350 followers, he occupied an area within the Kit Carson National Forest in New Mexico. They called it the Republic of San Joaquín, after the name of an ancient land grant at that spot. When police and rangers approached, the *aliancistas* "arrested" two rangers for trespassing and gave them a "suspended sentence."

As a result, federal charges were brought against Tijerina and others. The incident also created division among those who were struggling for Latino civil rights. The more militant Hispanics were delighted and encouraged by Tijerina's actions. The more moderate recoiled.

In 1967, after the arrest of several *aliancistas* who were planning to hold a meeting, Tijerina and an armed group attacked the courthouse in the town of Tierra Amarilla, New Mexico. They freed their arrested comrades, tried to make a citizen's arrest of the district attorney, and took two hostages during their getaway. They were chased by 600 troops and police in tanks and helicopters before being captured.

Free on bail while the cases went through the courts, Tijerina participated in several rallies and events of the civil-rights struggle, including the Poor People's March on Washington, D.C., in 1968.

In 1969, he tried another takeover of the Kit Carson National Forest. In this episode, he was charged with pointing a gun at officers who allegedly threatened his wife. He also tried to make citizen's arrests of various officials, including Warren Burger, who was then-U.S. president Richard Nixon's nominee for chief justice of the Supreme Court.

Tijerina, defending himself in court, obtained a verdict of not guilty in the Tierra Amarilla case, based on his right to make a citizen's arrest, but he did get a two-year sentence for the national forest takeover. The case reached the Supreme Court (by then Burger had been confirmed as chief justice), which declined to overturn the sentence. Tijerina served time in prison in 1970 and 1971, including seven months in solitary confinement. After his release, he was forbidden to hold office in the Alianza for a further five years.

In later years, he advocated nonviolent methods. The general tone of the civil rights movement across the United States had become less combative by then, so his change suited the times. Even so, he found his support dwindling as newer figures took his place. In 1999, a ceremony was held at the University of New Mexico to honor Tijerina when he contributed his papers to the university library's Center for Southwest Research.

Further Reading

Blawis, Patricia Bell. *Tijerina and the Land Grants.* New York: International Publishers, 1971.

Nabokov, Peter. *Tijerina and the Courthouse Raid.* Albuquerque: University of New Mexico Press, 1969.

Tijerina, Reies Lopez. *They Called Me "King Tiger": My Struggle for the Land and Our Rights.* Houston: Arte Público Press, 2000.

Tizol, Juan (1900–1984) *jazzman*

Puerto Rican Juan Tizol composed two of the classic melodies in the history of jazz, *Caravan* and *Perdido.* He was bandleader Duke Ellington's right-hand man.

Born in the Puerto Rican capital, San Juan, on January 22, 1900, Tizol came from a family that was active in business, law, and music. Of the musicians in the family, the best known until Juan came along was his uncle Manuel Tizol, director of the San Juan Symphony Orchestra and of the San Juan municipal band. Under his uncle's guidance, Juan received a traditional musical education and joined the symphony orchestra as a valve trombonist, choosing the more common instrument of the time. The valve trombone is played by pressing valves, like other brass instruments. With the slide trombone, now more familiar, the sound is controlled instead by sliding lengths of brass tubing. But even though the slide trombone gained in popularity, Tizol remained a valve trombonist all his working life.

Tizol went to Washington, D.C., in 1920 with a Puerto Rican band that had won a contract to play at the Howard Theatre on the black vaudeville circuit. He remained there, performing not only at the theater but also, occasionally, with various jazz bands in Washington and in New York. To supplement his income as a musician, he opened a delicatessen in Washington, D.C.

In 1929 jazz giant Edward Kennedy "Duke" Ellington hired Tizol to play trombone in his orchestra in New York. For more than 30 years, Tizol alternated between the Ellington and the Harry James bands: he was with Ellington from 1929 to 1944, with James until 1951, with Ellington from 1951 to 1953, with James from 1954 to 1959, and with Ellington again from 1960 to 1961. Tizol also performed for brief stints with other jazz orchestras and as a studio musician, while shuttling back and forth between his two main employers.

Ellington in particular found that he could rely on Tizol's fine musicianship. Tizol seldom played trombone solos, yet he was highly valued as a rock-solid ingredient of the overall orchestral sound. He was also adept at other musical work. He would write out parts for each player, based on musical ideas that

Ellington expressed in general terms. When Ellington was away, Tizol led orchestra rehearsals.

Tizol's major contribution to jazz history was his musical compositions: he wrote many tunes for the orchestra, often with a distinctively Latin and/or exotic tinge. He was thus instrumental in occasionally bringing those sounds to jazz in the 1930s.

Caravan was written by Tizol and sold to Ellington's business manager for a flat fee of $25 in the standard practice of the time. The tune, as arranged by Ellington, was recorded in 1937 and became an Ellington signature. Established as a jazz perennial, *Caravan* is often referred to as a Tizol-Ellington composition or even simply as an Ellington tune. The same fate befell other works by Tizol, such as *Perdido* (meaning "Lost"), *Pyramid, Moonlight Fiesta, Lost in Meditation, Bakiff, Azure,* and *Admiration.* Ellington, Tizol declared, "took credit for everything I did." However, once *Caravan* became a runaway success—equaled by few others in Ellington's career—Tizol did receive a share of the royalties. Legally, he was no longer entitled to them because of the terms of the original sale.

After 1961, Tizol retired to Los Angeles and later to Las Vegas, where he spent the remainder of his life. He emerged from retirement only once, in 1964, recording the album *Big Bands!* with the jazzman Louis Bellson. He died 20 years later, in 1984.

Further Reading

Collier, James Lincoln. *Duke Ellington.* New York: Oxford University Press, 1987.

Kernfeld, Barry, ed. *The New Grove Dictionary of Jazz.* London: Macmillan Press, Ltd., 1988.

Kinkle, Roger D. *The Complete Encyclopedia of Popular Music and Jazz 1900–1974.* New Rochelle, N.Y.: Arlington House, 1974.

Space Age Pop Music. "Juan Tizol." Available online. URL: http://home.earthlink.net/~spaceage-pop/tizol.htm. Downloaded October 11, 2000.

❧ Treviño, Lee (Lee Buck Treviño)
(1939–) *golfer*

Lee Buck Treviño is credited not only with a remarkable array of victories on the golf course, but also with helping turn golf from an exclusive sport of rich Anglo people to one open to everyone. He is well known for making generous contributions to charity.

Treviño won at least one major tournament a year for 14 years in a row. He won the U.S. Open, the British Open, and Canadian Open all in the same year, 1971—in fact, within the same month.

Later, when competing on the senior circuit, he became the first senior golfer with bigger earnings in a year than that year's leader of the regular (under-50) golfing tour.

According to *Golf Magazine's Encyclopedia of Golf,* Treviño has done "everything but walk across the water." He even bounced back to the golfing circuit after being hit by lightning while on the green. He is called "Super Mex" by an enthusiastic legion of fans known as "Lee's Fleas."

Treviño was born in the outskirts of Dallas on December 1, 1939. He was raised by his mother, who was a maid, and his grandfather, who had arrived in the United States from Mexico and worked as a gravedigger. He lived in a house without water or electricity. He has joked that the shack was "rent-free, and we even had a lake behind the house." But most important was the golf course alongside. Lee's entire life revolved around the game. As a child, he would pick up balls that landed off the course and return them in exchange for some pocket money. After finishing seventh grade, he had to give up his schooling to go to work full time, caddying and helping to maintain the greens. In his spare time, Treviño taught himself the game. He was only six when he fashioned a two-hole course in his yard. He began to play with an old golf club that he had found and shortened to fit his size.

The result of his self-teaching was a swing that has been described as "highly unorthodox" or, less kindly, as "a horribly flat baseball swing." However, it does put the ball where Treviño wants it to go.

Even when Treviño joined the marines (he served for four years), he found himself playing golf. He was stationed in Okinawa, and the officers there enjoyed playing with the skilled, cheerful enlisted man. Treviño was promoted to sergeant for, as he puts it, "swinging my clubs with the colonels."

After his Marine Corps years, Treviño went back to Texas and took jobs as a golf club pro. He then began to play on the professional golf circuit, uncertainly for a few years and then with a meteoric rise. In 1967, a year when he had trouble finding $20 for the application to enter the U.S. Open, he finished fifth and was named Golf Rookie of the Year. The following year, he not only won the U.S. Open but was the first golfer in history to play every one of the four rounds of the tournament under par.

He was the Professional Golf Association's (PGA) biggest moneymaker in 1970. Treviño also established himself as a crowd pleaser, with a steady flow of jokes and comments and a ready grin even under high pressure.

In 1971, he won the U.S. Open again, the Canadian and British Opens, plus three other events (he was to win the British Open again in the following year, and the Canadian Open in 1977 and 1979). He received many honors in 1971: PGA Player of the Year, *Sports Illustrated* Sportsman of the Year, *Golf Magazine* Player of the Year, Associated Press Male Athlete of the Year, Gold Tee Award, Vardon Trophy, Hickock Belt, and British Broadcasting Corporation International Sports Personality of the Year.

In 1975, three golfers, including Treviño, were hit by a bolt of lightning while playing together in a tournament. They survived but sustained injuries. In Treviño's case, he was left with a severe back problem, requiring operations and other treatment. It seriously affected his game. Nevertheless, he was soon winning trophies again.

Between 1978 and 1981, Treviño was inducted into the Texas Golf Hall of Fame, American Golf Hall of Fame, and World Golf Hall of Fame. He retired from professional golf in 1985 with career earnings of more than $3 million.

In 1989, he joined the senior tour and by the middle of the following decade had added another $5 million. As always, he shared his earnings with diverse philanthropic organizations.

He accumulated more than a score of senior tour victories to add to the 30 he racked up on the regular tour and was named Senior Tour Player of the Year in 1990, 1992, and 1994. Treviño has also been a commentator for NBC.

Among other career highlights are wins in both the PGA Championship and the World Series of Golf in 1974, the Canadian PGA in 1979, the Tournament of Champions in 1981, and the PGA Championship again in 1984. He was a member of the U.S. Ryder Cup team six times, including one stint as captain in 1985. As of 2000, he ranked 40th in scoring average on the Senior PGA tour.

Further Reading

Jackson, Robert B. *"Supremex."* New York: Henry Z. Walck, 1973.

Emery, David, ed. *Who's Who in International Golf.* New York: Facts On File, 1983.

Martínez, Al. *Rising Voices: Profiles of Hispano-American Lives.* New York: New American Library, 1974.

PGA Tour. "Lee Trevino Bio, Stats, and Results." Available online. URL: http://www.pgatour.com/players/intro/2213.html. Downloaded October 11, 2000.

Treviño, Lee. *They Call Me Super Mex.* New York: Random House, 1982.

———. *The Snake in the Sandtrap and Other Misadventures on the Golf Tour.* New York: Holt, Rinehart, and Winston, 1985.

Van Riper, Guernsey. *Golfing Greats: Two Top Pros.* Champaign, Ill.: Garrard Publishing Co., 1975.

U

Unanue, Joseph A. (Joseph Andrew Unanue) (1925–) *businessperson*

Joseph A. Unanue took his father's food company, Goya Foods, and turned it into the biggest Hispanic-owned business in the United States and a textbook example of a well-organized, carefully led family corporation. By the end of the 20th century the net worth of the family was estimated at close to $500 million, while the company's annual sales were almost $700 million. "When Goya cooks up an expansion, you know it's a recipe for economic success," declared New York state governor George Pataki in 1998 when the company announced construction of a multimillion-dollar distribution center in Long Island, New York. The strategy and methods that transformed the company from a small local supplier of ethnic food products into a nationwide brand are studied at many business schools.

Unanue's Spanish-born father, Prudencio, arrived in the United States in 1915, after first having gone to Puerto Rico in 1904. His first business venture involved importing Spanish foods from Spain, but the advent of the Spanish Civil War made it impossible for him to continue. Undeterred, in 1936 he and his wife Carolina founded Goya Foods in New York to import the flavors of home for immigrants from Caribbean nations, adding products from Spain again as soon as possible.

The company, which is headquartered in Secaucus, New Jersey, has more than a dozen food distribution and manufacturing facilities across the United States, the Caribbean, and Spain, with a total of over 2,000 employees. It continues entirely in family hands; second- and third-generation Unanues head its diverse operations and locations.

At the top is Prudencio's son Joseph, born in New York on March 13, 1925, and holder, like each of his three brothers, of a mechanical engineering degree, which he obtained at the Catholic University of America in Washington, D.C. Joseph's brother Frank is president of Goya de Puerto Rico, Inc.; another brother died, and the fourth sold his holdings to Joseph and Frank, who between them own half of the company. The remaining half is divided among tens of other Unanues.

Joseph A. Unanue joined the business after U.S. Army service in World War II. For more than a quarter of a century, he labored in its diverse divisions until inheriting the company presidency in 1976 on the death of his father.

Unanue's business strategy has been to expand catering to the tastes of Mexican immigrants and their descendants—which differ from those of Puerto Ricans, Cubans, Dominicans, and others from the Caribbean area—and also by marketing to nonethnic buyers—for instance, health-conscious consumers interested in low-cholesterol bean products.

Unanue has carried out this growth—which has led his firm to enter the Forbes 500 ranking of companies, reaching post 353 in 1999—at a careful pace. As *Forbes* noted in 1984, "the Unanues are not ambitious hotshots with something personal to prove. No big risks for them. These are solid, long-term builders who move in an orderly, conservative rhythm."

Joseph Unanue is an active civic leader both in the United States and in Puerto Rico, in a tradition of service inaugurated by Prudencio and Carolina Unanue. Scores of community and other organizations receive his backing, from the Metropolitan and Guggenheim museums and Boys Club of America to the Ballet Hispánico and the Puerto Rican Day Parade.

In recognition of this service he has been the recipient of a large number of honors, including the Ellis Island Medal of Honor (1994), a knighthood in the Sovereign Order of the Knights of Malta, the National Hispanic Achievement Award, and two Man of the Year citations by the National Conference of Christians and Jews.

Further Reading

Tardiff, Joseph C., and Mpho Mabundo, eds. *Dictionary of Hispanic Biography.* Detroit: Gale Research, 1996.

Valdez, José (1925?–1945) *soldier*

A private in the U.S. Army during World War II José F. Valdez gallantly covered a retreat by his comrades during an attack by Nazi forces. He was the key factor in turning back the enemy attack, despite a mortal wound.

Valdez was born about 1925 in Governador, New Mexico, and joined the army in Pleasant Grove, Utah. His heroic act took place in France during the last year of the war. It entered the annals of military history through the posthumous award of a Congressional Medal of Honor.

In late January 1945 near Rosenkrantz in France, an advance by U.S. soldiers was met by a strong Nazi counterattack. Private First Class Valdez was involved in the action as a member of Company B, 7th Infantry, 3rd Infantry Division. His six-man patrol was posted approximately 500 yards to the front of the main body of U.S. troops.

A German tank made the first attempt at attack in their area, which was close to a woodland. Valdez saw the tank when it was 75 yards away. He directed volleys of fire at it with his automatic rifle. The tank, possibly uncertain of the size of the forces facing it, retreated.

The next bid was made by a group of three Nazi soldiers, carefully reconnoitering while trying to re-

main unseen. They arrived within 30 yards of Valdez's position when the two sides saw each other. Valdez faced them and in a vicious exchange of gunfire managed to kill all three.

At this point the enemy abandoned small, exploratory moves and launched an attack against Valdez and his comrades with more than 200 men. The Nazis advanced with guns firing and attempted to surround the half-dozen GIs. The soldier leading Valdez's patrol decided that there was no option but to retreat. Without hesitation, Valdez offered to cover the others "despite the terrible odds," as the Medal of Honor citation notes.

In the face of the concentrated enemy firepower on their position, the escape toward the U.S. army lines proved extremely risky, but the protection offered by Valdez's covering fire allowed all five to reach their goal alive. Three of them were wounded, and the other two were unscathed.

However, while covering their retreat, Valdez was pierced right through his midbody by an enemy bullet; this only briefly interrupted him. Realizing that the lives of the others depended on him, he somehow ignored the wound and resumed firing. When all five others had retreated, Valdez used his field telephone to call for artillery barrages against the enemy. By remaining at his exposed position, he was able to direct the aim of the U.S. artillerymen precisely.

It was not until he saw the Germans finally retreat under the accurate pounding that Valdez left his post. Unable to walk, he crawled back, only to die of his injuries.

Further Reading

The Committee on Veterans' Affairs, United States Senate. *Medal of Honor Recipients 1863–1978.* Washington, D.C.: U.S. Government Printing Office, 1979.

Valdez, Luis M. (Luis Miguel Valdez)

(1940–   ) *theatrical impresario*

A major force in the Hispanic theater, Luis M. Valdez founded and runs an organization called El Teatro Campesino (The Peasant Theater). Through it, he has done more than anybody else to make the theater, at a grassroots level, a tool for social and political change for Chicanos. He is also the writer and director of the major movie hit *La Bamba,* along with his many other accomplishments in literature and show business. His career ranges from work among the poor and powerless to commercially successful undertakings within mainstream U.S. culture.

Throughout his diverse career runs a unifying strand—his struggle to gain recognition and respect for Hispanics in U.S. life. Referring to the Indian and Spanish roots of the Chicano presence in the United States, Valdez has emphasized, "We did not, in fact, come to the United States at all. The United States came to us."

Luis Valdez (not related to soldier José VALDEZ) was born on June 26, 1940, in Delano, California. This town in the heart of migrant farmworker territory was later chosen by César CHÁVEZ for the launching of his campaign to organize the farmworkers. Valdez participated in that campaign through the medium of the theater.

Like other children of migrant laborers, Luis and his nine brothers and sisters had scattershot schooling. He was working in the fields when he was still a first-grader. Eventually, he graduated from high school in San Jose and won a scholarship to San Jose State University, from which he graduated with a B.A. degree in English in 1964. The year before, he had written a play, *The Shrunken Head of Pancho Villa,* that was produced by the university's drama department.

From college Valdez moved to the San Francisco Mime Troupe. A highly political group of actors during a time of rising opposition to the Vietnam War and of other 1960s causes, the experience gave Valdez a background in techniques of popular theater that he would further develop himself.

The following year, 1965, Valdez returned to his native Delano to work with César Chávez; Valdez's contribution to the unionization struggle was to help teach farmworkers about their rights and their possibilities if they united. To do this, he founded El Teatro Campesino and reached out to the laborers with simple, short plays. He created a new genre, or form, that he called *actos* (acts, sketches, events). Because of his work, grassroots theater became a favorite medium of expression for Chicanos in the drive for greater self-awareness and civil rights. Eventually, he launched a network of Hispanic drama groups in many states.

Valdez has been hailed not only as an innovator but as an organizer, creating structures to help others attain higher achievements. With time, El Teatro Campesino expanded its interests beyond the farm unionization struggle. In consequence, Valdez moved it from Delano to other locations. Since 1969, it has remained in San Juan Bautista, California, as a production enterprise. However, its stage company frequently tours the United States and Europe.

Valdez has spent considerable time teaching theater on campuses, including Fresno State College and the University of California at Berkeley, Santa Cruz, and Irvine. The plays he has written and produced include *La Quinta Temporada* (*The Fifth Season,* 1966); *Huelguistas* (*Strikers,* 1970), *Dark Root of a Scream* (1971), *Zoot Suit* (1978), and *I Don't Have to Show You No Stinking Badges* (1986). In 1969, Valdez produced and wrote the screenplay for a filmed version of Rodolfo "Corky" GONZALES's epic poem, *I Am Joaquín.* A number of his plays have been shown on television.

Zoot Suit proved to be especially successful in California. Based on incidents of violent persecution of Mexican Americans in California at the time of

World War II, it ran for a year in Los Angeles. It failed on Broadway, however, where no Chicano had ever written and produced a play before. In 1982, Valdez made a film version of *Zoot Suit,* which he wrote and directed.

The biography of Ritchie VALENS, a Mexican-American rock idol, was the basis of Valdez's *La Bamba* (1987). The movie was released as an experiment that yielded unexpectedly good results. There were three versions in the United States: one in English, one in Spanish, and one in English with Spanish subtitles. *La Bamba* was the biggest movie box-office moneymaker in the United States at the time of its release. Consequently, it was seen a breakthrough for Hispanics in U.S. culture, and its soundtrack, created by the Los Angeles Chicano rock band Los Lobos (The Wolves), became a hit in its own right.

Valdez acted in such films as *Which Way Is Up?* (1978) and coedited a 1972 book, *Aztlán: An Anthology of Mexican American Literature.* He performed in the movie *Flight in the Fields* (1997). Recent projects include a film on César Chávez for Warner Brothers.

Recognition for Valdez's work has included a Rockefeller Foundation fellowship, an Obie Award (1968), an Emmy Award (1973), three Los Angeles Drama Critics Awards between 1969 and 1978, a San Francisco Bay Critics Circle Best Musical Award, and a Golden Globe nomination.

Further Reading

Keller, Gary D, ed. *Chicano Cinema: Research, Reviews and Resources.* Tempe, Ariz.: Bilingual Review Press, 1988.

Lomelí, Francisco A., and Carl R. Shirley, eds. *Dictionary of Literary Biography: Chicano Writers, First Series.* Detroit: Gale Research, Inc., 1989.

❧ Valens, Ritchie (Richard Valenzuela)

(1941–1959) *singer*

The first Mexican American to become a pop music idol, Ritchie Valens was killed in a plane crash when he was only 17 years old. Almost three decades after his death, he was the subject of a popular movie biography, *La Bamba.*

Born in the town of Pacoima, California, on May 13, 1941, Richard Valenzuela was in high school when he launched his career as a rock musician, using the name Ritchie Valens. Valens grew up in the heyday of rock 'n' roll. He wrote a song, "Come On, Let's Go," which a music company executive liked and had him record. In 1958 it became one of the 50 best-selling records in the country.

Next, he recorded "Donna," a song he had written for Donna Ludwig, his high school girlfriend. Her father objected to her relationship with the darker-skinned Mexican American Valens. "Donna" became the number-two record hit in the United States. On the "B" side of that single, Valens recorded "La Bamba," his version of a Mexican folk song. It also was a success (number 22 on the charts), although it was somewhat obscured at the time by the attention given to "Donna."

Valens began to tour the United States as a rock 'n' roll legend in the making. At the beginning of 1959, he was on tour with rockers Buddy Holly, J. P. "Big Bopper" Richardson, and a backup group of musicians. Holly chartered a small airplane to go from one show in Iowa to another in North Dakota.

The weather was bad and the temperature freezing. The plane only had room for four passengers plus the crew, and competition to get a seat was strong because the others would have to travel on the tour bus. Valens got his seat by flipping a coin with one of Holly's band members. The plane crashed in a cornfield right after takeoff. All on board were killed. Valens had been three months short of his 18th birthday.

In *La Bamba,* a biographical film, Ritchie Valens was played by actor Lou Diamond Phillips (who is part Hispanic, Scottish, Irish, Hawaiian, Filipino, and Cherokee). Created by director Luis VALDEZ, the film earned $55 million in U.S. and Canadian ticket sales. Because of the movie, a new generation embraced not only the figure of Valens but also the title song. The soundtrack used music by the Los Lobos group as well as by guitarist Carlos SANTANA, among others. Los Lobos's version of "La Bamba," made for the movie, went on to become the number-one hit in the United States, as did the soundtrack album. No other song sung entirely in Spanish had reached that slot before.

Further Reading

Mendheim, Beverly. *Ritchie Valens: The First Latin Rocker.* Tempe, Ariz.: Bilingual Review Press, 1987.

Simon, Tim. "Ritchie Valens Page." Available online. URL:http://www.tsimon.com/valens.htm. Downloaded October 11, 2000.

Stambler, Irwin. *The Encyclopedia of Pop, Rock and Soul.* New York: St. Martin's Press, 1989.

Valenzuela, Fernando (1960–)
baseball player

Fernando Valenzuela is considered to be one of the best pitchers in baseball history. A Mexican who spoke no English when he appeared on the United States scene, his performance was greeted with an enthusiasm that was soon dubbed "Fernandomania." In 1981, he was the first rookie to receive the Cy Young Award; in 1983, he became the first baseball player to win a million dollars in arbitration; in 1986, he established a record of 44.1 innings in a row without an earned run.

Fernando Valenzuela was born to a family of farmworkers in Navajoa, Sonora state, Mexico, on November 1, 1960, the youngest of his parents' 12 children. He developed a roly-poly appearance that has been described as "Ruthian," a reference to baseball legend George Herman "Babe" Ruth. As in Ruth's case, Valenzuela's plump physique disguised his unusual playing skills. Although he is also good at bat, Valenzuela's specialty is pitching a left-handed screwball. This reverse-curve ball proved so hard to hit that, echoing an old hit song title "Hernando's Hideaway," it was termed "Fernando's fadeaway."

One of his elder brothers was also a baseball player, and Fernando emulated him by dropping out of high school to play baseball full time. He quickly distinguished himself in the Mexican League. In 1979 he was signed by the Los Angeles Dodgers, where he learned to throw his screwball. In 1981, he had his first full major league season. He tied the record for rookies by achieving eight shutouts, with seven victories in a row, and led the league with 180 strikeouts. The culmination of his rookie year came when he helped the Dodgers win the World Series.

All at once, he was National League Rookie Player of the Year, National League Player of the Year, *The Sporting News* Major League Player of the Year, and National Writers' Association of America National League Rookie Player of the Year, as well as bagging the Cy Young Award.

Valenzuela was named to the National League All-Star team five times. In 7.2 All-Star innings, his earned run average (ERA) was 0.00, with nine strikeouts. In 1986, he had five consecutive All-Star strikeouts, tying the league record set by Carl Hubbell. He won a Gold Glove that year, and a Silver Bat was awarded to him in 1983. In a 13-year career spent mainly with the Dodgers and then with the California Angels and Baltimore Orioles, he was 149–128 with a 3.45 ERA.

In 1994, Valenzuela left the United States to pitch for the Mexican League's Jalisco Cowboys, with whom he was 10–3. That same year, he returned to the United States to play for the Philadelphia Phillies.

In 2000, when http://www.SportsYA.com, an interactive Spanish-language sports site, carried out a vote among Internet users for the best Hispanic baseball players of the 20th century, Valenzuela easily came in first in the category of left-handed starting pitchers.

Further Reading

Gloeckner, Carolyn. *Fernando Valenzuela.* Mankato, Minn.: Crestwood House, 1985.

Littwin, Mike. *Fernando!* New York: Bantam, 1981.

———. *Fernando Valenzuela, the Screwball Artist.* Chicago: Children's Press, 1983.

Vallbona, Rima de (Rima Gretel Rothe) (1931–) *writer*

A distinguished literary figure, Rima de Vallbona was born in San José, Costa Rica, on March 15, 1931, the fourth of six children. She has lived, written, and taught in Texas since the 1960s. Though both her parents were born in Costa Rica, her paternal grandfather immigrated to Costa Rica from Germany, hence her German middle and last names, *Gretel* and *Rothe*.

Rothe's father made his living in the real estate business, but he had strong literary and artistic interests. He gave his daughter the name of Rima the bird girl, a character in *Green Mansions* by Argentine-British author W. H. Hudson.

During World War II, many Germans and descendants of Germans—including Rothe's father—were interned in camps in Costa Rica. In 1940, her father died in a camp, from natural causes. (According to one version, he was murdered.) Vallbona's mother became mentally disturbed following her husband's death. This interfered with Rothe's upbringing and almost forced her to abandon school. However, she managed to stay and graduated in 1948.

She had been studying French in Costa Rica, and—always a bright student—she won a scholarship to continue her studies in Paris. She obtained her certification as a French teacher from the University of Paris in 1953. In Paris, she also met her future husband, a Spaniard, Carlos de Vallbona. She moved to Spain, began her teaching career there, and attended the University of Salamanca, one of the world's oldest (founded in 1218). She earned a diploma in Spanish philology (language study) from that school in 1954. Later, she returned to her native country and, again while working as a teacher, studied at the University of Costa Rica, receiving her M.A. degree in 1962.

She then moved to the United States to join her fiancé. They married and settled in Houston. Rima de Vallbona joined the faculty of the University of St. Thomas in that city in 1964. This began a long association with St. Thomas, where she was made a full professor in 1978. She has also been a visiting professor at the University of Houston and at Rice University in that same city. In 1981, she received a D.M.L. degree from Middlebury College in Vermont.

The volume of Vallbona's writing has not been large; however, she has been highly praised for its literary quality and sensitivity. Her work centers on women's and children's experiences. Religiosity is another of her themes.

Her novels and collections of short stories include, among others, *Noche en Vela* (*Sleepless Night*, 1968), *Polvo del Camino* (*Dust from the Road*, 1971), *La Salamandra Rosada* (*The Pink Salamander*, 1979, which also encompasses poems), *Las Sombras Que Perseguimos* (*The Shadows We Chase*, 1983), *Cosecha de Pecadores* (*Harvest of Sinners*, 1989), and *Mundo, Demonio y Mujer* (*World, Demon and Woman*, 1991).

Vallbona is also known for her research in Latin American literature. In her early days in the United States, she had been told by a professor that this field was "unworthy of such detailed investigation."

She has been an executive or member of the Cultural Arts Council of Houston, the board of contributing editors of *The Americas Review,* and several other institutions and publications. The author has won U.S., Latin American, and Spanish literary awards that include the Jorge Luis Borges Short Story Prize (1977), Latin American Novel Prize (1978), and SCOLAS Literary Prize (1982).

In 1999, the University of St. Thomas staged a three-day symposium in honor of Vallbona.

Further Reading

Kanellos, Nicolás, ed. *Biographical Dictionary of Hispanic Literature in the United States.* Westport, Conn.: Greenwood Press, 1989.

Vallejo, Mariano G. (Mariano Guadalupe Vallejo) (1808–1890)
government official

When California still belonged to Mexico, General Mariano G. Vallejo was one of the wealthiest landowners there and one of the territory's most powerful officials. He became a leader of the faction that worked for California's entry into the United States, but when California became a U.S. state, Vallejo was repaid with a short, brutal imprisonment. After his release, he obtained some small measure of power, but he never regained his land. The city of Vallejo, California, is named after him. At his invitation, it was briefly the capital of the state.

Mariano Vallejo came from an influential family in Mexico's remote territory of Upper (Alta) California at the time when Mexico was ruled by Spain and was called New Spain. He was born in the territory's capital, Monterey, on July 7, 1808.

When he was 10 years old, his hometown was successfully attacked by an Argentine expedition led by Hipólito BOUCHARD. The goal was to claim independence from Spain. The incident is said to have helped shape his thinking in later years, including his decision to enter public life. He believed that in this way he could help determine the destiny of his land.

Vallejo became a military cadet at the age of 15, serving at Monterey's *presidio* (fort). By that time, Mexico had already become an independent country.

It was an era when it was common to combine political and military positions. When he was 19 years old and a young officer, he was also elected as a Californian legislator. In the same year, 1827, he received a new military post, the presidio in San Francisco. He rose to become its commander four years later, at age 23. In 1829, he saw military action, quelling a mutiny by the Indians at the San José mission.

His roles multiplied in the years that followed. The Mexican government in 1833 began to secularize the Indian missions. This meant putting them under civilian instead of religious administration. It also meant that the Indians at the missions were free to leave if they wished, and most of them did. During this transition, Vallejo was appointed to run two missions, San Francisco Solano and San Rafael Arcángel. In the same year, he rose to military chief of the northern half of the province.

He was also appointed commander of a force sent to inspect a Russian base not far from San Francisco: Rossiya, or Fort Ross. Vallejo decided that the Russians there were hunters who posed no threat save to sea otters in the area, which they wiped out. Nevertheless, for added security, Vallejo increased Mexican colonization of the area, creating new settlements.

In 1834 he became a member of the national congress, but he did not pursue this position and remained in California. While in California, he acquired large tracts of land as they became open to private development. The secularization of the missions had opened mission land to private ownership, and most of the land that had belonged to the San Francisco Solano Mission in the Sonoma Valley was bought by Vallejo. He made his home there.

As he increased his wealth—soon holding as much as 250,000 acres of land—Vallejo also participated in political uprisings. His aim, like that of other wealthy "Californios," was to secure local govern-

ments that would defend his interests against the faraway national government in Mexico City. These wealthy landowners saw the national government as uninterested and unhelpful.

In 1836, one such political rebellion succeeded in making Vallejo's nephew California's governor. This nephew was Juan Bautista Alvarado, who had led the revolt. Two years later, Governor Alvarado appointed Vallejo overall military commander of California. In the 1840s, however, the general and the governor began to disagree about U.S. immigration into California. The dispute came as more and more Anglos were arriving. Vallejo assisted the newcomers in establishing themselves, believing that Californios would fare better as part of the United States than as part of Mexico, but despite these views, Vallejo was one of the victims of the Bear Flag Revolt of 1846. Anglo settlers and the U.S. troops that arrived with them had been tolerated. These Anglos had presented themselves as geographical and scientific explorers but then rebelled against Mexican rule. They turned on all Mexicans indiscriminately. They confiscated land, looted, and committed murders.

In the aftermath of this revolt, Vallejo and a brother were arrested and imprisoned at Sutter's Fort. They were held for two months under harsh and humiliating conditions before they were finally freed.

When Mexico lost the war with the United States and lands including California had been turned over to the United States, Vallejo's standing improved. He helped draft the state's constitution in 1849 and was elected one of the new state's first senators in 1850. He also worked for the U.S. government as an Indian agent.

In 1851, Vallejo offered to give land to California for the state to set up its capital. The state government agreed. Vallejo, the town created on his donated tract, was California's capital briefly in 1852 and 1853.

Land disputes would plague Mariano Vallejo and occupy much of his time and energy for the rest of his life. But he did find time to write a history of California, as well as to pursue ranching and several other projects. One of his projects was a farsighted plan for a railroad to link California with Mexico City.

In 1855, a court declared Vallejo's land titles from the pre-U.S. takeover to be valid. Despite this, he was unable to keep the land. Eventually, all but 280 acres were taken from him. Vallejo pursued a succession of lawsuits to try to regain or hold onto his land, but these proved to be not only useless but ruinous. He died in 1890.

Further Reading

McKittick, Myrtle M. *Vallejo, Son of California.* Portland, Ore.: Binford & Mort, 1944.

Webster's American Military Biographies. Springfield, Mass.: Merriam, 1978.

The West Film Project and Weta. "People in the West: Mariano Vallejo." Available online. URL: http://www.pbs.org/weta/thewest/wpgs400/w4vallej.htm. Downloaded October 11, 2000.

❧ Vargas, M. Sando, Jr. (Jay Vargas)
(1940–) *soldier*

Marine captain (later major) Jay Vargas overcame severe wounds to rally his troops to victory in a three-day battle during the Vietnam War. He also carried several of his wounded men to safety. The U.S. Congress awarded him the Medal of Honor, calling his actions "conspicuous gallantry and intrepidity at the risk of his life above and beyond the call of duty." Vargas made a highly unorthodox request—that his award not be written and recorded in military records under his real name. The president granted his request, and so Vargas's medal was dedicated to his recently deceased mother, Italian-born immigrant Maria Teresa Sandini and inscribed to M. Sando Vargas, Jr.

Jay Vargas was born on July 29, 1940, in Winslow, Arizona. His ancestry on his father's side is Mexican. He joined the Marine Corps in Winslow.

One of the most significant experiences of his early military life took place in 1964. As a second lieutenant serving in Okinawa, Vargas was extremely impressed when he witnessed a meeting of five winners of the Congressional Medal of Honor. Before that incident, he had never met a Medal of Honor recipient. He could not have known that in 1968 he would join their ranks.

Vargas became a captain and commanded Company G, 2nd Battalion, 4th Marines, 9th Marine Amphibious Brigade. The unit was involved along with others in a vicious battle for the village of Dai Do in South Vietnam. Another Medal of Honor was earned during this battle, also by a captain, James Livingston.

The fight against hostile troops entrenched in the village resulted in great losses before surviving enemy troops withdrew from the area. It was a prolonged, back-and-forth battle. The U.S. Marines took, lost, and regained the position several times. The village itself was completely destroyed.

Vargas was wounded on each of the three days of the battle. Nevertheless, he refused medical assistance and continued to lead the fight, even when, in one hit, a piece of shrapnel became embedded under his scalp. He was repeatedly responsible for organizing the U.S. troops, including some from other units, into defense perimeters. He also maintained their morale and efficiency throughout the battle. Vargas's Medal of Honor citation notes his "expert leadership" in maneuvering troops.

For the U.S. troops the worst part of the battle came during a night when they were forced to entrench themselves in the village cemetery following a withering enemy counterattack. Vargas and his men had to improvise foxholes by yanking corpses from new graves.

That night, Vargas received radio communication from top U.S. officers, including the overall U.S. commander in South Vietnam, General William Westmoreland. These officers called to lend support to a group of men whom they feared were virtually lost. Yet, at dawn, the soldiers had not only held out, but were also able to stage a counterblow.

Vargas ignored the pain of his mounting injuries and carried a half-dozen wounded men, one by one, across exposed ground to safer positions where they could receive medical care. Vargas not only had to carry his comrades but also to fight his way ahead in close combat. He is credited with killing eight of the enemy in this way.

Vargas also had luck, in addition to pluck and unwavering determination, on his side. One of the men he rescued was the colonel commanding the 2nd Battalion; as Vargas was carrying him on his back, he was confronted by an enemy straight ahead. In the split second that the soldier aimed his rifle, Vargas stumbled. His weapon, a pistol, went off wildly. The bullet bounced off a wall and hit the enemy soldier.

Further Reading

The editors of the Boston Publishing Company. *Above and Beyond: A History of the Medal of Honor From the Civil War to Vietnam.* Boston, Mass.: 1985.

The Committee on Veterans' Affairs, United States Senate. *Medal of Honor Recipients 1863–1978.* Washington, D.C.: U.S. Government Printing Office, 1979.

U.S. Army Center of Military History. "AFIS Hispanic Heritage—Medal of Honor Winners—Vargas." Available online. URL: http://www. defenselink.mil/specials/hispanic/vargas.html. Downloaded October 11, 2000.

❦ Vázquez de Coronado, Francisco
(1510–1554) *explorer*

In 1540–42, Francisco Vázquez de Coronado led one of the epic feats of exploration in world history: He covered much of the ground of what today are the states of Arizona, New Mexico, Texas, Oklahoma, and Kansas. A detachment from this expedition discovered the Grand Canyon. Meanwhile Vázquez de Coronado and his main group were the first white men to encounter the Great Plains, their herds of bison, and the nomadic Indian nations who lived off the bison.

Some historical evidence indicates that the first birth of a European in what became United States territory took place during this trek. The mother was one of the women on the expedition, which had set out not only to explore but also to start colonies in the area.

Vázquez de Coronado was born around 1510 in the city of Salamanca, Spain. In 1535, he traveled to New Spain (Mexico) with Antonio de Mendoza, whom the king of Spain had appointed as the first viceroy of that land.

In the Americas, Vázquez de Coronado's career advanced rapidly for two reasons: first, he proved adept at quashing rebellions, be they among Indian serfs or among black slaves; second, he married Doña Beatriz de Estrada, the granddaughter of King Ferdinand the Catholic—her father, an illegitimate son of Ferdinand, was one of the most powerful men in New Spain.

In 1538, at the approximate age of 28, Vázquez de Coronado received a major appointment from Mendoza: governor of New Galicia, the northernmost province of New Spain at the time. Vázquez de Coronado sent a small group to explore the uncharted lands to the north of New Galicia. Nothing was known of that territory except what was recorded by the explorer Alvar NÚÑEZ CABEZA DE VACA, who in 1536 had been found there after wandering, lost, with three companions, including the Moroccan slave Esteban. Esteban was made one of Vázquez de Coronado's advance men. He was killed by the Zuñi Indians at a place called Hawikuh. This was one of the permanent Indian villages that the Spaniards came to call *pueblos.*

Another scout, Friar Marcos de Niza, returned with a fantasy-filled tale: that Hawikuh (which he had not actually entered) was in reality Cíbola, one of a legendary group of Seven Cities of Gold that the conquistadores were eager to find. Viceroy de Mendoza consequently set an exploration program in motion and put Vázquez de Coronado at its head.

The main body of this expedition left New Galicia in 1540. It included some 300 Europeans and as many as 1,000 Indians who reportedly volunteered for the trip. They set off with thousands of head of cattle, sheep, and pigs.

From the participants' point of view, the trek was a vast failure. None of the Spanish expeditions were ever to discover a single wealthy city anywhere in America north of Mexico. The pueblos were found to be very poor communities, and the teepee villages of the Great Plains Indians were even poorer.

After reaching Hawikuh, the first disappointment, Vázquez de Coronado sent one group northwest; they would discover the Grand Canyon. He himself went east and then northeast, first conquering other pueblos and then continuing further into the continent's heartland.

Impatient at the slow pace of the expedition, advancing with its animals and other supplies, Vázquez de Coronado traveled ahead with a smaller group. In addition to Cíbola, he was searching for Quivira, another fabled land of fabulous riches. But nowhere on this trip did the Spaniards even find it worth it to set up a colony. The fruits of the expedition were only a greatly expanded knowledge of the geography and of the peoples of the area. It is possible that some members of the expedition reached as far as present-day Nebraska.

Vázquez de Coronado left a bitter legacy among the Pueblo Indians he encountered. He was ruthless when they attempted to protect themselves from the Spaniards. He did however manage to bring most of his party, including the Indian auxiliaries, back alive, which was a highly unusual feat for expeditions of the time. They returned to Mexico in 1542 after a 4,000-mile round-trip trek.

In an official investigation that followed the expedition, Vázquez de Coronado was charged with cruelty toward the Indians he had encountered, but he was found not guilty.

He returned to governing New Galicia and was later charged with violence against the Indians there. This time, he was found guilty. He lost the post and had to pay a fine of 600 gold pesos.

Vázquez de Coronado next obtained a seat in the administrative council of Mexico City, which he held until his death in 1554.

Further Reading

Bolton, Herbert E. *Coronado, Knight of Pueblos and Plains.* Albuquerque: University of New Mexico Press, 1964.

Jensen, Malcolm. *Francisco Coronado.* New York: Watts, 1974.

Pedro de Castañeda de Nagera. *The Journey of Coronado.* Ann Arbor, Mich.: University Microfilms, 1966.

Stein, Conrad. *Francisco de Coronado.* Chicago: Children's Press, 1992.

Syme, Ronald. *Francisco Coronado and the Seven Cities of Gold.* New York: Morrow, 1965.

The West Film Project and Weta. "The Journey of Coronado." Available online. URL: http://www.pbs.org/weta/thewest/wpages/wpgs610/coronal.htm. Downloaded October 11, 2000.

Velásquez, William Cárdenas
("Willie") (1944–1988) *activist*

Willie Velásquez created and ran an unparalleled drive to give Hispanics in the United States greater political power through voting. He spearheaded a process that convinced millions to vote and thousands to run for office. He also filed scores of successful lawsuits to reshape election districts more fairly. He thus changed the face of U.S. politics for Hispanics, though he never held political office.

Velásquez was born on May 9, 1944, in San Antonio, Texas, the son of a butcher. While San Antonio would remain his home base for life, his work made him well known in U.S. political circles and in the Mexican-American community simply as "Willie."

He graduated from college in 1966 and plunged into Hispanic civil rights activism. He began graduate studies in 1968 but dropped out in order to work full time as an activist. Still, Velásquez retained a lifelong interest in intellectual study and had a particular fondness for classical Greek writings. He was noted for being as likely to quote Aristotle as a contemporary politician in order to make his point.

After leaving graduate school, Velásquez participated in an effort, led by civil rights pioneer César CHÁVEZ, to unionize farmworkers in Texas. He also helped found, or participated in the early operation of, a number of Hispanic civil rights organizations, including the Mexican American Legal Defense and Education Fund (MALDEF) and the Southwest Council of La Raza (the race), which later became the National Council of La Raza.

However, in time, Velásquez began to believe that many of the existing organizations, particularly La Raza, were too quixotic. He felt that they were more concerned with dramatically establishing a position than with obtaining practical results, and Velásquez was interested in the outcome. He thought that the key to results for Hispanics was voting power.

If many Hispanic Americans did not vote, he decided, it was not because of apathy or ignorance but because of a feeling that they could not win. This could change if the numbers of voters grew large enough. To help achieve this, he founded the Southwest Voter Registration Education Project in 1974.

Known as SVREP, or more often just as Southwest Voter, the new group employed a variety of tactics in its drive to empower Hispanics. One was to keep activities at grassroots level, maintaining close contact with individuals and with small community organizations. Another was to encourage people not only to vote but also to enter the political process as candidates. A third tactic was to conduct and then publish serious research into the voting patterns and the voting potential of Hispanics and the potential of Hispanic candidates.

In his work, Velásquez cooperated with groups such as MALDEF to bring lawsuits to redraw many election districts. These districts were often found to have been shaped in a way that diluted Hispanic voting power. An example was the joining of a heavily Hispanic downtown city area with largely Anglo suburbs to create a single voting district.

In the 14 years that Velásquez led SVREP, it was credited with spectacular results: Hispanic voter registration in the United States rose from 3 million to 5 million; half of that increase—a jump of 1 million—was directly attributed to Southwest Voter. Hispanics went from having the lowest voter-registration rate among U.S. minorities to the highest, and the number of Hispanics in political office doubled to 3,200. A large part of this increase took place in Texas, where Southwest Voter had concentrated its initial efforts. The group gradually expanded, aiming particularly at California, where the existing voting structure was found to be even more biased against Chicanos than in Texas.

Under Velásquez's guidance, SVREP launched hundreds of redistricting lawsuits and won 85 of them. These achievements came despite strong resistance; in Rock Springs, Texas, for example, he was told to stop his voter-registration drive and leave town by sunset.

The director of Mexican-American studies at the University of Texas, Rodolfo de la Garza, declared Velásquez to be "the single most important political actor since César Chávez, and in terms of representational politics, the most important ever. Henry CISNEROS (who was elected mayor of San Antonio in 1981) owes Willie in a direct way. All these guys (Hispanic politicians) owe Willie."

In 1981, on a sabbatical, Velásquez became a university lecturer, teaching at the Institute of Politics of Harvard University's John F. Kennedy School of Public Affairs.

In 1988, Michael Dukakis asked Velásquez to be his deputy campaign manager when he ran for the Democratic Party nomination for president of the United States. At that time, Velásquez was diagnosed with cancer. With the doctors believing that he had six months to a year to live, Velásquez accepted Dukakis's offer. However, he died three weeks later.

Velázquez, Nydia Margarita
(1953–) *government official*

Nydia Velázquez in 1992 became the first Puerto Rican woman to win a seat in the U.S. Congress, representing a New York City district.

A veteran of voter registration drives among Hispanics, like the Atrévete (Dare To Do It) crusade launched in 1987, Velázquez is also a tireless campaigner for the rights and welfare of all minorities.

Nydia Velázquez *(Congressional Hispanic Caucus)*

She is proud to point out that New York's Chinese community named her the biggest defender of immigrant groups in general.

Her rise to congresswoman began in the sugarcane fields of Puerto Rico. Nydia Margarita Velázquez is one of nine children of a cane cutter, butcher, and local politician from the Puerto Rican town of Yabucoa. She was born there on March 23, 1953, and grew up in a small house alongside the cane fields.

She was the first in her family to finish high school, and she did so by the age of 15. She then went immediately to the University of Puerto Rico in Río Piedras to earn a degree in political science at 21, graduating magna cum laude. On a scholarship, she continued her studies at New York University and obtained a master's degree two years later, in 1976, again in the field of political science.

Velázquez began her career as an educator. First, she taught school in Puerto Rico; then, after earning her master's degree in New York, she was a lecturer in political science at the University of Puerto Rico in Humacao; finally, she was a professor in the department of Black and Puerto Rican studies at the City University of New York's Hunter College. (This back-and-forth movement between Puerto Rico and New York established a pattern that she continued when she entered politics.)

Velázquez began to put her political science education into practice in 1983. She had a commitment to improve the lives of the poor and others on the margins of society—a sense of obligation that she attributes to her father's example. As assistant to a former congressman who sought her advice on immigration matters, she testified about immigration before Congress. After that, she served on the New York City Council. In 1986, she headed Puerto Rico's Migration Division Office, within the island's Department of Labor and Human Resources. Three years later, she was back in New York, this time as head of the Department of Puerto Rican Community Affairs in the United States.

In 1991, Velázquez created an AIDS research and education campaign in the Hispanic community, Hispanos Unidos Contra el SIDA (Hispanics United Against AIDS).

The 1990 census led to the redrawing of many election districts to reflect the increased presence of minorities among the population. This helped Velázquez in a hard-fought but successful campaign to be elected to the U.S. House of Representatives in 1992. In Congress, she continues battling for progressive causes. In 1998, Velázquez received 84 percent of the vote for return to Congress. Velázquez was reelected again in 2000.

Further Reading

U.S. House of Representatives. "Congresswoman Nydia M. Velázquez's Home Page." Available online. URL: http://www.house.gov/velazquez. Downloaded October 11, 2000.

Telgen, Diane, and Jim Kamp, eds. *Notable Hispanic American Women.* Detroit: Gale Research, Inc., 1993.

❧ Vélez, Lupe (María Guadalupe Vélez de Villalobos) (1908–1944) *actress*

Lupe Vélez provided the perfect example of the motion picture industry's "fiery Latina" character. She also personified the part in real life, becoming celebrated for relationships with such actors as Gary Cooper, Ronald Colman, John Gilbert, and Johnny Weissmuller.

María Guadalupe Vélez de Villalobos was born on July 18, 1908, in San Luis Potosí, Mexico. She received a convent education—according to some sources, in San Antonio, Texas. She is also believed to have known only a few words of English when she made her way to Hollywood as a nightclub chorus dancer.

In 1926, she was discovered by a movie industry talent scout and offered parts in film shorts. One of these was *Sailors Beware* (1927), with the comedians Laurel and Hardy. Her first feature film was *The Gaucho* (also 1927). She played the female lead opposite Douglas Fairbanks Sr. in the title role. With this successful movie, Vélez came into permanent demand to play hot-blooded women. Vélez was billed as the Mexican spitfire, and the characters she was given to play were always as ready to scratch and kick as to kiss.

Shortly after her arrival in Hollywood, movies began to incorporate soundtracks. Her voice became scratchy when excited, and she retained a strong Hispanic accent and tended to create funny mix-ups with words. Rather than rule out a movie career in the talkies, these factors pushed her in the direction of comedy. In comedy roles, her mistakes with words were often written purposefully into the scripts.

In 1929, she played opposite Gary Cooper in *The Wolf Song* and she and Cooper began a real-life romance. This delighted the movie gossip magazines, which later followed every one in a long series of Vélez romances with Hollywood leading men.

She married Johnny Weissmuller, the famous screen Tarzan. The union soon became a rocky one—the couple tended to quarrel noisily in public,

reinforcing Vélez's reputation as a temperamental Hispanic—and ended five years later.

In the 1930s and 1940s, she also made a handful of motion pictures in Britain and in Mexico. Her movie appearances include *Tiger Rose* (1929), *Half-Naked Truth* (1932), *Hot Pepper* (1933), *Strictly Dynamite* (1934), *Gypsy Melody* (1936), and *The Girl From Mexico* (1939). During World War II, Lupe Vélez appeared in a series of comedies built around the Mexican spitfire character: *Mexican Spitfire, Mexican Spitfire at Sea, Mexican Spitfire Sees a Ghost,* and *Mexican Spitfire's Blessed Event.*

The actress was not play-acting in her stormy romantic liaisons. The fact that Cooper had eventually

Lupe Vélez struggling with Leo Carrillo in *Honolulu Lu* *(Cabrera Archive)*

chosen not to marry her hurt her deeply. In 1944, a similar situation with an obscure French actor—worsened by the fact that she was pregnant—led her to commit suicide by taking an overdose of sleeping pills.

Further Reading

Conner, Floyd. *Lupe Vélez and Her Lovers.* New York: Barricade Books, 1993.
MacIntyre, Diane, and The Silent Majority. "Lupe Vélez." Available online. URL: http://www.mdle.com/ClassicFilms/FeaturedStar/perfor81.htm
Woll, Allen L. *The Latin Image in American Film.* Los Angeles: UCLA Latin American Center Publications, 1980.

❧ Villa-Komaroff, Lydia (Lydia Villa)
(1947–) *scientist*

A notable molecular biologist, working on the biochemistry of organic molecules, on genes and on cells, Lydia Villa-Komaroff has carried out major research in such fields as brain development, as well as having been one of the first scientists to work in the area of cloning. During her career she has perceived little discrimination as a Hispanic but has faced considerable hurdles as a woman delving into fields previously dominated by men. They have not kept her from making award-earning progress in those areas.

A descendant of Mexican immigrants, Lydia Villa was born in Las Vegas, New Mexico, on August 7, 1947. Her paternal grandfather is reputed to have been saved from execution during the Mexican Revolution by the fact that the revolutionary leader Pancho Villa discovered they had the same last name, and told him to "have many sons" to carry it.

The future scientist, who was raised in Santa Fe, New Mexico, was the eldest of six children. Both her parents were teachers—the first college graduates in each of their families—and they fully supported her early-blooming ambition to lead a life in science. One of Villa-Komaroff's earliest memories is of her mother reading to her children from an encyclopedia, which her father told Lydia contained everything she wanted to know.

Lydia Villa-Komaroff *(Courtesy of Jack Demuth Photography)*

The young girl's talent became noticeable early. The National Science Foundation awarded Villa-Komaroff a scholarship for college-level laboratory work in Texas during summer vacations in high school.

In praising her parents for their support, Villa-Komaroff stresses their acceptance of her going to college in faraway Seattle, since Mexican-American families, especially in those days, feared the dispersal of their children, more so in the case of women.

Villa-Komaroff went to the University of Washington in Seattle in 1965. Her intention was to study chemistry, but a university counselor ruled that chemistry was not a field for women. Chemistry's loss was biology's gain, because she decided to take biology as a major instead. In 1967 she switched to Goucher College in Towson, Maryland, where she graduated with an A.B. degree three years later, the year she also married Anthony Komaroff, a doctor. Her move to the other coast of the United States was due to her having been engaged to Komaroff when his own studies took him to Washington, D.C. Villa had set her sights on Johns Hopkins University, also in Maryland, but at that time it would not take women students, referring them instead to its sister institution, Goucher.

After their marriage, the couple moved to Boston, where Lydia continued her studies at the Massachusetts Institute of Technology (MIT). At MIT she found she was able to ignore the attitude of some sexists who objected to women scientists, and she received a Ph.D. in cell biology in 1975, having done advanced research on the virus that causes polio. Only two Mexican-American women before her had ever become doctors in scientific fields.

Next came three years of postdoctoral work at Harvard. Entering the controversial area of taking genes from one species and inserting them into another in the search for medical cures for humans, she announced a major discovery in 1978—that bacteria could be manipulated so as to cause them to manufacture insulin, a human hormone that is essential in the treatment of diabetes. The research had been banned between 1976 and 1977 out of safety fears.

Villa-Komaroff then went to work at the University of Massachusetts Medical School, moving on to Harvard in 1985. During these years, in addition to her teaching duties, she carried out far-reaching research on brain cells and related matters. She also taught and conducted research at the Children's Hospital in Boston.

Villa-Komaroff was the subject of a TV documentary, *DNA Detective,* broadcast in 1995. During the course of her career, Villa-Komaroff has patented several discoveries.

In 1996, Northwestern University named her vice president and put her in charge of all its research and graduate studies.

Villa-Komaroff received the Helen Hay Whitney Foundation fellowship in 1975–78, the Goucher College Alumnae Achievement Award in 1981, and the Hispanic Engineer National Achievement Award in 1992, among other honors.

Further Reading

Ambrose, Susan, et al. *Journeys of Women in Science and Engineering: No Universal Constraints.* Philadelphia: Temple University Press, 1997.

Hall, Stephen. *Invisible Frontiers: The Race to Synthesize a Human Gene.* New York: Atlantic Monthly Press, 1987.

American Men and Women of Science. New York: R. R. Bowker, 1999.

St. John Jetty. *Hispanic Scientists.* Mankato, Minn.: Capstone Press, 1996.

Villa-Komaroff, Lydia. "SACNAS Biography." Available online. URL: http://www.sacnas.org/bio/vilkomid.html. Downloaded October 11, 2000.

✺ Villalpando, Catalina Vásquez "Cathi" (1940–) *government official*

"Cathi" Villalpando has held high office in the Republican Party and in the U.S. government, including the post of treasurer of the United States. She has also had a successful business career.

Villalpando was born in San Marcos, Texas, on April 1, 1940. Her father, who had emigrated from Mexico, was a hardware store clerk. After the birth of Cathi, five other children followed.

Following her schooling in her hometown, Villalpando took courses at the Austin College of Business, Southern Methodist University in Dallas, and three other colleges. She began to take a succession of jobs in private business, beginning as a clerk in a jewelry store and ending as vice president of an oil company in Dallas and senior vice president of a communications company in Atlanta.

Villalpando changed her party affiliation from Democrat to Republican in 1969. This came when she held a staff job at the Republican Party offices in Austin. In the years that followed, she invested her time, energy, and talent in party work. In turn, this led to the vice presidency of the Republican National Hispanic Assembly of Texas.

From 1969 to 1979, Villalpando was assistant to the regional director of the Community Services Administration. In 1979, she helped set up VP Promotions, a private company to lend assistance to small businesses owned by minorities.

In the 1980s, she worked first for George H. W. Bush and then for Ronald Reagan in their presidential campaigns. When Reagan became president, Villalpando went to Washington to participate in the inauguration and transition. Reagan appointed her special assistant for Hispanic affairs in the Executive Office of the President, Public Liaison Office, in 1983. Five years later, George H. W. Bush, who had succeeded Reagan as president, appointed Villalpando treasurer of the United States.

Cathi Villalpando is the holder of special achievement awards from several government agencies. She has also been appointed to the U.S. Commission on Civil Rights.

Further Reading

Meier, Matt S. *Mexican American Biographies.* Westport, Conn.: Greenwood Publishing Group, 1988.

Villegas, Ysmael (ca. 1925–1945)
soldier

An army staff sergeant during World War II, Ysmael Villegas carried out a relentless one-man charge against a row of Japanese foxholes in the Philippines. He took them out, one by one, in the face of withering enemy fire. Though this heroic action cost him his life—leading to a posthumous decoration with the Congressional Medal of Honor—it provided an example and took his troops to victory in that battle.

Villegas was born about 1925 in Casa Blanca, California, and joined the United States Army in the same town. He had reached the rank of staff sergeant when his unit—Company F, 127th Infantry, 32nd Infantry Division—took part in what would be his last battle.

The hilltop on the Villa Verde Trail on the island of Luzon in the Philippines in March 1945, toward the end of the war, was full of enemy foxholes that stood in the way of Company F's advance. Villegas's men were raked by gunfire from Japanese soldiers both in the foxholes and in a series of interconnected caves.

To move among his troops, to organize the attack, and to raise the morale of the unit, Villegas disregarded a hail of fire, exploding grenades, and demolition-charge explosions. "Inspired by his gallantry, his men pressed forward to the crest of the hill," reads the citation accompanying his Medal of Honor.

The fire from the Japanese foxholes continued. Under these circumstances, Villegas on his own initiative made his frontal, running charge. As bullets filled the air around him, Villegas rushed the first foxhole and shot and killed the soldier inside. Without stopping, he ran to the next and did the same again. Fire was concentrating ever more fiercely on his movements, but he charged the third foxhole and again killed the occupant.

Still unscathed despite the sheets of gunfire from the entrenched Japanese troops, Villegas reached a fourth foxhole and killed a fourth enemy soldier. Displaying what is officially recorded in U.S. military history as "heroism and indomitable fighting spirit," the Mexican-American staff sergeant dashed forward again and conquered his fifth foxhole.

Then he ran ahead toward the sixth; this time, he never reached it. His troops, however, now surged forward to follow his example and, Villegas's citation concludes, "swept the enemy from the field."

Further Reading

The Committee on Veterans' Affairs, United States Senate. *Medal of Honor Recipients 1863–1978.* Washington, D.C.: U.S. Government Printing Office, 1979.

W

Welch, Raquel (Jo-Raquel Tejada)
(1940–) actress

In the 1960s, Raquel Welch became the reigning beauty queen of Hollywood, a title held in the 1940s by Rita HAYWORTH and in the 1950s by Marilyn Monroe. With this honor, she found that she had a lifetime battle on her hands, namely, to demonstrate that beauty does not mean brainlessness or the inability to act. Gradually proving herself, particularly in comedy roles, Welch later gave acclaimed performances on stage and in television dramas. She is also a nightclub singer and has written a successful fitness and beauty book.

Welch was the name of her first husband. Her Hispanic ancestry has become better known over time. In 1982, in talking about her role as an Indian squaw in a TV epic, *The Legend of Walks Far Woman,* Welch explained that she had a personal interest in Native Americans, pointing out that her father was Bolivian and that she has some Indian ancestry. On another occasion she approached the editor of a Spanish-language movie magazine in New York and told him that she feels Hispanic and regrets not speaking Spanish better.

Though born in Chicago, on September 5, 1940, Jo-Raquel Tejada grew up in La Jolla, California. Her father, Armando Tejada, had immigrated from Bolivia to the United States to pursue a career as an aeronautical engineer. Her mother, Josephine Hall, who was born in the United States of British ancestry, met Tejada when she took college courses in the Spanish language.

When Welch was two, the family moved to California. By the age of 14, her good looks encouraged her to enter beauty contests, which she promptly won.

Soon after finishing high school, she married a former schoolmate, James Welch. They had two children, including a daughter, Tahnee, who later also began an acting career. By the age of 21, however, Raquel Welch was divorced.

She made her living as a model, TV weather girl, and cocktail waitress, first in Dallas and then, as of 1963, in Hollywood. Her training for a career in show business included seven years of ballet lessons and drama studies at San Diego State College.

In 1964 she obtained a small role in an Elvis Presley movie, *Roustabout.* Three other small parts followed and, in 1966, her first leading role in *Fantastic Voyage.*

The same year saw the release of *One Million Years BC,* a film that gave her her second leading role.

Raquel Welch *(Cabrera Archive)*

It became her stepping-stone to sudden fame. Nobody took its story of prehistoric people and monsters seriously; however, photos and posters of Raquel Welch wearing a light, furry costume that was billed as history's first bikini flooded the world.

Other movies followed, several of them filmed in Britain: *Bandolero!* (1968), *100 Rifles* (1969), *Myra Breckinridge* (1970), *The Three Musketeers* (1973), *The Four Musketeers (The Revenge of Milady)* (1974), *The Wild Party* (1975), and *The Prince and the Pauper* (1976). She won a best actress Golden Globe award for her performance in *The Three Musketeers.*

Outspoken in her quest for better roles, her relationship with Hollywood studios was turbulent. In 1980, she was dropped from the cast of a movie being made by MGM; Welch considered the firing unjustified, and sued the studio for breach of contract. She won the lawsuit and collected huge sums in damages. However, movie offers were scarce after that.

In 1982, she was asked to replace the leading lady, actress Lauren Bacall, in a Broadway musical, *Woman of the Year.* Welch achieved a personal tri-umph in this play, receiving the highest praise from the critics. In 1990, she actually became Woman of the Year in real life, receiving that award from the Los Angeles Hispanic Women's Council.

On television, in addition to her role in *The Legend of Walks Far Woman,* she was so effective playing the unglamorous TV-movie role of a terminally ill woman in *Right to Die* (1987) that she was awarded a Golden Globe nomination.

A book written by the actress, *The Raquel Welch Total Beauty and Fitness Program* (1984), met with success. She also put out two exercise videos, *Raquel: Lose 10 Lbs in 3 Weeks* and *Body and Mind: Total Relaxation and Stress Relief Program.*

As a singer, Welch has performed in her own act in Las Vegas. Welch's recent film work has included *Chairman of the Board* and *What I Did for Love,* both in 1998.

Further Reading

Mr. Showbiz. "Mr. Showbiz Celebrities: Raquel Welch Biography." Available online. URL: http://mrshowbiz.go.com/people/raquelwelch. Downloaded October 10, 2000.

Haining, Peter. *Raquel Welch: Sex Symbol to Superstar.* New York: St. Martin's Press, 1984.

❧ Williams, William Carlos
(1883–1963) *writer*

William Carlos Williams is considered to be one of the greatest poets in U.S. literature. He is known not only for his own body of work but also for the influence he exerted on later generations. He won a Pulitzer Prize (in 1963, posthumously—he died that same year) for his book *Pictures from Brueghel and Other Poems.*

The son of a British father and a Puerto Rican mother, Williams lived virtually his entire life in the town of Rutherford, New Jersey. He worked there as a doctor and wrote about what he saw there and in the neighboring city of Paterson. Through his writing, he turned life in those apparently ordinary towns into a vital reference point in modern poetical imagery. In so doing, he proved to all U.S. writers that it was not necessary to be in Paris, as many thought in the first half of the century, or New York to be in the forefront of literature.

He was born in Rutherford on September 17, 1883. His English immigrant father, a businessman, saw to it that he obtained the best possible education, both in the United States and in Europe, where Williams traveled in the early 1900s.

The biggest influence on his future as a man of letters, however, was exerted by his mother. A cultivated woman who had studied art in Paris, she had Dutch, French, and Jewish as well as Spanish ancestry. Her full name was Raquel Hélène Rose Hoheb, but she was always called Elena, the Spanish equivalent of the French Hélène, and she spoke Spanish to her children.

Unlike her son, Elena tended to chafe at the cultural level of Rutherford. She welcomed house guests from the world over, who aroused the future writer's intellectual curiosity. Elena Hoheb Williams also lied about her age and was found, after her death in 1949, to have lived to be 110 years old, rather than the 101 she admitted to.

William Carlos Williams graduated as an M.D. from the University of Pennsylvania in 1906. He then did graduate work in pediatric medicine in Leipzig, Germany, but by 1910, he was back in Rutherford, the town where he died 53 years later.

At the University of Pennsylvania, Williams met Ezra Pound. The great poet influenced him, and Williams is often grouped with Pound as one of the key creators of modern U.S. poetry.

Williams did almost all of his writing in English, although he did turn to Spanish for one of his first distinctive works, *Al Que Quiere!* (*To Him Who Wants It!*, 1917).

Williams's goal in poetry was to capture concrete images of daily existence. He used everyday speech and broke with all rigid poetical forms. He made the form of the poem follow what he wanted to say, rather than shape what he wanted to say into an established pattern of rhythms, stresses, and rhymes. He was also known as an extremely artful craftsman, whose every word and pause was chosen with the greatest care, for maximum concision and effect.

Williams's masterpiece was *Paterson,* a long poem in five books that appeared separately between 1946 and 1958. They were reprinted together in 1963. In this epic work, he employs the device of imagining the city as a living person, lying down alongside the Passaic River.

Other books of poetry by William Carlos Williams include *Spring and All* (1923), *An Early Martyr and Other Poems* (1935), *The Collected Later Poems* (1950, revised in 1963), *The Desert Music and Other Poems* (1954), and *Journey to Love* (1955).

Williams is also regarded as a major writer of prose, both fiction and nonfiction. Among his novels are *A Voyage to Pagany* (1928), *White Mule* (1937), *In the Money: White Mule, Part II* (1940), and *The Build-Up* (1952).

Collections of short stories include *The Knife of the Times and Other Stories* (1932) and *Life Along the Passaic River* (1938). He also wrote plays, including *A Dream of Love* (1948) and *Tituba's Children* (1950).

In the American Grain (1925), a collection of essays about various significant figures in the history of the Americas, is Williams's most important work of nonfiction. Also of note is *Selected Essays* (1954).

In addition to the Pulitzer Prize, Williams was awarded the *Dial* Award in 1926 and the National Institute and American Academy of Arts and Letters Gold Medal in 1963; between these were the National Book Award, Library of Congress and American Academy of Poets fellowships, Bollingen Prize, and Brandeis University Creative Arts Medal.

In 1952, he was appointed Consultant in Poetry to the Library of Congress. However, political pressure related to the era's anticommunist hysteria kept him from serving in this prestigious post. Though never thought to have been a communist, Williams was suspected of harboring radical political thoughts. This suspicion was reinforced by his having published a poetry book called *The Pink Church* in 1949. Politically speaking, *pink* was a poorly timed word choice in that the word itself was associated with sympathy to communism.

Further Reading

Asher, Levi. "William Carlos Williams." Available online. URL: http://www.charm.net/~brooklyn/People/WilliamCarlosWilliams. Downloaded October 10, 2000.

Breslin, James E. *William Carlos Williams: An American Artist.* New York: Oxford University Press, 1970.

Guimond, James. *The Art of William Carlos Williams: A Discovery and Possession of America.* Urbana, Ill.: University of Illinois Press, 1968.

Mariani, Paul. *William Carlos Williams: A New World Naked.* New York: McGraw-Hill, 1981.

Mazzara, Jerome. *William Carlos Williams.* Ithaca, N.Y.: Cornell University Press, 1973.

Weaver, Mike. *William Carlos Williams.* Cambridge, England: Cambridge University Press, 1971.

Whitaker, Thomas R. *William Carlos Williams.* New York: Twayne, 1968.

Whittemore, Reed. *William Carlos Williams: Poet From Jersey.* Boston: Houghton Mifflin, 1975.

Williams, William Carlos. *The Autobiography of William Carlos Williams.* New York: Random House, 1951.

Z

Zavala, Lorenzo de (1788–1836)
government official

One of the leaders of the Texan secession from Mexico, Lorenzo de Zavala was vice president of the Republic of Texas, chosen by unanimous vote. Though he was a wealthy landowner, Zavala was, from earliest youth, a liberal thinker who repeatedly paid for this position with imprisonment and exile.

His desire for Texas independence was driven by opposition to the authoritarian, centralist government of Mexico at the time. Headed by the military ruler Antonio López de Santa Anna, this government had trampled on the liberal and federalist Mexican constitution of 1824. Zavala not only defended that constitution, but he had helped to draft it.

Born on October 3, 1788, Lorenzo de Zavala belonged to a prosperous family in the Mexican province of Yucatán. Originally, he planned to become a priest, and he later studied to be a doctor. However, although Zavala did practice medicine during some periods, he devoted most of his life to politics. He was also a historian of Mexican politics.

His first political office, in 1811, was as secretary of the city council of Yucatán's capital, Mérida, the town where he was born. Three years later, he was elected to the parliament in Madrid, but his liberal ideas led to three years of imprisonment in Mexico before he even had the chance to leave for Spain. He got a second chance, though. This time he successfully served in Spain's parliament during a brief period of freer government there before Mexico declared its independence.

When the newly independent Mexico wrote its constitution in 1823, Zavala was one of the members of the assembly that created this charter.

In the late 1820s and early 1830s, Zavala held a succession of government posts in Mexico, including congressman, state governor, Mexican finance minister, and envoy to France. He also received a large land grant in the Mexican state of Texas. It was an agitated period in Mexican politics, and at one point Zavala exiled himself from the country, spending part of this time north of the border.

Santa Anna became president in 1833. Two years later, as his rule became increasingly dictatorial, Zavala quit his last government position, that of minister to France. He settled in Texas and immediately began to encourage both the local Mexicans and the many new Anglo arrivals from the United States to cut all links with Mexico City.

Zavala was the most popular Mexican politician among the Anglo settlers and was elected to two assemblies in a row, the Consultation and the independence convention. He actively participated in all the stages that led to forming the Texas republic. His signature is on the Texan declaration of independence and on the constitution of the new country.

In a brief period of Anglo-Mexicano harmony during Texas's first flush of independent life, Lorenzo de Zavala became Texas's vice president in 1836. Yet, he had only a few months left to live. Illness forced him to resign after a half-year in office, and he died a few weeks later.

Further Reading

Lee, Roger A. "The History Guy: Lorenzo de Zavala (1788–1836)." Available online. URL: http://www.historyguy.com/lorenzo_de_zavala.html. Downloaded October 10, 2000.

Meier, Matt S. *Mexican American Biographies*. Westport, Conn.: Greenwood Publishing Group, 1988.

BIBLIOGRAPHY

Acuña, Rodolfo. *Occupied America—A History of Chicanos.* New York: HarperCollins, 1988.

Bloom, Harold, ed. *Hispanic American Writers.* Philadelphia: Chelsea House, 1998.

Cabán, Pedro, et al. *The Latino Experience in U.S. History.* Paramus, N.J.: Globe Fearon, 1994.

Cárdenas, Don, and Suzanne Schneider, editors. *Chicano Images in Film.* Denver: Denver International Film Festival, 1981.

Chabrán, Richard, and Rafael Chabrán. *The Latino Encyclopedia.* New York: Marshall Cavendish, 1996.

Cockroft, James D. *Latinos in Béisbol: The Hispanic Experience in the Americas.* Danbury, Conn.: Franklin Watts, 1996.

———. *Hispanics in the Making of the United States.* Danbury, Conn.: Franklin Watts, 1995.

Culligan, Judy. *Macmillan Profiles: Latino Americans.* New York: Macmillan, 1999.

Fernández-Flores, Darío. *The Spanish Heritage in the United States.* Madrid, Spain: Publicaciones Españolas, 1968.

Fernández-Shaw, Carlos M. *The Hispanic Presence in North America: From 1942 to Today,* Updated Edition. New York: Facts On File, 1999.

Foster, David William, ed. *Sourcebook of Hispanic Culture in the United States.* Chicago: American Library Association, 1982.

Gillan Straub, Deborah, ed. *Hispanic American Voices.* Detroit: UXL, 1997.

Hadley-García, George. *Hispanic Hollywood: The Latins in Motion Pictures.* Secaucus, N.J.: Citadel Press, 1990.

Kanellos, Nicolás. *Hispanic Firsts: 500 Years of Extraordinary Achievement.* Detroit: Gale Research, 1997.

———. *The Hispanic-American Almanac.* Detroit: Gale Research, 1993.

———. *Biographical Dictionary of Hispanic Literature in the United States.* Westport, Conn.: Greenwood Press, 1989.

Kanellos, Nicolás and Bryan Ryan, eds. *Hispanic American Chronology.* New York: UXL, 1996.

Kanellos, Nicolás and Claudio Esteva-Fabregat. *Handbook of Hispanic Cultures in the United States.* Houston: Arte Público Press, 1994.

Keller, Gary D. *Hispanics and United States Film: An Overview and Handbook.* Tempe, Ariz.: Bilingual Press, 1994.

Machamer, Gene. *Hispanic American Profiles.* New York: Ballantine, 1996.

Martínez, Al. *Rising Voices: Profiles of Hispano-American Lives.* New York: New American Library, 1974.

Martínez, Julio A. *Chicano Scholars and Writers: A Bio-Bibliographic Directory.* Metuchen, N.J.: Scarecrow Press, 1979.

Meier, Matt S. *Mexican American Biographies: A Historical Dictionary, 1836–1987.* Westport, Conn.: Greenwood Press, 1988.

Meier, Matt S., Conchita Franco Serri, and Richard A. García. *Notable Latino Americans.* Westport, Conn.: Greenwood Press, 1997.

Meier, Matt S., and Feliciano Rivera. *Mexican Americans, American Mexicans: From Conquistadors to Chicanos.* New York: Hill and Wang, 1993.

Meier, Matt S., and Feliciano Rivera. *Dictionary of Mexican American History.* Westport, Conn.: Greenwood Press, 1981.

Miller, Randall M., ed. *Ethnic Images in American Film and Television.* Philadelphia: The Balch Institute, 1978.

Moore, Joan, and Harry Pachón. *Hispanics in the United States.* Englewood Cliffs, N.J.: Prentice-Hall, 1985.

Morey, Janet. *Famous Hispanic Americans.* New York: Cobblehill, 1996.

Morey, Janet, and Wendy Dunn. *Famous Mexican Americans.* New York: E. P. Dutton, 1989.

Nagel, Rob, and Sharon Rose, eds. *Hispanic American Biography.* New York: UXL, 1995.

Newton, Clarke. *Famous Mexican Americans.* New York: Dodd, Mead, 1972.

Notable Hispanic American Women. Detroit: Gale Research, 1993.

Novas, Himilce. *The Hispanic 100: A Ranking of the Latino Men and Women Who Have Most Influenced American Thought and Culture.* New York: Carol, 1995.

Reyes, Luis. *Hispanics in Hollywood: An Encyclopedia of Film and Television.* New York: Garland, 1994.

Richard, Alfred C. *The Hispanic Image On the Silver Screen: An Interpretive Filmography From Silents Into Sound.* New York: Greenwood, 1992.

Roberts, John Storm. *The Latin Tinge: The Impact of Latin American Music on the United States.* Tivoli, N.Y.: Original Music, 1985.

Rodríguez, Clara E. *Puerto Ricans: Born in the U.S.A.* Boulder, Colo.: Westview Press, 1991.

Rodríguez Owsley, Beatrice. *The Hispanic American Entrepreneur: An Oral History of the American Dream.* New York: Twayne, 1992.

Samora, Julián, and Patricia Vandel Simon. *A History of the Mexican American People.* Notre Dame, Ind.: University of Notre Dame Press, 1977.

Shorris, Earl. *Latinos: A Biography of the People.* New York: Avon, 1992.

Sinnott, Susan. *Extraordinary Hispanic Americans.* Chicago: Children's Press, 1991.

St. John, Jetty. *Hispanic Scientists.* Mankato, Minn.: Capstone Press, 1996.

Sowell, Thomas. *Ethnic America: A History.* New York: Basic Books, 1981.

Telgen, Diane, and Jim Kamp, eds. *Latinas! Women of Achievement.* Detroit: Visible Ink, 1996.

Tardiff, Joseph C., and L. Mpho Mabunda, eds. *Dictionary of Hispanic Biography.* New York: Gale Research, 1996.

Unterburger, Amy L., and Jane L. Delgado, eds. *Who's Who Among Hispanic Americans.* Detroit: Gale Research, 1994–95.

Varona, Frank de. *Hispanics in American History.* Englewood Cliffs, N.J.: Globe Book, 1989.

Weyr, Thomas. *Hispanic USA.* New York: Harper & Row, 1988.

Woll, Allen L. *The Latin Image in American Film.* Los Angeles: UCLA Latin American Center Publications, 1980.

Entries by
Area of Activity

ACTIVISM
Baca, Judith
Chávez, César
Colón, Jesús
Flores, Patrick
Galarza, Ernesto
García, Héctor Pérez
Gonzales, Rodolfo "Corky"
Gutiérrez, José Ángel
Hernández, Antonia
Huerta, Dolores
Martínez, Antonio José
Martínez, Vilma S.
Mas Canosa, Jorge
Moreno, Luisa
Tijerina, Reies López
Velásquez, William Cárdenas
   "Willie"

ART
Baca, Judith
Botero, Fernando
Carrasco, Barbara
Gamboa, Harry, Jr.
Gómez-Peña,
   Guillermo

Jiménez, Luis
Marisol

ARCHITECTURE
Pelli, César

BALLET
Bocca, Julio
Bujones, Fernando
Herrera, Paloma
Limón, José

BUSINESS
Bañuelos, Romana Acosta
Goizueta, Roberto C.
Lorenzo, Frank
Ortega, Katherine D.
Rebozo, Charles Gregory "Bebe"
Unanue, Joseph A.

DISCOVERY, EXPLORATION
AND CONQUEST
Álvarez de Pineda, Alonso
De Soto, Hernando
Menéndez de Avilés, Pedro
Narváez, Pánfilo

Núñez Cabeza de Vaca, Álvar
Ponce de León, Juan
Serra, Junípero
Vázquez de Coronado, Francisco

EDUCATION
Cortines, Ramón
Escalante, Jaime
Rivera, Tomás

FASHION
Adolfo
De la Renta, Oscar
Herrera, Carolina

FILM, THEATER AND TELEVISION
Almendros, Néstor
Arnaz, Desi
Banderas, Antonio
Blades, Rubén
Carrera, Barbara
Carrillo, Leo
Carter, Lynda
Christian, Linda
Coca, Imogene
Colón, Miriam

Cristal, Linda
Del Río, Dolores
Díaz, Cameron
Estévez, Emilio
Ferrer, José
Ferrer, Mel
García, Andy
Gavin, John
Hayworth, Rita
Hayek, Salma
Juliá, Raúl
Jurado, Katy
Lamas, Fernando
López, Jennifer
Marín Richard Anthony
   "Cheech"
Meléndez, Bill
Miranda, Carmen
Montalbán, Ricardo
Moreno, Antonio
Moreno, Rita
Nava, Gregory
Novarro, Ramón
Olmos, Edward James
Peña, Elizabeth
Pérez, Rosie
Principal, Victoria
Quinn, Anthony
Rivera, Chita
Rivera, Geraldo
Roland, Gilbert
Rodríguez, Paul
Romero, César
Sheen, Charlie
Sheen, Martin
Smits, Jimmy
Valdez, Luis M.
Vélez, Lupe
Welch, Raquel

FITNESS
Principal, Victoria
Welch, Raquel

GOVERNMENT
Apodaca, Jerry

Archuleta, Diego
Badillo, Herman
Baird, Lourdes
Cavazos, Lauro F.
Chávez, Dennis
Chávez, Linda
Cisneros, Henry
De la Garza, Eligio "Kika"
Díaz-Balart, Lincoln
Gálvez, Bernardo de
Gavin, John
González, Henry B.
Hidalgo, Edward
Larrazolo, Octaviano
Luján, Manuel, Jr.
Martínez, Bob
Medina, Harold
Menéndez, Bob
Miró, Esteban Rodríguez
Molina, Gloria
Montoya, Joseph M.
Muñoz Marín, Luis
Muñoz Rivera, Luis
Novello, Antonia
Ortega, Katherine D.
Peña, Federico
Ros-Lehtinen, Ileana
Roybal, Edward R.
Roybal-Allard, Lucille
Sánchez, Loretta
Suárez, Xavier L.
Telles, Raymond
Vallejo, Mariano G.
Velázquez, Nydia
   Margarita
Villalpando, Catalina Vázquez
   "Cathi"
Zavala, Lorenzo de

HISTORY
Castañeda, Carlos E.

JOURNALISM
Ramírez, Francisco P.
Rivera, Geraldo
Salazar, Rubén

LAW ENFORCEMENT
Rodríguez, Matt L.

LITERATURE
Alegría, Fernando
Algarín, Miguel
Allende, Isabel
Álvarez, Julia
Anaya, Rudolfo A.
Cabrera, Lydia
Cisneros, Sandra
Colón, Jesús
Goldemberg, Isaac
Gonzales, Rodolfo "Corky"
González, Celedonio
Hernández Cruz, Víctor
Hijuelos, Oscar
Hinojosa-Smith, Rolando
Kanellos, Nicolás
Mohr, Nicholasa
Moraga, Cherríe
Piñero, Miguel
Rivera, Tomás
Salas, Floyd
Soto, Gary
Thomas, John Peter "Piri"
Vallbona, Rima de
Williams, William Carlos

MEDICINE
Novello, Antonia
Ochoa, Severo

MILITARY
Álvarez, Everett, Jr.
Archuleta, Diego
Benavídez, Roy P.
Bouchard, Hipólito
Chacón, Rafael
Chaves, Manuel
De la Garza, Emilio, Jr.
Farragut, David
Fernández Cavada, Federico
García, Macario
Gómez, Edward
González, Alfredo

Herrera, Silvestre
Jiménez, José
Longoria, Félix
López, Baldomero
López, José
Lozada, Carlos
Martínez, Benito
Martínez, Joe P.
Obregón, Eugene
Ortega, John
Pérez, Manuel, Jr.
Rubio, Eurípides
Seguín, Juan N.
Valdez, José
Vargas, M. Sando, Jr.
Villegas, Ysmael

MUSIC

Anthony, Marc
Arrau, Claudio
Arroyo, Martina
Báez, Joan
Blades, Rubén
Carey, Mariah
Carr, Vikki
Casals, Pablo
Cruz, Celia
Cugat, Xavier
Domingo, Plácido
Estefan, Gloria
Feliciano, José
Garcia, Jerry
Gormé, Eydie
Hernández, Rafael
Iglesias, Enrique

Iglesias, Julio
López, Jennifer
López, Trini
Machito
Martin, Ricky
Mata, Eduardo
Mendoza, Lydia
Migenes-Johnson, Julia
Puente, Tito
Ronstadt, Linda
Santana, Carlos
Schifrin, Boris Claudio "Lalo"
Secada, Jon
Selena
Tizol, Juan
Valens, Ritchie

PHILOSOPHY

Santayana, George

SCIENCE AND ENGINEERING

Álvarez, Luis Walter
Alvariño de Leira, Ángeles
Ayala, Francisco
Colmenares, Margarita
Dallmeier, Francisco
Molina, Mario
Ochoa, Ellen
Ocampo, Adriana
Villa-Komaroff, Lydia

SPACE TRAVEL

Chang-Díaz, Franklin
Gutiérrez, Sidney
Ochoa, Ellen

SPIRITUAL TEACHING

Castañeda, Carlos

SPORTS

Alomar, Roberto
Aparicio, Luis
Canseco, José
Casals, Rosemary
Clemente, Roberto
Cordero, Ángel, Jr.
De la Hoya, Oscar
Fernández, Mary Joe
Flores, Tom
Gonzales, Richard Alonzo "Pancho"
López, Nancy
Lucero-Schayes, Wendy
Ortiz-Del Valle, Sandra
Plunkett, Jim
Rodríguez, Juan "Chi Chi"
Salas, Floyd
Salazar, Alberto
Sosa, Sammy
Treviño, Lee
Valenzuela, Fernando

RELIGION

Flores, Patrick
Martínez, Antonio José
Serra, Junípero

WILD WEST

Baca, Elfego
Cortina, Juan Nepomuceno
Murieta, Joaquín

Entries by Country of Heritage

ARGENTINA
Bocca, Julio
Bouchard,
    Hipólito
Cristal, Linda
Herrera, Paloma
Lamas, Fernando
Pelli, César
Schifrin, Boris Claudio
    "Lalo"

BOLIVIA
Escalante, Jaime
Welch, Raquel

BRAZIL
Miranda, Carmen

CHILE
Alegría, Fernando
Allende, Isabel
Arrau, Claudio

COLOMBIA
Botero, Fernando
Ocampo, Adriana

COSTA RICA
Chang-Díaz, Franklin
Vallbona, Rima de

CUBA
Adolfo
Arnaz, Desi
Bujones, Fernando
Cabrera, Lydia
Canseco, José
Cruz, Celia
Díaz, Cameron
Díaz-Balart, Lincoln
Estefan, Gloria
Fernández Cavada, Federico
Ferrer, Mel
García, Andy
Goizueta, Roberto C.
González, Celedonio
Hijuelos, Oscar
Juliá, Raúl
Machito
Mas Canosa, Jorge
Menéndez, Bob
Peña, Elizabeth
Peña, Federico

Rebozo, Charles Gregory "Bebe"
Romero, César
Ros-Lehtinen, Ileana
Salazar, Alberto
Secada, Jon
Suárez, Xavier L.

DOMINICAN REPUBLIC
Álvarez, Julia
De la Renta, Oscar
Fernández, Mary Joe
Sosa, Sammy

ECUADOR
Baird, Lourdes

EL SALVADOR
Casals, Rosemary

GUATEMALA
Moreno, Luisa

MEXICO
Álvarez, Everett, Jr.
Anaya, Rudolfo A.
Apodaca, Jerry

Archuleta, Diego
Baca, Elfego
Baca, Judith
Báez, Joan
Bañuelos, Romana Acosta
Benavídez, Roy P.
Carr, Vikki
Carrasco, Barbara
Carrillo, Leo
Carter, Lynda
Castañeda, Carlos E.
Cavazos, Lauro F.
Chacón, Rafael
Chaves, Manuel
Chávez, César
Chávez, Dennis
Chávez, Linda
Christian, Linda
Cisneros, Henry
Cisneros, Sandra
Colmenares, Margarita
Cortina, Juan Nepomuceno
Cortines, Ramón
De la Garza, Kika
De la Hoya, Oscar
Del Río, Dolores
Flores, Patrick
Flores, Tom
Galarza, Ernesto
Gamboa, Harry
García, Héctor Pérez
García, Macario
Gavin, John
Gómez-Peña, Guillermo
Gonzales, Ricardo Alonso
    "Pancho"
Gonzales, Rodolfo "Corky"
González, Alfredo
González, Henry B.
Gutiérrez, José Ángel
Gutiérrez, Sidney
Hayek, Salma
Hernández, Antonia
Herrera, Silvestre
Hidalgo, Edward
Hinojosa-Smith, Rolando

Huerta, Dolores
Jiménez, José
Jiménez, Luis
Jurado, Katy
Larrazolo, Octaviano
Limón, José
Longoria, Félix
López, José
López, Nancy
López, Trini
Luján, Manuel, Jr.
Marín, Richard Anthony
    "Cheech"
Martínez, Antonio José
Martínez, Benito
Martínez, Joe P.
Martínez, Vilma
Mata, Eduardo
Meléndez, Bill
Medina, Harold
Mendoza, Lydia
Montalbán, Ricardo
Molina, Gloria
Molina, Mario
Montoya, Joseph M.
Moraga, Cherríe
Murieta, Joaquín
Novarro, Ramón
Nava, Gregory
Obregón, Eugene
Ochoa, Ellen
Olmos, Edward James
Ortega, Katherine
Plunkett, Jim
Quinn, Anthony
Ramírez, Francisco P.
Rivera, Tomás
Rodríguez, Juan "Chi Chi"
Roland, Gilbert
Rodríguez, Matt L.
Rodríguez, Paul
Ronstadt, Linda
Roybal, Edward R.
Roybal-Allard, Lucille
Salas, Floyd
Salazar, Rubén

Sánchez, Loretta
Santana, Carlos
Seguín, Juan N.
Selena
Soto, Gary
Telles, Raymond
Tijerina, Reies López
Treviño, Lee
Valdez, José
Valdez, Luis M.
Valens, Ritchie
Valenzuela, Fernando
Vallejo, Mariano G.
Vargas, M. Sando, Jr.
Velásquez, William Cárdenas
    "Willie"
Vélez, Lupe
Villa-Komaroff, Lydia
Villalpando, Catalina Vázquez
Villegas, Ysmael
Zavala, Lorenzo de

NICARAGUA
Carrera, Barbara

PANAMA
Blades, Rubén

PERU
Castañeda, Carlos
Goldemberg, Isaac

PUERTO RICO
Algarín, Miguel
Alomar, Roberto
Anthony, Marc
Arroyo, Martina
Badillo, Herman
Clemente, Roberto
Colón, Jesús
Colón, Miriam
Cordero, Ángel, Jr.
Feliciano, José
Ferrer, José
Hernández, Rafael
Hernández Cruz, Víctor

Kanellos, Nicolás
López, Jennifer
Lozada, Carlos
Martin, Ricky
Migenes-Johnson, Julia
Mohr, Nicholasa
Moreno, Rita
Muñoz Marín, Luis
Muñoz Rivera, Luis
Novello, Antonia
Ortiz-Del Valle, Sandra
Pérez, Rosie
Piñero, Miguel
Puente, Tito
Rivera, Chita
Rivera, Geraldo
Rubio, Eurípides
Smits, Jimmy
Thomas, John Peter "Piri"
Tizol, Juan
Velázquez, Nydia Margarita
Williams, William Carlos

SPAIN
Almendros, Néstor

Álvarez, Luis Walter
Álvarez de Pineda, Alonso
Alvariño de Leira, Ángeles
Ayala, Francisco
Banderas, Antonio
Casals, Pablo
Coca, Imogene
Cugat, Xavier
De Soto, Hernando
Domingo, Plácido
Estévez, Emilio
Farragut, David
Gálvez, Bernardo de
García, Jerry
Gormé, Eydie
Hayworth, Rita
Iglesias, Enrique
Iglesias, Julio
Lorenzo, Frank
Lucero-Schayes, Wendy
Martínez, Bob
Menéndez de Avilés, Pedro
Miró, Esteban Rodríguez
Moreno, Antonio
Narváez, Pánfilo

Núñez Cabeza de Vaca, Álvar
Ochoa, Severo
Ortega, John
Ponce de León, Juan
Santayana, George
Serra, Junípero
Sheen, Charlie
Sheen, Martin
Unanue, Joseph A.
Vázquez de Coronado,
    Francisco

VENEZUELA
Aparicio, Luis
Carey, Mariah
Dallmeier, Francisco
Herrera, Carolina
Marisol

UNKNOWN OR UNCERTAIN
De la Garza, Emilio, Jr.
Gómez, Edward
López, Baldomero
Pérez, Manuel, Jr.
Principal, Victoria

ENTRIES BY
YEAR OF BIRTH

1400s
Alvarez de Pineda, Alonso
De Soto, Hernando
Narváez, Pánfilo
Núñez Cabeza de Vaca, Álvar
Ponce de León, Juan

1500s
Menéndez de Avilés, Pedro
Vázquez de Coronado, Francisco

1700s
Bouchard, Hipólito
Gálvez, Bernardo de
Martínez, Antonio José
Miró, Esteban Rodríguez
Serra, Junípero
Zavala, Lorenzo de

1800–1849
Archuleta, Diego
Chacón, Rafael
Chaves, Manuel
Cortina, Juan Nepomuceno
Farragut, David
Fernández Cavada, Federico

Murieta, Joaquín
Ortega, John
Ramírez, Francisco P.
Seguín, Juan N.
Vallejo, Mariano G.

1850–1899
Baca, Elfego
Carrillo, Leo
Casals, Pablo
Castañeda, Carlos E.
Chávez, Dennis
Hernández, Rafael
Larrazolo, Octaviano
Medina, Harold
Moreno, Antonio
Muñoz Marín, Luis
Muñoz Rivera, Luis
Novarro, Ramón
Santayana, George
Williams, William Carlos

1900–1904
Arrau, Claudio
Cabrera, Lydia
Colón, Jesús

Cugat, Xavier
Tizol, Juan

1905–1909
Coca, Imogene
Del Río, Dolores
Galarza, Ernesto
Limón, José
Miranda, Carmen
Moreno, Luisa
Ochoa, Severo
Roland, Gilbert
Romero, César
Vélez, Lupe

1910–1914
Álvarez, Luis Walter
Ferrer, José
García, Héctor Pérez
Hidalgo, Edward
Machito
Rebozo, Charles Gregory
    "Bebe"

1915–1919
Alegría, Fernando

Alvariño de Leira, Ángeles
Arnaz, Desi
Ferrer, Mel
González, Henry B.
Hayworth, Rita
Lamas, Fernando
Meléndez, Bill
Mendoza, Lydia
Montoya, Joseph M.
Quinn, Anthony
Roybal, Edward R.
Telles, Raymond

1920–1924
Christian, Linda
Cruz, Celia
García, Macario
González, Celedonio
López, José
Martínez, Joe P.
Montalbán, Ricardo
Pérez, Manuel, Jr.
Puente, Tito

1925–1929
Badillo, Herman
Bañuelos, Romana Acosta
Castañeda, Carlos
Cavazos, Lauro F.
Chávez, César
De la Garza, Eligio "Kika"
Flores, Patrick
Gavin, John
Gonzales, Richard Alonzo
    "Pancho"
Gonzales, Rodolfo "Corky"
Herrera, Silvestre
Hinojosa-Smith, Rolando
Jurado, Katy
Longoria, Félix
López, Baldomero
Luján, Manuel, Jr.
Pelli, César
Salazar, Rubén
Thomas, John Peter "Piri"
Tijerina, Reies López

Unanue, Joseph A.
Valdez, José
Villegas, Ysmael

1930–1934
Adolfo
Almendros, Néstor
Aparicio, Luis
Apodaca, Jerry
Ayala, Francisco
Botero, Fernando
Clemente, Roberto
Cortines, Ramón
De la Renta, Oscar
Escalante, Jaime
Goizueta, Roberto C.
Gómez, Edward
Gormé, Eydie
Huerta, Dolores
Marisol
Martínez, Benito
Martínez, Bob
Moreno, Rita
Obregón, Eugene
Ortega, Katherine D.
Rivera, Chita
Salas, Floyd
Schifrin, Boris Claudio "Lalo"
Vallbona, Rima de

1935–1939
Álvarez, Everett, Jr.
Anaya, Rudolfo A.
Arroyo, Martina
Baird, Lourdes
Benavídez, Roy P.
Cristal, Linda
Flores, Tom
Herrera, Carolina
López, Trini
Mas Canosa, Jorge
Mohr, Nicholasa
Rivera, Tomás
Rodríguez, Juan "Chi Chi"
Rodríguez, Matt L.
Rubio, Eurípides

Treviño, Lee

1940–1944
Algarín, Miguel
Allende, Isabel
Báez, Joan
Carr, Vikki
Cordero, Ángel, Jr.
Domingo, Plácido
Garcia, Jerry
Gutiérrez, José Ángel
Iglesias, Julio
Jiménez, Luis
Juliá, Raúl
Lorenzo, Frank
Martínez, Vilma
Mata, Eduardo
Molina, Mario
Novello, Antonia
Rivera, Geraldo
Roybal-Allard, Lucille
Sheen, Martin
Valdez, Luis M.
Valens, Ritchie
Vargas, M. Sando, Jr.
Velásquez, William Cárdenas
    "Willie"
Villalpando, Catalina Vásquez
Welch, Raquel

1945–1949
Baca, Judith
Blades, Rubén
Casals, Rosemary
Chávez, Linda
Cisneros, Henry
Colón, Miriam
De la Garza, Emilio, Jr.
Feliciano, José
Goldemberg, Isaac
González, Alfredo
Hernández, Antonia
Hernández Cruz, Víctor
Jiménez, José
Kanellos, Nicolás
Lozada, Carlos

Marín, Richard Anthony
  "Cheech"
Migenes-Johnson, Julia
Molina, Gloria
Nava, Gregory
Olmos, Edward James
Peña, Federico
Piñero, Miguel
Plunkett, Jim
Ronstadt, Linda
Santana, Carlos
Suárez, Xavier L.
Villa-Komaroff, Lydia

1950–1954
Carrera, Barbara
Chang-Díaz, Franklin
Cisneros, Sandra
Dallmeier, Francisco
Díaz-Balart, Lincoln
Gamboa, Harry, Jr.
Gómez-Peña, Guillermo
Gutiérrez, Sidney
Hijuelos, Oscar
Menéndez, Bob

Moraga, Cherríe
Ortiz-Del Valle, Sandra
Principal, Victoria
Ros-Lehtinen, Ileana
Soto, Gary
Velázquez, Nydia

1955–1959
Bujones, Fernando
Carrasco, Barbara
Carter, Lynda
Colmenares, Margarita
Estefan, Gloria
García, Andy
López, Nancy
Ocampo, Adriana
Ochoa, Ellen
Peña, Elizabeth
Rodríguez, Paul
Salazar, Alberto
Smits, Jimmy

1960–1964
Banderas, Antonio
Canseco, José

Estévez, Emilio
Lucero-Schayes, Wendy
Pérez, Rosie
Sánchez, Loretta
Secada, Jon
Valenzuela, Fernando

1965–1969
Alomar, Roberto
Anthony, Marc
Bocca, Julio
Hayek, Salma
Sheen, Charlie
Sosa, Sammy

1970–1979
Carey, Mariah
De la Hoya, Oscar
Díaz, Cameron
Fernández, Mary Joe
Herrera, Paloma
Iglesias, Enrique
López, Jennifer
Martin, Ricky
Selena

INDEX

Boldface numbers indicate entries.
Italic numbers indicate photographs.

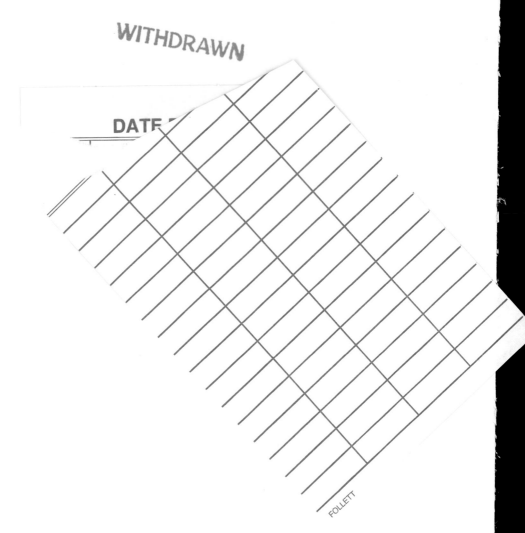